financial accounting, reporting, and analysis

financial accounting, reporting, and analysis

jennifer maynard

OXFORD
UNIVERSITY PRESS

UNIVERSITY PRESS

Great Clarendon Street, Oxford, OX2 6DP,
United Kingdom

Oxford University Press is a department of the University of Oxford.
It furthers the University's objective of excellence in research, scholarship,
and education by publishing worldwide. Oxford is a registered trade mark of
Oxford University Press in the UK and in certain other countries

© Jennifer Maynard 2013

The moral rights of the author have been asserted

Impression: 1

British Library Cataloguing in Publication Data

Data available

978-0-19-960605-4

Printed in Italy by
L.E.G.O. S.p.A.—Lavis TN

To Lars and Isobel for their constant support, and to Arthur and Mog, who have sometimes hindered rather than helped, but who have kept me company during the long hours at the computer.

CONTENTS IN BRIEF

Preface   xiv

How to use this book   xvi

How to use the Online Resource Centre   xviii

Acknowledgements   xx

Part 1   Introduction

Chapter 1   Financial reporting and accounting   3

Part 2   Financial reporting in context

Chapter 2   The financial reporting system   53
Chapter 3   Corporate governance, sustainability, and ethics 84
Chapter 4   Published financial statements of companies   125
Chapter 5   Interpretation of financial statements   184

Part 3   Income statement reporting issues

Chapter 6   Reporting performance   233
Chapter 7   Revenue   280
Chapter 8   Earnings per share   310
Chapter 9   Taxation   340

Part 4   Statement of financial position reporting issues

Chapter 10 Property, plant and equipment   375
Chapter 11 Intangible assets   419
Chapter 12 Current assets   454
Chapter 13 Liabilities   490
Chapter 14 Leasing   521

Part 5   Consolidated financial statements

Chapter 15 Subsidiaries   559
Chapter 16 Associates, joint arrangements, and statements of cash flow 617

Part 6   Conclusion

Chapter 17 Interpretation of financial statements revisited 659

Terminology converter   699

Glossary   700

Index   707

CONTENTS IN FULL

Preface	xiv
How to use this book	xvi
How to use the Online Resource Centre	xviii
Acknowledgements	xx

Part 1 — Introduction

Chapter 1 — Financial reporting and accounting — 3

1.1	Financial reporting	4
1.2	The difference between profit and cash flow	11
1.3	Qualitative characteristics	13
1.4	Financial accounting	17
1.5	Limited companies' financial statements	23
1.6	Accruals principle	27
1.7	Prudence	33
1.8	Pulling everything together	37

Part 2 — Financial reporting in context

Chapter 2 — The financial reporting system — 53

2.1	High quality financial reporting	54
2.2	Companies legislation	57
2.3	International accounting standards	59
2.4	The International Accounting Standards Board (IASB)	65
2.5	Principles based international financial reporting standards (IFRSs)	67
2.6	The conceptual framework	71
2.7	The consequences of global IFRS adoption	77
2.8	The future of IFRS	79

Chapter 3 — Corporate governance, sustainability, and ethics — 84

3.1	A wider financial reporting system	85
3.2	Corporate governance	87
3.3	The UK Corporate Governance Code 2010	92

3.4	Reporting of corporate governance	106
3.5	Corporate sustainability	107
3.6	Ethics	114
Chapter 4	**Published financial statements of companies**	**125**
4.1	Key financial statements	126
4.2	IAS 1 *Presentation of Financial Statements*	127
4.3	Structure and content of financial statements	131
4.4	Statement of financial position	132
4.5	Statement of comprehensive income	137
4.6	Statement of changes in equity	148
4.7	Statement of cash flows	150
4.8	Notes to the financial statements	161
4.9	Proposed changes to the presentation of financial statements	170
Chapter 5	**Interpretation of financial statements**	**184**
5.1	Where does an interpretation begin?	185
5.2	Overview of financial statements	189
5.3	Ratio analysis	196
5.4	Profitability ratios	198
5.5	Liquidity ratios	203
5.6	Efficiency ratios	206
5.7	Gearing	209
5.8	Investor ratios	211
5.9	Limitations in ratio analysis	216
Part 3	**Income statement reporting issues**	
Chapter 6	**Reporting performance**	**233**
6.1	Underpinning principles of performance	234
6.2	One-off, unusual items	237
6.3	Discontinued operations and non-current assets held for sale	241
6.4	Operating segment reporting	252
6.5	Related party disclosures	263
Chapter 7	**Revenue**	**280**
7.1	Issues with revenue	282
7.2	IAS 18 *Revenue*	285
7.3	ED 2011/6 *Revenue from Contracts with Customers*	294

Chapter 8	Earnings per share	310
8.1	Earnings per share (EPS)	311
8.2	Earnings	313
8.3	Shares	317
8.4	Diluted earnings per share	322
8.5	Disclosure of EPS	330
8.6	Future changes to IAS 33	333

Chapter 9	Taxation	340
9.1	Taxation on companies' profits	341
9.2	Current tax	343
9.3	Deferred tax	346
9.4	The effect of accounting for deferred tax	357
9.5	Is the approach of IAS 12 *Income Taxes* to accounting for deferred tax appropriate?	359
9.6	Disclosures	360
9.7	Users' interpretation of tax	365

Part 4	**Statement of financial position reporting issues**	

Chapter 10	Property, plant and equipment	375
10.1	Significance of property, plant and equipment	376
10.2	Definition of property, plant and equipment	377
10.3	Recognition of property, plant and equipment	378
10.4	Initial measurement of property, plant and equipment	380
10.5	Subsequent measurement—depreciation	383
10.6	Subsequent measurement—alternative models	388
10.7	Impairment of assets	394
10.8	Derecognition of property, plant and equipment	402
10.9	Investment properties	403
10.10	Non-current assets held for sale	405
10.11	Disclosures	405
10.12	Understanding property, plant and equipment information	409

Chapter 11	Intangible assets	419
11.1	Why is accounting for intangibles important?	420
11.2	Issues in accounting for intangible assets	421
11.3	IAS 38 *Intangible Assets*	423
11.4	Initial measurement	426
11.5	Intangible assets acquired in a business combination	427

11.6	Financial reporting in practice	430
11.7	Internally generated intangible assets	431
11.8	Measurement of an intangible asset after recognition	437
11.9	Disclosures	442
11.10	What do the accounting treatment and disclosures of intangible assets mean to the user?	446
11.11	Does this mean the current accounting and reporting of intangible assets is acceptable?	448
11.12	The current IASB position	449

Chapter 12	**Current assets**	**454**
12.1	Definition of and significance of current assets	455
12.2	Inventories	456
12.3	Receivables	464
12.4	Construction contracts	467

Chapter 13	**Liabilities**	**490**
13.1	Accounting for liabilities	491
13.2	Provisions	494
13.3	Contingent liabilities	501
13.4	Issues with IAS 37 and its future	507
13.5	Events after the reporting period	509

Chapter 14	**Leasing**	**521**
14.1	Off balance sheet financing	522
14.2	Leases	525
14.3	Accounting for leases in lessees' financial statements	530
14.4	Accounting for leases in lessors' financial statements	538
14.5	Sale and leaseback transactions	545
14.6	Future accounting for leases	548

Part 5	**Consolidated financial statements**	

Chapter 15	**Subsidiaries**	**559**
15.1	Categorisation of investments	560
15.2	Control	564
15.3	Exemptions from the preparation of consolidated financial statements	568
15.4	Consolidation techniques	568
15.5	Goodwill on acquisition	576

15.6	Consolidated statement of financial position after acquisition date	582
15.7	Acquisition of preference shares and other financial instruments in the subsidiary	585
15.8	Intragroup transactions and balances	587
15.9	Consolidated income statement	592
15.10	Consolidated statement of changes in equity	595
15.11	Disclosures in the financial statements	599

Chapter 16 Associates, joint arrangements, and statements of cash flow 617

16.1	Associate companies	618
16.2	Joint arrangements	629
16.3	Consolidated statements of cash flow	633

Part 6 Conclusion

Chapter 17 Interpretation of financial statements revisited 659

17.1	Interpretation of financial statements in the context of material covered in the textbook	660
17.2	A CORE approach	661
17.3	The effect of recognition and measurement issues, and accounting policies on interpretation	667
17.4	Case study	672
17.5	Industry statistics—use of databases	688

Terminology converter	699
Glossary	700
Index	707

PREFACE

This textbook on financial accounting, reporting, and analysis is aimed principally at level two undergraduate students on specialist accounting and finance degree programmes, although it may be relevant for postgraduate courses in financial statement analysis. It is assumed that all readers will have completed an introductory financial accounting course, and may go on to study more advanced financial reporting courses. There is, however, an introductory chapter which revises the main topics covered in introductory financial accounting courses and textbooks, and this provides a foundation on which the remainder of the textbook's material is built. The textbook's basis is international financial reporting standards issued by the International Accounting Standards Board (IASB).

One key issue with a second year undergraduate course in financial reporting is how to take students from basic financial accounting, which usually focuses on the preparation of the main financial statements, to an understanding of the complexities and many subtleties of financial reporting. Financial reporting is about communicating financial information about a business entity to its users. This is mirrored by this textbook's main aim—to enable readers to understand and interpret the financial statements of business entities—mainly companies. Inevitably, this requires understanding of detailed technical material and terminology, and an objective of this textbook is to ensure students become familiar with, and confident in, the use of this material and language. However, in all this complexity, the overarching objective of financial reporting should not be lost.

This textbook also seeks a balance between the sometimes conflicting needs of financial reporting courses. On the one hand these may seek to attract professional accountancy body exemptions, but, on the other, they need to be theoretical enough and include sufficient critical perspective to meet the demands of academic benchmarking requirements. Thus, the technical material is current and comprehensive, but not so much so that the main points are swamped in a mass of detail. The financial accounting and reporting methods are discussed in relation to underpinning frameworks and principles, and always in the context of what they mean for the user.

So the textbook takes as its foundation the IASB's decision-usefulness objective of financial reporting, which is to provide financial information about a reporting entity that is useful to users in making decisions. Discussion of the more technical topics then uses a model which addresses three questions:

- How is the financial accounting done?
- Why is the accounting done in the way that it is?
- What does this mean for the user?

(So that material is not presented in an artificial manner, the explanations and discussions of the topics integrate these questions.)

How the financial accounting is done, is the technical, preparing element, essential for professional accountancy body requirements. The textbook discusses the significant aspects of international financial reporting standards using clear explanations, which are supported by short explanatory examples and longer worked examples, and backed up by a comprehensive glossary.

Why the accounting is done in the way that it is, is the understanding element. Accounting methods are linked back to underpinning concepts and principles, and this provides the more critical perspective. It is set in the context of the financial reporting governance framework, and chapters in the textbook examine why this takes the form it does today, and also consider what future developments there are likely to be.

What it means for the user is the key interpretation theme of the textbook, and, in addition to this question being addressed in individual chapters, there are two chapters devoted to interpretation. The first of these, early on in the textbook, provides details of basic interpretative tools, which are referred to in later chapters. Full interpretation can only be achieved properly by understanding both the interrelationships of all financial statements taken together and the basis of individual figures, so the final chapter pulls together much of the material covered by all previous chapters. It illustrates this by the use of a detailed case study—an interpretation of the financial statements of J Sainsbury plc.

The final objective of this textbook is to show its readers that financial reporting is a real, live subject. Business entities have to address questions about how they account for and present the results of their increasingly complex financial and other transactions, and what information the users of their financial reports will want. Thus, what information is disclosed by entities is discussed in all chapters and illustrated by the financial reporting in practice examples. Readers will be able to understand how the detailed material they have studied is ultimately reported by entities.

Jennifer Maynard
September 2012

How to use this book

Chapter introduction

Each chapter opens with a concise outline of the chapter contents,
including key definitions.

Learning objectives

A bulleted outline of the main concepts and ideas indicates what
you can expect to learn from each chapter.

Key issues checklist

Use this checklist for each chapter to chart your progress with the
accounting issues—great for helping you to plan your revision.

Terminology

Accounting concepts are highlighted where they are first
explained and definitions are collated in a convenient glossary at
the back of the book along with a handy 'Terminology converter'
that clarifies equivalent terms.

Reminder

Refresh your memory of essential financial accounting terms and
concepts with these short reminder points.

Financial reporting in practice

Understand how the theory relates to financial reporting in
practice with frequent extracts from real-world annual reports
from organisations such as Sainsbury's, Rolls-Royce, British
Airways, and Lloyds TSB.

Illustrative examples

Regular examples of how to account for particular transactions and items, as well as example statements, help support your learning.

Worked examples

Detailed worked examples walk you through the calculation and presentation of figures required for financial statements.

Summary of key points

Linked to the learning objectives, each chapter concludes with a summary of the most important concepts you need to take away from it.

Further reading

Extend your knowledge with this annotated further reading section.

Graded questions

Test and consolidate your knowledge with end-of-chapter questions graded into 3 levels of difficulty:

- do a quick test of your ability;
- then develop your understanding as you build confidence with the accounting methods;
- finally, take it further by applying everything you have learned in the chapter to more complex scenarios.

Check your progress by accessing the full set of answers available on the Online Resource Centre where you can also watch walk-through solutions to key questions.

How to use the Online Resource Centre

Make the most of this package by accessing your FREE online supplementary learning materials at: **www.oxfordtextbooks.co.uk/orc/maynard/**

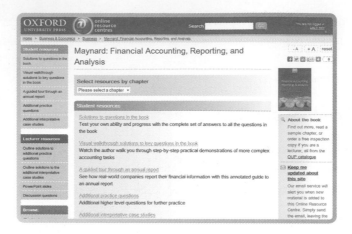

Student resources

Free and open-access material available:

Complete set of solutions to the questions in the book

Test your own ability and progress with the complete set of answers to all the questions in the book.

Walk-through solutions to key questions in the book

Watch the author walk you through step-by-step practical demonstrations of more complex accounting tasks.

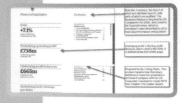

A guided tour through an annual report

See how real-world companies report their financial information with this annotated guide to an annual report.

Additional practice questions

Go that extra mile in consolidating your understanding by practising these higher-level additional questions.

Additional interpretative case studies

Develop your interpretative skills with these extra case studies.

Study skill tips

Read the author's tips for success in your accounting studies.

Lecturer resources
Free for all registered adopters of the textbook:

PowerPoint slides

Accompanying each chapter is a suite of customisable slides, fully integrated with the textbook, to be used in lecture presentations.

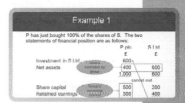

Outline solutions to the additional interpretative case studies

The outline answers to the additional case studies can be used in assignments and seminar preparation.

Discussion questions for seminar use

A set of stimulating questions to help lecturers plan group discussions.

Don't forget that all of these resources can be uploaded to your institution's Virtual Learning Environment to allow students to access them directly!

Author acknowledgements

Firstly, I would like to thank Kirsty Reade and the commissioning team at Oxford University Press who sent me an original proposal for a second year undergraduate textbook which must have been sufficiently enticing for me to decide that I would like to be involved in the project. I ended up being the author.

Secondly, I would like to thank the Higher Education development team at OUP and, in particular, Eleanor Chatburn, my development editor. Throughout the development of the book the team has always been helpful and encouraging, and kept faith in me when I fell behind on deadlines.

Thirdly, I would like to thank former and present colleagues who, through conversations about financial accounting and reporting, and how to best teach and deliver the subject, have provided inspiration, ideas, and examples.

Finally, I must thank anyone who recognises examples I have used in this textbook as their own and whom I have not acknowledged. Over 18 years of teaching financial accounting and reporting I have inevitably gathered, accumulated, and adapted examples, the original sources of which have now been lost.

Publisher acknowledgements

The publisher is grateful to the following reviewers who have contributed to development of the text:

Ifigenia Georgiou, Aston University

Penny Young, University of Bolton

Venancio Tauringana, Bournemouth University

Jing Li, Bradford University

Sumohon Matilal, University of Essex

Petros Vourvachis, University of Exeter

Suzanne McCallum, University of Glasgow

Salma Ibrahim, Kingston University

Chris McMahon, Liverpool John Moores University

Martin Kelly, Queen's University Belfast

Deb Lewis, Swansea University

John Wyett, University of East Anglia

Phang Soon Yeow, University of Malaya

Dimitrios Gounopoulos, University of Surrey

The publisher wishes to thank the following organisations for permission to reproduce copyright material:

International Financial Reporting Standards (IFRS) and International Accounting Standards Board (IASB) material is reproduced by kind permission of IFRS Foundation. Copyright © 2012 IFRS Foundation. All rights reserved. No permission to reproduce or distribute.

Extracts from the *UK Corporate Governance Code* are adapted and reproduced with the kind permission of the Financial Reporting Council. Copyright © Financial Reporting Council (FRC). All rights reserved. For further information, please visit www.frc.org.uk or call +44 (0)20 7492 2300.

Extracts from *Handbook of Code of Ethics for Professional Accountants* of the International Ethics Standards Board for Accountants are reproduced with permission of International Federation of Accountants (IFAC) http://www.ifac.org/publications-resources.

J Sainsbury plc, Tesco plc, Nestlé Group, Next plc, Marks and Spencer plc, Lenzing AG, Vodafone Group plc, Arsenal Holdings plc, GKN plc, Rolls-Royce plc, Marstons plc, Kingfisher plc, Barclays plc, JD Wetherspoon plc, British Airways plc, Balfour Beatty plc, Lloyds Banking Group plc, Shire plc, Ahold, Greene King plc, Dixons Retail plc. The opinions expressed are those of the author.

Figure 2.4 adapted from IFRS Foundation, IASB, *Who we are and what we do*, revised February 2012. Available from http://www.ifrs.org/. Copyright © 2012 IFRS Foundation. All rights reserved. No permission to reproduce or distribute.

Figure 3.3 from Institute of Chartered Accountants in England and Wales (ICAEW), *Reporting with Integrity: Abstract 2007* http://www.icaew.com/. Reproduced with permission of ICAEW.

Figure 17.1 reprinted from *Management Accounting Research*, 1993, 4, Moon, P. and Bates, K., 'Core analysis in strategic performance appraisal', pp139–152, Copyright © 1993, with permission from Elsevier.

The publishers would be pleased to make suitable arrangements to clear permission for material reproduced in this book with any copyright holders whom it has not been possible to contact.

Part 1
Introduction

Chapter 1   Financial reporting and accounting

1

Financial reporting and accounting

➤ Introduction

Financial reporting is concerned with the reporting of financial information about an entity to interested users. For profit-making entities, users require information about their financial position, including liquidity, and about their financial performance, which results in changes in the financial position. For companies and, in particular, public limited companies, financial reporting regulations are complex and onerous.

Financial accounting is about the systems and methods used to produce the financial statements. For all entities the basis of financial accounting is the double-entry bookkeeping system from which the key financial statements—the **statement of financial position** and income statement—are derived. Other financial statements are also produced for the users of different entities, such as the statement of cash flows and the statement of changes in equity.

This chapter provides a summary of the main issues covered in introductory financial accounting texts and courses, and which are concerned with the preparation of the main financial statements. The chapter focuses on limited companies. This will provide a sound foundation on which the complexities of financial reporting can be built in later chapters.

★ Learning objectives

After studying this chapter you will be able to:

- understand who the main users of financial information are and the type of information they require to help them make decisions
- explain the characteristics of financial information which makes it useful
- carry out double-entry bookkeeping for simple transactions
- produce a trial balance from the nominal ledger
- understand the main period-end accounting adjustments required and account for these
- draw up in good form from trial balance, including the main period-end adjustments, a statement of financial position and an income statement for a sole trader and limited company, and, in addition, for a company a statement of changes in equity.

✔ Key issues checklist

- ❏ Financial reporting as the provision of decision-useful information to users—who the users are, what needs they have, and how the financial information is used.
- ❏ Qualitative characteristics of financial information.
- ❏ Financial accounting as the preparation of the financial reports.
- ❏ Underpinning concepts—business entity, historic cost, accruals, and prudence.
- ❏ Accounting systems, including double-entry bookkeeping and the trial balance.
- ❏ Share capital and accounting for dividends.
- ❏ Accounting for accruals and prepayments, depreciation, and bad and doubtful debts.
- ❏ The preparation of the main financial statements—the statement of financial position, the income statement, and, for companies, the statement of changes in equity—from trial balance and including adjustments for accruals and prepayments, depreciation, and bad and doubtful debts.

1.1 Financial reporting

Financial reporting is concerned with the reporting of financial information about an entity to external interested parties. Entities can take many forms. Generally, there are business entities deemed to be concerned with making profits, which range from sole traders, through partnerships and small **companies** to large and complex multinational corporations; and there are entities less concerned with profit-making, such as government organisations, charities, clubs, and societies. Whatever form a business takes, or whatever its legal status, it reports the financial affairs only of itself; this is one of the underpinning concepts of financial reporting—that of the **separate business entity**.

Business entities started as fairly simple affairs funded and run by an individual or small group of individuals, and, in this context, the reporting of financial information needed to satisfy the requirements of the owners only. The owners required information about the financial results and position of the business in which they had invested in order for them to assess their investment and make decisions about future investment. As businesses grew, more investment was required, ownership widened, and management of the business was devolved to others. In this context the owners needed to be able to assess whether this was being carried out satisfactorily. Financial reporting therefore assumed a role of assessment of **stewardship**.

Investment provided by others can be on a perpetual basis (share ownership in companies) or on a fixed-term basis. This latter lender/creditor group also requires financial reports about their investment. Their principal needs differ, however, from the owners, as they mainly require information about the security of their loan—will it be repaid when it is due, will the business pay the servicing charges when due, what security is there if the business defaults on any part of the agreement?

In today's global environment, with the many different types of business entity, there is a wide range of external groups of people who are interested in businesses' financial information. Financial reporting to external users is generally backward-looking, reporting on what has happened in the past. Contrast this with the management of a business, the internal user, who will require financial information in order to run and control their business effectively and efficiently. In addition to financial information about what has happened management will need information which is forward-looking, concerning planning for the future.

So who are the external users and what information do they want? The answer to this lies in asking who deals with business entities and *for what purpose* these users want the information—what are they going to do with it, what course of action will they take having obtained the information, what decisions will they take? This is the key issue that drives financial reporting today—the **decision-usefulness** of financial information.

1.1.1 User groups

Figure 1.1 shows the main external groups of people who are likely to be interested in the financial statements provided by a business entity.

The main decisions they will take using financial information and the information needed to take these decisions are shown in Table 1.1.

1.1.2 Main financial statements

Although it can be seen that different users require different information, by considering mainly the needs of the investors, lenders and other creditors, many of the needs of other users will be satisfied. The common requirements can be summarised as information relating to the financial position and **liquidity** (the ability to have cash available to pay amounts due) of the entity, and information about the financial performance, which results in changes

Figure 1.1 **The external users of financial statements**

in the financial position. Thus, entities provide financial information in three key financial statements to satisfy these information needs. These financial statements need to be produced regularly, and so entities will draw them up at least annually.

Statement of financial position (balance sheet)

This statement shows the resources a business has (**assets**), the claims against those resources (**liabilities**), and the residual ownership interest (**capital**) at a particular point in time.

An asset is a resource controlled by the entity as a result of past events (in other words, the event giving rise to the control of the resource must have happened before the date at which the statement is drawn up) and from which future economic benefits are expected to flow to the entity.

A liability is a present obligation of the entity arising from past events, the settlement of which is expected to result in an outflow of resources embodying economic benefits.

Capital (termed **equity** for a company) is the residual interest in the assets of the entity after deducting all its liabilities and represents the owners' investment in the entity. Capital of a business increases if the entity makes profits and reduces if the entity makes losses. If the owner invests more in the business or takes resources out of the business for personal use, then the capital will also increase and decrease respectively.

These three **elements** are linked by the basic accounting equation:

$$\text{ASSETS} = \text{CAPITAL} + \text{LIABILITIES}$$

The statement of financial position can help users identify the business's financial strengths and weaknesses, its liquidity and solvency, its needs for additional investment, and how successful it will be in obtaining this financing. Information about different types of asset and liability, for example distinguishing those that are continuously circulating as **working capital**

Table 1.1 External users' decisions and the financial information they require

User group	Decisions	Financial information required
Investors	Continuation of investment? Withdrawal of investment? Increase investment?	Return from investment Ability to pay amounts to investors Value of investment Performance of management Risk in investment
Lenders	Lend or not? Interest rate to be charged? Security required?	Ability to repay loans when due Ability to pay interest when due Security for loans
Suppliers	Sale of goods or services to the entity? Prices to be charged?	Ability to pay amounts owing when due Future of business for further supply
Customers	Purchase from the business?	Whether the business is a secure source of supply for repeat purchases and after-sales care
Employees	Continuation of employment?	Long-term future and stability of business Ability to provide appropriate level of remuneration Retirement and other benefits Employment opportunities
Government	HMRC — has the business paid the appropriate taxes it owes? Other departments/agencies—has the business carried out its business properly and made appropriate information available?	Business profits Employee details Various reports and statistics
The public	Variety of decisions, including whether the business should be contributing to the local economy or whether it should be investigated because its practices are harmful to the environment	Various reports and statistics

from those used in the entity's long-term operations, will assist in this analysis. Thus, the statement of financial position usually shows different types of assets and liabilities under four main categories:

Non-current assets   Those assets held for long-term use.

Current assets   Those assets continuously changing as business is conducted.

Current liabilities	Where the obligation is due for settlement within a short time frame, usually taken as one year.
Non-current liabilities	Where the obligation is due for settlement usually after one year.

The basis of valuation of the assets and liabilities is **historic cost**, i.e. for an asset the purchase price, although, as seen in later chapters, certain assets and liabilities are or may be (where a business has a choice) valued using alternative methods.

 ## Example statement

Business XXX

Statement of financial position at accounting period end date

	£
ASSETS	
Non-current assets	
Property, plant and equipment	XX
Intangible assets	XX
	XX
Current assets	
Inventories	XX
Receivables	XX
Prepayments	XX
Bank and cash	XX
	XX
TOTAL ASSETS	**XX**
CAPITAL	XX
LIABILITIES	
Non-current liabilities	
Long-term loans	XX
	XX
Current liabilities	
Bank overdraft	XX
Payables	XX
Accruals	XX
	XX
TOTAL LIABILITIES	XX
TOTAL CAPITAL AND LIABILITIES	**XX**

Income statement (profit and loss account)

This statement shows the financial performance of a business over an accounting period by depicting the effects of transactions and other events when they occur, even if the resulting cash receipts and payments occur at a different time or in a different accounting period. This is termed **accrual accounting**. The income statement includes income earned and net of expenses incurred over the accounting period, resulting in net profit.

Income is increases in the economic benefits during the accounting period arising from revenues from, for example, sales, fees, interest, and rent, and from other gains, such as those arising from the sale of a non-current asset.

Expenses are decreases in economic benefits during the accounting period encompassing expenses that arise in the normal course of business, such as cost of sales, salaries and wages, heat and light, and insurance, and other losses, such as those resulting from flood damage or changes in exchange rates. Expenses are usually grouped under categories such as cost of sales, overhead expenses, and finance costs, with a subsidiary profit being calculated after each category of expenses has been deducted so that different levels of return from differing groups of activities can be ascertained.

Information about the financial performance helps users understand the return that the business has generated from its resources, and provides an indication of how effectively and efficiently these have been managed. Financial performance measured on the accrual basis provides a better basis for assessing the business's past and future performance than information about cash receipts and payments.

 Example statement

Business XXX

Income statement for the accounting period

	£
Revenue	XX
Cost of sales	(XX)
Gross profit	XX
Overhead expenses	(XX)
Profit from operations	XX
Finance costs	(XX)
Profit before tax	XX
Tax*	(XX)
Profit for the accounting period	**XX**

* Note it is only companies, as separate legal entities from their owners, that show the tax charged on their profits in the income statement, as it is the company that is liable for this.

For limited companies the income statement forms part of the **statement of comprehensive income**, which is discussed in Chapter 4.

Statement of cash flows

This statement provides information about the financial performance of a business measured solely in terms of cash receipts and payments. It shows the inflows and outflows of cash, and monetary assets deemed to be equivalent to cash (such as short-term deposits) over the accounting period. The inflows and outflows are classified under different types of activity, resulting in an increase or decrease in **cash and cash equivalents**. The different activities that a business conducts include those related to its main operations, acquiring or selling non-current assets, borrowing or repaying debt, receiving additional investment, and distributing cash to the owners.

Information about cash flows helps users assess the ability of the business to generate future net cash inflows, and evaluate its liquidity or solvency.

The preparation and presentation of a **statement of cash flows** for a company is covered in Chapter 4.

1.1.3 Statement of changes in equity

Limited companies are required to produce an additional financial statement—a **statement of changes in equity**—which provides information about changes in the equity (share capital and reserves) balances over the accounting period.

 Example statement

Company XXX

Statement of changes in equity for the accounting period

	Share capital £	Share premium £	Other reserves £	Retained earnings £	Total £
Balance at start of period	XX	XX	XX	XX	XX
Issues of share capital	XX	XX			XX
Profit for the period				XX	XX
Dividends paid				(XX)	(XX)
Other changes			XX	XX	XX
Balance at end of period	XX	XX	XX	XX	XX

1.2 The difference between profit and cash flow

As indicated in the previous section, financial performance can be measured either in terms of profits according to accrual accounting or in terms of cash flows. Essentially, the difference between the measures is one of timing, in other words in which period the effect of the transaction is included.

 Worked example 1.1: to show the difference between profit and cash flows

On 1 January 20X7 Giles starts his own business by investing £8,000 of his own money and getting a business contact to lend the business £2,000 for 5 years, on which interest will be paid at 5% p.a. Giles rents an office space and pays £1,000 for furniture and equipment. During the first year the business purchases goods for resale for £6,000, of which £5,500 had been paid by 31 December 20X7. The business makes sales of £5,000 on credit and £1,500 for cash, and Giles' credit customers have paid £4,000 by 31 December 20X7. Office running costs paid during the year total £2,200, and Giles takes £1,000 out of the business for personal expenses. At the year end goods which had cost £2,000 are still on hand.

Required:
Draw up financial performance statements for Giles' business for the year ended 31 December 20X7:

(i) On the accruals basis

(ii) On a cash basis.

(i) Giles' business income statement for the year ended 31 December 20X7

		£
Sales	(5,000 + 1500)	6,500
Cost of sales	(6,000 − 2000)	(4,000)
Gross profit		2,500
Overhead expenses		(2,200)
Profit from operations		300
Loan interest	(5% × 2000)	(100)
Net profit		£200

Notes

1 The office furniture and equipment is not included in the income statement as this is an asset (**depreciation**—see section 1.6.2—has been ignored in this example).

2 The cost of sales is the cost of the goods that have actually been sold.

3. The loan interest is included in the income statement even though it has not been paid because it is an expense that has been incurred in the year.

(ii) Giles' business statement of cash flows for the year ended 31 December 20X7

		£	£
Cash receipts			
Owner's investment			8,000
Loan			2,000
From sales	(1,500 + 4,000)		5,500
			15,500
Cash payments			
Furniture and equipment		1,000	
Goods for resale		5,500	
Office running costs		2,200	
Owner's personal expenses		1,000	
			(9,700)
Net cash inflow			£5,800

Notes

1 This statement includes all the year's transactions on a cash basis. The resulting net cash inflow is equivalent to the cash balance at 31 December 20X7, as, in this example, there is no opening cash balance at 1 January 20X7.

2 A company would group cash receipts and payments according to the activity type.

It can be seen that net profit and net cash flow result in very different figures because they are providing different measures of performance and resulting changes in different resources. The statement of financial position summarises the resources of the business at the end of the year.

Giles' business statement of financial position at 31 December 20X7

		£	£
Assets			
Furniture and equipment			1,000
Inventory			2,000
Receivables	(5,000 – 4,000)		1,000
Cash			5,800
			£9,800

Capital			
Initial investment			8,000
Net profit			200
Withdrawals			(1,000)
			7,200
Liabilities			
Loan		2,000	
Loan interest		100	
Payables	(6,000 – 5,500)	500	2,600
			£9,800

1.3 Qualitative characteristics

Users of financial statements need financial statements to help in making their decisions. This means that the information contained in the statements needs to be **relevant** to their decisions and it must **faithfully represent** what it purports to represent. Without these two **fundamental qualitative characteristics**, the information will not be useful.

Some financial information is better than other financial information. For example, information about a business that can be meaningfully compared with another business will be more useful than information that is in a completely different form or prepared according to an alternative basis. Also, information that is supported by facts is more reliable than that based on estimates. So information that is **comparable**, **verifiable**, **timely**, and **understandable** will improve the usefulness of relevant and faithfully represented financial information. These are termed **enhancing qualitative characteristics**. These are illustrated in Figures 1.2 and 1.3, and discussed in sections 1.3.1 to 1.3.6.

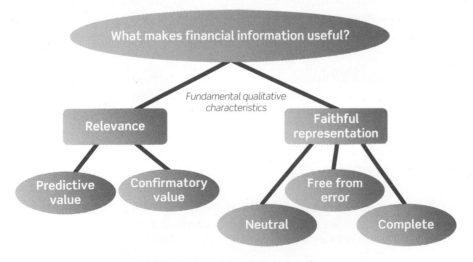

Figure 1.2 Fundamental qualitative characteristics

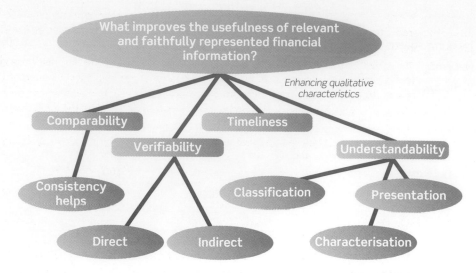

Figure 1.3 Enhancing qualitative characteristics

1.3.1 Relevant financial information

Relevant financial information can make a difference to decisions made by users. Users need information that confirms or changes their evaluations about a business, and that can also be used in making predictions about future outcomes. Thus, for information to be relevant it must have confirmatory value, predictive value, or both.

 Example of relevant information

An investor wishes to invest in a growing company. Relevant financial information would include sales revenues. Revenue information for the past few years can be used for predicting revenues in future years. The current year's revenue can also be compared with revenue predictions that were made in the past for the current year. The results of the comparisons can help the investor correct and improve the processes that are used to make future predictions.

Information is material if its omission or misstatement influences the decision made by a user. So **materiality** is an aspect of relevance that relates to the nature or size, or both, of the information.

 Example of materiality

Relevant financial information for the investor interested in investing in a business that makes a certain level of return on sales will include sales revenues and profit. A business makes sales of £10 million and reports profits at £1,010,000. The return on sales for this business is 10.1% (1.01 million/ 10 million).

If the investor requires this return to be 10%, they would have a very low quantitative materiality threshold, as a reduction in profit of only £10,000 would change their decision. However, an investor requiring a return of only 5% or more would have a much higher materiality threshold.

Another investor may choose not to invest in businesses that trade with other businesses in certain countries for religious or ethical reasons. Consequently, information about the location of the trading partners will affect the investment decision made and this information is deemed material to this investor. However, another investor may not be concerned about this and the information is, therefore, not material.

Materiality is therefore specific to a certain situation or business, and quantitative thresholds or the nature of material items cannot be defined.

1.3.2 Faithful representation

For information to faithfully represent what it purports to represent it should be as complete as possible, neutral, and free from error. Complete information will include all aspects of the item to enable the user to understand what is being depicted and may require some narrative explanations.

 Example of completeness

A complete depiction of a group of non-current assets would include, at a minimum, a description of the nature of the assets in the group (e.g. land and buildings, machinery, fixtures and fittings, motor vehicles), numerical values for each type of asset, and an explanation of what the numerical values represent (e.g. original cost, depreciated cost or fair value).

Neutral information is without bias. In other words, it should not be slanted, weighted, emphasised, de-emphasised, or otherwise manipulated to increase the likelihood that the information will be received favourably or unfavourably by users.

Not all financial information can be completely accurate. Many areas of financial accounting require estimates to be made, for example the expected lives of non-current assets in order to calculate depreciation or the amount owed for electricity at the end of an accounting period. The actual lives or amounts owed may turn out to be different from the estimates made, but this does not mean that the financial information is inaccurate. Users will require financial information to be as free from error as possible, and require information about where and how estimates have been made, and any limitations of the estimating process. Provided that the processes to derive the estimates are reasonable and applied without error, the information presented about these items is still faithful.

1.3.3 Comparable information

Users' decisions involve choosing between alternatives, for example in which company an investment should be made. Information is therefore more useful if it can be compared with similar information about another business. This does not mean that identical or uniform accounting methods have to be used from one business to another, for example all businesses having to depreciate their buildings over 50 years. However, a valid comparison will require the same basis of accounting to be used, and the same information and explanations about like items to be presented from one business to the next.

1.3.4 Verifiable information

Verifiability helps assure users that information faithfully represents what it purports to represent and relates to how sound the evidence for particular information is. The better the evidence, the more reliable the information. Information that is completely verifiable could be, for example, sales revenue for a simple business, where this could be verified by summing all sales invoices and deducting credit notes. Information that is estimated may not be able to be directly verified, and so users will require information about how the estimates have been made and any underlying assumptions.

1.3.5 Timely information

Generally, the older the information is, the less useful it is. However, there may be a trade-off between providing timely information and ensuring it is as verifiable as possible.

 Example of verifiability versus timeliness

A business may have incurred expenses for electricity and telecommunications during the accounting period, but not yet received the actual supplier invoices which would confirm the amounts incurred and owing at the end of the period. There may be pressure from users requiring information about the financial period as early as possible so that they can make decisions. To meet the users' demands, the business will have to make estimates of the expenses incurred—information which could be more verifiable if the business waited until the actual invoices had been received and accounted for.

1.3.6 Understandable information

Information should be classified, characterised, and presented clearly and concisely in order to make it understandable. Financial information about some transactions and items is inherently complex and not easy to understand. Although exclusion of this information may make the financial statements easier to understand, it would also make them incomplete and misleading.

A basic premise in determining how understandable information is that it is assumed that the users have a reasonable knowledge of business and economic activities, and they will review and analyse the information diligently. However, it is acknowledged that even a well-informed user may need to seek expert advice to understand particularly complex financial transactions.

1.3.7 Cost constraint

The provision of financial information imposes costs on businesses, which are borne, ultimately, by investors through lower returns. These users want high quality, useful information to enable them make the best decisions possible. In the context of investments in publicly traded companies on capital markets, this will result in more efficient functioning of these markets and a lower cost of capital for the economy as a whole. Hence, there has to be a trade-off between the benefits of businesses reporting particular information and thoroughly considering its qualitative characteristics with the costs incurred to provide and use such information.

1.4 Financial accounting

Financial accounting is concerned with the preparation of financial statements. Methods have been developed over centuries in order to record financial transactions and produce these statements in a systematic manner.

Figure 1.4 provides a representation of a simple accounting system. This type of system would not only produce two of the key financial statements, the statement of financial position and the income statement, but also provide detailed information about some of the aggregate figures that would be included in these statements. This would aid management in running and controlling the business.

The heart of the accounting system is the **nominal ledger** from which the financial statements are drawn up. Every system will include a nominal ledger. Most basic accounting systems will also include receivables and payables ledgers, which provide details of the account

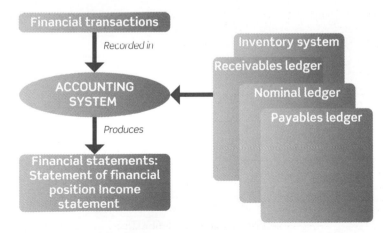

Figure 1.4 The financial accounting system

balances of all customers and suppliers, plus, if the business trades goods, some form of inventory control system.

1.4.1 The nominal ledger

The nominal ledger comprises all the accounts of the business in which are recorded all the individual financial transactions. Each account is effectively labelled as being one of five types of account, with the type of account determining whether its balance appears in the statement of financial position or in the income statement. The types of account and examples of different accounts corresponding to the label are as follows.

Statement of financial position accounts

Account type	Examples of accounts
Asset	Property, plant, and machinery; motor vehicles; computer software; inventory; accounts receivable; bank and cash
Liability	Bank overdraft, accounts payable, loan
Capital	Share capital, share premium, retained profits and losses, dividends paid

Income statement accounts

Account type	Examples of accounts
Income	Sales, rent receivable, interest receivable
Expense	Wages and salaries, heat and light, telephone, insurance, motor expenses, depreciation, bad debts, interest

Each nominal ledger account has two sides—a **debit** side and a **credit** side:

| DEBIT | CREDIT |

1.4.2 Double-entry bookkeeping

Transactions are recorded in the accounts in the nominal ledger by **double-entry bookkeeping**. This method, which has been in existence for centuries, recognises that every transaction affects two (or more) accounts. If only two accounts are affected by the transaction, one account will be debited and the other account will be credited with the same monetary amount. If more than two accounts are affected, the total of the debit entries will equal the total of the credit entries. This ensures that the statement of financial position equation always balances:

$$ASSETS = CAPITAL + LIABILITIES$$

The rules of double-entry are shown in Figure 1.5.

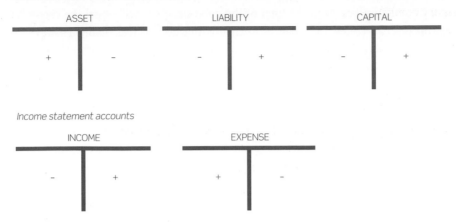

Statement of financial position accounts

ASSET   +   –

LIABILITY   –   +

CAPITAL   –   +

Income statement accounts

INCOME   –   +

EXPENSE   +   –

Figure 1.5 The rules of double-entry bookkeeping

A '**+**' indicates an account *increases* as a result of the transaction. This will mean a debit or credit entry, dependent upon whether the '**+**' is on the debit or credit side of the account.

A '**–**' indicates an account *decreases* as a result of the transaction. This will mean a debit or credit entry, dependent upon whether the '**–**' is on the debit or credit side of the account.

 Example of double-entry bookkeeping

	Transaction	Accounts increased or decreased	Resulting double-entry
1	The owner of a business pays £10,000 into the business bank account	Capital increases and bank increases	Debit: bank Credit: capital
2	The business purchases a motor vehicle on credit	Motor vehicles increase and accounts payable increase	Debit: motor vehicles Credit: accounts payable
3	The business sells goods on credit	Sales increase and accounts receivable increase	Debit: accounts receivable Credit: sales
4	The business pays wages	Wages increase and bank decreases	Debit: wages Credit: bank
5	The business pays a supplier from whom goods had been purchased on credit	Accounts payable decrease and bank decreases	Debit: accounts payable Credit: bank
6	The business receives a loan	Bank increases and loan increases	Debit: bank Credit: loan

1.4.3 The trial balance

When the financial statements are required to be prepared, businesses will determine the balance on each account—a net debit or a net credit. A listing of all account balances, which is called a **trial balance**, is drawn up.

The trial balance is a half-way house in the preparation process. If double-entry book-keeping has taken place, then the total of the debit balances will equal the credit balances, and businesses can review the balances to ensure they appear reasonable. However, the trial balance will not show whether the recording of transactions has been completely accurately done, for example a transaction may have been omitted entirely, or the wrong accounts may have been debited or credited.

1.4.4 Financial statements

As each account is labelled as either a statement of financial position account or an income statement account, these financial statements can be drawn up from the trial balance.

 Worked example 1.2: to show the drawing up of financial statements from a trial balance

Suraya's business trial balance at 31 December 20X8 is as follows:

	Debit £	Credit £
Capital		101,177
Plant and machinery	56,152	
Fixtures and fittings	35,040	
Inventories at 1 January 20X8*	15,450	
Receivables	43,415	
Payables		29,327
Bank		10,526
Sales		296,483
Purchases*	175,962	
Rent	6,397	
Heat and light	26,730	
Wages and salaries	36,389	
Insurance	11,978	
Drawings	30,000	
	437,513	437,513

Inventories at 31 December 20X8 were counted and valued at £16,070.*

* Note this business has recorded the inventories it purchased during the year in a purchases account, which is an expense account. A separate inventory account is maintained which is a statement of financial position account. The balance on this account in the trial balance represents inventories at the start of the accounting period. Inventories on hand at the end of the year have to be counted, valued, and accounted for as an adjustment to the trial balance figures.

Required:

Draw up the income statement for the year ended 31 December 20X8 and the statement of financial position at that date for Suraya's business.

Identifying each account in the trial balance as either an income statement account (income and expense accounts) or a statement of financial position account (asset, liability, and capital accounts) gives:

	Debit £	Credit £	
Capital		101,177	
Plant and machinery	56,152		
Fixtures and fittings	35,040		
Inventories	15,450		
Receivables	43,415		Income
Payables		29,327	statement
Bank		10,526	accounts
Sales		296,483	
Purchases	175,962		
Rent	6,397		
Heat and light	26,730		
Wages and salaries	36,389		
Insurance	11,978		
Drawings	30,000		
	437,513	437,513	

Inventories at 31 December 20X8 were counted and valued at £16,070.

	Debit £	Credit £	
Capital		101,177	
Plant and machinery	56,152		
Fixtures and fittings	35,040		
Inventories	15,450		Statement
Receivables	43,415		of financial
Payables		29,327	position
Bank		10,526	accounts
Sales		296,483	
Purchases	175,962		
Rent	6,397		

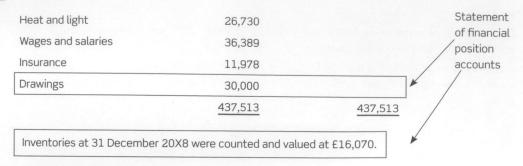

Heat and light	26,730	
Wages and salaries	36,389	
Insurance	11,978	
Drawings	30,000	
	437,513	437,513

Statement of financial position accounts

Inventories at 31 December 20X8 were counted and valued at £16,070.

The financial statements are drawn up as follows.

Suraya's business

Income statement for the year ended 31 December 20X8

	£	£
Sales		296,483
Cost of sales		
Opening inventories	15,450	
Purchases	175,962	
	191,412	
Closing inventories	(16,070)	(175,342)
Gross profit		121,141
Expenses		
Rent	6,397	
Heat and light	26,730	
Wages and salaries	36,389	
Insurance	11,978	
		(81,494)
Net profit		£ 39,647

Suraya's business

Statement of financial position at 31 December 20X8

	£	£
Non-current assets		
Plant and machinery		56,152
Fixtures and fittings		35,040
		91,192

Current assets		
Inventories	16,070	
Receivables	43,415	
		59,485
Total assets		£ 150,677
Capital		
Opening capital		101,177
Net profit for year		39,647
		140,824
Drawings		30,000
		110,824
Current liabilities		
Bank overdraft	10,526	
Payables	29,327	
		39,853
Total capital and liabilities		£ 150,677

1.5 Limited companies' financial statements

Worked example 1.2 demonstrates financial statements for a sole trader. Many businesses start out in the form of a sole trader, but, as they grow, they incorporate as a **private limited company**. The word 'limited' or 'Ltd' will appear in the business name. This means the capital of the business will be in the form of share capital and there can be more than one owner, called **shareholders**, who will each hold a number of shares in the company.

There are many reasons why businesses incorporate, but the most important of these is probably the limited liability status. This means a company has a separate legal identity from the owners and the owners' liability is limited to the amount they have invested. One consequence of this is that if the company collapses with amounts owing, the creditors cannot pursue the shareholders personally to settle the company's debts.

If a private limited company wishes to raise capital on stock markets and have its shares traded publicly, it will need to fulfil certain statutory requirements, register as a **public limited company**, or 'plc', and then apply to be listed. This is an onerous undertaking, as there will be increased scrutiny of the company and additional information, financial and otherwise, will have to be made public.

The basic underpinning financial accounting for private and public companies is the same. In the following sections, unless specifically stated, references to companies apply, therefore, to both private and public companies.

1.5.1 Company financial accounting

Double-entry bookkeeping and the basic format of the financial statements is the same for companies as for sole traders. However, there are some important differences which arise from the limited liability status.

1   Companies issue shares to their investors. The statement of financial position becomes:

$$ASSETS = EQUITY + LIABILITIES$$

Where equity consists of **share capital** and **reserves**, one of which is **retained earnings**, which accumulates the profits and losses the company makes.

(See further details of shares in section 1.5.2.)

2   There is separation of ownership and management. The shareholders are the owners and they appoint **directors** to run the company (although directors are often also shareholders in the company they are managing). The shareholders' return is in the form of **dividends**, which are paid out of retained earnings.

3   Directors are employees of company and receive remuneration, which is shown as an expense in the income statement.

4   Companies have to pay tax on the profits they make, which are chargeable to corporation tax. The tax is shown as a reduction of profits in the income statement.

5   Companies have to prepare additional financial statements for reporting purposes—a statement of changes in equity and a statement of cash flows.

6   Companies' legislation is extensive and, in the UK, is covered by the Companies Act 2006. Part of this relates to financial statements. In addition, all companies have to follow **accounting standards** when preparing their financial statements for reporting purposes. Private limited companies follow UK financial reporting standards (called **Statements of Standard Accounting Practice (SSAPs)** or **Financial Reporting Standards (FRSs)**); public listed companies follow international financial reporting standards (called **International Accounting Standards (IASs)** or **International Financial Reporting Standards (IFRSs)**). It cannot be emphasised enough how detailed and complex these financial reporting requirements are.

(See Chapter 2 for further details.)

1.5.2 Shares and share capital

There are two types of share capital: **equity (or ordinary) shares** and **preference shares**. A comparison of these two types can be summarised as shown in Table 1.2.

Table 1.2 Equity and preference shares

Equity shares	Preference shares
Ordinary shareholders are ultimate owners of company	There are two main types of preference share: • **irredeemable preference shares**, which is part of the equity • **redeemable preference shares**, which is treated as a non-current liability
A vote is attached to each share	No votes are attached to shares
There is no entitlement to a dividend—the amount of dividend can vary	Most preference shares give entitlement to a fixed rate dividend

The **authorised share capital** is the maximum amount of share capital that can be issued. It is disclosed in the financial statements.

When a company is first formed the initial value at which shares are issued is called the **nominal (or par) value**.

 Example of the nominal value of shares

Four friends decide to form a company. They each agree to supply £5,000 to provide the initial capital. What is the nominal value of the equity share capital?

The nominal value can be chosen as any amount, so it could be set at £5,000 per share. Each friend would therefore hold one share. However, this may not be the best nominal value to choose as the shareholders will be unable to sell part of their investment— it will be all or nothing. All new issues of (the same class of) shares will also have to be in units of £5,000, which is a large amount per investor. It is better to have share capital in small units, for example 20,000 shares of £1 nominal value, or 40,000 50p shares, or 200,000 10p shares, etc.

Once a company starts trading (and making profits), the value of shares at which they can be traded and issued may increase. This value is called the **market value**.

 Example of share premium

A company with 50,000 £1 equity shares, whose market value is £1.50, wishes to raise £300,000 by a new issue of the same class of share.

How many shares will the company issue, and how would this be accounted for?

No. of shares issued   = $\dfrac{£\,300,000}{£1.50}$

          =   200,000

Each share is issued at a premium of 50p:

	Per share £	Total £
Share capital	1.00	200,000
Share premium	0.50	100,000
Cash raised	1.50	300,000

Share premium is a reserve which is part of the equity in the company.

1.5.3 Dividends

Dividends are paid out of **distributable profits**. They may be paid in two stages—interim dividends are paid during the year, usually after half-year results become available, and final, or proposed, dividends are paid after the year end.

The description of preference shares indicates the level of fixed dividend to be paid, for example 6% £1 irredeemable preference shares means each preference shareholder will receive 6p per share for the year. Dividends on equity shares are paid at the directors' discretion and, for public companies, there are large policy implications surrounding this decision which may affect the market value of the company.

 Example of the calculation of ordinary and preference dividends

A company whose issued share capital is:

    £200,000 in 50p equity shares

    £100,000 in 8% £1 irredeemable preference shares

proposes the following dividends:

- the preference dividend
- a dividend of 5p per equity share.

What are the total dividends proposed?

	£
Preference dividend	
8% × £100,000	8,000
Ordinary dividend	
No. of equity shares × 5p	
(200,000 × 2 = 400,000) × 5p	20,000
Total dividend	28,000

Dividends paid during a financial year are shown as a reduction in retained earnings in the statement of changes in equity.

Redeemable preference shares are, in essence, the same as a long-term loan, as the amount invested in the company will eventually have to be paid back to the shareholder (in other words, redeemed) and there is a fixed rate of dividend. They are therefore accounted for as a liability on the statement of financial position and, to match this classification, dividends paid on these shares are accounted for as a finance cost in the income statement.

1.6 Accruals principle

1.6.1 Accruals and prepayments

As explained in the previous sections the income statement shows income earned net of expenses incurred over the accounting period, resulting in net profit. Income and expenses are included according to the accruals principle, that is when the underlying transaction occurs, and not on the basis of cash receipts and payments. The principle results in the expenses included in the income statement being those which match with the revenues generated by them and which match to the relevant accounting period. This leads to some expenses having to be accounted for before they are actually paid (accrued expenses or accruals) or expenditure having to be carried forward to a subsequent accounting period (prepaid expenses or prepayments).

 Worked example 1.3: of an accrual

Steyn Ltd has a year end of 31 December. The company has paid electricity bills covering the period 1 January to 31 October 20X8 amounting to £450. On 8 February 20X9 the business receives a bill for £150 covering the period 1 November 20X8 to 31 January 20X9.

Required:
What is the electricity expense (incurred) in 20X8?

Steyn Ltd will have to estimate the proportion of the £150 bill that relates to the financial year ended 31 December 20X8, i.e. how much electricity was incurred in the two months November and December 20X8. Unless there is other strong evidence to suggest otherwise, a time apportionment is considered a reasonable estimate, hence $2/3 \times £150 = £100$ will be estimated as the electricity expense for these two months. Figure 1.6 shows this calculation.

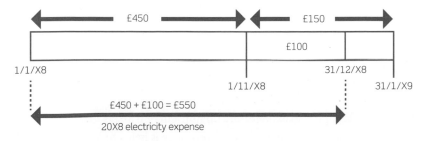

Figure 1.6 A timeline to time-apportion expenses

This £100 is owed at 31 December 20X8 and is therefore a liability. It is an accrual and will be included in current liabilities on the statement of financial position.

It can be seen from Example 1.3 that the effect of accounting for an accrual is to increase the expense and to show a liability. This translates into double-entry bookkeeping as:

Debit   Expense account

Credit   Accrual

 ## Worked example 1.4: of a prepayment

Steyn Ltd also makes rent payments of £5,000 during the year ended 31 December 20X8, which covers the period 1 January 20X8–31 March 20X9.

Required:

What is the rent expense for the year 20X8?

Steyn Ltd needs to determine how much of the total payment relates to 20X8. The total payment covers 15 months, of which 12/15 relates to 20X8: $12/15 \times £5,000 = £4,000$. Figure 1.7 shows this calculation.

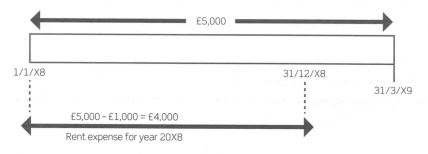

Figure 1.7 A timeline to time-apportion expenses

£1,000 of the payment relates to 20X9 and needs to be carried forward as a prepayment. It is an asset as the business will gain future economic benefits from the occupancy of the premises and will be included in current assets on the statement of financial position.

This example shows that the effect of accounting for a prepayment is to decrease the expense and to show an asset. This translates into double-entry bookkeeping as:

Debit   Prepayment

Credit   Expense account

1.6.2 Depreciation

The accruals principle applies to expenditure on non-current assets. Each time a non-current asset is used the cost of this is matched to the revenues it helps to generate. The accounting method used to do this is called depreciation and it can be thought of as spreading the cost of the asset over the years it is used, as shown in Figure 1.8.

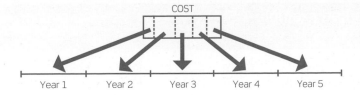

Figure 1.8 Depreciation: spreading the cost over the years a non-current asset is used

The application of depreciation results in non-current assets carrying amounts on the statement of financial position being reduced each accounting period. In the nominal ledger accounts, an income statement depreciation account records the expense and an additional statement of financial position accumulated depreciation account is used to record the total depreciation written off each asset. The double-entry to record annual depreciation is therefore:

Debit   Depreciation expense

  Credit   Accumulated depreciation

At the end of an accounting period, the (credit) balance on the accumulated depreciation account is netted off with the (debit) balance on the asset's cost account to give the carrying amount, called the **net book value**. Note, the net book value does not represent any other value, such as market value or resale value—it is the residual **carrying amount** of the asset after deducting accumulated depreciation.

In order to apply depreciation a business needs to determine an asset's cost, and estimate its expected useful life and expected residual value. This has to be done for all assets except for freehold land, where the estimated life is deemed to be unlimited. Freehold land is therefore not depreciated and, where a business has freehold property as a non-current asset, the buildings and land costs have to be separated.

The next question is how the asset is going to be used, as this will determine the depreciation method to be used. Although there are a number of methods of depreciation, the two main methods used by businesses are:

Straight-line   where the asset is used the same every year

Reducing balance   where the use of the asset reduces over the years

Less common methods include sum-of-digits and units of production. A business should select the method that best reflects the pattern of usage of an asset and, once selected, it should be applied consistently from one accounting period to the next unless altered circumstances justify a change.

1.6.3 Straight-line depreciation

A fixed amount is written off the carrying amount of the asset each year; in other words, the depreciation expense each year is the same.

Worked example 1.5: to show the calculation of straight-line depreciation

Rochford & Sons purchases a machine that costs £50,000. The business estimates it will use the machine for 10 years and, at the end of this time, the machine will be sold for £5,000.

Required:

Calculate the annual depreciation expense and the accounting effect of the depreciation.

$$\text{Annual depreciation expense} = \frac{\text{Cost} - \text{Estimated residual value}}{\text{Estimated life}}$$

$$= \frac{£50,000 - £5,000}{10}$$

$$= £4,500$$

Straight-line depreciation can also be expressed as a percentage, which is derived from the life. So this machine is depreciated at 10% straight-line:

$$\text{Annual depreciation expense} = 10\% \times (£50,000 - £5,000)$$

$$= £4,500$$

Statement of financial position balances will be as follows:

	Cost £	Accumulated depreciation £	Net book value £
Year 1	50,000		
Depreciation expense		4,500	45,500
Year 2			
Depreciation expense		4,500	
		9,000	41,000
Year 3			
Depreciation expense, etc.		4,500	
		13,500	36,500
Year 10			
Depreciation expense		4,500	
		45,000	5,000

1.6.4 Reducing balance depreciation

Under this method a fixed percentage is written off the reduced carrying amount (net book value) of the asset each year. This results in the annual depreciation expense reducing each year.

A business requires the cost and estimates of the expected life and residual value in order to calculate the fixed percentage from the formula:

$$1 - \sqrt[n]{(r/c)}$$

Where c is the cost, r is the estimated residual value, and n is the estimated life.

Given the percentage, the accounting is the same as for straight-line depreciation.

Worked example 1.6: to show the calculation of reducing balance depreciation

Rochford & Sons also purchases a motor vehicle for £20,000. Depreciation is to be charged at the rate of 25% on the reducing balance.

Required:
Calculate the annual depreciation expense and the accounting effect of the depreciation.

	Cost £	Accumulated depreciation £	Net book value £
Year 1	20,000		
Depreciation expense (25% × 20,000)		5,000	15,000
Year 2			
Depreciation expense (25% × 15,000)		3,750	
		8,750	11,250
Year 3			
Depreciation expense (25% × 11,250) etc.		2,813	
		11,563	8,437

Note the annual depreciation expense reducing each year.

1.6.5 Disposal of non-current assets

If a non-current asset is sold, the difference between the sale proceeds and the net book value of the asset gives rise to a profit or loss on sale, which is included in the income statement.

The double-entry bookkeeping requires a disposals account, to which is transferred the net book value (cost and accumulated depreciation) of the asset disposed of and the sales proceeds. The balance on this account will be the profit or loss on disposal.

1 Transfer original cost of asset to a disposals account

Debit	Disposals	} with original cost
Credit	Asset cost	}

2 Transfer accumulated depreciation to disposals account

Debit	Accumulated depreciation	} with accumulated
Credit	Disposals	} depreciation

3 Account for proceeds (if any)

Debit	Bank
Credit	Disposals

Worked example 1.7: to show the accounting for the disposal of a non-current asset

The balances on the machinery account and machinery accumulated depreciation accounts of Haslam Ltd at 1 January 20X9 were £58,000 and £32,000 respectively. The business scraps a piece of machinery on 31 October 20X9 and sells the parts for £1,000. The machinery had originally cost £6,000 on 1 January 20X3. The business's depreciation policy for machinery is straight-line at 10%, with a full year's depreciation charged in the year of acquisition and none in the year of disposal.

Required:

Show the double-entry bookkeeping for the disposal of the machinery and the resulting figures that would appear in the financial statements of Haslam Ltd for 20X9.

The double-entry bookkeeping for the disposal is as follows:

1 Transfer original cost of asset to a disposals account

		£	£
Dr	Disposals	6,000	
Cr	Asset cost		6,000

2 Transfer accumulated depreciation to disposals account

		£	£
Dr	Accumulated depreciation	3,600	
Cr	Disposals		3,600

Accumulated depreciation at date of sale = 6 years × (10% × £6,000)

3 Account for proceeds

		£	£
Dr	Bank	1,000	
Cr	Disposals		1,000

The balance on the disposals account is the profit or loss on disposal—in this case a loss of £1,400—which is an expense in the 20X9 income statement.

Disposals account

Cost	6,000	Accumulated depreciation	3,600
		Proceeds	1,000
		Loss on disposal	1,400
	6,000		6,000

Assuming there are no further transactions in machinery in 20X9, the remaining machinery is depreciated in the usual way:

		£	£
Dr	Depreciation expense	5,200	
Cr	Accumulated depreciation		5,200

Depreciation = 10% × Cost of remaining assets

= 10% × (58,000 – 6,000)

The resulting balances on the machinery cost and accumulated depreciation accounts are as follows:

Cost				**Accumulated depreciation**			
Bal. b/f	58,000	Disposal	6,000	Disposal	3,600	Bal. b/f	32,000
		Bal. c/f	52,000	Bal. c/f	33,600	Deprecn.	5,200
	58,000		58,000		37,200		37,200
Bal. b/f	52,000					Bal. b/f	33,600

The net book value of the machinery at 31 December 20X9 – 52,000 – 33,600 = £18,400.

1.7 Prudence

A business that overstates its profits or the value of its net assets does not provide useful information to users. For many years the fundamental concept of **prudence** underpinned financial accounting in order to counter the excessive over-optimism of some owners or managers in reporting financial results and positions. Broadly, this stated that where estimations were made, or choices existed, businesses should choose lower values when considering assets and profits, and higher values when considering losses and liabilities.

However, businesses have used the prudence concept in certain situations to undervalue net assets and profits, and, in the same way that overvaluation of business results and financial positions are undesirable, undervaluation of these amounts does not provide useful information to users.

Prudence has not been included in the discussion of the characteristics that make financial information useful earlier in the chapter as, essentially, it creates bias. For financial information to be represented faithfully, the values placed on assets and liabilities should be realistic and honest—in certain circumstances this may mean that being conservative about estimates could provide more useful information to some users.

1.7.1 Receivables, and bad and doubtful debts

For accounts receivable to be represented faithfully, a business needs to consider that the amount does not only represent an amount owed by a customer or other party, but also that it represents the actual economic benefit expected to flow to it in the future, in other words how much cash is expected to be received. If there is any question over this amount then the business will need to adjust the amount shown as receivables.

Firstly, any debts that are definitely not going to be received are written off—these are termed bad debts and are included as an expense. The double-entry bookkeeping is:

Debit   Bad debt expense

  Credit   Accounts receivable

Secondly, the business must then take an honest review of its remaining receivables and, if there is doubt about whether any amounts will be collected, the accounts receivable figure must be reduced to reflect this. In practice, a business will usually identify specific customers and/or invoices over which there is doubt, but it may consider its history of debt collection and estimate that there will be a certain percentage of debts that will probably not be collected. A doubtful debt, whether specific or general, is a subjective judgement.

Doubtful debts are not written off receivables. Instead, the accounting requires the creation of a provision for doubtful debts account, which records both specific and general provisions, and whose balance is netted off with accounts receivable in the statement of financial position. The balance on the provision account is maintained at the required amount, with any changes passing through the income statement bad debt expense. The double-entry bookkeeping is as follows:

1   To create a provision for doubtful debts
    Debit   Bad debt expense
     Credit   Provision for doubtful debts

2   To increase the provision for doubtful debts in subsequent accounting periods
    Debit   Bad debt expense   } with increase only
     Credit   Provision for doubtful debts   }

3   To decrease the provision for doubtful debts in subsequent accounting periods
    Debit   Provision for doubtful debts   } with decrease only
     Credit   Bad debt expense   }

Worked example 1.8: to show the accounting for bad and doubtful debts

(a) Barney starts trading on 1 January 20X2 and, during the year ended 31 December 20X2, makes total credit sales of £110,000 and collects cash from credit customers amounting to £95,900. The following debts are found to be bad and are written off on the dates shown:

30 April	Customer A	£220
31 August	Customer B	£130
31 October	Customer C	£50

On 31 December 20X2 the schedule of receivables, amounting to £13,700, is examined and it is decided to make a general provision for doubtful debts of £440.

(b) During 20X3 Barney makes credit sales of £205,600 and receives payments from credit customers of £192,400. The business also writes off bad debts totalling £1,200. At 31 December 20X3 accounts receivable total £25,700. Barney has identified two customers owing £500 in total as doubtful and decides to make a general provision of 5% against the remainder.

Required:

Show the accounting for Barney's bad and doubtful debts, and the resulting figures which will appear in the year's financial statements for the years 20X2 and 20X3.

(a) 20X2

On the dates the business identifies the bad debts it will record the write-offs as follows:

		£	£
Debit	Bad debt expense	400 (in total)	
Credit	Accounts receivable		400

At 31 December 20X2, the business will create a provision for doubtful debts as follows:

		£	£
Debit	Bad debt expense	440	
Credit	Provision for doubtful debts		440

The resulting figures in the financial statements at 31 December 20X2 relating to receivables, and bad and doubtful debts will be as follows:

Income statement

	£
Bad debts written off	400
Provision for doubtful debts	440
Bad debt expense	840

Statement of financial position

Current assets:	£	£
Inventory		X
Accounts receivable	13,700	
Less: provision for doubtful debts	(440)	
	13,260	
Prepayments		X
Bank		X

The amount expected to be collected from customers

(b) 20X3

The bad debts will be written off as follows:

		£	£
Debit	Bad debt expense	1,200	
Credit	Accounts receivable		1,200

At 31 December 20X3 the business calculates how much the provision for doubtful debts should be, and whether this increases or decreases the provision already maintained.

	£
Specific provision	500
General provision 5% × (25,700 – 500)	1,260
Provision for doubtful debts required at 31 December 20X3	1,760
Provision for doubtful debts at 31 December 20X2	440
Increase in provision	1,320

This increase will be recorded as follows:

		£	£
Debit	Bad debt expense	1,320	
Credit	Provision for doubtful debts		1,320

The resulting figures in the financial statements at 31 December 20X3 relating to receivables, and bad and doubtful debts will be as follows:

Income statement

	£
Bad debts written off	1,200
Increase in provision for doubtful debts	1,320
Bad debt expense	2,520

Statement of financial position

Current assets:	£	£
Inventory		X
Accounts receivable	25,700	
Less: provision for doubtful debts	(1,760)	
		23,940
Prepayments		X
Bank		X

1.8 Pulling everything together

The previous sections on accruals and prepayments, depreciation, and bad and doubtful debts provide examples of accounting adjustments that businesses have to make every time they require an income statement and statement of financial position to be drawn up. Many other adjustments will be required, some of which may result from correction of errors and all will have to be posted to the nominal ledger by means of a journal entry (i.e. the double-entry bookkeeping), so that the financial statements are in accordance with the books and records. Other accounting adjustments will be explained in subsequent chapters as more detailed financial reporting requirements in specific areas are examined.

However, at this stage, in order to provide a sound basis for an understanding of how three of the main financial statements are prepared, a comprehensive example follows. This requires the preparation of an income statement, statement of changes in equity and statement of financial position for a company from trial balance, and including main period-end accounting adjustments. Further examples are provided in the end-of-chapter exercises.

 Worked example 1.9: to show the preparation of financial statements from trial balance including year end adjustments

The following trial balance was extracted from the books of Mayfield Ltd at 31 December 20X5:

	Dr	Cr
	£000	£000
Issued share capital:		
400,000 50p equity shares		200
100,000 10% £1 irredeemable preference shares		100
Share premium		40
Retained earnings		90
Equity dividend paid	48	
Preference dividend paid	4	

Administration expenses	150	
Selling and distribution expenses	170	
Interest expense	6	
Investment income		8
Accounts receivable	80	
Provision for doubtful debts at 1 January 20X5		6
Accounts payable		56
Short term investments	70	
Non-current assets cost:		
Premises	400	
Machinery	160	
Motor vehicles	64	
10% Loan		120
Accumulated depreciation at 1 January 20X5		
Premises		40
Machinery		48
Motor vehicles		24
Inventory at 1 January 20X5	42	
Cash and bank	32	
Purchases	144	
Sales		638
	1,370	1,370

Adjustments for the following are required at the year end:

1 The closing inventory was valued at cost at £48,000

2 Salesmen's commission, which is included in selling and distribution expenses, for December of £10,000 had not yet been accounted for

3 Administrative expenses included a payment of £12,000 for insurance for the period 1 September 20X5 to 31 August 20X6

4 The loan was taken out in 20X3 and is due for repayment in 20X8. Its interest rate is fixed at 10%

5 The company's depreciation policies are as follows:

Buildings	Straight-line over 20 years
Machinery	Straight-line at 20%
Motor vehicles	25% on reducing balance

The buildings cost is £200,000

6 It was decided to maintain the provision for doubtful debts at 5% of year end accounts receivable

7 The directors propose to:

(a) Provide for £20,000 corporation tax

(b) Pay the remaining preference dividend

(c) Pay a final dividend on the equity shares of 10p per share.

Required:

Prepare Mayfield Ltd's:

(i) Income statement for the year ended 31 December 20X5

(ii) Statement of changes in equity for the year ended 31 December 20X5

(iii) Statement of financial position at 31 December 20X5.

Solution

Step 1

Identify which accounts in the trial balance belong in which financial statement, for example share capital balances are statement of financial position balances and will be shown in equity. Note that the preference shares are irredeemable, so they will be part of equity.

Step 2

Work out what adjustments are required in respect of the additional information.

1 This is closing inventory and will be included in costs of sales in the income statement and current assets in the statement of financial position.

2 This is an expense relating to the year which has not yet been paid—it is an accrual.

		£	£
Dr	Selling and distribution expenses	10,000	
Cr	Accruals		10,000

3 Part of the period covered by the insurance falls in the following financial year, hence this is a prepayment. The prepayment is calculated as $8/12 \times 12,000 = £8,000$. Insurance is an administration expense.

		£	£
Dr	Prepayments	8,000	
Cr	Administration expenses		8,000

4 Total loan interest for the year $= 10\% \times 120,000 = £12,000$. The trial balance interest expense account shows that only £6,000 has been paid and accounted for. Therefore, the remaining £6,000 must be accrued.

		£	£
Dr	Interest expense	6,000	
Cr	Accruals		6,000

5   Depreciation for the year needs calculating:

Buildings	200,000/20	=	£10,000
Machinery	20% × 160,000	=	£32,000
Motor vehicles	25% × (64,000 − 24,000)	=	£10,000

The adjustment will be:

		£	£
Dr	Depreciation expense	52,000	
Cr	Accumulated depreciation		
	Premises		10,000
	Machinery		32,000
	Motor vehicles		10,000

6   Provision for doubtful debts required at 31 December 20X5:

	£
5% × 80,000	4,000
Provision for doubtful debts at 1 January 20X5	6,000
Decrease in provision	2,000

The adjustment required is:

		£	£
Dr	Provision for doubtful debts	2,000	
Cr	Bad debts expense		2,000

7   (a) The corporation tax is a deduction from profits shown in the income statement and, as it will not have been paid yet, it is also a liability to be shown in the statement of financial position:

		£	£
Dr	Tax expense	20,000	
Cr	Tax liability		20,000

(b) and (c) The equity and preference dividends proposed at the year end are not accounted for in the 20X5 financial statements. It is only the dividends paid in the year, and shown in the trial balance, that are included in the statement of changes in equity.

Step 3

Draw up pro-forma financial statements and insert the figures from the trial balance, adjusted, as necessary, by step 2.

Mayfield Ltd

Income statement for the year ended 31 December 20X5

	£000	£000
Sales		638
Cost of sales		
Opening inventory	42	
Purchases	144	
	186	
Closing inventory	(48)	
		138
Gross profit		500
Expenses		
Administration expenses (150 – 8)	142	
Selling and distribution (170 + 10)	180	
Decrease in provision for doubtful debts	(2)	
Depreciation		
Premises	10	
Machinery	32	
Motor vehicles	10	
		(372)
Profit from operations		128
Investment income		8
Interest expense		(12)
Profit before tax		124
Corporation tax		(20)
Profit for the year		104

Mayfield Ltd

Statement of changes in equity for the year ended 31 December 20X5

	Equity share capital £000	Preference share capital £000	Share premium £000	Retained earnings £000	Total £000
Balance at 1 Jan 20X5	200	100	40	90	430
Profit for the year				104	104
Dividends paid					
Equity				(48)	(48)
Preference				(4)	(4)
Balance at 31 Dec 20X5	200	100	40	142	482

Mayfield Ltd

Statement of financial position at 31 December 20X5

	£000	£000	£000
Non-current assets	Cost	Acc depn	NBV
Premises	400	50	350
Machinery	160	80	80
Motor vehicles	64	34	30
	624	164	460
Current assets			
Inventory		48	
Accounts receivable	80		
Less: provision for doubtful debts	(4)		
		76	
Short-term investments		70	
Prepayments		8	
Cash and bank		32	
			234
Total assets			694
Equity			
Equity share capital			200
Preference share capital			100
			300
Share premium			40
Retained earnings			142
			482
Non-current liabilities			
Loan			120
Current liabilities			
Accounts payable		56	
Accruals	(10 + 6)	16	
Taxation		20	
			92
Total equity and liabilities			694

Summary of key points

Businesses report financial information to interested users in the form of standard financial statements, the main statements being:

- the statement of financial position, which shows the resources a business has, the claims against those resources, and the residual interest of the investors at a particular point in time
- the income statement, which shows the net profit the business has made over a period of time
- the statement of cash flows, which shows the cash inflows and outflows of a business over a period of time, resulting in a net increase or decrease in the cash or near-cash resources
- the statement of changes in equity (companies only), which shows the changes in the investors' interest over a period of time.

These statements provide most users with the financial information that they require in order to make decisions about their involvement with the business. In particular, they provide the principal users of company financial statements, in other words the investors (shareholders), potential investors, lenders, and other creditors, with information to help them assess the returns that they can expect from their investment and changes in the value of their investment. In order for financial information to be truly useful, it should exhibit certain characteristics, the fundamental ones being that the information should be relevant to the decisions that need to be made and faithfully represent the underlying transactions or items. If the information is also comparable, verifiable, timely, and understandable it will be more useful.

In order for businesses to produce financial statements regularly, all, except perhaps the very smallest, will maintain a financial accounting system. The heart of this is the nominal ledger, in which double-entry bookkeeping takes place. This system ensures that all financial transactions and items are recorded in a methodical manner and so that the two key statements—the statement of financial position and the income statement—can be drawn up easily.

Financial statements are drawn up in accordance with various principles, such as accruals and historic cost. This requires the financial statements to include not only the financial transactions that have occurred throughout an accounting period, but also the effect of adjustments made at period-end, such as depreciation, accruals and prepayments, and changes to any provision for doubtful debts.

 ## Further reading

IASB (International Accounting Standards Board) (2010) *Conceptual Framework for Financial Reporting*. London: IASB (Introduction, Chapters 1 and 3).

 ## Questions

● Quick test

1   For a sole trader, identify which nominal ledger accounts will be affected by the following transactions, and state whether the accounts will be increased or decreased as a result of the transaction.

	£
(a) Owner started business by paying into a business bank account	15,000
(b) Loan received	5,000
(c) Motor car purchased for cheque	8,000
(d) Goods purchased on credit from supplier Hall	2,250
(e) Goods sold on credit to customer White	1,645
(f) Cheque paid for office expenses	340
(g) Goods sold for cash to customer Black	1,300
(h) Goods purchased on credit from supplier Marks	1,200
(i) Credit note issued for goods returned by White	245
(j) Credit note received from Hall for return of faulty goods	300
(k) Cheque paid for car insurance	195
(l) Cheque paid to Hall	1,125
(m) Wages paid in cash	250
(n) Owner withdrawals to cover personal expenses	500
(o) Cheque received from White	900
(p) Cheque paid to Marks after deducting a £50 cash discount	1,150
(q) Payment made on loan	1,500

(NB—loan of £5,000 has interest @ 10% p.a. and is being repaid in £1,000 instalments.)

2   Enter the transactions given in Question 1 in the nominal ledger accounts of the business using double-entry bookkeeping, balance off the accounts, and extract a trial balance.

3   Draw up the income statement for the year ended 30 June 20X4 and statement of financial position at that date for P. Glass's business from the following trial balance.

	Dr £	Cr £
Inventory at 1 July 20X3	2,368	
Sales		19,647
Purchases	13,874	
Returns inwards	205	
Returns outwards		322
Salaries and wages	4,206	
Rent	300	
Insurance	76	
Motor expenses	554	
Office expenses	328	
Heat and light	160	
General expenses	325	
Carriage inwards	250	
Discounts allowed	68	

Premises	5,000	
Motor vehicles	1,800	
Fixtures and fittings	450	
Trade receivables	3,704	
Trade payables		2,731
Cash at bank		1,710
Drawings	1,200	
Capital at 1 July 20X3	_____	10,458
	34,868	34,868

(Note: inventory at 30 June 20X4 was valued at £2,946.)

●● Develop your understanding

4   The trial balance of Lytax at 31 December 20X2 is as follows:

	£	£
Capital at 1 January 20X2		68,000
Five-year loan		15,000
Land and buildings	67,000	
Plant and machinery	38,000	
Fixtures and fittings	21,300	
Accumulated depreciation at 1 January 20X2		
Land and buildings		12,000
Plant and machinery		8,100
Fixtures and fittings		5,300
Receivables	9,000	
Bank		1,000
Payables		8,400
Discounts allowed	700	
Purchases	79,500	
Heat and light	1,300	
Insurance	1,400	
Wages and salaries	24,200	
Inventory at 1 January 20X2	7,800	
General expenses	1,200	
Bad debts	700	
Provision for doubtful debts		300
Drawings	25,000	
Sales	_____	159,000
	277,100	277,100

The following information needs to be taken into account before the accounts can be finalised:

(a) Inventory was valued at £8,000 at the close of business on 31 December 20X2

(b) The owner took goods for his own use during the year. The cost of these was £1,500, and they have not been accounted for

(c) Interest on the loan at 8% p.a. has not been paid for the year ended 31 December 20X2

(d) Wages and salaries owing at 31 December 20X2 amounted to £400

(e) The figure for insurance includes a premium of £1,000 for the period 1 July 20X2 to 30 June 20X3

(f) The provision for doubtful debts required at 31 December 20X2 is 5% of receivables

(g) The business's depreciation policies are:

Buildings	Straight-line over 50 years
(Buildings element in the land and buildings cost is £40,000)	
Plant and machinery	15% straight-line
Fixtures and fittings	5% reducing balance.

Required:

Prepare Lytax's income statement for the year ended 31 December 20X2 and a statement of financial position at that date.

5 Porter Ltd is a company with total authorised share capital of £2,000,000 divided into £500,000 of 6% irredeemable preference share capital and £1,500,000 ordinary share capital.

Porter's trial balance at 31 May 20X6 has been extracted and is reproduced below:

	£000	£000
Preference share capital: £1 shares		500
Ordinary share capital: 50p shares		600
Retained earnings at 1 June 20X5		336
Inventory at 1 June 20X5	1,071	
Sales		4,377
Purchases	2,225	
Wages and salaries	808	
Motor expenses	164	
Rent	210	
General distribution costs	81	
General administration expenses	79	
Debenture interest	28	
Royalties receivable		42
Directors' remuneration	185	
Bad debts	31	
Plant and machinery at cost	1,750	
Motor vehicles at cost	320	

Accumulated depreciation at 31 May 20X5:

Plant and machinery		504
Motor vehicles		145
Trade receivables	781	
Trade payables		498
Bank		43
Provision for doubtful debts		29
Preference dividend paid	30	
Ordinary dividend paid	89	
Corporation tax paid	76	
VAT payable		54
7% debentures		800
	7,928	7,928

The following information is also relevant:

(a) Included in general administration expenses is a £24,000 insurance premium for the year ended 31 December 20X6

(b) An electricity invoice for £6,000 for the quarter ended 30 June 20X6 was received on 6 July and has not yet been accounted for

(c) Inventory at 31 May 20X6 was valued at £1,123,000

(d) A provision against specific doubtful debts of £34,000 is required at 31 May 20X6

(e) Total corporation tax for the year ended 31 May 20X6 has been agreed with the HM Revenue & Customs at £102,000

(f) The directors wish to provide for the following at 31 May 20X6:

   (i) Directors' bonuses of £36,000

   (ii) Auditors' fees of £12,000

   (iii) Any debenture interest due

(g) The company's depreciation policies are as follows:

Plant and machinery	10% straight line
Motor vehicles	35% reducing balance

Required:

Prepare the income statement and statement of changes in equity for Porter Ltd for the year ended 31 May 20X6 and a statement of financial position at that date.

●●● Take it further

6 Falmouth plc has an authorised share capital of £2,000,000 divided into 3,000,000 ordinary shares of 20p and 500,000 12% redeemable preference shares of £1.

The following trial balance has been extracted from the accounting records at 30 June 20X1:

	Debit £000	Credit £000
50p ordinary shares (fully paid)		500
12% £1 preference shares (fully paid)		200
8% debentures		400
Retained earnings 1 July 20X0		368
Freehold land and buildings (cost)	860	
Plant and machinery (cost)	1,460	
Motor vehicles (cost)	440	
Accumulated depreciation at 1 July 20X0:		
Freehold buildings		40
Plant and machinery		444
Motor vehicles		230
Inventory at 1 July 20X0	380	
Sales		6,590
Purchases	4,304	
Final dividends for year end 30 June 20X0:		
Ordinary	40	
Interim dividends for year end 30 June 20X1:		
Preference	12	
Ordinary	16	
Debenture interest	16	
Wages and salaries	508	
Light and heat	62	
Bad debt expense	30	
Other administration expenses	196	
Receivables	578	
Payables		390
Provision for doubtful debts		20
Corporation tax paid	112	
Bank	156	
	£ 9,182	£ 9,182

The following information needs to be dealt with before the financial statements can be completed:

(a) Inventories at 30 June 20X1 were valued at £440,000 (cost)

(b) Other administration expenses include £18,000 paid in respect of a machinery maintenance contract for the 12 months ending 30 November 20X1. Light and heat does not include an invoice of £12,000 for electricity for the quarter ending 3 July 20X1, which was paid in August 20X1

(c) The directors wish to provide for:

  (i)   any debenture interest due

  (ii) directors' bonuses of £24,000

  (iii) the year's depreciation

(d) The provision for doubtful debts required at 30 June 20X1 is £24,000

(e) During the year ended 30 June 20X1, a customer whose receivables balance of £8,000 had been written off in previous years paid the full amount owing. The company credited this to receivables

(f) The debentures have been in issue for some years

(g) Corporation tax of £256,000 is to be charged on the profits

(h) During the year a piece of machinery, which had originally cost £320,000 and had been owned by the company for 6 years, was scrapped. Proceeds received were £40,000. These have been incorrectly credited to the plant and machinery cost account

(i) The buildings element of the freehold land and buildings cost is £400,000.

  Depreciation methods and rates are as follows:

Buildings	Straight-line over 50 years
Plant and machinery	10% straight-line
Motor vehicles	33% reducing balance

Required:

Prepare the income statement and statement of changes in equity of Falmouth plc for the year ended 30 June 20X1 and a statement of financial position at that date.

Visit the Online Resource Centre for **solutions** to all these end of chapter questions plus visual walkthrough solutions. You can test your understanding with extra questions and answers, explore additional case studies based on real companies, take a guided tour through a company report, and much more. Go to the Online Resource Centre at **www.oxfordtextbooks.co.uk/orc/maynard/**

Part 2

Financial reporting in context

Chapter 2   The financial reporting system

Chapter 3   Corporate governance, sustainability, and ethics

Chapter 4   Published financial statements of companies

Chapter 5   Interpretation of financial statements

2

The financial reporting system

➤ Introduction

As defined in Chapter 1, financial reporting is concerned with the reporting of financial information about an entity to interested users. For financial markets to function efficiently, the financial information provided needs to be of the highest quality, and this requirement is equally applicable to non-listed companies whose shares are not publicly traded. The previous chapter discussed various characteristics that are required to make financial information useful, such as relevance and faithful representation. However, on their own, these are insufficient to ensure that the information is of the highest quality, as corporate scandals over the years have demonstrated. Thus, rules and regulations governing how financial information is provided have evolved and are still evolving.

This chapter explains the accounting rules and regulations that govern published financial reports of companies, who sets and influences these rules and regulations, and the authority they have. The main player in this is the International Accounting Standards Board (IASB), which sets international accounting standards. Its convergence programme with the US's Financial Accounting Standards Board (FASB) is key to the development of global financial reporting systems that will produce high quality financial statements.

★ Learning objectives

After studying this chapter you will be able to:

- appreciate the importance of appropriate regulation
- explain the main elements of the regulatory framework of financial reporting for all companies in the UK, both listed and unlisted, and describe who the bodies are that set the regulation
- understand what international accounting standards are, their importance, their principles-based underpinning, the processes by which they are produced, and to which companies they are applicable internationally
- discuss the IASB/FASB convergence project in relation to the goal of achieving a set of high quality global accounting standards.

✔ Key issues checklist

- ❑ Investors' and the capital markets' need for high quality financial information.
- ❑ The need for legislation and accounting standards to contribute to high quality information in the context of UK listed and non-listed companies.
- ❑ UK companies legislation.
- ❑ 'True and fair'.
- ❑ International accounting standards (generic term to include both IASs and International Financial Reporting Standards (IFRSs)), and their development and use globally.
- ❑ The IASB—its development, authority, and accountability.
- ❑ Financial reporting systems in the USA, and the convergence project between the FASB and IASB.
- ❑ The principles, judgement-based approach to international accounting standards.
- ❑ The IASB's underpinning *Conceptual Framework*, and the IASB/FASB convergence project to update this.
- ❑ The elements of financial statements, and recognition and measurement principles relating to these.
- ❑ Fair value.
- ❑ The consequences of global adoption of international accounting standards.
- ❑ The future of global adoption.

2.1 High quality financial reporting

As discussed in Chapter 1, the objective of financial reporting is:

> ...to provide financial information about the reporting entity that is useful to existing and potential investors, lenders and other creditors in making decisions about providing resources to the entity.

(IASB, 2010a)

In today's global environment, most public listed companies will be operating in many different countries, and will probably have their shares listed on a number of international stock markets. The investors, lenders, and other creditors will be multinational, and will require high quality financial information that they can compare easily across international boundaries.

High quality financial information will ensure that investors and lenders have trust in it, which will give them confidence to make good investment decisions, and thus enhance the liquidity and efficiency of capital markets. Efficient capital markets help reduce companies' costs of capital, and therefore improve returns and contribute to wealth-creation for the economic good.

However non-listed companies and small- and medium-sized entities (SMEs) constitute approximately 95% of companies in the world, and the provision of high-quality financial information about them is just as important as for publicly traded companies. These companies produce financial statements which are used by their investors, who may be venture capitalists, but, particularly, by lenders, such as banks and suppliers, and also by employees, government departments, and others outside the company. All these users would lose confidence if information was not high quality. In addition, the companies' access to capital, which is vital to their continuance and growth, and the economies of the countries in which they reside, would become even more difficult.

The global financial crisis of 2008 placed a particular focus on the quality of financial information provided by companies, with popular sentiment calling for companies, in this case in the financial sector, and their auditors to improve financial reporting. This is nothing new—history is littered with examples of such calls following financial scandals or major company collapses. Some more recent examples of this include Maxwell, Barings Bank, and Polly Peck in the UK in the 1980s and 1990s, and, more recently, Enron and WorldCom in the USA in the 2000s. But heads of government at the G20 summit in April 2009 also called for transparency and accountability to be strengthened, sound regulation to be enhanced, integrity in financial markets to be promoted, and the reinforcement of international cooperation.

2.1.1 What ensures high quality financial reporting?

As discussed in Chapter 1, it is necessary for financial information to be relevant, and to faithfully represent the financial position and performance to enable quality decisions to be taken. If these characteristics are exhibited, together with those of comparability, verifiability, timeliness and understandability, the quality of financial reporting will be enhanced.

However, these attributes are only part of the financial reporting system. For the system to be reliable, and to produce what the users require, regulation to govern this has had to evolve, and, for financial reporting, this is both statutory (in the UK, companies legislation) and includes the **audit**, and mandatory (accounting standards). For companies which have public accountability additional requirements are specified by listing rules.

Although the main purpose of financial reporting is decision-usefulness, it is also about showing the results of the stewardship of management, in other words the accountability of management for the resources entrusted to it. It may be argued that the financial statements and detailed breakdown of figures contained therein provide the information that users need to make decisions and to assess stewardship. However, today, users are becoming more concerned with *how* companies achieve wealth-creation through how they are run, how relationships with investors are managed, and with long-term sustainability matters, such as the impact of the companies' affairs on the environment or local community. Thus, financial reporting extends to the areas of corporate governance, corporate social responsibility, and ethical issues. Again, in these areas regulation to govern this has had to evolve. These issues are discussed in more detail in Chapter 3.

2.1.2 The regulatory framework of financial reporting

If the financial statements of UK publicly listed companies are considered first, Figure 2.1 illustrates the main sources of regulation of these.

For non-listed UK companies, the regulations are not very different, as Figure 2.2 illustrates.

IASB   International Accounting Standards Board

FASB   US Financial Accounting Standards Board

ASB   UK Accounting Standards Board

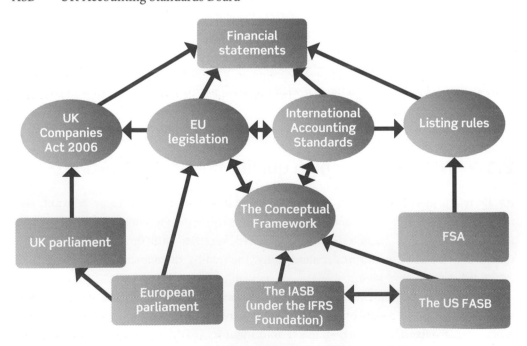

Figure 2.1 Regulatory framework of financial reporting (UK listed companies)

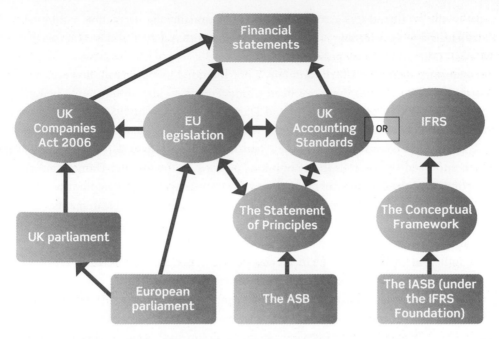

Figure 2.2 Regulatory framework of financial reporting (UK non-listed companies)

FSA   **Financial Services Authority**

IFRS   International Financial Reporting Standards

2.2 Companies legislation

In the UK statutory regulation is contained in Companies Acts and also in directives of the European parliament. The overriding requirement of Companies Act 2006 is that annual accounts are to be prepared which:

> ...give a true and fair view of the assets, liabilities, financial position and profit or loss...
>
> *(s.393, UK Companies Act 2006)*

2.2.1 True and fair

The evolution of the company with its limited liability status gave rise to legislation governing its conduct and accountability. This included the requirement for companies to produce financial statements for its members (shareholders). From 1900 in the UK these financial statements (at this date a balance sheet only) were required to show a 'true and correct' view of the company's state of affairs. In 1947, following recommendations by the **Institute of Chartered Accountants in England and Wales** (the ICAEW), one of the UK's professional accountancy bodies, the requirement was changed to 'true and fair', and was extended to apply to the profit and loss account. True and fair remains the overriding requirement of today's legislation concerning accounts in the Companies Act 2006 and it is on this that the external auditors ultimately provide their opinion.

A statutory definition of true and fair is not included in legislation; however, various statements as to its meaning have been produced—the most authoritative being legal opinions written by Lord Hoffmann and Dame Mary Arden in 1983 and 1984, respectively, and by Dame Mary Arden in 1993. A more recent opinion is that of Martin Moore QC, which was commissioned by the **Financial Reporting Council** (FRC) in 2008, and which endorsed the analysis in the opinions of Lord Hoffmann and Dame Mary Arden and confirmed the centrality of the true and fair requirement to the preparation of financial statements in the UK. This legal opinion confirms that financial statements that have been prepared in accordance with relevant accounting standards will 'prima facie' give a true and fair view.

As indicated in Chapter 1, financial accounting is not an exact science; estimates are required to be made, such as in determining the expected useful life of a non-current asset or in judging whether a customer will pay its debts. As demonstrated in further chapters, there are many other areas which require judgements to be made, based on opinion, and, inevitably, differences exist between one person's opinion and another's. This is possibly why the word 'correct' was replaced by 'fair' in company law. The application of true and fair can be taken to mean that financial statements should be accurate and comprehensive to within acceptable limits; where estimates and opinions are required, professional, informed, and reasonable judgement should be exercised; they should contain sufficient information in quantity and quality to satisfy the reasonable expectations of the users.

2.2.2 Other requirements

The Companies Act 2006 states that companies should prepare their financial statements in accordance with the applicable accounting framework, which, for listed companies and groups, is in accordance with international accounting standards, as specified by Article 4 of the 'IAS Regulation':

> ...for each financial year starting on or after 1 January 2005, companies governed by the law of a Member State shall prepare their consolidated accounts in conformity with the international accounting standards ... if, at their balance sheet date, their securities are admitted to trading on a regulated market of any Member State...
>
> *(Regulation (EC) no. 1606/2002 of the European Parliament and of the Council of 19 July 2002)*

For non-listed companies the applicable accounting framework is companies legislation, and the financial statements should consist of a balance sheet and profit and loss account with accompanying explanatory notes. Various provisions concerning whether group accounts should be prepared are also given—these are discussed in more detail in Chapter 15.

All financial statements must be approved by the board of directors and signed on behalf of the board by a director of the company on the company's balance sheet.

2.3 International accounting standards

Mandatory regulation governing financial statements is in the form of accounting standards and most of the chapters of this textbook are based on the detail contained in these.

2.3.1 Terminology

Clarification is needed in this area in relation to terminology, much of which is very similar. Firstly, international accounting standards (IASs) and international financial reporting standards (IFRSs) have the same meaning, and generic reference to either term will encompass both IASs and IFRSs. The reason for the different terms is explained later.

Secondly, international accounting standards are the accounting standards issued by the International Accounting Standards Board (IASB). The IASB has also issued an IFRS for small- and medium-sized entities (the IFRS for SMEs), which is a set of international accounting standards tailored for smaller companies. As referred to earlier, different accounting standards are used by different types of company and in different countries. Those used by non-listed companies in the UK are issued by the UK's **Accounting Standards Board (ASB)**, and are called statements of standard accounting practice (SSAPs) and financial reporting standards (FRSs). There is also a Financial Reporting Standard for Smaller Entities (FRSSE), which contains simplified standards for companies defined as small according to Companies Act 2006. In the USA accounting standards are called financial accounting standards (FASs) and are issued by the US **Financial Accounting Standards Board (FASB)**. Other countries will also have their own version of an accounting standards board and their own domestic standards.

Thirdly, a generic term—**generally accepted accounting principles (GAAP)**—is often used. This is used to refer to the standard framework of accounting guidelines used in any given jurisdiction. GAAP includes the accounting standards, and any other conventions and rules followed in the preparation of the financial statements.

This is summarised in Figure 2.3.

2.3.2 Accounting standards

Accounting standards are the 'instruction manual' of accounting. They are authoritative statements of how particular types of transaction and other events should be reflected in financial statements, and are there to answer the question 'how' should something be accounted for? As mentioned previously, compliance with accounting standards is necessary for financial statements to show a true and fair view.

Accounting methods have to evolve constantly to cope with, for example, changing opinions on relevant valuation methods, or new financial transactions or items such as complex financial derivatives, or changes in emphasis in what makes financial information really useful. Thus, accounting standards are constantly being withdrawn or revised, or new standards are issued. The last decade has seen an unprecedented level of change in accounting standards, particularly international standards, as discussed in the following sections.

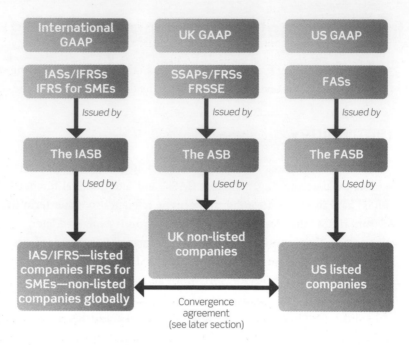

Figure 2.3 Accounting frameworks

2.3.3 UK accounting standards

In the UK accounting standards have been in issue since 1970 when the first body to produce them was formed, the Accounting Standards Steering Committee, a predecessor of the current ASB. Prior to this, accounting practice was considered a matter for the accounting profession, which also oversaw auditing firms. From 1942, the ICAEW produced its *Recommendations on Accounting Principles* for the information of its members. However, these were not binding and during the 1960s there was growing disquiet over UK companies publishing audited financial statements which were subsequently found to be materially incorrect.

Two particular cases triggered calls for action to be taken—GEC's takeover of AEI Ltd in 1967 and Pergamon Press Ltd's 1968 audited accounts.

In the AEI takeover, AEI produced a forecast profit figure of £10 million for 1967, on which its auditors provided assurance that it was reasonable and fair. After the takeover, GEC produced the actual accounts for AEI for 1967, largely from the same information, which showed a loss for the year of £4.5 million. £5 million of the difference of £14.5 million in the two profit figures was attributed to a change in facts, but the remaining £9.5 million, some of which related to inventory and work-in-progress valuations, arose from differences in judgement of the two teams of accountants.

Pergamon Press's 1968 audited accounts showed a profit of approximately £2 million. However, an independent investigation by another professional firm of accountants suggested that the profit should be reduced by £1.5 million as a result of differences in opinion over valuations.

The obvious question of how different accountants could arrive at such different profit figures was raised and, as a result, the Accounting Standards Steering Committee (ASSC) was formed from the main professional accounting bodies in the UK and Ireland:

- The Institute of Chartered Accountants in England and Wales (ICAEW)
- The Institute of Chartered Accountants of Scotland (ICAS)
- The Institute of Chartered Accountants in Ireland (ICAI)
- The Association of Certified Accountants (now the **Association of Chartered Certified Accountants** or ACCA)
- The Institute of Cost and Management Accountants (now the **Chartered Institute of Management Accountants** or CIMA).

The Chartered Institute of Public Finance and Accountancy (CIPFA) joined later.

The Committee's objective was 'to develop definitive standards for financial reporting' and it issued the first Statement of Standard Accounting Practice (SSAP 1) on Accounting for the Results of Associated Companies in January 1971. Companies and auditors were required to apply the standards or explain any departures from their application. For the next 19 years the Accounting Standards Committee (ASC—the 'Steering' was dropped from its title) issued 25 SSAPs until, in 1990, the ASB, a subsidiary body of the newly established Financial Reporting Council (FRC), took over its work. The ASB adopted the existing SSAPs, but any new accounting standards that it issued were given the title Financial Reporting Standards (FRSs).

Many SSAPs and FRSs have been reissued over the past decade to bring them into line with international accounting standards, which are discussed in section 2.3.4. The ASB has been consulting for a number of years on the future of UK GAAP for non-listed companies and are currently considering pulling together all existing standards, with updates as necessary, into one overriding standard. This would be broadly consistent with international standards (in particular the IFRS for SMEs), but allow for UK legal requirements.

2.3.4 International Accounting Standards (IASs) and the International Accounting Standards Board (IASB)

A discussion of international accounting standards and their use can only be carried out in the context of a discussion of the development of the body that issues them.

IASs have been in issue since 1973 when the International Accounting Standards Committee (IASC) was formed as a result of an agreement by accountancy bodies in nine countries—Australia, Canada, France, Germany, Japan, Mexico, the Netherlands, the UK and Ireland, and the USA—and these countries constituted the board of IASC at that time. The original intention of the IASC was to issue accounting standards with which the members should use 'best endeavours to ensure compliance'. External auditors were encouraged to report cases of non-compliance. The IASC issued its first standard, IAS 1 *Disclosure of Accounting Policies*, in 1974.

Although, over the next 15 years or so, the IASC expanded as accountancy bodies from other nations joined the organisation, and it began to hold discussions with national standard-setters, the accounting standards issued by local setters always took precedence. However, IASs were useful to companies in countries that did not have fully established financial reporting systems. Research in the early 1980s demonstrated that IASs had not changed national standards in developed countries and were only really codifying generally accepted practice. Pressure from these countries, particularly the USA and the UK, ensured that by 1982 there was agreement that IASs would not override national standards.

Significant events that triggered a greater acceptance of IASs globally were German reunification following the collapse of the Soviet Union in 1989, and the agreement of a list of core IASs by the International Organisation of Securities Commissions (IOSCO) in 1993. Following these events a number of Continental European companies started to adopt IASs for consolidated financial statements purposes and, in 1998, laws were passed in Belgium, France, Germany, and Italy to permit large companies to use IASs domestically.

2.3.5 US acceptance of IASs

While Europe was moving swiftly towards acceptance of IASs in 2000, with the European Commission announcing plans to require IASC standards for all European Union (EU) listed companies from no later than 2005, the key global player, the USA, was hesitating over the development of a set of accounting standards which would attract widespread international support. Possibly, the USA perceived that the EU wanted a politically-based financial reporting structure, while the EU may have been concerned that the USA wanted to fashion IASs on US GAAP. The impasse was broken as a result of a number of events.

Firstly, the IASC restructured itself in 2000 with a new constitution and wider membership, and the IASB became the body with responsibility for setting accounting standards, which were designated IFRSs. Sir David Tweedie, formerly the Chair of the UK's ASB, became Chairman of the new IASB, and immediately instituted a thorough review and update of all inherited IASs, which, he admitted, were second-rate. Secondly, in 2000 IOSCO, which includes the USA's Securities and Exchange Commission (SEC), recommended that its members allow multinational issuers to use 30 IASs in cross-border offerings and listings.

Finally, the commitment to the use of IASs by all EU listed companies was a clear message to the whole world of the significance of IASs for the future. From 1 January 2005 more than 7,000 companies were required to prepare their financial statements in accordance with IASs as opposed to their national GAAP.

These events had enormous significance. The New York Stock Exchange (NYSE) is the largest capital market in the world, which leads to it being very attractive to companies wishing to raise capital and for their global profile. In order to list on the NYSE or NASDAQ (National Association of Securities Dealers Automated Quotations, the USA's electronic screen-based equity securities trading market), foreign companies were required to either produce a set of financial statements prepared in accordance with US GAAP, which would be in addition to the financial statements prepared under their national GAAP, or to produce reconciliations of net profit and shareholders' equity from their national GAAP to US GAAP, with full details of differences. Either of these requirements imposes a large costly burden on companies.

Although this requirement remained for the time being, a major step forward was taken in 2002 with the IASB and the FASB signing the 'Norwalk Agreement', which committed the boards to work together to remove differences between IFRSs and US GAAP, and to coordinate their future work programmes. Then, in 2006, a 'Memorandum of Understanding' was drawn up between the two bodies, which set out a joint work programme to be completed by 2011. This was based on three principles:

1   Convergence was to be achieved by the development of high quality, common standards over time

2   Rather than eliminating differences between a FAS and an IAS, a new common standard should be developed

3   If standards needed replacing, new standards should be developed jointly.

Short-term projects to remove the variety of individual differences between US GAAP and IASs were agreed, with target completion dates by the end of 2008. In 2008 the two boards identified a series of priorities and milestones to complete the remaining major joint projects by June 2011, emphasising that the goal of joint projects was to produce common, principle-based standards.

As a result of progress on the Memorandum of Understanding, and also acceptance that the EU move to IAS in 2005 had generally been successful, in November 2007 came the (earlier than expected) decision of the US SEC to remove the requirement of reconciliation from home GAAP, which, in many cases, meant IFRS, to US GAAP for non-US companies listing in the USA.

Finally, in August 2008, the SEC produced a roadmap which would permit US companies to use IFRS domestically by 2014, with a decision to be taken by 2011 on whether the use of IFRS was 'in the public interest'.

Since then, events have intervened, such as the financial crisis and global recession, the Obama administration taking power in the USA, changes in the leadership at the SEC, and estimates of corporate costs of conversion to IFRS being large. Consequently, there has been a perceived fall in the momentum towards full acceptance of the adoption of IFRS.

However, pressure on the USA for adoption remains. In 2009, the G20 leaders called on 'international accounting bodies to redouble their efforts to achieve a single set of high quality, global accounting standards within the context of their independent standard setting process . . .'. Since 2001, almost 120 countries have required, or permitted, the use of IFRSs, with all major economies, including significant emerging ones, such as China, India, and Brazil, establishing timelines to converge with, or adopt, IFRSs in the near future. See Table 2.1 for an outline of IFRS use around the world.

Table 2.1 IFRS use around the world

G20 country	Status for listed companies
Argentina	Required for fiscal years beginning on or after 1 January 2012
Australia	Required for all private sector reporting entities and as the basis for public sector reporting since 2005
Brazil	Required for consolidated financial statements of banks and listed companies from 31 December 2010 and for individual company accounts progressively since January 2008
Canada	Required from 1 January 2011 for all listed entities and permitted for private sector entities including not-for-profit organisations
China	Substantially converged national standards
European Union	All member states of the EU are required to use IFRSs as adopted by the EU for listed companies since 2005
France	Required via EU adoption and implementation process since 2005
Germany	Required via EU adoption and implementation process since 2005
India	Converging with IFRSs, date to be determined
Indonesia	Convergence process ongoing; a decision about a target date for full compliance with IFRSs is expected to be made in 2012
Italy	Required via EU adoption and implementation process since 2005
Japan	Permitted from 2010 for a number of international companies; decision about mandatory adoption expected around 2012
Mexico	Required from 2012
Republic of Korea	Required from 2012
Russia	Required from 2012
Saudi Arabia	Required for banking and insurance companies. Full convergence with IFRSs currently under consideration
South Africa	Required for listed entities since 2005
Turkey	Required for listed entities since 2008
United Kingdom	Required via EU adoption and implementation process since 2005
United States	Allowed for foreign issuers in the US since 2007; target date for substantial convergence with IFRSs is 2012 and decision about possible adoption for US companies expected in 2012

Source: IFRS Foundation, IASB, *Who we are and what we do*, February 2012.

In addition, the position is now that US GAAP is used only by domestic US companies. All foreign companies listing on the US markets can choose IFRS, which has broad global acceptance. Indeed, US companies are *required* to use US GAAP—at present they cannot even elect to use IFRS!

The SEC has considered taking a 'condorsement' approach whereby some international standards would be endorsed by the FASB and adopted into US GAAP or converged where the FASB is not comfortable with endorsement without additional convergence. Many involved consider that the decision to fully adopt IFRS for US companies will be taken eventually, but it will be a prolonged, cautious, and incremental process.

2.4 The International Accounting Standards Board (IASB)

Although an explanation of how the predecessor body, the IASC, was formed has been provided in section 2.3.4, it is important to understand what the current IASB is and what authority it has. It is an independent accounting standard-setting board, part of the IFRS Foundation, and overseen by a geographically and professionally diverse body of trustees, who are publicly accountable to a Monitoring Board of public capital market authorities. The structure is shown in Figure 2.4.

The IFRS Foundation is a not-for-profit, private sector body that raises funds to support the operations of the IASB as an independent accounting standard-setter. It is funded by a wide range of market participants from across the world's capital markets through the establishment of national financing regimes, proportionate to a country's relative Gross Domestic Product, that charge a levy on companies or provide an element of publicly supported financing.

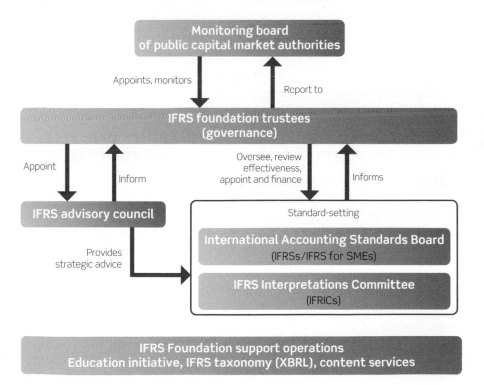

Figure 2.4 International Financial Reporting Standards (IFRS) Foundation, International Accounting Standards Board (IASB), *Who we are and what we do*, January 2012

There are currently 14 members of the IASB, who have a diverse range of accounting and finance backgrounds, and the board is chaired by Hans Hoogervorst (formerly the UK's Sir David Tweedie) from the Netherlands with vice chair Ian Mackintosh (from New Zealand). The board aims to represent all member countries, but it is interesting to note that of the current members four are from the USA, four are from Europe and only three are from Asia (India, China, and Japan respectively), so it could be questioned whether it is truly representative.

The objectives of the IFRS Foundation are:

● to develop a single set of high quality, understandable, enforceable and globally accepted international financial reporting standards through its standard-setting body, the IASB;

● to promote the use and rigorous application of those standards;

● to take account of the financial reporting needs of emerging economies and small and medium-sized entities; and

● to bring about convergence of national accounting standards and IFRSs to high quality solutions.

(IFRS Foundation, The Organisation)

The IASB engages closely with its stakeholders around the world, including investors, analysts, regulators, business leaders, accounting standard-setters, and the accountancy profession. It claims to follow thorough, open, and transparent processes in standard-setting with the publication of consultative documents, such as discussion papers and exposure drafts, for public comment. All meetings of the IASB are held in public and via webcast.

The IFRS Interpretations Committee (formerly called the IFRIC) is the interpretative body of the IASB. Its mandate is to review, on a timely basis, widespread accounting issues that have arisen from the practical application of current IFRSs and to provide authoritative guidance, through the publication of IFRICs, on those issues. The Interpretation Committee follows the same transparent, thorough and open due process, with its meetings open to the public and via webcast.

2.4.1 The development of international financial reporting standards (IFRSs)

IFRSs are developed through an international consultation process, the 'due process', which involves interested individuals and organisations from around the world. The due process comprises six stages:

1   Setting the agenda

2   Planning the project

3   Developing and publishing the discussion paper (DP)

4   Developing and publishing the exposure draft (ED)

5   Developing and publishing the standard (IFRS)

6   Two-year post-implementation review.

Round-table discussions are held in locations around the world while the project is being developed with comment periods allowed after stages 3 and 4.

The IASB sets itself an annual work plan with target dates for publication stages. In practice, these often differ, particularly if there are numerous comments from stakeholders which question the proposals. For example, an unprecedented number of comment letters was received following the publication of the ED on *Leases* in August 2010 and, although this was one of the key convergence projects due for completion by June 2011, a new accounting standard is not expected until 2013.

2.4.2 International financial reporting standard (IFRS) for small- and medium-sized entities (SMEs)

There is general agreement that many IFRSs are long, very detailed, and complex, and are suitable mainly for listed companies. This is inevitable, as they have to address accounting for the type of tough and complex matters in which these companies engage. Small companies and their users have complained for years that many IASs and IFRSs are not relevant for the type of business transactions and decisions that they make. The IASB has been working on a major project to address this since 2003 and, in 2009, finally issued its IFRS for SMEs.

This is a self-contained standard, containing accounting for all areas considered applicable for smaller companies. It simplifies many of the principles and choices contained in full IFRSs and significantly reduces disclosure requirements. It is designed for any size company globally that is required to produce financial statements and that does not have public accountability (publicly accountable companies should be using full IFRS), and focuses on ensuring that key information about cash flows, liquidity, and solvency is provided.

According to the IASB, 95% of companies globally are eligible to use the IFRS for SMEs, and 68 jurisdictions have either adopted the standard or indicated or proposed a plan to adopt it within the next 3 years.

The UK is considering adopting it, with some modifications, for all non-listed companies, except those small companies which can use the FRSSE. The ASB is currently consulting on this.

2.5 Principles based international financial reporting standards (IFRSs)

The objective of the IASB is to produce high quality financial reporting standards, and some discussion has been included at the start of this chapter as to how high quality financial reporting can be achieved. One of the main features of IFRSs, which contributes to their high quality, is that they are considered to be **principles based** and consistent with an underpinning conceptual framework.

Financial reporting in practice 2.1 | Enron

One issue which came to light in the Enron case was the accounting treatment of special-purpose entities (SPEs) in which Enron had invested and in which the company had 'hidden' much of its debt. The SPEs were 'off balance sheet', in other words they did not appear in the company's consolidated financial statements and, therefore, neither did the debt.

Enron, in agreement with its auditors, Arthur Anderson, had accounted for these SPEs in accordance with a specific 'rule' contained within US accounting standards relating to ownership interest and, as the 'rule' appeared to have been applied appropriately, the debt was not disclosed.

Even though financial statements in the USA are signed off as 'presenting fairly' the financial position and results, financial reporting systems in the USA accept that this essentially means that all accounting rules set out in the accounting standards have been followed correctly. Whether the financial statements reflected the economic substance of Enron's investment in the SPEs—the company essentially controlled them—was considered less important.

There has been much discussion over the past decade or so of what is meant by principles based accounting standards, mainly in comparison with so-called **rules based accounting standards**. Broadly speaking, the US accounting standards are said to be rules based and the perceived superiority of the IASB's principles based standards came to the fore particularly after the collapse of the US energy giant, Enron.

Claims that an 'Enron-type' of corporate collapse could not happen in jurisdictions that had principles based financial reporting systems were really expressing the point that the financial statements produced by these systems are said to faithfully represent the economic reality of businesses and their transactions. Faithful representation is discussed in Chapter 1—it is one of the fundamental characteristics of financial information that makes it useful. This concept, together with the idea that accounting should be in accordance with the economic or commercial reality of a transaction, is very much tied to the themes also discussed previously in relation to the meaning of true and fair.

🛈 **Reminder of true and fair** *Accurate as far as reasonably possible, with professional, informed, and reasonable judgement exercised.*

IFRSs encompass the principle of **substance over form**, in other words accounting for a transaction according to its commercial substance rather than its legal form.

 Example of substance over form

A business leases a machine. The business does not legally own this asset, as title is held by the leasing company. However, the business will use the machine to produce goods in the same manner as any machine which it legally owns.

The commercial substance of the **lease** arrangement is that the business has a resource—an asset—from which it will generate revenues; therefore, the financial statements should reflect the asset, together with all other assets, on its statement of financial position, even though it does not legally own the asset.

Note: accounting for leases is discussed in detail in Chapter 14.

Also key to a principles based system is the exercise of professional judgement rather than the identification of the rule that directs how a transaction should be recorded. Judgement should be reasonable in the light of the facts and circumstances present at the time it is made. Those who are unhappy with this approach justify their disquiet by suggesting this can lead to inconsistency and lack of comparability, which is one of the enhancing characteristics of financial information. Concerns are also expressed that subjective judgement rather than the application of rules could increase the risk of lawsuits. Perhaps the litigious nature of US society has, in part, contributed to the numerous rules that comprise US accounting standards. However, a robust and mature financial reporting system should ensure that accountants and auditors making these judgements are highly trained and experienced. Sufficient disclosure of the nature of the judgement that has been exercised should also enable users to understand how it has influenced the financial information.

Principles based accounting standards address broader areas than rules based standards, which are therefore more numerous, as rules for each specific element of accounting need to be provided. This latter system creates complexity and lack of clarity.

Although there are currently 41 accounting standards (28 extant IASs and 13 IFRSs), 16 IFRICs and 8 further statements of interpretation (SICs), this compares with over 100 extant FASs issued by the US FASB together with up to 48 FASB interpretations and numerous technical bulletins. IASs and IFRSs cover broad areas of accounting (see list in section 2.5.1), and all follow the same format:

- the objective and scope of the standard are outlined
- terms used in the standard are defined
- the accounting methods are explained
- required disclosures are specified
- if necessary, illustrative examples and implementation guidance are provided
- the basis for conclusions is given.

Principles based standards are also more flexible and adaptable. If a standard does not deal with a specific item or transaction, preparers of financial statements can refer to the underpinning principles and exercise judgement. This contrasts with rules based standards which create 'bright lines' or a much more 'black and white' approach.

From this discussion it can be appreciated why there have been difficulties in the convergence programme between the IASB and the FASB, and why the time frame to produce a new standard is so long.

2.5.1 Current international accounting standards (IASs)

The following is a list of current international accounting standards at the time of publication. Up-to-date lists can be found on the IFRS website (www.ifrs.org).

IAS 1   Presentation of Financial Statements

IAS 2   Inventories

IAS 7	Statement of Cash Flows
IAS 8	Accounting Policies, Changes in Accounting Estimates and Errors
IAS 10	Events after the Reporting Period
IAS 11	Construction Contracts
IAS 12	Income Taxes
IAS 16	Property, Plant and Equipment
IAS 17	Leases
IAS 18	Revenue
IAS 19	Employee Benefits
IAS 20	Accounting for Government Grants and Disclosure of Government Assistance
IAS 21	The Effects of Changes in Foreign Exchange Rates
IAS 23	Borrowing Costs
IAS 24	Related Party Disclosures
IAS 26	Accounting and Reporting by Retirement Benefit Plans
IAS 27	Consolidated and Separate Financial Statements
IAS 28	Investments in Associates
IAS 29	Financial Reporting in Hyperinflationary Economies
IAS 32	Financial Instruments: Presentation
IAS 33	Earnings per Share
IAS 34	Interim Financial Reporting
IAS 36	Impairment of Assets
IAS 37	Provisions, Contingent Liabilities and Contingent Assets
IAS 38	Intangible Assets
IAS 39	Financial Instruments: Recognition and Measurement
IAS 40	Investment Property
IAS 41	Agriculture
IFRS 1	First-time Adoption of International Financial Reporting Standards
IFRS 2	Share-based Payment
IFRS 3	Business Combinations
IFRS 4	Insurance Contracts
IFRS 5	Non-current Assets Held for Sale and Discontinued Operations
IFRS 6	Exploration for and Evaluation of Mineral Resources
IFRS 7	Financial Instruments: Disclosures
IFRS 8	Operating Segments
IFRS 9	Financial Instruments
IFRS 10	Consolidated Financial Statements

IFRS 11   Joint Arrangements

IFRS 12   Disclosure of Interests in Other Entities

IFRS 13   Fair Value Measurement

2.6 The conceptual framework

One feature of a principles based financial reporting system is that it is underpinned by a conceptual framework to provide the broad principles on which accounting standards can be built. Without the guidance provided by an agreed framework, standard-setting could end up being based on individual concepts developed for each standard separately and therefore lack coherence. The USA already has a number of 'Concepts Statements' providing a theoretical underpinning to its standards and, in 1989, the IASC, the predecessor committee of the IASB, published its underpinning conceptual *Framework for the Preparation and Presentation of Financial Statements* (the *Framework*). As the IASB and FASB began to work together to converge their standards it became apparent that having two frameworks was causing difficulties, even though they were fairly similar. So, from 2004, the two boards started on a long-term convergence project to develop a common conceptual framework. The objective of this project is to create a sound foundation for future accounting standards that are principles-based, internally consistent, and internationally converged.

The purpose and status of the *Conceptual Framework* is given in its introduction as setting out the concepts that underlie the preparation and presentation of financial statements for external users. Aims are:

(a) to assist the Board in the development of future IFRSs and in its review of existing IFRSs;

(b) to assist the Board in promoting harmonisation of regulations, accounting standards and procedures relating to the presentation of financial statements by providing a basis for reducing the number of alternative accounting treatments permitted by IFRSs;

(c) to assist national standard-setting bodies in developing national standards;

(d) to assist preparers of financial statements in applying IFRSs and in dealing with topics that have yet to form the subject of an IFRS;

(e) to assist auditors in forming an opinion on whether financial statements comply with IFRSs;

(f) to assist users of financial statements in interpreting the information contained in financial statements prepared in compliance with IFRSs; and

(g) to provide those who are interested in the work of the IASB with information about its approach to the formulation of IFRSs.

(IASB, 2010a)

The *Conceptual Framework* is not an accounting standard and the requirements of any standard will always override the contents of the *Conceptual Framework* should there be a conflict.

The convergence project is split into eight phases each dealing with different principles:

A   Objectives of financial reporting and qualitative characteristics

B   Definitions of elements, recognition and de-recognition

C   Measurement

D   Reporting entity concept

E   Boundaries of financial reporting, and presentation and disclosure

F   Purpose and status of the framework

G   Application of the framework to not-for-profit entities

H   Remaining issues, if any.

By July 2012 only stage A has been completed with the IASB, in September 2010, issuing two replacement chapters in its *Framework* dealing with the objectives of financial reporting and the qualitative characteristics, while the FASB has replaced two of its 'Concepts Statements'. As of March 2010 an ED of *The Reporting Entity* chapter had been published, with a comment period available up to July 2010. Since then the project has been paused with the IASB and FASB concentrating on more urgent convergence projects. However, following initial feedback to the review of its future work programme, which was initiated in July 2011, the IASB has indicated that the *Conceptual Framework* project will be restarted.

New IFRSs are currently being developed at the same time as the *Conceptual Framework* and, from a practical point of view, this also creates issues—how can new standards be written if their very underpinning is not yet agreed? It remains to be seen whether there will have to be a large revision of accounting standards once the complete *Conceptual Framework* has been finalised.

2.6.1 Objectives of financial reporting and qualitative characteristics

The objectives of financial reporting and qualitative characteristics (the characteristics of financial information that make it useful) are largely discussed in Chapter 1. To summarise, the objectives emphasise the decision-usefulness objective of financial reporting:

> ...to provide financial information about the reporting entity that is useful to existing and potential investors, lenders and other creditors in making decisions about providing resources to the entity. Those decisions involve buying, selling or holding equity and debt instruments, and providing or settling loans and other forms of credit.
>
> *(IASB, 2010a, OB2)*

Note that the **primary user group** is defined as investors, lenders, and creditors; the reason for this is that these are the resource providers in capital markets, and have the most critical and immediate need for the information in financial reports. Other users, as set out in

Chapter 1, are acknowledged, but the *Conceptual Framework* sets out that financial reporting is not directed primarily towards these other groups, as otherwise 'the *Conceptual Framework* would risk becoming unduly abstract or vague' (BC1.14).

As mentioned previously, assessment of the stewardship function of financial reporting is also given as an objective:

> To assess an entity's prospects for future net cash inflows, existing and potential investors, lenders and other creditors need information about the resources of the entity, claims against the entity, and how efficiently and effectively the entity's management and governing board have discharged their responsibilities to use the entity's resources. Examples of such responsibilities include protecting the entity's resources from unfavourable effects of economic factors such as price and technological changes and ensuring that the entity complies with applicable laws, regulations and contractual provisions. Information about management's discharge of its responsibilities is also useful for decisions by existing investors, lenders and other creditors who have the right to vote on or otherwise influence management's actions.
>
> *(IASB, 2010a, OB4)*

The extract also identifies the main need of the primary user group—that of being able to assess an entity's future net cash inflows. This will determine the returns they receive from, and market price increases in, their investment, which, in turn, will assist them in decisions about providing resources to the entity. Information about the resources of the entity, claims against the entity, and changes in the resources and claims refer to the type of financial statement that entities produce (the statement of financial position, statement of comprehensive income, statement of cash flows, and statement of changes in equity), as discussed in Chapter 1, although they are not defined as such in the objectives chapter. This information will help the users assess the entity's future net cash flows.

The principles basis of financial reporting is emphasised in the objectives chapter by the statement that, to a large extent, financial reports are based on estimates, judgements, and models, rather than exact depictions, with the concepts underlying these being established in the *Conceptual Framework*.

The qualitative characteristics of useful financial information explained in the *Conceptual Framework* are those discussed in Chapter 1.

🌑 **Reminder of qualitative characteristics** *The fundamental characteristics, without which the information would be useless, are relevance and faithful representation. Information is enhanced by the characteristics of comparability, verifiability, timeliness, and understandability.*

This chapter of the *Conceptual Framework* also acknowledges that cost imposes a constraint on useful financial reporting, with the necessary costs of financial reporting having to be justified against the benefits, and that this is a subjective assessment.

2.6.2 Other chapters of the *Conceptual Framework*

[Note: the remainder of this section will change as new sections of the Conceptual Framework are published.]

Currently, the remaining text of the *Conceptual Framework* consists of the relevant sections of the IASB's 1989 *Framework for the Preparation and Presentation of Financial Statements*, with the exception of a new chapter clarifying the reporting entity.

2.6.3 The reporting entity

As the reporting entity has been referred to in the Objectives chapter, a definition is required in order to define the boundaries of financial reporting. This is proposed as:

> ...a circumscribed area of economic activities whose financial information has the potential to be useful to existing and potential equity investors, lenders, and other creditors who cannot directly obtain the information they need...

> *(FASB, 2010)*

This encompasses single entities, portions of single entities, and also combinations of entities where one entity controls another.

The remaining sections of the *Framework* are as follows.

2.6.4 Going concern assumption

Financial statements are normally prepared on the assumption that an entity is a **going concern** and will continue in existence for the foreseeable future. If the entity intends to liquidate or materially curtail the scale of its operations, the financial statements may have to be prepared on a different basis, possibly by valuing the assets and liabilities on a break-up basis.

2.6.5 The elements of financial statements

The elements, or broad classes of financial effects and transactions, are next defined, with principles setting out both when they can be included in the financial statements, plus the value at which they can be recognised (see Figure 2.5).

Definitions of the five elements of financial statements, as given in the *Framework*, have been discussed in Chapter 1. **Recognition** of the elements relates to both the depiction of the item in words and by a monetary amount. Essentially, an element should be recognised if:

(a) it is probable that any future economic benefit associated with the item will flow to, or from, the entity

(b) the item has a cost or value that can be measured with reliability.

Note the subjective terms used here, such as 'probable' and 'measure with reliability'. This implies that the application of this principle may rely upon estimates and the exercise of professional judgement. Discussion of how these terms are applied to specific areas of accounting will be discussed in subsequent chapters.

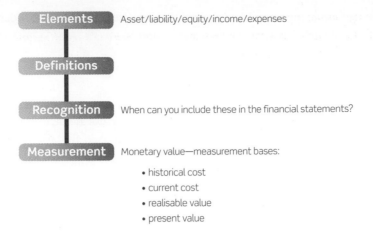

Figure 2.5 The International Accounting Standards Board's (IASB) *Framework for the Preparation and Presentation of Financial Statements:* **the elements of financial statements**

Measurement refers to the valuation methods applied to the elements. The *Framework* provides examples of four bases, which may be employed in different degrees and in varying combinations—historical cost, current cost, realisable value, and **present value**—although it specifies that historical cost is the most commonly used basis. Definitions of these terms are as follows.

Historical cost
: Assets – the amount of cash or cash equivalents paid or the fair value of the consideration given to acquire them at the time of their acquisition

  Liabilities – the amount of proceeds received in exchange for the obligation, or in some circumstances, at the amounts of cash or cash equivalents expected to be paid to satisfy the liability in the normal course of business

Current cost
: Assets – the amount of cash or cash equivalents that would have to be paid if the same or an equivalent asset was acquired currently

  Liabilities – the undiscounted amount of cash or cash equivalents that would be required to settle the obligation currently

Realisable (settlement) value
: Assets – the amount of cash or cash equivalents that could currently be obtained by selling the asset in an orderly disposal

  Liabilities – their settlement values, i.e. the undiscounted amounts of cash or cash equivalents expected to be paid to satisfy the liabilities in the normal course of business

Present value
: Assets – the present discounted value of the future net cash inflows that the item is expected to generate in the normal course of business

  Liabilities – the present discounted value of the future net cash outflows that are expected to be required to settle the liabilities in the normal course of business

(IASB,1989: para. 4.55)

Again, the applicable measurement basis will be discussed in relation to a particular area and the resulting elements of accounting in later chapters.

2.6.6 Fair value

Many recent IFRSs require the use of **fair value**, which is not defined specifically in the *Framework*. The IASB/FASB convergence project has addressed this in one of its projects with the publication of IFRS 13 *Fair Value Measurement* in 2011.

Fair value is a measurement basis that has become extremely important over the past decade and has received much publicity, some not particularly favourable. The growth of its use can be explained partially by the emphasis on decision-usefulness as the main objective of financial reporting, with fair value being considered more applicable for, for example, many **financial assets** and liabilities, and providing more relevant information to users than historical cost.

 Example of relevance

A business holds property for investment purposes. Which measurement basis would be more relevant for the users of the business's financial statements—the purchase price or the current market value (fair value)?

Current market values would provide information about whether the investment strategies were providing adequate returns. If the properties were valued at historic cost, this information would not be available.

Many IFRSs require some elements to be measured at fair value; however, its use has been added to IFRSs piecemeal and inconsistently over the years, leading to diversity in practice. The 2008 financial crisis (which some of the more extreme critics claim was exacerbated by the use of fair values by financial institutions) highlighted the need for clear guidance in this area and added impetus to the convergence project. The IFRS does not specify when fair value is to be used—a particular standard on a certain area of accounting will state this—but it establishes a single source of guidance for how fair value should be measured and it requires enhanced disclosures about how the degree of subjectivity in the methods is used. This adds relevant information for users, as they are able to assess the degree of reliability of the values.

The IFRS defines fair value as:

> The price that would be received to sell an asset or paid to transfer a liability in an orderly transaction between market participants at the measurement date.

(IASB, 2011)

Fair value is therefore an 'exit price'.

A fair value measurement assumes that the transaction to sell the asset or transfer the liability takes place either:

(a) in the *principal market* for the asset or liability; or

(b) in the absence of a principal market, in the most advantageous market for the asset or liability.

(IASB, 2011, para. 16)

The most advantageous market is the market that maximises the amount that would be received to sell the asset or that minimises the amount that would be paid to transfer the liability, after taking into account transaction costs and transport costs.

The assumptions used in arriving at a fair value (referred to in the standard as the 'inputs') are classified in a hierarchy that categorises the data they are based on, and whether this is observable (e.g. available market data) or non-observable (e.g. some model such as Black–Scholes). The higher the level, the less subjective and therefore the more reliable fair value can be said to be.

Level 1 inputs   Quoted prices in active markets for identical assets and liabilities that the entity can access at the measurement date.

Level 2 inputs   Inputs other than quoted prices included in level 1 that are observable either directly or indirectly.

Level 3 inputs   Inputs not based on observable market data (unobservable inputs), but which should reflect the assumptions the market participants would use when pricing the asset or liability, including assumptions about risk.

Entities are required to make full disclosure of these levels for all assets and liabilities which use fair value as the measurement model.

It should be stressed that although some commentators believe that fair value is the *only* measurement basis used in today's company financial statements, this is not the case. The IASB state categorically that the main basis is historical cost, but that other bases are more appropriate for certain assets and liabilities. In essence, this results in a mixed valuation model approach.

2.7 The consequences of global IFRS adoption

There is no doubt that as businesses operate increasingly in a global market, and with the internationalisation of capital markets, a common financial reporting language is needed so that communication with investors and other users is improved. The growing complexity of some financial transactions requires a strong financial reporting system to respond, so that the accounting is carried out in a consistent and understandable manner. Users require consistent and comprehensive accounting standards which are based on clear principles and sound professional judgement, rather than complex rules and guidance. This will enable the financial statements to reflect the underlying economic reality of companies' affairs.

Global adoption IFRSs should provide all these benefits, and, indeed, most research shows that the preparers and users of financial statements prepared under IFRS are benefitting. Companies are able to attract capital from a larger pool of investors, which drives down their cost of capital, and facilitates cross-border mergers and acquisitions activity, and strategic investment.

Surveys of, and other research conducted into, EU listed companies following the 2005 move to IFRS have shown that, in general, adoption went well, with an improvement in the quality of financial statements and subsequent reductions in the cost of capital, although this is not uniform across all EU countries. It should be noted, however, that measures of 'quality' and 'cost of capital' are subjective and can be influenced by many other factors. Fears over the use of fair values appeared to be unfounded; although, again, it should be noted that prior to the switch to IFRS, the EU had negotiated that a modified version of IAS 39 *Financial Instruments: Recognition and Measurement* be adopted following many continental European banks' objections to the requirements for **hedge** accounting. A general criticism of IFRSs was the volume and complexity of disclosures required—the average length of companies' annual reports increased significantly, which continues to be an issue. However, others counter this by suggesting that greater disclosure has enhanced the transparency of financial and risk exposure information.

Global adoption of IFRSs does attract further criticism, particularly since the credit crisis. The use of fair values required banks to revalue downwards many of their **financial instruments**, with complainants claiming that these were then artificially low values which would recover in the future. Greater earnings volatility also results as changes in fair value from one year end to the next pass through profit or loss. There are also issues with the number of alternative accounting treatments permitted by some standards (e.g. measurement models for **property, plant and equipment**, and **investment property**; pension fund actuarial differences; and proposals for accounting for leased assets by lessors), which will be examined in more detail in later chapters. In addition, some critics claim that in creating a global monopoly for a single set of accounting standards, more harm than good will result for the efficient functioning of organisations and markets, and some competition in accounting standard-setting would be beneficial. Quite how this might work in practice is questionable.

One common theme that has emerged from recent research is that the benefits of IFRS adoption depend on a country's enforcement mechanisms for ensuring proper application of IFRS. These vary from country to country; even in Europe they are delegated to a national level. In the UK, for example, the preparation of financial statements is only part of the financial reporting system, with the audit, listing rules, corporate governance, and regulation of these playing their part in ensuring that the financial statements provide high quality information. Specifically, in relation to appropriate application of IFRS (and companies legislation), the **Financial Reporting Review Panel** (FRRP), a body of the FRC, was set up to examine the published annual reports of companies for compliance, either through its own selection procedures or following complaints from the public, press, or City. Where it appears that requirements have not been followed and the financial statements are defective in some way, the panel has powers to require remedial action to be taken, which could be the company withdrawing the accounts and reissuing them. It should be stressed that in the

UK this is fairly rare and a less extreme sanction could require correction of the error in the comparative figures in the next set of financial statements.

2.8 The future of IFRS

The year 2011 was crucial for the future of IFRS globally. The IASB/FASB nine-year convergence project came to an end with the publication of some major revised accounting standards in the areas of consolidated financial statements and financial instruments, and the issue of the fair value standard, although the revenue recognition and leasing standards are still not finalised. At this point Sir David Tweedie's tenure as Chair of the IASB came to an end and Hans Hoogervorst replaced him. A period to enable implementation and review of the new standards has followed. Although other projects are still ongoing with new standards in the pipeline, the IASB is undertaking a consultation on its future work programme. Although not yet finalised, the feedback to this exercise is suggesting the development of a broader research and development programme that supports a smaller and more focused standards-level programme. The conceptual framework project will also be restarted. The IFRS Foundation is committed to countries fully adopting IFRS, with convergence seen as an intermediary step. Working relationships with counties in convergence processes, including the USA, will reflect this aim. It is also likely that the rise of the 'BRIC' economies will influence the IASB's development.

One of the most critical decisions will be that of the USA and whether it fully adopts IFRSs for domestic listed companies. IFRSs will not be able to be a truly global system if the USA does not do this. It is suggested that if the USA does not adopt IFRS, the structure of the IASB, with its significant number of US members, would have to change, and this could even lead to the coalition of countries supporting the IASB falling apart. A further consequence could be that US companies would become isolated, losing easy access to global capital markets, and the USA would no longer play the large influential role it currently enjoys.

 ## Summary of key points

In order for high quality financial information to be available which will assist the efficient functioning of global capital markets, high quality systems to produce this are required. These have evolved over time, with different countries developing their own methods based on their economies, legal systems, professional bodies, and culture, etc.

Any financial reporting system needs to determine the overall aim of financial statements and the methods of accounting used in their preparation. In the UK the overriding concept of 'true and fair' has been required for financial statements since the middle of the twentieth century. Following a number of prominent accounting scandals, accounting standards, which specified methods of accounting for certain transactions and events, began to be developed by the ASC, an independent body set up for the purpose by the existing professional accounting bodies. Other capital economies also developed their own GAAP.

However, in today's global economy with multinational companies, international markets, and cross-border listings, a common language to be used in financial accounting is increasingly necessary to ensure that users have the information they require for the type of decisions they make. Thus, the use of a set of global accounting standards, which are accepted by markets in different jurisdictions, has become increasingly important.

The IASC, an independent international body, had already produced some accounting standards for international use, although they were not widely accepted. The main impetus for more international use came from a reorganisation of the IASC in 2000, which became the IASB, acceptance of the use of IASs from IOSCO in the early 2000s, and then the requirement from 1 January 2005 for all listed European companies to use them. Since the recent global financial crisis the leaders of the G20 nations have called for the use of high quality international standards. Although there are issues with the change, more and more countries have now switched to the use of international accounting standards, and, very importantly, the IASB and the US FASB have been engaged in a project to converge their two sets of standards since 2002. The final key step in achieving a truly global set of standards requires the US markets to accept their use for all US domestic companies—they currently do accept cross listings prepared under IAS/IFRS.

International accounting standards are principles based, where sound professional judgement in their application is vital, with an underpinning conceptual basis, and there has been much discussion about the relative merits of such a system over rules based standards, which is what US GAAP has tended towards. Currently, the IASB and FASB are working towards the development of a converged conceptual framework, which will be truly principles based.

Although the IASB/FASB convergence project officially came to an end in 2011, the joint work continues, and it is highly likely that in the next five or six years, the USA will have completely converted to the use of IASs.

 ## Further reading

DiPiazza, S. A., Flynn, T., McDonnell, D., Quigley, J. H., Samyn, F. and Turley, J. S. (2008) *Principles-based accounting standards*. Presented at the 4th Global Public Policy Symposium, January 2008. Available at: http://wwwgrantthornton.com/staticfiles/GTCom/files/services/Audit%20and%20assurance%20services/Assurancepublications/PBAS_White_Paper.pdf (accessed 30 September 2012). Why read? A discussion of the importance of principles-based accounting standards from the leaders of the top accountancy firms.

International Accounting Standards Board (IASB) (2010) *Conceptual Framework for Financial Reporting*. London: IASB (Introduction, Chapters 1 and 3).

International Financial Reporting Standards (IFRS) Foundation. (2012) *About the IFRS Foundation and the IASB*. Available at: http://www.ifrs.org/The+organisation/IASCF+and+IASB.htm (accessed 23 July 2012).

 ## Bibliography

AccountingWeb (2010) *Dissidents Call for 'Rethink' on IFRS*. Available at: http://www.accountingweb.co.uk/ (accessed 30 September 2012).

ASB (Accounting Standards Board) (2010) *The Future of Financial Reporting in the United Kingdom and Republic of Ireland*. London: ASB.

Bruce, R. (2008) *Discussing the Credit Crunch*. Interview with Sir David Tweedie and John Smith, IFRS Foundation Insight Q1/Q2 2008. Available at: http://www.ifrs.org/Archive/INSIGHT-journal/Q1-and-Q2-2008/Documents/INSIGHT_Q1Q208_lowres.pdf (accessed 30 September 2012).

Bruce, R. (2011) *Europe and IFRSs: Six Years On*. London: IFRS Foundation.

Bullen, H. G. and Crook, K. (2005) *A New Conceptual Framework Project*. Available at: http://www.fasb.org/ (accessed 30 September 2012).

DiPiazza, S. A., Flynn, T., McDonnell, D., Quigley, J. H., Samyn, F. and Turley, J. S. (2008) *Principles-Based Accounting Standards*. Presented at the 4th Global Public Policy Symposium, January 2008. Available at: http://wwwgrantthornton.com/staticfiles/GTCom/files/services/Audit%20and%20assurance%20services/Assurancepublications/PBAS_White_Paper.pdf (accessed 30 September 2012).

FASB (Financial Accounting Standards Board) (2010) Exposure Draft, *Conceptual Framework for Financial Reporting: The Reporting Entity*. Norwalk, CT: FASB.

FRC (Financial Reporting Council) (2011) *Project on 'True and Fair'*. Available at: http://www.frc.org.uk/ (accessed 30 September 2012).

Flint, D. (1982) *A True and Fair View in Company Accounts*. Monograph. Edinburgh: ICAS.

G20 (2009) *Declaration on Strengthening the Financial System*. London: G20.

Hoffmann, L., QC and Arden, M. H. (1983) *Legal Opinion Obtained by Accounting Standards Committee of True and Fair View, with Particular Reference to the Role of Accounting Standards*. London: Accounting Standards Committee.

IASB (1989) *Framework for the Preparation and Presentation of Financial Statements*. London: IASB.

IASB (International Accounting Standards Board) (2010a) *Conceptual Framework for Financial Reporting 2010*. Introduction and Chapters 1 and 3. London: IASB.

IASB (International Accounting Standards Board) (2010b) Exposure Draft, *Measurement Uncertainty Analysis Disclosure for Fair Value Measurements*. London: IASB.

IASB (International Accounting Standards Board) (2010c) Comprehensive Project Summary, *Developing common fair value measurement and disclosure requirements in IFRS and US GAAP*. London: IASB.

IASB (International Accounting Standards Board) (2010d) *A Guide to the IFRS for SMEs*. London: IASB.

IASB (International Accounting Standards Board) (2011) IFRS 13 *Fair Value Measurement*. London: IASB.

IASB (International Accounting Standards Board) and FASB (Financial Accounting Standards Board) (2002). *The Norwalk Agreement*. Norwalk, CT: IASB and FASB.

IASB (International Accounting Standards Board) and FASB (Financial Accounting Standards Board) (2006) *A Roadmap for Convergence between IFRSs and US GAAP – 2006–2008, Memorandum of Understanding*. London: IASB and FASB.

ICAEW (Institute of Chartered Accountants in England and Wales) *Knowledge Guide to UK Accounting Standards*. Available at: http://www.icaew.com (accessed 1 October 2012).

ICAEW (Institute of Chartered Accountants in England and Wales) (2010) *Business Models in Accounting: The Theory of the Firm and Financial Reporting*. London: ICAEW.

ICAS (Institute of Chartered Accountants of Scotland) (2006) *Principles not Rules, A Question of Judgement*. Edinburgh: ICAS.

IFRS (International Financial Reporting Standards) Foundation (2007) *The EU two years after the adoption of IFRSs*. IFRS Foundation Insight Q4 2007. London: IFRS.

IFRS (International Financial Reporting Standards) Foundation. *About the IFRS Foundation and the IASB*. Available at: http://www.ifrs.org/ (accessed 1 October 2012).

IFRS (International Financial Reporting Standards) Foundation and IASB (International Accounting Standards Board) (2012) *Who We Are and What We Do*. London: IFRS and IASB.

J Sainsbury plc.(2010) *Annual Report and Financial Statements, 2010*. London: J Sainsbury plc.

Li, S. (2010) Does mandatory adoption of international financial reporting standards in the European Union reduce the cost of capital?, *The Accounting Review*, 85(2): 607–636.

Moore, M. QC (2008) *The True and Fair Requirement Revisited: Opinion*. London: Financial Reporting Council.

Pijper, T. (2009) IFRS in Europe – not yet an unqualified success, *International Accountant*, 45(Feb/Mar): 6–7.

Pitt, H. (2010) Following the road to IFRS convergence, *Compliance Week*. Available at: http://www.complianceweek.com (accessed 3 October 2012).

Singleton-Green, B. (2011) Who calls the tune?, *Accountancy*, 147(1410): 104.

Soderstrom, N. S. and Sun, K. J. (2007) IFRS adoption and accounting quality: a review, *European Accounting Review*, 16(4): 675–702.

Tweedie, D. (2011) *The Future of Financial Reporting, Convergence or Not?* Speech to the US Chamber of Commerce, March 2011. Washington, DC.

UK Companies Act 2006 (2006) Available at: http://www.legislation.gov.uk/ (accessed 9 August 2012).

Questions

● Quick test

1   High quality financial information is important to everyone. Of the various reasons that support this conclusion which ones seem most important to you and why?

2   Explain why neutrality is a key ingredient of high quality financial reporting. How might non-neutral financial information be harmful to investors?

●● Develop your understanding

3   Should usefulness in decision-making be the predominant objective of financial reporting or does stewardship (accountability) still have a role?

4   How important are accounting standards in ensuring the quality of financial information in the marketplace? What other functions or roles must be carried out for the financial reporting system to be considered high quality?

5   Discuss how the International Accounting Standards Board's *Conceptual Framework* contributes to high quality corporate reporting.

6   Critically evaluate whether the 'substance over form' concept, inherent in international accounting standards, results in financial statements that are fairly stated.

7   The IASB's *Conceptual Framework* sets out the concepts that underlie the preparation and presentation of financial statements that external users are likely to rely on when making economic decisions about an entity. Also contained within the *Framework* are the definitions of, and recognition criteria for, the five elements related to the financial position and performance of the entity, plus explanations of the qualitative characteristics which make the information provided in the financial statements useful to users.

(a) Discuss the purpose and authoritative status of the *Framework*.

(b) Using examples of items in an entity's financial statements, critically evaluate why the definitions and recognition criteria of the five elements and the details of the qualitative characteristics are of particular importance to the users of an entity's financial statements.

8   If an uncertain future event will determine whether *any* economic benefits flow to or from the entity, can an asset or a liability be recognised? What if the entity can influence whether that future event occurs?

Visit the Online Resource Centre for solutions to all these end of chapter questions plus visual walkthrough solutions. You can test your understanding with extra questions and answers, explore additional case studies based on real companies, take a guided tour through a company report, and much more. Go to the Online Resource Centre at **www.oxfordtextbooks.co.uk/orc/maynard/**

3

Corporate governance, sustainability, and ethics

➤ Introduction

Today, high quality financial information is more than just relevant and faithfully representational financial statements which are, principally, prepared for shareholders and lenders. A high quality financial reporting system needs to be transparent, to provide information about how the financial results and position have been achieved, and to enable the assessment of the long-term success of the business. Many other stakeholders, such as customers, suppliers, and the public, as well as the shareholders and lenders, are increasingly interested in this information; therefore, issues such as who runs the company, how it is run and governed, what the company's environmental and social policies are, and how shareholders are involved in the company, need to be explained. This can be seen in a listed company's annual report, where approximately half of the report is devoted to narrative information, some of which explain the financial data, but much of which addresses the above issues of concern to this wider stakeholder group.

This chapter considers in further depth why this information is provided, the regulation, if any, that governs the information, and the principles that underpin it.

Learning objectives

After studying this chapter you will be able to:

- understand the wider issues that the provision of high quality financial information encompasses
- understand what corporate governance is, its significance, and the issues the subject covers
- explain the five key areas of corporate governance included in the Financial Reporting Council's (FRC) *UK Corporate Governance Code 2010*
- explain the reporting requirements with regard to corporate governance
- understand the increasing significance of corporate sustainability issues for companies and their stakeholders
- explain how and why corporate sustainability issues may be reported
- understand how ethical behaviour is integral to the financial reporting chain.

✔ **Key issues checklist**

- ❑ Definitions of, and issues covered by, corporate governance.
- ❑ Stewardship and agency theories.
- ❑ The consequences of poor corporate governance.
- ❑ The UK's approach to regulation of corporate governance—principles based on 'comply or explain'.
- ❑ The development of the FRC's *UK Corporate Governance Code 2010*.
- ❑ The board of directors and regulation that governs their actions.
- ❑ The five key areas of corporate governance included in the *UK Corporate Governance Code*—leadership, effectiveness, accountability, remuneration, and relations with shareholders.
- ❑ The external audit and the relationship of the auditor to the audit committee.
- ❑ The reporting requirements with regard to corporate governance.
- ❑ The issues corporate sustainability encompasses, mainly environmental and social.
- ❑ The increasing significance of these issues for companies and their stakeholders.
- ❑ How corporate sustainability may be reported.
- ❑ Why ethical behaviour is important.
- ❑ Ethics in business—the link from the individual to the organisation.
- ❑ Ethics in professional accountancy bodies.

3.1 A wider financial reporting system

As discussed in Chapter 2, investors in and lenders to listed companies require high quality financial information on which to base their decisions and in which they can have confidence. Financial reporting systems in the UK therefore ensure that financial statements are prepared according to companies legislation and international financial reporting standards (IFRS) and are audited by a regulated firm of professional accountants in accordance with audit regulation. However, other issues, in addition to financial matters, are becoming increasingly important for investors, for example how a company is managed and run, whether its behaviour is ethical, the long-term sustainability of the business, and its attitude to the environment and local communities. Thus, reporting systems should be thought of in a wider sense as they need to provide information that encompasses these matters. As for financial statements, users need to have confidence in this information; thus, in the UK this has resulted in the development of other regulation concerned with corporate governance and social responsibility matters.

Figure 3.1 represents the relationships of the interested parties in companies and the reports they produce.

If a typical UK listed company's annual report is obtained, the user will find that it contains, on average, over 100 pages, with approximately half (the front half) being narrative reports. These might include the following:

- chairman's/chief executive's statement
- directors' report
- business review

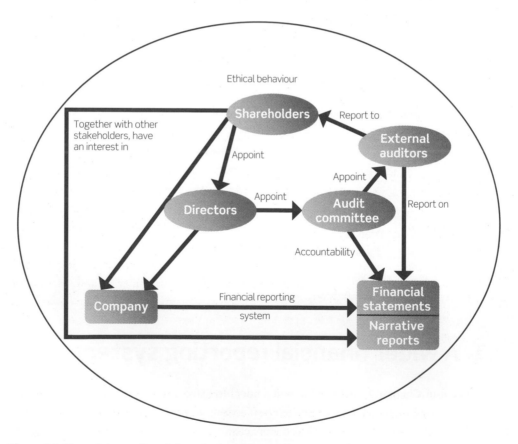

Figure 3.1 Financial reporting: interested parties

- directors' remuneration report
- statement of corporate governance
- statement of corporate responsibility.

(Note: Chapter 4 discusses the format and content of the actual financial statements contained in the second half.)

Some of these narrative reports provide an analysis of the numbers in the financial statements; others deal with corporate governance and social and environmental issues—all have grown in length over the past two decades. Some of the narrative reports are required by statute; others from listing requirements; others contain information provided voluntarily. They will vary in style and approach from company to company, but one key feature is that most of this information is not audited, in other words there is no independent assurance that the information is 'true and fair'. (The external auditor of the financial statements is only required to ensure that the information does not conflict with the financial statements.)

All of this therefore raises a number of questions:

- Do these reports provide the information that users increasingly want?
- What, if any, regulations govern the information contained in these reports?
- Can users have confidence in this information?
- Is the information comparable from company to company?
- Is this the best way of providing this information?

3.2 Corporate governance

3.2.1 Definition

The significance of corporate governance has grown enormously over the last 20 years, driven mainly by high profile corporate collapses and, more recently, the financial crisis. The continuous stream of media reports and articles have highlighted many issues, such as regulation and the inability of regulators to control how banks and other large corporations conduct their business, remuneration levels, risk, and the link between risk and reward, fraud, and dishonesty. Many of these issues stem from a lack of accountability of, and trust in, the management of companies and can be summarised in a definition that encapsulates what corporate governance is about:

> The system by which companies are directed and controlled.
>
> *(Cadbury, 1992)*

The roots of corporate governance are in stewardship and the principal–agent problem, with more recent stakeholder theories underpinning the role and behaviour of companies in society today. Stewardship describes the role the management of a company (the board of directors) are delegated by the investors (the shareholders). The directors are accountable to the investors and are expected to provide them with open and honest reports about the direction in which the company is being taken, and whether they are discharging their duties properly. The assumption is that the directors are acting in the best interest of the shareholders, which may be the maximisation of wealth.

However, this separation of ownership and control can result in the goals of the shareholders (the principal) and the directors (the agent) conflicting. The principal–agent problem assumes that the directors will pursue their own personal objectives, for example the maximisation of their own remuneration or short-term profits, rather than the long-term wealth of the company and its shareholders. To be able to do this, the directors can rely on the fact that they have information that is not available to shareholders, or, in other words, information asymmetry.

The relationship between the shareholders and directors is therefore key in corporate governance, as seen in updated definitions of the purpose of corporate governance following recent changes to regulation in this area.

> The role of corporate governance is to protect and advance the interests of shareholders through setting the strategic direction of a company and appointing and monitoring capable management to achieve this.
>
> *(Walker Review, 2009)*

> The purpose of corporate governance is to facilitate effective, entrepreneurial and prudent management that can deliver the long-term success of the company.
>
> *(FRC, 2010a)*

3.2.2 The role of reporting in corporate governance

Good corporate governance therefore requires that shareholders have trust in the directors. This will come from the directors being properly accountable to the shareholders, in other words providing an account of how they have fulfilled their responsibilities so that the shareholders can evaluate their performance. Financial reporting systems that produce high quality financial statements are part of this system of accountability, but more information is needed than just the numbers. From the various definitions given in the previous section, it can be seen that corporate governance requires details of both how shareholders' wealth has been, and will be, created and how it is, and will be, protected.

> Through reporting and auditing, chartered accountants support transparency and the flow of reliable information between management, boards, shareholders, regulators and other stakeholders.
>
> *(ICAEW, 2007)*

3.2.3 The consequences of ineffective corporate governance

The past 20 years have seen a significant number of high-profile corporate collapses, including Maxwell (1991, UK), Barings Bank (1995, UK), Enron (2001, USA), Parmalat (2003,

Italy), and Lehman Brothers (2008, USA). While these cannot be attributed to single issues, all exhibit some aspect of corporate governance failure. Of course, the consequences of these collapses do not just impact the company, its investors, and employees—all stakeholders (including those in the supply chain, pensioners, and customers) have suffered losses. The demise of Lehmans, as part of the credit crisis, has had worldwide implications.

Details of two of these cases are provided to illustrate their lack of effective corporate governance.

Financial reporting in practice 3.1 — Maxwell (1991, UK)

Robert Maxwell headed up a complex corporate media empire which was based around two key public companies: Maxwell Communication Corporation and Mirror Group Newspapers. The empire was built up through the 1970s through lavish spending on media companies and high levels of borrowings. In November 1991 Robert Maxwell's body was found floating in the Atlantic ocean near his luxury yacht—a verdict of 'accidental drowning' was delivered. Once the banks called in their loans, it was discovered that £272 million had been stolen from the two public companies' pension funds to prop up the business empire. As a result, the corporate empire collapsed losing the shareholders an estimated £1 billion. Maxwell's sons, who held key positions in various companies, ended up in court, but the case against them collapsed through technical complexities.

Subsequently, the corporate governance issues were identified as follows:

- there was lack of segregation of positions of power—Maxwell (allegedly a bully) was both Chief Executive Office (CEO) and Chairman
- the non-executive directors did not perform a proper independent function
- the pension fund trustees failed to examine Maxwell's financial affairs in sufficient detail
- auditors did not appear to observe the transfers of funds from the pension funds to the companies
- many years previously, in 1969, the then Department for Trade and Industry had considered that Maxwell was 'not to be a person who can be relied upon to exercise proper stewardship of a publicly quoted company', yet he remained in his position.

Financial reporting in practice 3.2 — Enron (2001, USA)

Enron was a Houston-based energy company, founded by Kenneth Lay, who became both CEO and Chairman. The company started as an oil and gas exploration business, but ended up as the world's largest energy trading company. By the time of its demise, it was involved predominantly in trading financial derivatives and energy contacts. The company exhibited phenomenal success and growth—in 1997 it reported sales of $4 billion; by 2000 sales had grown to more than $100 billion. By February 2001 its stock market value was $60 billion, which made it the seventh largest US company at the time. Enron pursued aggressive (and what were subsequently found to be fraudulent) earnings recognition policies, including forward contracts, financial derivatives, etc., and used US rules based accounting standards to avoid accounting for special-purpose entities, in which it had invested, to hide its debt and losses.

(continued)

(continued)

Once the energy markets fell, Enron's losses eventually caught up with the company, and it had to report some large write-offs. Then in August 2001 the chief operating officer, Jeff Skilling, resigned unexpectedly. In response to these events the financial markets started to get nervous and sell shares. Enron's share price fell and fell and its credit rating was cut to 'junk bond' status. Numerous class action lawsuits were filed against company, whilst the company was also accused of insider trading. Enron finally filed for Chapter 11 bankruptcy in December 2001.

The collapse of Enron has had enormous repercussions globally, not least in that it triggered the demise of one of the world's largest professional accountancy firms, Arthur Anderson, which was the company's auditor. The US's Sarbanes–Oxley Act, which governs all manner of internal and external financial accounting and reporting issues, was also a direct result of the scandal. The causes were numerous, but the following can be said to be related to corporate governance:

- there was unfettered power in the hands of the CEO—who was also the Chairman (and who, by some accounts, was a 'cult leader')
- the board of directors were shown to be of poor moral character
- the non-executive directors did not detect the fraudulent activities
- there were conflicts of interest involving members of the internal audit committee, which did not perform its functions of internal control and of checking the external auditing function properly
- the external auditors' independence was compromised by the fact that they earned $millions from non-audit services.

The more recent credit crisis can also be considered to have its roots in poor corporate governance, with a lack of effective control mechanisms to curb excessive risk-taking by financial institutions. Remuneration schemes for bankers, on which there has been much focus, are accused of encouraging short-termism, and failing to manage the interconnection between business risk and incentives. Boards of directors, non-executive directors, and supervisory bodies have also been accused of comprehending neither the nature nor scale of the risks, and weaknesses have been identified in the reporting of risk. (There are parallels here between the credit crisis and the collapse of Barings Bank in the UK in 1995, when a 'rogue trader' was found to be responsible for bringing down the bank as a result of the risky trading in which he was involved, but which was not questioned by his superiors until it was too late.)

3.2.4 The UK's approach to corporate governance

Principally, the UK's approach to corporate governance has been reactionary, with the approach of the government or other authoritative bodies being to commission reports into corporate collapses or other prominent financial scandals, and then to draft or redraft regulation in the area. In 1992 the Cadbury Committee was set up by the FRC, the London Stock Exchange, and the accountancy profession to 'help raise the standards of corporate governance in financial reporting and auditing by setting out clearly the responsibilities of those involved'. Since then there have been numerous reviews and reports into various corporate governance issues, which have culminated in the FRC's *Combined Code* and, which, following the latest revision, is now called the *UK Corporate Governance Code 2010*.

A summary of the various reports is given in Table 3.1.

Table 3.1 Corporate governance reports in the UK since 1992

Date	Review/report	Focus of review
1992	Cadbury	Comprehensive: Operation of the main board of directors Audit and remuneration subcommittees Non-executive directors Auditing and the relationship with the external auditor Shareholder relations
1995	Greenbury	Directors' remuneration
1998	Hampel	Implementation of Cadbury and Greenbury Approach to corporate governance should be to *contribute to* business prosperity
1998	Combined Code	Amalgamated Cadbury, Greenbury, and Hampel
1999	Turnbull	Internal controls (updated in 2005)
2003	Higgs	Non-executive directors
2003	Tyson	Recruitment and development of non-executive directors
2003	Smith	The audit committee (updated in 2008)
2004	A practical guide	Implementation of corporate governance
2006, 2008 and 2009	Combined Code	Revisions and updates
2009	Turner	Causes of global financial crisis Regulation and supervisory approaches Bankers' remuneration and risk-taking
2009	Walker	Banking sector Risk management Remuneration incentives Effectiveness of the board of directors—skills and expertise, performance of subcommittees Role of institutional shareholders
2010	UK Corporate Governance Code	Revision of Combined Code, incorporating Walker recommendations
2010	UK Stewardship Code	Engagement between companies and institutional investors

The approach to corporate governance in all these reports has maintained the overriding one set out by Cadbury—that this should be principles based rather than rules based, with the reporting being based on a 'comply or explain' approach. The Financial Services Authority (FSA) listing rules require companies to include a statement on whether, and how they have, complied with the latest set of corporate governance regulations or to explain why they have not complied. The *UK Corporate Governance Code* stresses that good corporate governance practices should be ingrained in businesses as an aspect of their codes of ethics. Detailed regulation may unnecessarily constrain business practice and innovation, and could lead to a 'tick-box' mentality. Businesses should pay more attention to the spirit of the code rather than its letter.

3.3 The UK Corporate Governance Code 2010

The *UK Corporate Governance Code* sets out corporate governance principles and recommendations (described as provisions). The context of the Code has not been changed from Cadbury:

> Corporate governance is the system by which companies are directed and controlled. Boards of directors are responsible for the governance of their companies. The shareholders' role in governance is to appoint the directors and the auditors and to satisfy themselves that an appropriate governance structure is in place. The responsibilities of the board include setting the company's strategic aims, providing the leadership to put them into effect, supervising the management of the business and reporting to shareholders on their stewardship. The board's actions are subject to laws, regulations and the shareholders in general meeting.
>
> *(FRC, 2010a)*

The five areas dealt with by the Code are:

A   Leadership

B   Effectiveness

C   Accountability

D   Remuneration

E   Relations with shareholders.

3.3.1 The board of directors

Sections A and B deal with the board of directors, considered the 'apex of the internal control system' (Jensen, 1993). Directors are appointed by the shareholders and are therefore accountable to them (as discussed in an earlier section), but corporate governance principles require that they are responsible for the long-term success of the company, which will involve relations with all stakeholders. This principle ties in with directors' duties, as specified in the Companies Act 2006, section 172. The implication here is that directors' duties are no longer just about acting in the best interests of the company, but that they should act for the good of society at large—good corporate governance as part of a wider corporate social responsibility.

Section 172: Duty to promote the success of the company

1   A director of a company must act in the way he considers, in good faith, would be most likely to promote the success of the company for the benefit of its members as a whole, and in doing so have regard (amongst other matters) to:

(a) the likely consequences of any decision in the long term,

(b) the interests of the company's employees,

(c) the need to foster the company's business relationships with suppliers, customers and others,

(d) the impact of the company's operations on the community and the environment,

(e) the desirability of the company maintaining a reputation for high standards of business conduct, and

(f) the need to act fairly as between members of the company.

(Companies Act, 2006, s.172)

The *UK Corporate Governance Code* attempts to address the classic disciplinary problem of constraining versus enabling as it relates to a board of directors, in other words how they are prevented from pursuing undesirable actions while, at the same time, given the appropriate encouragement to act productively. Thus, the Code deals with structural issues, how the board is managed and lead, how appointments are made, and how it should operate. The provisions are split under leadership and effectiveness headings.

3.3.2 Leadership

The main principles of the Code are as follows:

- Every company should be headed by an effective board which is collectively responsible for the long-term success of the company.

- There should be a clear division of responsibilities at the head of the company between the running of the board and the executive responsibility for the running of the company's business. No one individual should have unfettered powers of decision.

- The chairman is responsible for leadership of the board and ensuring its effectiveness on all aspects of its role.

- As part of their role as members of a unitary board, non-executive directors should constructively challenge and help develop proposals on strategy.

(FRC, 2010a)

The chairman, required to be independent on appointment, is considered to have an absolutely crucial role in ensuring good corporate governance. The chairman and CEO, who is responsible for the actual running of the company's operations, are required to be different people, to avoid the problems of Maxwell and Enron, with the chief executive not being able to move to the role of chairman. This is different from the typical US model, where there is still no such required separation of duties, despite Enron.

The structure of the board of directors of a typical UK company is unitary, with the non-executive directors being part of this main board, rather than comprising a second board. Cadbury first recommended that there should be at least three non-executive directors on a board and set out their role. The Higgs Report in 2003 (following the Enron and Parmalat scandals) raised the prominence of this role by making what were considered at the time quite radical proposals, but which are now incorporated into the *UK Corporate Governance Code*. The Code requires that for all FTSE 350 companies at least half the board should comprise independent non-executives.

The position of a non-executive director is tricky. There is inherent conflict in that the intention is for them to both contribute expertise, but, at the same time, be scrutinising the performance of the executive directors. Higgs recommended that they be remunerated adequately for their work. This, together with the fact that many non-executive directors are already executive directors of other companies, leads to the perception that their independence may be compromised. Research into whether, and how, non-executives have contributed to good corporate governance is mixed, with some showing that they act as effective monitors of management, with share prices reacting positively to their appointment, while other research has found a negative effect on financial performance. In spite of this they are generally considered a pillar of good corporate governance.

3.3.3 Effectiveness

The main principles of the Code are as follows:

- The board and its committees should have the appropriate balance of skills, experience, independence and knowledge of the company to enable them to discharge their respective duties and responsibilities effectively.

- There should be a formal, rigorous and transparent procedure for the appointment of new directors to the board.

- All directors should be able to allocate sufficient time to the company to discharge their responsibilities effectively.

- All directors should receive induction on joining the board and should regularly update and refresh their skills and knowledge.

- The board should be supplied in a timely manner with information in a form and of a quality appropriate to enable it to discharge its duties.

- The board should undertake a formal and rigorous annual evaluation of its own performance and that of its committees and individual directors.

- All directors should be submitted for re-election at regular intervals, subject to continued satisfactory performance.

(FRC, 2010a)

This section of the Code deals with the composition of the board, elections and re-elections to the board, and the development of the board as a body to take the company forward. A board should be of appropriate size so that it can discharge its duties properly; a balance has to be struck between one large enough to include all necessary expertise, but one that is not too large so that decision-making becomes cumbersome.

A nominations committee, comprising mainly non-executive directors, is required to lead the process for board appointments, and there should be appropriate procedures in place and provision of support to ensure both new and existing directors are properly introduced to, and receive up-to-date information about, the company and their role, and can refresh their skills. The *UK Corporate Governance Code* introduced new requirements for all directors of FTSE 350 companies to be subject to annual election by shareholders, to replace a system where only some of the directors were re-elected each year by rotation, and for the annual performance evaluations to be conducted by an external facilitator at least once every three years. The chairman is encouraged to comment on the effectiveness of the board in his/her report, which is usually contained in the company's annual report.

3.3.4 Accountability

Accountability encompasses financial and business reporting, as well as risk management, internal control, and audit-related matters. The main principles of the Code are as follows:

- The board should present a balanced and understandable assessment of the company's position and prospects.
- The board is responsible for determining the nature and extent of the significant risks it is willing to take in achieving its strategic objectives. The board should maintain sound risk management and internal control systems.
- The board should establish formal and transparent arrangements for considering how they should apply the corporate reporting and risk management and internal control principles and for maintaining an appropriate relationship with the company's auditor.

(FRC, 2010a)

Directors are already required to produce a statutory report for the company's annual report, the contents of which are governed by sections 416 and 417 of Companies Act 2006, with s.417 setting out the requirements of the business review:

Section 417: Contents of directors' report: business review

1 Unless the company is entitled to the small companies' exemption, the directors' report must contain a business review.

2 The purpose of the business review is to inform members of the company and help them assess how the directors have performed their duty under section 172 (duty to promote the success of the company – see above).

3 The business review must contain—

(a) a fair review of the company's business, and

(b) a description of the principal risks and uncertainties facing the company.

4 The review required is a balanced and comprehensive analysis of—

(a) the development and performance of the company's business during the financial year, and

(b) the position of the company's business at the end of that year, consistent with the size and complexity of the business.

5 In the case of a quoted company the business review must, to the extent necessary for an understanding of the development, performance or position of the company's business, include—

(a) the main trends and factors likely to affect the future development, performance and position of the company's business; and

(b) information about—

(i) environmental matters (including the impact of the company's business on the environment),

(ii) the company's employees, and

(iii) social and community issues, including information about any policies of the company in relation to those matters and the effectiveness of those policies; and

(c) information about persons with whom the company has contractual or other arrangements which are essential to the business of the company.

If the review does not contain information of each kind mentioned in paragraphs (b) (i), (ii) and (iii) and (c), it must state which of those kinds of information it does not contain.

6 The review must, to the extent necessary for an understanding of the development, performance or position of the company's business, include—

(a) analysis using financial key performance indicators, and

(b) where appropriate, analysis using other key performance indicators, including information relating to environmental matters and employee matters.

"Key performance indicators" means factors by reference to which the development, performance or position of the company's business can be measured effectively.

7 Where a company qualifies as medium-sized in relation to a financial year, the directors' report for the year need not comply with the requirements of subsection (6) so far as they relate to non-financial information.

8 The review must, where appropriate, include references to, and additional explanations of, amounts included in the company's annual accounts.

(Companies Act, 2006, s.417)

These requirements can be seen to mainly satisfy that of the *UK Corporate Governance Code* for a 'balanced and understandable assessment of the company's *position*', but its emphasis is on the financial year that has passed, rather than providing an assessment of the company's 'prospects', as also required by the Code.

3.3.5 Accountability: risk

At the time of the financial crisis many criticisms focused on the banks' poor reporting of the risks to which they were exposed, despite this being a requirement of the business review. Critics claimed that risks detailed in annual reports are often generic risks of merely being in business rather than explaining the factors that may affect the ability of the company to achieve its strategic objectives, or how the company manages its exposure to the risks it faces. Following the financial crisis, the UK's Department for Business, Innovation and Skills (BIS) has consulted on the future of narrative reporting, which includes the statutory business review. Details of its current proposals are detailed in section 3.4.

Walker's 2009 report also addressed risk and many of his recommendations have been incorporated in the *UK Corporate Governance Code*. The emphasis in the reporting of risk on 'what keeps the executives awake at night' may deliver a more rigorous review of risk. The provisions recommend that discussion of risk and uncertainties should be linked to disclosures of the company's 'business model', in other words details of the basis on which the company generates or preserves value over the longer term.

3.3.6 Accountability: internal controls

Although internal controls are often thought of in terms of financial controls, they serve a wider purpose—that of safeguarding shareholder value, as defined in Turnbull's updated 2005 report:

> Internal control facilitates the effectiveness and efficiency of operations, helps ensure the reliability of internal and external reporting and assists compliance with laws and regulations.
>
> *(FRC, 2005)*

Financial controls incorporate policies and procedures to ensure:

- the safeguarding of assets
- the prevention and detection of fraud and error
- the accuracy and completeness of the accounting records
- the timely preparation of reliable financial information.

They include approval procedures, segregation of duties, the granting of appropriate authority for access to assets and records, checks on accuracy, the reviewing of control accounts and trial balances, and reconciliations.

The maintenance of a sound system of internal controls may assist the management of risk, and the board of directors, through its audit committee, is required to ensure that there are effective internal controls in place. Many corporate collapses can be attributed in part to failures of internal controls.

3.3.7 Accountability: the audit committee

One of the main board's subcommittees, the audit committee has been identified as 'a cornerstone of effective corporate governance' (Spira, 2006). It was recommended by Cadbury in 1992 and widely adopted by UK companies. Audit committees have an extremely important and wide remit of overseeing the integrity of a company's financial affairs, encompassing financial reporting, risk management, internal controls, and monitoring the audit and the independence of the auditors.

The *UK Corporate Governance Code* requires the composition of the committee to comprise at least three independent non-executive directors, at least one of whom has recent and relevant financial experience; for example, it is desirable they have a professional accountancy qualification. The composition of the committee has been shown to be critical to the reliability of financial reporting systems—the more independent non-executive directors, the less the likelihood of financial fraud or earnings management. However, this is recognised as creating some practical problems, as the pool of available, suitability-qualified non-executives, who can commit sufficient time, is relatively small.

3.3.8 Accountability: the audit

The audit committee has prime responsibility for monitoring the company's relationship with the external auditors. The external audit is part of the chain of corporate governance and, as outlined by Cadbury in 1992:

> The annual audit is one of the cornerstones of corporate governance ... The audit provides an external and objective check on the way in which the financial statements have been prepared and presented.

It is a mechanism to increase shareholders' confidence in the financial statements, and contributes to the monitoring and control of directors. Failure of the audit function was a major contributor to the Maxwell and Enron collapses, and the 'big four' auditors of the UK's financial institutions were criticised in the March 2011 House of Lords Economic Affairs Committee report into the UK audit market, with their 'complacency' and 'dereliction of duty' said to have contributed to the financial crisis.

> We do not accept the defence that bank auditors did all that was required of them. In the light of what we now know, that defence appears disconcertingly complacent. It may be that the Big Four carried out their duties properly in the strictly legal sense, but we have to conclude that, in the wider sense, they did not do so.

> *(House of Lords Economic Affairs Committee, 2011, para. 198)*

The objective of an audit is to enable the auditor to express an opinion whether the financial statements are prepared, in all material respects, in accordance with an applicable reporting framework, in other words, in the UK, in accordance with IFRSs and companies legislation. The opinion is expressed that the financial statements show a 'true and fair' view, and thus provides reasonable, but not absolute, assurance of this.

A significant and ongoing problem for the accounting profession is that of the **expectations gap**—the role of the auditor often being misunderstood, even by financially sophisticated individuals. Investors frequently believe that the audit provides more assurance than is actually the case or that it provides assurance on different issues from those actually reported on. The audit report has changed its standard wording a number of times over the past 20 years as attempts to clarify this situation, with the auditors' responsibilities and those of the directors being set out in various forms. However, an audit is a complex procedure, and it is difficult to convey exactly what the auditor does and on what they have based their opinion in a clear, succinct manner that does not lead to further complexity and possible misunderstanding.

The current standard audit report is illustrated in *Financial reporting in practice 3.3.*

Financial reporting in practice 3.3   Marks and Spencer plc, 2012

Independent auditors' report to the members of Marks and Spencer Group plc

We have audited the financial statements of Marks and Spencer Group plc for the 52 weeks ended 31 March 2012 which comprise the Consolidated income statement, the Consolidated statement of comprehensive income, the Consolidated and Company statements of financial position, the Consolidated statement of changes in equity and Company statement of changes in shareholders' equity, the Consolidated cash flow information and Company statement of cash flows and the related notes. The financial reporting framework that has been applied in their preparation is applicable law and International Financial Reporting Standards (IFRSs) as adopted by the European Union and, as regards the parent company financial statements, as applied in accordance with the provisions of the Companies Act 2006.

Respective responsibilities of directors and auditors

As explained more fully in the Directors' Responsibilities Statement, the directors are responsible for the preparation of the financial statements and for being satisfied that they give a true and fair view. Our responsibility is to audit and express an opinion on the financial statements in accordance with applicable law and International Standards on Auditing (UK and Ireland). Those standards require us to comply with the Auditing Practices Board's Ethical Standards for Auditors.

This report, including the opinions, has been prepared for and only for the Company's members as a body in accordance with Chapter 3 of Part 16 of the Companies Act 2006 and for no other purpose. We do not, in giving these opinions, accept or assume responsibility for any other purpose or to any other person to whom this report is shown or into whose hands it may come save where expressly agreed by our prior consent in writing.

(continued)

(continued)

Scope of the audit of the financial statements

An audit involves obtaining evidence about the amounts and disclosures in the financial statements sufficient to give reasonable assurance that the financial statements are free from material misstatement, whether caused by fraud or error. This includes an assessment of: whether the accounting policies are appropriate to the Group's and the parent company's circumstances and have been consistently applied and adequately disclosed; the reasonableness of significant accounting estimates made by the directors; and the overall presentation of the financial statements. In addition, we read all the financial and non-financial information in the Annual report and financial statements 2012 to identify material inconsistencies with the audited financial statements. If we become aware of any apparent material misstatements or inconsistencies we consider the implications for our report.

Opinion on financial statements

In our opinion:

- the financial statements give a true and fair view of the state of the Group's and of the parent company's affairs as at 31 March 2012 and of the Group's profit and Group's and parent company's cash flows for the 52 weeks then ended;
- the Group financial statements have been properly prepared in accordance with IFRSs as adopted by the European Union;
- the parent company financial statements have been properly prepared in accordance with IFRSs as adopted by the European Union and as applied in accordance with the provisions of the Companies Act 2006; and
- the financial statements have been prepared in accordance with the requirements of the Companies Act 2006 and, as regards the Group financial statements, Article 4 of the IAS Regulation.

Opinion on other matters prescribed by the Companies Act 2006

In our opinion:

- the part of the Remuneration report to be audited has been properly prepared in accordance with the Companies Act 2006; and
- the information given in the Directors' report for the financial year for which the financial statements are prepared is consistent with the financial statements.

Matters on which we are required to report by exception

We have nothing to report in respect of the following:

Under the Companies Act 2006 we are required to report to you if, in our opinion:

- adequate accounting records have not been kept by the parent company, or returns adequate for our audit have not been received from branches not visited by us; or
- the parent company financial statements and the part of the Remuneration report to be audited are not in agreement with the accounting records and returns; or
- certain disclosures of directors' remuneration specified by law are not made; or
- we have not received all the information and explanations we require for our audit.

Under the Listing Rules we are required to review:

- the directors' statement, in relation to going concern;
- the parts of the Corporate Governance Statement relating to the Company's compliance with the nine provisions of the UK Corporate Governance Code specified for our review; and
- certain elements of the report to shareholders by the Board on directors' remuneration.

Stuart Watson (Senior Statutory Auditor) for and on behalf of PricewaterhouseCoopers LLP
Chartered Accountants and Statutory Auditors
London
21 May 2012

All audits are governed by regulation, which are legal (Companies Act 2006), mandatory (auditing standards issued by the **Auditing Practices Board (APB)**, a subsidiary of the FRC), and professional body requirements. Auditors must be members of a Recognised Supervisory Body (RSB) (e.g. the ICAEW is a RSB), which has procedures for monitoring auditors and codes of professional ethics. The APB also issues ethical standards concerning independence, objectivity and integrity.

These last items are issues that are at the heart of corporate governance and its relationship with the audit and auditors, and are not new. The Co-ordinating Group on Audit and Accounting Issues in the post-Enron aftermath raised them as issues which needed review and, more specifically, listed the following:

- audit partner rotation
- audit firm rotation
- auditor and client relationships
- auditor's economic dependence on a single client
- non-audit services for audit clients
- disclosure of audit/non-audit fees
- transparency of audit firms.

Some of these are addressed, for example, by audit partners of listed companies being required to change every five years (APB Ethical Standard 3), although the firm does not change; auditors being required to ensure that any non-audit services they provide do not compromise their independence (APB Ethical Standard 5); and disclosures of fees charged for audit and non-audit services. The audit committee plays a key role in managing these issues and the overall relationship with the auditor, and is required by the *UK Corporate Governance Code* to review and monitor the auditor's independence and objectivity, and the effectiveness of the audit process.

In 2010 the FRC produced a report, *Effective Company Stewardship*, to address some of the perceived shortcomings in the effectiveness of the stewardship role of boards and audit committees, and have suggested a number of developments in the conduct of the audit, for example:

- auditors need to have increased scepticism in their exercise of professional judgement, which is fundamental to the quality of every audit
- greater transparency in dialogue is needed between the audit committee and the auditors so that the committee understands how the auditor has reached his/her opinion. The committee needs to openly challenge the auditors to enhance its understanding of where and how professional judgement has been employed
- audit committees need to exercise greater oversight over provision of non-audit services
- there needs to be better dialogue between supervisors, regulators, and auditors in the financial sector
- the audit report (currently a pro-forma statement) should be expanded to clarify the scope of the audit and the work done to reach the audit opinion
- there should be greater liaison between investors and the auditors.

Following the House of Lords Economic Affairs Committee report referred to earlier, these issues will, no doubt, be reviewed again; in addition, the European parliament is looking at measures to widen the audit market. Changes are anticipated by the accountancy profession.

3.3.9 Remuneration

Probably the most contentious and widely commented on area of corporate governance, remuneration levels of directors achieved prominence in the mid-1990s with media reports of eye-wateringly large remuneration packages, which seemed unconnected to the financial successes of the companies.

 Examples of excessive remuneration levels

Cedric Brown of British Gas achieved notoriety in 1995 when a pig named Cedric was paraded outside the AGM as his large remuneration package was agreed.

Sainsbury's chairman, Sir Peter Davis, received a bonus of £2.4 million in 2004, a year when profits at the company fell.

Fred Goodwin, the subsequently de-knighted chairman of Royal Bank of Scotland, received a basic salary and bonuses totalling £15.5 million between 2003 and 2007, but what caused an outcry, in particular, was his pension pot of more than £16 million when he agreed to 'retire' from the bank in 2008 following a disastrous takeover of Dutch banking group ABN Amro.

From 2000 to 2010 the average pay ratio of a FTSE 100 chief executive officer to an average employee working in the company has nearly doubled—from 47 times to 88 times.

Bob Diamond, the former CEO of Barclays, was to have been awarded a bonus for 2011, thought to be £3 million, when return on shareholders' equity fell—he admitted returns were 'unacceptable'.

It is perhaps no wonder that companies and, to a certain extent, institutional investors, complain that the corporate governance debate is often hijacked by questions about remuneration.

The debate over remuneration, stemming from the principal–agent problem, often centres on the balance between fixed and variable elements of remuneration, with the variable elements used as a mechanism to incentivise the directors to improve corporate performance. How much, and the level, of directors' remuneration should be in the form of basic salary (the fixed element) and how much in the form of bonuses and share options (short- or long-term variable elements) causes much controversy. One view is that directors have been unduly incentivised to maximise their companies' profits in the short-term because the focus of many institutional shareholders is on short-term results. This may be because the institutional shareholders themselves are incentivised by short-term aspects of their own remuneration systems. This is clearly counter to the spirit of corporate governance. However, there is evidence that pressure from other shareholders is growing in this area and, from the mid-1990s, changes in the balance of directors' remuneration towards more long-term performance-related pay has resulted.

The principles of the *UK Corporate Governance Code* relating to remuneration are as follows:

- Levels of remuneration should be sufficient to attract, retain and motivate directors of the quality required to run the company successfully, but a company should avoid paying more than is necessary for this purpose. A significant proportion of executive directors' remuneration should be structured so as to link rewards to corporate and individual performance.

- There should be a formal and transparent procedure for developing policy on executive remuneration and for fixing the remuneration packages of individual directors. No director should be involved in deciding his or her own remuneration.

(FRC, 2010a)

The performance-related elements should be stretching and designed to promote the long-term success of the company in line with the company's objectives and risk policies. If a long-term incentive scheme is a share option scheme, the options should not be exercisable for at least three years. Shareholders are required to approve new schemes, but they do not actually have legal power over the level of directors' remuneration. Currently, shareholders have an advisory vote only at a company's AGM, although the proposals from the Department of BIS detailed later may change this.

The Code goes on to advise that the total potentially available rewards should not be excessive, but what is excessive or not is, of course, indefinable. One method of measuring this is by comparison with other companies, but the Code says this should be used with caution, as it is a means of merely ratcheting up general levels of remuneration.

Another subcommittee of the board of directors, the remuneration committee, has responsibility for setting remuneration for the executive directors and the chairman. They also advise on, and monitor, senior management's remuneration. Transparency in this area is strengthened by companies legislation, with the Companies Act 2006 requiring an extensive directors' remuneration report, some of which is audited. A summary of the disclosures is as follows.

- For each director—a summary of performance conditions regarding share options and long-term incentive schemes; an explanation of why they were chosen; and a summary of the methods to be used in assessing whether they have been met. The relative importance of elements that are, or are not, linked to performance are to be explained.

- A performance graph showing total shareholder return for the company for the last five financial years compared with that of a relevant broad equity market index.
- Details of directors' service contracts, including potential early termination payments.
- Audited details for each director of their remuneration, interests, and movements in share options, interests in long-term incentive schemes, pension details. Payments to past directors.

Despite the *UK Corporate Governance Code* and companies legislation disclosure requirements, there is a general consensus that directors' remuneration levels continue to be at extraordinarily high levels. In the UK the government has stepped in and recent proposals put forward by the department of BIS address some of the issues. The proposals include:

- giving shareholders more control, e.g. a binding vote on:
  - future pay policy
  - remuneration notice periods in excess of one year
  - exceptional exit payments
- more use of clawback provisions
- simplification of, and transparency in, the make-up of directors' remuneration
- provision of information on how executive pay relates to employees' salaries
- increasing the diversity of remuneration committees.

3.3.10 Relations with shareholders

Satisfactory engagement between company boards and investors is crucial to the UK's corporate governance regime. Although institutional investors' ownership of UK listed companies is reducing as international ownership increases, it still accounts for approximately 40% of listed company ownership, which is a significant minority.

> Given the weight of their votes, the way in which institutional shareholders use their power to influence the standards of corporate governance is of fundamental importance. Their readiness to do this turns on the degree to which they see it as their responsibility as owners, and in the interest of those whose money they are investing, to bring about changes in companies when necessary, rather than selling their shares.

> *(Cadbury Report, 1992: 50)*

Various reviews have considered institutional investors' relationships with their investee companies and have concluded that the engagement is less than satisfactory, with their actions sometimes in opposition to corporate governance principles.

> It is often said that [pension fund] trustees put fund managers under undue pressure to maximise short-term investment returns, or to maximise dividend income at the expense of retained earnings; and that the fund manager will be reluctant to support board proposals which do not immediately enhance the share price or the dividend rate.... We urge trustees to encourage investment managers to take a long view.
>
> *(Hampel Report, 1998: 41)*

Lord Myners also conducted a review in 2001 into pension fund trustees' roles and responsibilities, and found that many pension fund trustees lacked the necessary investment expertise to act as strong and discerning customers of the investment consultants and fund managers who sold them services. There was insufficient focus on the potential for adding value through active shareholder engagement.

Effective engagement was a key theme of the Walker Review in 2009 and, at the same time, the FRC commissioned a study into this area. Both resulting reports concluded that a more proactive approach to engagement was required, otherwise there was the danger of legislation, which was contrary to the principles-based approach to corporate governance. The engagement needed to be two-way, transparent, and with constructive dialogue conducted not just at set-piece meetings, such as the annual general meeting (AGM) and results announcements, but at other times with the chairman and non-executive directors.

As a result of these reviews, section E of the *UK Corporate Governance Code* has been updated and the FRC has produced a *UK Stewardship Code* (2010), as illustrated by Figure 3.2.

The principles of the *UK Corporate Governance Code* relating to relations with shareholders are as follows:

- There should be a dialogue with shareholders based on the mutual understanding of objectives. The board as a whole has responsibility for ensuring that a satisfactory dialogue with shareholders takes place.

- The board should use the AGM to communicate with investors and to encourage their participation.

(FRC, 2010a)

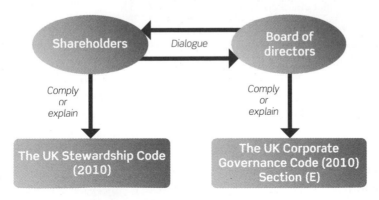

Figure 3.2 Shareholder engagement and the relevant Codes

The *UK Stewardship Code* sets out the role of institutional shareholders. They should recognise their stewardship responsibilities, with transparency on how they have achieved this. Internally, they need to ensure that those involved in fund management and corporate governance liaise effectively. They should be active in giving feedback on governance and other issues to their investee companies, using suitably qualified personnel to conduct this dialogue, to ensure governance issues do not build up. The level of pre-1990s voting by institutional shareholders at AGMs was fairly low and although it has been increasing since, this Code stipulates that they should use their votes at AGM 'thoughtfully' and be encouraged to disclose their level of voting.

3.4 Reporting of corporate governance

The reporting of corporate governance issues is governed by the FSA's *Disclosure and Transparency Rules*. These require a listed company to include a corporate governance statement in its directors' report. This statement must contain a reference to:

1   the corporate governance code to which the issuer is subject; and/or

2   the corporate governance code which the issuer may have voluntarily decided to apply; and/or

3   all relevant information about the corporate governance practices applied beyond the requirements under national law.

(FSA Handbook, 2012: Corporate governance statements, DTR 7.2.2)

To the extent that a company departs from that corporate governance code, it must explain which parts of the code it departs from and the reasons for doing so (DTR 7.2.3 (1) (b))—the 'comply or explain' approach.

In addition to these requirements the disclosure rules specify that the corporate governance statement should include a description of:

●   the main features of the issuer's internal control and risk management systems in relation to the financial reporting process (DTR 7.2.5)

●   the composition and operation of the issuer's administrative, management, and supervisory bodies and their committees (DTR 7.2.7).

In practice, corporate governance statements in companies' annual reports add significantly to the length of the narrative information, as they usually include mini-biographies of the directors, explanations of how the board of directors functions, which subcommittees exist and how they have operated, how the company has managed risk and internal controls, the relationship it has with its auditors and shareholders, and an extensive directors' remuneration report. The information focuses mainly on systems and procedures.

The FRC's 2010 *Effective Company Stewardship* report is concerned with the growth of narrative reporting and how corporate governance matters are reported. It suggests a number of improvements based on the principle that the directors should take full responsibility for ensuring that, viewed as a whole, the annual report should provide a fair and balanced report on their stewardship. The report wants to encourage companies to report on a bespoke basis, as boilerplate disclosures are considered of little use, with more description of the steps the directors have taken to ensure:

● the reliability of all information included

● transparency about the activities of the company and any associated risks.

The department of BIS consulted widely with stakeholders and has produced proposals, which have strong support from user groups, for companies to produce a strategic report backed up by an annual directors' statement. The strategic report would be concise and separate out from the remainder of the published company data the strategic, headline information that all investors would wish to see. The annual directors' statement would contain the remainder of the information and by default would be online.

3.5 Corporate sustainability

The purpose of the corporate governance issues discussed so far are 'to facilitate effective, entrepreneurial and prudent management that can deliver the long-term success of the company' (FRC, 2010a: 1). Although much of the focus of corporate governance is on the relationship between the company, its directors, and shareholders, this is now widening to encompass all stakeholders. How a company's actions affect or are perceived by all stakeholders is becoming increasingly important.

Long-term success undoubtedly means companies have to find means of increasing profits and company value; ways this can be achieved include brand enhancement, the use of more efficient processes, and effective management of risk. All of these have been cited by companies as reasons for the adoption of sustainability practices, which have rapidly been moving up the corporate agenda in the last few years. In the past, corporate sustainability was a niche activity for companies, such as IBM, which established a corporate environmental policy in 1971 and, indeed, its roots are in environmental reporting. Although environmental concerns remain at the top of the sustainability agenda today, this has developed to now include social and ethical issues, such as how human capital is valued in an entity, how intellectual capital is managed, and the impact of an entity's operations on society as a whole. These issues are also referred to under the heading of corporate social responsibility, but the term corporate sustainability is superseding this to indicate a broader approach to environmental and social business practices.

It is difficult to define corporate sustainability concisely as it involves many different issues, but it should be seen as part of a continuing process of building long-term value. Everything a business does should help improve the business's reputation, and encourage customers and other stakeholders to stay involved with it. It also encompasses the continuing commitment by businesses to behave ethically and responsibly, and to contribute to economic development, while improving the quality of life of its workforce and their families, as well as of the local community and society at large. Corporate sustainability emphasises the need for companies to adopt a coherent approach to a range of stakeholders, including investors, employees, suppliers, and customers, and to be accountable to them for their actions.

 Examples of how corporate sustainability can be practised

1 *Choice of suppliers*

Companies should deal with suppliers who practise corporate sustainability themselves. Trading with suppliers who pollute the environment could be as irresponsible as doing so yourself. Customers may perceive companies which favour suppliers who demonstrate responsible policies more favourably. Using local suppliers as much as possible helps companies support their community and this action also reduces energy and carbon emissions from deliveries. Companies should examine their suppliers' employment, health and safety, and environmental practices. Companies should also treat its suppliers fairly, particularly smaller businesses that rely on them. For example, being paid on time can make a big difference to a small business.

2 *How customers are treated*

Companies should have effective communication with customers, telling them openly and honestly about their products and services. Customers are increasingly concerned about the wider impact of supply chains, e.g. on local workforces and environments.

3 *How employees are treated*

For the responsible business, this means doing more than simply complying with legal requirements. A company's reputation can be damaged by being associated with businesses that abuse the rights of their own workers.

4 *The effect of the business on the local community*

Local customers are an important source of sales. By improving their reputation, companies may find it easier to recruit employees locally. A good relationship with local authorities can also make companies' lives easier, e.g. some local authorities prefer to award contracts to businesses with a record of community involvement. There are many ways companies can get involved, e.g. by supporting a local charity or by sponsoring a local event.

5 *The effect of the business on the environment*

Companies should use resources more efficiently and reduce pollution and waste. A company's reputation can be damaged by being associated with businesses that abuse their local environment.

3.5.1 What is driving corporate sustainability?

A 2010 global survey of companies' attitudes towards, and practices and processes in the area of, corporate sustainability carried out by KPMG, one of the big four accountancy firms, in cooperation with The Economist Intelligence Unit, revealed that a majority of the companies surveyed had a corporate sustainability strategy. The key factors driving this were regulation, brand enhancement, risk management, and also a means of cost reduction. This latter factor had been seen as a barrier to progress on sustainability only a few years previously. However, there are a number of ways in which corporate sustainability can now be seen to help cut costs. For example:

- compliance with regulatory requirements ensures reduced litigation costs. Also it is often cheaper to change processes in advance of regulation that requires the changes

- reducing resource use, waste, and emissions helps the environment and cuts utility bills and waste disposal costs

- a good reputation makes it easier to recruit employees. Employees may stay longer, reducing the costs and disruption of recruitment and retraining. Employees are better motivated and more productive

- understanding the wider impact of the business can help in the development of new products and services. Waste implications can be built into the design of new products and production processes.

Reduced costs from good sustainability practices therefore improve business performance, and result in stronger customer loyalty and motivated employees. A reputation as a responsible business that behaves ethically to its suppliers, customers, employees, local community, and society will also boost the corporate image. Sustainability is also seen by some companies as a source of innovation and new business opportunity, and can be a means of company or product differentiation, which, in turn, can lead to an improved share price. Some investors will actively seek environmentally and socially responsible companies.

Although corporate sustainability is undoubtedly increasing in importance for many companies, others continue to have poor internal knowledge about the issues. For many companies other, more pressing matters arising from the current economic environment—short-term financial pressures and lack of credit from banks—head their concerns.

3.5.2 Environmental and social responsibility

Corporate sustainability grew out of environmental responsibility, and this issue still tops the sustainability agenda and is likely to continue to do so in the coming years. For example, a majority of companies report that they have improved their energy efficiency, reduced packaging and waste, or taken other steps to reduce the environmental footprint of their products, and cut either greenhouse gas emissions or other pollutants. KPMG's research highlighted the fact that companies expect legislation to limit carbon emissions at some point and would welcome certainty as to whether this will be enacted. For this reason, many have taken steps in this area before any legislation comes into force.

However, the social aspect of corporate sustainability is also important, and includes companies ensuring that human rights and workers' rights are not abused, that companies have ethical supply chains, and that they do not carry out irresponsible marketing of their products and services. Many abuses of workers' rights in large global retailers' supply chains have been reported over the years, for example workers being forced to work more than 60 hours a week, receiving low wages, working in poor conditions, the use of child labour, cases of harassment, or companies ignoring health and safety legislation. Such retailers, among them Nike, Gap, Marks and Spencer, Next, Tesco, and Sainsbury, have attempted to improve ethical standards within their supply chains through codes of conduct policed by regular visits from ethical auditors. Despite such efforts, poor working conditions, low wages, and abuse of those attempting to join workers' groups or unions often continues.

Some companies will demonstrate their commitment to ethical supply chains by retailing Fairtrade products. Fairtrade is an organised social movement that aims to help producers in developing countries make better trading conditions and promote sustainability. The movement advocates the payment of a higher price to producers, as well as higher social and environmental standards. It focuses, in particular, on exports from developing countries to developed countries, most notably handicrafts, coffee, cocoa, sugar, tea, bananas, cotton, flowers, and gold.

3.5.3 Corporate sustainability today

The Global Reporting Initiative (GRI), a networked-based organisation, defines the goal of sustainable development broadly as follows:

> ...to meet the needs of the present without compromising the ability of future generations to meet their own needs.

(GRI, 2006)

Businesses and organisations all have an important role to play in achieving this goal. As they create new opportunities to generate prosperity through global trade, knowledge-sharing, and access to technology they should recognise that these opportunities are not available for an ever-increasing human population, where millions face poverty and hunger. So sustainable development for businesses is about developing new and innovative ways in which their operations, products, and services impact the earth, people, and economies to ensure this goal is achieved.

3.5.4 Reporting of corporate sustainability

The reporting of corporate sustainability is part of a company's accountability to its stakeholders. In addition, the benefit of enhanced reputation and image is not possible without effective communication of performance on sustainability, and so this is becoming more important for companies. However, there is no regulation governing the reporting, other than that required by accounting standards. For example, IAS 37 *Provisions, Contingent Liabilities and Contingent Assets* requires disclosures of provisions for future costs of rectifying environmental damage or the decommissioning of certain assets used, say, in the extraction of oil (see Chapter 13 for a full discussion of this accounting standard). IAS 1 *Presentation of Financial Statements* also encourages companies to disclose abnormally large items, which may be environmental fines and penalties, separately, otherwise their results would appear distorted. (Chapter 4 discusses this further.)

The Companies Act business review requires information about:

(i) environmental matters (including the impact of the company's business on the environment),

(ii) the company's employees

(iii) social and community issues

including information about any policies of the company in relation to those matters and the effectiveness of those policies. However, these requirements may be considered rather vague. This is recognised by the Department for BIS, which is reviewing narrative reporting and it is likely that the requirements for sustainability reporting will be extended.

One of the inherent problems of reporting in this area is that of what measures can be reported to show a company's performance and whether improvement has been made. For example, how does a business measure their impact on environment? Basic measures like greenhouse gas emissions, and energy and water consumption are able to be counted, and there are methods by which a carbon footprint can be calculated, but many other sustainability issues are unable to be reduced to figures; thus, measurement of progress proves difficult.

The GRI has pioneered the world's most widely-used sustainability reporting framework by setting out principles and performance indicators that companies and other organisations can use to report their economic, environmental, and social performance. The latest (third) version of their *Sustainability Reporting Guidelines*, known as the *G3 Guidelines*, was published in 2006 and is designed to be used by organisations of any size, sector, or location. It contains general and sector-specific content that has been agreed by a wide range of stakeholders around the world.

The *G3 Guidelines* are based on principles, which include materiality, stakeholder inclusiveness, completeness, balance, comparability, accuracy, timeliness, reliability, and clarity. Some of these are similar to the principles (qualitative characteristics) that make financial information useful. However, the guidelines are non-mandatory and what is reported is not audited, thus there is the danger that companies may cherry-pick the guidelines to paint the organisation in as favourable a light as possible. Various high-profile UK companies do follow the guidelines, including Astra Zeneca, Body Shop International, British Airways, BT, Vodafone, and Sainsbury's.

GRI is currently consulting on a new version of its guidelines, G4, which it is anticipated will be available in 2013. The proposals are based on the principles of materiality and clarity, and will include guidelines for companies to report on issues such as the management's approach to sustainability and the link between governance, remuneration, and sustainability performance.

KPMG's 2010 research found that just over one-third of the companies surveyed had issued at least one public report on sustainability performance—these may have been within the 'narrative' part of the companies' annual reports, or some companies choose to issue separate sustainability reports, which can be much more comprehensive and often contain detailed quantitative data. These are companies which are clearly indicating the importance of corporate sustainability to them; such companies may also have a corporate sustainability committee as one of its sub-board committees.

Companies are also encouraged to report properly in this area through recognised reporting awards. ACCA, for example, has sponsored an award since 1991—initially called an Environmental Reporting Award, but now termed a Sustainability Reporting Award—which judges companies on completeness, credibility, and communication criteria.

Financial reporting in practice 3.4   J Sainsbury plc, 2010

Sainsbury's goal, as indicated in its 2010 annual report, is to deliver an ever improving quality shopping experience for its customers with great products at fair prices. It aims to deliver healthy, safe, fresh, and tasty food by setting five values—all of which are connected to corporate sustainability. These values are referred to throughout the narrative reports, which include a comprehensive corporate responsibility review. This includes the following table, although further details are provided in the review.

Corporate responsibility review

Commitments and progress

Value	Commitment	Progress
Best for Food and Health		
Healthier baskets for customers	We will make the most popular items in our customers' baskets healthier, focusing on products that contribute the most saturated fat, salt or sugar to the UK diet, to deliver a real impact on the nation's health.	**Ongoing** — we continue to make the most popular items in our customers' baskets healthier.
Sourcing with Integrity		
Being best for British	We will source great-tasting British products when in season, wherever these meet our customers' expectations for quality and authenticity.	**Achieved and Ongoing** — we remain committed to supporting UK farmers and continue to source British products, both when in season and in certain categories all year round.
Being number one supermarket for animal welfare	We will offer the widest range of higher welfare products of any UK retailer.	**Achieved** — we offer both the widest range of Freedom Food higher welfare products and sell more than any other UK retailer.

Sourcing responsibly and ethically	We will be the largest UK retailer of Fairtrade products (by sales value).	**Achieved** — we are now the world's largest retailer of Fairtrade by value.

Respect for our Environment

Reducing energy	We will reduce our CO2 emissions per square metre by 25% by 2012, against a 2005/06 baseline.	**Ongoing** — our commitment on refrigeration, Eco-stores and reset programme are helping us to progress towards this target.
Reducing packaging	We will reduce our own brand packaging weight relative to sales, by 33% by 2015 against a 2009 baseline.	**Ongoing** — making progress both incrementally through packaging redesign and through packaging innovation like milk bags.
Reducing food waste	We will have all supermarkets and depots connected to a zero food waste to landfill programme by the end of 2009.	**Achieved** — we now have all of our supermarkets and depots connected to a zero food waste to landfill programme.
Reducing waste	We will have all supermarkets and depots connected to a zero waste to landfill programme for operational waste by the end of 2010.	**Ongoing** — making progress by using our back-hauling process more efficiently and ISO14001 at depots.

Making a Positive Difference to our Community

Generating a positive economic impact on communities	We will provide 6,500 new Sainsbury's jobs in 2009/10, through our planned opening of 28 supermarkets and 55 new convenience stores.	**Achieved** — over 6,500 new Sainsbury's jobs were created by opening 38 new supermarkets and 51 new convenience stores.
Supporting local communities	We will launch our Local Charity of the Year scheme, linking every store, Sainsbury's depot and our support centres to a local charity partner each year.	**Achieved** — we have supported over 750 local charities through the scheme this year and donated over £1 million to local charities.

A Great Place to Work

Supporting the development of our colleagues	We will provide over 10,000 colleagues with job opportunities, skills and qualifications through our 'You Can' programme by 2010.	**Ongoing** — we are making progress against our target of providing 10,000 colleagues with job opportunities, skills and qualifications through 'You Can'. To date, around 9,150 colleagues have taken part in 'You Can'.

3.6 Ethics

A couple of words have been used a number of times in the preceding discussions of corporate governance and corporate sustainability, which are at the heart of the two issues and without which a company cannot hope to achieve success in the areas. The words are 'ethical behaviour'.

3.6.1 Ethics in business

Ethical behaviour is considered by some to be of critical importance in maintaining confidence in capital markets. It is fundamental to an organisation's reputation, trustworthiness, and long-term performance, and underpins high quality information that is fit for purpose. Structures, systems, and procedures can be, and have been, established to ensure good corporate governance and good corporate sustainability within organisations, but without ethical and moral integrity these are meaningless. If the two case studies of Maxwell and Enron detailed earlier in the chapter are returned to, it can be seen that despite established structures, reporting systems, and procedures (admittedly some of them flawed), a common thread was the lack of honesty, principally from the man at the top of both empires. If leaders do not demonstrate ethical behaviour, it is difficult for it to be truly embedded in an organisation. Integrity should be instilled at all levels in a business, from leadership tone, through strategy, policies, information, and culture.

> Corporate governance is about what the board does and how it sets the values of the company...
>
> *(FRC, 2010a)*

However, despite regulators, governments, and the public being increasingly concerned about integrity in business, there are wide variations in perceptions of what it actually means and how it can be put into practice. Although integrity is essentially a personal quality, it plays its part in ethical behaviour if it is a joint endeavour of individuals, organisations and professions, including the accounting profession.

The ICAEW's 2007 paper, *Reporting with Integrity*, based on literature of modern moral philosophy, put forward five key aspects of integrity in an individual:

- moral values
- motives
- commitments
- qualities
- achievements.

The report suggests that an individual of integrity is guided by moral values and motives, which are translated into commitments. In turning these commitments into achievements, an individual draws on qualities such as rationality, open-mindedness, and perseverance. The individual's integrity is demonstrated by certain behavioural characteristics, for example being honest and truthful, being fair, and complying with laws.

The question is how these traits of an individual can be promoted through an organisation. In a company, as part of their strategy, oversight and risk-management responsibilities, the directors need to assess their company's approach and commitment to integrity. To be a truly ethical company, integral behaviour needs to be instilled, no matter what the other competing goals are. The company values, standards of behaviour, and support mechanisms need to reinforce and encourage integrity at all levels. So a company needs a robust framework that links the individuals that work for it to a common view of the company's moral values, motives, commitments, qualities, and achievements.

Reporting with Integrity suggests that there are five interconnected drivers of organisational integrity: leadership, strategy, policies, information and culture, and provides examples of how these may be put into practice, as given in Table 3.2.

Table 3.2 Drivers and practical examples of organisational integrity

Driver	Methods by which these may be put into practice
Leadership	Setting the right tone at the top Practising what is preached Signalling that integrity is important to performance and reputation
Strategy	Promoting integrity as integral to the company's strategy Devoting resources and management time Discussing integrity issues at board meetings and acting on the discussions Instilling integrity as part of risk management Ensuring business strategy does not conflict with integrity
Policies	Having a Code of Conduct that incorporates integrity and outlines expected behaviour Providing effective training and support Including discussion of behaviour in appraisals Linking rewards to integral behaviour Providing guidance on conflicts of interest
Information	Monitoring performance Ensuring a proper process for gathering information on the company's commitment to integrity Discussing and acting on this information
Culture	Encouraging employees to voice any concerns without fear of reprimand Encouraging employees to make decisions that are aligned with the company's values Monitoring and disciplining employees who behave without integrity

Figure 3.3 Framework for promoting organisational integrity. This article was first published in Reporting with Integrity: Abstract 2007. Reproduced with permission of ICAEW.

Thus, a framework for promoting integrity in a complex organisation can be represented as shown in Figure 3.3.

3.6.2 Do business ethics pay?

Ethics, if considered as a fundamental underpinning to corporate governance and long-term sustainability, will be of benefit to businesses for the reasons discussed in this chapter. A key question is whether it pays in terms of profitability. The Institute of Business Ethics (IBE) conducted research into whether companies exhibiting commitment to business ethics improved their financial performance. A sample of FTSE 350 companies were divided into those that demonstrated a commitment to ethical behaviour by providing training programmes to reinforce their code of ethics to their employees and those that merely disclosed that they had a code of ethics. The research concluded that in the five years from 2001 to 2005, the first group of companies, who were committed to embedding ethical values into business practice, demonstrated a better financial performance than the second group of companies. (Financial performance was measured by some common ratios—return on capital employed, return on assets (see Chapter 5)—and total return and market value added.) The study also found that accounting-based measures were more influenced by business ethics than market-based indicators.

The results of this research are thus consistent with assertions that companies with demonstrable ethics programmes do benefit financially. Confidence is instilled in their stakeholders, which facilitates reputation building, enhances relations with bankers and investors, helps attract better employees, increases goodwill, better prepares the companies for external changes, and, generally, results in better run companies.

3.6.3 Ethics in professional bodies

As part of the chain of ethical reporting, a company's own accountants, the directors and members of the audit committee, and the external auditor need to exhibit ethical behaviour. Many of these individuals will be professionally qualified accountants, who, through membership of a professional accountancy body, are required to abide by their body's Code of Ethics. Although not a new phenomenon, ethics has become an increasingly important aspect of professional accountancy bodies' standards in recent years, particularly post-Enron, as the public spotlight has been turned on the professions. Thus, all the major UK bodies have their own Codes of Ethics. As the ICAEW states, its code applies to all members, students, affiliates, employees of member firms, and, where applicable, member firms in all of their professional and business activities, whether remunerated or voluntary.

These codes are generally based on the **International Federation of Accountants** (IFAC's) *Handbook of the Code of Ethics for Professional Accountants*. IFAC is a New York-based global organisation for the accountancy profession that is committed to protecting the public interest by developing high-quality international standards, promoting strong ethical values, encouraging quality practice, and supporting the development of all sectors of the profession around the world. The organisation develops and promotes international standards in the areas of auditing and assurance, quality control, ethics, accounting education, and public sector accounting, and has as members national accountancy organisations, such as the UK's ICAEW and CIMA.

IFAC's *Code of Ethics* is principles based rather than rules based, which brings all the advantages of such an approach, as discussed in Chapter 2, in relation to accounting standards. Examples and guidance are provided for many practical situations. The five key principles guiding the code are as follows:

1 *Integrity*
   To be straight forward and honest in all professional and business relationships

2 *Objectivity*
   To not allow bias, conflict of interest or undue influence of others to override professional or business judgements

3 *Professional competence and due care*

   To maintain professional knowledge and skill at the level required to ensure competent professional services based on current developments in practice, legislation and techniques

   To act diligently in accordance with applicable technical and professional standards

4 *Confidentiality*

   To refrain from disclosing confidential information acquired as a result of professional and business relationships without proper and specific authority to disclose unless *there is a* legal or professional right or duty to disclose

   To refrain from using confidential information acquired as a result of professional and business relationships for personal advantage or the advantage of third parties

5   *Professional behaviour*
      Obligation to comply with relevant laws and regulations and avoid any action that discredits the profession

(IFAC, 2012)

The Code discusses threats facing professional accountants, such as those arising from financial or other interests, lack of evaluation of the results of judgements made or services performed, compromises to objectivity, having too long or close a relationship with a client or employer, and intimidation from others which would affect the work performed. Safeguards that can be put in place are either created by the profession, legislation or regulation, for example educational, training, and experience requirements for entry into the profession, continuing professional development requirements, disciplinary procedures and external reviews, or may exist in the work environment.

Ethical requirements for professional accountants in practice and those in business are then set out in more detail. For the accountant in practice, these cover the following areas:

- professional appointment
- conflicts of interest
- second opinions
- fees and other types of remuneration
- marketing professional services
- gifts and hospitality
- custody of client assets
- objectivity—all services
- independence—audit and review engagements
- independence—other assurance engagements.

 Example of principles based codes relating to auditor independence

The provision of non-assurance services to audit clients:

290.156   Firms have traditionally provided to their audit clients a range of non-assurance services that are consistent with their skills and expertise. Providing non-assurance services may, however, create threats to the independence of the firm or members of the audit team. The threats created are most often self-review, self-interest and advocacy threats.

290.157   New developments in business, the evolution of financial markets and changes in information technology make it impossible to draw up an all-inclusive list of non-assurance services that might be provided to an audit client. When specific guidance on a particular non-assurance service is not included in this section, the conceptual framework shall be applied when evaluating the particular circumstances.

290.158   Before the firm accepts an engagement to provide a non-assurance service to an audit client, a determination shall be made as to whether providing such a service would create a threat to independence. In evaluating the significance of any threat created by a particular non-assurance service, consideration shall be given to any threat that the audit team has reason to believe is created by providing other related non-assurance services. If a threat is created that cannot be reduced to an acceptable level by the application of safeguards, the non-assurance service shall not be provided.

(IFAC, 2012)

The ethical requirements for the accountant in business are briefer and encompass:

● potential conflicts

● preparation and reporting of information

● acting with sufficient expertise

● financial interests

● inducements.

The IFAC has also produced a lengthier good practice guide, *Defining and Developing an Effective Code of Conduct for Organisations* (2007), which defines key principles for organisations on which to base their ethics' policies and internal codes.

Although ethics is now incorporated into professional accountancy bodies' professional qualifications, and it is included within continuing professional development (CPD) requirements, some research has indicated that the various codes have had little practical effect. It suggests that most professional accountants will gain experience of ethics from on-the-job situations and will not necessarily consult their professional body's theoretical code. Other research suggests that rather than serving public interest, the various ethical codes tend to serve the interests of the profession, so that it can hide behind them if a financial scandal involving poor ethical behaviour occurs.

 ## Summary of key points

A financial reporting system needs to provide high quality and transparent information to all stakeholders, who are interested in a wide range of corporate issues other than the financial results and position. It has been demonstrated many times through high-profile corporate collapses and scandals, and latterly the global financial crisis, how important the question of how a company has achieved its results is, and how crucial an effective system of control and regulation over the financial reporting chain is. Ethical behaviour and honest accountability from all involved are at the heart of this. The ultimate goal of companies is that of wealth creation and protection, with the focus on the long-term success and sustainability.

Many aspects of what a company must and may not do, what the duties of its directors and auditors are, and what must be reported are governed by statutory legislation in the form of Companies Act 2006. However, regulation over how a company runs its affairs, in other words corporate governance, has developed in the UK through principles based regulation, developed by the FRC, largely as a result of high-profile corporate collapses or public disquiet. This has culminated in the publication of the *UK Corporate Governance Code 2010*, which addresses key areas relating to 'how a company is directed and controlled'—the leadership and effectiveness of the board of directors, their accountability and remuneration, and the relations with shareholders. The section dealing with accountability discusses the relationship with the external auditors. The audit is governed by its own statutory legislation, and professional and other regulations, including ethics, and is a key link in the financial reporting chain.

The requirements of the *UK Corporate Governance Code* are based on the stewardship principle of directors of companies being accountable to shareholders; however, other stakeholders are increasingly interested in these issues, together with information about the long-term sustainability of companies. Corporate sustainability encompasses issues of ethical environmental and social behaviour, and a growing number of companies are embracing corporate sustainability practices as a means to long-term success.

The reporting of the corporate governance principles of the *UK Corporate Governance Code* is based on the principle of 'comply or explain', although the FSA's Disclosure Rules and Transparency Rules do require listed companies to provide information about their corporate governance practices. As yet, there is little regulation governing the reporting of corporate sustainability matters, and so there is wide variation in the quantity and quality of reporting practices here; however, this may well change as additional legislation is introduced.

Further reading

FRC (Financial Reporting Council) (2010) *The UK Approach to Corporate Governance.* Available at: http://www.frc.org.uk/corporate/ (accessed 3 October 2012).

FRC (Financial Reporting Council) (2010) *UK Corporate Governance Code 2010.* Available at: http://www.frc.org.uk/corporate/ukcgcode.cfm (accessed 3 October 2012).

ICAEW (Institute of Chartered Accountants in England and Wales) (2007) *Reporting with Integrity: Abstract.* Available at: http://www.icaew.com/en/technical/financial-reporting/information-for-better-markets/ifbm-reports/reporting-with-integrity (accessed 3 October 2012). Why read? The ICAEW's thoughts on what integrity is and why it is important in reporting on businesses' activities.

KPMG (2010) *Corporate Sustainability: A Progress Report*, 2010. Switzerland: KPMG. Why read? Evidence of the growing significance of corporate sustainability issues to businesses from a global survey conducted by one of the leading accountancy firms.

Bibliography

Butler, S. (2010) Workers can fight for their own rights, *Drapers Magazine,* March.

Cable, V. (2012) *Executive Remuneration.* Speech to Social Market Foundation. London, 24 January 2012.

Cadbury, A. (1992) *The Report of the Committee on the Financial Aspects of Corporate Governance.* Available at: http://www.ecgi.org/codes/documents/cadbury.pdf (accessed 3 October 2012).

Deloitte LLP. (2010) *Swimming in Words: Surveying Narrative Reporting in Annual Reports*. London: Deloitte.

Department of Business, Innovation and Skills (BIS) (2012) *The Future of Narrative Reporting: The Government Response*. London: Department of BIS.

Department of Business, Innovation and Skills (BIS) (2012) *Executive Remuneration Discussion Paper: Summary of Responses*. London: BIS.

Fairtrade Foundation. [website] http://www.fairtrade.org.uk/ (accessed 7 October 2012).

Fédération des Experts Comptables Européens (FEE) (2003) *A Conceptual Approach to Safeguarding Integrity, Objectivity and Independence Throughout the Financial Reporting Chain*. Brussels: FEE.

Fédération des Experts Comptables Européens (FEE) (2009) *Integrity in Professional Ethics: A Discussion Paper*. Brussels: FEE.

FRC (Financial Reporting Council) (2005) *Internal Control: Revised Guidance for Directors on the Combined Code*. London: FRC.

FRC (Financial Reporting Council) (2010a), *UK Corporate Governance Code 2010*. Available at: http://www.frc.org.uk/corporate/ukcgcode.cfm (accessed 7 October 2012).

FRC (Financial Reporting Council) (2010b) *The UK Approach to Corporate Governance*. Available at: http://www.frc.org.uk/corporate/ (accessed 7 October 2012).

FRC (Financial Reporting Council) (2010c) *The UK Stewardship Code 2010*. London: FRC.

FRC (Financial Reporting Council) (2011) *Effective Company Stewardship: Enhancing Corporate Reporting and Audit*. London: FRC.

FSA (Financial Services Authority) (2012) *Disclosure Rules and Transparency Rules*. Available from http://fsahandbook.info/ (accessed 3 October 2012).

GRI (Global Reporting Initiative) (2012) *G4 Exposure Draft*. Available at: https://www.globalreporting.org/resourcelibrary/G4/G4-Exposure-Draft.pdf (accessed 7 October 2012).

GRI (Global Reporting Initiative) (2006) *G3 Sustainability Reporting Guidelines*. Available at: https://www.globalreporting.org/resourcelibrary/G3-Sustainability-Reporting-Guidelines.pdf (accessed 7 October 2012).

The Hampel Committee on Corporate Governance (1998) *The Final Report*. Available at: http://www.ecgi.org/documents/hampel_index.htm (accessed 7 October 2012).

IBE (Institute of Business Ethics) (2007) *Does Business Ethics Pay? – Revisited*. Executive summary. Available at: http://ibeorg.rits-ds.co.uk/userfiles/dbep_revisited.pdf (accessed 7 October 2012).

ICAEW (Institute of Chartered Accountants in England and Wales) (2004) *Sustainability: The Role of Accountants*. London: ICAEW.

ICAEW (Institute of Chartered Accountants in England and Wales) (2007a) *Reporting with Integrity*. London: ICAEW.

ICAEW (Institute of Chartered Accountants in England and Wales) (2007b) *Dialogue in Corporate Governance: Beyond the Myth of Anglo-American Corporate Governance. Emerging Issues*. London: ICAEW.

ICAEW (Institute of Chartered Accountants in England and Wales) (2007c) *Instilling Integrity in Organisations*. London: ICAEW.

ICAEW (Institute of Chartered Accountants in England and Wales) (2007d) *Reporting with integrity*. London: ICAEW.

ICAEW (Institute of Chartered Accountants in England and Wales) (2011) *Code of Ethics*. Available at: http://www.icaew.com/ (accessed 7 October 2012).

IFAC (International Federation of Accountants) [website] http://www.ifac.org/About/Acitivities.php.

IFAC (International Federation of Accountants) (2007) *Defining and Developing an Effective Code of Conduct for Organizations*. New York: IFAC.

IFAC (International Federation of Accountants) (2012) *Handbook of the Code of Ethics for Professional Accountants*. Available at: http://www.ifac.org/publications-resources (accessed 7 October 2012).

J Sainsbury plc. (2010). *Annual Report and Financial Statements, 2010*. Available at: http://www.j-sainsbury.co.uk/investor-centre/reports/2010/annual-report-and-financial-statements-2010 (accessed 7 October 2012).

Jensen, M. C. (1993) The modern industrial revolution, exit, and the failure of internal control systems, *Journal of Finance*, 48, 831–880.

KPMG (2010) *Corporate Sustainability: A Progress Report*, 2010. Switzerland: KPMG.

McPhail, K. and Walters, D. (2009) *Accounting and Business Ethics*. Abingdon: Routledge.

Marks and Spencer Group plc (2012) *Annual Report, 2012*. London: Marks and Spencer Group plc.

Next plc (2012) *Corporate Responsibility Report*. Available at: http://www.nextplc.co.uk/corporate-responsibility.aspx (accessed 7 October 2012).

Solomon, J. (2010) *Corporate Governance and Accountability*, 3rd edn. Chichester: Wiley.

Spira, L. (2006) Black boxes, red herrings and white powder, UK audit committees in the 21st century, *Journal of International Banking Regulation*, 7(1): 180–188.

UK Companies Act 2006. [website] http://www.legislation.gov.uk/ (accessed 7 October 2012).

UK House of Lords Economic Affairs Committee (2011) *Auditors: Market Concentration and their Role*. Available at: http://www.publications.parliament.uk/pa/ld201011/ldselect/ldeconaf/119/11902.htm (last accessed 7 October 2012).

Walker, D. (2009) *A Review of Corporate Governance in UK Banks and Other Financial Industry Entities: Final Recommendations*. Available at: http://webarchive.nationalarchives.gov.uk/+/www.hm-treasury.gov.uk/d/walker_review_261109.pdf (accessed 3 October 2012).

World Business Council for Sustainable Development (WBCSD) and UNEP Finance Initiative (2010) *Translating ESG into Sustainable Business Value*. Geneva: UNEP Finance Initiative and WBCSD.

 ## Questions

● Quick test

1 Comment on why corporate governance information is discussed in companies' annual reports.

2 Discuss the view that sustainability reporting recognises all corporate stakeholders.

●● Develop your understanding

3 Discuss how current developments in the project to update the IASB's *Conceptual Framework* relate to issues of accountability.

4 What role do ethics play in corporate governance?

5 Sustainability reporting is one issue in corporate governance. Some companies establish a subcommittee of the board to deal with sustainability issues. The audit function can also play

a role in sustainability reporting. Outline the arguments for and against a greater role for a dedicated subcommittee and the audit function in corporate sustainability reporting.

6   Accounting should contribute to the protection of the environment. Discuss whether this is a proper role for accounting and outline ways in which it could.

●●● Take it further

7   Obtain the GRI's 2006 *Sustainability Reporting Guidelines* from the GRI website at http://www. globalreporting.org. Discuss to what extent Sainsbury in its 2010 annual report (available from http://www.j-sainsbury.co.uk/index.asp?pageid=20) has met the GRI's three principal performance indicators in its sustainability reporting.

8   Next plc includes the following introduction to its corporate responsibility report on the company website (http://www.nextplc.co.uk/corporate-responsibility.aspx).

Financial reporting in practice 3.5	Next plc's Introduction to Corporate Responsibility Report January 2012

For NEXT, corporate responsibility (CR) means addressing key business-related social, ethical and environmental impacts in a way that aims to bring value to all our stakeholders, including our shareholders. This year's report illustrates how the focus areas of our CR programme support our business approach of acting responsibly whilst we continue to grow. Our approach is to manage our business and the measures we employ to ensure we operate both successfully and responsibly.

Continuous improvement lies at the heart of our business and we are constantly looking for ways to ensure we run our business in a responsible way by:

● Acting in an ethical manner

● Developing positive relationships with our suppliers

● Taking care of our employees

● Being responsible for our impact on the environment

● Delivering support through charitable contributions

● Delivering value to our customers

NEXT faces similar CR challenges to many other major retailers as we continue to operate in a challenging commercial environment. We are committed to develop our business to be more sustainable and responsible, as we work within an increasingly complex set of issues that impact on our business, our customers, the suppliers we trade with, the environment and the communities in which we operate. We believe we are making good progress, but know we will have more challenges in the future. In a world where natural resources are becoming scarcer and energy and commodity costs are rising, it is essential we operate as efficiently as possible. Our business takes a long term view of what is right, and this approach has driven our continuous investment in tackling environmental challenges, and working to achieve positive development in the challenging area of social compliance. We are committed to working with our suppliers to help them understand and develop their businesses to be compliant to our Code of Practice requirements. By working directly with our suppliers we believe we are more consistent in our approach and are able to benefit from the value of establishing long-term relationships with them to help them achieve the requirements of our Code.

(continued)

(continued)

During the last year, whilst NEXT has continued to grow, we have been able to continue to deliver on our objectives of reducing our environmental impact and promoting good environmental practice. We are encouraged by the progress we have made reducing our carbon emissions, sending less waste to landfill and improving the efficiency of our vehicles. We have achieved:

- Energy: 5% reduction compared to last year; and 26% reduction in electricity consumption against 2007 baseline

- Waste: 10% more waste recycled compared to last year; and 85% of operational waste now recycled overall

- Distribution: 9% reduction compared to last year; and 8% decrease in litres of fuel used against 2007 baseline

Our CR programme touches on some big issues that are key to how we do business. We aim to be honest, open and balanced in our CR report, preferring to focus our attention on actions that continue to develop our approach and achievements. The report has been independently assured and key data assured by PricewaterhouseCoopers LLP, and their independent assurance statement can be found on page 41.

Andrew Varley
Group Property Manager – Main Board

Comment on this statement in relation to corporate governance and corporate sustainability requirements.

 Visit the Online Resource Centre for solutions to all these end of chapter questions plus visual walkthrough solutions. You can test your understanding with extra questions and answers, explore additional case studies based on real companies, take a guided tour through a company report, and much more. Go to the Online Resource Centre at **www.oxfordtextbooks.co.uk/orc/maynard/**

Published financial statements of companies

➤ Introduction

The usefulness of financial statements to users will be enhanced if they are comparable and understandable. There therefore needs to be some consistency in the presentation of the financial statements between different years of one company and between different companies. IAS 1 *Presentation of Financial Statements* sets out overall requirements for the presentation of the statements of financial position, comprehensive income and changes in equity, guidelines for their structure, and minimum requirements for their content. IAS 7 *Statement of Cash Flows* sets out the same requirements for the statement of cash flows. Valid comparisons also require users to have knowledge of companies' accounting methods, and so IAS 8 *Accounting Policies, Changes in Accounting Estimates and Errors* specifies further details of how companies should select and disclose the accounting policies that underpin their financial numbers.

This chapter examines the requirements of these three accounting standards, and illustrates how the financial statements are drawn up and presented through the use of examples and company annual reports.

★ Learning objectives

After studying this chapter you will be able to:

- draw up the four main financial statements in accordance with the requirements of IASs 1 and 7, including alternative presentations where permitted
- explain the underpinning principles relating to presentation contained in IAS 1
- understand the purpose and nature of notes to the financial statements
- understand the significance of accounting policies, when changes to these and accounting estimates can be made, and how this is presented.

✔ Key issues checklist

- ❏ Underpinning aim and principles of financial statement presentation.
- ❏ The minimum disclosures of the statement of financial position (IAS 1).
- ❏ The distinction between current and non-current assets and liabilities.
- ❏ The distinction between profit and loss, and other comprehensive income.
- ❏ The two alternative methods of presenting the statement of comprehensive income—as one statement or as two.
- ❏ The minimum disclosures required for the statement of comprehensive income (IAS 1).
- ❏ The alternative methods for presenting the income statement—analysing expenses by nature or function.
- ❏ The statement of changes in equity.
- ❏ The statement of cash flows—its aim and presentation.
- ❏ Cash flows from operating, investing, and financing activities.
- ❏ The two alternatives of deriving cash flows from operating activities—the direct and indirect methods.
- ❏ The purpose and types of notes to the financial statements.
- ❏ Accounting policies—the need for them and the areas requiring them.
- ❏ Accounting estimates and judgements.
- ❏ Changes in accounting policies.
- ❏ Changes in accounting estimates.
- ❏ Dealing with errors.
- ❏ Proposed changes to the presentation of financial statements as a result of the International Accounting Standards Board (IASB)/Financial Accounting Standards Board (FASB) convergence project.

4.1 Key financial statements

As discussed in Chapter 1 the users of financial statements require information relating to the financial position, financial performance, and cash flows of an entity in order to assist them in predicting the entity's future cash flows, and, in particular, their timing and uncertainty. Companies produce four key financial statements at least annually to satisfy the information needs of their investors and lenders—the statement of financial position, the statement of comprehensive income (which incorporates the **income statement** and other comprehensive income), the statement of cash flows, and the statement of changes in equity, which analyses the changes that have occurred over the financial year to the equity balances, which may not be easily discernible from the other financial statements.

One of the underpinning enhancing characteristics of financial information is that it should be comparable, both within an entity from year to year and from entity to entity. Thus, the financial statements need to be structured and presented in a similar manner from year-to-year and entity-to-entity, and contain the same type of information.

The international financial reporting standard that addresses these issues is IAS 1 *Presentation of Financial Statements*. This standard sets out the components of financial statements and minimum requirements for disclosure in the statements of financial position, comprehensive income, and changes in equity. These requirements for the statement of cash flows are specified in a different financial reporting standard, IAS 7 *Statement of Cash Flows*.

4.2 IAS 1 *Presentation of Financial Statements*

4.2.1 Present fairly

IAS 1 repeats some of the details contained in the IASB's *Conceptual Framework* (see discussion in Chapter 2) and expands on some of these. However, one requirement contained in IAS 1 not included in the *Framework* is that:

> Financial statements shall present fairly the financial position, financial performance and cash flows of an entity.

> *(IASB, 2007: para. 15)*

The key words here are 'present fairly'. Remember, for UK companies the statutory overriding requirement of financial statements is that they should show a 'true and fair' view, which is specified in Companies Act 2006. Thus, the IASB is including a similar requirement for all companies worldwide that use international financial reporting standards. For UK companies the phrases 'true and fair view' and 'present fairly' have been accepted as being the same.

Fair presentation requires the faithful representation of the effects of transactions, other events, and conditions in accordance with the definitions and recognition criteria for assets, liabilities, income, and expenses set out in the *Conceptual Framework*. In virtually all circumstances a company achieves a fair presentation provided it complies with all applicable International Financial Reporting Standards (IFRSs). UK legislation allows what is termed the 'true and fair override', which means that departure from the application of a standard is permitted if the alternative accounting treatment or disclosures ensure that the financial statements show a true and fair view. This is also permitted by IAS 1 where compliance with a requirement of an IFRS can be ignored if it would be so misleading that it would conflict with the objective of financial statements as set out in the *Conceptual Framework*. However, such departures are extremely rare.

4.2.2 Underpinning principles

IAS 1 specifies that, apart from cash flow information, the basis of accounting is the accruals basis; this is used in the recognition criteria of elements in the financial statements.

🛈 Reminder *The elements are assets, liabilities, equity, income and expenses.*

The standard confirms that financial statements should be prepared on a going concern basis, unless management intends to liquidate the entity or to cease trading, or has no realistic alternative but to do so. This requirement is clarified by explaining that management must make an assessment of the company's ability to continue as a going concern and, in doing so, it should take into account all available information about the future which is at least, but not limited to, 12 months from the end of the reporting period. The extent of the review period is a matter of judgement based on facts and circumstances.

If no material uncertainties that may cast significant doubt upon a company's ability to continue as a going concern have been identified, then going concern is presumed in the preparation of the financial statements. For listed companies a statement is made that this is the case.

🛈 Reminder *Materiality was discussed in relation to relevance in Chapter 1.*

Financial reporting in practice 4.1	**Next plc, 2011**

This statement on going concern is included in Next's corporate governance report.

Going concern

The Group's business activities, together with the factors likely to affect its future development, performance and position are set out in the Directors' Report and Business Review on pages 3 to 22. The Directors' Report also describes the Group's financial position, cash flows and borrowing facilities, further information on which is detailed in the financial statements. Information on the Group's financial management objectives, and how derivative instruments are used to hedge its capital, credit and liquidity risks is provided in Notes 28 to 32 of the financial statements.

The directors report that, having reviewed current performance and forecasts, they have a reasonable expectation that the Group has adequate resources to continue its operations for the foreseeable future. For this reason, they have continued to adopt the going concern basis in preparing the financial statements.

If there is doubt about a company's ability to continue as a going concern, IAS 1 requires disclosure of the material uncertainties that management is aware of. Clearly, this includes an assessment of exposure to risks and uncertainties.

Following the financial crisis and subsequent times of recession, going concern has become a particularly important issue in relation to ensuring that financial reporting systems produce high quality information which is faithfully representative. The auditors of financial institutions which collapsed during the financial crisis, such as Northern Rock, were criticised during the House of Lords Economic Affairs Committee 2010 investigation into 'Auditors: Market concentration and their role' for making little mention of issues to do with going concern.

The UK's Financial Reporting Council (FRC) launched an inquiry into going concern and liquidity risks headed by Lord Sharman, which produced its final report and conclusions in June 2012. These set out that the going concern assessment process should be integrated with the directors' business planning and risk management processes, and not be seen as a separate exercise. The assessment process should always be transparent and not just carried out or reported on when there are heightened risks. Going concern should have an appropriate definition, and there should be clarity as to the thresholds to be used and the purposes of the required disclosures, which are all consistently understood in an international arena. If these recommendations are followed through, they will change procedures relating to going concern carried out by directors, the audit committee and auditors, and disclosures are likely to be enhanced.

4.2.3 Materiality and aggregation

Companies have to account for large numbers of transactions and other events every day, and determine how their accounting systems are to record these. This requires aggregation of the transactions and items into classes according to their nature or function, and a condensing of this data into the line items that make up the financial statements. IAS 1 requires companies to present separately each material class of similar items; this may be on the face of the financial statements or, if considered not sufficiently material for this, the item is, or items are, disclosed in the notes to the financial statements.

 Examples of aggregation

1 Companies have numerous tangible non-current assets which they use to generate their revenues and profits. These assets are aggregated into different classes, such as property, machinery, fixtures and fittings, and motor vehicles, as users of the financial statements do not need to know the values of all the individual assets. Information about the total values of each class is useful for the users and thus needs to be disclosed, but probably not on the face of the statement of financial position, where the key information is the value of the tangible non-current assets in aggregate. Thus, the breakdown of non-current assets showing the totals of the different classes will be in a note to the financial statements.

2 A company will have hundreds of overhead expense categories. Details of all of these would not be useful to users of financial information as this would be superfluous information. They are therefore aggregated on the face of the statement of comprehensive income, either according to the function of the expense (is it a cost of sale expense, or a distribution cost or an administrative expense?), or according to the nature of the expense (what type of expense is it, e.g. raw material used, employee cost, depreciation?).

Although IAS 1 specifies the minimum requirements for which line items are required to be shown on the face of the financial statements, it does not specify recognition, measurement, and disclosure requirements for specific transactions and other events. These are dealt with by other IFRSs and are discussed in later chapters. IAS 1 does not prevent companies from presenting other line items if they choose to do so, but companies have to consider the qualitative characteristic of understandability, and ensure that the overall message needing to be conveyed about the financial results or position is not lost in extra information. Users may find that IAS 1 financial statements are less comparable from company-to-company; indeed, this is one of the criticisms of the standard, but this is being addressed in an ongoing IASB/FASB convergence project (see further discussion of this later in the chapter).

4.2.4 Offsetting

In order for users to understand the substance of a transaction or other event, sufficient information about it needs to be presented. If a transaction gives rise to both an asset and a liability, which are material, these should be shown separately, and not netted off. The term used in IAS 1 for this is 'offsetting'. The same applies to transactions which give rise to both income and expenses; offsetting of these items is not allowed by IAS 1.

 Example of where offsetting is not permitted

A company acquires a non-current asset under a lease. The substance of this transaction is that the company has a resource, an asset, and a liability for the amounts due under the lease agreement. Even though they are associated, the asset and the liability are shown separately and not netted off on the statement of financial position as both have separate cash flow implications.
  (Note: accounting for leases is discussed in full in Chapter 14.)

 Example of where offsetting is permitted

A retailer sells a motor vehicle, which has a net book value of £2,000, for £1,500. This transaction is incidental to the main revenue-generating activities of the company and the substance of the transaction is the net result of the disposal of the asset. The company therefore does not have to disclose the revenue received from the sale of £1,500 separately from the value of the asset that has been sold; the amounts can be netted off and the resulting loss on sale of £500 accounted for as a single item.

4.2.5 Comparative information and consistency

When a user examines a set of financial statements, probably one of the first things they wish to do is to compare key figures to the previous year to see what changes have occurred. This will also assist in assessment of trends for predictive purposes. (Methods of interpretation are discussed in more depth in Chapters 5 and 17.) It is important that these financial statements are readily available and so IAS 1 requires comparative information in respect of the previous period for all amounts reported on in the current year's financial statements. This would include both quantitative, and relevant narrative and descriptive information.

Clearly, the information needs to be comparable, and so the presentation and classification of items should be retained from one reporting period to the next. If there is a significant change in the company's operations and the directors believe that a different presentation and classification would be more appropriate, a change in classification or presentation can be made. The reasons for this change and its impact on the financial statements must be explained fully in the notes to the financial statements so that the user can clearly understand the change made. The issue of a new or revised IFRS may also require a change in presentation. If there are changes, then the comparative information has to be reclassified unless it is impracticable to do so.

4.3 Structure and content of financial statements

IAS 1 defines a complete set of financial statements as comprising:

(a) a statement of financial position as at the end of the period;

(b) a statement of profit or loss and other comprehensive income for the period;

(c) a statement of changes in equity for the period;

(d) a statement of cash flows for the period;

(e) notes, comprising a summary of significant accounting policies and other explanatory information; and

(f) a statement of financial position as at the beginning of the earliest comparative period when an entity applies an accounting policy retrospectively or makes a retrospective restatement of items in its financial statements, or when it reclassifies items in its financial statements.

In revisions of IAS 1 in 2007 and 2011 the names of the financial statements were amended to those given in the aforementioned list; however, companies are still permitted to use the names balance sheet, statement of comprehensive income, and cash flow statement, and, indeed, many UK companies still do. Note that the new title for the statement of comprehensive income is a very recent amendment and therefore not yet widely used. Its use has not yet been endorsed for companies listed in the European Union (EU). For these reasons, the name 'statement of comprehensive income' is used throughout this textbook to refer to this particular statement.

For clarification, all financial statements and the notes must:

- be clearly identified with the name of the reporting company
- state whether the financial statements are for a single company or a group of companies
- show the date of the end of the reporting period
- show the currency in which the financial statements are presented
- state whether the amounts are in single units, thousands, or millions.

Minimum information to be presented for the statements of financial position, comprehensive income, and changes in equity are discussed in the following section.

4.4 Statement of financial position

Reminder *The statement of financial position (or balance sheet) represents the fundamental accounting equation:*

$$Assets = Equity + Liabilities \quad or \quad Assets - Liabilities = Equity$$

An IAS 1 statement of financial position does not specify in which form the statement of financial position should be drawn up; it merely lists the minimum line items which should be disclosed on the face of the statement:

(a) property, plant and equipment;

(b) investment property;

(c) intangible assets;

(d) financial assets (excluding amounts shown under (e), (h), and (i));

(e) investments accounted for using the equity method;

(f) biological assets;

(g) inventories;

(h) trade and other receivables;

(i) cash and cash equivalents;

(j) the total of assets classified as held for sale and assets included in disposal groups classified as held for sale in accordance with IFRS 5 *Non-current Assets Held for Sale and Discontinued Operations*;

(k) trade and other payables;

(l) provisions;

(m) financial liabilities (excluding amounts shown under (k) and (l));

(n) liabilities and assets for current tax, as defined in IAS 12 *Income Taxes*;

(o) deferred tax liabilities and deferred tax assets, as defined in IAS 12;

(p) liabilities included in disposal groups classified as held for sale in accordance with
     IFRS 5;

(q) non-controlling interests, presented within equity; and

(r) issued capital and reserves attributable to owners of the parent.

4.4.1 Current and non-current classifications

IAS 1 also requires that both assets and liabilities are classified as current or non-current
unless the company chooses a presentation based on liquidity, where all assets and liabilities are presented in order of liquidity. The distinction between non-current and current
is important as it provides information about net assets that are circulating continuously as
working capital as opposed to those used in the company's long-term operations. The liquidity presentation, however, is relevant for financial institutions as such organisations do not
supply goods or services within a clearly identifiable operating cycle.

Broadly, a current asset is one that a business holds primarily for trading purposes and
expects to realise, sell, or consume in its normal operating cycle (see Figure 4.1), for example
inventory and trade receivables. A current liability is also one held primarily for trading purposes and which the business expects to settle within its normal operating cycle, for example
trade payables. The usual period for the realisation of a current asset or the settlement of a
current liability is 12 months after the end of the reporting period, but if these are items held
primarily for trading purposes and it is expected that realisation or settlement will be after
the 12-month period, they are still classified as current.

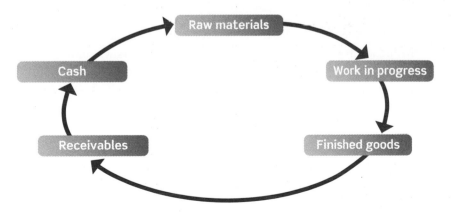

Figure 4.1 The operating cycle for a manufacturer

4.4.2 Presentation

The actual presentation of the statement of financial position, in other words the order of items, and where subtotals and totals are drawn, is not prescribed by IAS 1. Many UK companies, used to rigid Companies Act requirements prior to the 2005 change to IFRS, still present their statements of financial position vertically according to the second form of the balance sheet equation shown at the start of this section, thus arriving at a 'total' of net assets which equates to total equity; continental European companies tend to use the first form and may show a horizontal presentation with assets listed on the left-hand side, and liabilities and equity on the right.

Further line items may be included on the face of the statement of financial position if the judgement is that the items are sufficiently material. In addition, further subclassifications of the line items presented should be disclosed in the notes to disaggregate the figures on the face of the statement. These disclosures are determined largely by the relevant IFRSs, but also by the size, nature, and function of the amounts involved.

 Examples of subclassifications

1   Different classes of property, plant and equipment are disaggregated in accordance with IAS 16 *Property, Plant and Equipment*

2   Inventories are disaggregated into subclassifications, such as goods for sale, production supplies, materials, and work in progress, in accordance with IAS 2 *Inventories*.

3   Receivables does not have its own international accounting standard, but it is usual for these to be disaggregated into subclassifications of trade receivables, receivables from related parties, and prepayments.

4.4.3 Share capital

As share capital also does not have its own international accounting standard, IAS 1 provides details of the disclosures required for this line item so that users will have an understanding of the different classes of share capital the company has and, for each class, the numbers of shares authorised, issued, fully paid or not fully paid, shares reserved for issue under options or other contracts for sale, their par value, and details of any rights, preferences, and restrictions.

4.4.4 Financial reporting in practice

The following company example demonstrates the application of the IAS 1 requirements for a statement of financial position for the UK high street fashion retailer, Next.

Financial reporting in practice 4.2 | Next plc, 2011

Consolidated Balance Sheet as at 29 January 2011

	Notes	2011 £m	2010 £m
ASSETS AND LIABILITIES			
Non-current assets			
Property, plant & equipment	9	**592.4**	577.2
Intangible assets	10	**46.5**	47.4
Interests in associates	11	**5.1**	4.0
Other investments	12	**1.0**	1.0
Defined benefit pension surplus	21	**55.7**	–
Other financial assets	15	**24.3**	22.7
		725.0	652.3
Current assets			
Inventories	13	**368.3**	309.0
Trade and other receivables	14	**645.6**	616.6
Other financial assets	15	**4.1**	8.6
Cash and short term deposits	16	**49.3**	107.0
		1,067.3	1,041.2
Total assets		**1,792.3**	1,693.5
Current liabilities			
Bank overdrafts	17	**(10.2)**	(4.7)
Unsecured bank loans	17	**(115.0)**	–
Trade and other payables	18	**(544.6)**	(550.3)
Other financial liabilities	19	**(54.7)**	(93.6)
Current tax liabilities		**(108.4)**	(109.5)
		(832.9)	(758.1)
Non-current liabilities			
Corporate bonds	20	**(471.2)**	(520.9)
Defined benefit pension deficit	21	–	(49.5)
Provisions	22	**(13.3)**	(13.4)
Deferred tax liabilities	6	**(23.4)**	(3.7)
Other financial liabilities	19	**(2.6)**	(4.4)
Other liabilities	23	**(216.5)**	(210.1)
		(727.0)	(802.0)

(continued)

(continued)

Total liabilities		**(1,559.9)**	(1,560.1)
Net assets		**232.4**	133.4
EQUITY			
Share capital	24	**18.1**	19.1
Share premium account		**0.8**	0.7
Capital redemption reserve		**11.8**	10.8
ESOT reserve		**(138.6)**	(78.2)
Fair value reserve		**(3.2)**	5.1
Foreign currency translation reserve		**4.6**	4.7
Other reserves	25	**(1,443.8)**	(1,443.8)
Retained earnings		**1,782.6**	1,615.2
Shareholders' equity		**232.3**	133.6
Non-controlling interest		**0.1**	(0.2)
Total equity		**232.4**	133.4

Financial reporting in practice 4.3 illustrates the disclosures for share capital.

Financial reporting in practice 4.3   Marks and Spencer plc, 2010

25 share capital and reserves

	2010		2009	
	Shares	**£m**	**Shares**	**£m**
Authorised ordinary shares of 25p each	3,200,000,000	800.0	3,200,000,000	800.0
Allotted, called up and fully paid ordinary shares of 25p each:				
At start of year	1,577,794,919	394.4	1,586,478,423	396.6
Shares issued on exercise of share options	4,521,662	1.1	2,217,763	0.5
Shares purchased in buy-back	–	–	(10,901,267)	(2.7)
At end of year	1,582,316,581	395.5	1,577,794,919	394.4

Issue of new shares

4,521,662 (last year 2,217,763) ordinary shares having a nominal value of £1.1 m (last year £0.5 m) were allotted during the year under the terms of the Company's schemes which are described in note 12. The aggregate consideration received was £12.4 m (last year £5.3 m).

Share buy-back

Last year 10,901,267 ordinary shares having a nominal value of £2.7 m were bought back and subsequently cancelled during the year in accordance with the authority granted by shareholders at the Annual General Meeting in July 2007. The aggregate consideration paid was £40.9 m.

4.5 Statement of comprehensive income

As indicated in section 4.3, the name of this key performance statement was changed to 'statement of profit or loss and other comprehensive income' by the IASB in its project on the presentation of other comprehensive income, which concluded in June 2011. IAS 1 now uses the new name. However, throughout the textbook it is referred to as the statement of comprehensive income.

4.5.1 What is comprehensive income?

Total comprehensive income is the change in equity that has arisen from all transactions other than with the owners in their capacity as owners. It includes both profits or losses, and **other comprehensive income**. The statement of profit or loss, and other comprehensive income will show total comprehensive income as the bottom line.

 Examples of other comprehensive income items

In the year 20X7 a company makes a profit after tax of £500,000. During the year the company issued new shares for £2 million and paid dividends of £200,000.

This will result in the following changes to the company's equity over 20X7:

1   An increase of £500,000 from the profits made

2   An increase of £2 million from the issue of new shares

3   A decrease of £200,000 from the payment of dividends.

Items 2 and 3 are transactions with the shareholders in their capacity as owners of the business. The statement of comprehensive income will therefore include only the transactions making up the profits after tax of £500,000.

However, suppose the company holds some financial assets which are valued at fair value (market value), and these increase in value over the course of 20X7 by £100,000.

The asset values on the statement of financial position have increased by £100,000 and, in order for the balance sheet equation to hold, equity will also increase by £100,000. Thus, the statement of comprehensive income needs to include this amount as this is not a transaction with the shareholders. Depending on the type of financial asset, the increase will be included either as part of profit and loss, or as other comprehensive income. (The IFRSs that deal with financial instruments specify in which part of the statement of comprehensive income the increase would be included.)

IAS 1 provides the following examples of other comprehensive income items:

- revaluation gains and losses
- actuarial gains and losses on defined benefit plans (other than those recognised in profit or loss, and those not recognised)
- gains and losses on the translation of financial statements into the presentation currency
- gains and losses on the re-measurement of available-for-sale financial assets
- the effective portion of gains and losses on hedging instruments in a cash flow hedge.

Most of these items are beyond the scope of this textbook; however, the first item detailed in the list, revaluation gains and losses on non-current assets, is explained in Chapter 10.

4.5.2 Presentation

A company may present its statement of comprehensive income in one of two ways:

1   A single statement that includes the items making up profit or loss (effectively an income statement) followed by items of other comprehensive income

2   As two separate statements—a statement showing profit or loss (i.e. the income statement) and a second statement which starts with net profit or loss for the period, and includes the items of other comprehensive income.

If the financial statements are for a group of companies, both net profit or loss and net other comprehensive income must be allocated between that attributable to:

(a) non-controlling interests

(b) owners of the parent company.

This is discussed in more detail in Chapter 15.

As for the statement of financial position, IAS 1 specifies the minimum line items that have to be presented on the face of the profit or loss section of the statement of comprehensive income, which are fairly minimal.

(a) Revenue;

(b) Gains and losses arising from the derecognition of financial assets measured at amortised cost;

(c) Finance costs;

(d) Share of the profit or loss of associates and joint ventures accounted for using the equity method;

(e) If a financial asset is reclassified so that it is measured at fair value, any gain or loss arising from a difference between the previous carrying amount and its fair value at the reclassification date (as defined in IFRS 9);

(f)   Tax expense; and

(g)   A single amount comprising the total of discontinued operations.

The other comprehensive income section presents line items for amounts of other comprehensive income in the period, classified by nature and grouped into those that, in accordance with other IFRSs:

(a)   will not be reclassified subsequently to profit or loss; and

(b)   will be reclassified subsequently to profit or loss when specific conditions are met.

This is discussed further in section 4.5.7.

Many companies will elect to include other line items to show an analysis of the figures making up the totals and subtotals in the statement, and this is required when they are material and relevant to an understanding of the company's financial performance. These may include one-off items that are outside normal trading or business activities, or items that are material owing to their size in a particular period. These items are often referred to as **exceptional items**, although IAS 1 does not use this term. IAS 1 provides the following examples of circumstances which would give rise to separate disclosure of items of income and expense:

(a)   Write-downs of inventories to net realisable value or of property, plant and equipment to recoverable amount, as well as reversals of such write-downs;

(b)   Restructurings of the activities of an entity and reversals of any provisions for the costs of restructuring;

(c)   Disposals of items of property, plant and equipment;

(d)   Disposals of investments;

(e)   Discontinued operations;

(f)   Litigation settlements; and

(g)   Other reversals of provisions.

However, it is apparent from Financial reporting in practice 4.4 that companies will choose such disclosures according to their circumstances.

| Financial reporting in practice **4.4** | J Sainsbury plc, 2010 |

J Sainsbury plc's financial statements provide an analysis of profit before tax of £733 million on the face of its income statement, analysing its profit before tax into what the company describes as 'underlying profit before tax', i.e. profit from its core supermarket activities, and other items of profit and loss. This will assist users in understanding how the company achieved its profits in a particular year and provide more comparable information from one year to the next.

(continued)

(continued)

Group income statement for the 52 weeks to 20 March 2010

	Note	2010 £m	2009 £m
Revenue	4	**19,964**	18,911
Cost of sales		**(18,882)**	(17,875)
Gross profit		**1,082**	1,036
Administrative expenses		**(399)**	(420)
Other income		**27**	57
Operating profit	5	**710**	673
Finance income	6	**33**	52
Finance costs	6	**(148)**	(148)
Share of post-tax profit/(loss) from joint ventures	14	**138**	(111)
Profit before taxation		**733**	466
Analysed as:			
Underlying profit before tax		**610**	519
Profit on sale of properties	3	**27**	57
Investment property fair value movements	3	**123**	(124)
Financing fair value movements	3	**(15)**	(10)
IAS 19 pension financing (charge)/credit	3	**(24)**	24
One-off item: Office of Fair Trading dairy inquiry	3	**12**	–
		733	466
Income tax expense	8	**(148)**	(177)
Profit for the financial year		**585**	289

4.5.3 Income statement

The income statement (which is the statement of profit or loss), whether presented as a separate statement or as part of the statement of comprehensive income, includes items of income and expense recognised in a period according to the accruals principle. A company can choose one of two methods for analysing its expenses according to which provides information that is reliable and more relevant—an analysis either by their nature or by their function within the company.

4.5.4 Nature of expense method

This can be thought of as analysing an expense by its type and may be simple to apply because the expenses do not have to be allocated to different functions across the business. An example of this form of income statement is as follows.

Example statement

Business XXX

Income statement for accounting period (expenses analysed by nature)

	£	£
Revenue		XX
Other income		XX
Changes in inventories of finished goods and work in progress	XX	
Raw materials and consumables used	XX	
Employee benefits expense	XX	
Depreciation and amortisation expense	XX	
Other expenses	XX	
Total expenses		(XX)
Profit before tax		XX

The choice of this method will depend on a company's history and industry, but typically some engineering and manufacturing companies use this presentational format. One key figure which is not disclosed by this analysis is gross profit, which such companies may not wish their competitors to see.

Financial reporting in practice 4.5 | **GKN plc, 2009** |

GKN plc is a global engineering company providing technology and engineering for automotive, aerospace, and off-highway manufacturers. It uses the earlier-mentioned analysis for expenses in its 2009 financial statements.

Consolidated Income Statement: for the year ended 31 December 2009

	Notes	2009 £m	2008 £m
Sales	2	4,223	4,376
Trading profit		129	201
Restructuring and impairment charges		(144)	(153)
Amortisation of non-operating intangible assets arising on business combinations		(24)	(10)

(continued)

(continued)

Profits and losses on sale or closures of businesses		2	
Change in value of derivative and other financial instruments		76	(124)
Operating profit/(loss)	3	39	(86)
Share of post-tax earnings of joint ventures	14	21	6
Interest payable		(67)	(66)
Interest receivable		3	19
Other net financing charges		(50)	(3)
Net financing costs	4	(114)	(50)
Profit/(loss) before taxation		(54)	(130)
Taxation	5	15	10
Profit/(loss) from continuing operations		(39)	(120)
Profit after taxation from discontinued operations	6	5	13
Profit/(loss) after taxation for the year		(34)	(107)

Note 3 to the income statement provides the analysis of expenses.

3 Operating profit

The analysis of the components of operating profit is shown as follows:

(a) Trading profit

	2009 £m	2008 £m
Sales by subsidiaries	4,223	4,376
Operating costs and other income		
Change in stocks of finished goods and work in progress	(82)	18
Raw materials and consumables	(1,756)	(1,737)
Staff costs (note 10)	(1,224)	(1,232)
Reorganisation costs (i):		
Redundancy and other amounts	(3)	(5)
Impairment of plant and equipment		(1)
Depreciation of property, plant and equipment (ii)	(193)	(165)
Impairment of plant and equipment	(2)	
Amortisation of intangible assets	(11)	(10)
Operating lease rentals payable:		
Plant and equipment	(13)	(12)

Property	(29)	(23)
Impairment of trade receivables	(4)	(6)
Amortisation of government grants	1	2
Net exchange differences on foreign currency transactions	7	3
Other costs	(785)	(1,007)
	(4,094)	(4,175)
Trading profit	129	201

4.5.5 Function of expense method

Referred to also as the 'cost of sales' method, this is the more common method seen in companies as it is considered to provide more relevant information to the users than the nature of expense method. However, the allocation of expenses to different functions may be considered arbitrary and involve considerable judgement. An example of this form of income statement is as follows.

 Example statement

Business XXX

Income statement for accounting period (expenses analysed by function)

	£
Revenue	XX
Cost of sales	(XX)
Gross profit	XX
Other income	XX
Distribution costs	(XX)
Administrative expenses	(XX)
Other expenses	(XX)
Profit before tax	XX

IAS 1 requires companies that choose this method to provide additional information on the nature of some expenses in the notes to the financial statements, for example depreciation, and **amortisation** expenses and employee benefits costs.

Worked example 4.1: to show different methods of drawing up the income statement

Oakthorpe plc is a manufacturing company and its trial balance at 31 March 20X6 includes the following balances:

		Debit £	Credit £
Sales			175,335
Inventories at 1 April 20X5			
Raw materials		1,675	
Finished goods (FG)		1,005	
Purchases of raw materials		92,895	
Wages and salaries:	production staff	18,600	
	other staff	15,315	
Insurance		3,400	
Telecommunications costs		2,820	
Hire of plant and machinery		1,550	
Depreciation expense:	buildings	1,000	
	plant and machinery	2,400	
	motor vehicles	520	
Other expenses:	distribution	6,250	
	administrative	8,520	

Inventories of raw materials and finished goods at 31 March 20X6 are valued at £2,200 and £960 respectively. There is no work in progress (WIP).

Required:

In so far as the information permits, draw up the statement of comprehensive income for Oakthorpe plc for the year ended 31 March 20X6 showing expenses analysed (i) by nature and (ii) by function.

(i) Analysis of expenses by nature

	Changes in inventories of WIP & FG £	Employee benefits £	Raw materials & consumables £	Other expenses £
Opening inventories	1,005		1,675	
Purchases of raw materials			92,895	
Wages and salaries:				
Production staff		18,600		
Other staff				15,315

Insurance				3,400
Telecommunications costs				2,820
Hire of plant and machinery				1,550
Other expenses:				
Distribution				6,250
Administrative				8,520
Closing inventories	(960)		(2,200)	
	45	18,600	92,370	37,855

Oakthorpe plc
Statement of comprehensive income for the year ended 31 March 20X6

	£
Revenue	175,335
Changes in inventories of finished goods and work in progress	(45)
Raw materials and consumables used	(92,370)
Employee benefits expense	(18,600)
Depreciation and amortisation expense (1,000 + 2,400 + 520)	(3,920)
Other expenses	(37,855)
Profit before tax	22,545

(ii) Analysis of expenses by function

	Cost of sales £	Distribution costs £	Admin expenses £
Opening inventories (1,675 + 1,005)	2,680		
Purchases of raw materials	92,895		
Wages and salaries:			
Production staff	18,600		
Other staff			15,315
Insurance			3,400
Telecommunications costs			2,820
Hire of plant and machinery			1,550
Depreciation	2,400	520	1,000
Other expenses		6,250	8,520
Closing inventories (960 + 2,200)	(3,160)		
	113,415	6,770	32,605

Oakthorpe plc
Statement of comprehensive income for the year ended 31 March 20X6

	£
Revenue	175,335
Cost of sales	(113,415)
Gross profit	61,920
Distribution costs	(6,770)
Administrative expenses	(32,605)
Profit before tax	22,545

4.5.6 Statement of comprehensive income pro forma

A full statement of comprehensive income with profit and loss expenses analysed by function is shown in the following example statement.

 Example statement

XXX plc

Statement of comprehensive income for the year ended 31 December 20X7

	20X7 £000
Revenue	390,000
Cost of sales	(245,000)
Gross profit	145,000
Other income	20,667
Distribution costs	(9,000)
Administrative expenses	(20,000)
Other expenses	(2,100)
Finance costs	(8,000)
Share of profit of associates[1]	35,100
Profit before tax	161,667
Income tax expense	(40,417)
Profit for the year from continuing operations	121,250
Loss for the year from discontinued operations[2]	–
Profit for the year	121,250

Other comprehensive income:

Gains on property revaluation	933
Share of other comprehensive income of associates[1]	400
Income tax relating to components of other comprehensive income	(267)
Other comprehensive income for the year, net of tax	1,066
Total comprehensive income for the year	122,316
Profit attributable to:	
Owners of the parent	97,000
Non-controlling interests[1]	24,250
	121,250
Total comprehensive income attributable to:	
Owners of the parent	97,659
Non-controlling interests[1]	24,657
	122,316

[1] Associates and non-controlling interests, and their accounting treatment are explained in Chapters 15 and 16.
[2] Discontinued operations and their accounting treatment are explained in Chapter 6.

4.5.7 Why have a statement of comprehensive income?

The net income of simple entities that deal with day-to-day trading transactions related to the selling of a product or service is measured by net profit according to the accruals basis. For these entities the only changes to equity, apart from transactions with the owners, arise from the net profit or loss, and an income statement suffices to show this. However, once changes in asset valuations from the end of one year to the next need to be accounted for as a result of some assets and liabilities being permitted to be measured using bases other than historic cost (such as when non-current assets are revalued), the presentation of the effect of these changes on equity has had to be addressed. These changes are sometimes referred to as *unrealised* gains or losses (as opposed to *realised* gains and losses, which are profit and loss items) although these terms are not used in IFRSs.

Prior to the current version of IAS 1, these changes were accounted for purely as a change in equity and were included only in the statement of changes in equity (see section 4.6). However, the definitions of income and expenses as given in the IASB's *Conceptual Framework* (see Chapter 1) mean that the IASB consider there are no clear principles that can be used to separate income and expenses into two statements, and therefore they should all be included in one statement of comprehensive income. There is recognition, though, that the economic events that underpin income and expense items are different, and so there is the current distinction between profit and loss items, and other comprehensive income. The notion of profit or loss is fundamental to users, and it is also important in determining the key earnings per share ratio (discussed in detail in Chapter 8). This is a difficult area which the IASB may address in a future project.

Reminder *Income is increases in the economic benefits during the accounting period arising from revenues from and from other gains.*

Expenses are decreases in economic benefits during the accounting period encompassing expenses that arise in the normal course of business, such as cost of sales, salaries and wages, heat and light, and insurance, and other losses.

Two criticisms of other comprehensive income, which have been addressed recently by the IASB in its *Presentation of Items of Other Comprehensive Income (Amendments to IAS 1)* issued in June 2011, were:

- the lack of distinction between different items in other comprehensive income
- the lack of clarity in the presentation of such items.

Some items included in other comprehensive income can have a considerable effect on the overall financial performance of an entity and are accounted for initially as other comprehensive income, but are subsequently reclassified as profit and loss items (i.e. they pass through the income statement). This is often referred to as 'recycling'. The amendments now require the grouping of items in other comprehensive income on the basis of whether they are reclassified or not in order to make clear the effects these items may have on profit or loss in the future.

However, the overarching purpose of the statement of comprehensive income is to provide information about the financial performance of an entity. Chapter 5 discusses on which line items users may focus in their interpretation of performance.

4.6 Statement of changes in equity

Shareholders are the principle users of financial statements and their investment in the net assets of a company is represented by the equity balances. Changes in net assets result in, or are caused by, changes in equity. The statement of changes in equity analyses all these changes so that the shareholders can more readily discern what has caused the change in their investment from the end of one accounting period to the end of the next.

The statement reconciles the opening and closing equity balances shown in the statement of financial position by including net comprehensive income from the statement of comprehensive income together with all transactions with the owners in their capacity as owners. IAS 1 expands on this by specifying that the following information should be shown in the statement of changes in equity.

(a) total comprehensive income for the period, showing separately the total amounts attributable to owners of the parent and to non-controlling interests;

(b) for each component of equity, the effects of retrospective application or retrospective restatement recognised in accordance with IAS 8 (see section 4.8.3 below); and

(c) for each component of equity, a reconciliation between the carrying amount at the beginning and the end of the period, separately disclosing changes resulting from:

(i) profit or loss;

(ii) other comprehensive income; and

(iii) transactions with owners in their capacity as owners, showing separately contributions by and distributions (i.e. dividends) to owners and changes in ownership interests in subsidiaries that do not result in a loss of control.

The amount of dividends paid to the owners during the period and the related amount of dividends per share should be disclosed either in the statement or in a disclosure note.

An example of a statement in changes of equity is given in the following statement. This uses the figures from the statement of comprehensive income given in the previous example statement, and includes a change in accounting policy (which is discussed in more detail later in this chapter), an issue of shares, and payments of dividends.

 Example statement

XXX plc

Statement of changes in equity for the year ended 31 December 20X7

	Ordinary share capital £000	Preference share capital (irredeemable) £000	Share premium £000	Retained earnings £000	Revaluation surplus £000	Total £000	Non-controlling interest[1] £000	Total equity £000
At 1 January 20X7	550,000	30,000	10,000	161,300	1,600	752,900	48,600	801,500
Changes in accounting policy	–	–	–	400		400	100	500
Restated balance	550,000	30,000	10,000	161,700	1,600	753,300	48,700	802,000
Issue of share capital	50,000	–	10,000	–	–	60,000	–	60,000
Final dividends on ordinary shares	–	–	–	(12,000)	–	(12,000)	–	(12,000)
Final dividends on irredeemable shares	–	–	–	(3,000)	–	(3,000)	–	(3,000)
Total comprehensive income for the year	–	–	–	97,000	659	97,659	24,657	122,316

Transfer to retained earnings	–	–	–	200	(200)	–	–	–
At 31 December 20X7	600,000	30,000	20,000	243,900	2,059	895,959	73,357	969,316

These closing balances are the figures that will be shown on the statement of financial position at 31 December 20X7.

¹ Non-controlling interests and their accounting treatment are explained in Chapter 15.

4.7 Statement of cash flows

'Cash is the life blood of any organisation.' Cash is needed to conduct operations, pay obligations, and provide a return to investors. Users make decisions about whether to provide resources to a business and, as stated in the IASB's *Conceptual Framework* (discussed in Chapter 2), this is based on an assessment of an entity's prospects for future net cash inflows. Information about how a business generates and uses cash is therefore of prime importance to users of financial information.

A statement of cash flows on its own will not provide sufficient financial information for users. However, used in conjunction with the rest of the entity's financial statements, it will provide information that should enable the users to evaluate the changes in the business's net assets, its financial structure, including its liquidity and solvency, and its ability to adjust its cash flows in order to adapt to changing circumstances and opportunities. Any financial statement reports historic information and historical cash flow information is often used as an indicator of the amount, timing, and certainty of future cash flows.

Cash is also much more 'real' than profits, which are reported on the basis of accruals, and require estimates and judgements. Many corporate collapses of seemingly profitable businesses have occurred because the businesses have simply run out of cash. It was as a result of some high-profile company failures in the early 1990s, such as the Bank of Credit and Commerce International, that standard-setters introduced the requirement for companies to include a statement of cash flows in their financial statements. In 1994 IAS 7 *Cash Flow Statements* was issued by the IASC, which was retitled *Statement of Cash Flows* by the IASB in 2007.

4.7.1 Example of a simple statement of cash flows

A statement of cash flows essentially details all cash flowing into a business net of all cash flowing out of a business, with the net cash flow reconciling opening cash balances with closing cash balances. It should be noted that cash is taken to mean cash-in-hand and bank balances, although this is defined more precisely by IAS 7 (see section 4.7.2).

Worked example 4.2: to show the difference between profit and cash flows (taken from Chapter 1)

On 1 January 20X7 Giles starts his own business by investing £8,000 of his own money and getting a business contact to lend the business £2,000 for 5 years, on which interest will be paid at 5% p.a. Giles rents office space and pays £1,000 for furniture and equipment. During the first year the business purchases goods for resale for £6,000, of which £5,500 had been paid by 31 December 20X7. The business makes sales of £5,000 on credit and £1,500 for cash, and Giles's credit customers have paid £4,000 by 31 December 20X7. Office running costs paid during the year total £2,200, and Giles takes £1,000 out of the business for personal expenses. At the year end goods which had cost £2,000 are still on hand.

Required:
Draw up a financial performance statement on a cash basis for Giles' business for the year ended 31 December 20X7.

Giles' business statement of cash flows for the year ended 31 December 20X7

	£	£
Cash inflows (receipts)		
Owner investment		8,000
Loan		2,000
From sales (1,500 + 4,000)		5,500
		15,500
Cash outflows (payments)		
Furniture and equipment	1,000	
Goods for resale	5,500	
Office running costs	2,200	
Owner's personal expenses	1,000	
		(9,700)
Net cash flow		5,800
Cash balance at 1 January 20X7 *		–
Cash balance at 31 December 20X7		5,800

* This is zero in this example as the business started on 1 January. The resulting net cash flow is therefore equivalent to the cash balance at 31 December 20X7.

4.7.2 IAS 7 *Statement of Cash Flows*

A statement of cash flows in this form is not particularly useful; users need to know from which business activities the cash flows have arisen. The format of the IAS 7 statement of cash flows groups net cash flows under three activities (see Table 4.1).

Table 4.1 Format of IAS 7 statement of cash flows

Activity	Definition	Examples
Operating	Principal revenue-producing activities of the entity and other activities that are not investing or financing activities. They generally result from transactions that determine profit or loss	• Receipts from the sale of goods • Payments to suppliers for goods and services • Payments to employees • Income tax payments and refunds
Investing	The acquisition and disposal of long-term assets and other investments not included in cash equivalents. Essentially, this is expenditure on resources intended to generate future income and cash flows	• Payments for, and receipts from the sale of, long-term tangible and **intangible assets** • Payments for, and receipts from the sale of, equity or debt instruments in other companies
Financing	Activities that result in changes in the size and composition of the equity and borrowings of the entity. This cash flow information assists in predicting future cash outflows to the providers of capital	• Receipts from the issue of shares, debentures, loans, bonds, and other short and long-term borrowings • Repayments of amounts borrowed • Repayments under a finance lease

Interest and dividends received and paid should be disclosed separately, and there is choice of the activity under which they can be presented.

Interest paid	Usually operating, but may be financing
Interest received	Usually investing, but may be operating
Dividends received	Usually investing, but may be operating
Dividends paid	Usually financing, but may be operating

Cash is termed 'cash and cash equivalents', and these terms are defined as follows.

Cash	Cash on hand and demand deposits
Cash equivalents	Short-term, highly liquid investments that are readily convertible to known amounts of cash and which are subject to an insignificant risk of changes in value

Cash equivalents are held for the purpose of meeting short-term cash requirements rather than for investment purposes. For example, a deposit account with a maturity of three months or less. Bank overdrafts that are repayable on demand are classified as cash and cash equivalents, as they usually form an integral part of a business's cash management, as opposed to bank borrowings, which are generally considered to be financing activities. There is clearly some discretion here and so IAS 7 requires companies to disclose how it defines its cash and cash equivalents, and to provide a reconciliation of these balances in the statement of cash flows to those in the statement of financial position.

Financial reporting in practice 4.6 | Vodafone Group plc, 2010

Vodafone's financial statements for the year ended 31 March 2010 include the following disclosure note relating to how it defines cash and cash equivalents.

18. Cash and cash equivalents

	2010 £m	2009 £m
Cash at bank and in hand	745	811
Money market funds	3,678	3,419
Repurchase agreements	–	648
Cash and cash equivalents as presented in the statement of financial position	**4,423**	**4,878**
Bank overdrafts	(60)	(32)
Cash and cash equivalents as presented in the statement of cash flows	**4,636**	**4,846**

Bank balances and money market funds comprise cash held by the Group on a short-term basis with original maturity of three months or less. The carrying amount of these assets approximates their fair value.

4.7.3 Direct and indirect methods of reporting cash flows from operating activities

IAS 7 permits companies a choice as to how they present cash generated from operating activities.

Direct method   Major classes of gross cash receipts and gross payment are disclosed. Recommended by IAS 7.

Indirect method   Adjusts the company's profit or loss before tax for finance costs and investment income, the effects of non-cash transactions, and deferrals or accruals of past or future operating receipts and payments (i.e. the changes in inventories and operating receivables and payables).

The usual method chosen by UK companies as it is easier to produce from financial accounting records.

Worked example 4.3: to show the calculation of cash generated from operating activities using both methods

Extracts from the financial statements for Dewberry plc for the year ended 30 June 20X6 are as follows.

Income statement for the year ended 30 June 20X6

	£000	£000
Revenue		21,000
Opening inventory	500	
Purchases	16,400	
	16,900	
Closing inventory	1,500	
Cost of sales		(15,400)
Gross profit		5,600
Expenses (including depreciation of £395)		(3,370)
Interest		(200)
Profit before tax		2,030
Corporation tax		(520)
Profit for the year		£ 1,510

Balances from the statement of financial position at 30 June

	20X6 £000	20X5 £000
Current assets		
Inventory	1,500	500
Receivables	2,680	890
Current liabilities		
Payables	1,100	680

Required:

Calculate the cash generated from operating activities using:

(i) The direct method

(ii) The indirect method.

(i) Cash generated from operating activities using the direct method

	£000	£000
Cash received from customers:		
Sales	21,000	
– Closing receivables	(2,680)	
+ Opening receivables	890	
		19,210
Cash paid to suppliers of goods:		
Purchases	16,400	
– Closing payables	(1,100)	
+ Opening payables	680	
		(15,980)
Cash paid to employees and other suppliers:		
Expenses from income statement	3,370	
– Non-cash expenses: depreciation	(395)	
		(2,975)
Cash generated from operating activities		£ 255

Note: if a breakdown of cost of sales was not provided, cash paid to suppliers of goods would have to be calculated as follows:

	£000
Cost of sales	15,400
+ Closing inventories	1,500
– Opening inventories	(500)
– Closing payables	(1,100)
+ Opening payables	680
Payments to suppliers	15,980

(ii) Cash generated from operating activities using the indirect method

		£000
Profit before tax		2,030
Add back interest expense		200
Add back non-cash expenses: depreciation		395
Change in inventory: increase	(1,500 –500)	(1,000)
Change in receivables: increase	(2,680 –890)	(1,790)
Change in payables: increase	(1,100 –680)	420
Cash generated from operating activities		£ 255

The reconciliation of profit before tax to cash generated from operating activities provides very useful information to users of the financial statements about the cash management of the company; this will be explored in more detail in the Chapters 5 and 17 on financial statement analysis. The reconciliation is shown as a disclosure note to the statement of cash flows. A full pro-forma for this is as follows.

 Example statement

Company XXX plc

Reconciliation of profit/loss before tax to cash generated from operations for the year ended 31 December 20XX

	£
Profit/(loss) before tax	X
Finance costs	X
Investment income	(X)
Depreciation charge	X
Amortisation charge	X
Loss/(profit) on disposal of non-current assets	X/(X)
(Increase)/decrease in inventories	(X)/X
(Increase)/decrease in trade and other receivables	(X)/X
(Increase)/decrease in prepayments	(X)/X
Increase/(decrease) in trade and other payables	X/(X)
Increase/(decrease) in accruals	X/(X)
Increase/(decrease) in provisions	X/(X)
Cash generated from operations	X

Note carefully which way round the brackets are shown in relation to whether the items of working capital have increased or decreased.

4.7.4 Full statement of cash flows

A complete pro-forma statement of cash flows follows; this has been adapted from the example given in IAS 7.

Example statement

Company XXX plc

Statement of cash flows for the year ended 31 December 20XX

	£m	£m
Cash flows from operating activities		
Cash generated from operations	2,730	
Interest paid	(270)	
Income taxes paid	(900)	
Net cash from operating activities		1,560
Cash flows from investing activities		
Purchase of property, plant and equipment	(900)	
Proceeds from sale of property, plant and equipment	20	
Interest received	200	
Dividends received	200	
Net cash used in investing activities		(480)
Cash flows from financing activities		
Proceeds from issue of share capital	250	
Proceeds from issue of long-term borrowings	550	
Repayment of long-term borrowings	(300)	
Dividends paid	(1,290)	
Net cash used in financing activities		(790)
Net increase in cash and cash equivalents		290
Cash and cash equivalents at beginning of period		120
Cash and cash equivalents at end of period		£ 410

An example of the preparation of a full statement of cash flows from the statement of profit or loss and opening and closing statements of financial position is now demonstrated by continuing the example for company Dewberry plc used in Worked example 4.3.

> **Worked example 4.4:** to show the preparation of a statement of cash flows

The statement of comprehensive income can be taken to be the income statement given in Worked example 4.3 (i.e. there is no other comprehensive income).

The statement of changes in equity and full statements of financial position are given.

Statement of changes in equity for the year ended 30 June 20X6

	Ordinary Share Capital £000	Share Premium £000	Retained Earnings £000	Total £000
Balance at 1/7/X5	400	-	600	1,000
Issue of share capital	200	15		215
Profit for year			1,510	1,510
Dividends paid			(500)	(500)
Balance at 30/6/X6	600	15	1,610	2,225

Statements of financial position at 30 June 20X6 and 20X5

	20X6 £000	20X5 £000
Property, plant and equipment		
Cost	2,190	1,310
Accumulated depreciation	895	500
	1,295	810
Current assets		
Inventory	1,500	500
Receivables	2,680	890
Bank	-	60
	4,180	1,450
Total assets	5,475	2,260
Equity		
Share capital	600	400
Share premium	15	-
Retained earnings	1,610	600
	2,225	1,000
Current liabilities		
Bank overdraft	1,810	-
Payables	1,100	680
Taxation	280	320
	3,190	1,000
Non-current liabilities		
Long-term loan	60	260
Total liabilities	3,250	1,260
Total equity and liabilities	5,475	2,260

Required:

Prepare the statement of cash flows for Dewberry plc for the year ended 30 June 20X6.

Step 1

Calculate the net cash flow during the year from the opening and closing cash, and cash equivalent balances.

In this example cash and cash equivalents comprises an opening bank asset balance and a closing bank overdraft.

		£000
Balance at 1 July 20X5		60
Net cash outflow	(balancing figure)	(1,870)
Balance at 30 June 20X6		(1,810)

Step 2

Unless specified otherwise, calculate cash generated from operations by using the indirect method, i.e. by reconciling profit before tax to cash generated from operations.

This has already been done in Worked example 4.3.

Step 3

Set out the pro-forma statement of cash flows, identifying or calculating figures for each line item as necessary.

In this example the following calculations are required:

(a) Interest paid

Check whether there are accruals for interest payable in the opening and closing statements of financial position. In the absence of these, the interest paid figure will be the interest expense or finance charges figure from the income statement. In this example this is given in Worked example 4.3 as £200,000.

(b) Income taxes paid (note: in the UK, this means corporation tax paid)

Under UK pay-and-file systems, large companies pay corporation tax on account and settle the final amount owing for a financial year once this has been agreed with HM Revenue and Customs after the end of the year.

Corporation tax paid in the year ended 30 June 20X6 will therefore be the final 20X5 tax liability plus that part of the 20X6 tax paid on account. The amount paid for 20X6 will be the difference between the amount charged to profit and loss (given in Worked example 4.3) and the amount still owing at 30 June 20X6.

		£000
Final 20X5 tax liability		320
20X6 tax paid on account	(520 – 280)	240
		560

(c) Purchase of property, plant and equipment

In the absence of any disposals of property, plant and equipment the purchases will be the difference between the closing and opening cost balances.

	£000
Cost at 30 June 20X6	2,190
Cost at 30 June 20X5	1,310
Purchases	880

(d) Long-term borrowings

Look to see whether the balance has increased or decreased over the year. An increase represents the issue of further long-term debt, whereas a decrease represents a repayment of the debt.

	£000
Balance at 30 June 20X5	260
Balance at 30 June 20X6	60
Repayment of loan	200

(e) Any issue of shares and dividends paid will be shown in the statement of changes in equity. The complete statement of cash flows can now be drawn up.

Dewberry plc

Statement of cash flows for the year ended 30 June 20X6

	£000	£000
Cash flows generated from operating activities	255	
Interest paid	(200)	
Income taxes paid	(560)	
Net cash from operating activities		(505)
Cash flows from investing activities		
Purchase of property, plant and equipment	(880)	
Net cash used in investing activities		(880)
Cash flows from financing activities		
Proceeds from issue of share capital	215	
Repayment of long-term borrowings	(200)	
Dividends paid	(500)	
Net cash used in financing activities		(485)
Net decrease in cash and cash equivalents		(1,870)
Cash and cash equivalents at beginning of period		60
Cash and cash equivalents at end of period		£(1,810)

4.7.5 Other disclosures

Companies should disclose, together with a commentary by management, any other information likely to be of significance to users. This may include the following:

● restrictions on the use of or access to any part of cash equivalents

● the amount of borrowing facilities which are not drawn but are available

● cash flows which increased operating capacity compared with cash flows which merely maintained operating capacity.

Companies may also have investing and financing activities which do not have a direct impact on current cash flows although they do affect the capital and asset structure of an entity. If these 'non-cash transactions' are material, they should also be disclosed. Examples include:

● the acquisition of assets either by assuming directly related liabilities or by means of a finance lease

● the acquisition of an entity by means of an issue of equity shares.

Financial reporting in practice 4.7	Marks and Spencer plc, 2010

In its 2010 financial statements, Marks and Spencer notes that it had 'exceptional operating cash outflows primarily relating to the utilisation of the provision for UK restructuring'.

4.8 Notes to the financial statements

The four key financial statements occupy, at most, four or five pages in an annual report. The notes may run to 50 pages or more! The purpose of them is to amplify the information given in the financial statements and to disaggregate figures so that users have a full understanding of what each line item represents, its measurement basis, and, in some cases, how it has been derived.

IAS 1 specifies that the notes' aims are to:

(a) present information about the basis of preparation of the financial statements and the specific accounting policies used;

(b) disclose the information required by IFRSs that is not presented elsewhere in the financial statements; and

(c) provide information that is not presented elsewhere in the financial statements, but is relevant to an understanding of any of them.

As can be seen in the financial reporting in practice illustrations used throughout this textbook, notes are cross-referenced from the related line item in the particular financial statement, and they should be presented in a systematic manner to aid understanding and ease of use. The recommended order in which they are presented is as follows.

(a) A statement of compliance with IFRSs;

(b) A summary of significant accounting policies applied (see section 4.8.1 below);

(c) Supporting information for items presented in the statements of financial position and of comprehensive income, in the separate income statement (if presented), and in the statements of changes in equity and of cash flows, in the order in which each statement and each line item is presented; and

(d) Other disclosures, including:

(i) contingent liabilities (see Chapter 13) and unrecognised contractual commitments, and

(ii) non-financial disclosures, for example, the entity's financial risk management objectives and policies.

Financial reporting in practice 4.8 | Rolls-Royce plc, 2009

A typical statement by a company of compliance with IFRSs is provided by Rolls-Royce in the notes to its financial statements for the year ended March 2009.

Basis of preparation and statement of compliance

In accordance with European Union (EU) regulations, these financial statements have been prepared in accordance with International Financial Reporting Standards (IFRS) issued by the International Accounting Standards Board (IASB), as adopted for use in the EU effective at December 31, 2009 (Adopted IFRS). The Company has elected to prepare its parent company accounts under UK Generally Accepted Accounting Practices (GAAP).

The financial statements have been prepared on the historical cost basis except where Adopted IFRS requires the revaluation of financial instruments to fair value and certain other assets and liabilities on an alternative basis – most significantly post-retirement scheme liabilities are valued on the basis required by IAS 19 *Employee Benefits.*

The Group's significant accounting policies are set out below. These accounting policies have been applied consistently to all periods presented in these consolidated financial statements and by all Group entities.

The preparation of financial statements in conformity with Adopted IFRS requires the use of certain critical accounting estimates and judgements. The directors consider the potential key areas of judgements required to be made in applying the Group's accounting policies to be:

● A large proportion of the Group's activities relate to long-term aftermarket contracts. The determination of appropriate accounting policies for recognising revenue and costs in respect of these contracts requires judgement, in particular (i) whether an aftermarket contract is linked, for accounting purposes, to the related sale of original equipment and (ii) the appropriate measure of stage of completion of the contract.

- Where the Group participates in the financing of original equipment, judgement is required to determine whether revenue should be recognised or whether the transaction results in the consolidation of a special purpose financing entity.
- As set out in note 8, the Group has significant intangible assets. The decision as to when to commence capitalisation of development costs and whether sales of original equipment give rise to recognisable recoverable engine costs is a key judgement.
- As set out in note 22, the Group has contingent liabilities in respect of financing support provided to customers. Judgement is required to assess the likelihood of these crystallising, in order to assess whether a provision should be recognised.

4.8.1 Accounting policies

Accounting policies are defined in IAS 8 *Accounting Policies, Changes in Accounting Estimates and Errors* as the specific principles, bases, conventions, rules, and practices applied by an entity in preparing and presenting financial statements. The fundamental principle of accruals is accepted as being inherent in financial accounting and does not have to be explained, but if there are conditions which determine when certain items can be recognised and, in particular, which measurement bases have been used for items, users need to be informed of these matters. Some IFRSs specify the relevant accounting policy that should be used; others allow alternative accounting methods, in which case disclosure of the method chosen is required. In the absence of an IFRS that applies specifically to a transaction or event, management may be required to develop and apply a policy. The guiding principle is that accounting policies need to be formulated and disclosed if they assist users in understanding how a transaction or other event and condition is reflected in the financial statements. Accounting policies should ensure that the resulting financial information exhibits the fundamental characteristics of relevance and faithful representation, as discussed in Chapter 1. IAS 1 requires disclosure of all accounting policies.

 Examples of transactions and events requiring an accounting policy

These items will be discussed in more detail in later chapters; they are given here to illustrate the type of issue that would give rise to an accounting policy.

1 For property, plant and equipment, which measurement basis has been used for which class of asset—historic cost or fair value—could be used.
2 How inventory has been valued.
3 For companies such as those in the telecommunications industry, how and when revenue is recognised from the many different types of contracts they sell.
4 For companies which have significant transactions in foreign currencies, how foreign exchange gains and losses are accounted for.

4.8.2 Estimates, judgements, and risks

It should be noted that in applying accounting policies, estimates are often used—the terms 'policies' and 'estimates' should not be confused, although it may be difficult to distinguish them. For example, for property, plant and equipment, the accounting policy would be the measurement basis, which could be depreciated historic cost. In applying this policy, estimates of expected useful life, residual value, and pattern of usage have to be made to determine depreciation.

Many accounting policies produced by companies in their annual reports tend to regurgitate standard wording used in the related IFRS and appear similar from company to company. What is of more interest, and following the financial crisis, the focus of more attention, is the discussion of the areas where significant management judgement has had to be exercised in the process of applying the company's accounting policies that could significantly affect the amounts recognised in the financial statements. IAS 1 requires these judgements to be disclosed in the accounting policies

 Examples of transactions and events where judgement has to be exercised

Again, these items will be discussed in more detail in later chapters, but they are given here for illustration.

1 Whether a sale of goods is a financing arrangement and does not give rise to revenue.

2 Whether there is sufficient evidence to permit the capitalisation of development expenditure.

3 Whether a company controls another company and should account for its investment as a subsidiary.

Management also has to exercise subjective judgement where the determination of the carrying amount of some assets and liabilities requires estimates to be made of the effects of uncertain future events. As the number of variables and assumptions affecting the future outcome of the uncertainty increases, these judgements become more subjective and complex, and the potential for material adjustments to the carrying amounts usually increases.

 Examples of items where estimates about the uncertainty of future events have to be made

1 In determining whether an item of property, plant and equipment is impaired, an estimate of future cash flows which would result from using the asset is needed.

2 The impact of advances in technology on inventory obsolescence.

3 The future outcome of litigation.

4 Future pension benefits accruing to existing employees in a defined benefit plan.

IAS 1 requires disclosure of information about the assumptions it makes about the future and other major uncertainties that have a significant risk of resulting in material adjustments to the carrying amounts of assets and liabilities within the next financial year. (One exception to this is where the determination of fair value uses recently observed market prices as the measurement basis, for example on share prices.) These disclosures may require sensitivity analyses using ranges of possible outcomes with associated probabilities and may be fairly lengthy. However, the objective is that users should understand where and how judgement has been exercised, where uncertainties exist, and the impact of both on the financial statements.

This is an area of financial reporting that is of particular concern as it links to a company's financial exposure to risk. The discussion on corporate governance in Chapter 3 suggested that the perceived lack of management in this area and inadequate reporting of risk were major issues in the recent financial crisis, and that there are moves to improve financial reporting in this respect. Any strengthening of discussions on risk would need to tie into the disclosures already required by IAS 1 about uncertainties in estimates and judgements made by management.

Financial reporting in practice 4.9

Next plc, 2011

Next plc includes a fairly brief note in the accounting policies in its 2011 financial statements (however, further detail and discussions are contained in the cross-referenced notes).

Significant areas of estimation and judgement

The preparation of the financial statements requires judgements, estimations and assumptions to be made that affect the reported values of assets, liabilities, revenues and expenses. The nature of estimation means that actual outcomes could differ from those estimates. Significant areas of estimation for the Group include the expected future cash flows applied in measuring impairment of trade receivables (Note 14), estimated selling prices applied in determining the net realisable values of inventories and the actuarial assumptions applied in calculating the net retirement benefit obligation (Note 21).

Financial reporting in practice 4.10

Marks and Spencer plc, 2010

Marks and Spencer's financial statements accounting policies include more detail and further explanation is also contained in the individual cross-referenced notes.

Critical accounting estimates and judgements

The preparation of consolidated financial statements requires the Group to make estimates and assumptions that affect the application of policies and reported amounts. Estimates and judgements are continually evaluated and are based on historical experience and other factors including

(continued)

(continued)

expectations of future events that are believed to be reasonable under the circumstances. Actual results may differ from these estimates. The estimates and assumptions which have a significant risk of causing a material adjustment to the carrying amount of assets and liabilities are discussed below:

A. Impairment of goodwill

The Group is required to test, at least annually, whether goodwill has suffered any impairment. The recoverable amount is determined based on value in use calculations. The use of this method requires the estimation of future cash flows and the choice of a suitable discount rate in order to calculate the present value of these cash flows. Actual outcomes could vary from those calculated. See note 13 for further details.

B. Impairment of property, plant and equipment and computer software

Property, plant and equipment and computer software are reviewed for impairment if events or changes in circumstances indicate that the carrying amount may not be recoverable. When a review for impairment is conducted, the recoverable amount is determined based on value in use calculations prepared on the basis of management's assumptions and estimates. See notes 13 and 14 for further details.

C. Depreciation of property, plant and equipment and amortisation of computer software

Depreciation and amortisation is provided so as to write down the assets to their residual values over their estimated useful lives as set out above. The selection of these residual values and estimated lives requires the exercise of management judgement. See notes 13 and 14 for further details.

D. Post-retirement benefits

The determination of the pension cost and defined benefit obligation of the Group's defined benefit pension schemes depends on the selection of certain assumptions which include the discount rate, inflation rate, salary growth, mortality and expected return on scheme assets. Differences arising from actual experiences or future changes in assumptions will be reflected in subsequent periods. See note 11 for further details.

E. Refunds and loyalty scheme accruals

Accruals for sales returns and loyalty scheme redemption are estimated on the basis of historical returns and redemptions and these are recorded so as to allocate them to the same period as the original revenue is recorded. These accruals are reviewed regularly and updated to reflect management's latest best estimates, however, actual returns and redemptions could vary from these estimates.

4.8.3 Changes in accounting policies

One of the qualitative characteristics said to enhance financial information is comparability; this also encompasses the idea of consistency. Companies are required to select internally consistent accounting policies and are, generally, not permitted to change their accounting policies from one year to the next. There are only two circumstances where this is allowed:

1   Where the change is required by an IFRS

2   If it results in the financial statement providing reliable and more relevant information, which is a voluntary decision by a company.

If there is a change in an accounting policy, IAS 8 specifies that this be applied **retrospectively**. In other words, the financial statements are drawn up as if this policy had always been applied. This implies that the opening balance of each affected component of equity has to be adjusted, and all affected comparative figures are restated.

IAS 8 does recognise that there may be circumstances where it is impracticable to determine the effect in a specific period or on a cumulative basis. Where this is the case the policy should be applied retrospectively to the earliest period for which it is practicable to do so.

In the rare circumstance where it is impracticable to restate retrospectively any financial results the new policy should be applied **prospectively**. This means that the effect of the change is recognised only from the date of the change and no restatement of previous years' results is required.

If a new accounting standard is issued, or one is revised, it will usually specify transitional provisions for the initial application. In the absence of this, the requirements mentioned previously should be followed.

Full disclosure of the effect of the change in accounting policy is required. Specifically the following should be included:

● nature of the change

● reasons for the change (e.g. why it results in more reliable and relevant information)

● amount of the adjustment for the current period and for each prior period presented for each line item

● amount of the adjustment relating to periods prior to those included in the comparative information

● the fact that comparative information has been restated or that it is impracticable to do so.

4.8.4 Changes in accounting estimates

As discussed earlier many figures in financial statements are based on estimates and although management should exercise its best professional judgement in making these, there will always be circumstances where estimates are revised as more relevant or reliable information becomes available. The fact that this happens does not undermine the reliability of financial information provided that relevant details of significant estimates are disclosed, as has been discussed previously.

By its nature, the revision of an estimate does not relate to previous accounting periods (nor is it correcting an error—see section 4.8.5). The effect of a change in an accounting estimate is therefore recognised prospectively and is included from the date of the change.

Typical examples where changes in accounting estimates occur include provisions for irrecoverable debts, inventory obsolescence, fair values of financial instruments, the useful lives of depreciable assets, and warranty provisions.

IAS 8 requires disclosures of the nature and amount of a change in an accounting estimate on the current accounting period and future accounting periods, unless the effect on the future is impracticable to estimate.

 Example of a change in the estimate of useful life

A machine originally cost £200,000. At the date of acquisition the machine's useful life was estimated at ten years and the residual value as zero. The annual straight line depreciation charge will be £20,000 and the carrying amount after 3 years will be £140,000.

If in the fourth year it is decided that as a result of changes in technology the remaining useful life is only three years (implying a total life of six years), then the depreciation charge in that year (and in the next two years) will be calculated by writing off the current carrying amount over the remaining useful life.

Annual depreciation will become $\dfrac{£140,000}{3} = £46,667$

The depreciation charge for the first three years is not restated.

The effect of the change is an increase in the annual depreciation charge from £20,000 to £46,667; this must be disclosed if considered material.

4.8.5 Errors

Even with good internal controls systems and external audits of financial statements, errors do occur from time to time. Irrespective of whether the error was intentional or fraudulent, or merely careless, IAS 8 deals with how to account for an error when it has been discovered. Obviously, if it is discovered in the same accounting period as when it happened, it should be corrected before the financial statements are issued to shareholders, but it may be discovered in a subsequent period.

If this is the case and it is considered material, then it is corrected retrospectively, as for a change in an accounting policy. In other words, comparative amounts for the prior period(s) presented in which the error occurred are restated and opening balances of the affected equity accounts are restated.

Whenever there is a retrospective restatement of financial statements, or when a company reclassifies items in its financial statements from one period to the next, IAS 1 requires presentation of a statement of financial position as of the beginning of the earliest comparative period.

Worked example 4.5: to show the retrospective correction of error

Alpha plc reported a profit in its income statement for the year ended 31 December 20X3 as follows:

	£
Sales	14,700
Cost of sales	(8,900)
Gross profit	5,800
Distribution and administrative expenses	(1,800)
Profit before tax	4,000
Tax	(1,200)
Profit after tax	2,800

In 20X4 the company discovered that some products sold during 20X3 had been included incorrectly in inventory at 31 December 20X3 at £1,100. In 20X4, the company's records show sales of £20,800, cost of goods of £13,600 (including £1,100 for the error in opening inventory), and distribution and administrative expenses of £3,700. The company's corporation tax rate was 30% for both 20X3 and 20X4.

Alpha's retained earnings at 1 January and 31 December 20X3 were £4,000 and £6,800 respectively. The company had £5,000 of share capital and no other equity balances in 20X3 and 20X4.

Required:
In so far as the information permits, draw up Alpha plc's income statement for the year ended 31 December 20X4, showing the 20X3 comparative statement, and the statement of changes in equity for the two years. Show any other disclosures.

Alpha plc

Extract from the income statement for the year ended 31 December 20X4

	20X4 £	20X3 (restated) £
Sales	20,800	14,700
Cost of sales	(12,500)	(10,000)
Gross profit	8,300	4,700
Distribution and administrative expenses	(3,700)	(1,800)
Profit before tax	4,600	2,900
Tax	(1,380)	(870)
Profit after tax	3,220	2,030

Alpha plc

Statement of changes in equity

	Share capital £	Retained earnings £	Total £
Balance at 1 January 20X3	5,000	4,000	9,000
Profit for the year ended 31 December 20X3 as restated	____	2,030	2,030
Balance at 31 December 20X3	5,000	6,030	11,030
Profit for the year ended 31 December 20X4	____	3,220	3,220
Balance at 31 December 20X4	5,000	9,250	14,250

Extract from notes

Some products that had been sold in 20X3 were incorrectly included in inventory at 31 December at £1,100. The financial statements of 20X3 have been restated to correct this error. The effect of the restatement on those financial statements is summarised as follows. There is no effect in 20X4.

	Effect on 20X3 £
(Increase) in cost of goods sold	(1,100)
Decrease in tax expense	330
(Decrease) in profit and equity	(770)

4.9 Proposed changes to the presentation of financial statements

4.9.1 IASB/FASB convergence project

The 2007 changes to IAS 1 were Phase A of a convergence project of the IASB and US FASB to develop a new standard for financial statement presentation. The objective of the project is to establish a global standard that will guide the organisation and presentation of information in the financial statements to improve the usefulness of the information provided in an entity's financial statements to help users in their decision-making.

The joint project was initiated to address users' concerns that existing requirements permit too many alternative forms of presentation, and that information in financial statements is highly aggregated and inconsistently presented, making it difficult to understand fully the relationship between an entity's financial statements and its financial results. For example, the structure of the statements of comprehensive income and cash flows are very different, with the former differentiating expense elements of performance either by nature or function, and the latter classifying cash flow financial performance under different types of activity. This means users have to reclassify and reconcile items and subtotals in the different statements to gain a full understanding of performance. There are also key differences in presentation between IFRS and US generally accepted accounting principles (GAAP), leading to difficulties of comparison.

To address these concerns the project's main proposals are for:

● cohesive financial statements that share a common structure, separately presenting operating, investing, and financing activities, as well as income tax and discontinued operations

● disaggregation in each financial statement, considering the function, nature, and measurement bases of items, with some disaggregation included in the notes

● more disaggregation of operating cash receipts and payments, and reconciliation of profit or loss from operating activities to cash flows from operating activities

● analyses of changes in asset and liability line items (including net debt)

● and disclosure of remeasurement information.

The proposals would improve the comparability and understandability of information presented in financial statements by imposing some degree of standardisation in the way that information is presented in the financial statements, particularly regarding how information is classified and the degree to which it is disaggregated.

Phase A of the project set out what constitutes a complete set of financial statements and the requirements for the presentation of comparative information. These provisions have been incorporated in this chapter.

4.9.2 Changes to the presentation of the key financial statements

Progress has been made in Phase B of the project, which addresses more fundamental issues for the presentation of information in the financial statements. The aims of this phase are:

1 To produce a standard to replace both IAS 1 and IAS 7

2 To address the presentation of other comprehensive income

3 To address the presentation of discontinued operations.

A discussion paper was published in October 2008 and received a high level of responses. The boards have been holding additional outreach activities before finishing and publishing an exposure draft, although a 'staff draft' of this that reflects tentative decisions made to date relating to the first aim was published in July 2010. The second and third aims are addressed in separate projects.

The tentative decisions that have been reached so far are based on the core principles of cohesiveness and disaggregation, which are defined as follows.

Cohesiveness   The relationship between items in the financial statements is clear. The financial statements complement each other as much as possible.

Disaggregation   Resources are separated by the activity in which they are used and by their economic characteristics.

A common structure for the statements of financial position, comprehensive income, and cash flows would be established in the form of required sections, categories, subcategories, and related subtotals. All three financial statements would display related information in the same sections, categories, and subcategories so that the information is more easily associated. The proposals are summarised in Table 4.2.

The statement of changes in equity would not include the sections and categories used in the other statement because this presents information solely about changes in items classified in the equity category in the statement of financial position.

The business section would include items that are part of an entity's day-to-day and other income-generating activities, and segregate them into operating and investing categories. The financing section would include items that are part of an entity's activities to obtain or repay capital, and segregate them into debt and equity categories. This structure, which separates the functional activities of a business, would assist users of financial statements who commonly analyse a business's performance independently of its capital structure. (See Chapter 5 for discussion of analytical methods.)

Table 4.2 Proposed structures of key financial statements

Statement of financial position	Statement of comprehensive income	Statement of cash flows
Business section	Business section	Business section
Operating category	Operating category	Operating category
Operating finance subcategory	Operating finance subcategory	
Investing category	Investing category	Investing category
Financing section	Financing section	Financing section
Debt category	Debt category	
Equity category		
	Multicategory transaction section	Multicategory transaction section
Income tax section	Income tax section	Income tax section
Discontinued operation section	Discontinued operation section, net of tax	Discontinued operation section
	Other comprehensive income, net of tax	

The proposals are based clearly on the principles behind the current presentation of the statement of cash flows and would change the presentation of the statement of financial position the most. Here, assets and liabilities would either be grouped under each section, category, or subcategory according to whether they were short or long term, or be presented in order of liquidity, depending on which provided the most relevant information. They would be disaggregated by measurement basis and/or by reference to the economic characteristics that distinguish them (i.e. their nature). In the statement of comprehensive income, an entity would disaggregate its income and expenses by function (i.e. the primary activities in which it is engaged, such as selling goods, providing services, manufacturing, advertising, marketing, business development, or administration). The direct method for the presentation of cash flows for all sections and categories would be used in the statement of cash flows, but the reconciliation of operating income to operating cash flows would still be required.

Overall, more line items and subtotals would be presented enabling easier comparison of effects across the financial statements. For example, users would be able to assess how operating assets and liabilities generate operating income and cash flows.

Although the IASB had an original target date for the publication of the new accounting standard of late 2011, the board chose to concentrate on producing other, more pressing standards by mid-2011. Phase B is currently paused until the board has completed its ongoing deliberations about its future work plan.

4.9.3 Presentation of discontinued operations

The other aims of Phase B of the convergence project relate to the presentation of other comprehensive income and the topic of discontinued operations. Work on the presentation of other comprehensive income has concluded with the amendments to IAS 1 issued in 2011 as discussed earlier. Discontinued operations are discussed in Chapter 6 and full discussion of the development of the proposed changes in this area is included there.

 ### Summary of key points

What constitutes the financial statements of a company and their presentation are set out in IAS 1 *Presentation of Financial Statements*. This accounting standard defines financial statements as:

- a statement of financial position
- a statement of comprehensive income
- a statement of changes in equity
- a statement of cash flows
- notes, comprising a summary of significant accounting policies and other explanatory information.

The minimum line items that must be disclosed for the statements of financial position, comprehensive income, and changes in equity are specified by the standard, which permits two alternative methods for drawing up the statement of comprehensive income. The format of the statement of cash flows is governed by IAS 7 *Statement of Cash Flows*; this also allows two alternative methods for companies to present cash flows from operating activities, and is not prescriptive about where dividend and interest cash flows are included. This flexibility and ensuing lack of comparability between companies is criticised by some users and is currently being addressed in an IASB/FASB convergence project, which aims to produce a new IFRS to replace both IAS 1 and IAS 7, and which contains proposals to significantly change the format of the statements to align related information across the statements under the same section and category headings.

The current IAS 1 also explains the underpinning principles on which financial statements are based, namely accruals and going concern, materiality and aggregation, and that items should not be offset.

Notes to the financial statements are extensive, much of which information is specified by individual accounting standards. The underpinning principle of notes, as explained in IAS 1, is to disaggregate the aggregated figures on the face of the main financial statements so that users have a full understanding of what each line item represents and the measurement bases used.

The notes should include a comprehensive set of accounting policies, and details of the criteria for selecting and changing these, together with the accounting treatment and disclosure of changes in accounting policies, changes in accounting estimates, and corrections of errors, are set out in IAS 8 *Accounting Policies, Changes in Accounting Estimates and Errors*.

Further reading

Bruce, R. (2007) *Let's talk. Why a project on Financial Statement Presentation?* IASB's INSIGHT. London: IASB. Why read? This article expands upon some of the ideas discussed in this chapter relating to the important proposed changes to financial statement presentation.

IASB (International Accounting Standards Board) (2007) IAS 1 *Presentation of Financial Statements*. London: IASB.

IASB (International Accounting Standards Board) (2004a) IAS 7 *Statement of Cash Flows*. London: IASB.

IASB (International Accounting Standards Board) (2004b) IAS 8 *Accounting Policies, Changes in Accounting Estimates and Errors*. London: IASB.

Bibliography

Bruce, R. (2007) *Let's talk. Why a project on Financial Statement Presentation?* IASB's INSIGHT. London: IASB.

FRC (Financial Reporting Council) (2009) *Going Concern and Liquidity Risk: Guidance for Directors of UK Companies*. London: FRC.

FRC (Financial Reporting Council) (2011)*The Sharman Inquiry: Going Concern and Liquidity Risks: Lessons for Companies and Auditors, Preliminary Report and Recommendations of the Panel of Inquiry*. London: FRC.

FRC (Financial Reporting Council) (2012) *The Sharman Inquiry: Going Concern and Liquidity Risks: Lessons for Companies and Auditors, Final Report and Recommendations of the Panel of Inquiry*. London: FRC.

GKN plc (2010) *Annual Report and Accounts, 2009*. Redditch: GKN.

IASB (International Accounting Standards Board) (2004a) IAS 7 *Statement of Cash Flows*. London: IASB.

IASB (International Accounting Standards Board) (2004b) IAS 8 *Accounting Policies, Changes in Accounting Estimates and Errors*. London: IASB.

IASB (International Accounting Standards Board) (2007) IAS 1 *Presentation of Financial Statements*. London: IASB.

IASB (International Accounting Standards Board) (2008) *Preliminary Views on Financial Statement Presentation*. Discussion paper. London: IASB.

IASB (International Accounting Standards Board) (2010) *Financial Statement Presentation: Staff draft of an exposure draft*. London: IASB.

IASB (International Accounting Standards Board) (2011) *Presentation of Items of Other Comprehensive Income (Amendments to IAS 1)*. Project summary and feedback statement. London: IASB.

ICAEW (Institute of Chartered Accountants in England and Wales) (2010) *IAS 1 Revised*. IFRS Factsheet. London: ICAEW.

Lloyds Banking Group plc (2011) *Annual Report and Accounts, 2010*. Edinburgh: Lloyds Banking Group.

Marks and Spencer plc (2010) *Annual Report and Financial Statements, 2010*. London: Marks and Spencer.

Nestlé S.A. (2011) *2010 Financial Statements*. Vevey: Nestlé.

Next plc (2011) *Annual Report and Accounts, 2011*. Enderby: Next.

Rolls-Royce plc (2010) Annual Report, 2009. London: Rolls-Royce.

Vodafone Group plc (2010) Annual Report, 2010. Newbury: Vodafone.

 ## Questions

● Quick test

1   A company's credit sales are £45,678 during 20X8. Accounts receivable at 1 January 20X8 are £4,602 and at 31 December 20X8 are £5,709. What cash has the company received from its credit customers during 20X8?

2   A company's cost of sales in its income statement for the year ended 31 October 20X5 is £105,066. Inventory at 31 October 20X4 is £6,430 and at 31 October 20X5 is £5,757. Accounts payable at 31 October 20X4 are £9,204 and at 31 October 20X5 are £8,580.

(a) What are the purchases for the year?

(b) Assuming all purchases are made on credit, what cash has the company paid to suppliers during the year?

3   A company's rent expense in its income statement is £35,100. Opening and closing prepayments are £8,460 and £9,000 respectively. What cash has the company paid for rent in the year?

4   A company's corporation tax charge in its income statement is £75,267. The liabilities for corporation tax at the end of the previous year and at the end of the current year are £34,609 and £41,957 respectively. What cash has the company paid for corporation tax during the year?

5   Information about a company's fixtures and fittings at 30 September in two successive years is as follows:

	20X1 £	20X0 £
Cost	143,201	126,587
Accumulated depreciation	76,613	64,293

(a) If the company did not sell any fixtures and fittings during the year ended 30 September 20X1

   (i)   What is the depreciation expense for the year?

   (ii) What cash did the company spend on fixtures and fittings during the year?

(b) During the year ended 30 September 20X1 the company sold some shelving for £3,500. This shelving had originally cost £24,500 and at the time of sale had accumulated depreciation of £14,700.

   (i)   What is the depreciation expense for the year?

   (ii) What cash did the company spend on fixtures and fittings during the year?

   (iii) What is the profit or loss on the sale of the shelving?

6   At 30 June 20X3 a company has issued £100,000 7% debentures. On 1 April 20X4 the company issues a further £50,000 of the same debentures.

   (a) What is the interest expense for the year ended 30 June 20X4?

   (b) (i) Assuming the company pays interest quarterly in arrears on the last day of each quarter (31 March, 30 June, 30 September, and 31 December) and the company pays all interest when it is due, what is the cash paid for interest in the year ended 30 June 20X4?

      (ii) If there is an accrual for interest at 30 June 20X3 and 20X4 of £1,750 and £2,625, respectively, what is the cash paid for interest in the year ended 30 June 20X4?

●● Develop your understanding

7   The following information relates to the activities of Pilot plc:

Statements of financial position at 31 March

	20X8		20X7	
	£000	£000	£000	£000
Non-current assets				
Freehold land at cost		780		700
Plant and equipment—cost	660		560	
Less: accumulated depreciation	296		230	
		364		330
		1,144		1,030
Current assets				
Inventory	498		356	
Receivables	304		330	
Bank	-		30	
		802		716
Total assets		£1,946		£1,746
Equity				
Equity £1 shares	550		400	
Share premium	210		160	

Retained earnings	490		376	
		1,250		936
Current liabilities				
Trade payables	230		240	
Corporation tax	90		120	
Bank overdraft	126		-	
	446		360	
Non-current liabilities				
6% debentures	250		450	
Total liabilities		696		810
Total equity and liabilities		£ 1,946		£ 1,746

Statement of comprehensive income for the year ended 31 March 20X8

	£000
Revenue	4,520
Cost of sales	(3,420)
Gross profit	1,100
Expenses	(766)
Profit before tax	334
Corporation tax	(150)
Profit after tax	£184

Statement of changes in equity for the year ended 31 March 20X8

	Share Capital £000	Share Premium £000	Retained Earnings £000	Total £000
Balance at 1 April 20X7	400	160	376	936
Issue of share capital	150	50		200
Profit for the year			184	184
Dividends paid			(70)	(70)
Balance at 31 March 20X8	550	210	490	1,250

You are informed that:

(a) Plant which originally cost £80,000 was sold for cash of £14,000. The profit/loss on disposal is included in expenses. Accumulated depreciation relating to the plant sold amounted to £58,000.

(b) The debentures were repaid on 30 September 20X7. Interest of £21 for the year was fully paid by 31 March 20X8 and is included in expenses.

Required:

(i)   Calculate the net increase/decrease in cash for the year ended 31 March 20X8.

(ii) Calculate the cash flow from operating activities using the indirect method (i.e. reconciling profit before tax to cash flow from operating activities).

(iii) Prepare the complete statement of cash flows for Pilot plc for the year ended 31 March 20X8 in accordance with IAS 7 *Statement of Cash Flows*.

(iv) Comment on the information provided by the statement of cash flows.

8   (Question 6 from Chapter 1 with the addition of property, plant and equipment revaluation) Falmouth plc has an authorised share capital of £2,000,000 divided into 3,000,000 ordinary shares of 50p and 500,000 12% redeemable preference shares of £1.

The following trial balance has been extracted from the accounting records at 30 June 20X1:

	Debit £000	Credit £000
50p ordinary shares (fully paid)		500
12% £1 preference shares (fully paid)		200
8% debentures		400
Retained earnings 1 July 20X0		368
Freehold land and buildings (cost)	860	
Plant and machinery (cost)	1,460	
Motor vehicles (cost)	440	
Accumulated depreciation at 1 July 20X0:		
Freehold buildings		40
Plant and machinery		444
Motor vehicles		230
Inventory at 1 July 20X0	380	
Sales		6,590
Purchases	4,304	
Final dividends for year end 30 June 20X0:		
Ordinary	40	
Interim dividends for year end 30 June 20X1:		
Ordinary	16	
Debenture interest	16	
Wages and salaries	508	
Light and heat	62	

Bad debt expense	30	
Other administration expenses	196	
Receivables	578	
Payables		390
Provision for doubtful debts		20
Corporation tax paid	112	
Bank	168	
	£ 9,182	£ 9,182

The following information needs to be dealt with before the financial statements can be completed.

(a) Inventories at 30 June 20X1 were valued at £440,000 (cost).

(b) Other administration expenses include £18,000 paid in respect of a machinery maintenance contract for the 12 months ending 30 November 20X1. Light and heat does not include an invoice of £12,000 for electricity for the quarter ending 3 July 20X1, which was paid in August 20X1.

(c) The directors wish to provide for:

(i) any debenture interest due

(ii) directors' bonuses of £24,000

(iii) the year's depreciation.

(d) The provision for doubtful debts required at 30 June 20X1 is £24,000.

(e) During the year ended 30 June 20X1, a customer whose receivables balance of £8,000 had been written off in previous years paid the full amount owing. The company credited this to receivables.

(f) The debentures have been in issue for some years.

(g) Corporation tax of £256,000 is to be charged on the profits.

(h) During the year a piece of machinery, which had originally cost £320,000 and had been owned by the company for 6 years, was scrapped. Proceeds received were £40,000. These have been credited incorrectly to the plant and machinery cost account.

(i) The buildings element of the freehold land and buildings cost is £400,000. Depreciation methods and rates are as follows:

Buildings   Straight-line over 50 years

Plant and machinery 10% straight-line

Motor vehicles   33% reducing balance

(j) At 30 June 20X1 the freehold land and buildings are revalued at £1,200,000, and this revaluation is to be incorporated into the financial statements.

Required:

Prepare the statements of comprehensive income and changes in equity of Falmouth plc for the year ended 30 June 20X1, and a statement of financial position at that date in accordance with IAS 1 *Presentation of Financial Statements*. Expenses are to be analysed by function.

● ● ● .Take it further

9   Birch plc manufactures alarm systems. Its trial balance at 31 March 20X9 showed the following
    balances.

	£	£
Freehold land and buildings		
Cost (land: £400,000)	1,120,000	
Accumulated depreciation at 31 March 20X8		691,200
Plant and equipment		
Cost	182,860	
Accumulated depreciation at 31 March 20X8		74,100
Retained earnings at 31 March 20X8		119,704
Equity share capital (£1 shares)		200,000
5% Preference share capital (50p irredeemable shares)		100,000
Share premium		130,000
Cash in hand	124	
Bank overdraft		2,820
Trade and other receivables	172,800	
Trade and other payables		111,580
Sales		660,340
Manufacturing costs		
Direct costs	269,120	
Overheads	107,340	
Wages and salaries	63,150	
Administrative expenses	138,010	
Distribution costs	7,020	
Costs of Product Y (see note (iv))	25,200	
Inventory at 31 March 20X8	9,120	
Provision for doubtful debts at 31 March 20X8		5,000
	2,094,744	2,094,744

The following additional information is available:

(i)   Inventory at 31 March 20X9 was valued at £7,570.

(ii) The finance director has estimated that the provision for doubtful debts at 31 March 20X9
      should be £7,000.

(iii) Wages and salaries should be apportioned 60% to administrative expenses and the
      remainder to distribution costs.

(iv) Costs of Product Y relate to the materials and labour costs incurred over the period 1 April
      20X8 to 31 December 20X8 relating to the development of a new type of alarm system

which Birch plc had started in the year ended 31 March 20X8. In this year the company had spent a total of £5,340, which was written off against the year's profits as part of cost of sales. On 30 September 20X8 the project was judged commercially viable and sales of the system commenced on 1 January 20X9. The marketing director estimates that it will take three years before a competitor launches a superior product. The materials and labour costs accrued evenly over the period from 1 April 20X8 to 31 December 20X8. (See Chapter 11 for accounting treatment.)

(v) On 30 September 20X8 the directors decided to sell a machine which had cost Birch plc £30,000 on 1 October 20X6. At 30 September 20X8 the machine met the criteria of IFRS 5 *Non-current Assets Held for Sale and Discontinued Operations* to be classified as 'held for sale', but no adjustments were made to the accounting records in respect of the machine at this date. The machine was expected to sell for £16,000, with selling costs of £60. A buyer was found on 6 March 20X9 at this price, although the sale was not completed until after the year end. (See Chapter 6 for accounting treatment.)

(vi) Depreciation on property, plant and equipment has yet to be charged. Birch plc charges depreciation as follows:

Type	Depreciation policy	Depreciation presented in
Freehold buildings	Straight-line basis over 50 years	20% in administrative expenses, 80% in cost of sales
Plant and equipment	Straight-line basis over 5 years	Cost of sales

(vii) At 31 March 20X9 the directors of Birch decided to incorporate a revaluation of freehold land and buildings into the financial statements. At this date the land and buildings were valued at £800,000.

(viii) The 5% preference share dividend for the year was declared on 31 March 20X9. No ordinary dividend is to be paid.

(ix) The income tax charge for the year has been estimated at £6,100.

Required:

Prepare the statements of comprehensive income and changes in equity for Birch plc for the year ended 31 March 20X9, and a statement of financial position as at that date in a form suitable for publication.

Note: (i) notes to the financial statements are not required and (ii) expenses should be analysed by function.

10 The statements of financial position of Hemmingway plc at 30 June 20X4 and 20X3, and a summary of the income statement for the year ended 30 June 20X4, are given as follows.

Statements of financial position at 30 June

	20X4		20X3	
	£	£	£	£
Non-current assets				
Land and buildings				
Cost	47,000		47,000	
Accumulated depreciation	(12,000)		(10,000)	

Plant and machinery				
Cost	36,000		29,100	
Accumulated depreciation	(17,000)		(12,600)	
		54,000		53,500
Investments at cost		7,500		6,000
		61,500		59,500
Current assets				
Inventory	12,631		11,412	
Receivables and prepayments	10,987		12,784	
Cash at bank	-		4,713	
		23,618		28,909
Total assets		£ 85,118		£ 88,409
Equity				
£1 equity shares	33,000		33,000	
Retained earnings	34,115		28,597	
		67,115		61,597
Current liabilities				
Bank overdraft	1,490		-	
Trade payables and accruals	10,713		9,812	
Corporation tax	3,000		4,000	
	15,203		13,812	
Non-current liabilities				
10% debentures	2,800		13,000	
Total liabilities		18,003		26,812
Total equity and liabilities		£85,118		£88,409

Summarised income statement for the year ended 30 June 20X4

	£
Profit before tax	10,518
Tax	(2,000)
Profit after tax	£ 8,518

You are given the following additional information:

(a) During the year certain items of machinery were disposed of for proceeds of £1,200. The machines had originally cost £4,000 and had a net book value at disposal of £500.

(b) The debentures were repaid on 30 September 20X3. All interest due has been paid.

Required:

Prepare a statement of cash flows for the year ended 30 June 20X4 in accordance with IAS 7.

11 Vodafone plc includes the following information in its 2010 annual report.

Financial reporting in practice **4.11** | Vodafone plc 2010 |

Critical Accounting Estimates

The Group prepares its consolidated financial statements in accordance with IFRS as issued by the IASB and IFRS as adopted by the European Union, the application of which often requires judgements to be made by management when formulating the Group's financial position and results. Under IFRS, the directors are required to adopt those accounting policies most appropriate to the Group's circumstances for the purpose of presenting fairly the Group's financial position, financial performance and cash flows.

In determining and applying accounting policies, judgement is often required in respect of items where the choice of specific policy, accounting estimate or assumption to be followed could materially affect the reported results or net asset position of the Group should it later be determined that a different choice would be more appropriate.

Management considers the accounting estimates and assumptions discussed below to be its critical accounting estimates and, accordingly, provides an explanation of each below.

The discussion below should also be read in conjunction with the Group's disclosure of significant IFRS accounting policies which is provided in note 2 to the consolidated financial statements, "Significant accounting policies".

Management has discussed its critical accounting estimates and associated disclosures with the Company's Audit Committee.

Discuss this statement in the context of the underpinning characteristics of financial information.

 Visit the Online Resource Centre for solutions to all these end of chapter questions plus visual walkthrough solutions. You can test your understanding with extra questions and answers, explore additional case studies based on real companies, take a guided tour through a company report, and much more. Go to the Online Resource Centre at www.oxfordtextbooks.co.uk/orc/maynard/

5

Interpretation of financial statements

➤ Introduction

Investors, lenders, and other creditors require information to help them make decisions about providing resources to a company. Other users will also use financial information to assist them in the decisions they make in relation to their interactions with a company. Many decisions are determined by the returns that the users gain from their investment, for example from dividends, by principal and interest payments, or from market price increases.

But how is this information ascertained from a complex set of financial statements that contains a wealth of information? How is return measured and evaluated? How are the returns of one company compared with another? How can it be evaluated whether a loan to a company will be repaid in the future?

This chapter provides details of a range of standard analytical techniques that can be applied in financial statement interpretation to help answer these sorts of questions. These techniques are used in all subsequent chapters to explain the implication of accounting methods specified by accounting standards for users' interpretation of the financial information provided.

The methods demonstrated in this chapter are just part of interpretation. At this stage it is about providing some tools that can be used. Full interpretation of financial statements requires an understanding of far more than some line-by-line comparisons and ratio calculations. For example, the bases for the recognition and measurement of different figures need to be understood, and, crucially, to be meaningful, any interpretation must be set in the context of the company's internal and external environments.

Interpretation of financial statements is returned to at the end of the textbook. At this point readers will have knowledge of the accounting and measurement methods used for many items and a greater understanding of the relationships between figures in the financial statements.

After studying this chapter you will be able to:

- interpret a set of simple financial statements using horizontal, vertical, and ratio analytical techniques for a variety of users
- understand key limitations of the analysis performed
- understand that an interpretation of a set of financial statements requires more than the use of the analytical techniques included in this chapter.

- ❏ Different users and their needs.
- ❏ The key question—'why?'.
- ❏ Obtaining an overview of financial statements through horizontal and vertical analyses.
- ❏ Calculations and interpretation of the main ratios in order to analyse profitability, liquidity, efficiency, gearing, and investor returns.
- ❏ The interrelationships of ratios.
- ❏ Limitations of ratio analysis.

5.1 Where does an interpretation begin?

5.1.1 Purpose of the analysis

Before any financial figures are considered, the purpose of the analysis must be established. Different users of financial statements will have different reasons for examining and analysing the financial statements, and will therefore focus on different aspects.

 Examples of different purposes of analysis

1 If a shareholder wishes to assess the ongoing returns they receive from their investment, they will focus on dividend payments and the quality of the profits the company is making to estimate what any future level of dividend may be.

2 Alternatively, a shareholder may be holding shares for growth in market value. This shareholder will be more interested in predicting future earnings or the quality of the asset base of the business.

3 A venture capital provider will be more concerned that profit levels and liquidity are sufficient to meet the servicing costs of their investment.

4 A bank lender will have the same concerns as the venture capital provider and may have set the company requirements for sufficient liquidity levels measured by financial ratios (referred to as covenants).

5   One company interested in purchasing another may be doing so for reasons of growth to expand its customer base, to acquire part of the production chain, or to acquire a brand name. The reasons will determine on which aspects of the financial performance and position the interpretation is particularly focused.

Thus, any analysis needs to be directed to the specific requirements of the user.

However, for the purposes of the example used in this chapter, a full financial analysis will be provided covering all aspects from different users' perspectives.

5.1.2 Business information

The type of business must always be noted before any analysis is performed and any particular internal information provided about the company. External information, such as that about how the industry is performing, the markets in which the company operates, competitive forces, general economic conditions, or exchange rates (if applicable), will all need to be taken into account in order to provide the context for the analysis.

How this is used will be discussed in more detail in Chapter 17 'Interpretation of financial statements revisited'.

5.1.3 The question 'why?'

Before any analytical techniques are explained, it must be emphasised that the most important question that can be asked is 'why?'. The analytical techniques applied to a set of published financial statements by an external user should be seen as a series of steps. If the question 'why?' is asked after each technique or calculation performed, this will lead to further analytical stages.

However, these techniques will not necessarily provide all the answers. Chapter 4, which discussed the information provided by published financial statements, explained that many figures are aggregated, with a detailed breakdown of the amounts that make up the disclosed balance not necessarily being available. Disclosures in the notes to the financial statements, where provided, will usually have to be used to enhance the analysis, but, even then, without internal management information, some questions will still go unanswered and educated guesses may have to be part of the analytical process.

5.1.4 Financial statements to be used for analysis

The following financial statements are to be used throughout this chapter in the application of the analytical techniques.

Worked example 5.1: to show the financial statements of a company

Sharples plc is a company that wholesales non-electrical office equipment, from pens and stationery to filing cabinets. The company has just one warehouse and, during 20X7, replaced much of its shelving, as well as investing in new computer equipment to maintain its inventory and other records.

In October 20X7 the company tendered for, and won, a contract to supply some goods to the local high street office supplies and stationery shop.

The financial statements for both 20X7 and the previous year are given as follows.

Sharples plc

Statements of comprehensive income for the years ended 31 December 20X7 and 20X6

	20X7	20X6
	£000	£000
Revenue	3,000	2,500
Cost of sales	(1,800)	(1,425)
Gross profit	1,200	1,075
Administration expenses	(544)	(453)
Distribution costs	(250)	(245)
Profit from operations	406	377
Finance costs	(66)	(60)
Profit before tax	340	317
Tax	(180)	(122)
Profit for the year	£ 160	£ 195

Statements of changes in equity for the years ended 31 December 20X7 and 20X6

	Equity share capital	Preference share capital	Retained earnings	Total
	£000	£000	£000	£000
Balance at 1 January 20X6	1,000	200	640	1,840
Profit for the year			195	195
Dividends paid			(95)	(95)
Balance at 31 December 20X6	1,000	200	740	1,940
Profit for the year			160	160
Dividends paid			(100)	(100)
Balance at 31 December 20X7	1,000	200	800	£ 2,000

Statements of financial position at 31 December 20X7 and 20X6

	20X7	20X6
	£000	£000
Non-current assets	2,320	2,080
Current assets		
Inventory	400	290
Receivables	450	350
Cash at bank	50	200
	900	840
Total assets	£ 3,220	£ 2,920
Equity		
Equity share capital (£1 shares)	1,000	1,000
10% irredeemable preference share capital (£1 shares)	200	200
Retained earnings	800	740
Total equity	2,000	1,940
Non-current liabilities		
10% debentures (20X9)	720	600
Current liabilities		
Payables	400	300
Tax	100	80
	500	380
Total equity and liabilities	£ 3,220	£ 2,920

Statements of cash flow for the years ended 31 December 20X7 and 20X6

	20X7	20X6
	£000	£000
Cash flow from operating activities		
Cash generated from operations	636	580
Interest paid	(66)	(60)
Taxation paid	(160)	(115)
Net cash from operating activities	410	405
Cash flow from investing activities		
Purchase of non-current assets	(600)	(180)
Proceeds from sale of non-current assets	20	10
Net cash used in investing activities	(580)	(170)

Cash flow from financing activities

Issue of debentures	120	-
Preference dividends paid	(20)	(20)
Equity dividends paid	(80)	(75)
Net cash from/(used in) financing activities	20	(95)
Net (decrease)/increase in cash	(150)	140
Cash and cash equivalents at beginning of year	200	60
Cash and cash equivalents at end of year	£ 50	£ 200

Reconciliation of profit before tax to cash generated from operations

	20X7	20X6
	£000	£000
Profit before tax	340	317
Add back: finance costs	66	60
depreciation	330	250
loss on sale of non-current assets	10	(17)
(Increase)/decrease in inventory	(110)	20
(Increase) in receivables	(100)	(40)
Increase/(decrease) in payables	100	(10)
Cash generated from operations	£ 636	£ 580

5.2 Overview of financial statements

5.2.1 Horizontal analysis

As given in Worked example 5.1, a published set of financial statements will include comparative figures. A good initial analytical technique is to compare key figures in the two sets of accounts, selecting those which are of particular interest for the purposes of the analysis. The aim of this, sometimes referred to as **horizontal analysis**, is to gain a 'feel' for the financial performance and position of the company at least for the later year compared with the previous year, and to start directing attention to areas which require additional investigation.

If figures are keyed or copied into a spreadsheet, changes in all figures can be easily calculated. Identification of which are the key figures and which are significant changes can then be made.

Absolute differences in figures are of little use unless they are put in the context of the actual figures themselves, so expressing the changes in percentage terms provides the necessary analytical information.

Worked example 5.2: to show horizontal analysis

Key figures and changes have been highlighted.

Statements of comprehensive income

	20X7	20X6	Change
	£000	£000	
Revenue	3,000	2,500	20%
Cost of sales	(1,800)	(1,425)	26%
Gross profit	1,200	1,075	12%
Administration expenses	(544)	(453)	20%
Distribution costs	(250)	(245)	2%
Profit from operations	406	377	8%
Finance costs	(66)	(60)	10%
Profit before tax	340	317	7%
Tax	(180)	(122)	48%
Profit for the year	£160	£195	-18%

Statements of financial position

	20X7	20X6	
	£000	£000	
Non-current assets	2,320	2,080	12%
Current assets			
Inventory	400	290	38%
Receivables	450	350	29%
Cash at bank	50	200	-75%
	900	840	7%
Total assets	£3,220	£2,920	10%
Equity			
Equity share capital	1,000	1,000	0%
10% preference share capital	200	200	0%
Retained earnings	800	740	8%
Total equity	2,000	1,940	3%
Non-current liabilities			
10% debentures	720	600	20%

Current liabilities

Payables	400	300	33%
Tax	100	80	25%
	500	380	32%
Total liabilities	1,220	980	24%
Total equity and liabilities	£3,220	£2,920	10%

Statements of cash flow

	20X7 £000	20X6 £000	
Cash flow from operating activities			
Cash generated from operations	636	580	10%
Interest paid	(66)	(60)	10%
Taxation paid	(160)	(115)	39%
Net cash from operating activities	410	405	1%
Cash flow from investing activities			
Purchase of non-current assets	(600)	(180)	233%
Proceeds from sale of non-current assets	20	10	100%
Net cash used in investing activities	(580)	(170)	241%
Cash flow from financing activities			
Issue of debentures	120	–	–
Preference dividends paid	(20)	(20)	0%
Equity dividends paid	(80)	(75)	7%
Net cash from/(used in) financing activities	20	(95)	121%
Net (decrease)/increase in cash and cash equivalents	£(150)	£ 140	-207%

Key points revealed by this overview are as follows.

Statements of comprehensive income

● Revenue shows an increase of 20%.

  ● How much of this is from the new contact obtained?

  ● Are there any other significant changes in customers or products sold?

● However, gross profit has increased by only 12% and profit from operations by only 8%.

● Conclusion—costs are proportionately much higher. Which costs and why?

● Profit after tax has fallen—the tax charge has disproportionately increased. Why?

Statements of financial position

- All assets and liabilities have increased except cash and net current assets.
- Increased business would lead to increases in net assets.
- Why has cash decreased?
- There has been no new equity funding, but additional debentures have been issued.

Statements of cash flow

- Large cash decrease in 20X7—this was an increase in 20X6.
- Main cause—investment in non-current assets.
- The reconciliation of profit before tax to operating cash flow reveals working capital increases.

5.2.2 Common size statements

Another way of providing an overview of the financial statements and the comparative figures is to produce common size statements, a technique referred to as **vertical analysis**. For each financial statement a key figure is identified, such as revenue for the statement of comprehensive income and total assets for the statement of financial position, and all other figures are expressed as a percentage of this figure. For the statement of comprehensive income, comparison of the two years provides information about how the levels of different costs and profits have varied, and, for the statement of financial position, details of changes in the capital structure of the business are revealed.

 Worked example 5.3: to show vertical analysis

Key figures have been highlighted.

Statements of comprehensive income

	20X7	20X6
Revenue	100%	100%
Cost of sales	60%	57%
Gross profit	**40%**	**43%**
Administration expenses	18%	18%
Distribution costs	8%	10%
Profit from operations	**13%**	**15%**
Finance costs	2%	2%
Profit before tax	**11%**	**13%**

	6%	5%
Tax	6%	5%
Profit for the year	**5%**	**8%**

Statements of financial position

	20X7	20X6
Non-current assets	72%	71%
Current assets		
Inventory	12%	10%
Receivables	14%	12%
Cash at bank	**2%**	**7%**
	28%	29%
Total assets	100%	100%
Equity		
Equity share capital	31%	34%
10% preference share capital	6%	7%
Retained earnings	25%	25%
Total equity	62%	66%
Non-current liabilities		
10% debentures	22%	21%
Current liabilities		
Payables	12%	10%
Tax	3%	3%
	16%	13%
Total liabilities	38%	34%
Total equity and liabilities	100%	100%

Key points revealed by this review are as follows.

Statements of comprehensive income

● Confirmation of the fall in all profits in relation to revenues.

Statements of financial position

● Not many significant differences in relative sizes of asset and liability balances, and financial structure over the two years except for confirmation of the fall in cash balances by the end of 20X7.

Note: the analysis has not been performed for the statements of cash flows, as identification of a meaningful key figure in relation to which all other figures could be expressed is questionable.

Common size statements are particularly useful in the comparison of cost and profit levels, and financial structures of companies in different industry sectors.

 Worked example 5.4: to show different companies' common size statements of financial position

The common size statements of financial position given as follows are of the following companies:

Company:	Incorporated in:	Industry:
Severn Trent	UK	Water services
Deutsche Bank	Germany	Financial institution
Nestlé	Switzerland	Food and household goods manufacturer
Tesco	UK	Supermarket

	A	B	C	D
	%	%	%	%
Land and buildings	2	15	25	64
Plant equipment and infrastructure assets	1	22	62	18
Intangible assets	–	11	–	5
Inventories	–	14	2	7
Receivables	78	22	5	2
Cash and securities	19	16	6	4
Total assets	100	100	100	100
Equity	5	41	35	47
Long-term loans	3	18	46	10
Short-term loans	–	17	8	8
Trade payables	91	16	1	28
Other liabilities	1	8	10	7
Total equity and liabilities	100	100	100	100

Required:
Identify which common size statement relates to which company.

	Company	Main reasons
A	Deutsche Bank	Low equity; very high receivables and payables; no inventories; low plant and buildings.
B	Nestlé	Medium inventories; high receivables; medium payables; medium land, buildings and plant.

| C | Severn Trent | High plant, equipment, and infrastructure assets; low inventories, receivables and payables. |
| D | Tesco | High land and buildings; medium plant and inventories; high payables; low receivables. |

5.2.3 Five-year data

An analysis is usually performed by users to help them make decisions about their interaction with the company. This will usually entail some prediction of what may happen in the future. Cleary, two years of figures does not provide sufficient information to predict the future, especially if there are one-off anomalies within either, or both, of the years. Listed companies do, though, provide five-year summaries (sometimes ten-year summaries) of key financial figures towards the back of their published annual report; thus, the techniques mentioned earlier can be extended to this data to establish a longer trend from which more reliable predictions of the future may be able to be made.

Two main methods to describe changes in figures over time can be used in analysis.

1 A year-on-year change in percentage terms.

2 A percentage change from a base year—index numbers can be used here.

 Worked example 5.5: to show trend analysis

Revenue and profit before tax figures for Sharples plc for the five years 20X3–20X7 are as follows.

	20X7	20X6	20X5	20X4	20X3
	£000	£000	£000	£000	£000
Revenue	3,000	2,500	2,100	1,700	1,300
Profit before tax	340	317	250	186	165

Required:
Describe the changes in the figures over the five years.

1 *Year-on-year percentage change*

	20X7	20X6	20X5	20X4	20X3
Revenue	20%	19%	24%	31%	–
Profit before tax	7%	27%	34%	13%	–

2 *Change from base year*—expressing each figure as an index number with 20X3 as the base year

	20X7	20X6	20X5	20X4	20X3
Revenue	231	192	162	131	100
Profit before tax	206	192	152	113	100

Method 1 shows that revenue has increased over the years, but the rate of increase has fallen. Profit before tax has also increased over the years, but the increase year-on-year is more erratic.

Method 2 establishes that both revenue and profit before tax have grown steadily over the five-year period and have more than doubled over the years.

5.3 Ratio analysis

In addition to reviewing and comparing individual line items, the relationships of different figures within a single set of financial statements are of importance and can provide much useful information to a user. A ratio can be calculated using any two or more figures, but, for the ratio to be useful, it must have meaning. For example, receivables and credit sales are related, and a ratio of one to the other will have some meaning, but a ratio of distribution costs to non-current assets will not make any sense.

Thus, there are some standard ratios that are used in financial analysis. Remember that different users require different information from financial statements, so will use different groups of ratios. Appropriate ratios should, therefore, be selected for the purposes of the particular analysis.

A ratio, once calculated, may have some meaning on its own, for example if year end receivables are 15% of the year's credit sales this gives some indication of the ability of the business to convert its sales into cash. However, to be really useful, a ratio should be put in context and related to some sort of reference point or standard. These points of reference might include:

- ratios from past years, to provide a standard of comparison
- ratios of other businesses in the same industry
- standards required by an interested organisation, e.g. a bank.

To properly interpret ratios, the make-up of the figures used in the ratios has to be considered. For example, is an aggregate of different figures being used and is this the same in the two ratios being compared? What are the valuation bases of the figures included in the ratio? It is also important to understand the relationship between ratios, as one ratio may give one interpretation of the state of the business, but this needs to be supported by other ratios.

Ratio analysis, used with the overview techniques explained, provides a useful tool in the interpretation of financial statements, but it is not the final answer to understanding what the accounts mean. It is emphasised again that ratios should always be put in the context of the business itself: What is the business's trade? How does it operate? Where is it located? Does it own property? What relationships does it have with customers, suppliers, competitors, and banks? Is it a company and, if so, is it private or public? What deals have been entered into or are about to be entered into?, etc. Only if all these facts are considered can a full understanding of the financial statements be achieved. However, it can provide pointers to areas of financial control and decision-making which need investigation—the key question 'why?' needs to be asked at every stage until it cannot be answered any more from the information the user has.

5.3.1 Categories of ratios

Ratios calculated commonly are divided into the different categories shown in Table 5.1 depending on what purpose or who they are likely to be used by.

Different ratios falling within each category are now explained and calculated for the example company, Sharples plc. An analysis of these ratios is also included. A summary of all ratio formulae and the calculations is included at the end of the sections on the different categories.

It is important to note that for some ratios there is no definitive formula and one definition can be considered as valid as another. Also, in any analysis using real data, there are many choices to be made about which figures to use in the selected ratio. In carrying out a ratio analysis it is vitally important to explain how the ratios have been defined and calculated with an explanation of why they have been calculated in that way. In addition, when comparisons are to be made, consistency in how the ratios have been calculated is necessary. (This is discussed in more detail in Chapter 17 where an interpretation of a 'real' company is performed.)

Table 5.1 Ratio categories and their principal users

Ratio category	Category definition	Principal user groups
Profitability	Effectiveness in generating profits	Investors, lenders, employees, suppliers, customers, government, and their agencies
Liquidity	Ability to meet liabilities when they fall due	Lenders, suppliers, investors, customers
Efficiency/activity	Effectiveness of use of business assets	Investors, suppliers
Gearing	Financial structure	Investors, lenders
Investor/stock market	Returns to investors	Investors

5.4 Profitability ratios

Ratios included in this category are:

- return on capital employed
- asset turnover
- net profit margin
- gross profit margin
- expenses as a percentage of sales.

Asset turnover is strictly an efficiency ratio; however, it is considered here because it is used in the interpretation of return on capital employed (ROCE).

5.4.1 Return on capital employed (ROCE)

$$\frac{\text{Net profit}}{\text{Capital employed}}$$

ROCE expresses the net profit of the business in relation to the capital employed by the business and is given as a percentage.

An existing, or potential, investor wishes to know what return is being generated from the use of the capital in the business. The percentage return could then be compared to returns which could be gained elsewhere simply, for example, from a bank deposit or building society. However, note that the risks in running a business are considerably greater than depositing money with a bank or building society, and an additional return to compensate for this is needed.

It is impossible to state categorically what represents a 'good' or 'bad' return, but comparison with previous years or the industry as a whole will reveal differences which require investigation and explanation. In a well-established business this ratio may be fairly constant or show a slight increase from year to year. It is influenced by the level of profitability in a particular year and whether there are any significant changes in the capital structure of the business.

There are variations in the calculation of this ratio which stem from how profit and capital employed are defined.

A basic definition is that capital employed is all long-term capital in a business—in a company this includes equity (the shareholders' funds) and long-term debt, including the current portion of long-term debt. The ratio then takes a profit figure generated from the use of this capital before the actual return to these providers of capital, in other words this would be profit before interest and tax (PBIT), sometimes called operating profit. So ROCE becomes:

$$\frac{\text{PBIT}}{\text{Equity} + \text{long-term debt}}$$

Other definitions of capital employed often seen are:

1	Equity + non-current liabilities (also equivalent to: Total assets – current liabilities)	Similar to the earlier definition, but includes other non-current liabilities, which are arguably not part of the long-term financing of the business, such as deferred tax or provisions
		The resulting ratio can also be called return on net assets (RONA)
2	Total assets	The interpretation of the ratio is slightly different as it considers the returns generated from the use of the assets, the business's resources, only

Capital employed at the start or the end of the year, or an average, can be used as long as a consistent approach is taken to all calculations.

Net profit can also be taken to exclude depreciation and amortisation in addition to interest—the result is referred to as EBITDA (earnings before interest, tax, depreciation, and amortisation). The reason why depreciation and amortisation are excluded is because, firstly, they depend on a business's chosen accounting policies, which can vary from company to company, and, secondly, they are non-cash expenses and so the resulting 'profit' numerator is closer to a 'real' profit figure based on cash flows.

Net profit may also exclude unusual or one-off items, or fair value changes that have passed through the statement of comprehensive income, as demonstrated by the following company example.

Financial reporting in practice 5.1   J Sainsbury plc, 2010

Sainsbury, in its 2010 annual report, includes 'pre-tax return on capital employed' as one of its key financial performance indicators, and defines this as:

> Underlying profit before interest and tax, divided by the average of opening and closing capital employed (net assets before net debt)...

where underlying profit is defined as:

> Profit before tax from continuing operations before any profit or loss on the sale of properties, investment property fair value movements, impairment of goodwill, financing fair value movements, IAS 19 pension financing element and one-off items that are material and infrequent in nature.

Taken simply as Net profit/Capital employed, ROCE can be subdivided into two further ratios, the results of each of which will influence the return achieved. These two ratios are asset turnover and net profit margin, and their product gives ROCE.

5.4.2 Asset turnover

$$\frac{\text{Revenue}}{\text{Capital employed}}$$

If capital employed is defined as equity plus long-term debt, and there are no other significant non-current liabilities, capital employed is equivalent to total assets net of current liabilities. For the purposes of this textbook, this will be referred to as net assets. However, note that the term 'net assets' is sometimes taken as total assets minus total liabilities (in other words, equity). So care must be taken in defining and interpreting ratios that use this term.

The asset turnover ratio shows the value of revenue generated per £1 of net assets employed in the year and is used to assess the efficiency of the use of net assets during the year. It is strictly an efficiency ratio; however, it is explained here because it is used in the interpretation of ROCE. Generally, a larger figure for this ratio indicates that higher volume of sales have been generated with more efficient use of assets.

Some businesses, particularly those in the retail trade, may break down this ratio further and consider revenues generated from only non-current assets:

$$\frac{\text{Revenue}}{\text{Non-current assets}}$$

This indicates the efficiency of their stores in generating revenues. However, this would be influenced particularly by valuation methods and depreciation policies for non-current assets.

5.4.3 Net profit margin

$$\frac{\text{Net profit}}{\text{Revenue}}$$

This expresses the profit the business has earned on its sales and is given as a percentage. The net profit should be defined in the same way as for ROCE, the best measure being PBIT, or it may exclude certain items as discussed earlier.

Ideally, this percentage should be similar from year to year and comparable with other businesses in the same industry. There are two main influences over this ratio—the gross profit earned and the overheads incurred.

5.4.4 Gross profit margin

$$\frac{\text{Gross profit}}{\text{Revenue}}$$

This measures the profit earned from the trading activities of the business—the buying (or manufacturing) and selling of goods or services—and is expressed as a percentage. For example, a gross profit of 30% means that for every £100 of sales a gross profit of £30 is earned.

Businesses monitor their gross profit margin extremely closely. Ideally, it should be the same from year to year, but many things will influence it including:

- fluctuations in purchase prices and manufacturing costs
- bad purchasing policy resulting in inventories being sold at a reduced profit or even a loss
- changes in the selling prices (e.g. cutting the selling margin)
- changes in the mix of sales
- inventory losses through theft or reduction in value.

Different types of businesses will have very different gross profit margins, for example a supermarket will have a much lower gross profit margin compared with a jewellery business. Even within a business different products will have very different gross profits, for example the supermarket's green grocery products' gross profit margin will be much lower than pre-packed meals or luxury items. Hence, the product mix's influence over the gross profit is important.

Whatever the type of business, gross profit needs to be sufficient to cover the expenses and to provide an acceptable level of net profit.

5.4.5 Expenses as a percentage of sales

$$\frac{\text{Expense item}}{\text{Revenue}}$$

This can be calculated for any expense individually or in total, and gives some idea as to whether the business has been controlling expenses in relation to the level of revenue achieved. It is expressed as a percentage.

Facts about the business—the type of property, whether it is a labour-intensive business or a highly computerised one, whether costs are fixed in nature or variable, whether they are directly related to revenues or not, etc.—will have much influence over these ratios; this should be considered when comparing different businesses, in particular. Within the same business these ratios should, ideally, stay the same from year to year or, as the business grows, the ratios may be expected to decrease as economies of scale are seen.

5.4.6 Relationship between profitability ratios

Figure 5.1 indicates the relationship between the profitability ratios. If, for example, the gross profit falls from one year to the next, this will cause a fall in net profit margin (everything else remaining the same). As an analysis is being conducted, the relationship between these ratios may be used to explain the cause of changes in ratios higher up the relationship tree.

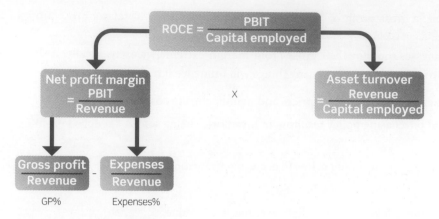

Figure 5.1 Relationship of profitability ratios

For example, if there is a decrease in net profit margin from one year to the next, the question that should be asked is: *why* has it decreased? If the gross profit margin is found to have fallen, this would go some way to explaining the decrease in the net profit margin. Likewise, the question 'why has ROCE increased?' can be analysed further by examining the changes in the two ratios net profit margin and asset turnover.

 Worked example 5.6: to show the calculation and interpretation of the profitability ratios

The profitability ratios are calculated for Sharples plc.

		20X7		20X6	
ROCE	$\dfrac{\text{PBIT}}{\text{Equity + long-term debt}}$	$\dfrac{406}{2,000 + 720}$	14.9%	$\dfrac{377}{1,940 + 600}$	14.8%
Asset turnover	$\dfrac{\text{Revenue}}{\text{Capital employed}}$	$\dfrac{3,000}{2,720}$	1.10	$\dfrac{2,500}{2,540}$	0.98
Net profit margin	$\dfrac{\text{PBIT}}{\text{Revenue}}$	$\dfrac{406}{3,000}$	13.5%	$\dfrac{377}{2,500}$	15.1%
Gross profit margin	$\dfrac{\text{Gross profit}}{\text{Revenue}}$	$\dfrac{1,200}{3,000}$	40.0%	$\dfrac{1,075}{2,500}$	43.0%
Administration expenses %	$\dfrac{\text{Administration expenses}}{\text{Revenue}}$	$\dfrac{544}{3,000}$	18.1%	$\dfrac{453}{2,500}$	18.1%
Distribution costs %	$\dfrac{\text{Distribution costs}}{\text{Revenue}}$	$\dfrac{250}{3,000}$	8.3%	$\dfrac{245}{2,500}$	9.8%

ROCE

● ROCE is fairly constant over the two years. Both PBIT and capital employed have increased in 20X7, but proportionately by the same rate. Both equity and long-term debt have increased.

- Is this a reasonable return for this type of business?
- A similar ROCE in each year masks other changes that have occurred.

	ROCE	=	Asset turnover	×	Net profit margin
20X7	14.9%	=	1.10	×	13.5%
20X6	14.8%	=	0.98	×	15.1%

- This breakdown shows that more sales have been generated from the use of assets (has the company been more efficient in 20X7?), but profitability as shown by the net profit margin has fallen.
- Overall capital (and net assets) have only increased marginally; revenue shows a large growth.

Net profit margin

- An analysis of what has caused the fall in the net profit margin is as shown:

	20X7	20X6
	%	%
Gross profit margin	40.0	43.0
Administrative expenses %	(18.1)	(18.1)
Distribution costs %	(8.4)	(9.8)
Net profit margin	13.5	15.1

- This shows it has been caused by a fall in gross profit margin from 43% to 40%, slightly mitigated by distribution costs being a smaller percentage of sales.
- The fall in gross profit margin could be as a result of any, or all, of the following:
  - increase in the cost of purchases (e.g. different suppliers, delivery charges, exchange rates) not passed on to customers
  - a reduction in sales prices (possibly unlikely)
  - special deals with the new high street customer in order to gain the contract
  - changes in the sales mix from higher margin goods to lower margin goods
  - stock damage, theft, or other losses.
- Has the company tried consciously to control distribution costs or have economies of scale had an impact as the company has grown?

5.5 Liquidity ratios

Ratios included in this category are:

- current ratio
- liquid ratio.

Liquidity is the ability of a business to meet its short-term liabilities as they fall due. Clearly, a business needs sufficient cash in order to be able to achieve this, but other assets which will turn into cash in the short-term as trading activities continue are also considered in the measure of liquidity. An analysis of the liquidity of a business therefore involves an assessment of what makes up working capital. Working capital is defined as net current assets (i.e. current assets—current liabilities) and is needed by all businesses in order to finance day-to-day trading activities. Many UK companies still present their statements of financial position in a format to show the key figure of working capital, although this is not specified by IAS 1 formats (see Chapter 4 for details of these).

Sufficient working capital enables a business to hold adequate inventories, allow a measure of credit to its customers, and to pay its suppliers as payments fall due. The amount of working capital required by a business will vary from business to business depending on:

- the nature of the business, e.g. a shop is likely to need less working capital than an engineering business because a shop has few, if any, trade receivables
- the size of the business, e.g. a small corner shop will need less working capital than a large department store.

5.5.1 Current ratio

$$\frac{\text{Current assets}}{\text{Current liabilities}}$$

This measures the balance of current assets and current liabilities, and is a measure of how easily a business can meet its current liabilities as they fall due; in other words, for every £1 of current liabilities how much is there in the form of current assets?

Although there is no ideal current ratio, an often quoted ratio is 2:1. However, the nature of the business will greatly influence the size of this ratio; these days many businesses work with a much lower ratio, even less than 1:1. Traditionally, retailers will have low current ratios because they deal mainly in sales for cash and so do not have large figures for receivables. A current ratio can be too high. If it is above, say, 3:1 the business may have too much cash tied up in inventories, or too many receivables, or too much cash sitting on a current bank account, or it is not benefitting from having enough trade payables.

5.5.2 Liquid ratio

$$\frac{\text{Current assets} - \text{Inventories}}{\text{Current liabilities}}$$

Also called the acid test or quick ratio, this is a more pertinent measure of the ability of a business to meet its liabilities as they fall due because it omits the least liquid current asset—inventories—from the numerator. Inventory has to be sold to customers who then have to pay before the asset converts to cash; some inventories may never be sold. Again, an often quoted minimum is 1:1, at which a business could pay the current liabilities on the statement of financial position from its receivables, if they were collected, and its cash balances. A figure below this might indicate that the business would have difficulty in meeting its liabilities. However, many businesses survive with a ratio well below this and, again, the level of the ratio is influenced by the nature of the business.

Financial reporting in practice 5.2 — Current and liquid ratios

The following are the current and liquid ratios for a selection of companies in different industries:

Company:	Industry:	Current:	Liquid:
Tesco plc, 2011	Supermarket	0.67	0.49
Marks and Spencer plc, 2010	High street retailer	0.80	0.48
Vodafone plc, 2010	Telecommunications	0.50	0.48
Rolls-Royce plc, 2010	Manufacturing	1.37	1.03
Balfour Beatty plc, 2010	Construction	0.83	0.60

5.5.3 Statement of cash flows

The statement of cash flows should also be used to assist in the interpretation of liquidity. The statement shows why cash and cash equivalent balances have increased or decreased over the year, and the different business activities where cash has been used or which have yielded cash. Significant cash receipts or payments figures should be identified, which together with the liquidity ratios, can provide some answers as to why liquidity may have increased or decreased, or why the liquidity position of one company differs from another.

In particular the reconciliation of profit before tax to cash generated from operating activities provides extremely useful information as to why cash flow differs from profits in day-to-day operating activities.

 Worked example 5.7: to show the calculation and interpretation of the liquidity ratios

The liquidity ratios are calculated for Sharples plc.

		20X7		20X6	
Current ratio	$\dfrac{\text{Current assets}}{\text{Current liabilities}}$	$\dfrac{900}{500}$	1.8	$\dfrac{840}{380}$	2.2
Liquid ratio	$\dfrac{\text{Current assets} - \text{Inventories}}{\text{Current liabilities}}$	$\dfrac{900 - 400}{500}$	1.0	$\dfrac{840 - 290}{380}$	1.4

- No apparent liquidity problems are indicated by these ratios with the company able to pay its liabilities as they fall due.

- Cash balances and the two liquidity ratios have fallen, but the company is still able to cover its current liabilities from its liquid assets (receivables and cash).

- The key question is why have cash balances fallen?

- The 20X7 statement of cash flows shows that there has been substantial investment in non-current assets (£600,000) with insufficient cash from operating activities to fund this and little from external sources (additional debentures of only £120,000 were issued)

5.6 Efficiency ratios

Ratios included in this category are:

- asset turnover (discussed in section 5.4.2)
- inventory turnover
- receivables collection period
- payables payment period.

One important issue arising from the earlier discussion on liquidity is the ability of a business to convert its current assets to cash to pay its liabilities. An understanding of the liquidity of a business must, therefore, include a study of the management of these conversion times, for example how long it takes to sell its inventories and collect the cash from its credit customers. The efficiency ratios provide figures which can help in this analysis.

5.6.1 Inventory turnover

$$\frac{\text{Inventories}}{\text{Cost of sales}} \times 365$$

This ratio shows the number of days inventories are held on average. Average inventory levels held over the year are the best measure to use in the calculation, but these will not be available from a set a financial statements. The average of opening and closing inventories can used as a substitute or, if opening inventories are not available, then inventories at the end of the year is the best figure available. The ratio can, alternatively, be stated as the number of times inventories are turned over, on average, each year by inverting the previous formula:

$$\frac{\text{Cost of sales}}{\text{Inventories}}$$

The nature of the inventories is crucial in interpreting this ratio, for example a greengrocer will have an inventory turnover of a few days, while a furniture shop's ratio may be 60–90 days. Nevertheless, inventory turnover should not be too long and review of the trend from year to year is important. Inventories sitting on a shelf unnecessarily tie up working capital which could be put to better uses. The business's inventory holding policies, for example just-in-time, make-to-order, and make-to-stock also have much influence over the ratio.

5.6.2 Receivables collection period

$$\frac{\text{Trade receivables}}{\text{Credit sales}} \times 365$$

This ratio shows, on average, how long credit customers take to pay for the goods sold to them. The denominator of the ratio should be credit sales only, but usually this is not available from the accounts, so revenue from sales or total revenue will have to be used instead. An average of opening and closing receivables may be used, but the year end receivables is often the figure included in the calculation.

The ratio calculated can be compared with the credit period the business allows to its customers—often 30 days, although 60 or 90 days is not uncommon—to see whether the business is efficient in its debt collection. Certainly, businesses do not wish to see this ratio increase from period to period; however, certain factors could influence it such as export sales or a very large sale just before the year end.

5.6.3 Payables payment period

$$\frac{\text{Trade payables}}{\text{Credit purchases}} \times 365$$

Similar in concept to the previous ratio, this shows how long, on average, it takes for a business to pay its credit suppliers. Often, the figure for credit purchases is not available from the financial statements, in which case it could be approximated by total purchases or cost of sales. Another issue with the ratio is that payables will include amounts owing to suppliers of services, for example electricity and telephone, so the numerator and denominator are internally inconsistent.

However, the ratio provides a useful indicator of the length of credit period taken from suppliers. While payables can be a useful source of short-term finance, delaying payment too long may cause problems with suppliers' relationships, or deter new suppliers from entering into business arrangements, so a business does not necessarily want this ratio to be as large as possible.

5.6.4 Working capital cycle

Figure 5.2 shows a simplified working capital cycle. This uses the earlier efficiency ratios and estimates the time taken to convert cash back into cash through the operating cycle, in other words the time from the payment of goods to the receipt of cash from the sale of these goods. The shorter this time, the lower the value of working capital required to be financed by the business.

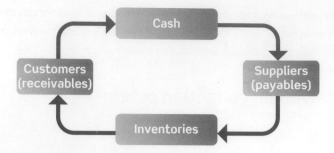

Figure 5.2 **The working capital cycle**

The length of the working capital cycle can be calculated as follows:

Inventory turnover + Receivables collection period − Payables payment period

Like all accounting ratios, a comparison needs to be made with previous years or another similar business. Businesses can reduce this time by:

- reducing inventories
- speeding up the receivables collection period
- slowing the rate at which suppliers are paid.

However these steps may have other consequences:

- reducing inventories may mean a poorer service is offered to customers, who may take their business elsewhere
- giving customers less time to pay may cause them to seek alternative suppliers who are offering better terms
- taking extra credit from suppliers may cause them to decline to supply goods.

 Worked example 5.8: to show the calculation and interpretation of the efficiency ratios

The efficiency ratios are calculated for Sharples plc.

		20X7		20X6	
			Days		Days
Inventory turnover	$\dfrac{\text{Inventories}}{\text{Cost of sales}} \times 365$	$\dfrac{400}{1,800} \times 365$	81	$\dfrac{290}{1,425} \times 365$	74
Receivables collection period	$\dfrac{\text{Receivables}}{\text{Revenue}} \times 365$	$\dfrac{450}{3,000} \times 365$	55	$\dfrac{350}{2,500} \times 365$	51
Payables payment period	$\dfrac{\text{Payables}}{\text{Cost of sales}} \times 365$	$\dfrac{400}{1,800} \times 365$	81	$\dfrac{300}{1,425} \times 365$	77
Working capital cycle		81 + 55 − 81	55	74 + 51 − 77	48

- The efficiency or working capital management ratios have all increased, indicating that the company is holding onto inventories longer, is taking longer to collect its receivables, and is taking longer to pay its payables.

- Why? Possible reasons may be:

  - the company is building up inventories to supply the new customer

  - other large orders are about to go out in early January 20X8

  - there is a large debt uncollected at the 20X7 year end

  - the company has negotiated longer payment terms with the new customer to gain business.

- The extension of the payables payment period has been negated by less efficient collection of receivables—the company must not risk upsetting its suppliers.

- Overall, the working capital cycle indicates less efficient cash management and may have contributed to the reduction in the liquidity of the company.

- This analysis is supported by the reconciliation of profit before tax to cash generated from operating activities. This indicates that although the company is generating a profit from its day-to-day activities, the cash generated from these has been reduced by the increases in the working capital items.

5.7 Gearing

Ratios included in this category are:

- gearing
- financial leverage
- interest cover.

Gearing (or leverage) is a measure of the balance between the two main types of long-term capital or funding in a business—that provided by equity (i.e. ordinary share capital and reserves) and that provided by debt (i.e. long-term loans, such as debentures).

As for many other ratios there are alternative ways of calculating a gearing ratio. Two basic gearing ratios are:

$$\frac{\text{Debt finance}}{\text{Equity}} \quad \text{or} \quad \frac{\text{Debt finance}}{\text{Debt finance} + \text{equity}}$$

Debt finance may be replaced by net debt, which reduces debt balances by positive cash and cash equivalent balances. The reason for this is that net debt is the figure that represents the outcome of treasury management policies.

| Financial reporting in practice **5.3** | J Sainsbury plc, 2010 |

Sainsbury, in its 2010 annual report, defines net debt as:

> ...the Group's borrowings (including accrued interest), bank overdrafts, interest bearing available-for-sale financial assets, fair value of derivatives and obligations under finance leases, less cash and cash equivalents.

An alternative way of viewing gearing is to consider how net assets are financed. If net assets are considered equivalent to capital employed, as discussed in section 5.4.2, this can be given by the financial leverage ratio:

$$\frac{\text{Capital employed}}{\text{Equity}}$$

and measures the proportion of assets that are financed by equity as opposed to debt.

Whichever way gearing is calculated, a company that has a high proportion of debt finance is considered highly geared, while a company that has mainly equity financing is considered a low-geared company.

A business that is highly geared is perceived as a riskier investment for the equity investor. This is because there is a greater chance that dividends to the ordinary shareholders will be reduced as profits are used to pay the fixed returns to the loan providers and preference shareholders first. In a highly-geared company the earnings per ordinary share (see section 5.8.2) can fluctuate enormously as profits fluctuate; investors are often wary of companies with large variations in key ratios from one year to the next. However, if the cost of borrowed capital is lower than the profits which can be earned on it, the earnings available to ordinary shareholders will rise as a consequence of additional borrowing.

5.7.1 Interest cover

$$\frac{\text{PBIT}}{\text{Finance costs}}$$

This ratio is of particular interest to lenders as it indicates the ability of the business to meet its debt-servicing costs from its profits. A low ratio may indicate the business will have difficulties meeting these requirements, which could, potentially, have serious consequences.

Worked example 5.9: to show the calculation and interpretation of the gearing ratios

The gearing ratios are calculated for Sharples plc.

		20X7		20X6	
Gearing	$\dfrac{\text{Net debt}}{\text{Equity}}$	$\dfrac{720-50}{2,000}$	33.5%	$\dfrac{600-200}{1,940}$	20.6%
Interest cover	$\dfrac{\text{PBIT}}{\text{Finance costs}}$	$\dfrac{406}{66}$	6.2	$\dfrac{377}{60}$	6.3

- Although gearing has increased, the company is not very highly geared.
- Both long-term borrowings (additional debentures issued) and equity have increased, but cash balances have fallen significantly—all contributing to the increase in gearing.
- Although the company issued more debentures, the company can comfortably meet its interest payments. As the company has fairly low gearing, the ordinary shareholders face little risk in their investment.

5.8 Investor ratios

Ratios included in this category are:

- return on equity (ROE)
- earnings per share (EPS)
- price/earnings ratio (P/E ratio)
- dividend per share
- dividend cover
- dividend yield
- total shareholder returns.

These are a group of ratios which apply to companies only, and in which a potential or existing equity investor will be particularly interested and may use to assess the success or failure of the investment.

5.8.1 Return on equity

$$\frac{\text{Profit attributable to ordinary shareholders}}{\text{Shareholders' funds (equity)}}$$

Profit attributable to ordinary shareholders is profit after tax and after preference dividends. Care must be taken if a company publishes a full statement of comprehensive income, as the profit figure excludes other comprehensive income.

This ratio, expressed as a percentage, measures the return to the equity (ordinary) shareholders on their investment. Profits are after the servicing costs of other forms of finance—this is what is left for the ordinary shareholder—but before the actual returns to them. Returns to shareholders can be either in the form of dividend distributions or through the growth of share price; the latter may result from companies reinvesting their profits. Thus, this ratio is assessing total return to the shareholders.

5.8.2 Earnings per share

$$\frac{\text{Profit attributable to ordinary shareholders}}{\text{No. of ordinary shares}}$$

This is a key ratio for investors. Companies are required to calculate and disclose EPS on the face of the statement of comprehensive income; the ratio has its own accounting standard, IAS 33 *Earnings per share*, which is examined in detail in Chapter 8. The ratio measures earnings available to the ordinary shareholder per share and is usually expressed as an amount in pence. Companies and investors like to see this value rising from year to year.

 Worked example 5.10: to show the effect of gearing on EPS

Companies Alpha and Beta have the same total capital as follows:

	Alpha	Beta
	£	£
Equity share capital (£1 shares)	1,000	4,000
Retained earnings	1,000	1,000
Long-term loans	4,000	1,000
	6,000	6,000

Assume the long-term loans have a fixed interest rate of 10% and a corporation tax rate of 30% on accounting profits.

Required:
Calculate and comment on the gearing ratio and earnings per share for each company for the three years when profits before interest and tax in each company were:

20X1   £400

20X2   £600

20X3   £1,000

	Company Alpha			Company Beta		
Gearing $\frac{\text{Debt}}{\text{Equity}}$	$\frac{4{,}000}{2{,}000} = 200\%$			$\frac{1{,}000}{5{,}000} = 20\%$		
	20X1	20X2	20X3	20X1	20X2	20X3
	£	£	£	£	£	£
PBIT	400	600	1,000	400	600	1,000
Interest	400	400	400	100	100	100
Profit before tax	–	200	600	300	500	900
Tax	–	60	180	90	150	270
Profit after tax	–	140	420	210	350	630
No. of ordinary shares	1,000	1,000	1,000	4,000	4,000	4,000
EPS	–	$\frac{140}{1{,}000}$	$\frac{420}{1{,}000}$	$\frac{210}{4{,}000}$	$\frac{350}{4{,}000}$	$\frac{630}{4{,}000}$
	–	14p	42p	5.25p	8.75p	15.75p

Alpha is a highly geared company, while Beta's gearing is fairly low. In a year of low profits, such as 20X1, Alpha's profits are wiped out by the interest it has to pay on its debt, leaving nothing for its equity investors. However, in more profitable years, Alpha's EPS is much higher than company Beta.

Note the large increases in company Alpha's EPS as profits increase over the years compared with Beta's more modest increases. As profit levels vary, Alpha's EPS will fluctuate more widely—an aspect that may deter equity investors.

5.8.3 Price/earnings ratio (P/E)

$$\frac{\text{Market price per share}}{\text{Earnings per share}}$$

Note: the market price of a share will only be available for listed companies and may not be disclosed in the annual report.

Quoted daily in the financial press, this ratio is a measure of market confidence in a company. It shows the number of times the market value of a share exceeds the earnings per share and indicates the number of years an investor would have to wait to recover his/her investment sum. For example, a P/E ratio of 10 implies 10 years until cumulative future EPS reaches the level of the current share price.

It might, therefore, be considered that a lower P/E ratio is better for the potential investor because they would have to wait fewer years to recoup their investment from earnings. However, a high P/E ratio implies investors are willing to pay a high multiple for expected earnings because of underlying strength and growth opportunities.

Any increase in the P/E ratio tends to indicate that either the market price of the share is rising more quickly than earnings or the earnings are falling in relation to the market price. The reasons for the change are important, but a number of factors might affect the market price unconnected to the performance of the business. For example, the ratio will rise if there is a general increase in share prices in the markets.

P/E ratios may also be calculated using analysts' forecasts of earnings rather than annual reported earnings.

5.8.4 Dividend per share

$$\frac{\text{Total ordinary dividends}}{\text{No. of ordinary shares}}$$

This is also required to be stated in the financial statements of a company—usually in a note. Care should be taken to ensure consistency in its calculation. Dividends accounted for in the statement of changes in equity are dividends paid, and comprises the previous year's final dividend and the current year's interim dividend (if one is paid). Total dividends for the current financial year (interim which has been paid and final which has been proposed) is the figure more usually used in the ratio. The final dividend for the current year will have to be identified from the notes to the financial statements.

Obviously, investors would wish to see the ratio rise year on year.

5.8.5 Dividend cover

$$\frac{\text{Profit after tax and preference dividends}}{\text{Total ordinary dividends}}$$

The above comments relating to dividends also apply to this ratio.

The ratio shows the number of times the funds available from a year's profits exceed the size of the ordinary dividend and is an indicator of the riskiness of the dividend. The greater the cover the more secure the dividend, while leaving substantial funds to be retained in the business for expansion or consolidation.

5.8.6 Dividend yield

$$\frac{\text{Dividend per share}}{\text{Market price per share}}$$

Expressed as a percentage, this ratio gives the actual dividend return for an investment in ordinary shares made at the latest market price.

5.8.7 Total shareholder returns

$$\frac{\text{Change in market share price} + \text{Dividend per share}}{\text{Opening market price per share}}$$

This ratio combines the two forms of return to an ordinary shareholder:

- the dividend
- capital growth (in the form of share price increases).

It expresses this as a percentage of the opening share price.

 Worked example 5.11: to show the calculation and interpretation of the investor ratios

The investor ratios are calculated for Sharples plc.

Assume that the market prices per share at 31 December 20X7, 20X6, and 20X5 are £1.80, £1.64, and £1.45 respectively.

		20X7		20X6	
Return on equity	Profit after tax and preference dividends / Equity	$\frac{160-20}{2,000}$	9.0%	$\frac{195-20}{1,940}$	9.0%
Earnings per share	Profit after tax and preference dividends / No. of ordinary shares	$\frac{160-20}{1,000}$	£ 0.14	$\frac{195-20}{1,000}$	£ 0.175
P/E ratio	Market price per share / Earnings per share	$\frac{1.80}{0.14}$	12.9	$\frac{1.65}{0.175}$	9.4
Dividend per share	Total ordinary dividends / No. of ordinary shares	$\frac{80}{1,000}$	£ 0.08	$\frac{75}{1,000}$	£ 0.075
Dividend cover	Profit after tax and preference dividends / Total ordinary dividends	$\frac{160-20}{80}$	1.75	$\frac{195-20}{75}$	2.33
Dividend yield	Dividend per share / Market price per share	$\frac{0.08}{1.80}$	4.4%	$\frac{0.075}{1.65}$	4.5%
Total shareholder returns	Change in share price + dividend per share / Opening share price	$\frac{(1.80-1.65+0.08)}{1.65}$	13.9%	$\frac{(1.65-1.45+0.075)}{1.45}$	19.0%

- Return on equity and earnings per share have both fallen owing to the fall in profit for the year, which, in turn, is a result of the abnormally looking large tax charge. Reasons for this are not evident from the financial statements.

- Despite this, the company has marginally increased the dividend per share, with the result that the dividend cover has fallen. However, dividends are still covered nearly twice by available profits. This ratio should be monitored closely, as shareholders looking for growth in the company and share price may be concerned that the ratio has fallen because of proportionately more of profits being paid out through dividends, possibly to maintain a stable dividend yield.

- The P/E ratio has increased significantly because the share price has risen, while EPS has fallen. This does indicate that the markets have confidence in the company, possibly because it has shown good growth in 20X7, and profitability and liquidity show no causes for concern.

- The increase in share price in 20X7 has not been as large as that in 20X6. This has resulted in the total shareholder returns being lower. Reasons for this are not apparent and would require details of the interpretation of the financial results for 20X6 in comparison to 20X5.

5.9 Limitations in ratio analysis

As demonstrated by the analysis of Sharples plc's financial statements, ratio analysis does not provide all the answers to why a business's financial performance and position has changed from one year to the next, or why it may differ from another business. Chapter 17, on interpretation of financial statements, demonstrates how a more detailed understanding of the recognition and measurement policies of figures in the financial statements will enhance the analysis. Consideration of external and internal factors, and the use of the additional narrative information provided in the financial statements are also included here. So, at this point in the textbook, interpretation is at a half-way stage.

However, there are some fundamental limitations of the ratio analysis techniques discussed so far, which will apply in most cases.

1 **Retrospective nature**

   As they are often calculated from the financial statements of a business, ratios are based on historical information, and conditions which affected their result may now not be relevant. For example, a large customer with a large outstanding balance may become insolvent, which would threaten the business with a large bad debt and also reduce sales in the future.

2 **Inflation**

   Inflation may also prove an issue as the basis for many figures in the financial statements is historical cost. As a result, comparison of figures from one year to the next may be impacted.

 Example of the inflationary effect over a number of years

Even if inflation is only 2% per annum, over a 5-year period prices will have risen by over 8%. Add in inflation in one of these years at 4%, and the 5-year increase becomes greater than 10%.

3   **Statement of financial position data**

Figures on the statement of financial position data may not represent the business's 'normal' position. For example, many businesses deliberately run down inventory levels at the year end in order to make its verification easier. Also, businesses with seasonal trade will have varying levels of working capital balances throughout the year, and a different interpretation will be gained depending on when the financial year end falls.

4   **Business-to-business comparisons**

The comparison of companies needs to be on a 'like with like' basis. Different businesses' financial statements will not, necessarily, be drawn up on the same basis owing to different accounting policies, for example in the area of depreciation.

Differences, such as the ownership of assets versus non-ownership, for example, owning property versus renting, or owning vehicles versus leasing, will affect profitability and the statement of financial position structure. Likewise, the balance between equity and debt financing will vary from company to company, and have implications for the analysis.

As discussed in Chapter 4, the aggregation of figures which appear in the financial statements may vary from business to business. For example, the interpretation of profitability will be affected by whether a business classifies expense items, such as motor expenses as a distribution cost or an administrative expense, or which overhead expenses it includes within cost of sales as opposed to administrative expenses.

5   **Combined operations**

For large organisations or groups of companies the key financial statements will aggregate financial figures from operations which differ radically in nature, for example manufacturing and retailing. This means it will be impossible to draw sensible conclusions from an analysis that uses these figures.

6   **Reliance on 'norms'**

Any interpretation should not rely too heavily on suggested norms for certain ratios or industry standards. For example, as discussed earlier, the current and liquid ratio norms will vary significantly depending on the nature of the business. There may be perfectly acceptable reasons why businesses are operating with different ratios.

 ## Summary of key points

This chapter has discussed some key analytical techniques used in the interpretation of financial statements. Different users are interested in different aspects of financial information, and therefore the analysis performed will vary according to its purpose. However any user performing an interpretation will be carrying out some form of comparison:

- within the same business from one year to the next, or over a number of years
- of one business to another
- of a business to industry norms.

The main analytical techniques are:

- horizontal analysis, which provides an overview of the financial performance and position
- ratio analysis, which takes two or more related figures within a set of financial statements to calculate a ratio, which is then used in comparisons.

Some ratios can be calculated in equally valid, but different ways, and care needs to be taken that, in interpretation, the basis of calculation is the same. This may not always be possible, particularly for business-to-business comparisons, where the aggregation of figures may differ.

In the interpretation of ratios, details of what makes up their component parts needs to be taken into account, as well as their interrelationships—no ratio can ever be interpreted in isolation. The most important question to be asked in any interpretation is 'why?', but this may never be fully answered, as it will require internal or detailed information, which is not available to external users. There are also certain inherent limitations to the analysis.

The techniques demonstrated are only part of a more complete analysis applied to a full set of financial statements. An enhanced interpretation will include consideration of external factors and other internal information about the business, which may be available from narrative reports contained in the published financial statements. Details of the recognition and measurement policies are also needed to fully interpret differences in financial items. These aspects will be incorporated in Chapter 17, which will also draw on the techniques demonstrated in this chapter.

 ## Bibliography

Balfour Beatty plc (2011) *Annual Report and Accounts, 2010*. London: Balfour Beatty.

J Sainsbury plc (2010) *Annual Report and Financial Statements, 2010*. London: J Sainsbury.

Marks and Spencer plc (2010) *Annual Report and Financial Statements, 2010*. London: Marks and Spencer.

Rolls-Royce plc (2010) *Annual Report, 2009*. London: Rolls-Royce.

Tesco plc (2011) *Annual Report and Financial Statements, 2011*. Cheshunt: Tesco.

Vodafone Group plc (2010) *Annual Report, 2010*. Newbury: Vodafone.

 ## Questions

Quick test

1   Snappy Ltd is a manufacturer and retailer of handbags. The following are extracts from the company's draft financial statements.

Income statements for the years ended 31 December

	20X7	20X6
	£000	£000
Revenue	3,900	4,300
Cost of sales	(2,652)	(2,795)
Gross profit	1,248	1,505
Distribution costs	(302)	(430)
Administrative expenses	(91)	(210)
Profit from operations	855	865
Finance costs	(4)	(15)
Profit before tax	851	850
Tax	(290)	(285)
Profit for the year	561	565

Statements of financial position at 31 December

	20X7	20X6
	£000	£000
ASSETS		
Non-current assets	770	810
Current assets		
Inventories	470	340
Trade and other receivables	470	360
Cash and cash equivalents	20	40
	960	740
Total assets	1,730	1,550
EQUITY AND LIABILITIES		
Equity		
Equity share capital	350	350
Retained earnings	790	325
Total equity	1,140	675
Non-current liabilities		
Borrowings	50	150
Current liabilities		
Trade and other payables	270	455
Taxation	240	270

Borrowings	30	–
	540	725
Total equity and liabilities	1,730	1,550

Required:

(a) Perform horizontal and vertical analyses on these financial statements.

(b) Comment on what this shows and identify the areas requiring particular investigation.

2 The income statements for the years ended 31 December 20X9 and 20X8, and the statements of financial position at these dates for Squirt Ltd are shown as follows.

Income statements for the years ended

	20X9	20X8
	£000	£000
Revenue	1,200	900
Cost of sales	(600)	(525)
Gross profit	600	375
Operating expenses	(300)	(225)
Operating profit	300	150
Interest	(60)	(15)
Profit before tax	240	135
Taxation	(90)	(45)
Profit for the year	150	90

Statements of financial position at 31 December

	20X9		20X8	
	£000	£000	£000	£000
Non-current assets		1,800		1,320
Current assets				
Inventory	300		360	
Trade receivables	96		66	
Cash			18	
		396		444
Total assets		2,196		1,764
Equity		1,653		1,592
Non-current liabilities				
Loan		300		75

Current liabilities			
Trade payables	180		97
Bank	63		–
		243	97
		2,196	1,764

(a) Calculate the following ratios for the company for each of the two years:
  (i)   Return on capital employed
  (ii)   Asset turnover
  (iii) Net profit margin
  (iv)   Gross profit percentage
  (v)   Current ratio
  (vi)   Liquid ratio
  (vii) Inventory turnover
  (viii) Receivables collection period
  (ix)   Payables payment period.
(b) Comment on the financial performance and financial position of Squirt Ltd based on these ratios.

●● Develop your understanding

3 Smokey plc, an engineering company, has approached its bank for a £5 million long-term secured loan to finance the rebuilding of part of its plant to comply with new regulations to control emissions.

You are a financial advisor in the bank and you have extracted the following information from the latest financial statements of the company.

Year ended 31 March	20X4	20X5
Return on capital employed	27%	30%
Gross profit margin	45%	47%
Net profit margin	18%	25%
Asset turnover	1.5	1.2
Inventory turnover	4.7 times	5.8 times
Receivables collection period	46 days	35 days
Payables payment period	26 days	34 days
Current ratio	0.9	1.2
Acid test (liquid) ratio	0.6	0.9

Required:

Write a report to your manager which:

(a) analyses the financial performance and position of the company based on these ratios

(b) recommends whether the bank should be willing to lend.

4 The statements of financial position and income statements for the year ended 30 June 20X6 of Gold Ltd and Silver Ltd, two companies in the same type of business, are given as follows.

Statements of financial position at 30 June 20X6

	Gold Ltd		Silver Ltd	
	£	£	£	£
Non-current assets: cost		90,000		30,000
Accumulated depreciation		30,000		10,000
		60,000		20,000
Current assets				
Inventories	85,500		30,000	
Receivables	33,000		20,000	
Cash	16,500		10,000	
		135,000		60,000
Total assets		£195,000		£ 80,000
Equity				
Equity share capital	142,500		45,000	
Retained earnings	7,500		5,000	
		150,000		50,000
Current liabilities		45,000		30,000
Total equity and liabilities		£195,000		£ 80,000

Income statements for the year ended 30 June 20X6

	Gold Ltd		Silver Ltd	
	£	£	£	£
Revenue		240,000		120,000
Opening inventory	58,500		20,000	
Purchases	171,000		85,000	
	229,500		105,000	
Closing inventory	(85,500)		(30,000)	
Cost of sales		(144,000)		(75,000)
Gross profit		96,000		45,000
General expenses		(84,000)		(39,000)
Profit before tax		12,000		6,000

Taxation	(3,000)	(1,000)
Profit for the year	£ 9,000	£ 5,000
Dividends paid	£ 6,000	£ 1,500

You may assume that inventories have increased evenly throughout the year.

Required:

(a) Calculate the following ratios for each company:

  (i) Return on capital employed

  (ii) Asset turnover

  (iii) Net profit margin

  (iv) Gross profit margin

  (v) Current ratio

  (vi) Liquid (acid test) ratio

  (vii) Inventory turnover

  (viii) Receivables collection period

  (ix) Payables payment period.

(b) Discuss the main conclusions drawn from a comparison of the ratios calculated for each company.

5 Micawber & Sons, an unincorporated business founded approximately 20 years ago, is in the retail trade. Since then, the business has shown increasing profits. Summarised financial statements for the last two completed financial years are as follows.

Income statements for the years ended 31 December

	20X6	20X5
	£000	£000
Revenue	940	800
Cost of sales	(583)	(480)
Gross profit	357	320
Expenses	(259)	(222)
Interest	(20)	(6)
Profit for the year	78	92

Statements of financial position at 31 December

	20X6		20X5	
	£000	£000	£000	£000
Non-current assets				
Cost		1,227		807
Accumulated depreciation		546		404
		681		403

Current assets			
Inventory	240		150
Accounts receivable	33		23
Bank and cash	28		97
		301	270
Total assets		£ 982	£ 673
Capital		543	501
Non-current liabilities			
Long-term bank loan		280	60
Current liabilities		159	112
Total capital and liabilities		£ 982	£ 673

Required:

(a) Calculate the following ratios for Micawber & Sons for the financial year ended 31 December 20X6 (the ratios for year ended 31 December 20X5 have already been calculated):

		Year ended 31 December *20X5*
(i)	Return on capital employed	17.5%
(ii)	Net profit percentage	12.3%
(iii)	Gross profit percentage	40.0%
(iv)	Expenses as a percentage of revenue	27.8%
(v)	Asset turnover	1.4
(vi)	Current ratio	2.4
(vii)	Liquid ratio	1.1
(viii)	Inventory turnover	114 days
(ix)	Payables payment period	85 days

(b) Using the financial statements, together with the ratios in part (a), comment on the financial performance and position of Micawber & Sons for the year ended 31 December 20X6 in comparison with the previous year.

●●● Take it further

6   Deepa & Co. is an unincorporated family business and wholesaler, importing silk fabric from Far Eastern countries, and selling on to specialist curtain and upholstery retailers. During the year ended 31 December 20X1 the business entered into a new contract with the local branches of a national retail chain. The business also expanded its warehouse and automated its office processes in the year.

Summarised financial statements for 20X1 and 20X0 for the business are as follows.

Income statements for the years ended 31 December

	20X1		20X0	
	£	£	£	£
Revenue		382,100		289,800
Cost of sales		(275,150)		(194,170)
Gross profit		106,950		95,630
Administrative expenses	45,235		44,240	
Distribution costs	16,430		14,680	
Interest	1,875		–	
		(63,540)		(58,920)
Profit for the year		43,410		36,710

Statements of financial position at 31 December

	20X1		20X0	
	£000	£000	£000	£000
Non-current assets		130,000		78,750
Current assets				
Inventory	24,650		15,600	
Accounts receivable	22,850		11,275	
Bank and cash	3,750		11,700	
		51,250		38,575
Total assets		181,250		117,325
Capital		77,760		73,350
Non-current liabilities				
5% bank loan, repayable 20X5		50,000		-
Current liabilities				
Accounts payable		53,490		43,975
Total capital and liabilities		181,250		117,325

Required:

(a) Calculate the following ratios for Deepa & Co. for the financial years ended 31 December 20X1 and 20X0:

    (i)   Return on capital employed

    (ii) Net profit percentage

    (iii) Gross profit percentage

    (iv) Administrative expenses as a percentage of revenue

(v) Distribution costs as a percentage of revenue

(vi) Asset turnover.

(b) Using both the summarised financial statements and the ratios from part (a) produce a report that provides an analysis of the financial performance of Deepa & Co. for the year ended 31 December 20X1 in comparison with the previous year.

(c) Give details of any other information you would require to improve your analysis of the financial performance of the business, providing reasons for the requirement.

7 The following financial data is available for Ash plc:

Extracts from statements of financial position at 31 March

	20X5	20X4	20X3
	£000	£000	£000
Equity			
Equity share capital (20p shares)	6,000	5,000	5,000
6% irredeemable preference share capital (£1 shares)	1,000	1,000	1,000
Share premium	5,500	1,200	1,200
Retained earnings	2,610	1,890	2,270
Total equity	15,110	9,090	9,470
Non-current liabilities			
7% debentures (20X8)	5,000	5,000	3,000
Current liabilities	7,140	7,530	6,180
Total equity and liabilities	27,250	21,620	18,650

Retained earnings columns from statements of changes in equity for the years ended 31 March

	20X5	20X4	20X3
	£000	£000	£000
At start of year	1,890	2,270	1,700
Profit for the year	4,230	2,180	2,880
Dividends paid	(3,510)	(2,560)	(2,310)
At end of year	2,610	1,890	2,270

Extracts from the income statements for the years ended 31 March

	20X5	20X4	20X3
	£000	£000	£000
Profit before tax	6,040	3,200	3,960
Tax	(1,810)	(1,020)	(1,080)

Profit after tax	4,230	2,180	2,880
	20X5	**20X4**	**20X3**
Market price per equity share	72p	58p	60p

Ash plc issued the additional debentures on 1 September 20X3 and the new equity shares on 1 April 20X4.

Required:

(a) Calculate the following ratios for Ash plc for the years ended 31 March 20X5, 20X4, and 20X3:

    (i) Return on equity

    (ii) Earnings per share

    (iii) Price earnings

    (iv) Dividend per share

    (v) Dividend cover

    (vi) Dividend yield

    (vii) Gearing.

(b) On the basis of the ratios calculated in part (a), produce a report for a potential equity investor, advising whether to invest in the company or not.

8   The financial statements of Mono plc for 20X7 and 20X6 are as follows.

Statements of financial position at 31 December

	20X7	20X6
	£000	**£000**
Non-current assets		
Freehold premises	3,875	4,025
Plant and equipment	2,607	2,167
	6,482	6,192
Current assets		
Inventories	1,435	2,625
Receivables	3,900	2,277
Cash	13	198
	5,348	5,100
Total assets	11,830	11,292
Equity		
Equity share capital (50p ordinary shares)	1,000	1,000
Share premium	350	350
Retained earnings	5,979	5,864
	7,329	7,214
Non-current liabilities		
9% Redeemable debenture stock 20X7–20Y1	2,000	2,500

Current liabilities		
Payables	2,501	1,578
Total equity and liabilities	11,830	11,292

Income statements for the years ended 31 December

	20X7	20X6
	£000	£000
Revenue	11,450	10,874
Profit before tax	434	721
Taxation	(119)	(178)
Profit after tax	315	543
Dividends proposed and paid	200	200
Year end share price	£3.15	£ 4.20

Notes to the accounts

1   Analysis of operating profit

	20X7	20X6
	£000	£000
Revenue	11,450	10,874
Cost of sales	(6,764)	(6,351)
Gross profit	4,686	4,523
Administrative expenses	(4,072)	(3,577)
Operating profit	614	946

2   Operating profit is stated after charging:

	20X7	20X6
	£000	£000
Depreciation	890	750
Auditor's remuneration	55	50
Leasing charges	95	115
Director's emoluments	135	120

3   Interest paid

	20X7	20X6
	£000	£000
Payable on debenture stock	180	225

Required:

Analyse the financial performance of Mono plc as an investment prospect during the two years of 20X6 and 20X7.

 Visit the Online Resource Centre for solutions to all these end of chapter questions plus visual walkthrough solutions. You can test your understanding with extra questions and answers, explore additional case studies based on real companies, take a guided tour through a company report, and much more. Go to the Online Resource Centre at **www.oxfordtextbooks.co.uk/orc/maynard/**

Part 3

Income statement reporting issues

Chapter 6   Reporting performance

Chapter 7   Revenue

Chapter 8   Earnings per share

Chapter 9   Taxation

6

Reporting performance

This chapter discusses how financial performance is presented by, and may be evaluated, from the statement of profit or loss and other comprehensive income. (Note: throughout the chapter this is referred to as the statement of comprehensive income. The statement of profit or loss part is referred to as the income statement.) A published statement of comprehensive income for large multinational corporations contains aggregated figures for the many different segments of the business. For a complete evaluation of the performance of the business, details of the performance of the individual segments are needed. The financial performance shown in the statement is also only for one year, and one-off or less regularly occurring events can have an enormous impact on the figures. These events may be within the control of the business, such as decisions to close or curtail parts of the business, or outside its control. Any analysis performed will have to take account of the effect of such events.

The interpretation of performance is therefore not straightforward, and users also need to bear in mind that any profit or loss figure shown in the statement of comprehensive income is not exact, and is influenced by estimates and judgements made by the company's management and the accounting policies selected. These may not necessarily be related directly to income and expense figures, but could still affect them.

Disclosures are required by certain accounting standards to assist users in understanding the performance of a company; this chapter will discuss how this information can help in the assessment.

★ Learning objectives

After studying this chapter you will be able to:

- understand how the evaluation of the performance of a company, as given by the statement of comprehensive income, has to take into account the effect of underpinning financial accounting principles, management's judgements and estimates, and other significant items and transactions that have occurred during the financial reporting period
- account for non-current assets held for sale and discontinued operations
- produce disclosures required for operating segments and understand how the information may be used in an analysis of performance
- understand the significance of the disclosures required for related party transactions.

✔ Key issues checklist

- ❏ The accruals concept.
- ❏ Management's influence over reported profit and loss through estimations, judgements, and choice of accounting policies.
- ❏ Exceptional, one-off or significant items, how they may be reported, and their impact on performance.
- ❏ Accounting for non-current assets classified as held for sale—International Financial Reporting Standard (IFRS) 5.
- ❏ Accounting for discontinued operations—IFRS 5.
- ❏ Issues with accounting for discontinued operations.
- ❏ Disclosures required for operating segments—IFRS 8.
- ❏ Issues raised by the management approach taken by IFRS 8.
- ❏ Disclosures required for related parties and related party transactions—International Accounting Standard (IAS) 24.
- ❏ How and why these issues affect an analysis of financial performance, as given by the statement of comprehensive income.

6.1 Underpinning principles of performance

As seen in Chapter 5, the analysis of performance is based frequently on measures of profit taken from the statement of comprehensive income. All existing and potential investors will use profit or earnings figures in their assessment of the performance of a business and for future predictions so that they can more readily understand the returns that have been, or will be, generated by the business. It is therefore important that these figures are reliable and that sufficient, relevant information is provided about their make-up.

6.1.1 Accruals concept

🛈 **Reminder** *The statement of comprehensive income consists of an income statement, which shows a break-down of net profit made during the financial year, and a statement of other comprehensive income. This second part of the statement includes items such as surpluses arising from the revaluation of properties and may be presented as a separate statement. Full discussion of the statement of comprehensive income is included in Chapter 4.*

The statement of comprehensive income is based on the accruals concept. At a basic level this means items are accounted for in the period in which the underpinning transaction occurred and not when the related cash flow occurs. Financial performance measured on the accruals basis provides a better basis for assessing a business's past and future performance than information about cash receipts and payments, which can be determined by other factors and may not be directly comparable from one year to the next.

IAS 1 *Presentation of Financial Statements* explains the accruals concept by specifying that when it is used 'an entity recognises items as assets, liabilities, equity, income and expenses (the elements of financial statements) when they satisfy the definitions and recognition criteria for those elements in the [*Conceptual*] *Framework*' (para. 28). In other words, net comprehensive income, which is the difference between income and expenses, is determined by the criteria for when these items can be recognised; these are given in the *Conceptual Framework* as follows.

Income is recognised in the statement of comprehensive income when the increase in the future economic benefits related to an increase in an asset or a decrease of a liability can be measured reliably. (Note: income and revenue are discussed in detail in Chapter 7.)

Expenses are recognised in the statement of comprehensive income when a decrease in the future economic benefits related to a decrease in an asset or an increase of a liability can be measured reliably. Revenues and expenses that result directly and jointly from the same transactions or other events should be recognised simultaneously. This is commonly referred to as 'matching'. However, the application of the matching concept does not allow the recognition of items in the statement of financial position that do not meet the definition of assets or liabilities.

6.1.2 Balance sheet approach to profit recognition

The recognition criteria for income and expenses mentioned in section 6.1.1 indicate that their net result, i.e. profit, is determined largely by changes in the recognition and measurement of assets and liabilities. This is why the International Accounting Standards Board's (IASB) decision-usefulness approach to financial reporting has acquired the label of a 'balance sheet approach'.

The recognition in profit of simple day-to-day transactions and items, such as sales and purchases on credit, and accounting for usual overhead expenses and depreciation, does not change with these definitions. However, there is much critical debate about the effect of other transactions on profit that results from this approach. Such transactions include the change in the value of financial assets and liabilities, which are measured at fair or market value, being included as either income or expense, or the recognition of revenue from more complex arrangements.

Although some of these items may be disclosed separately in other comprehensive income and can be identified easily, others are included in the income statement part of the statement of comprehensive income. The interpretation of performance, as given by a net profit figure, will, therefore, be affected. The actual accounting for those items which are within the scope of this textbook are discussed in later, relevant chapters.

6.1.3 Estimates, judgement, and choices of accounting policies

As is evident from discussion in previous chapters, financial accounting is not an exact science. Many, if not most, figures included in the statements of comprehensive income and financial position are based on management's judgement. Examples include:

- depreciation—estimates of useful lives and residual values
- estimates of accrued expenses
- provisions for doubtful debts
- fair values of assets and liabilities requiring this valuation base, particularly where market values are unavailable
- inventory obsolescence
- capitalisation of internal development costs—the point at which certain criteria have been met, such as whether a market exists for the product or service being developed
- the financial impact of ongoing legal cases or industrial tribunals.

Estimates of figures required for the statement of financial position, for example a provision for doubtful debts, affect profit and loss directly.

Is there a problem with this? International accounting standards are principles based and inherent in this is the necessity for professional judgement. It is assumed that users will be able to understand the implication of this, provided sufficient information is given about where these judgements have been made, and that this is clear and concise. Remember, understandability is an enhancing characteristic of financial information and implies that, although users do not have to be financial experts, they should have a reasonable knowledge of business and economic matters, and also know when to seek the help of a financial expert.

The section on accounting policies in Chapter 4 discusses the disclosures that companies are required to make regarding estimates and judgements, and provides some company examples. Detailed disclosures of the recognition and measurement methods and policies are also required by certain accounting standards to aid users' understanding, and these will be examined in the relevant chapters.

The more sceptical user may consider that companies produce the financial results and performance that they want, and hide behind the use of estimates and professional judgement as a justification. Undoubtedly, financial directors can, and do, 'tweak' their judgements to produce the financial figures they require for a variety of reasons (to meet bank covenants, to ensure the company credit rating is not affected adversely, to ensure earnings per share is in line with market expectations, etc.). However, there are other ways of 'massaging' earnings, including asking suppliers to delay delivery of goods and shipping large orders out just prior to the year end. The auditors will take their own professional view on whether the financial statements can still be said to be 'fairly stated'. No financial reporting system can eliminate this.

The even more sceptical user will also cite major corporate collapses, such as Enron and WorldCom, to suggest that earnings figures of companies are completely fictional. The evolution of financial reporting systems, particularly over the past 20 years, has included the development and acceptance of international accounting standards and corporate governance mechanisms. These attempt to ensure that financial statements do represent faithfully companies' financial performance and position, and that these sorts of events do not happen again. As discussed throughout this textbook, this development is continuing.

6.2 One-off, unusual items

One-off or unusual items are sometimes referred to as exceptional items. Although this term is not one that is used by the IASB, it used to be included in UK generally accepted accounting principles (GAAP), which allowed companies to classify one off or non recurring material items which had affected the year's performance (not necessarily adversely) as exceptional, and disclose them separately on the face of the income statement. The argument for separate disclosure of items, such as the costs of restructuring activities, or large changes in asset valuations, or the results of litigation, is to aid the user of financial statements to understand the performance of the regular underlying business without these items and to ensure a 'true and fair' view is presented.

IAS 1 *Presentation of Financial Statements* only specifies the minimum disclosures that have to be made on the face of the main financial statements; it does not prevent a company from including other items it considers will make the information provided by the financial statements more relevant to the user. Indeed, the standard requires that such items should be disclosed if they are material and relevant to an understanding of the company's financial performance, and provides examples of items which may be included.

Some UK companies, in particular, therefore have various presentations of their income statements, as shown by the following examples. The first has already been used in Chapter 4, but it is worth repeating here.

Financial reporting in practice 6.1

J Sainsbury plc, 2010

J Sainsbury plc, in its 2010 financial statements, has provided an analysis of its profit before tax of £733 million on the face of its income statement, analysing its profit before tax into what the company describes as 'underlying' profit before tax, i.e. profit from its core supermarket activities, and other items of profit and loss. This will assist users in understanding how the company achieved its profits in a particular year and provide more comparable information from one year to the next.

Group income statement

for the 52 weeks to 20 March 2010	Note	2010 £m	2009 £m
Revenue		19,964	18,911
Cost of sales	4	(18,882)	(17,875)
Gross profit		1,082	1,036
Administrative expenses		(399)	(420)
Other income		27	57
Operating profit	5	710	673
Finance income	6	33	52
Finance costs	6	(148)	(148)
Share of post-tax profit/(loss) from joint ventures	14	138	(111)
Profit before taxation		733	466
Analysed as:			
Underlying profit before tax		610	519
Profit on sale of properties	3	27	57
Investment property fair value movements	3	123	(124)
Financing fair value movements	3	(15)	(10)
IAS 19 pension financing (charge)/credit	3	(24)	24
One-off item: Office of Fair Trading dairy inquiry	3	12	–
		733	466
Income tax expense	8	(148)	(177)
Profit for the financial year		585	289

Financial reporting in practice **6.2**   **Arsenal Holdings plc, 2010**

Arsenal Holdings' view of relevance and understandability results in it separating out the results of player trading from its other activities. These other activities comprise the football-related business and results from property transactions. The company defines player trading as primarily the amortisation of the costs of acquiring player registrations, any impairment charges, and profit on disposal of player registrations. Financial results from player trading are less comparable from one year to the next as they depend, in part, on one or two significant transfers of players.

Consolidated profit and loss account: for the year ended 31 May 2010

	Note	Operations excluding player trading £'000	Player trading £'000	Total £'000
Turnover of the group including its share of joint ventures		381,262	460	381,722
Share of turnover of joint venture		(1,866)	-	(1,866)
Group turnover	3	379,396	460	379,856
Operating expenses		(319,272)	(25,033)	(344,305)
Operating profit/(loss)		60,124	(24,573)	35,551
Share of joint venture operating result		463	-	463
Profit on disposal of player registrations		-	38,137	38,137
Profit on ordinary activities before finance charges		60,587	13,564	74,151
Net finance charges				(18,183)
Profit on ordinary activities before taxation				55,968
Taxation				5,024
Profit after taxation retained for the financial year				60,992

Other, predominantly UK, companies use the columnar format for separating exceptional items from all other operations, as shown by JD Wetherspoon's income statement.

Financial reporting in practice 6.3   **JD Wetherspoon plc, 2010**

This income statement shows that exceptional items have caused a reduction of overall profit. Profits from normal operating activities therefore appear higher. The question remains whether companies would choose this explicit voluntary disclosure if exceptional items had increased profits?

(continued)

(continued)

Income statement for the 52 weeks ended 25 July 2010

	52 weeks ended 25 July 2010 Before exceptional items £000	52 weeks ended 25 July 2010 Exceptional items (note 3) £000	52 weeks ended 25 July 2010 After exceptional items £000	52 weeks ended 26 July 2009 Before exceptional items £000	52 weeks ended 26 July 2009 Exceptional items (note 3) £000	52 weeks ended July 2009 After exceptional items £000
Revenue 1	996,327	–	996,327	955,119	–	955,119
Operating costs	(896,314)	(10,557)	(906,871)	(858,118)	(21,920)	(880,038)
Operating profit 2	100,013	(10,557)	89,456	97,001	(21,920)	75,081
Finance income 5	16	–	16	336	–	336
Finance costs 5	(29,014)	–	(29,014)	(31,182)	–	(31,182)
Fair value gain on financial derivatives 5	–	–	–	–	794	794
Profit before taxation	71,015	(10,557)	60,458	66,155	(21,126)	45,029
Income tax expense 6	(19,680)	–	(19,680)	(20,954)	1,224	(19,730)
Profit for the year	51,335	(10,557)	40,778	45,201	(19,902)	25,299

Note 3 discloses the nature of the exceptional items.

3 Exceptional items

	52 weeks ended 25 July 2010 £000	52 weeks ended 26 July 2009 £000
Operating items		
Impairment of property and fixed assets	10,557	15,951
Property-related disposals and write-offs	–	4,404
Litigation costs	–	1,565
Operating exceptional items	10,557	21,920
Non-operating items		
Fair value gain on derivatives	–	(794)
Total exceptional items	10,557	21,126
Tax on exceptional items	–	(1,224)
	10,557	19,902

The exceptional charge of £10,557,000 relates to the impairment of property, plant and equipment following a review of the company's assets, as required under IAS 36.

Under the impairment review, each cash-generating unit is reviewed for its **recoverable amount**, determined as being the higher of its fair value less costs to sell and its value in use. This resulted in an impairment charge of £10,557,000.

During the previous year, included within the £15,951,000 charge in respect of impairment of property and fixed assets was a charge of £6,527,000 relating to the impairment review of the company's assets, and £9,424,000 relating to a one-off depreciation adjustment.

Property-related disposals and write-offs in the previous year relate to one non-trading unit which was disposed of and three additional non-trading units that management decided to sell, resulting in a charge to the income statement arising from the reduction of their book value to their fair value. Also included are aborted property costs on several sites which management decided not to pursue. This resulted in a charge of £4,404,000.

Litigation costs of £1,565,000 in the previous year related to legal action against the company's former estate agents, Van de Berg.

6.3 Discontinued operations and non-current assets held for sale

Users will use historic trends in profit or loss to make predictions about future performance. In order for the forecasting techniques to be as good as possible which earnings are sustainable need to be identifiable. Information about items which may affect future results is therefore important. One of these is whether a company has discontinued a part of its business and how much of its current earnings relate to this, and will, therefore, not be present in the future. Businesses may dispose of the assets of discontinued operations and users also need to be able to evaluate the financial effect of such disposals on the results for the year.

The accounting standard that addresses these issues is IFRS 5 *Non-current Assets Held for Sale and Discontinued Operations*, which was issued in 2004 as part of the IASB/Financial Accounting Standards Board (FASB) convergence project.

One aspect of the accounting for discontinued operations is how the disposal of the assets within the discontinued part of the business is dealt with. If the assets have not been disposed of by the end of the financial period, they may be classified as held for sale. Therefore, as the IFRS does, exactly what an asset held for sale is and how this is accounted for will be examined first. Note that assets held for sale may not arise exclusively from a discontinued operation, although in many instances they do.

Note that Chapter 10 deals with accounting for non-current assets. Although the main accounting treatment for assets held for sale will be discussed here in this chapter, complete understanding of some of this material may only be achieved when this later chapter has been read.

6.3.1 What is a non-current asset held for sale?

A non-current asset or a group of non-current assets to be disposed of in a single transaction (termed a 'disposal group') are classified as held for sale if their carrying amounts (in other words, the amount at which they are included in the financial statements) will be recovered principally through a sale transaction rather than through continuing use. This requires the following criteria to be met:

- management is committed to a plan to sell
- the asset or disposal group is available for immediate sale in its present condition
- an active programme to locate a buyer has been initiated
- the asset or disposal group is being actively marketed for sale at a price that is reasonable in relation to its current fair value
- the sale is highly probable and is expected to be completed within a year from the date of classification
- it is unlikely that significant changes will be made to the plan or it will be withdrawn.

There must, therefore, be formal commitment to disposal with evidence of positive steps taken towards this before the year end. It is possible that the sale may not be completed within one year, but the delay must be due to circumstances outside the company's control. In this case, the classification as held for sale will still be applicable.

 Example of criteria for classification as held for sale

The directors of a company have agreed, in a board meeting, to sell a building and have instructed the chief administrative officer to start looking for a buyer. They wish to sell the building for £3 million, even though the current market prices indicate a value of £2.5 million. The company will continue to use the building until other, suitable property has been found and no staff will be relocated until this is the case.

The building will not be classified as held for sale because the situation fails to meet the criterion of being available for immediate sale—staff will remain in the building until new premises have been found. In addition, it does not appear that an active programme to locate a buyer has been initiated yet—only internal instructions to an officer to 'start looking for a buyer'. In addition, the sale price would, at present, not be considered reasonable in relation to its fair value (market price).

The same criteria apply to an asset or disposal group that is held for distribution to the owners.

Any non-current assets or disposal groups that are to be 'abandoned', for example because the assets have reached the end of their useful lives or as a result of a company winding up certain operations, are not classified as held for sale as their carrying amount will be recovered through use (and not a sale). Hence, the accounting for these assets just continues as normal under the relevant accounting standard (see Chapter 10).

Non-current assets that become idle because they are taken out of use temporarily because, for example, current market conditions cause businesses to reduce their operating capacity, are not classified as abandoned. They may be classified as part of a discontinued operation if the relevant criteria are met.

Some non-current assets are acquired exclusively with the intention of re-selling them. These are classified as held for sale at the acquisition date only if it is anticipated that the sale will occur within one year and that it is highly likely that any of the other criteria not met at acquisition will be within a short time period—usually taken as three months.

Certain non-current assets are also outside the scope of IFRS 5 and their accounting treatment is according to the relevant accounting standard, as detailed as follows:

(a) deferred tax assets (IAS 12 *Income Taxes*)

(b) assets arising from employee benefits (IAS 19 *Employee Benefits*)

(c) financial assets within the scope of IFRS 9 *Financial Instruments*

(d) non-current assets that are accounted for in accordance with the fair value model in IAS 40 *Investment Property*

(e) non-current assets that are measured at fair value less costs to sell in accordance with IAS 41 *Agriculture*

(f) contractual rights under insurance contracts as defined in IFRS 4 *Insurance Contracts.*

6.3.2 Accounting for a non-current asset classified as held for sale

Immediately prior to the classification of a non-current asset or disposal group as held for sale they are measured in accordance with the applicable IFRS (usually IAS 16 *Property, Plant and Equipment*, as detailed in Chapter 10). On classification, the asset or disposal group is measured at the lower of carrying amount and fair value less costs to sell. Fair value is defined in IFRS 13 as 'the price that would be received to sell an asset in an orderly transaction between market participants at the measurement date' and assumes that the market is the principal, or most advantageous, market available, and the sale is under current market conditions.

The accounting treatment means that if the expected net selling price is lower than the carrying amount, the asset is written down to this value—the expected amount to be realised from the asset. On this first classification of an asset as held for sale, if the expected net selling price is higher than the carrying amount, no adjustment is made.

If the sale is expected to occur in more than one year's time, the costs to sell are discounted to present value. Any increase in the present value of these costs as time passes (owing to the **unwinding of the discount rate**) is included as a finance cost in profit and loss.

If the fair value less costs to sell is less than the carrying amount, an **impairment loss** is recognised, and charged to profit and loss.

Worked example 6.1: to show the accounting for an asset classified as held for sale

Brea plc, which has a financial year end of 31 December, has an item of plant which meets the criteria to be classified as held for sale at 1 July 20X9. The original cost of the asset was £120,000 with an estimated useful life of 10 years and, at 1 January 20X9, had accumulated depreciation of £36,000. At 1 July 20X9 the fair value of the plant is £50,000 with costs to sell estimated at £4,000.

Required:
Show how this asset would be accounted for in the 20X9 financial statements.

Depreciation would be charged for the first 6 months of 20X9, i.e. $6/12 \times £120,000/10 = £6,000$.

At 1 July 20X9 the plant has a carrying amount (net book value) of $£120,000 - (£36,000 + £6,000) = £78,000$.

Fair value less costs to sell $= £50,000 - £4000 = £46,000$.

The asset would be written down to £46,000 and an impairment loss of $£78,000 - £46,000 = £32,000$ would be charged to profit and loss.

Once an asset or disposal group is classified as held for sale and remeasured, no further depreciation is charged, even if the asset is still being used in the business.

If the asset or disposal group is still held at the subsequent financial year end, the fair value less costs to sell must be estimated again and compared to the carrying amount. A further impairment loss may be recognised; however, if the fair value less costs to sell have increased, a gain may be recognised in profit and loss, but only up to the amount of any previous impairment losses that have been recognised.

Worked example 6.2: to show the accounting for subsequent estimation of fair value less costs to sell

Using the same details as Worked example 6.1, suppose that the plant is still held for sale at 31 December 20X9, and, at this date, the fair value and estimated costs to sell are respectively:

(a) £45,000 and £4,000

(b) £55,000 and £5,000.

Required:
For (a) and (b) show how the changes in fair value less costs to sell would be accounted for.

	(a) £	(b) £
At 31 December 20X9		
Fair value	45,000	55,000
Costs to sell	(4,000)	(5,000)
	41,000	50,000
Carrying amount (from above example)	46,000	46,000
Impairment (loss)/gain	(5,000)	4,000

Under (a) and (b) the plant would be revalued to £41,000 and £50,000 respectively. A further impairment loss of £5,000 would be recognised under scenario (a) and a gain of £4,000 would be able to be recognised under scenario (b), as this is less than the original impairment loss of £32,000.

6.3.3 Change of plans

If the criteria for an asset or disposal group to be classified as held for sale are no longer met, then the asset or disposal group ceases to be held for sale. In this case the asset must be remeasured at the lower of:

- the carrying amount immediately prior to its classification as held for sale, adjusted for any depreciation, amortisation, or revaluations that would have been recognised if it had not been classified as held for sale (in other words, on its original measurement basis as if the classification as held for sale and subsequent reclassification has never happened)

- its recoverable amount (this is the higher of fair value less costs to sell and recoverable amount, and is discussed in more detail in the section dealing with impairment in Chapter 10).

6.3.4 Disclosures

To enable the user to understand which non-current assets will be in use in the future to generate operating profits, assets which are classified as held for sale are disclosed separately on the face of the statement of financial position, usually below current assets. Further information is provided in the notes to the financial statements explaining what assets are held for sale, and the facts and circumstances of the anticipated sale.

The impairment losses and any gains do not have to be disclosed separately, but companies may choose to if they consider they are material.

Financial reporting in practice 6.4	BG Group plc, 2010

BG group plc works in cooperation with governments, partners, and other stakeholders to find, develop, and connect natural gas to markets worldwide. Its 2010 financial statements contain the following disclosures relating to assets classified as held for sale.

Accounting policies—assets held for sale

When an asset or disposal group's carrying value will be recovered principally through a sale transaction rather than through continuing use, it is classified as held for sale and stated at the lower of carrying value and fair value less costs to sell. No depreciation is charged in respect of non-current assets classified as held for sale.

(continued)

(continued)
Balance sheets

These include the following line items:

	Note	31 Dec 2010 $m	31 Dec 2009 Restated $m
Assets			
Assets classified as held for sale	18	227	–
Liabilities			
Liabilities associated with assets classified as held for sale	18	(104)	–

Note 18 Assets held for sale

The major classes of assets and liabilities classified as held for sale are as follows:

	31 Dec 2010 $m	31 Dec 2009 $m
Investments in joint venture entities	209	–
Cash and cash equivalents	18	–
Assets classified as held for sale	227	–
Trade and other payables	(7)	–
Borrowings	(97)	–
Liabilities associated with assets classified as held for sale	(104)	–
Net assets classified as held for sale[a]	123	–

(a) There were no currency translation adjustments in respect of the above assets and liabilities recorded in the consolidated statement of comprehensive income.

During 2010, BG Group committed to a plan to dispose of its indirect 40% interests in First Gas Holdings Corporation and FGP Corp which own the Santa Rita and San Lorenzo power stations in the Philippines, respectively. Accordingly, these businesses have been reclassified as held for sale as at 31 December 2010, with sales completion expected in 2011 subject to receiving necessary waivers and consents. The results of these businesses have been classified as discontinued operations, see note 8.

6.3.5 What is a discontinued operation?

The accounting for discontinued operations uses some of the issues and accounting methods relating to assets held for sale, but before this is explained the question that must be asked is what is a discontinued operation? How significant a part of a business does it have to be? A separate subsidiary company? A factory? A department? What is the distinction between a discontinued operation and the merger or reorganisation of parts of the business? Is it part of the business that has already been closed down in the year? Or is it one where there are plans to close it?

IFRS 5 defines a discontinued operation as:

A component of an entity that either has been disposed of or is classified as held for sale and:

(a)   represents a separate major line of business or geographical area of operations,

(b)   is part of a single co-ordinated plan to dispose of a separate major line of business or geographical area of operations, or

(c)   is a subsidiary acquired exclusively with a view to resale.

(IASB, IFRS, 2004: Appendix A)

A component of an entity comprises operations and cash flows that can be clearly distinguished, operationally, and for financial reporting purposes from the rest of the entity. The IFRS also terms this a **cash-generating unit**, which, in turn, is defined as 'the smallest identifiable group of assets that generates cash inflows that are largely independent of the cash inflows from other assets or groups of assets'. A cash-generating unit may also have some directly associated liabilities, for example if property is part of the unit there may be a related mortgage.

The business operation would therefore have to be seen as separate from other parts of the business and separate reporting of it would have to be possible. Examples would include a major product line, a factory, a retail outlet, or a development division.

The disposal of the business operation does not need to have actually happened in the financial period to be treated as a discontinued operation, but the criteria for being classified as held for sale as given earlier, need to be fulfilled.

6.3.6 Accounting for discontinued operations

The essential requirement is that anything to do with a discontinued operation is disclosed separately on the face of the statement of comprehensive income. This includes:

1   The profits or losses from the actual operation of the component during the year

2   Any gains or losses arising from the disposal of the component, or from any remeasurement to fair value less costs to sell.

A single figure of the overall profit or loss from these two items must be shown separately on the face of the statement of comprehensive income (in the income statement section) and, under the IAS 1 presentation, it is be included after tax, but before profit or loss for the year.

An analysis of this single figure into:

(i)   the revenue, expenses and pre-tax profit or loss of discontinued operations;

(ii)   the related income tax expense;

(iii) the gain or loss recognised on the measurement to fair value less costs to sell or on the disposal of the assets or disposal group(s) constituting the discontinued operation; and

(iv)   the related income tax expense

must be disclosed either on the face of the statement of comprehensive income or, more usually, in a note.

In addition, the net cash flows relating to the operating, investing, and financing activities of discontinued operations must be disclosed, either on the face of the statement of cash flows or as part of the disclosure note. All comparative figures are also adjusted to separate out results from these business components in the previous years, even though, at the time, they were not classified as discontinued operations. This is to ensure the impact on performance of the discontinuance is clear, and users can identify separately the trends in the results for the continuing operations.

 Worked example 6.3: to show the accounting for a discontinued operation

The income statement for Blacker plc for the year ended 31 March 20X6 is as follows:

	£000
Revenue	1,650
Cost of sales	(1,230)
Gross profit	420
Distribution costs	(150)
Administrative expenses	(210)
Profit before tax	60
Income tax expense	(20)
Profit for the year	40

As a result of the company deciding to outsource its manufacturing overseas the manufacturing division was classified as held for sale and, on 1 February 20X6, the criteria for being classified as a discontinued operation were judged to have been met.

The results of the division for the year were as follows (note: these are included in the preceding figures):

	£000
Revenue	380
Cost of sales	(290)
Distribution costs	(60)
Administrative expenses	(70)
Income tax effect	10

Required:
Ignoring the effect of remeasuring the assets of the division at fair value less costs to sell, redraw the income statement of Blacker plc for the year ended 31 March 20X6 in accordance with IFRS 5.

		£000
Revenue	(1,650 – 380)	1,270
Cost of sales	(1,230 – 290)	(940)
Gross profit		330
Distribution costs	(150 – 60)	(90)
Administrative expenses	(210 – 70)	(140)
Profit before tax		100
Income tax expense	(20 – (-10))	(30)
Profit for the year from continuing operations		70
Loss for the year from discontinued operations		(30)
Profit for the year		40

A disclosure note would show the detail of the discontinued operation:

	£000
Revenue	380
Cost of sales	(290)
Distribution costs	(60)
Administrative expenses	(70)
Income tax effect	10
Loss after tax	(30)

Financial reporting in practice 6.5 — Lenzing AG, 2010

Lenzing AG is an Austrian manufacturer of high-quality cellulose fibres for global textile and non-wovens industries. Its products range from special cellulose fibres to high-quality plastic polymer products. Its core fibres business is complemented by other activities in plastics, as well as engineering.

Income statement

Continuing operations	Note	2010 EUR '000	2009 EUR '000
Sales	(7)	1,766,323	1,217,993
Changes in inventories of finished goods and work in progress	(8)	(3,632)	(32,245)
Work performed by the Group and capitalized	(9)	33,839	31,411
Other operating income	(10)	43,525	35,152

(continued)

(continued)

Cost of material and purchased services		**(1,028,523)**	(685,143)
Personnel expenses	(11)	**(259,211)**	(234,784)
Amortization of intangible assets and depreciation of property, plant and equipment	(12)	**(102,523)**	(77,688)
Other operating expenses	(13)	**(217,870)**	(140,489)
Income from operations (*EBIT*)	(14)	**231,928**	114,207
Income from investments in associates	(15)	**1,411**	2,399
Other investment income	(16)	**1,716**	781
Finance costs	(16)	**(16,051)**	(13,909)
Allocation of profit or loss to puttable non-controlling interests		**(2,140)**	(561)
Income before tax (EBT)		**216,864**	102,917
Income tax	(17)	**(40,203)**	(22,994)
Profit for the year after taxes from continuing operations		**176,661**	79,923
Discontinued operations			
Result from discontinued operations	(5)	**(6,723)**	(13,120)
Profit for the year		**169,938**	66,803

Note 5 shows the required breakdown of the loss from discontinued operations into the operating results and the gain or loss recognised on the measurement to fair value less costs to sell of the assets.

Note 5: discontinued operations

To focus the resources on the core business cellulose fibres in the future, the plastics filaments business is sold to a consortium around the Global Equity Partners Group (GEP) for further streamlining of the portfolio. GEP acquires 100% of the shares in the two German companies Hahl Filaments GmbH/Munderkingen and Pedex GmbH/Affolterbach, in the US company Hahl Inc./Lexington and in the Czech company Hahl Filaments s.r.o./Plana, as well as in the related real estate and holding companies.

Discontinued operations are part of the segment Plastics Products.

The major parts influencing the result from discontinued operations are set out in the following table:

Result from discontinued operations	2010 **EUR '000**	2009 EUR '000
Revenue	**50,511**	37,504
Other income and expense	**(45,469)**	(39,991)
EBITDA	**5,042**	(2,487)
Depreciation and amortization	**(5,472)**	(7,672)
EBIT	**(430)**	(10,159)

Financial result	**(634)**	(930)
Income before tax	**(1,064)**	**(11,089)**
Attributable income tax	**(176)**	409
Income after tax	**(1,240)**	**(10,680)**
Result from measurement at fair value less costs to sell	**(4,877)**	0
Valuation adjustments and tax effects attributable to discontinued operations	**(606)**	(2,440)
Loss for the period	**(6,723)**	**(13,120)**

The carrying amounts were adjusted according to the agreed sales price. Expenses of EUR 24 thousand (2009: income of EUR 107 thousand) of other comprehensive income/expense (e.g. actuarial gains) are related to discontinued operations.

6.3.7 Judgement in classification

Although the classification of what constitutes a discontinued operation seems precisely set out in IFRS 5, in practice it is not necessarily straightforward. It requires the exercise of management's judgement, often of future events, which may not be entirely within their control.

 Examples of where the classification as a discontinued operation may not be straightforward

1 A manufacturer ceases production of a number of its product lines which are not selling in current economic conditions. What is meant by a 'major line of business'? How many product lines have to be ceased? What happens if economic conditions improve, which, in turn, may mean the product lines are reinstated?

2 A company merges a subsidiary company's operations into its own because its business is similar and then sells the subsidiary. The operations and cash flows of the subsidiary would be clearly distinguishable, but would this be a separate line of business?

Management may be tempted to classify continuing, but underperforming, operations as discontinued so that the performance of the continuing operations to be used in future forecasts appears 'better'. Some research indicates that this does happen.

6.3.8 Proposed changes to accounting for discontinued operations

Although IFRS 5 was issued by the IASB as part of its short-term convergence project with the US FASB, the boards' definitions of discontinued operations remained different. In their joint project on financial statement presentation, discussed in Chapter 4, the boards decided to develop common definitions of, and require, common disclosures about components of an entity that have been disposed of or are classified as held for sale. An exposure draft (ED) was issued in 2008 which, among other matters, aligned the definition of a discontinued operation to that of an operating segment, as defined in IFRS 8 *Operating Segments* (see section 6.4.1). However, respondents to the ED raised concerns, as some felt the definition would include operations that were too small and thus provide information of limited usefulness.

The IASB has listened to these comments, with the result that the definition of a discontinued operation will now probably not change much from the one currently in IFRS 5. A staff draft of a new exposure draft was published in July 2010; however, further progress towards a revised IFRS is dependent on the outcome of the IASB's agenda consultation.

6.4 Operating segment reporting

One of the main difficulties with interpreting the performance of a large company is that the figures on the face of the main financial statements are aggregated. Most listed companies are multinational, operating in several different economic environments, and providing a range of different products and services. Each product, service, or economic environment is subject to:

- different rates of profitability and growth
- different future prospects and opportunities
- different risks.

To fully understand the performance of a company as a whole, the information needs to be disaggregated into the different operations conducted, so that the effect of the performance of the different operations on the company can be determined. This will enable users to take appropriate actions if those parts of the business which are performing poorly can be identified from the financial statements. IFRS 8 *Operating Segments* was issued by the IASB in 2006 as part of its convergence programme with the US FASB, and replaced IAS 14 *Segment Reporting*. When issued, the standard was criticised widely, and this is discussed in section 6.4.5. The core principle of IFRS 8 is to:

> ...disclose information to enable users of its financial statements to evaluate the nature and financial effects of the business activities in which it engages and the economic environments in which it operates.

> *(IASB, IFRS 8, 2006: para. 1)*

This standard is therefore not about how to account for an item or transaction; it is about additional disclosures that companies are required to make in the notes to their financial statements to aid the interpretation of financial performance.

6.4.1 What is an operating segment?

The key issue to note is that management determines what an operating segment is for their company, but based on guidance set out in IFRS 8. This specifies that an operating segment is a component of a business:

(a) that engages in business activities from which it may earn revenues and incur expenses,

(b) whose operating results are regularly reviewed by the entity's chief operating decision maker to make decisions about resources to be allocated to the segment and assess its performance, and

(c) for which discrete financial information is available.

The business component may be a group of similar products or services, or a geographical location of production, or a geographical location of where sales are made, or be defined on an entirely different basis.

Start-up operations may also be classified as operating segments before they start earning revenues. However, other parts of a company may not be operating segments if they do not earn revenue, or they earn revenues that are only incidental to the activities of the company, for example a corporate headquarters. In particular, IFRS 8 excludes a company's pension schemes from being operating segments.

The chief operating decision-maker is used in the standard as a description of the role; a company does not have to have an individual employee with that title. In practice, the chief operating decision maker is a company's chief executive officer (CEO), but it may be the whole board of directors. To help companies determine what may be an operating segment, IFRS 8 suggests that an operating segment usually has an individual in charge, the segment 'manager'; again, the title is not important, it is the role that is. However, the standard acknowledges that companies will have different operational and management structures, and that some companies will have to determine their operating segments by reference to the core principle as given earlier.

6.4.2 Reportable operating segments

Disaggregated information about an operating segment is only required to be disclosed if certain size thresholds are reached. Only one of the following thresholds has to be reached.

1 Reported revenue, including both sales to external customers and intersegment sales or transfers, is 10% or more of the combined revenue, internal and external, of all operating segments.

2 The absolute amount of its reported profit or loss is 10% or more of the greater, in absolute amount, of (i) the combined reported profit of all operating segments that

did not report a loss and (ii) the combined reported loss of all operating segments that reported a loss.

3   The assets are 10% or more of the combined assets of all operating segments.

(Note: internal revenue would be that earned from transactions with other segments within the company or group.)

Operating segments that do not meet any of these thresholds should be combined with other operating segments if they have similar economic characteristics and their products, services, and operations are similar, and the aggregated figures tested for reportability. Management may also classify an operating segment as reportable, even if the thresholds are not reached, if it believes this information would be useful to users.

To ensure that sufficient detailed information is disclosed about the company's business activities, particularly where the activities are dispersed across many segments, the standard requires that if the total external revenue of the reportable segments constitutes less than 75% of the company's revenue, additional operating segments have to be identified as report-able, even if they do not meet the criteria detailed earlier. However, so that information does not become too detailed and at risk of losing its usefulness and understandability, IFRS 8 suggests that the maximum number of reportable segments should be ten. Reconciliations to total figures shown on the face of the main financial statements of all segmental information have to be provided.

A company has to ensure that all comparative information is adjusted to disclose the details of all segments which are classed as reportable in the current year. This works the other way as well, in that if a segment was reportable in the previous year and management still considers it significant in the current year, it will continue to be reportable even if it does not meet the criteria.

Worked example 6.4: to show the identification of reportable segments

Financial data relating to the operating segments of Drax plc is as follows:

Segment	External revenue £000	Profit/(loss) £000	Assets £000
A	2,000	250	1,500
B	400	(70)	1,100
C	3,000	300	1,900
D	1,500	(20)	600
E	50	(120)	400
	6,950	340	5,500

Required:

Identify the reportable segments of Drax plc. (Assume all revenue earned is external.)

Revenue threshold	10% × combined revenue	= 10% × 6,950	= £695
Profit/(loss) threshold	10% × combined profits	= 10% × 550	= £55
	10% × combined losses	= 10% × 210	= £21
	Profit threshold of £55 is greater		
Asset threshold	10% × combined assets	= 10% × 5,500	= £550

Do the segments meet the thresholds?

Segment	External revenue	Profit/(loss)	Assets
A	✓	✓	✓
B	✗	✓ *	✓
C	✓	✓	✓
D	✓	✗ *	✓
E	✗	✓ *	✗

* Ignore the loss in these segments and take the absolute figure for the threshold test.

All segments meet at least one of the threshold criteria, and therefore all segments are reportable.

6.4.3 Disclosures for reportable segments

The disclosure requirements are to enable users of the financial statements to evaluate the nature and financial effects of the business activities in which a company engages and the economic environments in which it operates. They are, therefore, fairly extensive.

Given that the approach taken in the determination of operating segments is based on management's decision, the factors that have been used to identify these are to be disclosed. This will include some information about how management has organised the business, for example whether this is around different products or services, or geographically, or based on different regulatory environments.

For each reportable segment the following information is then required to be disclosed:

- The types of products and services from which revenues are earned
- A measure of profit or loss
- The following items, if they are included, in the measure of profit or loss that is reported to the chief operating decision-maker

- External revenues
- Internal revenues
- Interest revenue
- Interest expense
- Depreciation and amortisation
- Other material items of income and expense
- The company's interest in the profit or loss of **associates**, and joint ventures
- Income tax expense

- A measure of total assets and liabilities if these are provided regularly to the chief operating decision-maker.

Further disclosures include:

- The basis for accounting for transactions between segments
- Explanations of the measurement of the reportable segments' profits or losses, and assets and liabilities, as provided to the chief operating decision-maker, including any changes
- Explanations of the differences between these measurement bases and those used for financial reporting purposes
- Any asymmetrical allocations, for example if depreciation is allocated to a segment without the related asset to that segment
- Reconciliations of revenues, measures of profit or loss, assets, and liabilities to the figures included in the financial statements.

Financial reporting in practice 6.6   Greene King plc, 2010

Greene King plc, a UK pub retailer and brewer, lists its main businesses as:

- retail, which includes managed pubs, restaurants, and hotels within England and Wales
- pub partners, which includes the operation of tenanted and leased pubs within England and Wales
- brewing
- a Scottish division encompassing all these activities, which is located in Scotland.

This is mirrored in the segment information note included in the following financial statements. This also shows the reconciliation of the segments' operating profits (the measures of profit) to net profit as reported in the company's income statement. (Details for 2010 only are shown.)

2 Segment information

The group has determined four reportable segments that are largely organised and managed separately according to the nature of products and services provided, brands, distribution channels and profile of customers. These are also considered to be the group's operating segments and are based on the information presented to the chief executive who is considered to be the chief operating decision maker.

Retail: Managed houses and restaurants in England and Wales.

Pub Partners: Tenanted houses predominantly in England.

Brewing Company: Brewing beer, marketing and selling, predominantly in England.

Belhaven: Our Scottish operation which includes managed and tenanted houses and brewing and selling beer.

Transfer prices between operating segments are set on an arm's length basis.

2010

	Retail £m	Pub Partners £m	Brewing Company £m	Belhaven £m	Corporate £m	Total operations £m
Segment revenue	589.2	145.1	143.2	154.6	–	1,032.1
Less: internal revenue	–	–	(45.3)	(2.7)	–	(48.0)
External revenue	589.2	145.1	97.9	151.9	–	984.1
Operating costs	(482.8)	(80.5)	(76.5)	(119.2)	(13.8)	(772.8)
Segment operating profit	106.4	64.6	21.4	32.7	(13.8)	211.3
Exceptional items						(31.3)
Net finance costs						(78.1)
Income tax expense						(22.0)
Net profit for the period						79.9
Balance sheet						
Segment assets	1,361.1	796.2	245.9	394.0	34.8	2,832.0
Unallocated assets*						91.4
	1,361.1	796.2	245.9	394.0	34.8	2,923.4
Segment liabilities	(69.9)	(13.1)	(37.0)	(32.4)	(53.4)	(205.8)
Unallocated liabilities*						(1,804.7)
	(69.9)	(13.1)	(37.0)	(32.4)	(53.4)	(2,010.5)
Net assets	1,291.2	783.1	208.9	361.6	(18.6)	912.9
Other segment information						
Capital expenditure – tangible assets	57.3	8.7	3.7	8.3	0.5	78.5
Capital expenditure – tangible assets						

(continued)

(continued)

acquired through business combinations	32.7	–	–	20.8	–	53.5
Capital expenditure – goodwill	3.1	–	–	2.8	–	5.9
Depreciation	35.5	7.2	4.2	5.7	0.5	53.1
EBITDA**	141.9	71.8	25.6	38.4	(13.3)	264.4

* Unallocated assets/liabilities include cash, borrowings, pensions, net deferred tax, net current tax, and derivatives.
** EBITDA represents earnings before interest, tax, depreciation and exceptional items and is calculated as operating profit before exceptionals adjusted for the depreciation charge for the period.

Management reporting and controlling systems

Management monitors the operating results of its strategic business units separately for the purpose of making decisions about allocating resources and assessing performance. Segment performance is measured based on segment operating profit or loss referred to as trading profit in our management and reporting systems. Included within the corporate column in the table above are functions managed by a central division.

No information about geographical regions has been provided as the group's activities are predominantly domestic.

6.4.4 Entity-wide disclosures

Owing to the many different ways of companies organising their businesses and determining their operating segments, there are some catch-all disclosures to ensure certain information is provided to users to meet the overriding aim of the standard. Some of these may already be met by the disclosures for the reportable segments, but, if not, the following additional information needs to be shown.

- External revenue for each product and service group
- Geographical information
  - External revenues
  - Non-current assets
- Reliance on major customers—revenue from each major customer, if it constitutes more than 10% of the company's revenues (the actual customer does not have to be identified).

Financial reporting in practice 6.7 | **Rolls-Royce plc, 2010** |

Rolls-Royce plc, in applying IFRS 8, has determined its operating segments along product groups (civil aerospace, defence aerospace, marine, and energy), and, given its customers are global, provides the following information in its segmental analysis note.

Geographical segments

The Group's revenue by destination is shown below:

	2010 £m	2009 £m
United Kingdom	1,594	1,458
Norway	486	443
Germany	413	488
Spain	231	233
Rest of Europe	1,251	1,109
USA	3,096	2,895
Canada	299	275
China	890	640
South Korea	355	301
Middle East and South East Asia	1,585	1,689
Rest of Asia	228	226
Africa	109	144
Australasia	153	230
Other	395	283
	11,085	10,414

In 2010, revenue (included in all reportable segments) of £1,131m was received from a single customer.

The carrying amounts of the Group's non-current assets, excluding financial instruments, deferred tax assets and post-employment benefit surpluses, by the geographical area in which the assets are located, are as follows:

	2010 £m	2009 £m
United Kingdom	2,925	2,764
North America	611	467
Nordic countries	908	824
Germany	625	574
Other	344	289
	5,413	4,918

6.4.5 Evaluation of IFRS 8

At the time it was issued IFRS 8 received much criticism and has continued to do so. Some of this may have been because it was largely based on the US standard dealing with operating segments, Statement of Financial Accounting Standard (SFAS) 131, rather than the then existing international standard, IAS 14. UK and European critics saw this as a political solution between the IASB and FASB, rather than the IASB selecting the best accounting methods for users.

The main criticisms concerned the management approach to the determination of defining an operating segment, the fact that detailed requirements for geographical disclosures had gone (IAS 14 required these), and that different accounting methods could be applied to segment information from that used in the remainder of the financial statements. The matter even reached the UK parliament, where a group of members of parliament called the standard 'totally unacceptable' by giving company directors too much choice about what they disclose and how they do it.

On one hand the approach taken by IFRS 8 means that comparability of key segment information from one company to another is now difficult (remember, comparability is an enhancing characteristic of financial information). Another doubt is whether publication of figures based on internal management accounting bases generates great benefit for investors if the figures differ from those based on IFRS. Others criticise the fact that only a minimum 75% of trading activity has to be analysed into segmental disclosures. Another issue (which was also present under IAS 14) is whether common costs should be allocated across segments, for example general building costs if a number of segments are based in the same property, or directors' remuneration costs.

On the other hand the use of the management approach has been claimed to have had an overall positive effect on the quality of the segment information, whose usefulness and relevance has increased, which outweighs any concerns expressed about the comparability of financial reports. Some interested parties have stated that the management approach ensures that the usefulness of information is improved because the results of business activities are presented 'through the eyes of management', which uses this information to make key decisions, allocate resources, and monitor performance. The information prepared using the management approach can also provide a better linkage between the financial statements and information reported in the operating and financial review, and other management commentaries, including assessments of risk.

The information should be able to be produced in a timelier manner and at a reduced cost as it is based on that already produced internally by the company. In addition, the geographical information required by IFRS 8 is said to address appropriately the global needs of users of financial statements for these disclosures.

The debate continues with the UK's Financial Reporting Review Panel (FRRP) in 2010 issuing a warning to some UK companies about how they are applying IFRS 8. Specific complaints have included:

- some companies with different divisions and significant operations in different countries reporting only one segment

- the operating analysis in the narrative reports differing from the operating segments included in the financial statements
- the measurement bases used in narrative reports and in the segmental information being different.

Some may suggest that this indicates management is trying to mislead the users of their financial statements or at least hide some of their activities, possibly those conducted overseas. However, there are no current plans by the IASB to revise IFRS 8 and the board is currently carrying out a post-implementation review.

6.4.6 How can segmental information be used?

If disclosures are within the spirit of the standard the information supplied provides the user with a breakdown of the different business activities of a company so that they can analyse which activities have the greatest effect upon the performance of the company as a whole. The relative size of each segment can be ascertained and, together with intersegment comparisons, including horizontal and some ratio analysis, this can provide some detailed understanding of the different segments' performance.

 Worked example 6.5: to show how operating segment disclosures may be used in analysis

Goodman plc has determined three reportable operating segments based upon three different product groups, A, B, and C. Details of revenues (which are all external), profits, and assets of each of the segments are shown as follows.

	Product Group A £m	Product Group B £m	Product Group C £m
Revenue			
UK sales	37	41	66
Export sales—Europe	123	15	43
Export sales—USA	76	3	91
	236	59	200
Profit before interest	38	23	42
Total assets	128	35	101

Required:
Apply analytical techniques to this information to enhance an interpretation of the financial performance of Goodman plc. Comment on the results of this analysis.

1   Establish the relative sizes of each segment:

	Product Group A	Product Group B	Product Group C	Total
Revenue				
UK sales	26%	28%	46%	100%
Export sales—Europe	68%	8%	24%	100%
Export sales—USA	45%	2%	53%	100%
Total revenue	48%	12%	40%	100%
Profit before interest	37%	22%	41%	100%
Total assets	48%	13%	38%	100%

2   The relative sizes of sales to different markets can also be established:

	Product Group A	Product Group B	Product Group C	Total
Revenue				
UK sales	16%	70%	33%	29%
Export sales—Europe	52%	25%	21%	37%
Export sales—USA	32%	5%	46%	34%
	100%	100%	100%	100%

Analysis of this information includes the following:

● although product group A produces the highest revenues, and has the highest related assets, it does not produce the highest profits, which are from product group C

● total sales to the three different markets are not significantly different, with European sales being the largest, followed by the USA and then the UK. The different economic environments of these geographical areas may have a bearing on these figures.

● the majority of export sales to Europe are of product group A, the majority of UK sales are of product group C, and product groups A and C have similar proportions of sales to the USA

● product group B sells mainly to the domestic market.

● product group B yields far less revenue than the other product groups at only 12% of total revenue, yet relative to this it contributes 22% of profit.

3   Some ratios which have meaning can be calculated and compared segment-to-segment:

	Product Group A	Product Group B	Product Group C	Total
Return on total assets				
(PBIT/total assets)	30%	66%	42%	39%
Net profit margin				
(PBIT/total revenue)	16%	39%	21%	21%
Asset turnover (Total revenue/total assets)	1.8	1.7	2.0	1.9

Analysis of, and questions raised by, this information include the following:

- although product group B is the smallest it is the most profitable by far by both measures of return on total assets and net profit margin. Should the company try to increase its business in these products? Or, given that the majority of this group's sales are to the UK market, are there conditions in the home market economic environment which lead to this result?
- despite its greater profitability, product group B has generated less revenue per £ of assets allocated to the group compared with the other products. Information about the nature of the product group is needed to assess this ratio
- product group A, despite having the largest revenues, is the least profitable. Can the company influence this or is it connected to the fact that the majority of the sales of this product group are to overseas customers?

6.5 Related party disclosures

6.5.1 The need for information

Discussion of IFRS 8 *Operating Segments* touched upon one issue which may affect the users' interpretation of the performance of a company—that of reliance on one or more significant customers. Disclosure of this is required by this standard. However, the performance of a company may also be influenced by the existence of transactions with individuals or other businesses which are related in some way to the company and where the transactions may not be (or not perceived to be) at arm's length or under normal commercial arrangements. The monetary value of such transactions may be different to other 'normal' ones. The company's financial position may also be influenced by the existence of outstanding balances with such related parties, for example, preferential payment arrangements may be present.

A transaction with a related party may not even have happened for the financial statements to have been affected. Where a relationship exists one company may be able to influence another company not to act, for example, a subsidiary company may be instructed not to carry out research and development, or to produce a product (such as the instruction from NewsCorp to the News of the World to cease production of its Sunday newspaper).

There is nothing inherently wrong about such transactions—they are a normal feature of business. For example, companies frequently conduct their activities through subsidiary or associate companies where the parent company has the ability to control, or significantly influence, decisions being made.

However, what is important is that the financial statements faithfully represent all transactions and that users have knowledge of all relevant information to enable them to evaluate whether the performance has been distorted by any transactions not on an arm's length basis. The users also need to be able to compare companies' performance and financial position, including assessments of the risks and opportunities facing the companies.

Examples of transactions which are not on normal commercial terms

1 Company B controls company A. Company A sells goods to company B at cost.
2 A company makes a loan to another company in which it has a significant investment at a preferential rate of interest.
3 A director of a company persuades the board of directors to award a contract to a company owned by her brother.

The IASB has had a standard relating to related parties for some years. The current revised version of IAS 24 *Related Party Disclosures* was issued in 2009 and sets out the information that companies are required to disclose about related parties and transactions with such parties. Note, like IFRS 8, it does not specify any accounting methods—it is a disclosure standard only— thus companies will have a note, or notes, relating to these matters in their financial statements.

6.5.2 What is a related party?

A related party can be a person or another business entity that is related to the company that is reporting its financial statements. Although IAS 24 provides what may appear to be clear-cut definitions of a related party, the emphasis of determining whether there is a related party relationship is very much on the substance of the relationship and not merely the legal form.

A person is related to the reporting company if any of the following apply:

(i) The person has control or joint control over the reporting company

(ii) The person has significant influence over the reporting company

(iii) The person is a member of the key management personnel of the reporting company or of a parent of the reporting company.

A close family member of the person concerned is also considered a related party. A close family member is defined as those family members who may be expected to influence, or be influenced by, the person in their dealings with the company and include:

(a) the person's children and spouse or domestic partner;

(b) children of the person's spouse or domestic partner; and

(c) dependants of the person or the person's spouse or domestic partner.

A business entity is considered to be related to the reporting entity if any of the following apply:

(i) The entity and the reporting entity are members of the same group (which means that each parent, subsidiary and fellow subsidiary is related to the others).

(ii) One entity is an associate or joint venture of the other entity (or an associate or joint venture of a member of a group of which the other entity is a member).

(iii)   Both companies are joint ventures of the same third party.

(iv)   One entity is a joint venture of a third entity and the other entity is an associate of the third entity.

(v)   The entity is a post-employment benefit plan for the benefit of employees of either the reporting entity or an entity related to the reporting entity. If the reporting entity is itself such a plan, the sponsoring employers are also related to the reporting entity.

(vi)   The entity is controlled or jointly controlled by a person identified as a related party.

(vii)   A person identified as a related party has significant influence over the entity or is a member of the key management personnel of the entity (or of a parent of the entity).

These criteria relate to the key question of what constitutes a group of companies—the relationships between different companies and how much control or influence one company exerts over another. At a basic level a group comprises a parent company which controls one or more subsidiary companies, through holding, directly or indirectly, more than 50% of the voting (equity) shares of the subsidiary. An associate company is one in which the reporting company can exert significant influence, and the rebuttable presumption is that this relationship is evidenced by the holding of between 20% and 50% of the voting shares of the associate. A joint venture is a company which is controlled jointly by two or more other companies. Do note that there are other indicators which may provide evidence of control or significant influence, and, indeed, exactly what is meant by control or significant influence needs to be defined and discussed. These matters are not necessarily straightforward, and they are discussed in Chapters 15 and 16, which deal with group financial statements.

Note, some relationships may appear to be close, but they are actually specified as not being related parties. They are as follows:

(a)   Two entities simply because they have a director or other member of key management personnel in common or because a member of key management personnel of one entity has significant influence over the other entity.

(b)   Two venturers simply because they share joint control over a joint venture.

(c)   (i)   Providers of finance,

     (ii)   trade unions,

     (iii) public utilities, and

     (iv) departments and agencies of a government that does not control, jointly control or significantly influence the reporting entity, simply by virtue of their normal dealings with an entity (even though they may affect the freedom of action of an entity or participate in its decision-making process).

(d)   A customer, supplier, franchisor, distributor or general agent with whom an entity transacts a significant volume of business, simply by virtue of the resulting economic dependence.

Worked example 6.6: to illustrate related parties

1   Xavier plc owns 75% of the equity shares of Yoyo plc and 18% of the equity shares of Zed plc.

2   Christie owns 25% of the equity share capital of Xavier plc and Bill is her husband.

3   Clive is a director of Xavier plc. He owns 60% of the equity shares of Alpen Ltd. Muriel is his partner who owns 10% of the equity shares of Bixit Ltd.

4   James works for Xavier plc as a manager, but he is not a director. Clare is his daughter.

5   Xavier plc has a pension scheme for its employees.

6   Xavier plc obtains approximately 30% of its main product from one overseas supplier.

Required:
Establish the related parties under each of the circumstances for company Xavier plc.

1   Xavier plc controls Yoyo plc, so Yoyo is a related party. However, Xavier plc does not control Zed plc and prima facie does not exert significant influence over the company as the shareholding is less than 20%. So, Zed plc is not a related party.

2   Christie is a related party unless it can be demonstrated that her shareholding does not give her significant influence over Xavier plc. If Christie is a related party then Bill, her husband, will also be.

3   Clive is a member of the key management personnel of Xavier plc and is therefore a related party. Clive controls Alpen Ltd, so Alpen is a related party. Muriel, Clive's partner, is considered a close family member of Clive and so is also a related party. Muriel does not control Bixit Ltd and is unlikely to exert significant influence with a shareholding of only 10%, so Bixit is not a related party.

4   James may or may not be a member of key management personnel of Xavier plc. If he is a related party, then so is Clare, his daughter.

5   The pension scheme is a related party.

6   The overseas supplier is not a related party.

6.5.3 What is a related party transaction?

A related party transaction is any transfer of resources, services, or obligations between the reporting company and a related party, irrespective of whether a price is charged.

6.5.4 Disclosures

These are fairly extensive and include the following:

1   Irrespective of whether there have been any transactions between them, all relationships between the company and its subsidiary companies must be disclosed. The company also needs to disclose the name of its parent, if any, and, if different, the ultimate controlling company.

2   Key management personnel compensation, which includes all employee benefits as defined in IAS 19 *Employee Benefits* and to which IFRS 2 *Share-based Payment* applies.

Although these two accounting standards are outside the scope of this textbook, broadly employee benefits means all forms of consideration paid or provided in return for services rendered to the company by the employee. IAS 24 requires this information categorised as:

(a) Short-term benefits (for example, wages, salaries, bonuses, holiday pay, National Insurance and benefits-in-kind)

(b) Post-employment benefits (for example, pensions and post-employment insurance)

(c) Other long-term benefits (for example, long-service leave, long-term disability benefits and deferred benefits)

(d) Termination benefits

(e) Share-based payment.

Reminder *As discussed in Chapter 3 in relation to corporate governance, extensive disclosures of directors' remuneration is already required by Companies Act 2006 for UK companies. The IAS 24 disclosures are covered mainly by these requirements and, if not, are usually added to the information provided in the narrative report.*

3   For all transactions with a related party separate disclosure of:

(a) The nature of the relationship

(b) Information about the transaction and any outstanding balances, including any provisions made if a debt is considered doubtful.

 Examples of the types of transactions that are disclosed if they are with a related party

1   Purchases or sales of goods (finished or unfinished).
2   Purchases or sales of property and other assets.
3   Rendering or receiving of services.
4   Leases.
5   Transfers of research and development.
6   Transfers under licence agreements.
7   Transfers under finance arrangements (including loans and equity contributions in cash or in kind).
8   Provision of guarantees or collateral.
9   Commitments to do something if a particular event occurs or does not occur in the future.
10   Settlement of liabilities on behalf of the entity or by the entity on behalf of that related party.

Financial reporting in practice 6.8

Included in the note relating to investments of the parent company, Kingfisher plc lists its principal subsidiary companies. It is interesting to note that it does not list them all on the grounds of excessive information, which may detract from relevance and understandability. Other related party transactions are detailed in a later note.

Notes to the consolidated financial statements 2011/2012

4 Investments

The Directors consider that to give the full particulars of all subsidiary undertakings would lead to a statement of excessive length. In accordance with Section 410(2)(a) of the Companies Act 2006, the information below relates to those Group undertakings at the financial year end whose results or financial position, in the opinion of the Directors, principally affect the figures of the consolidated financial statements of Kingfisher plc. Details of all subsidiary undertakings will be annexed to the next Annual Return of Kingfisher plc to be filed at Companies House.

	Country of incorporation and operation	% interest held and voting rights	Class of share owned	Main activity
B&Q plc[1]	Great Britain	100	Ordinary & special[2]	Retailing
B&Q Properties Limited	Great Britain	100	Ordinary	Property investment
Halcyon Finance Ltd[2]	Great Britain	100	Ordinary	Finance
Kingfisher Information Technology Services (UK) Limited[2]	Great Britain	100	Ordinary	IT services
Screwfix Direct Limited	Great Britain	100	Ordinary	Retailing
Sheldon Holdings Limited[2]	Great Britain	100	Ordinary	Holding company
Zeus Land Investments Limited	Great Britain	100	Ordinary	Holding company
B&Q Ireland Limited	Ireland	100	Ordinary	Retailing
Brico Dépôt S.A.S.[3]	France	100	Ordinary	Retailing
Castorama Dubois Investissements S.C.A.[3,4]	France	100	Ordinary	Holding company
Castorama France S.A.S.[3]	France	100	Ordinary	Retailing
Eurodépôt Immobilier S.A.S.[3]	France	100	Ordinary	Property investment
Immobilière Castorama S.A.S.[3]	France	100	Ordinary	Property investment
Kingfisher France S.A.S.[3]	France	100	Ordinary	Holding company

B&Q Asia Holdings Ltd[5]	Hong Kong	100%	Ordinary	Holding company
Kingfisher Asia Limited	Hong Kong	100%	Ordinary	Sourcing
B&Q (China) B.V.[5]	Netherlands	100%	Ordinary	Holding company
Castim Sp.z.o.o.[3]	Poland	100%	Ordinary	Property investment
Castorama Polska Sp.z.o.o.[3]	Poland	100%	Ordinary	Retailing
Castorama RUS LLC[6]	Russia	100%	Ordinary	Retailing
Euro Depot España S.A.U.[3]	Spain	100%	Ordinary	Retailing

[1] The special shares in B&Q plc are owned 100% by Kingfisher plc and are non-voting.
[2] Held directly by Kingfisher plc.
[3] Owing to local conditions, these companies prepare their financial statements to 31 January.
[4] Castorama Dubois Investissements S.C.A. is 100% owned, of which 45% is held directly by Kingfisher plc.
[5] Holding companies for the Group's Chinese retailing operations, which have a 31 December year end.
[6] Owing to local conditions, this company prepares its financial statements to 31 December.

36 Related party transactions

During the year, the Company and its subsidiaries carried out a number of transactions with related parties in the normal course of business and on an arm's length basis. The names of the related parties, the nature of these transactions and their total value are shown below:

£ millions	2011/12 Income/ (expense)	2011/12 Receivable/ (payable)	2010/11 Income/ (expense)	2010/11 Receivable/ (payable)
Transactions with Koctas Yapi Marketleri Ticaret A.S. in which the Group holds a 50% interest				
Commission and other income	0.9	1.0	1.0	0.8
Transactions with Hornbach Holding A.G. in which the Group holds a 21% interest				
Commission and other income	3.8	0.3	3.6	0.4
Other expenses	(0.3)	–	(0.2)	–
Transactions with Crealfi S.A. in which the Group holds a 49% interest				
Provision of employee services	0.1	–	0.1	–
Commission and other income	7.0	1.5	6.7	1.6
Transactions with Kingfisher Pension Scheme				
Provision of administrative services	1.1	–	1.4	0.1

Services are usually negotiated with related parties on a cost-plus basis. Goods are sold or bought on the basis of the price lists in force with non-related parties. (continued)

(continued)

The amounts outstanding are unsecured and will be settled in cash. No guarantees have been given or received. No provisions have been made for bad and doubtful debts in respect of the amounts owed by related parties.

The remuneration of key management personnel is given in note 8.

Other transactions with the Kingfisher Pension Scheme are detailed in note 27.

 ## Summary of key points

As the discussion in this chapter has shown, a company's performance, as shown by the statement of comprehensive income, is influenced by many factors:

- by the judgements and estimates made by management, which can arise from both simple and complex transactions and items
- by the accounting policies selected by management
- by any unusual material, exceptional, or one-off items that occur during an accounting period
- by the potential write-down of non-current asset values when they are classified as held for sale
- by discontinued operations
- by the fact that the performances of individual business segments are aggregated
- by the existence of related party relationships.

Various international accounting standards have been issued in order to specify how the accounting should be carried out or the additional disclosures required to be made for many of these factors. The aim of these standards is to ensure that the financial statements provide relevant information about the transactions undertaken by companies and that users understand the effect these have had, or may have, on the performance. Users are often assessing past performance in order to predict what may happen in the future and therefore need knowledge of any material items which will influence future results.

Some of these factors, and the application of the detailed provisions in the standards, rely upon management's interpretation and judgement; thus, there is always scope for some 'massaging' of results and how performance might be portrayed, however minor this may be. Remember, though, details of significant estimates and judgements that have been made also need to be disclosed. Users should therefore be provided with sufficient information to analyse the performance and assess what may have influenced the results.

 ## Further reading

IASB (International Accounting Standards Board) (2009) IAS 24 *Related Party Disclosures*. London: IASB.

IASB (International Accounting Standards Board) (2004) IFRS 5 *Non-current Assets Held for Sale and Discontinued Operations*. London: IASB.

IASB (International Accounting Standards Board) (2006) IFRS 8 *Operating Segments*. London: IASB.

Bibliography

Arsenal Holdings plc (2010) *Statement of Accounts and Annual Report* 2009/10. London: Arsenal Holdings.

BG Group plc (2011) *Annual Report and Accounts, 2010*. Reading: BG Group.

Bush, T. (2007) *IFRS 8: What is it Good For?* Available at: http://www.accountancyage.com (accessed 10 October 2012).

GAAPweb (2007) *MPs Criticise IFRS 8*. Available at: http://www.gaapweb.com/ (accessed 10 October 2012).

Greene King plc (2010) *Annual Report, 2010*. Bury St Edmonds: Greene King.

IASB (International Accounting Standards Board) (2004) IFRS 5 *Non-current Assets Held for Sale and Discontinued Operations*. London: IASB.

IASB (International Accounting Standards Board) (2006) IFRS 8 *Operating Segments*. London: IASB.

IASB (International Accounting Standards Board) (2007) IAS 1 *Presentation of Financial Statements*. London: IASB.

IASB (International Accounting Standards Board) (2009) IAS 24 *Related Party Disclosures*. London: IASB.

IASB (International Accounting Standards Board) (2010) *Conceptual Framework for Financial Reporting*. London: IASB.

J Sainsbury plc (2010) *Annual Report and Financial Statements, 2010*. London: J Sainsbury.

JD Wetherspoon plc (2010) *Annual Report and Accounts, 2010*. Watford: JD Wetherspoon.

Kingfisher plc (2012) *Annual Report and Accounts, 2011/12*. London: Kingfisher.

Lenzing Group (2011) *Annual Report 2010*. Lenzing: Lenzing Group.

Murphy, R. (2010) *IFRS in Trouble – Country-by-Country Reporting is the Answer*. Available at: http://www.taxresearch.org.uk/ (accessed 10 October 2012).

Next plc (2011) *Annual Report and Accounts, 2011*. Enderby: Next.

Robins, P. (2007) *IFRS 8 Operating Segments*. Available at: http://www2.accaglobal.com (accessed 10 October 2012).

Rolls-Royce plc (2011) *Annual Report, 2010*. London: Rolls-Royce.

Stockdyk, J. (2010) *FRRP Unhappy with IFRS 8 Dodgers*. Available at: http://www.accountingweb.co.uk (accessed 10 October 2012).

Questions

● Quick test

1   A company which prepares financial statements to 31 December classifies a non-current asset as held for sale on 1 September 20X2. The asset's carrying amount at that date is £20,000 and its fair value is £15,600, with estimated costs to sell of £600. The asset is sold in June 20X3 for £16,000 (net of costs). Calculate any **impairment losses** or gains that should be recognised in the company's income statement for the year ended 31 December 20X2 if the asset's fair value less costs to sell at 31 December 20X2 is:

(a) 14,000

(b) 17,000

(c) 22,000.

In each case, also calculate the profit or loss that should be recognised on the disposal of the asset in 20X3 and comment on the results shown.

2   Dewy plc is a company with six operating segments and no other activities except those of the six operating segments. It reports in accordance with the minimum requirements of IFRS 8.

Operating segment	Internal revenue £m	External revenue £m	Total revenue £m	Profit (loss) £m	Assets £m
Sparrow	50	940	990	310	80
Hawk	30	80	110	(50)	70
Eagle	–	400	400	130	570
Owl	240	220	460	80	120
Robin	50	160	210	(100)	80
Thrush	30	200	230	30	80
TOTAL	400	2,000	2,400	400	1,000

Required:

Explain whether each of the operating segments is a reportable segment.

3   Discuss whether the following relationships of Alpha plc constitute a related party relationship as defined by IAS 24:

(a) Beta is a separate entity in which one of Alpha's junior managers owns 10% of the share capital

(b) The daughter of a director of Alpha

(c) A director of Alpha owns 60% of the share capital of another entity called Gamma Ltd

(d) Miss Delta owns 25% of the share capital of Alpha

(e) A director of Alpha is also a director of Epsilon plc (which is independent of Alpha), but is not a shareholder in either entity

(f) Zeta Ltd is an entity owned by the niece of the finance director of Alpha.

4   Discuss the disclosures that would be required by IAS 24 in the financial statements of Black plc in respect of each of the following transactions.

(a) Black sells goods on credit to White Ltd, which is a company owned by the son of one of the directors of Black. At the year end there was a receivable of £100,000 owing from White to Black. The £100,000 was expensed to the income statement as it was considered as being non-recoverable. Debt collection costs incurred by Black were £4,000.

(b) Black purchased goods from Blue plc for £600,000, which was deemed to be an arm's length price. Black owns 40% of the ordinary share capital of Blue.

(c) An amount of £90,000 is due to one of Black's distributors, Red Ltd.

(d) A house owned by Black, with a carrying amount of £200,000 and a market value of £450,000, was sold to one of its directors for £400,000. Black guaranteed the loan taken out by the director to purchase the property.

●● Develop your understanding

5 During the year to 30 September 20X6 Price plc carried out a major reorganisation of its activities as follows.

(a) The only remaining manufacturing division of the company was closed down on 1 June 20X6. As a result of the closure Price's only activity will be in retail.

(b) Owing to fierce competition, on 31 August 20X6 it was decided to sell the only division that operated in Europe. The company was confident of a sale within the year. The sale actually took place on 20 January 20X7.

(c) The activities carried on by the research division were terminated during the period. This division was one of a number of smaller ones which operated from the same location as the main headquarters of Price. All these divisions use the same central accounting system and operating costs are allocated between them for the purpose of the management accounts.

The accounts for the year ended 30 September 20X6 were approved on 5 January 20X7.

Required:

Discuss how these events should be accounted for in the financial statements of Price plc for the year ended 30 September 20X6 in relation to IFRS 5 *Non-current Assets Held for Sale and Discontinued Operations*.

6 Bullfinch plc is an international hotel group whose sole business is that of operating hotels. The group reports to management on the basis of regions, these being Europe, South East Asia, and the Americas. The hotels are located in capital cities in these regions and the company sets individual performance indicators for each hotel based on its city location. The results of these regional segments for the year ended 30 June 20X9 are as follows.

| | Revenue | | Segment | Segment | Segment |
| | External | Internal | profit / (loss) | assets | liabilities |
Region	£m	£m	£m	£m	£m
Europe	200	3	(10)	300	200
South East Asia	300	2	60	800	300
Americas	500	5	105	2,000	1,400

There were no significant intersegment balances in the asset and liability figures.

Required:

(a) For an international company such as Bullfinch plc, discuss the purpose behind the requirements of IFRS 8 *Operating Segments*.

(b) Explain the principles in IFRS 8 for the determination of a company's reportable segments, and how these principles would be applied for Bullfinch plc, using the information given.

(c) Demonstrate how an analyst might use the segmental information and outline any conclusions that may be reached.

(d) Evaluate the usefulness of the segmental information, including in your answer details of other information that is required to be disclosed by IFRS 8 or would be considered useful for analytical purposes.

●●● Take it further

7 The following list of balances was extracted from the books of Crompton plc on 31 December 20X7:

	£	£
Sales		2,640,300
Administration expenses	220,280	
Selling and distribution costs	216,320	
Interest paid on loan stock	10,000	
Dividends received		2,100
Profit on sale of premises (see note 6)		40,000
Purchases	2,089,600	
Inventories at 1 January 20X7	318,500	
Bank		11,860
Trade receivables	415,800	
Provision for doubtful debts at 1 January 20X7		10,074
Loss on sale of business operation (see note 6)	8,800	
Trade payables		428,250
Corporation tax paid	32,500	
10% loan stock		200,000
Investments in other listed companies	20,000	
Office equipment	110,060	
Vehicles	235,000	
Equity share capital (£1 shares)		200,000
Retained earnings at 1 January 20X7		144,276
	£ 3,676,860	£ 3,676,860

The following information needs to be dealt with before the financial statements can be finalised:

1 Provide for the loan stock interest which is due for payment on 1 January 20X8

2 Provide for administration expenses paid in advance at 31 December 20X7 of £12,200 and distribution costs of £21,300 owing at this date.

3 The provision for doubtful debts is to be maintained at 3% of receivables

4 Inventories are valued at 31 December 20X7 at £340,600

5 The total corporation tax payable on the company's profits for 20X7 is estimated at £45,700

6 During the year, the company sold a material business operation with all activities ceasing on 28 February 20X8. The premises were sold separately, and gave a profit on sale of £40,000. The loss on sale of the remainder of the operation amounted to £8,800.

The operating results of the business segment were as follows (these figures are *included* in the relevant trial balance figures):

	£
Sales	180,634
Cost of sales	153,539
Administration expenses	20,240
Distribution costs	22,823
Corporation tax effect	3,500 reduction

8   In addition, the company is negotiating the sale of another business sector, which should be completed by 30 April 20X8. Relevant values of the assets of this sector at 31 December 20X7 are as follows:

	Book value £	Fair value less costs to sell £
Vehicles	43,554	20,000
Office equipment	16,566	5,000
Inventories	66,000	68,000

Required:

Prepare a statement of comprehensive income for the year ended 31 December 20X7 and a statement of financial position at that date, which comply, as far as the information allows, with relevant international accounting standards.

9   Next is a UK-based retailer offering exciting, beautifully designed, excellent quality clothing, footwear, accessories, and home products. Next distributes through three main channels: Next Retail, a chain of more than 500 stores in the UK and Fire, Next Directory, a home shopping catalogue and website with nearly 3 million active customers, and Next International, with more than 180 stores around the world. Next also has a growing website capability in more than 30 countries.

Other group businesses include:

- Next Sourcing, which designs, sources and buys Next-branded products
- Lipsy, which designs and sells its own branded younger women's fashion products through retail, Internet, and wholesale channels
- Ventura, which provides customer services management to clients wishing to outsource their customer contact administration and fulfilment activities.

Next's consolidated income statement for the financial year ended 29 January 2011 and the comparative 2010 statement are shown as follows. An extract from the company's balance sheet at 29 January 2011, plus the segmental analysis as disclosed in the 2011 financial statements, are also shown.

Financial reporting in practice 6.9 — Next plc

Consolidated income statement for the year ended 29 January 2011

	Notes	2011 £m	2010 £m
Revenue	1, 2	3,453.7	3,406.5
Cost of sales		(2,445.0)	(2,409.6)
Gross profit		1,008.7	996.9
Distribution costs		(223.2)	(232.1)
Administrative expenses		(214.7)	(236.6)
Other gains	2	2.2	0.7
Trading profit		573.0	528.9
Share of results of associates	11	1.8	0.9
Operating profit	3	574.8	529.8
Finance income	5	0.9	0.8
Finance costs	5	(24.3)	(25.3)
Profit before taxation		551.4	505.3
Taxation	6	(150.5)	(141.3)
Profit for the year		400.9	364.0

Extract from consolidated balance sheet at 29 January 2011

	Notes	2011 £m	2010 £m
ASSETS AND LIABILITIES			
Non-current assets			
Property, plant and equipment	9	592.4	577.2
Intangible assets	10	46.5	47.4
Interests in associates	11	5.1	4.0
Other investments	12	1.0	1.0
Defined benefit pension surplus	21	55.7	–
Other financial assets	15	24.3	22.7
		725.0	652.3
Current assets			
Inventories	13	368.3	309.0
Trade and other receivables	14	645.6	616.6

Other financial assets	15	**4.1**	8.6
Cash and short term deposits	16	**49.3**	107.0
		1,067.3	1,041.2
Total assets		**1,792.3**	1,693.5

Note 1. Segmental analysis

The results for the financial year are for the 52 weeks to 29 January 2011 (last year 53 weeks to 30 January 2010) with the exception of NEXT Sourcing, Ventura and certain other activities which relate to the calendar year to 31 January.

The Group's operating segments under IFRS 8 have been determined based on the management accounts reviewed by the Board of Directors. The Board assesses the performance of the operating segments based on profits before interest and tax, excluding equity settled share option charges recognised under IFRS 2 *Share Based Payments* and unrealised foreign exchange gains or losses on derivative instruments.

The activities and products and services of the operating segments are detailed in the Directors' Report on page 3 (given above). The Property Management segment holds properties which are sub-leased to other segments and external parties.

	External revenue		Internal revenue		Total revenue	
	2011 **£m**	2010 £m	**2011** **£m**	2010 £m	**2011** **£m**	2010 £m
NEXT Retail	**2,222.1**	2,274.2	**6.4**	5.2	**2,228.5**	2,279.4
NEXT Directory	**935.5**	873.2	-	-	**935.5**	873.2
NEXT International	**67.3**	64.2	-	-	**67.3**	64.2
NEXT Sourcing	**4.1**	3.5	**505.7**	529.9	**509.8**	533.4
NEXT Brand	**3,229.0**	3,215.1	**512.1**	535.1	**3,741.1**	3,750.2
Ventura	**156.0**	145.6	**4.6**	4.3	**160.6**	149.9
Property Management	**6.9**	6.3	**186.5**	181.9	**193.4**	188.2
Total segment revenues	**3,391.9**	3,367.0	**703.2**	721.3	**4,095.1**	4088.3
Other	**61.8**	39.5	**4.4**	2.8	**66.2**	42.3
Eliminations	-	-	**(707.6)**	(724.1)	**(707.6)**	(724.1)
	3,453.7	3,406.5	-	-	**3,453.7**	3406.5

Other revenues comprise sales by Lipsy and third party distribution activities.

(continued)

(continued)

	Segment profit	
	2011 £m	2010 £m
NEXT Retail	328.8	324.0
NEXT Directory	221.9	183.6
NEXT International	5.8	1.2
NEXT Sourcing	26.7	35.7
NEXT Brand	583.2	544.5
Ventura	8.0	6.0
Property Management	2.3	0.3
Total segment profit	593.5	550.8
Other activities (including central costs)	(10.9)	(13.2)
Share option charge	(11.8)	(9.4)
Unrealised foreign exchange gain	2.2	0.7
Trading profit	573.0	528.9
Share of results of associates	1.8	0.9
Finance income	0.9	0.8
Finance costs	(24.3)	(25.3)
Profit before tax	551.4	505.3

Transactions between operating segments are made on an arm's length basis in a manner similar to those with third parties.

Segment revenue and segment profit include transactions between business segments; these transactions are eliminated on consolidation.

	Property, plant and equipment		Capital expenditure		Depreciation	
	2011 £m	2010 £m	2011 £m	2010 £m	2011 £m	2010 £m
NEXT Retail	488.2	473.5	131.8	83.8	109.1	112.0
NEXT Directory	5.1	4.3	2.5	1.0	1.7	1.3
NEXT International	2.4	3.2	1.4	4.8	1.0	1.2
NEXT Sourcing	4.2	3.9	1.7	1.0	1.6	1.7
NEXT Brand	499.9	484.9	137.4	90.6	113.4	116.2
Ventura	11.1	12.7	2.2	2.4	3.5	5.2
Property Management	72.0	74.2	0.1	–	0.2	0.2
Other	9.4	5.4	4.6	5.6	1.3	0.7
Total	592.4	577.2	144.3	98.6	118.4	122.3

Analyses of the Group's external revenues (by customer location) and non-current assets (excluding investments, the defined benefit pension surplus, other financial assets and deferred tax assets) by geographical location are detailed below:

	External revenue		Non-current assets	
	2011 £m	2010 £m	2011 £m	2010 £m
United Kingdom	3,261.2	3,228.5	581.1	565.6
Rest of Europe	153.5	143.1	21.3	22.5
Middle East	21.7	23.6	4.6	4.5
Asia	9.8	9.5	31.4	32.0
Rest of World	7.5	1.8	0.5	–
	3,453.7	3,406.5	638.9	624.6

Required:

Produce an analysis of the performance of NEXT plc for the year ended 29 January 2011 using the segmental information as far as possible in this analysis.

Visit the Online Resource Centre for solutions to all these end of chapter questions plus visual walkthrough solutions. You can test your understanding with extra questions and answers, explore additional case studies based on real companies, take a guided tour through a company report, and much more. Go to the Online Resource Centre at www.oxfordtextbooks.co.uk/orc/maynard/

7

Revenue

➤ Introduction

Revenue is a key figure in any business's financial statements, widely used as a measure of the size of a business and in any assessment of its performance and prospects. Any misstatement of revenue has a significant impact on profit or loss. US studies have shown that over half of all financial statement frauds and restatements of previously published financial information have involved revenue manipulation. It is therefore important that the principles behind the recognition and measurement of revenue are applied consistently if financial statements are to present fairly the true economic activity of a business. This is particularly so given the complexities of modern business transactions.

International Accounting Standard (IAS) 18 *Revenue* is the current accounting standard to be applied when determining how and when revenue should be recognised, and IAS 11 *Construction Contracts* is applicable for the accounting for revenue arising from long-term construction contracts. IAS 18 sets out the principles mainly for the recognition of revenue arising from the sale of goods and the rendering of services, and provides illustrative examples of a number of different transactions.

However, the International Accounting Standards Board (IASB) has been working on a convergence project with the US Financial Accounting Standards Board (FASB) for a number of years to improve the accounting standards relevant to revenue and have produced an exposure draft (ED), *Revenue from Contracts with Customers*, for a new accounting standard which will replace both IAS 18 and IAS 11. Feedback received from the first exposure draft caused the IASB to reconsider some of its proposals; a second version of the ED was issued in November 2011. This provides a set of different principles to be applied in the recognition of revenue from IAS 18 and will apply to all contracts with customers whether short- or long-term. The final accounting standard is expected to be issued in the latter half of 2012.

This chapter discusses briefly the current accounting requirements given by IAS 18 and then considers the proposals in the latest ED.

★ Learning objectives

After studying this chapter you will be able to:

● understand the significance of revenue reporting to businesses and their users and the issues with this

● understand and apply the accounting methods for revenue recognition and measurement set out in current accounting standards IAS 18 *Revenue* and IAS 11 *Construction Contracts*

● explain the principles for revenue recognition and measurement proposed in the exposure draft ED/2011/6 *Revenue from Contracts with Customers*.

✔ Key issues checklist

❑ Definition of revenue.

❑ Key issues with revenue recognition.

❑ Accounting for revenue under IAS 18.

   ❑ Measurement of revenue.

   ❑ Fair value for interest-free credit periods.

   ❑ Recognition of revenue from the sale of goods.

   ❑ Transfer of the risks and rewards of ownership.

   ❑ Sale and repurchase agreements.

   ❑ Accounting for sales refunds.

   ❑ Recognition of revenue from the rendering of services—similarity to accounting for revenue from construction contracts according to IAS 11.

   ❑ Accounting for investment revenue—interest, dividends, and royalties.

   ❑ Other revenue raising transactions.

   ❑ Disclosures.

   ❑ Inadequacies of the accounting standard.

❑ Proposals for accounting for revenue from contracts with customers under ED/2011/6.

   ❑ Principles and five-step approach.

   ❑ Identification of the contract.

   ❑ Identification of the performance obligations.

   ❑ Recognition of revenue from the satisfaction of the performance obligations.

   ❑ Performance obligations satisfied over time.

   ❑ Performance obligations satisfied at a point in time.

   ❑ Determination of the transaction price.

   ❑ Allocation of the transaction price to the performance obligations.

   ❑ Changes in the transaction price.

   ❑ Onerous performance obligations.

   ❑ Accounting for contract costs.

   ❑ Disclosures.

☐ The effect of the ED's proposals.

☐ Current status of the revenue project.

7.1 Issues with revenue

Revenue is a topic of relevance to virtually all companies. A headline figure, it is one of the most crucial numbers used to assess a company's financial performance and position. A company's growth or contraction is often framed in terms of changes in revenue; numerous ratios employed in the interpretation of financial statements, for example net profit margin, gross margin, and asset turnover, use revenue in their calculation. Any interpretation of profit is affected by the reported revenue figures.

The issues relating to revenue recognition are explored in the following sections, but, first, revenue needs to be defined clearly.

7.1.1 Definition of revenue

Revenue is a subset of income. Income is defined in the IASB's *Conceptual Framework* as:

> . . . increases in economic benefits during the accounting period in the form of inflows or enhancements of assets or decreases of liabilities that result in increases in equity, other than those relating to contributions from equity participants.

In bookkeeping terms, an enhancement of an asset is a debit entry to an asset account; a decrease in a liability is a debit to a liability account. The other side of the double-entry must be a credit entry which results in an increase in equity. This cannot be from the shareholders, such as a share issue, so the credit to equity could arise from an increase in retained earnings or some other reserve, such as a **revaluation reserve**. (Note: revaluation reserves are discussed in detail in Chapter 10.)

Revenue is income that arises in the course of the ordinary activities of a business and includes sales, fees, royalties, rent, interest, and dividends. It excludes gains, which is the other subset of income and which includes gains from the sale of non-current assets, impairment gains, or gains from the revaluation of net assets to fair value at each statement of financial position date.

 Examples of revenue

Determine which of the following transactions gives rise to revenue and how much the revenue is in these cases.

1   A company sells goods for £1,200, including sales tax of £200.

Revenue = £1,000. Sales tax is collected by the company on behalf of the tax authorities (Revenue & Customs in the UK) and does not increase equity.

2 A company sells goods for £500 with a trade discount of £25. The customer is offered a further discount of £19 if payment is made within 30 days.

Revenue = £475. Trade discounts are netted off with selling price. Cash discounts are treated as an expense.

3 A company issues 100,000 £1 equity shares at £2 each.

Revenue = 0. This is a contribution from shareholders.

4 A manufacturing company, which is moving to a new factory, sells its old factory for £450,000.

Revenue = 0. Any profit on sale is treated as a gain in accordance with IAS 16.

7.1.2 Revenue recognition issues

One of the key issues relating to revenue is that of the timing of when it should be recognised, since under a single contract goods and services may be provided in the current and future periods. Profit is based on the underpinning accruals concept, which therefore means that revenue should be recognised in the period in which the transaction giving rise to the revenue occurs; in other words, the revenue must have been earned. This ties in to the IASB's *Conceptual Framework*, which specifies that revenue should be recognised:

> ...when it is probable that the economic benefits associated with the transaction will flow to the entity and these benefits can be measured reliably.

Consider the operating cycle for a manufacturing company as represented by Figure 7.1. The main question is at what point in this cycle revenue should be recognised?

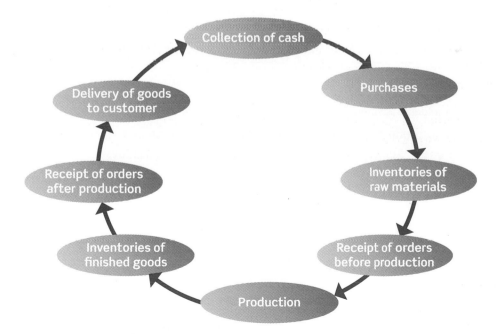

Figure 7.1 **The operating cycle for a manufacturing company**

Assuming that this figure does not relate to a long-term contract, such as a **construction contract** which spreads over a number of accounting periods, the usual point at which revenue is recognised according to the IASB's *Conceptual Framework* is when the goods are delivered to the customer. It is at this point that it is likely that economic resources will flow to the company, in other words the company will receive money. The sale price will usually have been determined by this stage, so these benefits can be measured reliably.

One way in which a company can increase its reported revenue, is to make the recognition point earlier in the cycle. This is an example of creative accounting, often referred to as aggressive earnings management.

 ## Examples of aggressive earnings management

There have been many real-life examples of companies pursuing aggressive earnings management, for example dot.com companies and Enron. In these companies revenue was recognised essentially on the promise of goods or services being delivered rather than when the goods were delivered or the services performed.

Enron also pursued other aggressive policies which related to how it measured its revenue from wholesale trading and risk-management in the supply of energy. It inflated its revenues by recording them at wholesale prices rather than just at service fee levels. The result of this was that between 1996 and 2000 Enron's revenues increased from $13.3 billion to $100.8 billion—an unprecedented rise of over 750% or 66% per year. At the time, the energy industry considered annual growth of 2–3% to be respectable.

Revenues can also be manipulated by companies which sell goods as follows:

- keeping 'the quarter open' to improve sales figures
- recording phoney sales and shipping products to, perhaps, an employee's premises where they are kept until requested by legitimate customers
- asking customers to accept additional products sooner than needed—often allowing them to delay payment beyond their usual credit period
- reducing production quality standards to meet volume goals and shipping products of poor quality knowing that they will be returned during the next quarter.

Not all companies engage in these practices, but internal control departments and auditors need to be alert to them, and design their testing accordingly to detect them and, if necessary, to advise on adjustments required to financial statements.

The arrangements businesses enter into to sell their products and services to customers have become ever more complex. One only has to consider a typical sale a telecommunications company makes, which will include any, or all, of the following elements: a mobile phone; a subscription to a particular network; calls and texts for a certain period, some of which will be 'free' to the customer and some of which, if unused, can be carried forward to another period; and various downloads, etc. The key question arising in this situation is how and when revenue should be recognised for the various elements of this transaction.

7.2 IAS 18 *Revenue*

7.2.1 Measurement of revenue

One of the criteria required for the recognition of revenue is that the economic benefits can be measured reliably. The economic benefit that flows to an entity from a revenue transaction is usually consideration in the form of cash, and the amount is generally agreed by negotiation between the seller and the buyer. Trade discounts and volume discounts are deducted from the amount of consideration. However, the accounting is more complex when long credit periods are allowed to customers or when the consideration is in a form other than cash.

IAS 18 specifies that 'the measurement of revenue should be at the fair value of the consideration received or to be received'.

ⓘ **Reminder** *Fair value is defined in IFRS 13 as 'the price that would be received to sell and asset or paid to transfer a liability in an orderly transaction between market participants at the measurement date'.*

In the case of deferred cash, the seller is effectively allowing an interest-free credit period to the buyer and the sale includes a form of financing arrangement. The fair value of the consideration is calculated by discounting the cash flows to their present value using an imputed rate of interest. The difference between the fair value and the nominal amount of the consideration is accounted for as interest revenue and recognised over the period it is earned.

 Example of accounting for revenue with an interest-free credit period

A furniture retailer sells goods to a customer for £2,500 on 1 January 20X0. Delivery will take place within 7 days and the company has given the customer an interest-free credit period of 12 months.

Required:
How would this transaction be accounted for according to IAS 18? Assume the retailer normally obtains finance at a cost of 10% per annum.

The fair value of the consideration = £2,500/1.1 = £2,273
This is recognised as the revenue from the sale of the furniture on 1 January 20X0.
The balance of £227 (£2,500 – £2,273) represents interest which is recognised over the 12-month credit period.
In terms of double-entry bookkeeping:
On 1 January 20X0

		£	£
Debit	Receivables	2,273	
Credit	Sales revenue		2,273

Interest revenue is recognised in the income statement as it is earned, probably each month, so by the end of 20X0:

		£	£
Debit	Receivables	227	
Credit	Interest revenue		227

The receivables account now has a balance of £2,500 which is cleared when the customer pays on 1 January 20X1.

When goods or services are exchanged for those of a similar nature and value, then no revenue is created (and no additional cost recorded) because all that is really taking place is the substitution of one good or service by something very similar. Such transactions are quite common in the sale of commodities like oil and milk where suppliers swap or exchange the products in order to fulfil demand in a particular location. However, when the goods or services are dissimilar, then these are transactions which generate revenue; this is measured at the fair value of the goods or services received adjusted by the amount of cash transferred.

7.2.2 Revenue transactions

If a revenue transaction has separately identifiable components, then these should be accounted for separately, and the revenue recognition and measurement criteria applied separately to each component.

 Example of the identification and accounting for separate components

On 31 March 20X0 Computing Solutions plc completes the handover of a new system to a client at an agreed price of £800,000. The price includes after-sales support for the next two years. The cost to Computing Solutions of providing this support is estimated at £48,000 per annum and the company earns a gross profit of 20% on similar support contracts. The customer pays the full £800,000 in May 20X0.

Required:
How should Computing Solutions account for this contract in its financial statements for the years ended 31 March 20X0, 20X1, and 20X2?

The sales price of £800,000 should be allocated between the sale of the equipment and the after-sales support.

Revenue from the sale of the equipment can be recognised as for the sale of goods (see section 7.2.3) when the equipment is transferred to the buyer.

The after-sales support revenue should be deferred and recognised over the next two years (i.e. years ended 31 March 20X1 and 20X2), and should include a reasonable element of profit. This can be computed by reference to similar contracts.

	£
Annual cost of providing support	48,000
Profit element 20/80 × 48,000	12,000

After-sales support revenue		60,000
Revenue to be recognised on handover of system		
Price		800,000
Less: two years of after-sales support revenue		(120,000)
		680,000

Financial statements for years ended 31 March	20X0	20X1	20X2
Income statements			
Sales revenue	680,000		
After-sales support revenue		60,000	60,000
Statements of financial position			
Current asset—receivables	800,000		
Current liability—deferred revenue	60,000	60,000	
Non-current liability—deferred revenue	60,000		

7.2.3 Revenue from the sale of goods

IAS 18 specifies five criteria, all of which have to be satisfied for revenue to be recognised from the sale of goods. These are as follows:

(a) The significant risks and rewards of ownership have been transferred from seller to buyer

(b) The seller no longer has management or control of the goods

(c) The amount of the revenue can be measured reliably

(d) It is probable that the economic benefits associated with the transaction will flow to the seller

(e) The costs incurred (or to be incurred) in respect of the transaction can be measured reliably.

The transfer of the risks and rewards of ownership is based on the 'substance over form' concept, and the question of whether they have been transferred requires all facts and circumstances of the individual sale to be considered. The risks of owning an asset may include possible losses resulting from the ultimate use of the goods or variable returns from the use of the goods as economic conditions alter. Rewards resulting from owning an asset include profitable returns or gains from an appreciation in value. However, for the majority of retail sales risks and rewards of ownership will be transferred when possession of the goods passes to the buyer or when the legal title is transferred.

If the company retains significant risks of ownership, the transaction is not deemed to be a sale and revenue is not recognised. Examples of this type of situation include the following:

- sale and repurchase agreements where on the transfer of goods to the buyer the seller concurrently agrees to repurchase the same goods at a later date

- when the seller retains some obligation for unsatisfactory performance which is outside a normal warranty cover

- if the receipt of the revenue from a particular sale depends on the buyer receiving revenue from his own sale of the goods

- when the goods are shipped subject to installation and the installation is a significant part of the contract which has not yet been completed by the seller. In this case revenue should not be recognised until the installation has been completed

- when the buyer has the right to return the goods and the seller is uncertain about the probability of the return.

 ### Example of a sale and repurchase agreement

A whisky distiller holds inventories for long periods. It sells some of its inventories to a finance company, with a binding obligation to repurchase the inventories in the future at a price equal to the repayment of original amount plus interest.

How should the distiller account for this transaction?

The legal position is that the assets have been sold. However, the commercial substance of the transaction is that the whisky distiller has retained the benefit and risks of holding the inventories. The company has also incurred an obligation according to the IASB's *Conceptual Framework* definition of a liability—effectively it has a loan on which it will pay interest. Thus, the accounting treatment is that no revenue is recognised on the transfer of goods and, instead, a liability is recorded:

Debit   Bank
  Credit   Loan liability

The appropriate amount of interest is accrued over the period of the loan. The inventories held by the finance company remain in the whisky distiller's financial statements.

It is possible for the seller to retain only an insignificant risk of ownership and for the sale and revenue to be recognised. Common examples include the following situations:

- where the seller retains title only to ensure collection of what is owed on the goods
- where an item may be returned and a refund provided.

Where refunds are a normal part of the sale transaction care needs to be taken in determining whether the sale is recognised. Compare the following two examples.

 ### Examples of sales refunds

1   Ginger plc sells goods on a 'sale or return' basis. The customer is entitled to return the goods to Ginger (and obtain a full refund) if they cannot be sold on to a third party within three months. When will the revenue be recognised?

Until they have been sold on by the customer, Ginger plc retains the risks and rewards of ownership. Revenue is recognised:

(a) Either when the goods are resold by the customer

(b) Or at the end of the three-month period if the customer chooses not to return them.

2 Blue Jeans plc, a retailer, offers a 12-month guarantee on all its products whereby a customer can return the product for whatever reason and receive a full refund. In the normal course of business it has been found that 1% per annum of sales is subject to such refunds.

When will the revenue be recognised?

In this case the retailer retains very little risk associated with the products and therefore revenue should be recognised when the sale is made. An accrual will be made for the expected returns.

The probability of the entity receiving the revenue arising from the transaction must be assessed. For example, in most cases, revenue in relation to credit sales is recognised before actual payment is received. However, where collectability is in doubt and recovery has ceased to be probable, the amount should be recognised as an expense resulting in an irrecoverable debt or a provision for doubtful debts being accounted for. Note that neither of these adjusts revenue previously recognised.

Matching of revenue and expenses is an underpinning concept in the calculation of profit meaning that revenue and expenses relating to the same transaction should be recognised at the same time. In some cases the expenses may need to be estimated at the date of sale. Where they cannot be estimated reliably, then revenue cannot be recognised and any consideration that has already been received is treated as the liability deferred revenue:

Debit   Bank
  Credit   Deferred revenue

 Example of the measurement of the costs associated with a sale

As part of its sales prices, Dixit plc, which sells electrical equipment, includes a year's warranty. When will the revenue from the sales be recognised?

The question arises whether the costs of providing the warranty can be estimated. This will include replacements or repair work carried out under the warranty. If there are past records which show the proportion of sales which result in warranty work and the costs of such work then a reliable estimate could be made of the costs, and the sale will be recognised.

Note: the accounting for the warranty is considered in detail in Chapter 13, which deals with provisions for such expenses.

7.2.4 Revenue from the rendering of services

The criteria for the recognition of revenue from a transaction involving the rendering of services, such as a maintenance contract for an item of machinery, are similar to those for the sale of goods as discussed previously. Some service arrangements spread over more than one year, for example the maintenance contract may be for a three-year period. Recognition of the revenue in this case is very similar to the accounting for a construction contract, which is addressed by IAS 11 *Construction Contracts* and discussed further in Chapter 12, with the key issue being how much revenue should be recognised in each accounting period. Payments and advances received from customers often do not reflect the services performed. As a result, it is normally inappropriate to recognise revenue based on payments received.

IAS 18 therefore specifies that if the outcome of the transaction involving the rendering of services can be estimated reliably, the associated revenue should be recognised by reference to the stage of completion of the transaction at the end of the accounting period. The outcome of a transaction can be estimated reliably when all of the following conditions are satisfied:

(a) The amount of revenue can be measured reliably

(b) It is probable that the economic benefits associated with the transaction will flow to the entity

(c) The stage of completion of the transaction at the end of the reporting period can be measured reliably

(d) The costs incurred for the transaction and the costs to complete the transaction can be measured reliably

The assessment of the stage of completion of the transaction is of key importance as this is also used to calculate the amount of revenue to be recognised in each accounting period. The following methods of assessing the stage of completion are suggested in IAS 18:

- surveys of work performed
- services performed to date as a percentage of total services to be performed
- the proportion that costs incurred to date bear to the estimated total costs of the transaction.

Companies should choose the best method that measures the revenue reliably.

If the overall outcome of a services transaction cannot be estimated reliably, then revenue is only recognised to the extent of those costs incurred that are recoverable from the customer. In other words, no profit is recognised for transactions at an early stage. However, there is no guidance as to at what stage of completion the outcome is deemed to be able to be estimated reliably. So judgement and estimates are required in the recognition of revenue from these long-term service arrangements and all circumstances would need to be considered to form these.

 Example to show revenue recognition from the rendering of services

Support Solutions plc enters into a fixed-price contract for £180,000 for the provision of services. At the end of 20X4, the first year of the contract, costs of £44,000 have been incurred and the remaining costs to complete the contract are estimated reliably at £88,000.

Required:

Calculate the revenue to be recognised in 20X4.

The project is profitable overall (total revenue £180,000, total costs £132,000), so no provision for a contract loss needs to be made.

As each of the total revenue, the costs incurred, and the remaining costs to complete can be estimated reliably, revenue can be recognised by the percentage of completion method.

The stage of completion can be calculated by using the proportion that costs incurred to date bear to the estimated total costs of the transaction = 44,000/132,000 = 33.3%

Revenue to be recognised in 20X4 = 33.3% × £180,000 = £60,000

Note: if the costs to complete the contract could not be estimated reliably, then revenue is only recognised to the extent of the costs incurred which are recoverable from the customer. In this example if all the costs incurred in 20X4 were considered recoverable, the revenue recognised would be restricted to £44,000 and no profit would be recognised.

7.2.5 Other revenue transactions

IAS 18 includes details of the accounting of some other specific investment revenue transactions—interest, dividends, and royalties—and provides further details of many other types of sources of revenue as illustrative examples (see Table 7.1). The basic principles of when revenue can be recognised apply to all of these:

Table 7.1 Other sources of revenue and their accounting treatment

Revenue source	Accounting treatment
Consignment sales	Under such arrangements, the buyer of the goods undertakes to sell them on, but on behalf of the original seller. So the buyer is effectively acting as an agent on behalf of the original seller. The original seller only recognises his/her sale when his buyer sells them on to a third party. This treatment also applies to sale and return transactions, but see previous examples.
Lay away sales	Under these arrangements the goods are only delivered once the final instalment has been received, so it is only then that the risks and rewards of ownership move from seller to buyer and revenue can be recognised.
Subscriptions to publications	Where a series of publications is subscribed to and each publication is of a similar value, for example a monthly magazine, revenue is recognised on a straight-line basis over the period in which the publications are despatched. Where the value of each publication varies, revenue is recognised on the basis of the sales value of the item despatched in relation to the estimated sales value of all items covered by the subscription.
Servicing fees included in the price of the product	When an item's sales price includes 'free' servicing, revenue in relation to that servicing should be deferred and recognised over the servicing period. The amount deferred should be sufficient to cover both the cost of servicing and a reasonable profit.
Advertising commissions	Media commissions, for example payment for a series of adverts, should be recognised when the related advertisement or commercial appears before the public.

(a) It is probable that the economic benefits associated with the transaction will flow to the entity

(b) These benefits can be measured reliably.

For investment income, the following recognition provisions apply:

1   Interest is recognised on a time proportion basis that takes into account the effective yield on the asset

2   Royalties are recognised on an accrual basis in accordance with the substance of the relevant agreement

3   Dividends are recognised when the shareholder's right to receive payment is established.

7.2.6 Disclosures

IAS 18 requires companies to disclose their accounting policies adopted for the recognition of revenue and for the amount of each significant category of revenue recognised during the period to be disclosed. In most company reports this information is already provided in the operating segment disclosure notes (see Chapter 6 for full details), so separate disclosures relating to revenue are not usually given. As discussed in Chapter 6, it is left to the companies to determine which are their significant revenue streams, which may result in comparisons between companies difficult for the user. However, IAS 18 does specify that revenue arising from the following should be disclosed:

(a) The sale of goods

(b) The rendering of services

(c) Interest

(d) Royalties

(e) Dividends

(f) Exchanges of goods or services within each category.

These disclosures may seem rather short and general, but, in practice, they can result in lengthy accounting policy notes. An example of this is given by the telecommunications company, Vodafone, in its 2011 financial statements.

| Financial reporting in practice **7.1** | Vodafone Group plc, 2011 |

Accounting policy – Revenue

Revenue is recognised to the extent the Group has delivered goods or rendered services under an agreement, the amount of revenue can be measured reliably and it is probable that the economic benefits associated with the transaction will flow to the Group. Revenue is measured at the fair value of the consideration received, exclusive of sales taxes and discounts.

The Group principally obtains revenue from providing the following telecommunication services: access charges, airtime usage, messaging, interconnect fees, data services and information provision, connection fees and equipment sales. Products and services may be sold separately or in bundled packages.

Revenue for access charges, airtime usage and messaging by contract customers is recognised as services are performed, with unbilled revenue resulting from services already provided accrued at the end of each period and unearned revenue from services to be provided in future periods deferred. Revenue from the sale of prepaid credit is deferred until such time as the customer uses the airtime, or the credit expires.

Revenue from interconnect fees is recognised at the time the services are performed.

Revenue from data services and information provision is recognised when the Group has performed the related service and, depending on the nature of the service, is recognised either at the gross amount billed to the customer or the amount receivable by the Group as commission for facilitating the service.

Customer connection revenue is recognised together with the related equipment revenue to the extent that the aggregate equipment and connection revenue does not exceed the fair value of the equipment delivered to the customer. Any customer connection revenue not recognised together with related equipment revenue is deferred and recognised over the period in which services are expected to be provided to the customer.

Revenue for device sales is recognised when the device is delivered to the end customer and the sale is considered complete. For device sales made to intermediaries, revenue is recognised if the significant risks associated with the device are transferred to the intermediary and the intermediary has no general right of return. If the significant risks are not transferred, revenue recognition is deferred until sale of the device to an end customer by the intermediary or the expiry of the right of return.

In revenue arrangements including more than one deliverable, the arrangements are divided into separate units of accounting. Deliverables are considered separate units of accounting if the following two conditions are met: (1) the deliverable has value to the customer on a standalone basis and (2) there is evidence of the fair value of the item. The arrangement consideration is allocated to each separate unit of accounting based on its relative fair value.

7.2.7 Criticisms of IAS 18

Although IAS 18 and IAS 11 set out broad principles for the recognition of revenue and provide some illustrative examples, between them they contain limited guidance on some topics. The guidance that is provided can be difficult to apply to complex transactions and some companies have turned to US GAAP to supplement the guidance. US generally accepted accounting principles (GAAP) contains numerous industry-specific requirements, but these can result in economically similar transactions being accounted for differently. Thus, much diversity in the recognition of revenue exists which is not helpful for users in using this all-important figure in their understanding and interpretation of financial statements.

In addition, some users have criticised the disclosure requirements as being inadequate for them to fully understand the estimates and judgements made by companies in recognising their revenues. In particular, they are concerned that the information disclosed is often of a 'boilerplate' nature, in other words formulaic and not specific to the particular company.

The IASB and US FASB have been working together since 2002 on a convergence project on revenue recognition. The aim is to produce a principles based approach which will make it easier to account for and analyse all situations giving rise to revenue. An ED for a new accounting standard to replace both IAS 18 and IAS 11 was issued in June 2010, which prompted much response. Reviewers considered that it was insufficiently clear in places and may have led to anomalous figures. As a result of this, and because the IASB and FASB consider revenue to be such an important topic, the boards revised some of their proposals and reissued a new ED in November 2011.

7.3 ED 2011/6 *Revenue from Contracts with Customers*

The objective of the proposed new accounting standard is to provide a robust and comprehensive framework for the recognition, measurement, and disclosure of revenue and some contract costs which will be applicable to, and therefore comparable, across all industries. Revenue is affected particularly by new commercial practices, which has given rise in the past to the development of case-by-case guidance and the new ED aims to reduce this need. It also aims to provide more useful information to users of financial statements through improved disclosure requirements.

The definition of revenue is not altered by these proposals. Also, the basic principle of revenue recognition is the same as the current IASs 18 and 11, in that revenue should be recognised as it delivers goods and services to a customer; however, the proposals remove the distinction between goods and services. The measurement of revenue should reflect the consideration which the seller expects to be entitled in exchange for the goods or services.

In order to achieve these principles a five-step approach should be applied to all contracts with customers as shown in Figure 7.2.

The first, second, and fifth steps deal with recognition, and the third and fourth steps are concerned with measurement. Discussion of these steps takes recognition first followed by measurement matters.

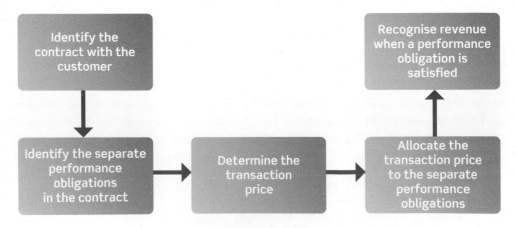

Figure 7.2 Five-step approach to the recognition of revenue

7.3.1 Identification of the contract with the customer

The new accounting standard would apply to all contracts with customers except those dealt with by other standards, such as leases, insurance contracts, and those within the scope of financial instruments. Essentially, a contract is an agreement between two parties that creates enforceable rights and obligations, with enforceability being determined by law. The contract may be written, oral, or implied by the business's customary practices. Contracts would mainly be accounted for individually unless they are clearly commercially related or dependent upon another, in which case contracts would be combined and accounted for as a single contract. There is also guidance for the case of modification of an existing contract to determine whether this constitutes a new contract or if the changes should be combined with what remains of the modified contract.

7.3.2 Identification of the separate performance obligations in the contract

The determination of the separate performance obligations in a contract is a key issue of the proposals as revenue is to be recognised when a performance obligation is satisfied. A performance obligation in a contract is a promise to transfer a good or a service to the customer. If the relevant goods or services are distinct, in other words if they are regularly sold separately or the customer benefits from their separate delivery, then the promised goods or services transfer is a separate performance obligation. However, the goods or services transferred may be highly interrelated or modified in accordance with the particular contract. In this case the goods and services are bundled together, and their promised transfer is treated as a single performance obligation.

 Examples of separate or bundled performance obligations

1   A company licences customer relationship management software to a customer. In addition, the contract promises to provide consulting services to significantly customise the software to the customer's information technology environment. The total consideration for the licence and the consulting services is £600,000.

   In this case the company is integrating the goods and services (the licence and the consulting services) into a combined item for which the customer has contracted. In addition, the software is customised significantly by the company in accordance with the specifications negotiated with the customer. Hence, the company would account for the licence and consulting services together as one performance obligation.

2   A company enters into a contract to design and build a hospital. The company is responsible for the overall management of the project and identifies various goods and services to be provided, including engineering, site clearance, foundation, procurement, construction of the building, piping and wiring, installation of equipment, and finishing.

The company would account for the bundle of goods and services as a single performance obligation because the goods or services are highly interrelated. Providing them to the customer also requires the company to provide a significant service of integrating the goods or services into the combined item—the hospital—for which the customer has contracted. In addition, the goods or services are modified significantly and customised to fulfil the contract.

7.3.3 Satisfaction of a performance obligation

Revenue is to be recognised when a performance obligation is satisfied so this step includes a number of important issues. The first issue dealt with is that the satisfaction is determined when the goods or services are transferred to the customer, and this is defined as when the customer obtains control of the goods or services. To help with the practical application of determining whether control is transferred, the second important issue is that a distinction is made between transfer either over time or at a point in time.

The transfer of control basis for the recognition of revenue has been generally accepted by respondents to the first ED as being appropriate. The 2011 ED contains guidance as to how this may be determined. Essentially, control is obtained if the buyer obtains the ability to use and obtain all of the benefits of receiving the goods or services. It also includes the ability to prevent other entities from using the goods or benefitting from the services. For many straightforward sales of goods where the current IAS 18 requires transfer of the significant risks and rewards of ownership for the recognition of revenue, the transfer of control will be the same in practice.

 Example of when control has transferred

A company enters into a contract to sell a product to a customer. The company uses a third-party carrier to deliver the product. The delivery terms of the contract are free on board shipping point, in other words legal title to the product passes to the customer when the product is handed over to the carrier. In accordance with the company's past business practices, it will provide the customer with a replacement product, at no additional cost, if a product is damaged or lost while in transit. The company has determined that its past business practices of replacing damaged products has implicitly created a performance obligation.

Here, the company has two performance obligations:

(i) to provide the customer with a product

(ii) to cover the risk of loss during transit.

The customer obtains control of the product at the point of shipment. Although it does not have physical possession of the product at that point, it has legal title and therefore can sell the product to or exchange it with another party. The company is also precluded from selling the product to another customer. The company would allocate a portion of the transaction price to the performance obligation to deliver the product and recognise this when the goods were handed over to the carrier.

The additional performance obligation for risk coverage does not affect when the customer obtains control of the product. However, it does result in the customer receiving a service from the entity while the product is in transit. Hence, the entity has not satisfied all of its performance obligations at the point of shipment. The remaining portion of the transaction price allocated to the performance obligation to provide risk coverage would be recognised as revenue as that performance obligation is satisfied.

Control may be transferred over time or at a point in time and therefore revenue is recognised over time or at a particular point. The ED provides provisions and guidance for control being transferred over time and companies need to determine whether these apply. If these are not fulfilled, then the performance obligation is deemed to be satisfied at a point in time.

7.3.4 Performance obligations satisfied over time

The transfer of control of goods or services over time will relate mainly to contracts for the construction of assets and the provision of services over time. There are two criteria; if either one of which is satisfied, revenue is recognised over time.

(a) The performance creates or enhances an asset (e.g. work in progress) that the customer controls

(b) The performance does not create an asset with alternative use to the company, and one of the following conditions is met:

   (i) The customer simultaneously receives and consumes the benefits as the company performs

   (ii) Another entity would not need to substantially re-perform the work if it took over part way through

   (iii) The company has the right to payment for performance completed to date and expects to fulfil the contract as promised.

An asset has alternative use if, both practically and contractually, it could be supplied to another customer.

The aim of recognising revenue over time is to depict the selling company's performance. This is achieved by selecting a method to measure the progress towards complete satisfaction of the relevant performance obligation. The method should be applied consistently to all similar circumstances and performance obligations. Specific methods are not given, but the ED includes discussion of what it terms output and input methods.

Output methods measure the progress towards the performance obligation on the basis of the value to the customer of the goods or services transferred, such as a survey of work completed to date or a milestone reached. These may provide the best method for measuring revenue, but, practically, may be difficult to achieve as relevant information may not be available. Input methods measure the progress towards the performance obligation on the basis of the selling company's efforts, such as resources consumed, labour hours worked, or costs incurred. These methods are easier to use, but may not relate directly to the transfer of control of goods or services to the customer.

The measurement of progress must be reasonably reliable. If significant information is unavailable, then revenue may not be able to be recognised. If the reasonably reliable test is not met, but costs incurred are expected to be recoverable, then revenue is recognised to the extent of these costs.

 Example of measuring the progress towards satisfaction of a performance obligation

A company enters into a contract with a customer to construct a building for £15 million over 2 years. The company estimates the total costs of the construction at £12 million. Assume, as discussed in a previous example, the contract is a single performance obligation because all of the promised goods and services in the contract are highly interrelated, and the construction company integrates these into the building for which the customer has contracted.

In order for the construction company to recognise revenue as the contract progresses it has to select a method to measure the progress towards the satisfaction of the performance obligation, i.e. the completion of the building.

Surveyors may, at stages, certify the stage the construction has reached. If so, these certifications can be used as an output method. For example, at the end of the first financial year in which construction took place, suppose the surveyor certifies that the value of work complete is £5 million. This figure will be used as the revenue recognised figure for this year's financial statements.

An alternative method may be based on inputs. For example, at the end of the first financial year in which construction took place, suppose total costs of the construction project are £2.4 million. Progress towards satisfaction of the performance obligation could be measured on the basis of costs incurred relative to total costs expected to be incurred, i.e. £2.4 million/£12 million = 20%. Revenue recognised in this year would be 20% × £15 million = £3 million.

Note 1: the method chosen would have to be applied consistently to this contract.

Note 2: these methods are similar to those used currently in accounting for construction contracts under IAS 11 (see Chapter 12 for full details).

7.3.5 Performance obligations satisfied at a point in time

If a performance obligation is not satisfied over time, a company satisfies the performance obligation at a point in time. Indicators of when the transfer of control of a promised asset, and thus the satisfaction of the performance obligation, has taken place may include the following:

(a) the company has a present right to payment for the asset;

(b) the customer has legal title to the asset;

(c) the company has transferred physical possession of the asset;

(d) the customer has the significant risks and rewards of ownership of the asset; and

(e) the customer has accepted the asset.

The proposals in the ED include further details as to how sales with a right of return, sales with warranties, repurchase agreements, consignment arrangements, bill-and-hold arrangements, and other variations on basic sale contracts should be accounted for. The details focus on the principle of when control of such goods has been transferred to the customer, with the measurement of the revenue reflecting the consideration which the seller expects to be entitled in exchange for the goods.

 Example of a sale with a right of return

A company sells 100 products for £100 each. The company's customary business practice is to allow a customer to return any unused product within 30 days and receive a full refund. The cost of each product is £60.

Past sales experience indicates that for every 100 sales, three products will be returned. The company further estimates that the costs of recovering the products will be immaterial and expects that the returned products can be resold at a profit. The company considers its past experience is predictive of the amount of consideration to which it will be entitled.

Upon transfer of control of the products, the company would recognise revenue on the basis of the amount of the consideration which it is reasonably assured of collecting. Revenue for the three products that it expects to be returned would therefore not be recognised. Consequently, the company would recognise:

(a) Revenue of 97 × £100 = £9,700 for the products expected not to be returned

(b) A refund liability for 3 × £100 = £300 for the products expected to be returned

The bookkeeping for these items would be:

		£	£
Debit	Accounts receivable	10,000	
Credit	Sales revenue		9,700
Credit	Refund liability		300

(c) An asset (inventory) of 3 × £60 = £180 for its right to recover products from customers on settling the refund liability would be accounted for. Hence, the amount recognised in cost of sales for 97 products is 97 × £60 = £5,820.

7.3.6 Determination of the transaction price

The third step in the approach to revenue recognition and measurement is that of determining the transaction price. The principle underpinning the price is that it is the amount of consideration a company expects to be entitled in exchange for transferring the promised goods or services. In the majority of cases this will be the price specified in the contract. However, there are a number of situations where this may have to be adjusted.

1   The consideration may be variable because of a range of items, such as discounts, rebates, refunds, incentives, performance bonuses, penalties, contingencies, and price concessions. In these cases the company has to estimate the transaction price, either:

(a)   by calculating the expected value, in other words the sum of probability-weighted amounts for a range of possible alternative consideration amounts

(b)   by using the most likely amount, in other words the amount of consideration for the single most likely outcome.

2   The time value of money has to be taken into account where there is a significant financing component to a contract. This arises where goods or services are transferred to a customer with payment by the customer being at a much later date. The objective is to recognise revenue at an amount that reflects what it would have been if the customer had paid at the time of transfer. The assessment of whether the financing component is significant is a matter of judgement. However, for practical purposes the ED has specified that an adjustment for the time value of money need not be done if the period between the transfer of the goods or services, and the expected receipt of all, or substantially all, of the consideration is one year or less.

The discount rate to be used in any time value calculation should reflect that which would be used in a separate financing transaction between the company and its customer at the inception of the contract.

3   If consideration is promised by the customer in a form other than cash, this is measured at fair value.

4   If the company providing the goods or services pays any consideration to the customer in cash or any other non-cash form which the customer can apply against the amount it owes, then this amount reduces the transaction price. The exception to this is if this consideration is for distinct goods or services that the customer transfers to the company, which would be accounted for as a normal purchase.

The issue of how the collectability of the consideration, in other words the issue of how provisions for doubtful debts, should be accounted has undergone a change between the two versions of the ED. With the increasing emphasis on the transparency of disclosures relating to risk in financial statements and annual reports—in this case a customer's credit-risk—the latest ED requires that any provision for non-collectability should be included in profit and loss, but not as an administrative expense. Instead, it should be presented as a separate line item adjacent to the revenue line item and presumably deducted from revenue to give some form of net revenue figure. This may lead to mismatching of revenues and expenses as a provision for non-collectability may relate to revenue recognised in previous accounting periods. In addition, it will have implications for the key figure of gross profit.

7.3.7 Allocation of the transaction price to the separate performance obligations

Once the transaction price has been determined, this is then allocated to each separate performance obligation to reflect the amount that the company would expect to be entitled to in exchange for satisfying each separate performance obligation. Companies would have to use, or estimate, the standalone selling price of the goods or services underlying each separate performance obligation at the time of the inception of the contract. For example, if a company sold the goods or services relating to a particular performance obligation separately to other customers in similar circumstances, this would give a standalone selling price.

If this is not available, a number of approaches to the estimate of the standalone selling price are given in the ED, which include an adjusted market-based assessment, a cost plus margin approach, or a residual approach. The latter should only be used where the standalone price is highly variable or uncertain, and is the difference between the total contract price and the sum of the observable standalone selling prices of the other performance obligations' goods or services.

7.3.8 Changes in the transaction price

The transaction price of a contract or performance obligation may change for a variety of reasons. If there is a change in the transaction price of the contract, this is allocated to the separate performance obligations on the same basis as the allocation of the original transaction price. Any changes are accounted for in the accounting period in which the change in the transaction price occurs, essentially, as a change in estimate (see Chapter 4 for full discussion of accounting for changes in estimates). So, if the change affects amounts allocated to an already satisfied performance obligation, additional revenue or a reduction in revenue is recognised in the year the change occurs—alterations are not made retrospectively.

7.3.9 Onerous performance obligations

Note that accounting for onerous contracts is currently addressed by IAS 37 *Provisions, Contingent Liabilities and Contingent Assets*, and which is discussed in Chapter 13.

An onerous performance obligation is one which is expected to be loss-making. The issue is only relevant for performance obligations satisfied over time where the time period is expected to be greater than one year.

The proper calculation that should be performed requires:

(a) The transaction to be price allocated to the performance obligation

(b) An estimate of the lowest cost of settling the performance obligation, which is given by the lower of:

  (i) The costs directly relating to satisfying the performance obligation

  (ii) The amount the company would have to pay not to execute the performance obligation (e.g. fines and/or penalties).

If (b) exceeds (a) the performance obligation is onerous and the company should recognise a liability and corresponding expense for the excess of (b) over (a).

This is similar to current accounting given by IAS 11 for construction contracts expected to make an overall loss. If a loss is foreseen, this should be recognised immediately. (See Chapter 12 for further details.) However, the proposed accounting methods in the ED are at the performance obligation level. A contract with a customer may be profitable overall, yet the requirements are for a loss and liability to be recognised for a portion of the contract.

7.3.10 Contract costs

Although this ED is concerned mainly with revenue recognition and measurement, it is due to replace IAS 11 *Construction Contracts*, which specifies the accounting methods for all aspects of a construction contracts, including their costs. The proposed new standard therefore includes a section which deals with contract costs.

The costs incurred by a company to fulfil a contract are recognised as an asset (work in progress or another asset, such as property, plant and equipment, or inventories) if all of the following criteria are met:

(a) the costs relate directly to a contract (or a specific anticipated contract);

(b) the costs generate or enhance resources of the company that will be used in satisfying performance obligations in the future; and

(c) the costs are expected to be recovered.

These costs include direct materials and labour, allocation of overhead costs that relate directly to the contract, such as management time, insurance, depreciation of tools and equipment, and incremental costs of obtaining a contract.

Costs which must be expensed when incurred include general administrative costs, costs of waste, and any costs relating to performance obligations that have already been satisfied, in other words costs relating to past performance.

Costs that are recognised as an asset are expensed (the ED uses the term amortised) on a systematic basis consistent with the pattern of transfer of the goods or services to which the asset relates. So, costs are recognised in profit and loss either over time or at a point in time.

If the carrying amount of any asset exceeds the consideration that the company expects to receive in exchange for the goods and services to which the asset relates, the asset amount is reduced, and the company recognises an impairment loss in profit and loss:

Debit   Impairment loss

 Credit   Work in progress asset

7.3.11 Disclosures

The proposed disclosures are more extensive and specific than the current disclosures required by IASs 18 and 11. Although the feedback received by IASB from preparers and auditors of financial statements was that the requirements may result in voluminous disclosures and possibly useful information for a company's competitors, the users of financial statements were broadly supportive of the requirements. The aim of the proposed disclosures is to help users understand the nature, timing, amount, and uncertainty of revenue and cash flows arising from contracts with customers, and the risks associated with future revenues.

To achieve this, a company would be required to disclose quantitative and qualitative information about the following:

(a) Its contracts with customers, including a reconciliation of contract balances. This would include a breakdown of revenue into categories to show how revenue is affected by economic factors, information about the company's performance obligations and details of any that are onerous. The reconciliation would include information to enable users to understand the changes from the opening to the closing balances.

(b) The significant judgements, and changes in judgements, made in applying the proposed requirements to those contracts. At a minimum this should include judgements relating to the timing of the satisfaction of performance obligations, and the transaction price and amounts allocated to performance obligations.

(c) Any assets recognised from the costs to obtain or fulfil a contract with a customer. This should include a reconciliation of the opening and closing balances of assets recognised from the costs incurred to fulfil a contract.

7.3.12 Effect of ED 2011/6 *Revenue from Contracts with Customers*

It is difficult to be precise about how the proposals will affect different companies and industries, but many companies will probably find that the provisions contained in the ED will not fundamentally change how they currently recognise revenue. For the sale of goods under straightforward contracts, revenue recognition currently depends on the transfer to the customer of the significant risks and rewards of ownership. The ED bases revenue recognition on the transfer of control, using the transfer of the risks and rewards as one indicator of this. In practice, the effect may be the same.

For services, under IAS 18, revenue recognition depends on the stage of completion of the contract. The ED would use the transfer of control model with revenue recognised over time. In practice, the effect may be similar, although there could be some significant differences, for example relating to set-up activities.

For construction contracts (see Chapter 12), under IAS 11 revenue recognition depends on the stage of completion of the contract activity. The ED would base revenue recognition on the transfer of control to the customer with revenue probably recognised over time. In practice, the effect may be the same, which is likely to please companies in the construction industry.

There may be changes to how some warranties are currently accounted for (for a full discussion of this see Chapter 13).

🛈 **Reminder** *Currently a liability is set up for the expected costs of fulfilling the warranty arrangement.*

The nature of warranties can vary significantly across industries and contracts with some providing assurance that the product complies with certain specifications and others providing the customer with a service in addition to this assurance. The nature of the warranty needs to be examined carefully to determine whether it should be accounted for as a separate performance obligation.

If so, the contract price would need to be allocated to this performance obligation, with the resulting effect that revenue would be deferred until the performance obligation were satisfied. If the customer has the option to purchase the warranty separately, then the promised warranty would be accounted for as a separate performance obligation. However, it is less clear whether a warranty provides the customer with a service and thus should be accounted for as a separate performance obligation; the ED suggests some factors which may indicate this.

If the warranty is not categorised as a separate performance obligation, it will be accounted for in accordance with IAS 37.

Companies in the telecommunications industry may be particularly affected. In addition, suppliers of high-tech equipment may have to consider carefully whether they are supplying a bundle of elements or multiple elements.

Example of industries which may be affected by the ED's proposals

1   A company in the telecommunications sector sells a smartphone and a two-year data plan to a customer under a single contract. It may have to change the way it allocates the price between the smartphone and the data plan, and the timing of when it recognises the revenue.

2   A company supplies a major software product together with associated services, such as customisation and integration, and a support package. The company will need to consider whether the separate elements are distinct performance obligations or whether the different elements can be bundled together into one performance obligation.

The IASB and FASB are currently reviewing comments received on this ED. The core principles are unlikely to change, but there are a number of areas that the boards have indicated they will review or provide further clarification on, including performance obligations satisfied over time, customer credit risk and collectability, the measurement of revenue where the consideration is variable, and onerous performance obligations. The final new accounting standard is expected shortly.

Summary of key points

Revenue is income which arises in the course of the ordinary activities of a business. It is a key headline figure for the majority of businesses, and used widely in users' interpretation and assessment of the business. The main issue in accounting for revenue is determining when it should be recognised.

Accounting for revenue is currently specified by IAS 18 *Revenue* with the requirements for revenue from construction contracts set out in IAS 11 *Construction Contracts*. IAS 18 sets out broad principles underpinning revenue recognition and measurement, and provides examples to illustrate how a few of the multitude of revenue contracts and arrangements that exist in today's complex global business environment should be accounted for. This guidance is considered somewhat limited.

According to IAS 18, revenue should only be recognised if the economic benefits can be measured reliably. It should be measured at the fair value of the consideration received or to be received. Revenue from the sale of goods is recognised mainly on the basis of the transfer of the risks and rewards of ownership, with revenue from the rendering of services recognised by reference to the stage of completion of the transaction at the end of the particular accounting period. This latter method of revenue recognition also applies to construction contracts according to IAS 11. Full discussion of accounting for construction contracts is given in Chapter 12.

Diverse and inconsistent revenue recognition practices have arisen and IASs 18 and 11 are currently considered to be inadequate to deal with these. The IASB and FASB have been working on a convergence project for a number of years to replace both these standards and the many US industry-specific guidance documents, and have issued a second version of an exposure draft on revenues from contracts with customers. The boards' wish is to produce a standard that will be wide enough to encompass the myriad diverse business arrangements that give rise to revenue. The proposals remove the distinction between revenue from the sale of goods and services, and construction contracts. The main principles underpinning, and the approach to accounting for, revenue are unlikely to change in the final accounting standard when this is finally published.

The proposals are for a five-step approach to revenue recognition and measurement. This requires a contract with a customer to be broken down into performance obligations, which are separately identifiable transfers of goods and services. The contract price is allocated to these performance obligations and revenue is recognised when a performance obligation has been satisfied. The satisfaction can be over time, when a suitable method for determining how revenue can be measured to reflect the performance of the selling company needs to be determined, or it is at a point in time. The amount at which revenue is recognised is based on the consideration which the seller expects to be entitled in exchange for the goods or services.

The ED also requires increased quantitative and narrative disclosures of the nature, timing, amount, and uncertainty of revenue and cash flows arising from contracts with customers, with an emphasis on the risks associated with future revenues. These disclosure proposals have been broadly welcomed by users of financial statements.

Further reading

IASB (International Accounting Standards Board) (2004a) IAS 18 *Revenue*. London: IASB.

IASB (International Accounting Standards Board) (2004b) IAS 11 *Construction Contracts*. London: IASB.

IASB (International Accounting Standards Board) (2011) Exposure Draft ED/2011/6 *Revenue from Contracts with Customers*. London: IASB.

Bibliography

Barden, P. (2012) *Revenue Recognition: One Step Further Towards a Converged Standard.* London: ICAEW By All Accounts.

IASB (International Accounting Standards Board) (2004a) IAS 18 *Revenue*. London: IASB.

IASB (International Accounting Standards Board) (2004b) IAS 11 *Construction Contracts*. London: IASB.

IASB (International Accounting Standards Board) (2011a) Exposure Draft ED/2011/6 *Revenue from Contracts with Customers*. London: IASB.

IASB (International Accounting Standards Board) (2011b) Exposure Draft ED/2011/6 *Revenue from Contracts with Customers*. Illustrative examples. London: IASB.

IASB (International Accounting Standards Board) (2011c) Exposure Draft ED/2011/6 *Revenue from Contracts with Customers*. Basis for conclusions. London: IASB.

IASB (International Accounting Standards Board) (2011d) Revised Exposure Draft Snapshot: *Revenue from Contracts with Customers*. London: IASB.

ICAEW (Institute of Chartered Accountants in England and Wales) (2012) *Revenue from Contracts with Customers FAQ*. London: ICAEW.

O'Donovan, B. (2011) *Recognise the Impact of Revenue Changes*. Available at: http://www.accountancyage.com (accessed 10 October 2012).

Vodafone Group plc (2011) *Annual Report, 2011*. Newbury: Vodafone.

 Questions

● **Quick test**

1   On 1 January 20X3 Furniture Warehouse plc sells a lounge suite to a customer for £2,000 with the amount being payable on 31 December 20X5. If the customer had paid in full on 1 January 20X3, the purchase price would have been £1,500.

Assuming an effective rate of interest of 10% per annum, and in accordance with IAS 18 *Revenue*, how would this transaction be accounted for in the financial statements of Furniture Warehouse plc for the years ended 31 December 20X3, 20X4, and 20X5?

2   Warwick Publishers plc commenced publication of a monthly magazine on 1 March 20X1, which it sells for £5 per issue. The company had received £54,000 in annual subscriptions by 30 June 20X1 and had produced 4 issues.

How should the company account for the annual subscription income in its financial statements for the year ended 30 June 20X1?

3   Grier plc sells computer software to Amos Ltd on 1 April 20X7 for £1.8 million, a price which includes the provision of a support service for 2 years. The total cost to Grier plc of providing this service is estimated at £150,000. Grier plc usually earns a gross margin of 25% on such contracts.

How should this transaction be accounted for in the income statement of Grier plc for the year ended 31 December 20X7 and the statement of financial position at that date according to IAS 18 *Revenue*?

●● Develop your understanding

4 Triad plc has a 31 December year end. The company sells goods to a customer on 1 January 20X7 on the understanding that the customer will pay £5,000 immediately and will then pay two further instalments of £5,000 each on 1 January 20X8 and 1 January 20X9.

Required:

Applying the provisions of IAS 18 *Revenue*, and assuming an effective interest rate of 10% p.a., calculate the amount of revenue that should be recognised in the years 20X7, 20X8, and 20X9, and the resulting accounting treatment of this transaction for the years ended 31 December 20X7, 20X8, and 20X9.

5 On 1 July 20X5, Morse plc sells goods worth £800,000 to Lewis plc for £500,000. The sales agreement states that Morse plc is entitled to repurchase the goods on 30 June 20X8 for £500,000 plus compound interest calculated at 10% per annum and it is expected that repurchase will, in fact, occur.

Required:

(a) Explain how the concept of substance over form applies to the sale of goods under IAS 18 *Revenue*.

(b) Discuss how Morse plc should account for this transaction on 1 July 20X5 according to IAS 18.

6 Priestly Bakers plc operates its retail outlets on a franchise basis. On 1 January 20X0 a new outlet was opened with a four-year franchise arrangement. The franchisee paid a fee of £600,000 to cover the initial services and with an additional annual fee of £90,000 commencing on 1 January 20X0 to cover marketing, managerial, and other support services provided by Priestly during the franchise period. Priestly has estimated that the cost of providing these services is £120,000 per annum and marks up other similar service contracts by 25%.

Required:

Discuss how this transaction would be accounted for in Priestly Baker plc's financial statements for the year ended 31 December 20X0.

7 Rightstore plc is a retailer that operates a customer loyalty programme. For every pound that a customer spends in any of the company's stores, they receive one point. Once a customer has accrued 1,000 points they are entitled to buy a free product to the value of £100 from any of Rightstore's department stores.

During August 20X8, the total sales price of items sold to loyalty card holders is £6,500. Prior experience has shown that 10% of customers do not redeem their points before they expire.

Required:

Show how Rightstore plc should account for the cash received of £6,500 in the month of August 20X8 according to IAS 18 *Revenue*.

●●● Take it further

8 Triangle plc is in the process of preparing its draft financial statements for the year to 31 March 20X2.

On 1 April 20X1 Triangle sold maturing inventory that had a carrying value of £3 million (at cost) to Factorall, a finance house, for £5 million. Its estimated market value at this date was in excess of £5 million. The inventory will not be ready for sale until March 20X3 and will remain on Triangle's premises until this date.

The sale contract includes a clause allowing Triangle to repurchase the inventory at any time up to 31 March 20X5 at a price of £5 million plus interest of 10% p.a. compounded from 1 April 20X1. The inventory will incur storage costs until maturity. The cost of storage for the current year of £300,000 has been included in trade receivables (in the name of Factorall). If Triangle chooses not to repurchase the inventory, Factorall will pay the accumulated storage costs on 31 March 20X5.

The proceeds of the sale have been debited to the bank and the sale has been included in Triangle's sales revenue.

Required:

Discuss how this item should be treated in Triangle's financial statements for the year ended 31 March 20X2 in accordance with IAS 18 *Revenue*. Your answer should quantify amounts where possible.

9   On 1 April 20X3, Bright Solutions plc, a company which provides industrial cleaning services, entered into an 18-month contract with a new customer. The contract price was agreed at £525,000 and total contract costs were estimated to be £400,000. The accounting policy of Bright Solutions is to consider the outcome of contracts to be capable of reliable estimation when they are at least 20% complete.

At 31 December 20X3 amounts relating to the contract were as follows.

	£
Certified sales value of work completed	367,500
Contract costs incurred	300,000
Invoices raised to customer	325,000
Progress payments received	287,500
Estimate of additional costs to complete contract	150,000

Required:

(a) Explain, with calculations where appropriate, how the amounts in respect of this contract should be presented in the income statement and statement of financial position of Bright Solutions plc for the year to 31 December 20X3 if the stage of completion of the contract is calculated with reference to:

(i)   Contract costs incurred as a proportion of total estimated contract costs

(ii) The certified sales value of the work completed as a proportion of the total contract price.

(b) Explain briefly why the two accounting policies result in different amounts in the 20X3 financial statements.

10 Just before the end of the financial year, a customer requested Murray plc to delay the delivery of 500,000 units of products until early the following year because, at the time, the customer did not have enough space to store the goods. The customer, however, indicated to Murray that it could still issue the invoice as if the goods had been delivered at the date specified in the purchase order and he agreed to settle the amount within 90 days of the invoice date under

the usual credit terms granted to him. Murray plc invoiced the customer before the year ended 31 December 20X8.

Pinkerton plc operates a logistics company. Customers place their orders with the company for airfreight or surface transportation services required. Pinkerton, in turn, places its order with the necessary carriers. Pinkerton can cancel its order with the carrier if its customers cancel their orders with the company. Pinkerton does not bear the risk of loss or other responsibility during the transportation process. Pinkerton can normally earn a margin of 10% on airfreight and 5% on surface transportation. The company's customers usually pay the gross amount to Pinkerton directly, while it pays the gross amount to the carriers.

Required:

Determine how the transactions of Murray plc and Pinkerton plc should be accounted for in accordance with IAS 18 *Revenue* in terms of the timing of recognition and the amounts to be included in their income statements.

Visit the Online Resource Centre for solutions to all these end of chapter questions plus visual walkthrough solutions. You can test your understanding with extra questions and answers, explore additional case studies based on real companies, take a guided tour through a company report, and much more. Go to the Online Resource Centre at **www.oxfordtextbooks.co.uk/orc/maynard/**

8

Earnings per share

➤ Introduction

Earnings per share (EPS) has been introduced in Chapter 5 as one of the key ratios that equity investors will use to assess the performance of a company and the return to them. As a component of the price earnings ratio, EPS is considered so important that it is required to be disclosed on the face of the statement of comprehensive income. For these reasons it is crucial that there is consistency in its calculation from company to company; it therefore, has its own international accounting standard (IAS), IAS 33 *Earnings per share*.

The main focus of this standard is the denominator of the EPS ratio, the number of shares used in its calculation, particularly where there are changes in equity share capital during the accounting period. Diluted EPS, which takes into account the future reduction or dilution of EPS from potential ordinary shares which are outstanding, is also dealt with by IAS 33, to ensure consistency in its calculation and related disclosures.

★ Learning objectives

After studying this chapter you will be able to:

- explain the significance of basic and diluted EPS as a measure of financial performance
- calculate basic and diluted EPS for a variety of situations, including changes in share capital, and where share options and convertible financial instruments exist
- understand the presentation and disclosure requirements for EPS.

✔ Key issues checklist

- ☐ Definition of basic EPS.
- ☐ The importance of EPS and its significance in relation to the price earnings ratio.
- ☐ The need for, and aims of, IAS 33 *Earnings per Share*.
- ☐ Definition and criticisms of earnings used in EPS.
- ☐ Alternative earnings figures.
- ☐ Different types of preference shares.
- ☐ The calculation of basic EPS where there are changes in share capital from issues and repurchases of shares at market price, bonus issues, and rights issues.
- ☐ What diluted EPS is.
- ☐ The calculation of diluted EPS where share options and warrants, convertible financial instruments, and contingently issuable shares exist.
- ☐ Dilutive and anti-dilutive potential shares and the effect on the calculation of diluted EPS.
- ☐ Presentation of EPS on the face of the statement of comprehensive income.
- ☐ Disclosures required.
- ☐ Proposed changes to IAS 33 *Earnings per Share*.

8.1 Earnings per share (EPS)

8.1.1 Definition

EPS is one of a number of measures that equity investors use to assess the performance of a company. It provides a measure of the earnings that are attributable (or available) to the ordinary shareholders on a per share basis. **Basic EPS** is given by the ratio:

$$\frac{\text{Profit / (Loss) attributable to ordinary equity holders}}{\text{Number of ordinary shares outstanding during the period}}$$

The profit or loss attributable to ordinary equity holders includes *all* items of income and expense recognised in an accounting period, and is after tax and after any preference dividends. It can be viewed as what is left for the ordinary shareholders after all other investors have had what is due to them. If there is a profit remaining, a company can use this to pay a dividend to its ordinary shareholders or retain for reinvestment. Thus, EPS is a measure of the wealth-creating abilities of a company.

8.1.2 Why is EPS important?

EPS is the denominator in the price earnings (PE) ratio:

$$\frac{\text{Market price per share}}{\text{Earnings per share}}$$

which, for listed companies, is published daily in the financial press. As discussed in Chapter 5, the PE ratio is a measure of the market's confidence in a company as it compares the price investors are required to pay to acquire an ordinary share in the company to the current earnings per share. Confidence can arise for a variety of reasons; examples include a company's past successes, or the fact that it has launched a new product or service, or has entered into new markets, or has completed a successful takeover. Confidence is not measurable from merely looking at the market price of shares or even from EPS on its own.

 Example of the use of the PE ratio

The following information is available for companies A and B, which both have £1 ordinary share capital:

	Company A	Company B
EPS	13.5p	9.2p
Market price per share	£1.14	£1.05

Both EPS and the market price per share are higher for company A, which may lead to a conclusion that company A has performed better and whose shares are more in demand compared to company B. However, a calculation of the PE ratio for both companies reveals:

	Company A	Company B
PE ratio	$\frac{114}{13.5} = 8.4$	$\frac{105}{9.2} = 11.4$

The PE ratio for company B is considerably higher, which means that investors are willing to pay 11.4 times the current earnings in this company compared with only 8.4 times to invest in company A. This indicates that the markets, in general, consider that company B's future prospects and earnings potential are better than company A—possibly for the sorts of reasons given earlier.

Of course, the PE ratio is not necessarily a true or accurate measure as market confidence, which affects share prices, can be misplaced.

Financial reporting in practice 8.1   the dot.com boom

In the late 1990s a new group of Internet-based companies were founded, which were commonly referred to as dot.com companies. Initially, these companies provided their services for free and therefore had little revenue as they were all about growing market share. The promise was that they could build enough brand awareness to charge profitable rates for their services later. It was all about 'getting big fast'.

A combination of a variety of factors at that time, including apparently realistic plans that the companies would eventually be profitable, low interest rates, the wide availability of capital from venture capitalists, and the pure novelty of such companies, created an environment in which many investors were willing to overlook traditional financial measures to assess companies, such as the PE ratio, in favour of confidence in technological advancements. Share prices in the dot.com companies rose and rose.

However, by 1999–2000 Western economies' growth began to slow down, interest rates began to rise, and share prices on stock markets started to fall. The dot.com boom was over, and many of these companies ceased trading as they had no profits and they ran out of cash.

8.1.3 The need for an accounting standard

A reliable and consistent calculation of EPS for companies is vital to ensure that there is some degree of reliability and comparability between companies' PE ratios. IAS 33 *Earnings per Share* was therefore issued with the aims of:

- prescribing the principles for the determination and presentation of EPS
- improving comparisons of performance between different companies in the same reporting period and between different reporting periods for the same company.

The standard recognises that EPS has limitations because of the different accounting policies that may be used for determining 'earnings'. Its focus is therefore on the determination of the denominator of the ratio to ensure consistency in this. Thus, it sets out how this should be calculated where there are changes in share capital in an accounting period.

Potential future issues of shares through, for example, share option schemes or convertible financial instruments, can have a significant effect on EPS. The standard addresses how the impact of such issues should be shown, as it sets out how diluted EPS should be calculated.

The significance of the EPS ratio is emphasised by the requirement for the disclosure of basic and diluted EPS on the face of the income statement. IAS 33 prescribes the disclosures required to enable users to fully understand the calculations of the ratios.

8.2 Earnings

8.2.1 Definition

The numerator of the EPS ratio is defined as profit or loss attributable to ordinary equity holders. It includes all income and expenses recognised in the financial year and is after tax. For a single company that produces a separate income statement, it will be the bottom line of this statement (profit or loss for the year) less any preference dividends, and will exclude any items included in other comprehensive income in the statement of comprehensive income.

For a group producing consolidated financial statements earnings excludes the non-controlling interests' share of the profit or loss.

⊕ **Reminder** *A consolidated income statement combines the profit and loss items of a parent company and its subsidiary companies, irrespective of whether the parent holds all the equity shares. If there are other investors in a subsidiary company who hold (usually) less than 50% of the equity share capital, they are termed the non-controlling interest. Their share of the profits or losses of the subsidiary is shown on the face of the consolidated income statement.*

Note: this is explained further in Chapter 15 dealing with consolidated financial statements.

 Example of earnings

An extract from Beta Holdings plc's income statement is given as follows. The company has both ordinary share capital and irredeemable cumulative preference share capital.

Extract from consolidated income statement

	£m
Profit from operations	65
Finance costs	(18)
Profit before taxation	47
Tax expense	(14)
Profit for the year	33
Attributable to:	
Shareholders of the parent	29
Non-controlling interests	4
	33

The statement of changes in equity includes:

		£m
Dividends:	Irredeemable preference	2
	Ordinary	6
		8

Earnings for the EPS calculation = £29m – £2m = £27 million.

8.2.2 Other definitions of earnings

As noted in section 8.1.3, earnings as a comparative performance measure is limited owing to different accounting policies being used in different companies. Thus, the question remains whether EPS is truly comparable from company to company. In addition, and as discussed in Chapter 6, earnings can be subject to some manipulation by companies, and there may be pressure for companies to maintain a steady upward trend in their EPS ratio or to avoid large fluctuations from year-to-year. However, the days are gone when earnings in the EPS calculation could exclude one-off or unusual items (which may have been referred to as extraordinary items). Basic EPS has to include all items recognised in profit and loss. Changes in fair value measurements from one year end to the next, and unexpected losses or write-offs can lead to volatility in profits and losses, and these will be included in this ratio.

Many companies therefore include in their financial statements additional EPS figures using alternative measures of profit. For example, some companies will present an additional EPS figure based on continuing operations only.

Financial reporting in practice 8.2   Lenzing AG, 2010

Lenzing AG is an Austrian manufacturer of high-quality cellulose fibres for global textile and non-wovens industries. Its products range from special cellulose fibres to high-quality plastic polymer products. Its core fibres business is complemented by other activities in plastics, as well as engineering. In 2010 it discontinued operations which were disclosed in its financial statements, as discussed in Chapter 6, and the company disclosed an additional EPS from its continuing operations as shown.

Income statement (extract)

	Note	2010	2009
Continuing operations		**EUR '000**	EUR '000
Profit for the year after taxes from continuing operations		176,661	79,923
Discontinued operations			
Result from discontinued operations	(5)	**(6,723)**	(13,120)
Profit for the year		**169,938**	66,803
Attributable to shareholders of Lenzing AG		159,118	64,369
Attributable to non-controlling interests		10,820	2,434
Earnings per share	(18)	**EUR**	EUR
From continuing operations and discontinued operations		**6.19**	2.50
From continuing operations		**6.45**	3.01

Other companies choose to show an additional EPS figure using a different definition of earnings.

Financial reporting in practice 8.3   J Sainsbury plc, 2010

The following extract from Sainsbury's income statement for the 52 weeks ended 20 March 2010 shows the company analysing its profit before tax into underlying profit from its core supermarket activities and other, less comparable (year-to-year), items. The company has shown basic EPS based on the final profit for the financial year of £585 million (2009: £289 million) and a further basic EPS based on this underlying profit figure as a measure of earnings.

It can be seen clearly that basic EPS has almost doubled from 2009 to 2010 as the profit for the financial year has; the underlying basic EPS is much more comparable over these two years and a better measure of the company's core business performance.

	Note	£m	£m
Profit before taxation		**733**	466
Analysed as:			
Underlying profit before tax		**610**	519
Profit on sale of properties	3	**27**	57
Investment property fair value movements	3	**123**	(124)
Financing fair value movements	3	**(15)**	(10)
IAS 19 pension financing (charge)/credit	3	**(24)**	24
One-off item: Office of Fair Trading dairy inquiry	3	**12**	–
		733	466
Income tax expense	8	**(148)**	(177)
Profit for the financial year		**585**	289
Earnings per share	9	**pence**	pence
Basic		**32.1**	16.6
Underlying basic		**23.9**	21.2

In its five-year data, Sainsbury's includes its underlying profit and underlying basic EPS, rather than profit and EPS, including all items of income and expense.

Five year financial record	2010	2009	2008	2007	2006
Underlying profit before tax	**610**	519	434	339	244
Increase on previous year (%)	**17.5**	19.6	28.0	38.9	2.5
Earnings per share					
Underlying basic (pence)	**23.9**	21.2	17.4	13.0	9.5
Increase on previous year (%)	**12.7**	21.8	33.8	36.8	21.8

8.2.3 Preference dividends

It is necessary to include a word of caution about preference dividends. There are different types of preference shares and different conditions under which they are issued, and it may not be a question of merely deducting a dividend that has been paid and included in the statement of changes in equity in order to calculate earnings for EPS. IAS 33 specifies that the amounts deducted in relation to preference dividends should be 'the after-tax amounts of preference dividends, differences arising on the settlement of preference shares, and other similar effects of preference shares classified as equity'. The treatments of these differences on the earnings figure to be used in EPS are shown in Table 8.1.

Note also that some redeemable preference shares are under *IAS 32 Financial Instruments: Presentation* treated either in full or in part as a liability. Any dividend on these shares is treated in full, or in part, as finance charge, and will already be deducted from profit before tax.

Table 8.1 Treatment of different types of preference share or issue conditions on earnings

Type of preference share/ issue condition	Treatment in earnings for EPS
Non-cumulative	Dividends declared in respect of the period
Cumulative	Dividend required for the period irrespective of whether they have been declared. Deduction does not include dividends paid or declared in respect of previous periods
Increasing rate*	Original issue discount or premium is amortised to retained earnings—this is treated as a dividend for EPS
Repurchased by company	Excess of fair value of consideration over carrying amount deducted
Repurchased by company	Excess of carrying amount over fair value of consideration is added to earnings
Convertible—early conversion	Excess of fair value of ordinary shares issued or other consideration over fair value of ordinary shares under original conversion terms deducted

* Dividend is not fixed because either it is initially lower to compensate the company for shares issued at a discount or it is higher later to compensate the investor for shares issued at a premium.

8.3 Shares

8.3.1 Definition

Basic EPS requires earnings to be divided by the weighted average number of ordinary shares outstanding during the period. This is to take account of changes in ordinary share capital during the period arising from shares issued and bought back. A time-weighting factor is applied, and although IAS 33 specifies that this should be measured in days, a reasonable approximation, such as months, can be used.

8.3.2 Issue and repurchase of shares at fair value

If the number of shares increases through some form of issue, the immediate effect on the EPS ratio will be a decrease. However, for an issue of shares at fair (market) value, the resources of the company are increased, and thus it would be expected that profits (earnings) will also increase over time. So for this form of share issue at fair value, a straightforward weighted average number of ordinary shares is calculated and used as the denominator in EPS as it is considered the EPS will not be reduced unfairly.

The same argument applies, but in reverse, for a company that repurchases its shares at fair value.

 Worked example 8.1: to calculate EPS where there is an issue and repurchase at market price

Cox plc has post-tax profits for the calendar years as follows:

20X1	£510,000
20X2	£650,000

The company's share capital of £1,000,000 consists of 2,000,000 50p ordinary shares in issue at 1 January 20X1. The company makes the following share transactions in 20X2:

31 May 20X2	Issues 800,000 further shares at market value
1 December 20X2	Purchases 250,000 of its own shares at market value

Required:
Calculate the EPS for disclosure in Cox plc's 20X1 and 20X2 financial statements.

$$20X1 \ EPS = \frac{\text{Profit after tax}}{\text{No. of shares in issue}}$$

$$= \frac{£510,000}{2,000,000}$$

$$= 25.5p$$

20X2 weighted average no. of shares

	Shares in issue	Time factor	
1 Jan–31 May	2,000,000	5/12	833,333
1 Jun–30 Nov	2,800,000	6/12	1,400,000
1 Dec–31 Dec	2,550,000	1/12	212,500
Weighted average			2,445,833

$$20X2 \ EPS = \frac{£650,000}{2,445,833}$$

$$= 26.6p$$

8.3.3 Bonus issue of shares

When a company makes a bonus issue of shares (sometimes called a capitalisation issue), there is no change to the resources of a company. In this case the company is giving away shares to its shareholders perhaps in lieu of a dividend, or to increase an undercapitalised company, or to widen the number of potential shareholders. The impact on EPS will be an automatic reduction, which seems inappropriate given that bonus issues are often made by successful companies.

IAS 33 addresses this by requiring that the weighted average number of ordinary shares outstanding before the issue be adjusted for the proportionate change in the number of shares outstanding, as if the bonus issue had happened at the beginning of the earliest period presented. In other words, EPS is calculated for the both the financial year in which the bonus issue was made and all other comparative periods presented in the financial statements using the increased number of shares.

 Worked example 8.2: to calculate EPS where there is a bonus issue

Pippin plc has post-tax profits for the calendar year as follows:

20X1	£180,000
20X2	£225,000

There are 600,000 ordinary shares outstanding at 1 January 20X1. On 1 October 20X2 the company makes a 2 for 1 bonus issue.

Required:
Calculate the EPS for disclosure in Pippin plc's 20X1 and 20X2 financial statements.

20X1 financial statements

$$20X1 \text{ EPS} = \frac{£180,000}{600,000}$$

$$= 30p$$

20X2 financial statements

For 20X2 EPS, there is no weighted average calculation. The number of shares outstanding is adjusted to assume that the bonus issue had occurred at beginning of the year. As 20X1 is presented as a comparative in the 20X2 financial statements, it is also assumed that the bonus issue had occurred at the start of this year.

A 2 for 1 bonus issue (2 shares are issued for every 1 share held) means that 1,200,000 shares will be issued.

$$20X2 \text{ EPS} = \frac{£225,000}{600,000 + 1,200,00}$$

$$= 12.5p$$

20X1 comparative EPS adjusted to:

$$\frac{£180,000}{1,800,000} \quad \text{OR} \quad \frac{£180,000}{600,000 \times 3^*}$$

$= 10p$

*The number of shares has increased by a factor of $3 = [(2 + 1) / 1]$.

Without the adjustment of the 20X1 comparative EPS it would have appeared there had been a large drop in EPS from 30p in 20X1 to 12.5p in 20X2. With the adjustment the comparison makes more sense (EPS is more fairly stated): 10p in 20X1 compared with 12.5p in 20X2.

8.3.4 Rights issue of shares

A rights issue of shares is an offer of shares to existing shareholders in some proportion to their holding at a reduced price. It is the most common method by which companies raise capital from a share issue. It can be thought of as combining the two elements—an issue of shares at full market price plus a bonus issue.

 Example of a rights issue

A company has 300,000 ordinary shares in issue. It makes a 2 for 3 rights issue to its existing share-holders, which is fully subscribed. The current market price per share is £4 and the shares are offered at £2.50 under the rights issue.

The company will issue 200,000 shares and (ignoring issue costs) will raise $200,000 \times £2.50 =$ £500,000. This may be considered equivalent to an issue of £500,000/£4 = 125,000 shares at full market price, plus a bonus issue of 200,000 − 125,000 = 75,000 shares.

The calculation of the weighted average number of shares outstanding therefore contains elements of the previous two EPS calculations—a time-weighting factor and an adjustment to the number of shares outstanding before the rights issue for the bonus element. This latter adjustment is achieved through the calculation and use of a 'bonus fraction', which is defined in IAS 33 as:

$$\frac{\text{Fair value per share immediately before the exercise of rights}}{\text{Theoretical ex-rights fair value per share}}$$

The theoretical ex-rights fair value per share is a weighted combined price of the shares immediately after the rights issues has happened. (Note: ex-rights means after the rights issue.) It is calculated by adding the aggregate market value of the shares immediately before the exercise of the rights to the proceeds from the rights issue and dividing by the number of shares outstanding after the exercise of the rights.

Worked example 8.3: to calculate EPS where there is a rights issue

Braeburn plc has post-tax profits for the calendar years as follows:

20X1	£30,000
20X2	£38,000
20X3	£45,000

The company has 500,000 shares outstanding before it makes a 1 for 4 rights issue. The exercise price is £5 and the last date to exercise rights is 1 March 20X2. The fair value of one ordinary share immediately before exercise is £11.

Required:
Calculate the EPS for disclosure in the company's 20X1, 20X2, and 20X3 financial statements.

20X1 EPS

$$= \frac{£30,000}{500,000}$$

$$= 6p$$

20X2 EPS

$$\text{Theoretical ex-rights fair value per share} = \frac{4 \times £11 + 1 \times £5}{4 + 1} = £9.80$$

Bonus fraction = 11/9.8 (better not to round at this stage)

No. of shares issued in 1 for 4 rights issue = 125,000

Weighted average number of shares including effects of 'bonus' element of rights issue:

	Shares in issue		Bonus fraction *	Time factor	
1 Jan–28 Feb	500,000	×	11/9.8	2/12	93,537
1 Mar–31 Dec	625,000			10/12	520,833
Weighted average					614,370

* Note that it is only the period prior to the rights issue that is multiplied by the bonus fraction.

$$\text{20X2 EPS} = \frac{£38,000}{614,370}$$

$$= 6.2p$$

The 20X1 EPS requires restating as there is a bonus element involved. This is achieved by multiplying the weighted average number of shares used in the 20X1 EPS calculation by the bonus fraction:

$$\text{Restated 20X1 EPS} = \frac{\text{Earnings}}{\text{Restated no. of shares}}$$

$$= \frac{£30,000}{500,000 \times 11/9.8}$$

$$= 5.3p$$

$$\text{20X3 EPS} = \frac{£45,000}{625,000}$$

$$= 7.2p$$

Summary

Disclosed in financial statements of year	EPS	Comparative
20X1	6p	Not available
20X2	6.2p	5.3p
20X3	7.2p	6.2p

8.4 Diluted earnings per share

8.4.1 What is diluted EPS?

Most listed companies will have a variety of financial instruments funding them, including convertible preference shares and convertible debentures and bonds. In addition, many employee remuneration packages (particularly those of directors and senior employees) will offer share options and warrants. All of these arrangements mean that at some date in the future additional equity shares may be issued either in lieu of paying off a debt or at a price which is fixed under the particular arrangement and which will be different from the market price at this date. (Note: the incentive for employee share options is for the option price to be lower than market at the date they are exercised.)

For existing ordinary shareholders reviewing EPS, this may not be good news, as the impact will be a reduction in or a dilution of EPS. However, this information is considered important for the investors and so diluted EPS is calculated and disclosed. It may be thought of as a 'worst-case' scenario which assumes all convertible instruments are converted, and all options and warrants exercised to give the maximum dilution of EPS. Unlike basic EPS, diluted EPS is not an exact figure based on actual events. It is a theoretical figure that accounts for future events which may or may not happen, or only partially happen.

Its calculation takes the numerator and denominator of the current basic EPS as the starting point and makes adjustments as follows.

Earnings	Adjustments made for the effect, including the tax effect, of any conversion of preference shares, debentures, and bonds into shares. Preference dividends and interest will no longer be payable, so should be added back to earnings.
Number of shares	Incorporates an assumed number of shares from the conversions of debt instruments, and exercise of options and warrants, which will be issued with no additional flow of resources into the company.

8.4.2 Share options and warrants

Share options and warrants are financial instruments that give the holder the entitlement to purchase shares at some point in the future at a predetermined price. Some resource will flow to the company when they are exercised, but the dilutive effect of these arrangements on EPS is where the exercise price is lower than the market price. A notional calculation of the number of shares issued at no consideration needs to be made. The market price is taken as the average market price during the year. Although IFRS 2 *Share-based Payment* is outside the scope of this textbook, note that if this applies to the share options, then the actual issue price should include the fair value of any goods or services to be supplied to the company by the employee under the option arrangement.

Worked example 8.4: to show the calculation of basic and diluted EPS where there are share options

Seville plc made post-tax profits of £1,200,000 in 20X1. The number of ordinary shares in issue during the year was 5 million, with the average market value per share being £4.00.

The company has share option schemes in existence, with 1 million shares issuable in 20X2 at an exercise price of £3.00 per share. There are no other goods or services to be supplied to the company under the option schemes.

Required:
Calculate the basic and fully diluted EPS figures for disclosure in Seville plc's 20X1 financial statements.

	Earnings £	Shares (million)	Per share
Post-tax profit	1,200,000		
Weighted average shares in issue		5	
Basic EPS (£1.2m/5m)			24p

No. of shares under option *		1
No. of shares issued at fair value (1m × £3.00/£4.00)*		(0.75)
	1,200,000	5.25
Diluted EPS (£1.2m/5.25m)		22.9p

* In other words, 1 m – 0.75m = 0.25m shares are treated as if they are to be issued for no consideration. These are added to the number of shares already issued for the diluted EPS calculation.

Where more than one basis of conversion exists, for example where share options are offered with their exercise at different dates and prices, the calculation assumes the most advantageous conversion rate or exercise price from the standpoint of the holder of the potential ordinary shares.

8.4.3 Convertible instruments

Where convertible debt is issued, IAS 32 *Financial Instruments: Presentation* requires that the proceeds received are split between being accounted for as a liability and as part of equity. The topic of financial instruments is outside the scope of this textbook, so examples given of convertible instruments will ensure sufficient information regarding this is provided. Whatever the interest rate of the actual debt instrument is, an effective interest rate has to be used for the recognition of interest payable in the income statement.

Details of this are needed as both earnings and the number of shares are adjusted in the diluted EPS calculation.

 Worked example 8.5: to show the calculation of basic and diluted EPS where there are convertible bonds

Gala plc has 10,000 ordinary shares in issue and has made post-tax profits of £1,000. The company has convertible 6% bonds of £1,000, with each block of £10 bonds convertible into 15 ordinary shares.

When the convertible bonds were issued originally, the proceeds were split between the equity component and the debt component, as required by IAS 32 *Financial Instruments: Presentation*. The liability component carried in the balance sheet at the start of the period is £800 and the effective interest rate is 8%.

Required:
Assuming a corporation tax rate of 25%, calculate the basic and fully diluted EPS figures for disclosure in Gala plc's financial statements.

$$\text{Basic EPS} = \frac{£1,000}{10,000}$$

$$= 10p$$

For diluted EPS adjust both earnings and the number of shares:

	£
Earnings	1,000
Add back interest saved on conversion (net of tax) 8% × £800 × (100 − 25)%	48
	1,048

No. of ordinary shares resulting from conversion: 1,500.

$$\text{Diluted EPS} = \frac{£1,048}{10,000 + 1,500}$$

$$= 9.1\text{p}$$

8.4.4 Contingently issuable shares

Contingently issuable ordinary shares are shares issuable for little, or no, cash or other consideration upon the satisfaction of specified conditions given in a contingent share agreement. There may be one condition, or a combination of conditions, that have to be fulfilled and these may include a certain level of profit that has to be reached, or a certain level for the future market price of shares or some other event, for example the opening of a specific number of retail stores.

If the conditions are satisfied then the shares will be issued and included in both the basic and diluted EPS calculations. If the conditions are not met, the number of contingently issuable shares included in the diluted EPS calculation is based on the number of shares that would be issuable if the end of the accounting period were the end of the contingency period.

 Worked example 8.6: to show the calculation of basic and diluted EPS where there are contingently issuable shares

Discovery plc has 1 million ordinary shares outstanding at 1 January 20X1. There were no options, warrants, or convertible instruments outstanding during the period. An agreement relating to a recent business combination provides for the issue of additional ordinary shares based on the following conditions:

● 5,000 additional ordinary shares for each new retail site opened during 20X1

● 1,000 additional ordinary shares for each £1,000 of consolidated profit in excess of £2 million for the year ended 31 December 20X1.

During the year Discovery opened two new retail sites on 1 May 20X1 and 1 September 20X1. The consolidated profit attributable to ordinary equity holders of the parent company for the year ended 31 December 20X1 was £2.9 million.

Required:
Calculate basic and diluted EPS for disclosure in Discovery plc's 20X1 financial statements.

Five thousand shares will be issued on both 1 May and 1 September for the new retail stores opened.

Although the year's profit exceeds £2 million, it is not certain that this will be achieved until the very end of the year. These contingent shares cannot, therefore, be issued before the end of the year.

Basic EPS

The weighted average calculation for the number of shares outstanding during the year is as follows:

	Shares outstanding	Time period	
1 January–30 April	1,000,000	4/12	333,333
1 May–31 August	1,005,000	4/12	335,000
1 September–31 December	1,010,000	4/12	336,667
Weighted average			1,005,000

$$\text{Basic EPS} = \frac{£2,900,000}{1,005,000} = £2.89$$

Diluted EPS

The number of shares added to the initial 1 million assumes that the end of the financial year is the end of the contingency period. A weighted average calculation for the number of shares is therefore not required.

No. of shares issued for opening of the two retail stores = $2 \times 5,000 = 10,000$

No. of shares issued for achieving profit target = $(900,000/1000) \times 1000 = 900,000$

No. of shares to include in diluted EPS = $1,000,000 + 10,000 + 900,000 = 1,910,000$

$$\text{Diluted EPS} = \frac{£2,900,000}{1,910,000} = £1.52$$

8.4.5 Dilutive and antidilutive potential ordinary shares

Diluted EPS must always be lower than basic EPS (or if the company has made a loss, the diluted loss per share will be higher) as it includes the effects of all dilutive potential ordinary shares. However, a conversion of a financial instrument or exercise of an option may not automatically dilute EPS, in which case this future event will not be included in the calculation. The potential ordinary shares in this situation are referred to as antidilutive. In order to determine whether potential ordinary shares are dilutive or antidilutive a company should use profit or loss from continuing operations attributable to the shareholders of the parent company as the control number. In other words, this is used as the earnings to determine whether the shares are dilutive or antidilutive).

Example of reason for the control number

A company's income statement shows the following (all figures are net of tax):

	£000
Profit from continuing operations	4,800
Loss from discontinued operations	(7,200)
Loss for the year	(2,400)

The company has 2,000,000 ordinary shares in issue and 400,000 potential ordinary shares outstanding.

$$\text{Basic loss per share} = \frac{£(2,400)}{2,000} = (120)\text{p}$$

Assuming the 400,000 potential shares outstanding have no effect on profit and loss, a calculation for whether these are dilutive or antidilutive using the total loss for the year would show:

$$\text{Diluted loss per share} = \frac{£(2,400)}{2,400} = (100)\text{p}$$

As the loss per share has been reduced, it appears that the potential shares outstanding are anti-dilutive and it would follow that no diluted EPS would be disclosed.

However, the control number is profit from continuing operations, and so the correct calculations and comparison should be as follows:

$$\text{EPS (based on profit from continuing operations)} = \frac{£4,800}{2,000} = 240\text{p}$$

$$\text{Diluted EPS (based on profit from continuing operations)} = \frac{£4,800}{2,400} = 200\text{p}$$

On these calculations EPS has been reduced by the inclusion of the potential shares outstanding, thus they are dilutive and a diluted EPS would be disclosed.

Companies may have any number of arrangements, including share options and convertible instruments. In determining whether the potential ordinary shares are dilutive or anti-dilutive, each arrangement that gives rise to potential shares must be considered separately rather than taking them all together. The order in which the arrangements are considered may affect whether they are dilutive. As the objective is to maximise the dilution of basic EPS, the order will take the most dilutive to the least dilutive. This is achieved by starting with the lowest 'earnings per incremental share' and then continuing in size order to the highest 'earnings per incremental share'.

Worked example 8.7: to show the order in which to include dilutive arrangements

Delaware plc has the following financial data for 20X3:

	£
Profit from continuing operations	16,400,000
Loss from discontinued operations	(4,000,000)
Profit for the year	12,400,000
Preference dividends	£6,400,000
No. of ordinary shares outstanding	2,000,000
Average market price of one ordinary share during the year	£75

The company has outstanding share options and convertible instruments as follows:

Share options	100,000 with exercise price of £60.
Convertible preference shares	800,000 shares with a par value of £100 entitled to a cumulative dividend of £8 per share. Each preference share is convertible to two ordinary shares.
5% convertible bonds	Nominal amount £100 million. Each £1,000 bond is convertible to 20 ordinary shares. There is no amortisation of premium or discount affecting the determination of the interest expense.

Assume the tax rate is 40%.

Required:
Calculate basic and diluted EPS for disclosure in Delaware plc's 20X3 financial statements.

Increase in earnings attributable to ordinary equity holders on conversion of potential ordinary shares

	Increase in earnings	Increase in number of ordinary shares	Earnings per incremental share
	£		£
Share options			
Increase in earnings	Nil		
Incremental shares issued for no consideration 100,000 × (£75 – £60)/£75		20,000	Nil
Convertible preference shares			
Increase in earnings			
800,000 × £8	6,400,000		
Incremental shares			
2 × 800,000		1,600,000	4.00

5% convertible bonds

Increase in earnings

£100,000,000 × 5% × (1 − 0.4)   3,000,000

Incremental shares

100,000 × 20   2,000,000   1.50

The order in which to include the dilutive instruments is therefore:

1   Share options

2   5% convertible bonds

3   Convertible preference shares.

Calculation of diluted EPS

Note: this is based on profit from continuing operations as shown in the previous example.

	Profit £	No. of ordinary shares	Per share £
Profit from continuing operations	16,400,000		
Preference dividends	(6,400,000)		
Profit attributable to ordinary shareholders	10,000,000	2,000,000	5.00
Share options	–	20,000	
	10,000,000	2,020,000	4.95 Dilutive
5% convertible bonds	3,000,000	2,000,000	
	13,000,000	4,020,000	3.23 Dilutive
Convertible preference shares	6,400,000	1,600,000	
	19,400,000	5,620,000	3.45 Anti-dilutive

Because diluted EPS is increased when taking the convertible preference shares into account, these shares are antidilutive and are ignored in the calculation of diluted EPS.

EPS figures disclosed are as follows (see section below for full requirements of disclosures):

	Basic EPS £	Diluted EPS £
Profit from continuing operations attributable to ordinary equity holders	5.00	3.23
Loss from discontinued operations attributable to ordinary equity holders	(2.00)[1]	(0.99)[1]
Profit attributable to ordinary equity holders	3.00[2]	2.24[2]

[1] Calculated as: $\dfrac{\text{Loss from discontinued operations}}{\text{No. of shares}}$ $\dfrac{£(4,000,000)}{2,000,000}$ $\dfrac{£(4,000,000)}{4,020,000}$

[2] Calculated as: $\dfrac{\text{Profit}}{\text{No. of shares}}$ $\dfrac{£(6,000,000)}{2,000,000}$ $\dfrac{£(9,000,000)}{4,020,000}$

8.5 Disclosure of EPS

Various EPS figures must be presented on the face of the statement of comprehensive income (or the income statement, if presented separately) for each class of ordinary shares that has a different right to share in the profit or loss for the accounting period. If the earnings figure is negative, a loss per share is disclosed. The disclosures are:

1   Basic and diluted EPS for profit or loss from continuing operations attributable to the ordinary equity holders of the parent company—these must be presented with equal prominence.

2   Basic and diluted amounts per share for any discontinued operations—these may be presented in the notes.

Companies may choose to present EPS figures using alternative definitions of earnings, as seen in the earlier Lenzing and Sainsbury examples. These figures must be calculated using the weighted average number of ordinary shares, as specified by IAS 33, and must include the related diluted EPS.

In the notes to the financial statements, the following disclosures are required:

(a) The amounts used as the numerators in calculating basic and diluted earnings per share, and a reconciliation of those amounts to profit or loss attributable to the parent company for the period. The reconciliation shall include the individual effect of each class of instruments that affects earnings per share.

(b) The weighted average number of ordinary shares used as the denominator in calculating basic and diluted earnings per share, and a reconciliation of these denominators to each other. The reconciliation shall include the individual effect of each class of instruments that affects earnings per share.

(c) Instruments (including contingently issuable shares) that could potentially dilute basic earnings per share in the future, but were not included in the calculation of diluted earnings per share because they are anti-dilutive for the periods presented.

(d) A description of ordinary share transactions or potential ordinary share transactions that occur after the reporting period and that would have changed significantly the number of ordinary shares or potential ordinary shares outstanding at the end of the period if those transactions had occurred before the end of the reporting period. For example, issues of shares for cash, or the conversion or exercise of potential ordinary shares into ordinary shares.

If a company has presented alternative EPS figures on the face of the statement of comprehensive income (or income statement), additional disclosures are required to indicate the basis on which the numerator(s) is (are) determined, including whether amounts per share are before tax or after tax. If an earnings figure is used that is not reported as a line item in the statement of comprehensive income, the company is required to show a reconciliation between the figure used and a line item that is reported in the statement of comprehensive income.

Financial reporting in practice 8.4 | Marks and Spencer plc, 2011

Like Sainsbury's, in its 2011 financial statements Marks and Spencer plc presents alternative EPS figures based on what it defines as its underlying profit. It therefore shows four EPS figures on its income statement—basic EPS, diluted EPS, underlying basic EPS, and underlying diluted EPS. The disclosure note showing the various reconciliations is as follows.

8 Earnings per share

The calculation of earnings per ordinary share is based on earnings after tax and the weighted average number of ordinary shares in issue during the year.

The underlying earnings per share figures have also been calculated based on earnings before profits and losses on the disposal of properties, impairment charges, pension credits arising on changes of the defined benefit pension schemes, and non-cash fair value movements in financial instruments, and costs relating to strategic changes that are not considered normal operating costs of the underlying business (see note 5). These have been calculated to allow the shareholders to gain an understanding of the underlying trading performance of the Group.

For diluted earnings per share, the weighted average number of ordinary shares in issue is adjusted to assume conversion of all dilutive potential ordinary shares. The Group has only one class of dilutive potential ordinary shares being those share options granted to employees where the exercise price is less than the average market price of the Company's ordinary shares during the year.

Details of the underlying earnings per share are set out below:

	2011 £m	2010 £m
Profit attributable to equity holders of the parent	**612.0**	526.3
(Less)/add (net of tax):		
Profit on property disposals	(2.9)	(8.1)
IAS 19 Ireland one-off pension credit	(9.4)	–
IAS 36 Impairment of investment property	6.3	–
IAS 39 Fair value movement of financial instrument	(54.3)	–
IAS 39 Recognition of embedded derivative	(15.1)	–
Strategic programme costs	11.5	–
Underlying profit attributable to equity holders of the parent	**548.1**	518.2
	Million	Million
Weighted average number of ordinary shares in issue	**1,577.1**	1,572.2
Potentially dilutive share options under Group's share option schemes	**15.6**	14.3
Weighted average number of diluted ordinary shares	**1,592.7**	1,586.5
	Pence	Pence
Basic earnings per share	**38.8**	33.5
Diluted earnings per share	**38.4**	33.2
Underlying basic earnings per share	**34.8**	33.0
Underlying diluted earnings per share	**34.4**	32.7

Financial reporting in practice 8.5 | Ahold, 2009

This illustration shows the disclosures where there are discontinued operations.

Ahold is an international food retailing group based in the Netherlands which operates leading supermarket companies in eastern Europe and the USA. Its 2009 income statement showed discontinued operations resulting from the sale of groups of stores to other operators. The company disclosed basic and diluted EPS based on total net profit and continuing operations, and showed amounts per share from discontinued operations in the disclosure note.

Extracts from the company's income statement and the EPS disclosure note are as follows.

Consolidated income statement

€ million	Note	2009	2008
Income before income taxes		1,014	989
Income taxes	10	(148)	(2 26)
Share in income of joint ventures	14	106	124
Income from continuing operations		972	887
Income (loss) from discontinued operations	5	(78)	195
Net income		894	1,082
Attributable to:			
Common shareholders		894	1,077
Non-controlling interests		–	5
Net income		894	1,082
Earnings per share	29		
Net income per share attributable to common shareholders			
Basic		0.76	0.92
Diluted		0.74	0.90
Income per share from continuing operations attributable to common shareholders			
Basic		0.82	0.76
Diluted		0.81	0.74
Weighted average number of common shares outstanding (in millions)			
Basic		1,180	1,174
Diluted		1,243	1,238

29 Earnings per share

	2009	2008
Earnings (€ million)		
Net income attributable to common shareholders for the purposes of basic earnings per share	**894**	1,077
Effect of dilutive potential common shares – reversal of preferred dividends from earnings	**32**	31
Net income attributable to common shareholders for the purposes of diluted earnings per share	**926**	1,108
Number of shares (in millions)		
Weighted average number of common shares for the purposes of basic earnings per share	**1,180**	1,174
Effect of dilutive potential common shares:		
Share options and conditional shares	**9**	9
Cumulative preferred financing shares	**54**	55
Weighted average number of common shares for the purposes of diluted earnings per share	**1,243**	1,238

€ million	2009	2008
Income from continuing operations, attributable to common shareholders		
for the purposes of basic earnings per share	**972**	887
Effect of dilutive potential common shares – reversal of preferred dividends from earnings	**32**	31
Income from continuing operations, attributable to common shareholders for the purposes of diluted earnings per share	**1,004**	918

Basic and diluted income per share from discontinued operations attributable to common shareholders amounted to negative €0.06 and negative €0.07 respectively (2008: €0.16 basic and €0.16 diluted). They are based on the income from discontinued operations attributable to common shareholders of negative €78 million (2008: €190 million) and the denominators detailed above.

8.6 Future changes to IAS 33

As part of the convergence project between the International Accounting Standards Board (IASB) and the Financial Accounting Standards Board (FASB), an exposure draft of proposed amendments to IAS 33 was published by the IASB in August 2008 in order to achieve convergence of the denominator in the EPS calculation, and to clarify and simplify the calculation of EPS where more complex financial instruments were involved. The key proposals were:

To achieve convergence:

1   A principle should be established to determine which instruments are included in the calculation of basic EPS. The weighted average number of ordinary shares should include only those instruments that give (or are deemed to give) their holder the right to share currently in profit or loss of the period, and if ordinary shares issuable for little, or no, cash or other consideration or convertible instruments do not meet this condition, they will not be included in basic EPS.

2   Contracts where a company is purchasing its own ordinary shares for cash or other financial assets through, for example gross physically settled written put options, forward purchase contracts, and mandatorily redeemable ordinary shares, should be treated as if the entity had already repurchased the shares.

3   The calculation of diluted EPS for participating instruments and two-class ordinary shares should include a test to determine whether a convertible financial instrument would have a more dilutive effect if conversion is assumed. The diluted EPS calculation should assume the more dilutive treatment.

Clarification and simplification of the calculation of EPS:

1   Profits or losses from changes in fair value for financial instruments measured at fair value through profit or loss should remain in the numerator of diluted EPS, as changes in fair value reflect the economic effect of such instruments on current equity holders for the period.

2   The calculation of the dilutive effect of options, warrants, and their equivalents should use the year end share price, rather than the average for the period.

3   For the calculation of diluted EPS an entity should assume that ordinary shares relating to forward contracts to sell an entity's own shares are sold and the effect is dilutive.

4   No adjustments should be required in calculating diluted EPS where there are contracts to repurchase an entity's own shares and contracts that may be settled in ordinary shares or cash owing to classification requirements of these items as financial instruments.

Responses to the exposure draft have been received by the IASB, but more urgent projects have taken precedence and currently the IASB states that this project will resume at some future date.

Summary of key points

Earnings per share is a key ratio used by equity investors as a measure of the performance and, to some extent, the wealth-creating abilities of a company. It calculates the profit or loss available to the ordinary shareholders on a per share basis. Its significance is emphasised by the requirement for companies to disclose basic and diluted EPS on the face of their statements of comprehensive income.

Consistency in its calculation from company to company is particularly important, as EPS is used in the price earnings ratio, which is published daily in the financial press and which provides some indication of markets' confidence in a company. Although published profit or loss available to the ordinary shareholders may be questioned as a truly comparable performance measure, IAS 33 *Earnings per Share* was issued to ensure the calculation of EPS has some degree of consistency. The accounting standard concentrates mainly on how the denominator is to be calculated where there are changes in the number of shares outstanding during the financial year from different types of share issue and repurchases of shares.

Companies also have many different types of arrangements involving share options and warrants, and convertible financial instruments, all of which mean that at some point in the future the number of ordinary shares will increase and thus dilute EPS. Given that investors are using EPS trends to help in forecasting, the impact of these arrangements on EPS is important, and thus diluted EPS, a theoretical figure, is required to be calculated and disclosed. IAS 33 gives guidance on the calculation of diluted EPS for many different types of these arrangements, and this chapter has provided examples of those that are within the scope of the textbook.

 ## Further reading

IASB (International Accounting Standards Board) (2005) IAS 33 *Earnings per Share*. London: IASB.

 ## Bibliography

Ahold (2010) *Annual Report, 2009*. Amsterdam: Ahold.

IASB (International Accounting Standards Board) (2005) IAS 33 *Earnings per Share*. London: IASB.

J Sainsbury plc (2010) *Annual Report and Financial Statements, 2010*. London: J Sainsbury.

Lenzing Group (2011) *Annual Report, 2010*. Lenzing: Lenzing Group.

Marks and Spencer plc (2011) *Annual Report and Financial Statements, 2011*. London: Marks and Spencer.

 ## Questions

● Quick test

1 On 1 January 20X8 a company with no subsidiaries had 3 million ordinary shares of £1 each in issue. On 1 May 20X8 the company made an issue of 1 million shares at full market price of £2 per share. On 30 September 20X9 the company made a 2 for 5 bonus issue.

The post-tax earnings of the company for the years ended 31 December 20X8 and 2009 were £750,000 and £1,200,000 respectively.

Calculate the EPS for the years ended 31 December 20X8 and 20X9, showing (where possible) comparatives for reporting purposes.

2   You are given the following information relating to Santos plc:

	£000	£000
Profit before tax		4,131
Tax		(1,629)
Profit after tax		2,502
Non-controlling interests		(90)
		2,412
Retained profits at 1 January 20X3		5,268
		7,680
Dividends: preference	45	
ordinary	669	(714)
Retained profits at 31 December 20X3		6,966

(i)   From 1 January 20X2 until 31 March 20X3 the issued share capital of Santos plc was as follows:

Ordinary 25p shares	£3,000,000
5% irredeemable preference shares of £1 each	£ 900,000

(ii) On 1 April 20X3 Santos made a 1 for 4 rights issue of ordinary shares at £1. The market price of an ordinary share of Santos on the last day of quotation cum rights was £1.50.

(iii) The earnings per share for the year ended 31 December 20X2 had been calculated at 15.0 pence.

In accordance with the requirements of IAS 33, you are required to:

(a) Calculate the EPS of Santos plc for the year ended 31 December 20X3

(b) Calculate the adjusted EPS of Santos plc for the year ended 31 December 20X2

(c) Show how the results of your calculations, together with any necessary notes, would be disclosed in the financial statements of Santos plc.

●● Develop your understanding

3   Discuss why earnings per share, as a measure of financial performance, is required to be disclosed on the face of the income statement and whether it is possible to distil the performance of a complex organisation into a single measure, such as earnings per share.

4   At 1 January 20X7 and 20X8 the issued share capital of Coombe plc comprised:

Ordinary share capital (20p shares)	£1,500,000
4% irredeemable preference share capital (£1 shares)	£ 600,000

On 1 September 20X8 Coombe made a rights issue of three new ordinary shares at a price of 90p per share for every two shares held. The offer was fully subscribed. The market price of Coombe's ordinary shares immediately prior to the offer was £1.65 each.

At the start of 20X9 the company offered a 1 for 3 bonus issues of shares to its ordinary shareholders in lieu of the 20X8 final ordinary dividend; 40% of shareholders accepted this offer on 31 March 20X9.

Coombe's profits after tax for the years ended 31 December were as follows:

20X7: £3,460,000

20X8: £2,300,000

20X9: £3,970,000.

Preference dividends were paid at the end of each quarter.

Required:

Calculate Coombe plc's earnings per share for disclosure in its financial statements for the years ended 31 December 20X8 and 20X9, including comparative figures.

5   An extract from the income statements of Longstone plc for the years ended 31 December 20X4 and 20X5 are set out as follows:

	20X4	20X5
	£000	£000
Profit from operations	4,030	4,890
Finance charges	(730)	(760)
Profit before tax	3,300	4,130
Taxation	(1,150)	(1,360)
Profit after tax	2,150	2,770

On 1 January 20X4 the issued share capital of the company was £4,600,000 in 6% irredeemable preference shares of £1 each and £4,140,000 in ordinary shares of 50p each.

On 1 October 20X4 the company made a rights issue of 50p ordinary shares in the proportion of 1 for every 5 shares held, at a price of £0.60. The market price for the shares on the last day of quotation cum rights was £0.90 per share.

On 1 May 20X5 the company raised £2,750,000 from an issue of ordinary shares at full market value of £1.10 per share.

The company has paid the full preference dividend each year.

Basic earnings per share for 20X3 was 20.5p.

Required:

Calculate the earnings per share figures for disclosure in Longstone plc's financial statements for the years ended 31 December 20X4 and 20X5, including comparative figures.

6   On 1 January 20X1 a company had in issue 6 million £1 ordinary shares and £7.5 million of 7% convertible redeemable loan stock, on which the conversion terms were:

On 31 December 20X4	40 ordinary shares for each £125 of loan stock
On 31 December 20X5	40 ordinary shares for each £130 of loan stock
On 31 December 20X6	40 ordinary shares for each £135 of loan stock

The liability component of the convertible redeemable loan stock was carried in the statement of financial position on 1 January 20X1 at £7.2 million and the effective interest rate 8.5%. The company pays tax at the rate of 20%.

The profit attributable to the ordinary equity holders for the year ended 31 December 20X1 was £1.5 million.

Calculate the basic and diluted EPS for the year ended 31 December 20X1.

●●● Take it further

7   EPS is generally regarded as a key accounting ratio for use by investors and others. Like all accounting ratios, however, it has its limitations.

Critically examine why EPS is regarded as so important and discuss its limitations for investors who are comparing the performance of different companies.

8   Berkeley plc, a company with no subsidiaries, has issued share capital at 31 December 20X6 of £2.4 million made up of £1.8 million in ordinary share capital and £0.6 million in 6% £1 irredeemable preference shares. The nominal value of its ordinary shares is 20p. The company's profit after tax for the year ended 31 December 20X6 was £846,000. There were no changes in share capital during 20X6.

From 20X5, the company has had an executive share option scheme which gives the company's directors the option to purchase a total of 500,000 ordinary shares for £1.50 each. These options are exercisable in 20Y0.

On 1 March 20X7 Berkeley raised £1.11 million from an issue of ordinary shares at full market value of £1.85 per share. During 20X7 the average market price of the ordinary shares was £2.10 per share. No further shares were issued in accordance with the executive share option scheme. The post-tax profit for 20X7 was £960,000.

On 1 May 20X8 Berkeley made a rights issue of one new ordinary share for every four ordinary shares held at £1.80 per share. The cum rights price on the last day of quotation cum rights was £2.50 per share.

The average market price per ordinary share in 20X8 was £2.60 per share and the post-tax profit was £1.25 million.

Required:

Calculate Berkeley plc's basic and diluted earnings per share figures for the years ended 31 December 20X7 and 20X8, including the comparative figures for both years.

9   The following financial statement extracts relate to Silver plc for the year ended 31 December 20X6.

Share capital at 31 December 20X6:	
Issued and fully paid ordinary shares of £1 each	12,500,000
7% convertible cumulative preference shares of £1 each	1,000,000

The net profit for the year 20X6 was £4,820,000.

The 7% convertible cumulative preference shares were issued on 1 January 20X4. There were no preference dividends in arrears in 20X5; however, preference dividends were not declared in the year 20X6. The cumulative preference shares are convertible into ordinary shares in the ratio of 20 cumulative preference shares to 3 ordinary shares. No shares have been converted in 20X6.

On 1 August 20X6, 3.6 million ordinary shares were issued at £4.50 each.

The company has a share option scheme whereby certain employees can subscribe for company shares. Options outstanding on 1 January 20X6 were as follows:

1.2 million ordinary shares at £2 each

2 million ordinary shares at £3 each

1 million ordinary shares at £4 each.

The options relative to the 1.2 million ordinary shares at £2 were exercised on 1 October 20X6. The average fair value of one ordinary share during the year was £5.

Silver issued £6 million of 6% convertible bonds on 1 January 20X5, and each £1,000 bond is convertible into 200 ordinary shares. The corporation tax rate applicable is 35%.

Required:

(i) Calculate the number of shares in issue at 1 January 20X6.

(ii) Calculate the basic and diluted earnings per share for the year ended 31 December 20X6.

10 On 1 January 20X3, Juno plc had the following capital and debt structure:

- 800,000 ordinary shares of £10 each

- 1,200,000 6% cumulative convertible preference shares of £1 each (1 year of dividends in arrears)

- £1,300,000 8% convertible bonds.

Each preference share is convertible to one ordinary share in 20X3 and every £10 nominal value of the bonds carries a right to convert into one ordinary share before 1 April 20X6.

Juno also issued two share options during 20X3. Option A was granted to directors to subscribe for 700,000 ordinary shares at £3.00 per share on 1 July, whereas option B was granted to key management personnel to subscribe for 500,000 ordinary shares at £6.00 per share on 1 August. Both options would be exercisable from 1 January 20X6.

On 1 May 20X3 Juno issued 300,000 additional ordinary shares at full market price. On 1 July 20X3, Juno declared and issued a bonus issue of 2 bonus shares for every 10 existing shares. On 1 October 20X3, an additional 400,000 shares were issued at full market price.

Net income (assuming no discontinuing operations) for the year ended 31 December 20X3 was £1,172,000. No dividends were declared during the year. The average market price of Juno's ordinary shares for 20X3 was £5.00 and the corporate tax rate in 20X3 was 15%.

Required:

(a) Compute the weighted average number of ordinary shares outstanding during 20X3.

(b) Compute the earnings per incremental share for each arrangement giving rise to potential ordinary shares (namely, options A and B, convertible preference shares, and convertible bonds), identifying whether they are dilutive or antidilutive.

(c) Using your answer to parts (a) and (b), compute basic earnings per share and diluted earnings per share for the year ended 31 December 20X3.

(d) Using the two options (A and B) in the question to illustrate your answer, discuss whether options are always included in calculating diluted earnings per share.

Visit the Online Resource Centre for solutions to all these end of chapter questions plus visual walkthrough solutions. You can test your understanding with extra questions and answers, explore additional case studies based on real companies, take a guided tour through a company report, and much more. Go to the Online Resource Centre at **www.oxfordtextbooks.co.uk/orc/maynard/**

9

Taxation

> ## ➤ Introduction

This chapter focuses on the tax relating to the profits or losses a company makes, the assets and liabilities a company has, and how this is accounted for. In the UK this is generally referred to as corporation tax, but, from an international accounting perspective, it is called income tax. It includes both current tax and deferred tax.

Every transaction a company undertakes has a tax consequence. As a result, income tax may be become payable or the amount due may be reduced; the effect may be on current tax payable or recoverable, or it may relate to tax amounts payable or recoverable in the future. This chapter will not cover in detail how such taxes are calculated as this will be different in every tax jurisdiction. It will, however, discuss the principles behind, and the accounting treatment of, the tax consequences of both transactions and other events which are recognised in a company's financial statements, and the future recovery and the settlement of assets and liabilities recognised in the statement of financial position.

International Accounting Standard (IAS) 12 *Income Taxes* is the accounting standard that explains and specifies the accounting treatment of current and deferred taxes, and sets out the presentation and disclosure requirements.

★ Learning objectives

After studying this chapter you will be able to:

● understand why accounting profits and taxable profits are not the same
● explain the components of companies' income tax—current and deferred tax
● understand why deferred tax balances are accounted for and the issues with this
● account for current tax and deferred tax in accordance with IAS 12 *Income Taxes*.

✔ Key issues checklist

❑ Tax on companies' profits.
❑ Definitions of current tax and deferred tax.
❑ Differences between accounting profit and taxable profit—permanent and temporary differences.
❑ Accounting for current tax.
❑ The tax base of assets and liabilities.
❑ Taxable and deductible temporary differences.
❑ Recognition of deferred tax liabilities and deferred tax assets.
❑ Tax rate to be used.
❑ Accounting for changes in deferred tax balances.
❑ Concepts underpinning the accounting for deferred tax.
❑ Alternative views.
❑ Disclosures.

9.1 Taxation on companies' profits

9.1.1 Introduction

Governments have an influence on the economic activity of a country by withdrawing money through taxes, which it then injects through public sector spending. Different countries will raise taxes in different ways, and have different rules and regulations which determine the amounts they collect. Within a particular country these will vary, as they depend on the stance of a particular government on social justice and the amounts of revenues it determines need to be raised. Governments will change taxes periodically to encourage or discourage certain types of individual and corporate activity, or to respond to issues in society. In the UK tax legislation is set by Parliament each year in the Finance Act.

Businesses' actions give rise to many different types of taxation. A business will deduct taxes from its employees' wages and salaries, and pay these to the government. In the UK these taxes are called pay-as-you-earn (or **PAYE**) and employees' **National Insurance** (NI). A business, in addition, has to pay a further amount of employers' National Insurance to the government. Businesses that are large enough are required to include tax on the selling price of their goods and services (although this does not apply to all goods and services) and then pay this tax to the government. In the European Union (EU) this is termed value added tax (or **VAT**). The VAT a business has been charged on goods and services it has acquired is deducted from the amount payable.

Companies have a separate legal identity from their owners (shareholders). Because of this, companies are liable for taxes charged on the profits and gains they make. In the UK this is referred to as corporation tax. Although not the largest revenue raiser for governments, this is still a significant tax. Statistics show that between 5% and 15% of total government revenue in developed countries is raised from taxes on corporate profits.

This chapter deals with the accounting for taxes on a company's profits or losses. This tax is called income tax in international financial reporting and refers to all domestic and foreign taxes on corporate profits. (However, note that in the UK the term income tax is usually taken to refer to tax on an individual's earnings.)

For all companies there are tax consequences of the transactions recognised in profit or loss. There are also tax consequences of transactions which are recognised outside profit and loss, for example property revaluations and other items recognised as other comprehensive income or items recognised directly in equity. These can be immediate, for example tax is payable or recoverable once the profit or loss has been recognised, but can also affect future tax payments. Accounting standard-setters have debated and changed methods of accounting for these tax consequences for many years, and IAS 12 *Income Taxes*, which was issued in 1996 by the International Accounting Standards Board's (IASB) predecessor body, the International Accounting Standards Committee (IASC), sets out the accounting treatment of these to ensure consistency of treatment. It does not specify how tax amounts are calculated, as these will be different according to each country's tax legislation, but takes the principle of the tax consequence, and specifies how and when the tax should be accounted for and the disclosures needed for the users to understand this.

Income tax includes both current tax and deferred tax, which are defined as follows:

Current tax   The amount of income taxes payable (or recoverable) in respect of the taxable profit (tax loss) for a period.

Deferred tax   An accounting measure representing income taxes payable or recoverable in the future relating to transactions that have already taken place.

9.1.2 Taxable profit or loss

The taxable profit (or loss) for a period will seldom be the same as profit for accounting purposes. Taxable profit will be determined in accordance with the rules established by the government or taxation authorities, and upon which taxes are payable (or recoverable). The differences between taxable and accounting profits are of two types.

1   **Temporary differences**—where income or expenses are recognised for both accounting and tax purposes, but in different time periods. For example, accounting requires the accruals basis for the recognition of expenses, such as pension contributions, but the expense is only deductible as a tax expense on a cash basis.

Another major temporary difference is depreciation. Depreciation for accounting purposes is an accounting mechanism to spread the cost of an asset on a systematic basis over the accounting periods expected to benefit from the use of the asset. It is judgemental, requiring estimates of the useful life, any residual value, and patterns of usage. For tax purposes depreciation is replaced by deductions allowed by taxation authorities (sometimes referred to as capital allowances or writing down allowances). These are often varied to encourage investment by companies in certain types of asset.

2   **Permanent differences**—where expenses are included for accounting purposes, but are never allowed to be deducted for tax purposes. For example, entertainment expenses, and donations to political parties and national charities.

9.2 Current tax

As detailed in section 9.1.1 current tax is the income tax payable or recoverable once the profit or loss has been recognised. It is based on taxable profit. To determine taxable profit companies produce a reconciliation of accounting profit (or loss) to taxable profit (or loss), which takes into account both temporary and permanent differences (see Worked example 9.1). Current tax is then calculated by applying the relevant corporation tax rate to the taxable profit. If tax is payable, this is recognised as an expense and a liability:

Debit   Income tax expense (income statement)

Credit   Current tax liability

Current tax may be recoverable for the following reasons:

(a) Amounts may already have been paid to the tax authorities in respect of current and prior periods which exceed the amounts due for these periods

(b) Tax losses may be able to be carried back to recover current tax of a previous period.

These give rise to a benefit, which can be recognised as a current tax asset, as the definition of an asset as given in the IASB's *Conceptual Framework* is met.

🛈 **Reminder** *An asset is a resource controlled by the entity as a result of past transactions and from which future economic benefits are expected to flow to the entity.*

In this case the accounting is:

Debit   Current tax asset

Credit   Income tax expense (income statement)

Worked example 9.1: to show the reconciliation of accounting profit to taxable profit

Lilliput plc's summarised income statement for the year ended 31 March 20X6 is as follows:

	£
Revenue	346,140
Cost of sales	(235,380)
Gross profit	110,760
Distribution and administrative expenses	(97,470)
Other income	12,000
Profit before tax	25,290

Included in the distribution and administrative expenses are the following items:

- depreciation of £36,500
- donations to a political party of £500
- contribution to company pension scheme accrued £5,000.

Other income represents dividends receivable from an overseas investment, which are taxable on receipt.

The capital allowances have been calculated as £27,300.

Required:

Produce the reconciliation of accounting profit to taxable profit for Lilliput for the year ended 31 March 20X6.

		£
Profit before tax		25,290
Add back:	Depreciation	36,500
	Donations to political party	500
	Accrued pension scheme contribution	5,000
		67,290
Deduct:	Dividends receivable	(12,000)
	Capital allowances	(27,300)
Taxable profit		27,990

The current tax liability or asset is measured using rates 'that have been enacted or substantively enacted by the end of the reporting period', and companies have to be aware of the time between the passing of tax legislation and when it is actually applicable. In the UK, corporation tax rates have been reducing for many years and are currently (in 2012) 24% for large companies (i.e. those with taxable profits greater than £1.5 million) or there is a small companies rate of 20%.

From a practical point of view, listed companies will usually publish their financial statements before they have agreed the final tax liability with the tax authorities. (In many cases, agreement of the amount payable or recoverable may take many months or years!) Thus, the tax liability or asset will be an estimate, the value of which requires management's and the auditor's expertise and judgement to be exercised. The amount actually settled will therefore differ from this estimate. As with other accounting estimates, and in accordance with IAS 8 *Accounting Policies, Changes in Accounting Estimates and Errors*, any over-/underestimates of tax are included in the tax expense in the period in which the final settlement or agreement is reached.

In the UK large companies have to make quarterly payments based on their estimate of the corporation tax payable for the year. Thus, any total liability will be reduced by these amounts. Other companies are required to pay their corporation tax within nine months and one day of the end of the accounting period.

 Worked example 9.2: to show the calculation of current tax

Verne plc estimates that current tax for the year ended 30 June 20X4 is £750,000. This figure takes into account new tax rates which were announced in March 20X4 and which are confidently expected to be enacted in August 20X4. If the new tax rates were to be disregarded the amount due would be £810,000. Verne has made payments on account totalling £390,000 during the year to 30 June 20X4 in relation to the current tax for the year.

Current tax for the year ended 30 June 20X3 was estimated at £620,000, but the final settlement was £590,000, which was paid on 29 March 20X5.

Required:
Calculate the current tax amounts which should be shown in the financial statements for the year ended 30 June 20X4 and show the resulting accounting entries.

Income statement expense	£
Current tax for y/e 30 June 20X4	750,000
Overestimate of current tax for y/e 30 June 20X3	
(590,000 – 620,000)	(30,000)
	720,000

Statement of financial position current liability	£
Current tax for y/e 30 June 20X4	750,000
Less: payments on account	(390,000)
	360,000

This can also be achieved through double-entry and T accounts.

At 1 July 20X3 there will be an opening credit balance on the tax liability account of £620,000 – £590,000 = £30,000 being the overestimate of tax for the year ended 30 June 20X3. This will be cleared to the tax expense account by:

		£	£
Dr	Tax liability	30,000	
Cr	Tax expense		30,000

The estimate of tax for the current year ended 30 June 20X4 will be based on the tax rates that are confidently expected to be enacted in August 20X4 and so will be £750,000. The double-entry for this is:

		£	£
Dr	Tax expense	750,000	
Cr	Tax liability		750,000

Payments on account will be posted as follows:

		£	£
Dr	Tax liability	390,000	
Cr	Bank		390,000

T accounts will give the final balances for the income statement (I/S) and statement of financial position (SoFP):

Tax expense (I/S)			
Tax liability	750,000	Tax liability	30,000
		I/S expense	720,000
	750,000		750,000

Tax liability (SoFP)			
Tax expense	30,000	Balance b/f	30,000
Bank	390,000	Tax expense	750,000
Balance c/f	360,000		
	780,000		780,000

9.3 Deferred tax

9.3.1 What is deferred tax?

Deferred tax is tax attributable to temporary differences. Temporary differences have been explained in the previous sections in terms of the timing difference between the accounting and tax recognition of income and expense. However, IAS 12 takes a statement of financial position approach to deferred tax and defines temporary differences as differences between the carrying amount of an asset or liability in the statement of financial position and its **tax base**. However, these different approaches do not give a different result. If a statement of financial position was drawn up with assets and liabilities using tax bases, and this was compared with the statement of financial position drawn up according to accounting rules, the difference in net assets value would be the same as the difference between taxable profit and accounting profit.

The tax base of an asset or liability is defined as the amount attributed to that asset or liability for tax purposes, and is explained further in section 9.3.3.

The tax attributable to temporary differences may give rise to a deferred tax liability or asset depending on whether the temporary differences are:

(a) *Taxable temporary differences*, which are temporary differences that will result in taxable amounts in determining taxable profit (tax loss) of future periods when the carrying amount of the asset or liability is recovered or settled.

 Taxable temporary differences give rise to deferred tax liabilities.

(b) *Deductible temporary differences*, which are temporary differences that will result in amounts that are deductible in determining taxable profit (tax loss) of future periods when the carrying amount of the asset or liability is recovered or settled.

 Deductible temporary differences give rise to deferred tax assets.

9.3.2 Approach to the recognition of deferred tax

The IAS 12 approach to the recognition and measurement of deferred tax requires the following steps to be taken which will be explained and illustrated in the following sections.

1 Determine the tax base of an asset or liability, and compare this to the carrying (accounting) amount.

2 If they are not the same, calculate the temporary difference, and determine whether this is a taxable or deductible difference.

3 Identify if there are any exceptions to the recognition of a deferred tax asset or liability.

4 Consider the recoverability of any deferred tax asset.

5 Establish the tax rate to be used in the measurement of deferred tax.

6 Account for the deferred tax, and present and disclose according to IAS 12.

9.3.3 Tax base of an asset or liability

The definitions of the tax base of an asset or liability given in IAS 12 are not straightforward. These definitions are given in Table 9.1.

Table 9.1 Defining the tax base as an asset or liability

Tax base	Definition
Asset	The amount that will be deductible for tax purposes against any taxable economic benefits that will flow to an entity when it recovers the carrying amount of the asset. If those economic benefits will not be taxable, the tax base of the asset is equal to its carrying amount.
Liability	The carrying amount, less any amount that will be deductible for tax purposes in respect of that liability in future periods. In the case of revenue which is received in advance, the tax base of the resulting liability is its carrying amount, less any amount of the revenue that will not be taxable in future periods.

Essentially, the tax base reflects the tax consequences that will occur when the carrying amount of the asset or liability is recovered or settled, in other words how much will be deducted for tax purposes when the asset is sold or the liability is paid?

 Examples of tax bases

1 A machine whose original cost was £100,000 is depreciated in accordance with normal accounting rules and has a net book value of £40,000. For tax purposes, writing down allowances (tax depreciation) of £30,000 have been allowed.

   Use of the machine will generate future economic benefits (revenues), which will be taxable. As the machine is used the remaining cost not already deducted for tax purposes will be deductible in the future either through tax depreciation or as a deduction on disposal. Hence, the tax base is the cost not already deducted of £100,000 – £30,000 = £70,000.

2 Income receivable of £40,000 included in current assets. This income is taxed on a cash basis.

   The tax statement of financial position will not include an asset for income receivable as the income is taxed when received. The tax base is therefore nil.

3 Trade receivables of £50,000.

   The related revenue has already been included in taxable profit so there will be no further taxable economic benefits. The tax base is equal to the carrying amount of £50,000.

4 Accrued overhead expenses of £15,000.

   The overhead expenses have already been deducted in arriving at taxable profit so there are no further future deductions. The tax base is equal to the carrying amount of £15,000.

5 An expense payable of £20,000 included in current liabilities. This expense is allowable for tax on a cash basis.

   The tax statement of financial position will not include a liability for interest payable as interest is taxed when paid. The tax base is therefore nil. Alternatively, applying the definition in IAS 12, there will be future deductions for the interest to be paid, so the tax base is £20,000 – £20,000 = nil.

6 A loan of £200,000 included in non-current liabilities.

   The repayment of the loan will have no tax consequences so the tax base is the carrying amount of £200,000.

9.3.4 Taxable and deductible temporary differences

Once the tax base of assets and liabilities have been established these are compared to the carrying amounts, and the differences are determined as either taxable or deductible, as given in Figure 9.1.

Typical examples of items giving rise to taxable and deductible temporary differences are provided in Table 9.2.

Under certain IFRSs assets may be revalued to fair value. Provided this does not adjust the tax base of an asset, the difference between carrying amount and tax base will change and give rise to a temporary difference, and, hence, to a deferred tax asset or liability.

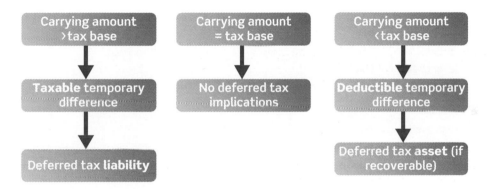

Figure 9.1 Taxable and deductible temporary differences

Table 9.2 Examples of taxable and deductible temporary differences

Taxable temporary differences	Deductible temporary differences
1 Royalty revenue—included in accounting profit on the accruals basis, but included in taxable profit on a cash basis.	1 Retirement benefit costs—deducted from accounting profit as service is provided by the employee, but deducted from taxable profits either when contributions are paid to the retirement fund or when the retirement benefits are paid.
2 Depreciation—deducted from accounting profit according to matching and estimates of expected life, residual value and pattern of usage. Deducted from taxable profit according to tax rules.	2 Research costs—recognised as an expense in accounting profit, but may not be permitted as a deduction for taxable profits until a later period.
3 Development costs—may be capitalised and amortised for accounting profit purposes, but deducted in full for taxable profit.	3 A liability recognised in a business combination—the related costs may be deducted from taxable profits in a later period.

Examples of taxable and deductible temporary differences

Using the tax base examples given in the previous example.

1   A machine whose original cost was £100,000 is depreciated in accordance with normal accounting rules and has a net book value of £40,000. For tax purposes, writing down allowances (tax depreciation) of £30,000 have been allowed.

Carrying amount = £40,000. Tax base = £70,000.

- Deductible temporary difference.
- Deferred tax asset.

2   Income receivable of £40,000 included in current assets. This income is taxed on a cash basis.

Carrying amount = £40,000; Tax base = nil.

- Taxable temporary difference.
- Deferred tax liability.

3   Trade receivables of £50,000.

Carrying amount = Tax base = £50,000.

- No deferred tax implications.

4   Accrued overhead expenses of £15,000.

Carrying amount = Tax base = £15,000.

- No deferred tax implications.

5   Expense payable of £20,000 included in current liabilities. This expense is allowable for tax on a cash basis.

Carrying amount = £(20,000); Tax base = nil.

Be careful with liabilities where there are differences between the carrying amount and the tax base. Treat the liability as a negative number. Here, the carrying amount is less than the tax base.

- Deductible temporary difference.
- Deferred tax asset.

6   A loan of £200,000 included in non-current liabilities.

Carrying amount = Tax base = £200,000.

- No deferred tax implications.

9.3.5 Exceptions to the recognition of deferred tax assets and liabilities

IAS 12 requires the recognition of deferred tax liabilities and assets for all taxable and deductible temporary differences, except for the following:

1   The initial recognition of goodwill in a business combination

2   The initial recognition of an asset or liability outside a business combination and in a transaction that does not affect accounting profit or taxable profit

3   Investments in subsidiaries and associates where the investor is able to control the timing of the reversal of any temporary differences and it is probable that the temporary difference will not arise in the foreseeable future.

As discussed in Chapter 15, which deals with consolidated financial statements, goodwill arising on the acquisition of a business is essentially the difference between the consideration and the investor's share of the fair value of the net assets acquired. In other words, it is a residual amount. Many tax authorities do not allow reductions in goodwill (through impairment) as a deductible expense for tax purposes nor do they permit deductions for goodwill when the business, to which goodwill relates, is disposed of. The tax base of goodwill in these jurisdictions is therefore nil. It could be argued that there would, therefore, be a taxable temporary difference. However, because goodwill is a residual amount, the recognition of a deferred tax liability in the goodwill computation would increase the carrying amount of goodwill (because the fair value of the net assets would reduce). This iterative calculation could continue in perpetuity. This would lead to lack of transparency; thus, any deferred tax liability is not recognised.

If a business acquired an asset through a transaction which was not a business combination, and which affected neither accounting nor taxable profits, a difference between the carrying amount and the tax base of the asset could still exist. It could be argued that a deferred tax liability (or asset) should be accounted for. However, this recognition would mean the carrying amount of the asset would have to be adjusted by the same amount, which would gross up the value of the asset. Again, this would lead to less transparency in the financial statements. Therefore, in these circumstances, the deferred tax liability or asset is not permitted to be recognised.

9.3.6 Recoverability of a deferred tax asset

Subject to the exceptions detailed previously, deferred tax liabilities are recognised in full. This is because deferred tax liabilities arise when the carrying amount of an asset exceeds its tax base. In other words, the amount of taxable economic benefits will exceed the amount that will be allowed as a deduction for tax purposes in the future. The company will, therefore, have future taxable profits, which makes it probable that economic benefits will flow from the company in the form of tax payments. Thus, the criteria for the recognition of a liability, as given in the IASB's *Conceptual Framework*, are satisfied.

 Reminder *A liability is recognised in the statement of financial position when it is probable that an outflow of resources embodying economic benefits will result from the settlement of a present obligation and the amount at which the settlement will take place can be reliably measured.*

Also, subject to the exceptions detailed previously, a deferred tax asset arises when there are deductible temporary differences which result from the tax base exceeding the carrying amount of an asset or liability. Alternatively, this can be viewed as future taxable profits being reduced as tax deductions are allowed, thus giving rise to future economic benefits. However, these economic benefits will only flow to a company if there are sufficient future taxable profits. Therefore, a deferred tax asset is only recognised when it is probable that taxable profits will be available; companies need to consider this and exercise judgement.

In order to do this, companies will need to identify how future taxable profits arise. Broadly, there are three main sources.

1   *The reversal of existing taxable temporary differences*

Taxable profits will increase when taxable temporary differences reverse. If they are expected to reverse in the same period as the deductible temporary differences and relate to the same taxation authority, the related deferred tax asset should be recognised.

2   *Future trading profits*

A company needs to consider whether its future operations will generate sufficient taxable profits. It also has to take into account whether there are unused tax losses which can be set against future taxable profits. This clearly requires use of budgets and forecasts, and includes making estimates and applying judgement.

3   *Tax planning opportunities*

Tax planning opportunities are actions which a company would take to realise a deferred tax asset. For example, a company may accelerate taxable income to an earlier period to ensure a tax loss does not expire, or make certain elections, if allowed by the tax jurisdiction, as to whether income is to be taxed on a receivable basis rather than received basis.

9.3.7 Tax rate to be used in measuring deferred tax

The recovery of a deferred tax asset or the settlement of a deferred tax liability may not occur for many years. However, as for current tax, the tax rates to be used in measuring deferred tax assets and liabilities are those expected to apply when the asset is realised or the liability is settled. This should be based upon tax rates and laws that have been enacted, or substantively enacted, at the statement of financial position date.

In some jurisdictions the tax rate may vary according to the manner in which the asset is recovered or the liability is settled. A company has to apply the appropriate rate according to its plans.

 Example of tax rate to use in the calculation of deferred tax

An item of property, plant and equipment has a carrying amount of £10,000 and a tax base of £6,000. A tax rate of 20% would apply if the item were sold and a tax rate of 30% would apply to other income.

The entity recognises a deferred tax liability of £800 ((£10,000 – £6,000) at 20%) if it expects to sell the item without further use, and a deferred tax liability of £1,200 (£4,000 at 30%) if it expects to retain the item and recover its carrying amount through use.

(From IAS 12)

9.3.8 Recognition of deferred tax

One of the underpinning principles of IAS 12 is that the tax effects of a transaction or other event should be consistent with the accounting for the transaction or event itself. Therefore, deferred tax is recognised as either income or expense, and included in profit or loss for the period:

Debit	Income tax expense	OR	Debit	Deferred tax asset
Credit	Deferred tax liability		Credit	Income tax income

Once a deferred tax liability or asset is created, the change in the required liability or asset is debited or credited to profit and loss in subsequent reporting periods.

 Examples of the accounting for deferred tax

Using the relevant tax base examples given in section 9.3.4 and assuming a tax rate of 25%.

1   A machine whose original cost was £100,000 is depreciated in accordance with normal accounting rules and has a net book value of £40,000. For tax purposes, writing down allowances (tax depreciation) of £30,000 have been allowed.

Carrying amount = £40,000. Tax base = £70,000.

- Deductible temporary difference.
- Deferred tax asset of 25% × (£70,000 – £40,000) = £7,500.

		£	£
Dr	Deferred tax asset	7,500	
Cr	Income tax expense		7,500

2   Income receivable of £40,000 included in current assets. This income is taxed on a cash basis.

Carrying amount = £40,000; Tax base = nil.

- Taxable temporary difference.
- Deferred tax liability of 25% × (£40,000 – nil) = £10,000.

		£	£
Dr	Income tax expense	10,000	
Cr	Deferred tax liability		10,000

3   No deferred tax implications.

4   No deferred tax implications.

5   Expense payable of £20,000 included in current liabilities. This expense is allowable for tax on a cash basis.

Carrying amount = £(20,000); Tax base = nil.

- Deductible temporary difference.
- Deferred tax asset of 25% × (£20,000 – nil) = £5,000.

		£	£
Dr	Deferred tax asset	5,000	
Cr	Income tax expense		5,000

6 No deferred tax implications.

An exception to this accounting treatment is where the underpinning transaction or event is recognised outside profit or loss. If this is the case, then the related deferred tax is also be recognised outside profit or loss. Examples include the surplus arising on the revaluation of a non-current asset, which is recognised in other comprehensive income, and adjustments to opening retained earnings from a change in accounting policy or error applied retrospectively, which are recognised directly in equity. Any deferred tax asset or liability arising from these items would be also included in other comprehensive income and equity respectively.

9.3.9 Right of offset

As companies will have both deferred tax liabilities and deferred tax assets, the question arises whether these can be netted off on the statement of financial position. One of the underpinning principles of presentation outlined in IAS 1 *Presentation of Financial Statements* (discussed in Chapter 4) is that companies should not offset assets and liabilities, as this leads to lack of transparency. However, it is permitted where another IFRS does allow it—deferred tax is one such area. There are restrictions on this though and IAS 12 states that the offset is only allowed if:

(a) the entity has a legally enforceable right to set off current tax assets against current tax liabilities; and

(b) the deferred tax assets and the deferred tax liabilities relate to income taxes levied by the same taxation authority on either:

  (i) the same taxable entity; or

  (ii) different taxable entities which intend to either settle or current tax liabilities and assets on a net basis, or to realise the assets and settle the liabilities simultaneously, in each future period in which significant amounts of deferred tax liabilities or assets are expected to be settled or recovered.

Deferred tax balances are never offset against current tax balances, as they relate to different issues.

Worked example 9.3: to show the calculation and recognition of deferred tax

Warrington plc commenced operations on 1 January 20X8. Its book and tax financial statements are consistent except for two items.

1   Warrington purchased a piece of equipment in 1 January 20X8 for £2,000. The equipment has a useful life of four years and is depreciated on a straight-line basis for accounting purposes. The tax authority allows the company to claim tax allowances for the cost of the asset over two years, also on a straight-line basis.

2   When Warrington sells products that have a warranty attached it records a warranty provision in its financial statements when the revenue is recognised (Dr Warranty expense; Cr Warranty provision). The tax authority does not allow a deduction for the warranty expense until cash is paid to settle a warranty claim. The warranty provision at 31 December 20X8 is estimated at £1,200.

Warrington recorded a net profit of £10,000 for its first year of trading before accounting for these two items. The tax rate in Warrington's jurisdiction is 40%.

Required:

Calculate and show the accounting for the current tax and deferred tax for Warrington plc for 20X8.

Before dealing with deferred tax, the *current tax* should be calculated.

	Accounting profit	Tax profit
	£	£
Net profit	10,000	10,000
Depreciation	(500)	(1,000)
Warranty provision	(1,200)	–
Profit before tax/taxable profit	8,300	9,000
Current tax 40% × £9,000	3,600	

		£	£
Debit	Income tax (I/S)	3,600	
Credit	Tax liability (SoFP)		3,600

Deferred tax

1   Determine the tax base of an asset or liability and compare this to the carrying amount.

2   If they are not the same, the temporary difference is calculated and whether this is a taxable or deductible difference is determined.

	Equipment	Warranty
	£	£
Carrying amount	1,500	(1,200)
Tax base	1,000	Nil
Taxable temporary difference	500	–
Deductible temporary difference	–	1,200
Deferred tax	Liability	Asset

3 Identify if there are any exceptions to the recognition of a deferred tax asset or liability.

The exceptions are not relevant in this example.

4 Consider the recoverability of any deferred tax asset.

Warrington is able to recognise at least £500 of the £1,200 deductible temporary difference related to the warranty provision because of the £500 taxable temporary difference related to the equipment. The recognition of the remaining deductible temporary difference depends on whether future taxable profits will be available. For the purposes of this example, assume the company does expect to make sufficient profits in the future from ongoing operations and is therefore able to recognise the entire deferred tax asset.

5 Establish the tax rate to be used in the measurement of deferred tax.

Assuming there have been no laws enacted that will change future tax rates, the present rate of 40% is used as the best estimate of the tax rate in force when the deferred tax liability will be settled and the asset realised.

		£
Deferred tax liability	40% × 500	(200)
Deferred tax asset	40% × 1,200	480

6 Account for the deferred tax and present and disclose according to IAS 12.

Given the deferred tax liability and asset arise for a single company, Warrington can offset these two balances on its statement of financial position. The accounting will therefore be:

		£	£
Debit	Deferred tax asset (SoFP)	280	
Credit	Income tax (I/S)		280

The full income statement for Warrington for the year ended 31 December 20X8 will appear as follows:

	£
Net profit	10,000
Depreciation	(500)
Warranty provision	(1,200)
Profit before tax	8,300
Income tax (3,600 – 280)	(3,320)
Profit for the year	4,980

On the statement of financial position at 31 December 20X8, the current tax liability of £3,600 will be included in current liabilities and a non-current deferred tax asset of £280 will be presented.

Note that the Warrington's effective tax rate (i.e. income tax expense divided by profit before tax) is now 40% (3,320/8,300), which is consistent with the tax rate in the company's jurisdiction. If only current tax had been included in the income statement, the effective tax rate would have been 3,600/8,300 = 43%. The deferred tax has had the effect of 'normalising' the effective tax rate; this issue is discussed further in section 9.4.

9.4 The effect of accounting for deferred tax

As shown by the Worked example 9.3, one effect of accounting for deferred tax is to 'normalise' the effective tax rate, so that a user looking at the income statement sees the income tax charge as approximating to the tax rate multiplied by profit before tax. (Note: they will never be exactly the same because of permanent differences, among other matters.) It could be argued that this makes the income tax figure in the income statement more relevant and understandable.

Extending this idea illustrates the further argument that accounting for deferred tax has the effect of 'income smoothing'. Worked example 9.4 shows this by considering a company's profits for more than one year.

 Worked example 9.4: to show the income smoothing effect of deferred tax

Belay plc has issued share capital of 2 million £1 equity shares. The company has exactly the same profit before tax for the three years to 31 December 20X4:

	20X2	20X3	20X4
	£000	£000	£000
Profit before tax (PBT)	2,000	2,000	2,000
Depreciation (included in above PBT)	600	600	600
Tax allowances on non-current assets	800	500	200

The depreciation and tax allowances relate to an asset which was acquired for £2,400 on 1 January 20X2. Assume that there are no other permanent or temporary differences, and that the rate of tax is 25% throughout the full period.

Required:

(a) Accounting only for current tax, calculate Belay's profit after tax and earnings per share (EPS) for the three years, and comment on these results.

(b) Repeat the calculations required in (a), but include accounting for deferred tax. Comment on the results.

(a) Current tax charge

	20X2	20X3	20X4
	£000	£000	£000
Profit before depreciation	2,600	2,600	2,600
Tax allowances on non-current asset	800	500	200
Taxable profits	1,800	2,100	2,400
Current tax (25% × taxable profits)	450	525	600

If only current tax is accounted for, the income statements would show:

	20X2	20X3	20X4
	£000	£000	£000
Profit before tax	2,000	2,000	2,000
Income tax	450	525	600
Profit after tax	1,550	1,475	1,400
EPS	78p	74p	70p

For a company with identical profits before tax for three years and no change in taxation rates, falling profits after tax and EPS certainly look strange, and, to users, would certainly lack transparency. Remember, tax allowances are not shown in the financial statements—these figures are used in the company's tax returns.

(b) Deferred tax

	20X2	20X3	20X4
	£000	£000	£000
Carrying amount of asset	1,800	1,200	600
Tax base	1,600	1,100	900
Taxable/(deductible) temporary difference	200	100	(300)
Deferred tax (liability)/asset (@ 25%)	(50)	(25)	75

In 20X2 the deferred tax liability would be set up:

		£000	£000
Debit	Income tax (I/S)	50	
Credit	Deferred tax liability		50

In 20X3 and 20X4 this balance is adjusted, with the change being accounted for in the income statement; so, for 20X3:

		£000	£000
Debit	Deferred tax liability	25	
Credit	Income tax (I/S)		25

For 20X4:

		£000	£000
Debit	Deferred tax liability	100	
Credit	Income tax (I/S)		100

The effect of including changes in deferred tax balances in the income tax charge is as follows:

	20X2	20X3	20X4
	£000	£000	£000
Current tax	450	525	600
Change in deferred tax	50	(25)	(100)
Income tax charge	500	500	500

The income statements and EPS are thus 'smoothed':

	20X2	20X3	20X4
	£000	£000	£000
Profit before tax	2,000	2,000	2,000
Income tax	500	500	500
Profit after tax	1,500	1,500	1,500
EPS	75p	75p	75p

9.5 Is the approach of IAS 12 *Income Taxes* to accounting for deferred tax appropriate?

As mentioned previously, methods of accounting for deferred tax have been changed over the years by different countries' accounting standard-setters. In the UK, accounting profit and taxable profit are determined relatively independently of each other. Deferred tax has always, therefore, been a significant accounting issue and there have been many changes, such as the question of whether deferred tax should be recognised in full or only partially. However, in countries where accounting and tax systems are closer, for example Germany, deferred tax has been less of an issue and deferred tax balances will be much smaller.

The IASB's approach to deferred tax is based on the principles behind the recognition of assets and liabilities. It is inherent in the recognition of assets or liabilities that a company expects to recover or settle the carrying amount of that asset or liability. If it is probable that recovery and settlement of the carrying amount will make future tax payments larger or smaller, then, with certain limited exceptions, the company should recognise a related deferred tax liability or asset. The IASB's discussion of an asset given in its *Conceptual Framework* explains that:

> ...the future economic benefit embodied in an asset is the potential to contribute, directly or indirectly, to the flow of cash and cash equivalents to the entity.

(IASB, 2010: para. 4.8)

Given this, it would be difficult to argue for the tax consequences of the future economic benefits of an asset being ignored in its measurement.

This can also be considered as the application of accruals or matching, one of the core underpinning concepts of financial reporting. On one hand, the IASB's approach requires the tax consequences of transactions and other events to be accounted for in the same way, and in the same accounting period that the transactions and other events are accounted for themselves.

On the other hand, the *Conceptual Framework*'s definition of a liability includes the requirement that there is a present obligation. A present obligation means that the event or transaction giving rise to the obligation has happened before the date of the statement of financial position. Critics of the IASB's approach to deferred tax argue that the reversal of taxable temporary differences may not result in future tax payments because of events that occur in the future, for example because of rolling capital investment programmes. A further argument is that tax is only payable when tax legislation requires it to be paid. However, this latter argument is contrary to the 'substance over form' principle that underpins much of the IASB's standard-setting.

Critics raise further objections to accounting for deferred tax by claiming it is difficult to understand. The IASB, in explaining its enhancing qualitative characteristic of understandability, states that the complexity of an event or a transaction should not be a barrier to any accounting treatment. Clear and comparable disclosures relating to how and where deferred tax has been accounted for, and its effect on the financial statements, are therefore very important to provide this understanding to users.

Industries that are particularly affected by large deferred tax balances are those which include assets on a fair value basis, as the difference between the accounting and tax bases is likely to be substantial.

9.6 Disclosures

Transparency in accounting for tax is critical and the disclosures required by IAS 12 are there to ensure this as far as possible. Companies will generally include a brief accounting policy relating to taxation.

The major components of the income statement tax charge should be disclosed, which will include:

- the current tax expense or income for the period
- adjustments relating to under- or overestimates of current tax from previous periods
- the amount of deferred tax expense or income relating to temporary differences
- the amount of deferred tax expense or income relating to changes in tax rates or legislation.

If income tax is recognised outside profit and loss, for example in other comprehensive income, the amount of tax relating to each component of other comprehensive income is disclosed separately.

An explanation of the relationship between the tax expense and accounting profit is also required, and a company can present this in two alternative ways:

1 A reconciliation between the tax expense and the figure obtained by multiplying accounting profit by the tax rate used

2 A reconciliation between the effective tax rate and the tax rate used.

This is often a key requirement of users who, as research shows, often ask why there is such a large difference between the statutory rate of tax of income tax and the amount companies actually pay to the tax authorities.

Financial reporting in practice 9.1 — Nestlé, 2010

Nestlé's 2010 detailed tax note shows this information. The company's profit before tax was CHF 38,067 million (2009: CHF 14,355 million). (Note: CHF denotes Swiss francs.)

Note 14 – Taxes

14.1 Taxes recognised in the income statement

In millions of CHF	2010	2009
Components of taxes		
Current taxes (a)	2,917	2,772
Deferred taxes	181	236
Taxes reclassified to other comprehensive income	248	87
Taxes reclassified to equity	(3)	(8)
Taxes from continuing operations	3,343	3,087
Taxes from discontinued operations	350	275
Total taxes	3,693	3,362
Reconciliation of taxes		
Expected tax expense at weighted average applicable tax rate	2,882	2,789
Tax effect of non-deductible or non-taxable items	(10)	(168)
Prior years' taxes	(129)	(17)
Transfers to unrecognised deferred tax assets	53	58
Transfers from unrecognised deferred tax assets	(20)	(44)
Changes in tax rates	9	(1)
Withholding taxes levied on transfers of income	353	340
Other, incl. taxes on capital	205	130
Taxes from continuing operations	3,343	3,087

(a) Current taxes related to prior years represent a tax expense of CHF 25 million (2009: tax income of CHF 45 million).

(continued)

(continued)

The expected tax expense at weighted average applicable tax rate is the result from applying the domestic statutory tax rates to profits before taxes of each entity in the country it operates. For the Group, the weighted average applicable tax rate varies from one year to the other depending on the relative weight of the profit of each individual entity in the Group's profit as well as the changes in the statutory tax rates.

14.2 Taxes recognised in other comprehensive income

In millions of CHF	2010	2009
Tax effects relating to		
Currency retranslations	195	(131)
Fair value adjustments on available-for-sale financial instruments	(11)	(43)
Fair value adjustments on cash flow hedges	21	(178)
Actuarial gains/(losses) on defined benefit schemes	63	442
	268	90

A company shall also disclose for each type of temporary difference the amount of deferred tax liability or asset, and the amount of deferred tax expense or income recognised in the income statement.

Financial reporting in practice 9.2   Marston's plc, 2010

Marston's has a policy of revaluation of its properties to fair value (see Chapter 10). The company therefore has a relatively large deferred tax liability (approximately 12% of its non-current liabilities) and clearly shows the different types of temporary difference. The company does not offset its deferred tax asset against its deferred tax liabilities as indicated as follows.

Note 22 Deferred tax

Net deferred tax liability

Deferred tax is calculated on temporary differences between tax bases of assets and liabilities and their carrying amounts under the liability method using a tax rate of 27% (2009: 28%). The movement on the deferred tax accounts is shown below:

	2010	2009
	£m	£m
At beginning of the period	113.9	141.8
Charged/(credited) to the income statement	5.9	(11.6)
Charged/(credited) to equity		
Impairment and revaluation of properties	(6.2)	(5.3)
Hedging reserve	(7.9)	(11.0)
Retirement benefits	0.1	—
At end of the period	105.8	113.9

The movements in deferred tax assets and liabilities (prior to the offsetting of balances within the same jurisdiction as permitted by IAS 12) during the period are shown below. Deferred tax assets and liabilities are only offset where there is a legally enforceable right of offset and there is an intention to settle the balances net.

Deferred tax liabilities

	Accelerated capital allowances £m	Revaluation of properties £m	Rolled over capital gains £m	Other £m	Total £m
At 4 October 2009	30.5	126.2	9.2	7.4	173.3
Charged/(credited) to the income statement	8.1	(1.3)	(1.8)	(0.8)	4.2
Credited to equity	—	(6.2)	—	—	(6.2)
At 2 October 2010	38.6	118.7	7.4	6.6	171.3

Deferred tax assets

	Pensions £m	Tax losses £m	Hedging reserve £m	Other £m	Total £m
At 4 October 2009	(9.9)	(23.3)	(21.5)	(4.7)	(59.4)
Charged/(credited) to the income statement	3.1	(0.1)	—	(1.3)	1.7
(Credited)/charged to equity	—	—	(7.9)	0.1	(7.8)
At 2 October 2010	(6.8)	(23.4)	(29.4)	(5.9)	(65.5)
Net deferred tax liability					
At 3 October 2009					113.9
At 2 October 2010					105.8

Deferred tax assets have been recognised in respect of all tax losses and other temporary differences where it is probable that these assets will be recovered.

Also key are disclosures relating to deferred tax assets and liabilities that have not been recognised, which emphasises transparency. In particular, where a deferred tax asset has not been recognised because it is unlikely that there will be future taxable profits available as the company has unused tax losses which it is carrying forward, the amount of the losses and their expiry date should be disclosed.

Financial reporting in practice 9.3   Nestlé, 2010

To illustrate this, see the note Nestlé includes in its 2010 financial statements.

Note 14 – Taxes

14.4 Unrecognised deferred taxes

The deductible temporary differences as well as the unused tax losses and tax credits for which no deferred tax assets are recognised expire as follows:

In millions of CHF	2010	2009
Within one year	56	48
Between one and five years	276	298
More than five years	1,648	1,279
	1,980	1,625

At 31 December 2010, the unrecognised deferred tax assets amount to CHF 544 million (2009: CHF 478 million).

In addition, the Group has not recognised deferred tax liabilities in respect of unremitted earnings that are considered indefinitely reinvested in foreign subsidiaries. At 31 December 2010, these earnings amount to CHF 13.3 billion (2009: CHF 20.8 billion). They could be subject to withholding and other taxes on remittance.

Accounting for income taxes requires many estimates and management judgements, and has to look forward. Although companies will include a brief accounting policy in relation to the recognition of current and deferred tax, many will also include income taxes in their disclosures of critical estimates and judgements.

Financial reporting in practice 9.4   Next plc, 2011

Next plc's 2011 financial statements include a comprehensive accounting policy relating to the recognition of taxes, which largely uses words from IAS 12.

Taxation

Current tax liabilities are measured at the amount expected to be paid, based on tax rates and laws that are enacted or substantively enacted at the balance sheet date.

Deferred tax expected to be payable or recoverable on differences at the balance sheet date between the tax bases of assets and liabilities and their carrying amounts for financial reporting purposes is accounted for using the balance sheet liability method. Deferred tax liabilities are generally recognised for all taxable temporary differences. Deferred tax assets are only recognised to the extent that it is probable that taxable profits will be available against which deductible temporary differences can be utilised.

Such assets and liabilities are not recognised if the temporary difference arises from goodwill or from the initial recognition (other than in a business combination) of other assets and liabilities in a transaction that affects neither the taxable profit nor the accounting profit. Deferred tax is not recognised in respect of taxable temporary differences associated with investments in subsidiaries and associates where the timing of the reversal of temporary differences can be controlled and it is probable that the temporary differences will not reverse in the foreseeable future. Deferred tax is calculated at the rates of taxation that are expected to apply when the asset or liability is settled, based on tax rates that have been enacted or substantively enacted by the balance sheet date, and is not discounted.

Taxation is charged or credited directly to equity if it relates to items that are credited or charged to equity; otherwise it is recognised in the income statement.

Financial reporting in practice 9.5   J Sainsbury plc, 2011

J Sainsbury plc does detail deferred tax as a particular area where significant judgements and estimates have been made, despite its deferred tax liability balance on the statement of financial position neither being particularly significant (approx. 6% of total non-current liabilities) nor if measured as a proportion of the company's income statement tax charge (12%).

Income taxes

The Group recognises expected liabilities for tax based on an estimation of the likely taxes due, which requires significant judgement as to the ultimate tax determination of certain items. Where the actual liability arising from these issues differs from these estimates, such differences will have an impact on income tax and deferred tax provisions in the period when such determination is made. Detail of the tax charge and deferred tax are set out in notes 8 and 21 respectively.

9.7 Users' interpretation of tax

Care needs to be taken by users when interpreting financial statements by using ratio analysis as to whether tax balances are included or not in the figures used for the ratios. Most performance ratios will use earnings or profit figures before tax, as it is argued that companies have little control over the tax that is charged on profits or tax that can be recovered if losses are made. This is true up to a point—companies do not set tax rates or determine tax legislation. However, companies can, for example, decide when they invest in non-current assets which will affect tax allowances given, and, through other tax planning means, minimise tax to be paid or influence when it will be due.

For ratios that use net assets figures (e.g. return on net assets) questions usually arise as to whether deferred tax balances should be included or excluded. Given that deferred tax balances arise from the difference between the carrying amount and the tax base of assets and liabilities, it may be appropriate to include these related tax balances, which are the tax consequence of having these balances. However, as mentioned previously, they could be excluded as the issue of whether the company has control over these tax consequences arises.

For ratios that use long-term financing, such as return on capital employed and gearing, there are issues over the definition of 'debt', as discussed in Chapter 5. Deferred tax liabilities, although disclosed in non-current liabilities, are not a long-term source of finance and should be not be included in such figures.

Summary of key points

Tax on a company's profit is referred to as income tax for international accounting purposes and comprises current tax and deferred tax. Current tax is tax payable or recoverable in respect of the taxable profit for a period, and its accounting is relatively straightforward. The amounts included in a company's financial statements are usually estimates and, once final agreement has been reached with the tax authorities, any changes in these estimates are accounted for in accordance with IAS 8.

Deferred tax is income tax either payable or recoverable in future periods in respect of temporary differences, and may also arise due to the carry forward of unused tax or unused tax credits. Temporary differences arise because some items or transactions are accounted for in a different period to the period in which the tax effect occurs. A key example of this is depreciation versus tax allowances for non-current assets. Temporary differences may be taxable or deductible, and result in deferred tax liabilities or deferred tax assets respectively. The IASB's approach, as specified in IAS 12 *Income Taxes*, is that all deferred tax liabilities are fully recognised, but that deferred tax assets are recognised only if it is probable that there are sufficient future taxable profits. This approach stems from the IASB's definitions of assets and liabilities, as set out in its *Conceptual Framework*. There are alternative views to this and alternative accounting treatments have been used in the past. The impact of accounting for deferred tax is that it makes the income tax figure in the income statement appear to relate more closely to the actual profit before tax and has a smoothing effect.

IAS 12 was revised in readiness for the 2005 EU requirement for the use of IFRSs, and there has only been one specific amendment since. The standard sets out fairly extensive disclosure requirements to ensure transparency in how the income statement tax figure and deferred tax balances have been arrived at. Deferred tax, in particular, is dependent on future plans and estimates, with judgement inherent in this. Users may have less understanding of tax than they do of accounting issues so the disclosures will be particularly important for them.

Further reading

IASB (International Accounting Standards Board) (2004) IAS 12 *Income Taxes*. London: IASB.

Bibliography

Abdela, M., Davids, K. and Jehle, N. (2009) Hidden Gems or Pure Fiction?, *Accountancy Magazine*, 143(1387): 63–64.

IASB (International Accounting Standards Board) (2004) IAS 12 *Income Taxes*. London: IASB.

IASB (International Accounting Standards Board) (2010) *Conceptual Framework for Financial Reporting*. London: IASB.

J Sainsbury plc (2011) *Annual Report and Financial Statements, 2011*. London: J Sainsbury.

Kingfisher plc (2011) *Annual Report and Accounts 2010/11*. London: Kingfisher.

Maloney, B. (2009) *IFRS News – Beginners' Guide: Nine Steps to Income Tax Accounting*. London: PricewaterhouseCoopers.

Marston's plc (2010) *Annual Report, 2010*. Wolverhampton: Marston's.

Nestlé S.A. (2011) *2010 Financial Statements*. Vevey: Nestlé.

Next plc (2011) *Annual Report and Accounts, 2011*. Enderby: Next.

 Questions

● Quick test

1   The following assets and liabilities appear in a company's statement of financial position at 31 March 20X6:

   (a) A motor lorry which cost £200,000 is shown at its carrying amount of £40,000. For tax purposes, its written down value is £60,000

   (b) A loan payable is shown at £120,000. The repayment of the loan will have no tax consequences

   (c) An account receivable is shown at £90,000. Of this amount, £50,000 has already been taxed, but the remaining £40,000 will be taxed in the accounting period in which it is received. The whole £90,000 has been included in accounting profit

   (d) An account payable is shown at £6,000. This relates to an expense which has already been deducted when computing accounting profit, but which will not be deducted for tax purposes until it is paid.

   Compute the tax base of each of these assets and liabilities, and identify any taxable or deductible temporary differences.

2   Markham plc acquires a machine for £200,000 on 1 January 20X2. The company estimates the useful life to be eight years with zero residual value, and adopts the straight-line basis of depreciation. The writing down allowance for tax purposes for this asset is 20% per annum on a reducing balance basis.

   Required:
   In relation to this machine, calculate the deferred tax asset or liability balance at each of Markham plc's financial year ends 20X2–20X9, and show the accounting entries which would be made.

●● Develop your understanding

3   The draft income statement of Hedley plc for the year ended 31 March 20X3 shows an income tax expense of £55,000. The draft statement of financial position shows a non-current liability of £280,000 for deferred tax, but does not show a current tax liability.

   Tax on the profit for the year ended 31 March 20X3 is estimated at £260,000. The figure in the draft income statement is the under-provision for the year ended 31 March 20X2. The carrying amount of Harrington's net assets at 31 March 20X3 is £1.4 million more than their tax base on that date. Assume a tax rate of 25%.

   Required:
   Restate the figures which should appear in relation to taxation in the company's income statement for the year ended 31 March 20X3 and in the statement of financial position at that date.

4   A company purchases an item of equipment on 1 January 20X1 for £48,000 which it estimates will have a seven-year useful life, at the end of which it is estimated it will be sold for £6,000. The company pays tax at 30% and the tax allowances for the equipment are as follows:

	£
20X1	12,000
20X2	9,000
20X3	7,000
20X4	5,000
20X5	4,000
20X6	3,000
20X7	2,000

The company had the same accounting profit before tax for each year of £80,000.
Assume that there are no other non-current assets, and that there are no differences between taxable profit and accounting profit other than those relating to depreciation

Required:
For each year determine the company's income tax figure that would be shown in the company's income statement and the deferred tax balance that would be disclosed on the company's statement of financial position.

5   The accounting policies of Kingfisher plc, in its 2011 financial statements, include the following:

> Deferred tax is the tax expected to be recoverable or recoverable on differences between the carrying amounts of assets and liabilities in the financial statements and the corresponding tax bases used in the computation of taxable profit and is accounted for using the balance sheet liability method.

You are required to explain this policy.

6   Deferred tax may be seen as an income-smoothing device which distorts the true and fair view. Explain the impact of deferred tax on reported income and justify its continued use.

●●● Take it further

7   Garrick plc's statement of financial position at 30 June 20X6 is as follows:

	£000
Assets	
Non-current assets	
Property, plant and equipment	10,000
Other intangible assets	5,000
Investments	10,500
	25,500
Current assets	
Trade receivables	7,000
Other receivables	4,600

Cash and cash equivalents	6,700
	18,300
Total assets	43,800
Equity and liabilities	
Equity	
Equity share capital	9,000
Revaluation surplus	1,500
Retained earnings	7,510
	18,010
Non-current liabilities	
8% Long-term borrowings	9,600
Deferred tax liability	3,600
Pension liabilities	4,520
	17,720
Current liabilities	
Current tax liability	3,070
Trade and other payables	5,000
	8,070
Total equity and liabilities	43,800

The following information is relevant to the above statement of financial position.

(i) The investments are shown at their fair value at 30 June 20X6. The original cost of the investments was £9 million. The difference between cost and fair value has been accounted for through the revaluation surplus. Taxation is payable on the sale of the investments.

(ii) Other intangible assets are development costs which were all allowed for tax purposes when the cost was incurred in 20X5.

(iii) Trade and other payables include an accrual for compensation to be paid to employees. This amounts to £1 million and is allowed for taxation when paid.

(iv) The tax bases of the other assets and liabilities are the same as their carrying amounts in the statement of financial position at 30 June 20X6 except for the following:

	£000
Property, plant and equipment	2,400
Trade receivables	7,500
Other receivables	5,000
Pension liabilities	5,000
8% long term borrowings	10,000

(v) Assume taxation is payable at 30%.

Required:

Calculate Garrick plc's deferred tax liability or asset at 30 June 20X6. Show how this would be dealt with in the financial statements at this date. (Assume that any adjustments do not affect current tax.)

8 Sapper plc has reported profit before tax for the two years ended 31 December 20X5 and 20X6 of £8,775,000 and £8,740,000 respectively. In 20X5 the enacted income tax rate was 40% of taxable profit. In 20X6 the enacted income tax rate was 35% of taxable profit.

The company made charitable donations of £500,000 and £350,000 in 20X5 and 20X6 respectively. Charitable donations are recognised as an expense when they are paid and are not deductible for tax purposes.

In 20X5, the company was notified by the relevant authorities that they intend to pursue an action against the company with respect to sulphur emissions. Although at December 20X6 the action had not yet come to court, the company recognised a liability of £700,000 in 20X5 being its best estimate of the fine arising from the action. Fines are not deductible for tax purposes.

In 20X2, the company incurred £1,250,000 of costs in relation to the development of a new product. These costs were deducted for tax purposes in 20X2. For accounting purposes, the company capitalised this expenditure and amortised it on the straight-line basis over five years. At 31 December 20X4, the unamortised balance of these product development costs was £500,000.

In 20X5, the company entered into an agreement with its existing employees to provide healthcare benefits to retirees. The company recognises as an expense the cost of this plan as employees provide service and recognised £2,000,000 and £1,000,000 as expenses in 20X5 and 20X6 respectively. No payments to retirees were made for such benefits in 20X5 or 20X6. Healthcare costs are deductible for tax purposes when payments are made to retirees. The company has determined that it is probable that taxable profit will be available against which any resulting deferred tax asset can be utilised.

Details of the company's building and motor vehicles cost, and accumulated depreciation for the years 20X5 and 20X6 are as follows:

	Building	Motor vehicles	Total
Cost	£000	£000	£000
Balance at 31/12/X4	50,000	10,000	60,000
Additions 20X5	6,000	–	6,000
Balance at 31/12/X5	56,000	10,000	66,000
Elimination of accumulated depreciation on revaluation at 1/1/X6	(22,800)	–	(22,800)
Revaluation at 1/1/X6	31,800	–	31,800
Balance at 1/1/X6	65,000	10,000	75,000
Additions 20X6	–	15,000	15,000
Balance at 31/12/X6	65,000	25,000	90,000
Accumulated depreciation			
Balance at 31/12/X4	20,000	4,000	24,000
Depreciation 20X5	2,800	2,000	4,800

Balance at 31/12/X5	22,800	6,000	28,800
Revaluation at 1/1/X6	(22,800)	–	(22,800)
Balance at 1/1/X6	–	6,000	6,000
Depreciation 20X6	3,250	5,000	8,250
Balance at 31/12/X6	3,250	11,000	14,250

Carrying amount

31/12/X4	30,000	6,000	36,000
31/12/X5	33,200	4,000	37,200
31/12/X6	61,750	14,000	75,750

Buildings are depreciated for accounting purposes at 5% a year on a straight-line basis and at 10% a year on a straight-line basis for tax purposes. Motor vehicles are depreciated for accounting purposes at 20% a year on a straight-line basis and at 25% a year on a straight-line basis for tax purposes. A full year's depreciation is charged for accounting purposes in the year that an asset is acquired.

At 1 January 20X6, the building was revalued to £65,000,000 and the company estimated that the remaining useful life of the building was 20 years from the date of the revaluation. The revaluation did not affect taxable profit in 20X6 and the taxation authorities did not adjust the tax base of the building to reflect the revaluation.

Required:

For the years 20X5 and 20X6 calculate the income tax figures that would be shown in Sapper plc's statement of comprehensive income and the deferred tax balances that would be disclosed on the company's statement of financial position.

 Visit the Online Resource Centre for solutions to all these end of chapter questions plus visual walkthrough solutions. You can test your understanding with extra questions and answers, explore additional case studies based on real companies, take a guided tour through a company report, and much more. Go to the Online Resource Centre at **www.oxfordtextbooks.co.uk/orc/maynard/**

Part 4
Statement of financial position reporting issues

Chapter 10 Property, plant and equipment

Chapter 11 Intangible assets

Chapter 12 Current assets

Chapter 13 Liabilities

Chapter 14 Leasing

10

Property, plant and equipment

➤ Introduction

Property, plant and equipment are essentially tangible non-current assets, such as land and buildings, plant and machinery, office equipment, and motor vehicles. It is often the largest item in monetary terms on the face of the statement of financial position, affects other figures in the financial statements, and underpins many accounting ratios. It is therefore important that financial statements communicate relevant and faithfully representational information about property, plant and equipment.

There are also inherent issues relating to the future when businesses acquire property, plant and equipment. This means that estimates and judgements are an integral part of accounting for property, plant and equipment.

The key accounting standard, which provides the framework for the accounting methods, is International Accounting Standard (IAS) 16 *Property, Plant and Equipment*. There are, however, a number of related issues dealt with by other accounting standards. These address how additional elements of the cost of an asset are determined, for example related interest costs and government grants. Additionally, IAS 36 *Impairment of Assets* deals with the crucial question of whether the carrying amount of an asset reflects the value to the business, and whether an asset is consequently deemed to be impaired or not.

Property held for investment purposes and other non-currents which are held for sale purposes are different categories of non-current asset requiring different accounting treatment and separate disclosure. How these are accounted for is addressed by two further accounting standards, IAS 40 *Investment Property* and International Financial Reporting Standard (IFRS) 5 *Non-current Assets Held for Sale and Discontinued Operations*.

After studying this chapter you will be able to:

● understand the issues relating to accounting for property, plant and equipment, and why and where judgements are required

● account for the acquisition, subsequent use of, and derecognition of property, plant and equipment, including the determination of cost, depreciation, and revaluations

● understand what impairment of non-current assets is and account for this issue

● define and account for investment properties and assets held for sale.

❏ Significance of property, plant and equipment.

❏ Definition of an asset and property, plant and equipment.

❏ Relationship to underpinning principles.

❏ Initial measurement—what is cost?

❏ Borrowing costs.

❏ Government grants.

❏ Subsequent costs.

❏ Depreciation—estimates, methods, and accounting.

❏ The two measurement models—historic cost and valuation.

❏ Impairment—what it is, why it is accounted for, and accounting treatments.

❏ Cash-generating units.

❏ Investment properties—definition of and accounting alternatives: the cost and fair value models.

❏ Assets held for sale—definition of and accounting for.

❏ Disclosures in published financial statements—what and why.

❏ Interpretation and the effect of alternative measurement models and estimates on financial information.

10.1 Significance of property, plant and equipment

Many industries, such as manufacturing and retailing, are described as capital intensive and therefore property, plant and equipment is often the largest group of assets on the businesses' statements of financial position. In these industries the cost and associated cash flows of items of property, plant and equipment will be monitored closely by users of the financial statements. Relevant and faithfully representational information about property, plant and equipment is therefore essential for users, as this will have significant implications for funding and future cash flows.

There may be pressures on businesses to enhance the figures for property, plant and equipment to improve the presentation of their statements of financial position. However, overstating the carrying amount of non-current assets, either intentionally or unintentionally, leads to the inflation of earnings. Inflated earnings have consequential effects on key performance indicators, such as earnings per share, return on capital employed, and gearing. The accounting standards relating to property, plant and equipment set out provisions to counter any such pressures.

10.2 Definition of property, plant and equipment

Expenditure in a business is generally either of a capital nature or related to ongoing expenses (revenue expenditure). The classification of expenditure as an asset or an expense often has to be based on judgement and will have a significant impact on the financial statements. The key question is where the 'debit' of the double-entry goes: either in the statement of financial position as an asset or in the income statement as an expense and reduction of profit. One of the main issues in the WorldCom scandal revolved around the inappropriate capitalisation of expenses.

Financial reporting in practice 10.1   WorldCom

At its peak, WorldCom was the second largest long distance telephone company in the USA. WorldCom grew largely by aggressively acquiring other telecommunications companies, most notably MCI Communications in 1998, and had ambitions to become the largest company in the industry. In 2000 the telecommunications industry suffered a downturn and the market prices for WorldCom's shares started to fall. Pressures from his business empires meant that the Chief Executive Officer (CEO), Bernard Ebbers, wanted WorldCom's share price to remain high. From 1999 to 2002 the company, under the direction of Ebbers and other company officers, used fraudulent accounting methods to mask its declining earnings by painting a false picture of financial growth and profitability to prop up the price of the company's shares.

The $3.8 billion fraud involved inflating profits by inappropriately capitalising expenses and inflating revenues with bogus accounting entries. The costs that were erroneously capitalised related to fees that WorldCom paid to other telecom companies for the right to access their networks.

The fraud was discovered by a small team of internal auditors which informed the audit committee and board of directors. The company filed for Chapter 11 bankruptcy protection in 2002.

Note: the auditors of WorldCom were Arthur Andersen.

The IASB's *Conceptual Framework*, which defines an asset as:

> ...a resource controlled by the entity as a result of past transactions and from which future economic benefits are expected to flow to the entity...

(IASB, 2010: para. 4.4)

is key in situations where judgement has to be applied, in particular the requirement for the expectation of future economic benefits. What this means is that for an item to be defined as an asset, it has to have the potential to contribute, directly or indirectly, to the flow of cash and cash equivalents to the company. IAS 16 *Property, Plant and Equipment* applies the Conceptual Framework's definition rigorously.

Property, plant and equipment are defined as tangible resources that are:

- held for use in the production or supply of goods or services, for rental to others, or for administrative purposes; and
- expected to be used during more than one financial year.

(IASB, 2004a: para. 6)

Property, plant and equipment are, therefore, non-current assets, and have physical form and are usually owned, but the legal right of ownership does not have to be present for control to be present. (Note: the accounting for property, plant and equipment which is leased is dealt with in Chapter 14.) Assets may be donated or provided by the government, for example as part of a programme to encourage economic growth in an area. However, property, plant and equipment are often purchased and the acquisition transaction must have occurred before the end of the financial year. The intention to purchase an asset, even if agreed and documented, does not give rise to an asset.

10.3 Recognition of property, plant and equipment

10.3.1 Initial recognition

The recognition criteria for property, plant and equipment in the financial statements as detailed in IAS 16 are the same as the requirements for the recognition of any of the elements of financial statements as set out in the *Conceptual Framework*:

- it is probable that any the future economic benefits associated with the asset will flow to the entity
- the cost of the asset can be measured reliably.

For many items classified as property, plant and equipment the related future economic benefits are clear to see. For example, a manufacturing business's machines are producing the products that will be sold to customers and the business will receive cash once the customers pay; the delivery vehicles are being used to transport the goods to the customers. Other items of property, plant and equipment may not directly increase future economic benefits. However, the property, furniture, and computer systems of the business and the motor vehicle driven by the chief financial officer are considered necessary for the business to obtain future economic benefits from its other assets and can, therefore, be recognised as property, plant and equipment.

10.3.2 Recognition of subsequent expenditure

Costs of acquiring an item of property, plant and equipment will include the purchase price, which can usually be readily ascertained, but there may be other costs associated with the acquisition. These include:

- costs of spare parts
- subsequent expenditure, for example future costs to improve or expand the capacity of the asset
- costs to replace part of or service the asset.

If the recognition criteria are met, this expenditure will be recognised as property, plant and equipment, but, if the criteria are not met, it will be written off to the income statement as an expense.

Recognition of subsequent expenditure as property, plant and equipment may lead to the different parts of a bigger asset being treated as separate components, with separate lives and depreciation being applied.

 Examples of recognition

Discuss whether the following items are property, plant and equipment, and, if so, whether they are able to be recognised in the financial statements.

1   A chemical manufacturer installs new chemical handling processes which are necessary to comply with environmental requirements for the production and storage of dangerous chemicals.

   Although these plant enhancements do not directly increase the future economic benefits of the manufacturer, they are able to be recognised as an asset because without them the business is unable to manufacture and sell chemicals.

2   On acquisition of a specialised item of machinery a manufacturer purchases spare parts for the motor that drives the machine. The motor is expected to run without needing replacement parts for 18 months.

   The spare parts are to be used only in connection with this particular machine, and the business expects to use them during more than one accounting year. It is assumed the cost is known. They can therefore be recognised as property, plant and equipment.

3   A business fits interior partitions into its general office space.

A business does this often as part of a restructuring programme or to enable its employees to work more efficiently. Thus, the business will derive future economic benefits from this building work. It is likely the partitions will be in place for more than one year and the cost can be established. They can therefore be recognised as property, plant and equipment.

4   A business repaints its warehouse.

The repainting expenditure only maintains the future economic benefits flowing from the use of the warehouse; there is no increase in the benefits originally identified when the warehouse was first acquired. This expenditure is therefore treated as repairs and maintenance, and is written off to profit and loss when incurred.

10.4 Initial measurement of property, plant and equipment

10.4.1 Cost

An item of property, plant and equipment is measured (*remember this means valued*) on its recognition at its cost. This comprises all costs directly attributable to bringing the asset to the location and condition necessary for it to be capable of operating in the manner intended by the business, and will include:

(a) The purchase price net of trade discounts

(b) Import duties and taxes

(c) Costs of site preparation

(d) Delivery and handling costs

(e) Construction, installation, and assembly costs

(f) Wages and salaries, and other employee benefits relating to the acquisition, construction, and installation of the asset

(g) Costs of testing whether the asset is working properly

(h) Professional fees.

If, as a result of having acquired the asset, a business has an obligation to dismantle and remove the item and restore the site on which it is located at the end of its use, an estimate of these costs will be included in the cost of the property, plant and equipment. This applies, for example, to oil exploration or drilling companies, where they are required to remove all drilling rigs and restore the land or sea bed to its original state. This obligation means that a provision, which is a liability, has to be accounted for:

Debit   Property, plant and equipment

  Credit   Non-current liability

and the measurement of this liability, and hence the amount added to the asset cost, will be on a discounted cash flow basis if the discounting is considered material. This will be discussed further in Chapter 13 which deals with accounting for provisions.

Once an asset is capable of operating as the business intended, any further costs relating to the asset are not capitalised as property, plant and equipment, even if the asset is not yet being operated or it is being operated, but not at full capacity. So, for example, losses incurred while the demand for the asset's output builds up and costs of reorganising the business's operations during this time are written off to profit and loss.

If an asset is constructed internally by a business, the same principles apply in determining its cost. However, any abnormal costs, for example related to wasted material, labour, or other resources, are not included. In practice this may be difficult to ascertain.

If an item of property, plant and equipment is acquired by an exchange of non-monetary assets, the cost of the asset is measured at fair value. There are two exceptions to this:

1   Where the exchange transaction lacks commercial substance, for example where two similar assets are exchanged

2   Where the fair value of neither asset exchanged can be measured reliably.

In these cases the cost of the acquired asset is measured at the carrying amount of the asset transferred.

10.4.2 Borrowing costs

Some items of property, plant and equipment take a substantial period of time to get ready for their intended use. The acquisition itself may take some time, if, for example, planning permission has to be obtained to enable the development of a plot of land, and then the asset may have to be constructed. A business in this position may fund the acquisition or construction itself, and take out some form of loan and incur finance and other charges in relation to this. Alternatively, a business may acquire a complete asset immediately ready for use. The cost of this asset would include financing costs incurred by the third party during the development phase.

To enhance comparability of these two situations, the asset in the former case described previously is called a **qualifying asset** and the borrowing costs that are directly attributable to the acquisition or construction of this qualifying asset form part of the cost of the asset. IAS 23 *Borrowing Costs* sets out the accounting treatment and requirements.

If a business borrows funds specifically for the purpose of obtaining a qualifying asset, it is straightforward to identify the borrowing costs. However, it may be difficult to identify a direct relationship between particular borrowings and a qualifying asset. For example, many businesses will coordinate their financing activities centrally, or a parent company in a group obtains the borrowing and lends out funds on various bases to the other groups companies. In this case the amount of borrowing costs that should be capitalised is calculated by reference to the weighted average cost of the general borrowings. This calculation excludes borrowings directly related to another qualifying asset.

Borrowing costs are capitalised from the commencement date until the date when substantially all the activities necessary to prepare the asset for its intended use are complete. The commencement date is the first date when all three of the following conditions are met:

(a) The company incurs expenditure on the asset

(b) The company incurs borrowing costs

(c) The company undertakes activities that are necessary to prepare the asset for its intended use.

Cessation of the capitalisation of the borrowing costs is when the asset is substantially available for use and not when the asset is actually used. So, if, for example, the move of the business to the property that has been constructed is delayed but the property is complete, the interest incurred during the period of the delay cannot be added to the cost of the property.

10.4.3 Government grants

Businesses may receive financial assistance from the government or government agencies for a variety of reasons and in various forms. For example:

- monetary assistance may be provided to stimulate employment or investment in particular geographical areas or for specific industries

- business start-up grants may be awarded

- governments may actually invest in the business (as the UK government has in financial institutions as a result of the financial crisis)

- tax breaks may be given or reductions in certain taxes allowed.

IAS 20 *Accounting for Government Grants and Disclosure of Government Assistance* was issued to ensure that companies which received government assistance and those which had not could be compared fairly, and that the companies' performances could be interpreted properly.

Government grants are a particular form of government assistance and are awarded 'in return for past or future compliance with certain conditions relating to the operating activities of the entity' (IASB, IAS 20 *Accounting for Government Grants and Disclosure of Government Assistance*, para. 3). They may include the actual transfer of an asset, such as a plot of land, or be in the form of cash to assist companies in the acquisition of non-current assets.

Government grants can be recognised when there is reasonable assurance that:

1   The company will comply with any conditions attached to the grant

2   The company will actually receive the grant.

The recognition of the grants follows the accruals or matching principle (called the 'income approach' in IAS 20), and should be included in profit and loss over the periods in which the company recognises the costs which the grants are intended to compensate. In relation to grants received for depreciating non-current assets the grants are recognised over the periods in which the asset is depreciated and on the same systematic basis as the depreciation is charged.

Table 10.1 shows the two alternative accounting methods by which this may be achieved.

On one hand, the net effect of the two accounting methods on profit is the same; however, the statement of financial position of a company choosing the netting-off method will be less comparable to companies who have not received grants. On the other hand, impairment (see later in chapter) may be less of an issue as the carrying amount of the asset is lower.

Table 10.1 Alternative methods for accounting for government grants

	Approach	Accounting	
1	**Deferred income approach**	Dr	Bank/cash
	Set up grant as deferred income (a liability on the statement of financial position)	Cr	Deferred income
	The income is recognised in profit and loss over the useful life of the asset corresponding to the method of depreciation used	Dr	Deferred income
		Cr	Income
2	**Netting-off method**	Dr	Bank/cash
	Deduct the grant from the cost of the asset	Cr	Asset
	The grant is recognised in profit and loss through the reduced depreciation		

10.5 Subsequent measurement—depreciation

Once an item of property, plant and equipment is available for use, all costs of using the resource need to be matched against the benefits the resource brings in. This includes the cost of the asset; the accounting mechanism by which this is done is depreciation. The allocation of the cost of an asset should be done on a systematic basis over its useful life. Owing to subsequent expenditure on an item of property, plant and equipment, the cost of the asset may comprise different parts. In this case, each part of the asset may have to be depreciated separately. For example, for an aircraft it may be appropriate to depreciate the airframe and the engines separately. This splitting of an asset into component parts is a key feature of IAS 16 and may provide specific challenges where property, plant and equipment, and intangible assets are linked closely, for example where a machine is preloaded with application software.

It is necessary here to define various terms used in connection with depreciation. Depreciation actually allocates the depreciable amount of an asset over its useful life.

Depreciable amount	Cost of asset (or other amount substituted for cost) less its *residual value*.
Residual value	Estimated amount that the entity would currently obtain from the disposal of the asset, net of costs of disposal, if the asset were already in the condition expected at the end of its *useful life*.
Useful life	The period over which an asset is expected to be available for use.
	Or:
	The number of production units expected to be obtained from the asset.

10.5.1 Accounting for depreciation

The effect of depreciation is to write down the cost (or other amount substituted for cost) for each accounting period. The resulting value of the asset is termed net book value or carrying amount. Businesses, however, need to keep the depreciation that accumulates on an asset in a separate account from the cost, as they are required to disclose both amounts (see section 10.11 for disclosure requirements). Depreciation is an expense charged to profit or loss, and so the basic bookkeeping is:

Debit   Depreciation expense

  Credit   Accumulated depreciation

Instead of being expensed depreciation may be capitalised as part of the cost of another asset. For example, suppose a crane owned by a business is used in the construction of a new building which the business will own and occupy. The depreciation expense of the crane is a directly attributable cost incurred in the construction of another asset, the building. Hence, the bookkeeping will be:

Debit   Building cost

  Credit   Crane accumulated depreciation

Depreciation should commence once an asset is available for its intended use, which may be different from when it is actually used, and ceases:

1   Either when the asset is classified as 'held for sale' (see section 10.10),

2   Or when the asset is derecognised, i.e. it is disposed of, or no future economic benefits are expected from its use or disposal.

A few further points about depreciation should be made. All assets classified as property, plant and equipment should be depreciated, except land as this has an unlimited useful life. Exceptions to this land exception are quarries and mines, which are depreciated as the land is consumed.

Depreciation is required even if the fair value of the asset exceeds its carrying amount. Arguably, companies such as breweries, which own chains of pubs, and hotel and leisure complexes, which maintain their assets in a good state of repair by carrying out frequent refurbishments, should not have to depreciate these assets. However, IAS 16 makes clear that it is only if the residual value exceeds the carrying amount that depreciation would not be required.

The future economic benefits of an asset are consumed mainly through its use. However, other factors may result in the reduction of the economic benefits and should, therefore, be taken into account when estimating the useful life. These factors could include:

- expected physical wear and tear
- level of maintenance
- technical or commercial obsolescence
- change in demand for the products produced by the asset.

10.5.2 Method of depreciation

The depreciation method chosen by the company should reflect the pattern in which the asset's future economic benefits are expected to be consumed by the company and be reviewed at least at each financial year end. Three alternative methods are mentioned in IAS 16:

- the straight-line method
- the diminishing (or reducing) balance method
- the units of production method.

Note that the standard does not specify that a company has to select one of these methods. Many companies choose the straight line method as they estimate the pattern of consumption of an asset to be similar from year to year.

 Worked example 10.1: to show the different depreciation methods

Details relating to a machine acquired by Quin plc are as follows:

Cost of machine	£25,000 purchased at the start of year 1
Expected useful life	4 years
Residual value	£5,000

The machine is to be used in production and the forecast output of the units is as follows:

Year 1	15,000 units
Year 2	10,000 units
Year 3	20,000 units
Year 4	5,000 units
	50,000

Required:

For each of the four years the asset is used, calculate the annual depreciation and the resulting figures that will appear in the financial statements for each of the following methods of depreciation:

(a) Straight-line

(b) Diminishing (reducing) balance

(c) Sum of digits

(d) Units of production.

(a) Straight-line method

Annual depreciation expense = Depreciable amount/useful life
= (£25,000 − £5,000)/4
= £5,000

Year	I/S expense £	Net book value £
1	5,000	25,000 − 5,000 = 20,000
2	5,000	20,000 − 5,000 = 15,000
3	5,000	15,000 − 5,000 = 10,000
4	5,000	10,000 − 5,000 = 5,000*

* Note the net book value at the end of year 4 is the expected residual value.

The depreciation expense is the same each year; thus, this method should be chosen if the pattern of consumption is similar each year.

(b) Diminishing (reducing) balance method

A constant proportion is written off the net book value each year. The appropriate proportion is obtained from the formula

$$1 - \sqrt[n]{(r/c)}$$

where c = cost, r = residual value, and n = useful life.

Substituting the appropriate values into the formula gives the proportion as
$1 - \sqrt[4]{(5,000/25,000)} = 0.331$, which will be rounded to 0.35 or 35% for this example.

Annual depreciation expense = 35% × net book value

Year	I/S expense £	Net book value £
1	35% × 25,000 = 8,750	25,000 − 8,750 = 16,250
2	35% × 16,250 = 5,688	16,250 − 5,688 = 10,562
3	35% × 10,562 = 3,697	10,562 − 3,697 = 6,865
4	35% × 6,865 = 2,403	6,865 − 2,403 = 4,462*

* The effect of rounding the answer given by the formula to 35% means that the net book value at the end of year 4 is £4,462 and not the expected residual value of £5,000.

The depreciation expense reduces each year, and thus this method should be used for assets whose use is greater in earlier years and then reduces.

(c) Sum of digits method

This is an approximation to the reducing balance method.

Annual depreciation expense = Depreciable amount × depreciation rate

Depreciable amount	= 25,000 − 5,000 = £20,000
Depreciation rate	= No. of years of useful life remaining/sum of digits
Sum of digits	= [n(n + 1)]/2 (where n = estimated useful life)
	= [4× (4 + 1)]/2 = 10

Year	Depreciation rate	I/S expense £	Net book value £
1	4/10	× 20,000 = 8,000	25,000 − 8,000 = 17,000
2	3/10	× 20,000 = 6,000	17,000 − 6,000 = 11,000
3	2/10	× 20,000 = 4,000	11,000 − 4,000 = 7,000
4	1/10	× 20,000 = 2,000	7,000 − 2,000 = 5,000

(d) Units of production method

Annual depreciation expense = Depreciable amount × depreciation rate

Depreciable amount	= 25,000 − 5,000 = £20,000
Depreciation rate	= Units of output produced in the period
	Total no. of units

Year	Depreciation rate	I/S expense £	Net book value £
1	15/50	× 20,000 = 6,000	25,000 − 6,000 = 19,000
2	10/50	× 20,000 = 4,000	19,000 − 4,000 = 15,000
3	20/50	× 20,000 = 8,000	15,000 − 8,000 = 7,000
4	5/50	× 20,000 = 2,000	7,000 − 2,000 = 5,000

This method matches exactly the consumption of the benefits of the machine to the expected production levels of the units and, given that these estimates have been made, is the best of the four methods to be chosen.

10.5.3 Changes in estimates

Although consistency in accounting from one year to the next is one of the underpinning principles of financial reporting, if the circumstances in a company change, then this should be reflected in the financial statements so that they faithfully represent these circumstances. Therefore, if a company decides that the original estimates of useful life or residual value or of how the asset was to be used need revising, it is permitted to do this. IAS 8 *Accounting Policies, Changes in Accounting Estimates and Errors* is then relevant (see discussion in Chapter 4). As these are changes in estimates (and not a change in accounting policy) the effect of the change is applied prospectively, i.e. from the date of change.

An example of a change in estimate of useful life is shown in Chapter 4, but here is another.

Example of a change in residual value

A company purchases an item of machinery on 1 March 20X2 for £50,000 and estimates the useful life to be 10 years with zero residual value. The company applies a straight-line depreciation method to its plant and machinery.

Owing to an increase in the price of scrap metal, on 1 March 20X6 the company revises its estimate of the residual value to £3,000.

Annual depreciation charged for years ended 28 February 20X3 – 20X6 = 50,000/10 = £5,000

Carrying amount of the machine at 28 February 20X6 = 50,000 – (4 × 5,000) = £30,000.

There are six years of useful life remaining.

Annual depreciation to be charged from 1 March 20X6 = (30,000 – 3,000)/6 = £4,500.

10.6 Subsequent measurement— alternative models

There are two alternative measurement models for property, plant and equipment—the cost model or the revaluation model—and companies can decide which one they should choose. Under the two models the carrying amount of an asset is defined as:

Cost model   Cost *minus* accumulated depreciation *minus* accumulated impairment losses.

Revaluation model   Fair value at date of revaluation *minus* accumulated depreciation *minus* accumulated impairment losses.

Note that impairment for both models is discussed in section 10.7. What constitutes cost has been discussed earlier, so the fair value model will now be dealt with.

10.6.1 Fair value

The fair value of an asset is defined in IFRS 13 *Fair Value Measurement* as:

> …the price that would be received to sell an asset in an orderly transaction between market participants at the measurement date.

(IASB, 2011: para. 9)

This standard sets out guidance in how the fair value for non-financial assets may be ascertained. Briefly, these are that when measuring fair value, the following must be considered:

- the condition, location, and any restrictions on sale of the asset being measured

- the principal (or most advantageous) market in which an orderly transaction would take place for the asset

- for a non-financial asset, the highest and best use of the asset, and whether the asset is used in combination with other assets or on a standalone basis
- the assumptions that market participants would use when pricing the asset.

Approaches to the determination of fair value include a market approach (based on market prices), a cost approach (based on the current cost of replacing the asset), and an income approach (using discounting techniques applied to the cash flows the asset is estimated to bring in). Chapter 2 discusses the hierarchy of methods.

⚠ Reminder *The 'fair value hierarchy' specifies three levels, with Level 1 being the preferable (most reliable) method if available:*

- *level 1—unadjusted quoted prices for identical assets in active markets*
- *level 2—other observable inputs for the asset, such as quoted prices in active markets for similar assets or quoted prices for identical assets in markets which are not active*
- *level 3—unobservable inputs developed by an entity using the best information available where there is little, or no, market activity for the asset at the measurement date.*

IAS 16 suggests that the fair value of land and buildings, and plant and equipment is usually determined from market-based evidence, such as appraisals undertaken by professionally qualified valuers. If there is no market-based evidence of fair value, possibly because assets have been customised by the business, this standard suggests that fair value be estimated using an income or depreciated replacement cost approach.

 Example of depreciated replacement cost

A company chooses the revaluation model for its land and buildings. Its headquarters building was acquired three years ago for £500,000 and the useful life at this time was estimated at 20 years. The company now wishes to revalue the building. A replacement cost for the building at current market prices is £600,000.

Fair value estimated by the depreciated replacement cost approach takes the replacement cost as the revalued 'cost' and applies the company's depreciation policy for the length of time the asset has been held.

Hence, the replacement cost is depreciated for three years and the resulting net book value is taken as the fair value of the asset:

Fair value = £600,000 – [3 × (£600,000/20)] = £510,000

In practice the process of estimating the fair value of an asset is difficult and requires extensive judgement. If professional valuers have been used this fact is disclosed together with extensive details of where and how fair value has been used in the financial statements. This information will assist users in assessing the reliability of the values stated.

10.6.2 Revaluation model

If a company selects the revaluation model, it cannot 'cherry-pick' which assets it chooses to revalue to increase asset values on the statement of financial position. IAS 16 requires that the class of property, plant and equipment to which the asset belongs is revalued. Typical classes would be:

- land
- land and buildings
- aircraft or ships
- machinery
- motor vehicles
- fixtures and fittings
- office equipment.

To ensure the financial information is relevant revaluations need to be made with sufficient regularity to ensure the carrying amount does not differ from an up-to-date fair value. In practice this means the frequency of revaluations depends upon changes in fair values. If the markets related to the assets are particularly volatile, this may mean that annual revaluation is required, but, for other assets, revaluations may only be necessary every 3–5 years.

10.6.3 Accounting for the revaluation model

On revaluation the asset's fair value is compared to its carrying amount.

1   If the fair value is greater than carrying amount, the difference is credited to a revaluation surplus account, which is an equity reserve:

Debit   Asset (carrying amount)

Credit   Revaluation surplus

The increase in revaluation is recognised in other comprehensive income in the statement of comprehensive income and it will also be shown in the statement of changes in equity.

The increase is recognised in profit and loss (i.e. the income statement) to the extent that it reverses any previous revaluation decrease which had been recognised in profit and loss.

2   If the fair value is less than the carrying amount, the difference is recognised as an expense in profit and loss:

Debit   Profit and loss

Credit   Asset (carrying amount)

If, however, a credit balance relating to the asset exists on the revaluation surplus account, the decrease in value is debited to the revaluation surplus to the extent this exists, recognised in other comprehensive income in the statement of comprehensive income, and is also shown in the statement of changes in equity:

Debit   Revaluation surplus

Credit   Asset (carrying amount)

The adjustment to the asset carrying amount can be achieved in two alternative ways:

(i) The accumulated depreciation on the asset is eliminated against the asset's cost (or revaluation) account and the resulting net book value in the cost account is then restated to the revalued amount. This method is often used for buildings

(ii) The asset's cost and accumulated depreciation accounts are both restated proportionately so that the resulting carrying amount (cost – accumulated depreciation) equals the revalued amount. This method is often used when the fair value is determined by using a depreciated replacement cost.

Following revaluation there are also two alternative accounting treatments for the revaluation surplus account:

(i) Its balance is transferred to retained earnings when the asset is derecognised

(ii) Its balance is transferred to retained earnings as the asset is used—the amount being transferred being the additional depreciation based on the revalued amount over the depreciation based on the cost (or previous revaluation).

It should be noted that this is a transfer between reserves and that the transfer in both alternatives does not pass through profit and loss.

 Worked example 10.2: to show the accounting for a revaluation

Squib plc, which has a 31 December year end, adopts the revaluation model for its plant and machinery. The company acquires one item of plant for £10,000 on 1 January 20X1. The plant is depreciated on a straight-line basis over its useful economic life, which is estimated to be five years. On 1 January 20X3 the company revalues the plant at its fair value of £9,600.

On 1 January 20X5 the plant is sold for £4,000. Any revaluation surplus is amortised to retained earnings as the plant is being depreciated.

Required:
Show the accounting entries for the transactions for the years 20X3 to 20X5.

The carrying amount of the asset at the date of revaluation of 1 January 20X3 needs to be established:

	£
Cost at 1 Jan 20X1	10,000
Depreciation expense for y/e 31 Dec 20X1	(2,000)
Depreciation expense for y/e 31 Dec 20X2	(2,000)
Net book value (NBV) at 1 Jan 20X3	6,000
Revalued amount	9,600
Surplus on revaluation	3,600

Method 1—elimination of accumulated depreciation account on revaluation

		£	£
Dr	Accumulated depreciation	4,000	
Cr	Asset cost		4,000
Dr	Asset cost	3,600	
Cr	Revaluation surplus		3,600

As a result of these entries the asset cost has a balance of £9,600—the revalued amount. This is depreciated over the remaining useful life of three years:

		£	£
Dr	Depreciation expense	3,200	
Cr	Accumulated depreciation		3,200

Each year the excess depreciation of £3,200 – £2,000 = £1,200 is transferred from Revaluation surplus to Retained earnings:

		£	£
Dr	Revaluation surplus	1,200	
Cr	Retained earnings		1,200

At the date of sale of 1 January 20X5 (two years later):
Asset revalued 'cost' account has a balance of   £9,600 Dr
Accumulated depreciation has a balance of   £6,400 Cr
Revaluation surplus has a balance of (£3,600 – £2,400)   £1,200 Cr

The accounting for the sale of the asset is as follows:

		£	£
Dr	Bank	4,000	
Dr	Accumulated depreciation	6,400	
Cr	Asset revalued amount		9,600
Cr	Profit on sale (balancing figure)		800

The remaining balance on the Revaluation surplus is transferred to Retained earnings:

		£	£
Dr	Revaluation surplus	1,200	
Cr	Retained earnings		1,200

Method 2—'grossing up' of cost and accumulated depreciation accounts

The asset's net book value of £6,000 is effectively increased by a factor of 1.6 to fair value of £9,600 (£6,000 × 1.6 = £9,600).

The asset's cost and accumulated depreciation accounts are increased by the same factor:

		£	£
Dr	Asset cost (£10,000 × 1.6 – £10,000)	6,000	
Cr	Accumulated depreciation		
	(£4,000 × 1.6 – £4,000)		2,400
Cr	Revaluation surplus		3,600

As a result:

Asset 'cost' account has a balance of   £16,000
Accumulated depreciation has a balance of   £6,400

The net book value of the asset = £9,600, which is the revalued amount.
The 'cost' continues to be depreciated over five years:

		£	£
Dr	Depreciation expense	3,200	
Cr	Accumulated depreciation		3,200

As for Method 1, each year the excess depreciation of £3,200 – £2,000 = £1,200 is transferred from the Revaluation surplus to Retained earnings:

		£	£
Dr	Revaluation surplus	1,200	
Cr	Retained earnings		1,200

At the date of sale 1 January 20X5 (2 years later):

Asset 'cost' account has a balance of   £16,000 Dr
Accumulated depreciation has a balance of   £12,800 Cr
Revaluation surplus has balance of (£3,600 – £2,400)   £1,200 Cr

The accounting for the sale of the asset is as follows:

		£	£
Dr	Bank	4,000	
Dr	Accumulated depreciation	12,800	
Cr	Asset 'cost'	16,000	
Cr	Profit on sale (balancing figure)		800

The remaining balance on the Revaluation surplus is transferred to Retained earnings:

		£	£
Dr	Revaluation surplus	1,200	
Cr	Retained earnings		1,200

10.6.4 Choice of revaluation model

The prices paid to acquire businesses may be significantly higher than their reported net asset values, reflecting significant changes in value which are not necessarily reflected in the financial statements. Many believe that the usefulness of financial statements is undermined unless the updated values for items of property are reflected in the financial statements. So one argument for a company choosing the revaluation model is that the method provides more up-to-date values of assets, and thus can be said to be more relevant than historic cost to investors in their decision making. (*Remember, relevance is one of the fundamental qualitative characteristics*.) For many years it has resulted in higher asset values, particularly for property. This has been useful for companies wishing to enhance their statements of financial position, especially if a company has net current liabilities or high gearing.

However, the resulting depreciation expense is higher, resulting in lower profits. There are also the additional costs of having to keep revaluations current and employing expert valuers. Recent revaluations of property may now be resulting in reductions as the property market has declined, which may also be causing a reduction in profits.

In the UK, surveys of companies have revealed that only a small proportion (less than 5%) actually use the revaluation model. Those that do tend to be in the brewing industry, with chains of pubs, or those with hotel and leisure complexes. These are the same industries that, prior to IAS 16, argued against the depreciation of property.

Financial reporting in practice 10.2　　　　| Marston's plc, 2010 |

Marston's plc is a brewery and pub retailer. In its 2010 financial statements it discloses the accounting policy for its properties:
Freehold and leasehold properties are initially stated at cost and subsequently at valuation. Plant and machinery and fixtures, fittings, tools and equipment are stated at cost.
　　Valuation of properties — Properties are revalued by qualified valuers on a sufficiently regular basis using open market value so that the carrying value of an asset does not differ significantly from its fair value at the balance sheet date. Substantially all of the Group's properties have been externally valued in accordance with the Royal Institution of Chartered Surveyors' Red Book and these valuations are performed directly by reference to observable prices in an active market or recent market transactions on arm's length terms. Internal valuations are performed on the same basis.

10.7 Impairment of assets

10.7.1 What is impairment?

In order to provide a fair view of a company's long-term resources, non-current assets should not be included in the statement of financial position at values in excess of what they are worth to the company, that is in excess of amounts the company can expect to recover through their use in the future. This recoverable amount is the amount the company could recover through either the use or the sale of the asset. Assets are therefore carried at the lower of their carrying amount and their recoverable amount. If the recoverable amount is less than the carrying amount, the asset is impaired, and an impairment loss is recognised:

Debit   Impairment loss

 Credit   Asset (carrying amount)

IAS 36 *Impairment of Assets*, which was issued in 1998 and then revised in 2004 as a result of the IASB's business combinations project, addresses accounting for the impairment of assets. It applies to property, plant and equipment, investment properties accounted for under the cost model, intangible assets and subsidiaries, associates, and joint ventures. It does not apply to inventories, assets arising from construction contracts, deferred tax assets, assets arising from employee benefits, or assets classified as held for sale (or included in a disposal group that is classified as held for sale) because other IFRSs are applicable to these assets.

10.7.2 When is an impairment test required?

An impairment test is the comparison of an asset's carrying amount with its recoverable amount. At each statement of financial position date a company is required to assess whether there are any indications that an impairment loss may have occurred. Only if there are such indications does the company need to perform the impairment test, in other words determine the recoverable amount of the asset and compare this to the carrying amount.

There are three exceptions to this—intangible assets with indefinite useful lives, intangible assets not yet available for use, and goodwill arising on consolidation. These must be tested annually for impairment. These are discussed further in Chapter 11.

Indications of impairment arise from factors both external and internal to the business and include the following.

External indicators:

- a decline in the market value for specific assets
- significant adverse changes in the technological, market, economic, or legal environment in which assets are used (e.g. in recessionary times)
- increases in market interest rates (because this affects **value in use**—see section 10.7.3)
- a decline in the company's market capitalisation, resulting in the company's net assets exceeding market capitalisation
- competitor actions.

Internal indicators:

- obsolesce or physical damage to an asset
- significant internal changes to the company's operations that may adversely affect an asset's remaining useful life or utility

- reorganisation of the business

- internal reporting data indicating that the economic performance of an asset is (or will become) worse than previously anticipated

- idle assets

- change of use of assets

- major loss of key employees

- poor asset performance or operating losses in the business where the assets are used.

When assessing internal factors a company should compare the cash flows associated with an asset, or group of assets, with those budgeted. For example, cash outflows may exceed budgeted figures due to higher than expected maintenance costs. Cash inflows may be lower than budgeted due to increased competition. Both would indicate potential impairment.

10.7.3 Impairment test

If an impairment test is required a company must determine the recoverable amount. The recoverable amount is defined as the higher of:

- the value in use of the asset

- the fair value less costs to sell of the asset.

This assumes a rational approach to what a business would do with an asset given the two values—it would either keep it (value in use) or sell it (fair value less costs to sell), i.e. it would choose whichever gives the higher amount.

The asset will be valued at the lower of its current carrying amount and the recoverable amount, as shown in Figure 10.1.

Fair value has been defined and discussed previously in this chapter (see section 10.6.1). Costs to sell include legal costs, stamp duty, taxes, removal costs, and other incremental costs of bringing the asset into a condition for sale, but exclude any reorganisation costs.

The value in use is the present value of the future cash flows expected to be derived from an asset. Estimates of future cash in- and outflows from the use and ultimate disposal of the asset need to be made, and an appropriate discount rate to be used has to be determined. Both of these require a great deal of judgement to be exercised and IAS 36 provides much guidance in this area to help ensure a consistent approach. For example, the cash flows should be based on recent budgets or forecasts for a maximum of five years, and if the expected useful life of the asset extends beyond this, a steady growth/decline rate in cash flows should be applied. The cash flows should exclude the effects of future restructurings or improving and enhancing the asset's performance. The discount rate to be used should be a pre-tax rate reflecting current market assessments of the time value of money and risks specific to the asset.

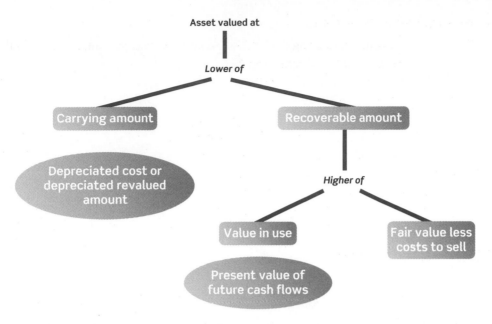

Figure 10.1 The impairment test

 Worked example 10.3: to show an impairment test

Idaho plc owns a machine which produces a range of products and, at 31 December 20X5, this has a book value of £123,000 (based on depreciated historic cost). In the past year Idaho's competitors have brought out similar, but more technologically advanced, products and the company believes this indicates that there may be evidence of impairment. The company estimates future cash inflows and outflows, based on the diminishing productivity expected of the machinery as new products are produced, and also increasing costs as follows:

Year	£ Revenues	£ Costs (excluding depreciation)
20X6	75,000	28,000
20X7	80,000	42,000
20X8	65,000	55,000
20X9	20,000	15,000
	240,000	140,000

The fair value of the machine is obtained from a prominent dealer and, after deducting estimated disposal costs, the net is estimated as £84,500.
  The company determines that a discount rate taking into account appropriate risks is 5%.

Required:
Carry out an impairment test on the machine and show the resulting accounting.

Carrying amount = £123,000

Fair value less costs to sell = £84,500

Value in use:

Year	Net cash flow	Discount factor	PV of cash flow
	£		£
20X6	47,000	0.952	44,744
20X7	38,000	0.907	34,466
20X8	10,000	0.864	8,640
20X9	5,000	0.823	4,115
Value in use			91,965

Value in use > FV less costs to sell:

- Recoverable amount = £91,965.

Recoverable amount < Carrying amount.

- Impairment loss of £123,000 – £91,965 = £31,035 needs to be accounted for:

Dr   Impairment loss (profit and loss)
Cr   Asset carrying amount

10.7.4 Accounting for the results of the impairment test

If the recoverable amount is greater than the current carrying amount, no adjustments are required.

If the recoverable amount is less than the carrying amount, the company accounts for this impairment loss as follows:

1   If the asset is valued under the cost model, the impairment loss is recognised in profit and loss:

Debit   Profit and loss

  Credit   Asset accumulated depreciation and impairment

2   If the asset is valued under the revaluation model, the impairment loss is written off directly against any revaluation surplus to the extent that it relates to the asset which is impaired, with any excess recognised in profit and loss:

Debit   Revaluation surplus

(Debit   Profit and loss)

  Credit   Asset accumulated depreciation and impairment

The impaired value, less any residual value is depreciated over the asset's remaining useful life, which may need to be reassessed at the date of impairment.

Worked example 10.4: to show the accounting for an impairment loss

Stag plc, which has a 31 December year end, acquired an item of property, plant and equipment on 1 January 20X4 for £50,000 for which it applies the revaluation model. The asset is depreciated on a straight line basis over its useful economic life of ten years (the assumed residual value is nil). On 1 January 20X5 it was established that the gross replacement cost* of the asset was £60,000. On 31 December 20X6, there are indications that the asset is impaired, an impairment test is carried out, and the recoverable amount at that date is estimated as £30,000.

* Gross replacement cost is the gross revalued amount of the asset *before* any depreciation is deducted (i.e. it is the equivalent 'original cost' on a revalued basis).

Required:
Show the accounting entries for the transactions for the years 20X5 and 20X6.

Account for the revaluation on 1 January 20X5

	£
Original cost at 1 Jan 20X4	50,000
Accumulated depreciation (1 year 20X4)	(5,000)
Net book value at 31 December 20X4	45,000

Using the grossing up method of revaluation, on revaluation the original asset cost is increased to the gross replacement cost (£50,000 is increased by a factor of 1.2 to £60,000).
The accumulated depreciation also increased by same factor (£5,000 × 1.2 = £6,000):

● Revalued amount of asset = £60,000 – £6,000 = £54,000.

		£	£
Dr	Asset cost	10,000	
Cr	Accumulated depreciation		1,000
Cr	Revaluation surplus		9,000
	(£54,000 – £45,000)		

Accounting entries in years 20X5 and 20X6

Each year:
Asset is depreciated at (£60,000/10 = £6,000 p.a.):

		£	£
Dr	Depreciation expense	6,000	
Cr	Accumulated depreciation		6,000

The additional depreciation of £1,000 is transferred from revaluation surplus to retained earnings:

		£	£
Dr	Revaluation surplus	1,000	
Cr	Retained earnings		1,000

At 31 December 20X6, balances on the relevant accounts are:

Asset cost	£60,000 Dr
Accumulated depreciation	£18,000 Cr
(NBV	£42,000)
Revaluation surplus (£9,000 – 2 × £1,000)	£7,000 Cr

Account for the impairment at 31 December 20X6

Carrying amount	= £42,000
Recoverable amount	= £30,000
● Impairment loss of	£12,000

This can be written off against the revaluation surplus to the extent it exists, with any balance to profit and loss:

		£	£
Dr	Revaluation surplus	7,000	
Dr	Income statement	5,000	
Cr	Accumulated depreciation and impairment		12,000

10.7.5 Cash-generating units

In practice it may be difficult to estimate the recoverable amount for a single asset. In this case the impairment test must be performed for the cash-generating unit (CGU) to which the asset belongs. Any impairment loss is allocated on a pro rata basis to the individual assets in the CGU.

A CGU is defined as the smallest identifiable group of assets that generates cash inflows which are largely independent of cash inflows from other assets or groups of assets. The identification of CGUs within a company will depend on how management monitors the company's operations. This may be, for example, by product lines, businesses, or individual locations, or by how management makes decisions about continuing or disposing of the company's assets and operations. This is extremely judgemental, but does require consistent treatment from year-to-year.

There are further complexities where assets are used by a number of different CGUs, for example a head or corporate office. An allocation of these assets' carrying amounts to the relevant CGUs should be made on a 'reasonable and consistent basis'.

10.7.6 Goodwill

As detailed in section 10.7.2, goodwill arising from a business combination and which is capitalised as an intangible asset is required to be tested annually for impairment. (See Chapter 15 for details of how this arises and is valued.) It is meaningless to test this goodwill as a separate asset, so the carrying amount is allocated to the CGUs expected to benefit from the synergies of the combination, and these CGUs are tested for impairment. This is discussed and illustrated further in Chapter 11.

10.7.7 Reversal of impairment losses

There is no such thing as an impairment gain. However, companies are required to assess at the end of each financial year whether there are any indications that a previously recognised impairment loss has decreased or may no longer exist. Essentially, indications of this are the opposite of the indications for impairment, as given in section 10.7.2. An impairment loss should only be reversed if there has been an increase in the asset's service potential. Essentially, this means it will only be reversed if there is a change in the estimates that were used to determine the asset's recoverable amount.

The reversal is recognised as:

Debit   Asset (carrying amount)

Credit   Profit and loss

but only to the extent that the increased carrying amount does not exceed the amount it would have been (after any subsequent depreciation) if no impairment loss had originally been recognised. Otherwise, this would amount to a revaluation. Note that impairment of goodwill is never reversed.

> **Worked example 10.5:** to show the reversal of an impairment loss

Jules plc has a CGU comprising two classes of asset. On 31 December 20X3 the CGU was found to be impaired, and an impairment loss of £35,000 was recognised and allocated pro rata to the assets. On 31 December 20X5 the assets' carrying values were:

	£000
Land and buildings	40
Plant and machinery	50
	90

At this date there are indications that the conditions giving rise to the original impairment have changed. The recoverable amount of the CGU is assessed as £120,000. Calculations indicate that if the original impairment had not occurred, the land and buildings would have a carrying amount of £52,000, and the plant and machinery £63,000.

Required:
Show the accounting for the reversal of the impairment loss at 31 December 20X5.

The difference between the carrying amount and the new recoverable amount is £30,000 (i.e. £120,000 – £90,000).

However, the total carrying amount of other assets if the original impairment had not occurred = £52,000 + £63,000 = £115,000.

This is the maximum carrying amount permitted for these assets, so the reversal of the original impairment loss is restricted to £115,000 – £90,000 = £25,000.

This would be allocated to the assets again on a pro rata basis.

Financial reporting in practice 10.3 | JD Wetherspoon plc, 2011

JD Wetherspoon plc includes the following accounting policy relating to impairment in its 2011 financial statements. This uses terminology from the accounting standard.

Impairment

At each reporting date, the Company assesses whether there is an indication that an asset may be impaired. If any such indication exists, or when annual impairment testing for an asset is required, the Company makes an estimate of the asset's recoverable amount. An asset's recoverable amount is the higher of an asset or CGU's fair value less costs to sell and its value in use; this is determined for an individual asset, unless the asset does not generate cash inflows which are largely independent of those from other assets or groups of assets. Where the carrying amount of an asset exceeds its recoverable amount, the asset is considered impaired and is written down to its recoverable amount. In assessing value in use, the estimated future cash flows are discounted to their present value using a pre-tax discount rate which reflects current market assessments of the time value of money and the risks specific to the asset. Impairment losses of continuing operations are recognised in the income statement in those expense categories consistent with the function of the impaired asset.

An assessment is made at each reporting date about whether there is any indication that previously recognised impairment losses may no longer exist or may have decreased. If such indication exists, the recoverable amount is estimated. A previously recognised impairment loss is reversed only if there has been a change in the estimates used to determine the asset's recoverable amount since the last impairment loss was recognised. If that is the case, the carrying amount of the asset is increased to its recoverable amount. That increased amount cannot exceed the carrying amount which would have been determined, net of depreciation, had no impairment loss been recognised for the asset in previous years. Such reversal is recognised in the income statement. After such a reversal, the depreciation charge is adjusted in future periods, to allocate the asset's revised carrying amount, less any residual value, on a systematic basis, over its remaining useful life.

10.8 Derecognition of property, plant and equipment

The terminology used in IAS 16 referring to the disposal of property, plant and equipment is derecognition. Essentially, it is about when the asset is removed from the statement of financial position and this will arise not only when the asset is disposed of, but also when there are no future economic benefits expected from its use or disposal. So an old piece of machinery in a corner of a factory that is no longer used and is going to be scrapped should be derecognised. Care must also be taken if a company has recognised replacement parts as part of the cost of an asset. When these are actually used to replace older parts, the older replaced parts must be derecognised.

The gain or loss arising from the derecognition of an item of property, plant and equipment is the difference between net disposal proceeds (if any) and the carrying amount of the item. This is accounted for as a gain, not revenue, and included in profit and loss.

The exception to this is if a business routinely sells items of property, plant and equipment, where the sale proceeds are classified as revenue, and the provisions of IAS 18 *Revenue* apply.

10.9 Investment properties

Businesses may hold property:

- to earn rentals
- for capital appreciation
- or both

rather than for use in the production or supply of goods and services, or for administrative purposes.

Examples of investment property include:

- land held for long-term capital appreciation
- land held for an undetermined future use
- buildings owned by the company and leased out under one or more operating leases*
- vacant buildings held by an entity to be leased out under one or more operating leases*
- property being constructed or developed for future use as investment property.

  * Operating leases are discussed in detail in Chapter 14.

In some cases it may be possible to treat part of a property as an investment property. For example, an entity may use a number of floors of a building as its head office and let out the rest. If these different parts can be separated the relevant section can be treated as an investment property.

IAS 40 *Investment Property* deals with the accounting for this class of asset. It specifically excludes certain types of property which are dealt with by other standards, as given in Table 10.2.

Table 10.2 Applicable accounting standards for different types of property

Type of property	Applicable IAS
Property intended for sale in the ordinary course of business	IAS 2 *Inventories*
Property being constructed or developed on behalf of third parties	IAS 11 *Construction Contracts*
Owner-occupied property	IAS 16 *Property, Plant and Equipment*
Property leased to another entity under a finance lease	IAS 17 *Leases*

10.9.1 Accounting for investment property

The holding of property as an investment will generate cash flows that are independent of the other assets held by the business, and therefore distinguishes investment property from owner-occupied property. The commercial purpose of holding such property being capital appreciation suggests that measuring investment property at a depreciated historical cost will not provide meaningful information for the users of the financial statements. Instead, it is widely accepted that market values would be more appropriate so that users can evaluate the success of property managers in creating this capital appreciation. However, the IASB has recognised that in some countries property markets are less developed than in others, and reliable market values may be difficult to obtain. Subsequent to initial acquisition, IAS 40 therefore permits investment properties to be accounted for under two alternative models:

- the cost model
- the fair value model.

The policy chosen should be applied consistently to all of company's investment property.

Although it does not recommend the fair value model, there are indicators that the IASB would prefer this model to be used. These include the requirement for disclosure of fair values for investment properties accounted for under the cost model. Also, it is highly unlikely that a company using the fair value model would change its accounting policy to the cost model.

The cost model is the same as under IAS 16 *Property, Plant and Equipment*, in that the investment property is measured at:

Cost *minus* Accumulated depreciation *minus* Accumulated impairment losses

Similar definitions of cost apply as in IAS 16.

The fair value model requires the investment property to be measured at fair value and this should be assessed at each statement of financial position date. Note this is not the same as the revaluation model available for property, plant and equipment. No revaluation equity reserve is created; instead, changes in fair value are accounted for through profit and loss. An implication of this is that no depreciation is charged.

Adoption of this model may cause volatility in reported profits for investment property-owning companies in addition to significant changes to return and gearing ratios. However, it is considered that the information provided about the capital appreciation is of key importance to users.

10.10 Non-current assets held for sale

Users will wish to assess the resources a company has not only now, but also in the future. This will require information about significant resources that are not going to be available for use in the future. Companies therefore need to provide details of assets where it is known that they are going to be disposed of and sold, in other words non-current assets held for sale.

This issue was discussed fully in Chapter 6 which dealt with reporting performance, as non-current assets are often classified as held for sale because they are part of a discontinued operation. IFRS 5 *Non-current Assets Held for Sale and Discontinued Operations* specifies the accounting treatment for these connected situations.

For the statement of financial position, non-current assets held for sale are disclosed separately from other non-current assets, and they are measured at the lower of carrying amount and fair value less costs to sell, with fair value as defined in IFRS 13 *Fair Value Measurement*.

Reminder IFRS 5 sets out criteria for the recognition of non-current assets as held for sale, including the requirements that management must have taken steps towards the sale of the assets, the assets must be available for immediate sale, and the sale must be expected within a year.

If the fair value less costs to sell is less than the carrying amount, an impairment loss is recognised, and charged to profit and loss.

Once an asset or disposal group is classified as held for sale and remeasured, no further depreciation is charged.

10.11 Disclosures

Accounting for property, plant and equipment deals with many different issues, and it is not surprising, therefore, that extensive disclosures are required. Given the many choices available to companies, it is crucial that accounting policies explain the measurement models selected by a company for its property, plant and equipment and investment properties so that there is a basis for comparability. Details of depreciation methods and useful lives or depreciation rates are required; the basis on which interest has been capitalised as part of the cost of assets and how government grants have been treated should also be provided. As seen earlier, companies also explain when and how they account for impairment, and, importantly, the related assumptions.

Sainsbury's has the following accounting policies relating to property, plant and equipment in its 2011 financial statements.

Property, plant and equipment

Land and buildings

Land and buildings are stated at cost less accumulated depreciation and any recognised provision for impairment. Properties in the course of construction are held at cost less any recognised provision for impairment. Cost includes the original purchase price of the asset and the costs incurred attributable to bringing the asset to its working condition for intended use. This includes capitalised borrowing costs.

Fixtures, equipment and vehicles

Fixtures, equipment and vehicles are held at cost less accumulated depreciation and any recognised provision for impairment. Cost includes the original purchase price of the asset and the costs attributable to bringing the asset to its working condition and its intended use.

Depreciation

Depreciation is calculated to write down the cost of the assets to their residual values, on a straight-line method on the following bases:

Freehold buildings and leasehold properties – 50 years, or the lease term if shorter
Fixtures, equipment and vehicles – 3 to 15 years
Freehold land is not depreciated
Buildings under construction are not depreciated.
Gains and losses on disposal are determined by comparing proceeds with the asset's carrying amount and are recognised within operating profit.

Investment property

Investment properties are those properties held for capital appreciation and/or to earn rental income. They are initially measured at cost, including related transaction costs. After initial recognition at cost, they are carried at their fair values based on market value determined by professional valuers at each reporting date. The difference between the fair value of an investment property at the reporting date and its carrying amount prior to re-measurement is included within the income statement but is excluded from underlying profit in order to provide a clear and consistent presentation of the underlying performance of Sainsbury's on-going business for shareholders. Currently, the only investment properties the Group holds are those contained within its joint ventures with Land Securities Group PLC and the British Land Company PLC.

Capitalisation of interest

Interest costs that are directly attributable to the acquisition or construction of qualifying assets are capitalised to the cost of the asset, gross of tax relief.

Non-current assets held for sale

Non-current assets are classified as assets held for sale and stated at the lower of the carrying amount and fair value less costs to sell if their carrying amount is to be recovered principally through a sale transaction rather than through continuing use. Non-current assets held for sale are not depreciated.

The main disclosure note relating to property, plant and equipment is of a standard format showing for each class of property, plant and equipment a reconciliation of the opening and closing cost (or revalued amount) and accumulated depreciation balances. This will detail all changes that have occurred in the year arising from:

- additions
- disposals
- acquisitions through business combinations
- revaluations
- depreciation charged
- impairments
- classification as held for sale.

Financial reporting in practice 10.5   Rolls-Royce plc, 2010

A typical disclosure note for property, plant and equipment is provided by Rolls-Royce plc in its 2010 financial statements.

Note 9 Property, plant and equipment

	Land and Buildings £m	Plant and equipment £m	Aircraft and engines £m	In course of construction £m	Total £m
Cost:					
At January 1, 2009	787	2,350	171	245	3,553
Exchange differences	(17)	(43)	(2)	(8)	(70)
Additions	22	94	20	155	291
Reclassifications	30	78	5	(113)	–
Transferred to assets held for sale	(12)	–	–	–	(12)
Disposals/write-offs	(4)	(92)	(31)	(3)	(130)

(continued)

(continued)

	Land and Buildings £m	Plant and equipment £m	Aircraft and engines £m	In course of construction £m	Total £m
At January 1, 2010	806	2,387	163	276	3,632
Exchange differences	6	16	–	1	23
Additions	11	94	35	221	361
Acquisition of businesses	17	7	–	–	24
Reclassifications	41	108	5	(154)	–
Disposals/write-offs	(4)	(74)	(14)	(2)	(94)
At December 31, 2010	877	2,538	189	342	3,946
Accumulated depreciation:					
At January 1, 2009	218	1,308	32	–	1,558
Exchange differences	(2)	(25)	(1)	–	(28)
Charge for the year	25	156	8	–	189
Impairment	4	1	–	–	5
Transferred to assets held for sale	(12)	–	–	–	(12)
Disposals/write-offs	(2)	(82)	(5)	–	(89)
At January 1, 2010	231	1,358	34	–	1,623
Exchange differences	4	11	–	–	15
Charge for the year	37	190	10	–	237
Disposals/write-offs	(1)	(62)	(2)	–	(65)
At December 31, 2010	271	1,497	42	–	1,810
Net book value:					
At December 31, 2010	606	1,041	147	342	2,136
At December 31, 2009	575	1,029	129	276	2,009
At January 1, 2009	569	1,042	139	245	1,995

Where a company has adopted the revaluation method, additional disclosures are required:

- the date of the revaluation
- whether an independent valuer was involved
- the methods and significant assumptions applied in estimating the fair values
- for each revalued class of property, plant and equipment, the carrying amount that would have been recognised had the assets been carried under the cost model
- the revaluation surplus, indicating the change for the period and any restrictions on the distribution of the balance to shareholders.

Financial reporting in practice **10.6**	Marston's plc, 2010

Marston's accounting policy for property, plant and equipment shown in Financial reporting in practice 10.2 states that the company adopts the revaluation method for its freehold and leasehold properties. The revaluation amounts are included in the property, plant and equipment note.

Additional information about the revalued properties is then provided.

Cost or valuation of land and buildings comprises:

	2010 £m	2009 £m
Valuation	1,645.4	1,610.0
At cost	114.7	105.7
	1,760.1	1,715.7

If the freehold and leasehold properties had not been revalued, the historical cost net book amount would be £1,285.7 million (2009: £1,243.2 million).

During the current and prior period a number of properties were revalued prior to their transfer to Marston's Pubs Limited. These revaluations generated an unrealised revaluation surplus of £3.3 million (2009: £3.0 million), a reversal of past revaluation surplus of £1.3 million (2009: £nil) and reversal of past impairments of £nil (2009: £0.3 million), a total increase in shareholders' equity/ property, plant and equipment of £2.0 million (2009: £3.3 million).

Extensive disclosures are required relating to impairment, including:

- amounts of impairments or reversals of impairment recognised
- details of the circumstances giving rise to the impairment
- details of the asset or CGU impaired
- whether the recoverable amount is value in use or fair value less costs to sell
- the bases of how these amounts have been estimated.

If a CGU includes goodwill or intangible assets with indefinite useful lives further details are required to explain the key assumptions used in estimating recoverable amount. Companies are also encouraged to provide sensitivity information about the level of changes required in assumptions before impairment would arise.

10.12 Understanding property, plant and equipment information

Once depreciation is understood, the figures relating to property, plant and equipment in the financial statements may, initially, seem straightforward to derive and inherently reliable. However, as seen in this chapter, the level of judgement required in recognition and measurement, and the choices available to companies for different accounting policies and methods, mean that there is a high level of complexity behind the figures presented. A full understanding of this requires a diligent approach by the user. Where intercompany comparisons are to be performed, users need to be very careful that they are comparing like-with-like, and they may need to make various adjustments in their calculations. As detailed in section 10.11, there are extensive disclosures so that the information to enable a user to do this is available.

10.12.1 Judgements

Companies are required to disclose areas where significant judgement has been exercised; impairment is frequently mentioned here. However, it is unlikely that all issues requiring judgement that relate to property, plant and equipment will be highlighted. The distinction between capital and revenue expenditure is not always clear-cut, and it will probably not be indicated in the financial statements where this has been considered. This distinction can have a significant impact on both profit and statement of financial position figures and many performance ratios. (Consider, for example, the inappropriate capitalisation of £10 million of repairs and maintenance expenditure on an asset with, say, estimated useful lives of 10 years.) The determination of the cost of an asset, or a part of an asset, may require judgement. The capitalisation of the appropriate amount of interest relating to qualifying assets where the borrowings are not related directly provides another example of where judgement is necessary.

Judgement is required in estimating the useful lives of property, plant and equipment. While property, plant and equipment manufacturers will often give guidance as to the maximum operating life of assets, the useful life is more likely to be determined by reference to the threat of new technology and changing patterns of demand for the assets' outputs. Businesses have to consider when new property, plant and equipment will make their existing assets an uneconomic way of producing goods. In addition, estimates of how long customers will buy the goods, before they move on to something new, will have to be made.

Residual values are often estimated as zero as it may be seen as prudent in the light of ever-changing technology. However, scrapping or decommissioning costs at the end of the assets' lives have to be considered and estimated; these judgements will affect the amounts charged for depreciation.

If a company adopts the revaluation method for a class of property, plant and equipment, fair values are required. While experts may be employed to provide these, there will be a great deal of judgement exercised for very individual, possibly custom-built, items of property, plant and equipment. Although it is argued that a revalued basis for property, plant and equipment provides more relevant information for users, the verifiability is lessened, which is a key enhancing qualitative characteristic.

Impairment is about ensuring that assets are not stated at more than they are worth to the business and that the reported values are generating positive returns. This assurance for the users is, of course, important, especially in adverse market and trading conditions, but accounting for impairment has led to volatility of earnings, of which users are wary. The determination of the recoverable amount of an asset requires extensive judgement to be exercised. Although users will see much information of how the estimates and judgements have been arrived at, including sensitivity analysis, again, the verifiability of the measurements is an issue. In recent years interest rates in most developed economies have been at low levels; however, even relatively modest increases in general interest rates could have a significant impact on the present value of projected cash flows. The combination of lower income streams, resulting from the economic downturn, and higher discount rates can have significant implications for asset measurement.

Finally, the classification of an asset as being held for sale is based entirely on management's intentions, which is highly judgemental. Interpretations of the guidance set out in IFRS 5 can also vary from company to company, and situation to situation. For example, what is really meant by management being committed to a plan to sell the asset; how verifiable should the evidence to support this be? Can a company be sure that an asset or disposal group will be sold within a year—particularly in a difficult economic environment?

Summary of key points

The definition of an asset in the IASB's *Conceptual Framework* as a resource from which future benefits are expected to flow, underpins the recognition criteria for costs to be accounted for as property, plant and equipment. Costs which can be capitalised are various; they may be incurred to get the asset into a condition ready for use; they may arise subsequent to the initial acquisition of the asset; they may include interest on borrowings taken out in order to fund the acquisition. Essentially, they are costs which would not be incurred unless the asset was being acquired. Government grants may be deducted from the cost or, alternatively, accounted for as deferred income.

Although few in the UK, some companies decide to subsequently value certain classes of property, plant and equipment (mainly property) using the revaluation model rather than basing measurement on the historic cost. The revaluation model uses fair value as the measurement basis, which is considered to provide more relevant information for users. The accounting for revaluations adds a reserve, the revaluation surplus, to equity and there are alternative ways of carrying out the bookkeeping. Once the revaluation model is adopted, assets must be revalued continually and revaluations may decrease, as well as increase. Companies have to weigh up carefully whether this is the best model for their business and users need to understand the financial implications. Additional disclosures are made to assist in comparisons with other companies. Whichever model is used, depreciation is the method by which the cost or revalued amount of the asset is systematically matched against the recognised benefits the asset brings.

Users need to be sure that the carrying amount of assets on the statement of financial position does not exceed a fair representation of their worth to a business. Companies are therefore required to be aware of any internal or external factors which may have reduced their value. If such factors are present, a test for the impairment of an asset, or a group of assets which collectively generate cash flows, is required. The comparison of carrying amount and recoverable amount may result in impairment losses being recognised in profit and loss. If the asset is valued using the revaluation model, the impairment loss is set against any revaluation surplus.

Some property, plant and equipment may be acquired for investment purposes. In this instance, users require information about capital appreciation or depreciation, and so different accounting rules are recommended so that these assets are included at up-to-date fair values.

Other property, plant and equipment may no longer be being used in the business, but be held for sale purposes. The future economic benefits will therefore be from sale proceeds; thus, different valuation methods are used for these assets.

Given the number of areas where estimates and judgements have to be applied, and alternative accounting methods that are available, there are extensive accounting policies and other disclosures to assist the user in understanding and interpreting property, plant and equipment figures.

 ## Further reading

IASB (International Accounting Standards Board) (2004a) IAS 16 *Property, Plant and Equipment.* London: IASB.

IASB (International Accounting Standards Board) (2004b) IAS 20 *Accounting for Government Grants and Disclosure of Government Assistance.* London: IASB.

IASB (International Accounting Standards Board) (2004c) IAS 36 *Impairment of Assets.* London: IASB.

IASB (International Accounting Standards Board) (2004d) IAS 40 *Investment Property.* London: IASB.

IASB (International Accounting Standards Board) (2004e) IFRS 5 *Non-current Assets Held for Sale and Discontinued Operations.* London: IASB.

IASB (International Accounting Standards Board) (2007) IAS 23 *Borrowing Costs.* London: IASB.

 ## Bibliography

Elstrom, P. (2002) How to hide $3.8 billion in expenses. *BusinessWeek* (8 July 2002).

IASB (International Accounting Standards Board) (2004a) IAS 16 *Property, Plant and Equipment.* London: IASB.

IASB (International Accounting Standards Board) (2004b) IAS 20 *Accounting for Government Grants and Disclosure of Government Assistance.* London: IASB.

IASB (International Accounting Standards Board) (2004c) IAS 36 *Impairment of Assets.* London: IASB.

IASB (International Accounting Standards Board) (2004d) IAS 40 *Investment Property.* London: IASB.

IASB (International Accounting Standards Board) (2004e) IFRS 5 *Non-current Assets Held for Sale and Discontinued Operations.* London: IASB.

IASB (International Accounting Standards Board) (2007) IAS 23 *Borrowing Costs.* London: IASB.

IASB (International Accounting Standards Board) (2010) *Conceptual Framework for Financial Reporting 2010.* London: IASB.

IASB (International Accounting Standards Board) (2011) IFRS 13 *Fair Value Measurement.* London: IASB.

ICAEW (Institute of Chartered Accountants in England and Wales) (2008) IFRS Factsheet, *Impairment: applying IAS 36.* London: ICAEW.

Marston's plc (2010) *Annual Report, 2010*. Wolverhampton: Marston's.

Pearson plc (2011) *Annual Report and Accounts, 2010*. London: Pearson.

Rolls-Royce Group plc (2011) *Annual Report, 2010*. London: Rolls-Royce.

J Sainsbury plc (2011) *Annual Report and Financial Statements, 2011*. London: J Sainsbury.

 Questions

● Quick test

1   Discuss whether the following items are property, plant and equipment, and, if so, whether they are able to be recognised in the financial statements.

   (a) A machine has broken down unexpectedly and the company spends £2,000 on its repair, including £800 for spare parts. Not all the parts are used and £100 worth is available for use by the company in the future.

   (b) The costs of relining a furnace after 8,000 hours of use amount to £20,000.

   (c) A company which owns an aircraft spends £60,000 on the major airworthiness inspection required by the Civil Aviation Authority after the mandatory number of hours flying.

   (d) A company has installed a new machine in a new factory and incurs costs of £3,000 relocating the production team to these premises.

2   Georgi plc sold a non-current asset on 7 July 20X5 for £200,000. The asset had been bought for £100,000 three years before, on 1 July 20X2, when it was estimated to have a life of 10 years. The company uses the revaluation model for this class of asset and, on 1 July 20X4, undertook a revaluation. At that date the fair value of this individual asset was deemed to be £150,000. The company uses the straight-line method of depreciation.

Required:

Show how this asset would be accounted for in the statements of comprehensive income and financial position for the years ended 30 June 20X3, 20X4, 20X5, and 20X6, indicating clearly the profit or loss on disposal.

3   Explain the difference between depreciation charges and charges for impairment of non-current assets.

4   An item of property, plant and equipment was acquired on 1 January 20X2 at a cost of £150,000. The useful life and residual value were estimated at 10 years and £15,000 respectively.

On 1 January 20X5 the asset was classified as held for sale. Its fair value was estimated at £60,000 and the costs to sell at £3,000.

The asset was sold on 30 June 20X5 for £57,000.

Required:

   (a) Show the accounting treatment for this asset at 1 January and 30 June 20X5, identifying clearly all entries in the income statement for the year ended 31 December 20X5.

   (b) How would your answers change if the sale proceeds on 30 June 20X5 were £48,000?

   (c) Rework the question with the fair value on classification as held for sale being estimated at £120,000, the costs to sell at £4,500, and the asset being sold for £115,000.

●● Develop your understanding

5 Sephco plc has recently purchased an item of plant, the details of which are:

	£
Basic list price of plant	240,000
Trade discount applicable to Sephco	12.5% on list price
Ancillary costs:	
Shipping and handling costs	2,750
Estimated preproduction testing	12,500
Maintenance contract for three years	24,000
Site preparation costs:	
Electrical cable installation	14,000
Concrete reinforcement	4,500
Own labour costs	7,500

Sephco paid for the plant (excluding the ancillary costs) within 4 weeks of order, thereby obtaining an early settlement discount of 3%.

Sephco had incorrectly specified the power loading of the original electrical cable to be installed by the contractor. The cost of correcting this error of £6,000 is included in the figure of £14,000.

The plant is expected to last for 10 years. At the end of this period there will be compulsory costs of £15,000 to dismantle the plant and £3,000 to restore the site to its original use condition. Assume a discount rate of 6%.

Required:

Calculate the amount at which the initial cost of the plant should be measured.

6 On 1 January 20X0 a company acquires a building for £336,000 and estimates its useful life as 12 years with a nil residual value. The company adopts the revaluation model for its property and on 1 January 20X2 and 1 January 20X7 undertakes two revaluations.

Required:

Show how the revaluation gain on 1 January 20X7 should be recognised in the financial statements if the revalued amounts were:

(a) On 1 January 20X2 £120,000 and on 1 January 20X7 £144,000

(b) On 1 January 20X2 £400,000 and on 1 January 20X7 £144,000.

7 Draytex plc has the following non-current assets at 1 January 20X7:

	Cost	Accumulated depreciation
	£000	£000
Freehold factory	2,880	288
Plant and equipment	3,936	514
Office fixtures and fittings	1,776	1,166
Motor vehicles	898	388
	9,490	2,356

You are given the following information for the year ended 31 December 20X7.

(a) The company's depreciation policies are as follows.

Factory (acquired on 1 January 20X2)	straight-line over 50 years
Plant and equipment	straight-line at 10%
Fixtures and fittings	straight-line at 20%
Motor vehicles	straight-line at 25%

(b) On 1 January 20X7 the factory was revalued to an open market value of £4.4 million and an extension costing £1 million became available for use. The directors have decided to adopt the revaluation model for buildings.

(c) Two cars costing £35,000 each were bought on 1 January 20X7. On this date plant and fittings for the factory extension were also acquired, costing £150,000 and £44,000 respectively.

(d) On 1 January 20X7 the directors decided to change the method of depreciating motor vehicles to 30% reducing balance to give a more relevant presentation of the results and of the financial position.

(e) When reviewing the expected lives of its non-current assets, the directors felt that it was necessary to reduce the remaining life of a 2-year-old grinding machine to 4 years when it is expected to be sold for £16,000 as scrap. The machine originally cost £596,000 and, at 1 January 20X7, had related accumulated depreciation of £116,000.

Required:

Prepare the disclosure notes for property, plant and equipment for the year ended 31 December 20X7 in accordance with relevant IFRSs.

●●● Take it further

8 The financial statements for the year ended 31 January 20X8 of Sacramento plc, an engineering company, included the following balances in respect of property, plant and equipment:

	Cost/valuation £	Accumulated depreciation £
Land and buildings	1,800,000	378,000
Plant and machinery	1,531,800	1,055,160
Office equipment	427,680	252,480

Sacramento has adopted the cost model for all of the assets with the exception of land and buildings in respect of which it has adopted the revaluation model.

Additional information:

1 Land is included in the figures at a valuation of £1,020,000.

All other items of property, plant and equipment are depreciated on a straight-line basis as follows:

Buildings	over 50 years
Plant and machinery	at a rate of 25% per annum on cost
Office equipment	at a rate of 20% per annum on cost

Sacramento charges depreciation on a monthly basis.

2 During January 20X9 Sacramento's structural engineer noticed some cracks appearing at one of the company's outlying workshops and, as a result, a full structural survey was carried out. It was discovered that the foundations of the workshop were insufficient to support some of the machinery which had been housed there. This workshop had cost £180,000 on 1 February 20X4 and had been revalued to £252,000 on 31 January 20X6. It is now estimated that its fair value is only £120,000 and that costs to sell would be £6,000. Its value in use has been estimated at £108,000.

3 On 1 December 20X8 the directors decided to sell a major piece of machinery. At that date a buyer had been identified and contracts were on the point of being exchanged, at an agreed price of £13,200. Selling costs were expected to be £1,800. The machine had not actually been sold by 31 January 20X9. This machine had cost £60,000 on 1 June 20X6.

Required:

(a) In respect of property, plant and equipment, show all the figures which would appear in Sacramento plc's statement of comprehensive income for the year ended 31 January 20X9 and in non-current assets on the statement of financial position at that date. (Show all workings.)

(b) Discuss how the accounting treatments of the property, plant and equipment of Sacramento plc apply the IASB's qualitative characteristics as set out in the *Conceptual Framework* (2010).

9 Perth plc was formed on 1 January 20X3 to provide delivery services for packages to be taken between the city and the airport. Details of Perth's non-current assets at 31 December 20X5 were as follows:

Tangible Assets			Intangible Assets	
	£	£		£
	Vehicles	*Buildings*		*Software*
Cost			Cost	
At 01.01.20X5	990,000	600,000	At 01.01.20X5	–
Additions	–	–	Additions	250,000
Disposals	–	–	Disposals	–
Revaluation	–	–	Revaluation	–
At 31.12.20X5	990,000	600,000	At 31.12.20X5	250,000
Accumulated depreciation			Accumulated amortisation	
At 01.01.20X5	132,000	–	At 01.01.20X5	–
Provided during the year	66,000	60,000	Provided during the year	25,000
Disposals	–	–	Disposals	–
Revaluation/impairment	–	–	Revaluation/impairment	–
At 31.12.20X5	198,000	60,000	At 31.12.20X5	25,000
NBV 01.01.20X5	858,000	600,000	NBV 01.01.20X5	–
NBV 31.12.20X5	792,000	540,000	NBV 31.12.20X5	225,000

The following information is also available:

1   The vehicles were acquired upon formation of Perth plc and are being depreciated on a straight-line basis over their useful economic life of 15 years (a zero residual value is estimated). As part of an expansion programme, Perth plc paid a cash price of £30,000 to acquire two new vehicles on 1 July 20X6. The vehicles needed some repairs for the elimination of rust (cost £2,300), major servicing to the engine (cost £480), and the replacement of all tyres (cost £690). Perth plc incorrectly specified the requirements of the tyres to be installed and the cost of £140 for correcting this error was included in the figure. As part of the expansion programme, Perth plc also decided to spend £15,000 on a marketing campaign to advertise and promote its services.

2   The buildings were acquired on 1 January 20X5 and are being depreciated on a straight-line basis over their useful economic life of ten years. On 1 January 20X6 the buildings were revalued. No fair value was available, but, instead, their gross replacement cost was established to be £700,000. Perth plc has a policy of amortising any revaluation surplus arising on the revaluation of non-current assets into retained earnings. On 31 December 20X7 there were indications that the buildings might be impaired so an impairment test was conducted. The value in use of the buildings was estimated to be £410,000, whereas their estimated net selling price was £380,000.

3   On 1 July 20X5 Perth plc acquired a logistics software package for £250,000 to allow customers to place and track their orders online. Owing to rapidly changing technology, management estimated a useful life of only five years and decided that straight-line amortisation was to be used. At 1 January 20X6 management was uncertain about the economic feasibility of the logistics process. Therefore, it decided to write-down the software to an estimated market value of £75,000 and to re-estimate its useful economic life at only 3 years.

Required:

Using the non-current assets schedule for the year ended 31 December 20X5 as a guide, prepare Perth plc's non-current assets schedule for the year ended 31 December 20X7. For each asset category show clearly your workings in all intermediate years and state any assumptions you make. All accounting adjustments should comply with the requirements of IAS 16 *Property, Plant and Equipment*, IAS 38 *Intangible Assets*, and IAS 36 *Impairment of Assets*.

10 Alpha plc and Beta plc are manufacturing companies, and Gamma plc is a property investment company. All three companies have recently acquired and disposed of freehold properties which were identical in every respect. Details of the properties are as follows:

1 January 20X3	Each company bought its property for £300,000. The buildings element in the cost of each property was estimated at £120,000 with an estimated useful life of 40 years.
30 June 20X4	The fair value of each property was estimated at £380,000 (including buildings element £160,000). The estimated remaining useful life at this date was revised to 50 years.
30 June 20X5	Following an impairment review each property was revalued at £290,000 (including buildings element £100,000).
30 Nov 20X5	Each property was sold for £320,000.

Alpha plc and Beta plc both use their properties for their business operations, and both provided a full year's depreciation (straight line) in the year of acquisition and none in the year of disposal. Alpha plc uses the revaluation model for its properties, whereas Beta plc uses the cost model.

Gamma plc leased its property to produce a rental income negotiated at arm's length.

All three companies have accounting periods ending on 30 June.

Required:

Show how the properties would be dealt with in the accounts for years ended 30 June 20X3–20X6 of each company separately. (The rental income of Gamma plc should be ignored.) You should answer in accordance with all relevant IASs.

11   Hybrid plc has two operating divisions, X and Y, which it has determined are CGUs. The carrying amounts of the assets within each CGU at 31 December 20X1 are as follows:

	Division X	Division Y
	£000	£000
Goodwill	8,000	1,000
Property, plant and equipment	36,000	10,000
Inventories and receivables	9,000	8,000

When carrying out the annual impairment test, Hybrid has estimated that the fair value less costs to sell of Division X is £28 million and of Division Y is £20 million.

The divisions' net cash flow forecasts for the next six years are as follows:

	Division X	Division Y
	£000	£000
20X2	8,000	3,200
20X3	9,000	2,400
20X4	7,200	3,600
20X5	9,600	4,000
20X6	6,000	4,500
20X7	12,000	4,800

Appropriate discounts rates for activities in Divisions X and Y are 12% and 10% respectively.

Required:

(a) Determine whether the divisions are impaired at 31 December 20X1.

(b) If the divisions are impaired, show the accounting for the impairment losses.

 Visit the Online Resource Centre for solutions to all these end of chapter questions plus visual walkthrough solutions. You can test your understanding with extra questions and answers, explore additional case studies based on real companies, take a guided tour through a company report, and much more. Go to the Online Resource Centre at **www.oxfordtextbooks.co.uk/orc/maynard/**

11

Intangible assets

> ## ➤ Introduction

An intangible asset is an identifiable non-monetary asset without physical substance. Examples include goodwill, patents, trademarks, licences, brands, intellectual property rights, customer relationships, and computer software. Businesses expend vast resources on intangible assets, and this chapter explains and illustrates when such assets should be recognised, and how they should be valued in the business's financial statements.

After studying this chapter you will be able to:

- understand the main accounting issues relating to intangible assets
- define what an intangible asset is, and distinguish between those purchased externally, acquired as part of a business combination, and internally generated
- explain how intangible assets are accounted for in accordance with International Accounting Standard (IAS) 38 *Intangible Assets* at the point of recognition and subsequently
- understand how the accounting treatments affect a user's interpretation of the financial statements
- discuss alternative methods which may be used in the reporting of intangible assets.

❑ Why is accounting for intangibles important?

❑ Recognition and measurement of assets from the International Accounting Standards Board's (IASB) *Conceptual Framework*.

❑ Recognition issues—control, identifiable, separable, future economic benefits, reliable measurement.

❑ Initial measurement at cost.

❑ Intangible assets acquired in a business combination measured at fair value (International Financial Reporting Standard (IFRS) 3 *Business Combinations*).

❑ Internally generated intangible assets—research and development phases, subsequent capitalisation of development costs if six criteria met.

❑ Cost or revaluation models allowed.

❑ Amortisation and impairment—finite or indefinite lives.

❑ Disclosures in financial statements.

❑ What do the accounting treatment and disclosures mean to the user?

❑ Other measures to provide information to users.

❑ The current IASB position.

11.1 Why is accounting for intangibles important?

In the latter part of the twentieth and in the twenty-first centuries more of the economic growth of companies is being driven by investments not in physical assets such as property, plant and equipment, but in non-physical or intangible items, such as intellectual capital, organisational and institutional assets, and reputation. The dot.com boom of the 1990s saw enormous growth in Internet and telecommunications companies, which has continued into the twenty-first century with large technology companies, such as Microsoft, Google, Samsung, and Nokia, playing an increasingly important role in the world's economy. Today's 'products' are increasingly intangible and the assets used to produce them are increasingly intangible. Even traditional companies are more reliant now on knowledge-based assets as a source of competitive advantage and to generate their wealth.

One indicator of the growing significance of intangible assets is the difference between the value of companies' net assets, as included in their statements of financial position (book value), and their stock market values. Over the 1990s surveys of companies in Europe and the USA demonstrated large increases in these **market-to-book** ratios, indicating growth in investment in intangibles and the values placed on them, which were not appearing on statements of financial position. Despite recent fluctuations in stock markets, large market-to-book ratios are still prevalent.

Examples of company market-to-book ratios

From their 2009 financial statements the following companies had market-to-book ratios of:

- Microsoft 5.4
- Google 5.4
- Nokia 2.5

The ability to identify, measure, and account for these intangible assets and, ultimately, provide sound information about them is of great importance to users of financial reports. It is argued that the lack of good reporting of intangibles could lead to systematic undervaluation by investors of the shares of companies, particularly intangibles-intensive enterprises, and higher costs of capital as the raising of finance for such companies is more difficult. It also adds to the question about the decision-usefulness of financial reporting.

11.2 Issues in accounting for intangible assets

An intangible asset in its broadest sense can be taken to include

> ...any resource that is both intangible (lacking physical substance) and of economic value to the firm. This includes all types of intellectual capital, including those items associated with the firm's human capital (the value of employee training, morale, loyalty, knowledge, etc.), process-related capital (the value of intangibles associated with information technology, production processes, etc.), and external relations (customer satisfaction, customer loyalty, business relationships, other components of brand values, etc.).
>
> *(Skinner, 2008).*

11.2.1 Recognition issues

The question of how to account for intangible assets has exercised accounting standard-setters for a long time, particularly the last 20–25 years. Businesses spend much money acquiring or developing the sorts of resources referred to in the previous section to improve their competitiveness and to grow, and one key question arises: is this type of expenditure an investment for the future or a general business cost? What this means in financial accounting terms is whether the expenditure is on an asset to be included in the statement of financial position (in other words the expenditure is capitalised) or whether the expenditure is written off as an expense in the income statement. Comparability is one of the qualitative characteristics of financial reporting, and the consistency of treatment of this expenditure between businesses, the consistency of the accounting treatment of expenditure on intangibles acquired in external transactions and those that are internally developed, are key concerns.

 Example of capitalisation versus write-off of expenditure

A company's draft financial statements for the year ended 31 December 20X5 show net profit before tax of £300,000 and net assets (defined here as total assets minus total liabilities) of £2.5 million. The company has not yet accounted for expenditure on intangible items of £100,000.

If this expenditure is capitalised, the accounting entries will be:

		£	£
Debit	Intangible asset	100,000	
Credit	Bank		100,000

If this expenditure is written off, the accounting entries will be:

		£	£
Debit	Sundry expenditure	100,000	
Credit	Bank		100,000

The resultant effect on the financial statements will be:

	Capitalisation £	Write-off £	Difference £
Net profit before tax	300,000	200,000	100,000 (33%)
Net assets	2,500,000	2,400,000	100,000 (4%)
Equity	2,500,000	2,400,000	100,000 (4%)

It can be seen from this example that if there is no proper guidance for the accounting treatment of this expenditure, there is scope for significantly different financial results and position to be reported. The impact on accounting ratios is examined in Worked example 11.6.

11.2.2 Measurement issues

Following on from the question of whether intangible assets can be recognised and included in the financial statements is the question of measurement or valuation. Given the nature of these assets and their uniqueness, regular trade in many of them is difficult; thus, there is a lack of reliable market values. The inclusion of intangible assets with poor or incomparable valuations will not assist the users of financial information.

11.3 IAS 38 *Intangible Assets*

The current IAS 38 *Intangible Assets* was issued by the IASB in March 2004 and has been reissued over the years as the nature of which intangible assets are significant to businesses has changed. From a historical perspective the focus was initially on the accounting treatment of research and development expenditure. With decision-usefulness of financial statements becoming a key principle of financial reporting, the standard had to address issues such as whether brands should be accounted for. Changes in the current version of the standard were concerned primarily with the accounting for goodwill and intangible assets acquired in business combinations.

Note that IAS 38 does not apply to:

(a) the recognition and measurement of exploration and evaluation assets (*see* IFRS 6 *Exploration for and Evaluation of Mineral Resources*).

(b) expenditure on the development and extraction of minerals, oil, natural gas and similar non-regenerative resources.

(c) intangible assets held by an entity for sale in the ordinary course of business (see IAS 2 *Inventories* and IAS 11 *Construction Contracts*).

(d) deferred tax assets (see IAS 12 *Income Taxes*).

(e) leases that are within the scope of IAS 17 Leases.

(f) assets arising from employee benefits (see IAS 19 *Employee Benefits*).

(g) financial assets as defined in IAS 32. Note - the recognition and measurement of some financial assets are covered by IFRS 10 *Consolidated Financial Statements*, IAS 27 *Separate Financial Statements* and IAS 28 *Investments in Associates and Joint Ventures*.

(h) goodwill acquired in a business combination (see IFRS 3 *Business Combinations*).

(i) deferred acquisition costs, and intangible assets, arising from an insurer's contractual rights under insurance contracts within the scope of IFRS 4 *Insurance Contracts*. IFRS 4 sets out specific disclosure requirements for those deferred acquisition costs but not for those intangible assets. Therefore, the disclosure requirements in this Standard apply to those intangible assets.

(j)   non-current intangible assets classified as held for sale (or included in a disposal group that is classified as held for sale) in accordance with IFRS 5 *Non-current Assets Held for Sale and Discontinued Operations*.

The standard addresses the accounting issues relating to intangible assets which arise when the model of recognition and measurement from the IASB's *Conceptual Framework* is imposed on this group of resources. As seen previously, the definition of an asset in the *Framework* is 'a resource controlled by the entity as a result of past events and from which future economic benefits are expected to flow to the entity' (para. 4.4). The *Framework* (para. 4.44) also states that for an asset to be recognised it must be probable that the future economic benefits will flow to the entity and that the asset's value must be able to be measured reliably. If these conditions are not met, then the expenditure incurred on acquiring the asset will be recognised as an expense in profit or loss.

IAS 38 deals with these issues by firstly defining an intangible asset as:

...an identifiable non-monetary asset without physical substance...

(IASB, 2004: para.8),

11.3.1 Identifiable

Note that the IAS 38 definition of an intangible asset inserts the word 'identifiable', and the standard explains that this has two meanings:

1   Either the asset is able to be separated from the business and sold, transferred, licensed, rented or exchanged either on its own or with other assets and liabilities; or

2   The asset arises from contractual or other legal rights, regardless of whether these rights are separable.

If an intangible asset, such as a customer list, a patent, a broadcasting licence, or software, is purchased by an entity, then it is separable and, therefore, identifiable. However, many intangible assets are not separate or saleable items. Examples of such items include employee loyalty, customer satisfaction, and certain brand names. These resources all interact to add value to a business and they cannot be identified uniquely. They cannot, therefore, be regarded as intangible assets in the financial statements of the entity.

11.3.2 Control

An intangible asset, like any other asset, also needs to be controlled by a business. This means that the business should have the power to obtain future economic benefits from the asset and restrict these benefits from other third parties. Control is usually evidenced by legal rights, which are enforceable in a court of law; however, this is not actually necessary for control to be evident.

Examples of control

1   Specific technical knowledge that will give rise to a future product or service has been developed by a business and has been patented. Future economic benefits will arise from the products or services that are protected by the legal right of the patent. The business is restricting the benefits of the knowledge to itself and therefore has control.

2   A business considers it has built up a loyal customer base over many years through quality and good customer relations, and expects the customers will continue to buy from the business. If there are no legal rights to protect this relationship, then the business has insufficient control over the expected economic benefits as the customers can decide to buy the products or services elsewhere. Therefore, the business lacks control.

11.3.3 Recognition

IAS 38 follows the *Framework* almost word-for-word in respect of recognition:

An intangible asset shall be recognised if, and only if:

(a)   it is probable that the expected future economic benefits that are attributable to the asset will flow to the entity; and

(b)   the cost of the asset can be measured reliably...

(IASB, 2004: para.21)

   If an intangible asset is acquired from an external source, the probability recognition criterion given in (a) is always considered to be satisfied. However, the principles-based nature of international accounting standards results in words, such as 'probable' being used, and so for internally-generated intangible assets the management of a business is required to use its best judgement to assess the degree of certainty of the flow of future economic benefits. The reasonableness and reliability of any assumptions will have to be considered.

 Example of probability criterion

A defence contractor has developed a new radar system for use in fighter aircraft which uses wide-angle microwaves. Initial experiments have been promising, but there is little immediate prospect of a saleable product because the transmitter is too large and heavy to install in an aeroplane.

   In the absence of any sales contacts, and the identification of design problems, the likelihood of any future economic benefits is considered fairly remote, and so this criterion is not met and no intangible asset can be recognised.

Reminder *When determining whether the cost of an intangible asset can be measured reliably, the attributes of reliability given in the Conceptual Framework (faithful represen-tation, freedom from bias, prudent estimation, if applicable, and completeness) must be considered.*

11.4 Initial measurement

If an intangible asset can be recognised, it will initially be recorded at cost.

If the asset is acquired for cash or in a normal credit transaction, then the purchase price can clearly be measured reliably and, as for tangible assets, the cost of the asset will include:

(a) Purchase price

(b) Import duties

(c) Non-refundable purchase taxes

(d) Deductions for trade discounts and rebates

(e) Directly attributable costs of preparing the asset for its intended use (e.g. labour costs, professional fees, and testing costs)

and exclude:

(a) Costs of introducing a new product or service (such as advertising costs)

(b) Costs of conducting business in a new location or with a new customer

(c) Administration and other general overheads

(d) Costs incurred while the asset which is ready for use has not yet been brought into use

(e) Initial operating losses incurred while the asset is being prepared for use.

 Worked example 11.1: to show initial costs

Bream plc purchases an online sales order control computer package for £150,000 from Xentov plc. Included in the purchase price is a maintenance agreement for 2 years, which is listed at £20,000. Bream plc employs the services of an external computer consultant to install and test the package; this costs £1,000. Costs incurred to train the staff in the use of the new package are £4,000 and costs relating to advertising the new system to customers are £2,500. There are a few delays during the switchover to the new system, caused by technical problems, and the company estimates that the costs of unproductive sales staff in this time amounted to £1,200 and potential lost orders would have yielded profits of £3,000.

Required:
Identify which of the items will be included in the cost of the intangible asset.

Initial cost of intangible asset computer software:

	£	
Purchase price	150,000	
Less: maintenance agreement	(20,000)	This item would be expensed over the subsequent two years.
Installation and testing	1,000	
	£131,000	

Staff training costs and the costs of advertising the new system to customers are specifically excluded from the cost of the asset by IAS 38, and costs and losses relating to the delays in implementation are not costs of bringing the asset to the condition necessary for it to be capable of operation, and so would be excluded from the initial cost.

11.5 Intangible assets acquired in a business combination

Consider now one key issue to do with intangible assets, which is addressed by IAS 38: how are intangible assets acquired in a business combination accounted for?

When one business acquires the net assets of another many intangible items will be included in the acquisition, some of which may already be recognised as intangible assets in the acquiree business's financial statements, but some of which may not. Prior to the current inclusion of the word 'identifiable' in the standard's definition of an intangible asset, acquiring companies would often subsume the value of these intangible assets acquired in goodwill arising on acquisition. Acquiring companies are required by IAS 38 to assess whether any of the intangible assets acquired are separable, and, if so, they must be recognised as an identifiable intangible asset in the group financial statements and not form part of the overall goodwill figure. This additional information about the different resources acquired is considered to enhance the usefulness of the financial statements.

 Worked example 11.2: to show the accounting for intangible assets acquired in a business combination and the resulting goodwill

Alpha plc acquires the whole of the net assets of company Beta Ltd for cash of £400,000, and Beta is dissolved. Immediately prior to the acquisition the statements of financial position of the two companies are as follows:

	Alpha £000	Beta £000
Non-current assets		
PPE	1,000	110
Intangible assets	–	30
Net current assets	1,050	90
	2,050	230
Non-current liabilities	450	40
	1,600	190
Equity		
Share capital	900	150
Share premium	300	–
Retained earnings	400	40
	1,600	190

In accounting for the acquisition, all identifiable net assets of Beta are required to be valued at fair value (defined in IFRS 13 *Fair Value Measurement* as the price that would be received to sell an asset or paid to transfer a liability in an orderly transaction between market participants at the measurement date). This may mean that some intangible assets not recognised in Beta's financial statements are now identified.

Suppose Beta Ltd has a five-year agreement to supply goods to one of its customers, Gamma Ltd. Both Beta and Alpha believe that Gamma will renew the agreement, which is not separable, at the end of the current contract. The agreement, whether cancellable or not, meets the contractual-legal criterion for determining whether an intangible asset can be considered identifiable. Additionally, because Beta has established its relationship with Gamma through a contract, not only the agreement itself, but also Beta's customer relationship with Gamma meet this criterion. This agreement will now be recognised as an intangible asset and its fair value will therefore need to be estimated.

Assume that the revaluation to fair values and the identification of the supply agreement leads to valuations of Beta's net assets as follows:

	Beta £000
Non-current assets	
PPE	160
Intangible assets	50
(including supply agreement)	
Net current assets	80
	290
Non-current liabilities	40
	250

Required:

Show the final statement of financial position of Alpha plc after its acquisition of Beta Ltd.

The difference between the purchase price of £400,000 and the fair values of the separable net assets acquired of £250,000 represents future economic benefits arising from these assets that have not been individually identified and recognised separately. This is defined as **goodwill** of £150,000, which is now recognised in the financial statements of the enlarged Alpha plc:

		£000
Non-current assets		
PPE	(1,000 + 160)	1,160
Intangible assets	(50)	50
Goodwill		**150**
		1,360
Net current assets	(1,050 – 400* + 80)	730
		2,090
Non-current liabilities	(450 + 40)	490
		1,600
Capital and reserves	(Co. Alpha)	
Share capital		900
Share premium		300
Retained earnings		400
		1,600

* Cash paid for Beta reduces the net current assets.

(See Chapter 15 for further explanation of accounting for business combinations.)

IFRS 3 *Business Combinations* provides many examples of intangible assets regularly acquired in business combinations which are to be regarded as identifiable because they meet one of the two necessary criteria. Examples include:

- marketing-related intangible assets, such as trademarks, newspaper mastheads, and Internet domain names

- customer-related intangible assets, such as customer lists and contacts, order backlogs, and non-contractual arrangements

- artistic-related intangible assets, such as copyrights to plays, books, magazines, song lyrics, photographs, and video and audio-visual material

- other contract-based intangible assets, such as licences, franchise agreements, construction permits, and employment contracts

- technology-based intangible assets, such as software, trade secrets, and databases.

Note that the terms 'brand' and 'brand name' are not included in these examples. This is because they are considered, from an accounting point-of-view, marketing terms, which encompass a group of complementary assets, such as a trademark and its related trade name, formulas, recipes, and technological expertise. A single intangible asset called a 'brand', representing these sorts of complementary assets, may be recognised if its fair value can be measured reliably and the assets that make up the group have similar useful lives. Some companies will refer to this as a 'brand'; others use the terminology of 'trade mark' or 'trade name'.

11.5.1 Fair value

The cost of intangible assets acquired in a business combination, as for tangible assets, and in accordance with IFRS 3 *Business Combinations*, is the fair value at the date of acquisition. IAS 38 states that if an intangible asset is able to be recognised there will be sufficient information available to measure its fair value. This will be in accordance with the guidance given in IFRS 13 *Fair Value Measurement*.

❗ Reminder *Fair valued is defined as 'the price that would be received to sell an asset or paid to transfer a liability in an orderly transaction between market participants at the measurement date'. Ideally, fair value can be obtained from observable prices or data, but, in the absence of this, unobservable data or financial models may have to be used. This leads to increased subjectivity.*

The fair value of an intangible asset may be more difficult to ascertain than that for a tangible asset, as more estimates may have to be made. If there is a range of possible outcomes with different probabilities, this uncertainty enters into the measurement of the asset's fair value.

Some assets may be grouped together as a single asset if their fair value as individual items cannot be estimated, but the fair value for the group can be.

 Example of assets grouped together for fair value

An acquiree company is a company bottling water from a single natural spring. The company has a registered trademark for the spring water.

The trademark and the actual spring cannot be sold separately, so the two intangible assets are grouped together as one asset in the group financial statements, for which the fair value is determined.

11.6 Financial reporting in practice

The following examples of the intangible assets in companies' financial statements demonstrate the diverse nature of what assets companies recognise and the uniqueness of such assets to individual businesses. As required by IAS 38, the companies disclose separately the additions to the categories of intangible assets from acquisitions of other companies and from external purchases.

Financial reporting in practice **11.1**	examples of different intangible assets recognised by companies

Nokia Corporation

This Finnish telecommunication company's statement of financial position at 31 December 2009 includes intangible assets of €8,076 million out of total assets of €12,125 million, comprising capitalised development costs (€143 million), goodwill (€5,171 million), and other intangible assets (€2,762 million), which includes patents, trademarks, licences, customer relationships, and developed technology.

Vodafone Group plc

The UK mobile network operator's statement of financial position at 31 March 2010 includes £22,420 million of intangible assets, excluding goodwill, out of total assets of £142,766 million. The principle categories of intangible assets are licence and spectrum fees, computer software, and others, including brands and customer bases.

Shire plc

This is a Jersey-registered specialty biopharmaceutical company. Its 31 December 2009 financial statements include intangible assets, excluding goodwill, of US$1,791 million out of total assets of US$4,618 million. The vast majority of these are intellectual property rights acquired relating to currently marketed products.

Rolls-Royce plc

Rolls-Royce produces power systems for civil and defence aerospace, marine and energy markets, and, in line with this, has intangible assets comprising development costs, certification costs and participation fees, recoverable engine costs, and software costs. Intangible assets at 31 December 2009 contribute £2,472 million of total assets of £15,422 million.

11.7 Internally generated intangible assets

So far, this chapter has concentrated on intangible assets that are acquired externally, either on their own or through a business combination. However, many intangible assets are ones which develop within a business as it operates and produces its goods or services. It is sometimes difficult to assess whether these internally generated intangible assets meet the identifiable and recognition criteria. Specifically, questions that must be asked are:

1   Can an internally generated asset be separated and sold from the business?
2   Can the costs of generating an asset internally be distinguished from the cost of maintaining or enhancing the business's internally generated goodwill or of running day-to-day operations?

Example of footballers as intangible assets

Consider a footballer, such as Michael Owen. Initially, he played for Liverpool FC after being trained through the club's youth training scheme. In common parlance he was an 'asset' to Liverpool and, ultimately, was sold for £8 million to Real Madrid in mid-2004. He transferred to Newcastle United in 2005 and then to Manchester United four years later, when his contract with Newcastle United expired. Clearly, Owen meets the separability (identifiable) criterion for an intangible asset. However, when recognition is considered for Liverpool FC, the question arises as to whether the development costs associated with this one particular star footballer can be identified reliably. Owen would have been one of a number of players going through the youth training programme, so costs associated solely with him would be difficult to separate out. In addition, it would be difficult to identify what type of costs should be associated with his development—coaching costs: yes; promotion: possibly; training overheads: more difficult to identify; and so on. So the recognition criteria cannot be fulfilled and footballers who have come up through a Club's ranks cannot be recognised as intangible assets.

However, once a footballer is sold to another Club, all identifiable and recognition criteria are satisfied:

- the footballer is separable
- the purchase cost is established.

Hence, there is inconsistency in recognition of the same 'asset' on football clubs' statements of financial position, dependent upon whether the player has come up through the ranks or been bought from another Club.

Financial reporting in practice 11.2 | Arsenal plc, 2008

This issue is explained clearly in the accounting policies of the 31 May 2008 financial statements of Arsenal plc.

Player costs

The costs associated with acquiring players' registrations or extending their contracts, including agents' fees, are capitalised and amortised, in equal instalments, over the period of the respective players' contracts. Where a contract life is renegotiated the unamortised costs, together with the new costs relating to the contract extension, are amortised over the term of the new contract. Where the acquisition of a player registration involves a non-cash consideration, such as an exchange for another player registration, the transaction is accounted for using an estimate of the market value for the non-cash consideration. Provision is made for any impairment and player registrations are written down for impairment when the carrying amount exceeds the amount recoverable through use or sale.

Profits or losses on the sale of players represent the transfer fee receivable, net of any transaction costs, less the unamortised cost of the player's registration.

The disclosure note relating to intangible assets also spells out:

The figures for cost of player registrations are historic cost figures for purchased players only. Accordingly, the net book amount of player registrations will not reflect, nor is it intended to, the current market value of these players nor does it take any account of players developed through the Group's youth system. The directors consider the net realisable value of intangible fixed assets to be significantly greater than their book value.

The accounting treatment set out in IAS 38 attempts to provide a solution to one of the key accounting issues in relation to recognition of an internally generated asset, and which was outlined as one of the key issues in accounting for intangible assets at the start of the chapter: is the expenditure an asset or should it be written off?

In addition to complying with the requirements for the recognition and initial measurement of an intangible asset, IAS 38 adds further requirements for the recognition of internally generated intangible assets. Entities are required to divide the generation of such assets into two phases:

(a) a research phase

(b) a development phase.

11.7.1 Research

Research can be defined as the obtaining of new knowledge, the search for application of this knowledge, and the search for, and design of, possible alternative materials, devices, products, processes, systems, or services. A business undertaking these sorts of activities cannot demonstrate that any intangible asset which may result will generate probable future economic benefits and so all such expenditure is recognised as an expense when it is incurred.

11.7.2 Development

Development is the application of research towards specific new or alternative materials, devices, products, processes, systems, or services. It can involve design, construction, and testing of preproduction or pre-use plants, models, and prototypes, involving new technology. For development costs to be recognised as an intangible asset six criteria have to be demonstrated by a business:

(a) the technical feasibility of completing the intangible asset so that it will be available for use or sale.

(b) its intention to complete the intangible asset and use or sell it.

(c)   its ability to use or sell the intangible asset.

(d)   how the intangible asset will generate probable future economic benefits. Among other things, the entity must demonstrate the existence of a market for the output of the intangible asset or the intangible asset itself or, if it is to be used internally, the usefulness of the intangible asset.

(e)   the availability of adequate technical, financial and other resources to complete the development and to use or sell the intangible asset.

(f)   its ability to measure reliably the expenditure attributable to the intangible asset during its development.

(IAS 38, 2004: para.57)

Note all six criteria have to be met, otherwise the expenditure is recognised as an expense when it is incurred, as for research costs. This may appear fairly clear-cut, but the terminology used (e.g. 'intention', 'ability', and 'technical feasibility') means that management's, and sometimes specialists', experience and judgement have to be relied upon in practical application. Some of the criteria are also forward-looking, so the recognition of development expenditure as an intangible asset is relying upon assessment of future plans. IAS 38 does provide some guidance as to how businesses may 'demonstrate' that these criteria are fulfilled, such as having prepared business plans which include the required resources or having lenders' indications of willingness to fund the plans.

Worked example 11.3: to show the application of the criteria necessary for capitalisation of development costs

1   Hayley plc, a textile manufacturer has incurred expenditure of £600,000 over the past 2 years on one project to develop unique bandaging to treat muscular injuries. Samples have been tested, appropriate clinical approval has been granted, and there have been strong expressions of interest from some hospitals and sports organisations. The company confidently expects that orders for the bandaging will start to be received in the following year, and sales and costs are included in the company's budgets.

Hayley has also purchased a machine to be used in its research laboratory for £2 million. The machine measures the tensile strength of different yarns the entity is developing and experimenting with, and is expected to be used for ten years. Hayley uses the straight-line method of depreciation for machinery.

Required:
Discuss the accounting treatment of the £600,000 development expenditure and the purchase of the machine according to IAS 38.

The £600,000 expenditure relates to a development project which appears to satisfy the six criteria stated in IAS 38:

(a)   if clinical approval has been granted the project must be technically feasible

(b)   and (c) the entity is clearly able to produce the bandaging and anticipates sales of the product

(d) a market exists, as evidenced by the interest shown by potential customers

(e) provided the budgets demonstrate that funding is available to support the project, resources are there to complete the development

(f) the entity appears to be able to identify the costs of development.

Costs of development can therefore be included in the statement of financial position as an intangible asset. The point at which this can be done is discussed in the following section.

The machine is a tangible asset and should be accounted for as property, plant and equipment, i.e. capitalised and depreciated in the normal way over its expected useful life. Depreciation of £200,000 per year will, therefore, need to be accounted for. As the machine has been acquired by the manufacturer to provide facilities for research and development, if it is used in development activities, the depreciation can be included as a development cost and capitalised if the aforementioned criteria for such projects are met. The depreciation of £200,000 will need to be allocated across the various projects; part of this expense may then be capitalised as development costs. The depreciation arising from the use of the machine on any projects which are not identified as development projects will be written off to profit and loss in the usual way.

So, if 40% of the machine usage is on development projects where all six criteria have been fulfilled, the accounting for the depreciation will be:

		£	£
Debit	Development (intangible asset)	80,000	
	Depreciation expense	120,000	
Credit	Accumulated depreciation		200,000

2   Gordons, a bakery, has spent £150,000, £120,000 ,and £75,000 over the past three successive years creating and promoting a range of its products under the brand name 'Simply Yummy!', and is now successfully selling these in its high-street shops.

During the most recent year the bakery acquired the business and assets of a sole trader. As part of the total acquisition price of £1,300,000 the bakery valued the brand 'Crunchie Munchies' at a fair value of £200,000.

Required:
Discuss and contrast the accounting treatment of the costs of promoting Gordons' own-brand products and the costs associated with the acquisition.

IAS 38 does not permit internally generated brands, mastheads, publishing titles, and customer lists to be recognised as intangible assets because expenditure on these items cannot be distinguished from the cost of developing the business as a whole (IAS 38 paras 63 and 64). The expenditure in developing the 'Simply Yummy' range is, therefore ,written off to profit and loss in its respective years.

However, a brand name acquired in a business combination can be recognised as an intangible asset provided its fair value can be measured reliably. The allocation of £200,000 of the purchase price for the brand name 'Crunchie Munchies' means the fair value has been identified and the bakery will include this as a separately identified intangible asset in its statement of financial position.

11.7.3 Cost of an internally generated intangible asset

A key point to note is that only new development expenditure is recognised as an intangible asset from the point of the fulfilment of the recognition criteria; there is no retrospective capitalisation of previously incurred costs.

Costs which can be capitalised typically include:

(i) costs of direct materials and services

(ii) wages and salaries and related costs

(iii) fees to register a patent or licence

(iv) amortisation of such patents or licences

but exclude general selling and administrative expenditure, and costs of training staff to operate the asset.

 Worked example 11.4: to show the accounting for the capitalisation of development costs

Wigton Manufacturers plc, a company with a 31 December financial year end, is developing a new production process and, during 20X5, incurred expenditure of £1,000,000. Wigton Manufacturers is able to demonstrate that at 1 December 20X5 the production process met the criteria for recognition as an intangible asset. Of the total expenditure £900,000 was incurred before 1 December 20X5, and the remainder was incurred between 1 December and 31 December 20X5. In 20X6 the entity incurred further expenditure of £2,000,000 on development of the process.

Required:
Show how the development costs will be accounted for in 20X5 and 20X6.

At the end of 20X5 the production process is recognised as an intangible asset at a cost of £100,000 as this is the expenditure incurred since the date when the recognition criteria were met, i.e. 1 December 20X5. The £900,000 incurred prior to this is recognised as an expense in profit and loss:

		£	£
Debit	Intangible assets (cost)	100,000	
	Development expense (I/S)	900,000	
Credit	Bank		1,000,000

During 20X6 all expenditure is capitalised:

		£	£
Debit	Intangible assets (cost)	2,000,000	
Credit	Bank		2,000,000

At the end of 20X6 the cost of production process recognised as an intangible asset is £2,100,000.

Rolls-Royce plc states that it follows the requirements of IAS 38 in the research and development accounting policy in its 2009 financial statements.

Financial reporting in practice 11.3 | Rolls-Royce plc, 2009

Research and development

In accordance with IAS 38 *Intangible Assets*, expenditure incurred on research and development, excluding known recoverable amounts on contracts, and contributions to shared engineering programmes, is distinguished as relating either to a research phase or to a development phase.

All research phase expenditure is charged to the income statement. For development expenditure, this is capitalised as an internally generated intangible asset only if it meets strict criteria, relating in particular to technical feasibility and generation of future economic benefits.

Expenditure that cannot be classified into these two categories is treated as being incurred in the research phase. The Group considers that, due to the complex nature of new equipment programmes, it is not possible to distinguish reliably between research and development activities until relatively late in the programme.

11.8 Measurement of an intangible asset after recognition

The accounting methods applied to an intangible asset once it has been recognised are very similar to those applied to tangible non-current assets. This makes sense, as both are long-term resources being used by a business to generate future benefits. A business can choose either the cost model or the revaluation model, with all assets in the same class using the same model. Accumulated amortisation and accumulated impairment losses are deducted to give the carrying amount.

If the revaluation model is chosen, all the assets in the class should be revalued at the same date, with the revalued amount being the fair value at this date. However, the use of the revaluation model is less common for intangible assets, as the determination of fair value generally requires an active market for the assets to exist. An active market means that items traded in the market are uniform, willing buyers and sellers are readily available, and prices are in the public domain. The very nature of many intangible assets leads them to be unique (e.g. brands, newspaper mastheads, patents and trademarks, and any internally generated asset) and any trading in them to be relatively infrequent. There may be an active market for some licences and quotas; nevertheless, most businesses use the cost model for intangible assets.

In the event that the revaluation model is used, there is no set time limit for when a new valuation has to be carried out or even a recommendation as to how long this should be. Again, it is because of the uniqueness of each intangible asset that businesses are required to revalue the assets only if the fair value differs materially from its carrying amount. This may result in annual revaluations for some asset classes; others will be far less frequently revalued.

 Reminder *The accounting for revaluation surpluses or deficits is the same as for tangible non-current assets:*

1   *If the asset's carrying amount is increased as a result of a revaluation, the increased amount is:*

(a) *recognised in other comprehensive income in the statement of comprehensive income*

(b) *credited to a revaluation surplus account in equity.*

However, if the increase reverses a previous revaluation decrease which had been recognised in profit and loss, the increase is credited to profit and loss, limited to the amount of the previous decrease. Any excess in increase is treated as before.

2   *If the asset's carrying amount is decreased as a result of a revaluation, the decrease is recognised in profit and loss.*

However, if there is a credit balance on a revaluation surplus account relating to the asset, the decrease, which is limited to the amount of this balance, is:

(a) *debited to the revaluation surplus account*

(b) *credited to the asset's carrying amount.*

Any excess in decrease is recognised in profit and loss.

3   *The balance on the revaluation reserve may be realised as the intangible asset used by the entity by transferring the difference between the amortisation charged on the revalued amount and the amortisation which would have been charged on the historic cost from the revaluation reserve to retained earnings. Note: this does not pass through profit and loss—it is an inter-reserve transfer.*

11.8.1 Amortisation and useful life

As for tangible non-current assets, the question arises as to what happens to the intangible asset's value once it has been capitalised. For tangible assets this results in depreciation being accounted for—to spread the cost or value of the asset over the periods expected to benefit from the asset's use—and it would seem logical to apply the same approach to intangible assets.

So, if the useful life of an intangible asset can be estimated or, in other words, it is finite, then the asset must be amortised from the point at which the asset is available for use. A similar accounting approach as that applied to tangible assets and depreciation is used. The actual estimation of the life of an intangible asset may be difficult and management will have to consider many factors, such as:

● technical or commercial obsolescence

● future changes in market demand for the products or services output from the asset

- the period of control over the asset
- typical product life cycles.

Financial reporting in practice 11.4   Shire plc, 2009

In its 2009 financial statements Shire plc indicates the factors it takes into account when estimating the useful life of its intangible assets:

Other intangible assets accounting policy

Other intangible assets principally comprise intellectual property rights for products with a defined revenue stream, and for business combinations completed subsequent to January 1, 2009 also include acquired IPR&D. Intellectual property rights for currently marketed products are recorded at cost and amortized over the estimated useful life of the related product, which ranges from five to 35 years (weighted average 18 years). IPR&D acquired through a business combination which completed subsequent to January 1, 2009 is capitalized as an indefinite lived intangible asset until the completion or abandonment of the associated research and development efforts. Once the research and development efforts are completed the useful life of the relevant assets will be determined, and the IPR&D asset amortized over this useful economic life.

The following factors are considered in estimating the useful lives of Other intangible assets:

- expected use of the asset;
- regulatory, legal or contractual provisions, including the regulatory approval and review process, patent issues and actions by government agencies;
- the effects of obsolescence, changes in demand, competing products and other economic factors, including the stability of the market, known technological advances, development of competing drugs that are more effective clinically or economically;
- actions of competitors, suppliers, regulatory agencies or others that may eliminate current competitive advantages; and
- historical experience of renewing or extending similar arrangements.

When a number of factors apply to an intangible asset, these factors are considered in combination when determining the appropriate useful life for the relevant asset.

Management also has to consider whether the intangible asset has any residual value. This is presumed to be zero unless there is a commitment by a third party to purchase the asset at the end of its useful life, or a residual value can be determined by the presence of an active market in the type of asset.

The depreciable amount, established as the difference between the cost or value of the asset and any residual value, is then written off on a 'systematic basis' over its useful life, taking into account the pattern of how it is going to be used. In practice most companies will use a straight-line basis. All estimates used to determine amortisation require review at the end of each financial period and, if these change, then the amortisation method and amount will alter from that point.

Examples of useful life

1   A direct-mail marketing company with a financial year end of 31 December purchases a customer list on 1 September 20X8 for £4,500. The company expects that it will be able to derive benefit from the information on the list for at least one year, but no more than three years. The first mail shot using the list is on 1 October 20X8.

The customer list would be amortised over management's best estimate of its useful life, say 18 months. Although the direct-mail marketing company may intend to add customer names and other information to the list in the future, the expected benefits of the acquired customer list relate only to the customers on the list at the date it was acquired. Amortisation would commence from the point at which the asset is available for use, in other words from 1 September 20X8. Amortisation charged to the income statement in 20X8 would amount to £1,000 (4/18 × £4,500). At the end of each reporting period the company would also assess whether there were any indications that the customer list may be impaired in accordance with IAS 36.

2   An airline company has acquired an airline route authority between two European cities. The route authority expires in three years and then may be renewed every five years. Route authority renewals are granted routinely at a minimal cost and, historically, have been renewed when the airline has complied with the applicable rules and regulations. The airline company intends to comply with these, and expects to provide service indefinitely between the two cities from its hub airports and expects that supporting infrastructure (airport gates, slots, and terminal facility leases) will remain in place at those airports for as long as it has the route authority. An analysis of the company's demand and cash flows supports these assumptions.

Because the facts and circumstances support the airline company's ability to continue providing air service indefinitely between the two cities, the intangible asset related to the route authority is treated as having an indefinite useful life. Therefore, the route authority would not be amortised until its useful life is determined to be finite. It would be tested for impairment in accordance with IAS 36 annually and whenever there is an indication that it may be impaired.

(From IAS 38 Illustrative examples.)

11.8.2 Impairment

Because intangible assets, by their nature, arise in very different ways and are individual, it may be difficult to assess the useful life of some assets. Any asset in this case is deemed to have an indefinite life and IAS 38 specifies that it shall not be amortised (para. 107). However, the asset must be tested each year for impairment, and also whenever there are indications that the asset is impaired, in accordance with IAS 36 *Impairment of Assets*.

🛈 **Reminder**   *As detailed previously in Chapter 10 for tangible non-current assets, a test for impairment means that the recoverable amount of the asset has to be determined (this is the higher of the asset's fair value less costs to sell and its value in use). The carrying amount of the asset is compared to the recoverable amount. If the recoverable amount is lower than the carrying amount, an impairment loss is recognised, either in profit and loss, or, if the asset is using the revaluation model and there is a revaluation surplus in relation to the asset, the loss can be debited to the surplus to the extent that it exists, with any excess recognised in profit and loss.*

In addition to the test for impairment, other conditions need to be reviewed each year to determine whether the indefinite useful life assessment of the asset is still appropriate. If a finite life can be subsequently estimated, then the asset must start to be amortised, and this is treated as a change in accounting estimate in accordance with IAS 8 *Accounting Policies, Changes in Accounting Estimates and Errors*. This is usually accompanied by a test for impairment to determine the carrying amount, as the conditions which indicate the asset now has a finite life often indicate the asset is impaired.

11.8.3 Goodwill

Goodwill acquired in a business combination is never amortised, but is tested each year for impairment. For the purpose of its impairment testing, the goodwill is allocated to the cash-generating units (CGUs) expected to benefit from the combination, which are then tested for impairment. Any impairment loss is allocated first to goodwill and then to the net assets of the CGU.

 Worked example 11.5: to show the accounting for impairment of goodwill

Peter plc acquired the whole of company Saul Ltd in 20X5 and the goodwill arising on acquisition was calculated at £200,000. Peter identifies the net assets of Saul as a CGU. No impairment losses or gains have previously been accounted for in relation to Saul, but, at 31 December 20X7, the recoverable amount of Saul was assessed to be £750,000. At this date, the carrying amount of net assets of Saul, excluding goodwill, was £850,000.

Required:
Show how the goodwill impairment is accounted for in the 20X7 financial statements of Peter plc.

	£
Carrying amount of CGU	
Carrying amount of identifiable net assets	850,000
Goodwill	200,000
	1,050,000
Recoverable amount	750,000
Impairment loss	300,000

The loss is recognised as an expense in profit and loss, and allocated to the net assets as follows:

	Goodwill £	Net assets of CGU £	Total £
Carrying amount	200,000	850,000	1,050,000
Impairment loss	(200,000)	(100,000)	(300,000)
New carrying amount	Nil	750,000	750,000

11.8.4 Derecognition

As for a tangible non-current asset, an intangible asset is derecognised either when it is disposed of, or when no future economic benefits are expected from its use or disposal. The gain or loss on derecognition is calculated as the difference between the proceeds from disposal, if any, and the carrying amount at the date of derecognition.

11.9 Disclosures

These are extensive and are very similar to those required for property, plant and equipment. Generally, there will be information provided in the company's accounting policies for each class of intangible asset about:

- whether the lives are indefinite or finite, and, if indefinite, the reasons for this assessment
- for assets with finite lives, the estimated useful lives and amortisation methods used.

A disclosure note breaking down the total carrying amount of intangible assets will contain a full reconciliation, by class of asset, of the opening and closing carrying amounts, which will include:

- additions, showing separately those acquired externally, those from internal development, and those acquired in a business combination
- assets classified as held for sale
- disposals
- increases/decreases arising from revaluations
- impairment losses or reversals of impairment losses recognised previously
- amortisation recognised during the period
- any other changes in the carrying amounts
- the gross carrying amount and accumulated amortisation at the beginning and end of the accounting period.

If any class of intangible asset uses the revaluation model, there are additional disclosures:

- the date(s) of revaluation(s)
- the carrying amount of revalued intangible assets
- the carrying amount that would have been recognised if the cost model had been applied to the class of asset
- the amount of the revaluation surplus relating to intangible assets at the beginning and end of the accounting period

- the methods and assumptions used in estimating the assets' fair values.

  Further disclosures include:

- the amount of research and development expenditure recognised as an expense during the accounting period

- the line item in the statement of comprehensive income in which amortisation of intangible assets is included.

Financial reporting in practice 11.5 | Vodafone plc, 2010

Vodafone Group plc's 2010 financial statements contain extensive information about its intangible assets, starting with the accounting policy.

Intangible assets

Identifiable intangible assets are recognised when the Group controls the asset, it is probable that future economic benefits attributed to the asset will flow to the Group and the cost of the asset can be reliably measured.

Goodwill

Goodwill arising on the acquisition of an entity represents the excess of the cost of acquisition over the Group's interest in the net fair value of the identifiable assets, liabilities and contingent liabilities of the entity recognised at the date of acquisition.

Goodwill is initially recognised as an asset at cost and is subsequently measured at cost less any accumulated impairment losses. Goodwill is held in the currency of the acquired entity and revalued to the closing rate at each end of reporting period date.

Goodwill is not subject to amortisation but is tested for impairment.

Negative goodwill arising on an acquisition is recognised directly in the income statement.

On disposal of a subsidiary or a jointly controlled entity, the attributable amount of goodwill is included in the determination of the profit or loss recognised in the income statement on disposal.

Goodwill arising before the date of transition to IFRS, on 1 April 2004, has been retained at the previous UK GAAP amounts, subject to being tested for impairment at that date. Goodwill written off to reserves under UK GAAP prior to 1998 has not been reinstated and is not included in determining any subsequent profit or loss on disposal.

Finite lived intangible assets

Intangible assets with finite lives are stated at acquisition or development cost, less accumulated amortisation. The amortisation period and method is reviewed at least annually. Changes in the expected useful life or the expected pattern of consumption of future economic benefits embodied in the asset is accounted for by changing the amortisation period or method, as appropriate, and are treated as changes in accounting estimates. The amortisation expense on intangible assets with finite lives is recognised in profit or loss in the expense category consistent with the function of the intangible asset.

(continued)

(continued)

Licence and spectrum fees

Amortisation periods for licence and spectrum fees are determined primarily by reference to the unexpired licence period, the conditions for licence renewal and whether licences are dependent on specific technologies. Amortisation is charged to the income statement on a straight-line basis over the estimated useful lives from the commencement of service of the network.

Computer software

Computer software comprises computer software purchased from third parties as well as the cost of internally developed software. Computer software licences are capitalised on the basis of the costs incurred to acquire and bring into use the specific software. Costs that are directly associated with the production of identifiable and unique software products controlled by the Group, and are probable of producing future economic benefits are recognised as intangible assets. Direct costs include software development employee costs and directly attributable overheads.

Software integral to a related item of hardware equipment is accounted for as property, plant and equipment.

Costs associated with maintaining computer software programs are recognised as an expense when they are incurred.

Internally developed software is recognised only if all of the following conditions are met:

- an asset is created that can be separately identified;
- it is probable that the asset created will generate future economic benefits; and
- the development cost of the asset can be measured reliably.

Amortisation is charged to the income statement on a straight-line basis over the estimated useful lives from the date the software is available for use.

Other intangible assets

Other intangible assets including brands and customer bases, are recorded at fair value at the date of acquisition. Amortisation is charged to the income statement on a straight-line basis over the estimated useful lives of intangible assets from the date they are available for use.

Estimated useful lives

The estimated useful lives of finite lived intangible assets are as follows:

- Licence and spectrum fees 3–25 years
- Computer software 3–5 years
- Brands 1–10 years
- Customer bases 2–7 years

The reconciliation of opening and closing carrying amounts of intangible assets is shown in the disclosure note relating to intangible assets:

Note 9. Intangible assets

	Goodwill £m	Licences and spectrum £m	Computer software £m	Other £m	Total £m
Cost:					
1 April 2008	91,762	22,040	5,800	1,188	120,790
Exchange movements	14,298	2,778	749	153	17,978
Arising on acquisition	613	199	69	130	1,011
Additions	–	1,138	1,144	–	2,282
Disposals	–	(1)	(403)	–	(404)
Change in consolidation status	(9)	(16)	–	–	(25)
31 March 2009	**106,664**	**26,138**	**7,359**	**1,471**	**141,632**
Exchange movements	(2,751)	62	(72)	326	(2,435)
Arising on acquisition	1,185	1,454	153	1,604	4,396
Change in consolidation status	(102)	(413)	(281)	(175)	(971)
Additions	–	306	1,199	19	1,524
Disposals	–	–	(114)	–	(114)
31 March 2010	**104,996**	**27,547**	**8,244**	**3,245**	**144,032**
Accumulated impairment losses and amortisation:					
1 April 2008	40,426	5,132	4,160	741	50,459
Exchange movements	6,630	659	569	126	7,984
Amortisation charge for the year	–	1,522	885	346	2,753
Impairment losses	5,650	250	–	–	5,900
Disposals	–	–	(391)	–	(391)
Change in consolidation status	–	(11)	–	–	(11)
31 March 2009	**52,706**	**7,552**	**5,223**	**1,213**	**66,694**
Exchange movements	(1,848)	(29)	(104)	64	(1,917)
Amortisation charge for the year	–	1,730	1,046	678	3,454
Change in consolidation status	–	(135)	(154)	(181)	(470)
Impairment losses, net	2,300	(200)	–	–	2,100
Disposals	–	–	(87)	–	(87)
31 March 2010	**53,158**	**8,918**	**5,924**	**1,774**	**69,774**
Net book value:					
31 March 2009	53,958	18,586	2,136	258	74,938
31 March 2010	51,838	18,629	2,320	1,471	74,258

(continued)

(continued)

For licences and spectrum and other intangible assets, amortisation is included within the cost of sales line within the consolidated income statement. Licences and spectrum with a net book value of £2,570 million (2009: £2,765 million) have been pledged as security against borrowings.

The net book value at 31 March 2010 and expiry dates of the most significant licences are as follows:

	Expiry date	2010 £m	2009 £m
Germany	December 2020	4,802	5,452
UK	December 2021	3,914	4,246
Qatar	June 2028	1,328	1,482
Italy	December 2021	1,097	1,240

11.10 What do the accounting treatment and disclosures of intangible assets mean to the user?

As seen in this chapter only certain intangible assets which meet the definition and recognition criteria set out by IAS 38 are actually included on a company's statement of financial position. The same type of asset may even be treated differently depending on whether it was internally generated or acquired externally, possibly through a business combination. Hence, a user of the financial statements could be said to get an incomplete picture of the resources that a company uses to generate its revenues and wealth. In addition, some businesses actively pursue strategies to develop their own intangible assets, which they see as the core success of their business, and which will never be capitalised. As Bill Gates of Microsoft highlighted:

> The law requires circa 40 pages of figures in the annual company report but these figures represent only 3% of the company's value and assets. The remaining 97% are the company's intangible assets.

Even if a company followed the requirements of IAS 38, the whole issue of accounting for intangible assets can be considered prone to 'earnings management', particularly if there is pressure on earnings. Management's judgement and estimations of future events, which may not be entirely in its control, are required to determine whether recognition criteria have been fulfilled. Alternative interpretations of these subjective criteria can be made, which may also lead to a different approach to capitalisation from one company to another, or even within the same company from one project to another.

As for tangible assets, two alternative measurement bases are available for intangible assets—the cost basis and the revaluation basis—which can lead to difficulties in comparability between companies. The revaluation model uses fair value, which, for intangible assets, can be particularly subjective.

The extensive disclosures will aid the comparability of different companies, but these show mainly what has been capitalised and subsequent treatment of these costs; there is less information on what has not been capitalised. Companies' financial statements generally quote the words of IAS 38 to explain accounting treatments, and will not explicitly show management's interpretations and decision-making processes.

So is this, therefore, a problem? Non-recognition of intangible assets will result in the understatement of net assets and capital employed, and variations in recognition methods will have an impact on these figures. Analysis of the financial performance of a company using ratios which include these items will clearly be affected.

 Worked example 11.6: to show the effect of capitalisation versus non-capitalisation of intangible assets on accounting ratios

Jenmark plc has its own internally generated brand, which it has spent years developing. Annual expenditure on maintaining the brand is £1 million and, as a result of this, the company's directors estimate that the brand has an indefinite useful life. Brand valuation experts have recently estimated the fair value of the brand at £15 million.

The financial statements of Jenmark properly excluding the brand as an intangible asset and also if the brand were recognised are shown as follows.

Note: if the brand were recognised, equity would be increased. As the brand has an indefinite life, there is no amortisation to be recognised. The annual expenditure on maintaining the brand remains an expense.

	Excluding brand	Brand recognised
Statement of financial position	£m	£m
Intangible assets	–	15
Other assets	<u>14</u>	<u>14</u>
	<u>14</u>	<u>29</u>
Equity	5	20
Long-term borrowings	3	3
Current liabilities	<u>6</u>	<u>6</u>
	<u>14</u>	<u>29</u>
Income statement		
Revenue	20	20
Profit before interest and tax	7	7

Required:

Calculate and comment on the following accounting ratios using the financial information including and excluding the recognition of the brand:

- return on capital employed
- return on assets
- net profit margin
- gearing.

		Excluding brand	Brand recognised
Return on capital employed	$\dfrac{\text{PBIT}}{\text{Capital employed}}$	88%	30%
Return on assets	$\dfrac{\text{PBIT}}{\text{Total assets}}$	50%	24%
Net profit margin	$\dfrac{\text{PBIT}}{\text{REVENUE}}$	35%	35%
Gearing	$\dfrac{\text{Debt}}{\text{Debt + Equity}}$	38%	13%

The two performance ratios—return on capital employed and return on assets—are much higher without the brand, but these ratios could be considered meaningless as the capital employed or assets do not reflect the 'true' resources of the company. Inclusion of the brand gives more meaningful ratios.

The net profit margin is unaffected and is therefore a good ratio to use when comparing companies' performances. Even if the brand had a finite life and amortisation were included in the income statement, profit before interest, tax, and amortisation is often taken as the measure of profit.

Although the gearing ratio looks much improved when the intangible asset is recognised, companies' borrowings depend, in part, on their ability to provide security in the form of tangible assets. Lenders will usually discount any intangible assets.

One of the initial issues set out at the beginning of the chapter was that non-recognition of intangible assets could lead to undervaluation of the shares of companies. It must be remembered that the purpose of a statement of financial position is not to provide a market value for a business, and stock market analysts understand this. Market values are based largely on earnings reported in the income statement and stock market analysts tend to ignore intangible assets actually included in statements of financial position.

11.11 Does this mean the current accounting and reporting of intangible assets is acceptable?

It is important for users of financial statements to have information about all resources an entity has available, including intangibles which are not recognised on the statement of financial position. However, adding intangibles to this statement, where it is difficult or too early to assess whether they may bring future benefits to the entity, or where their value is dubious, will not assist the relevance or reliability of financial statements.

Recent proposals for the reform of accounting for intangibles have been put forward by various international groups, including the chief executive officers (CEOs) of the world's six largest auditing firms, Meritum (a European Union-sponsored group of researchers), The Danish Ministry of Science Technology and Innovation, and Baruch Lev (an American accounting academic who has written widely on financial reporting for intangibles). None of these propose abandoning the accounting and reporting methods of current accounting standards; they all suggest that additional information should be disclosed. This information would require companies to identify and explain key intangibles which drive their business, and provide measures of these. For example, the ratio of the number of personal computers to the total number of employees could be used if information technology is critical to achieving the entity's objectives.

There are obvious problems with these voluntary disclosures—many would be industry or company-specific, and so would not be comparable; they would be subjective and their reliability would be called into question; and companies would probably not wish to disclose information which may be helpful to competitors and be costly to produce. However, to make these sorts of disclosures mandatory would also be problematic as some form of standardisation would be required, which would be impossible across all industries and, possibly, meaningless for some. The ability to audit the information would also be very difficult and the additional information would add to the length of company annual reports.

11.12 The current IASB position

Currently, the IASB is contemplating undertaking an active project on the accounting for identifiable intangible assets (excluding goodwill) jointly with the Financial Accounting Standards Board (FASB) and a project proposal was put forward in December 2007. The project proposed addressing concerns that the current accounting requirements lead to inconsistent treatments for some types of intangible assets depending on how they arise. Specifically, the project would address:

- the initial accounting for identifiable intangible assets other than those acquired in a business combination (with a particular focus on, but not limited to, internally generated identifiable intangible assets)
- the subsequent accounting for all identifiable intangible assets.

However, the IASB decided not to add a project on intangible assets to its active agenda in December 2007 because of the large demand of such a project on its limited resources. The project has yet to be recommenced.

Summary of key points

Intangible assets are key resources of businesses, and the question of whether, and how, they should be included in financial statements to enable users to have reliable and comparable information about the entity is an important one. Recognition and measurement are key issues for intangibles owing to the assets' nature, with subjective judgements often required.

IAS 38 defines an intangible asset as an identifiable non-monetary asset without physical substance; common examples are computer software, patents, copyrights, trademarks, customer lists, licences, quotas, and franchises. An intangible asset must be separable, or arise from contractual or other legal rights, and, to be recognised, it must be probable that future economic benefits will flow to the entity and the cost must be capable of being measured reliably.

Intangible assets may be purchased from an external source when they are measured initially at cost; be acquired as part of a business combination when they are measured initially at fair value; or be internally generated. In the latter case only expenditure arising in the development phase can be recognised as an intangible asset and this only if certain criteria are met.

The accounting for recognised intangible assets is similar to that for property, plant and equipment, with the cost and valuation models being available, amortisation being required for intangible assets with finite lives, and annual impairment testing required for assets with indefinite lives and for goodwill. The accounting treatment for impairment losses is the same as for property, plant and equipment, although testing for impairment of goodwill requires the allocation of goodwill to related CGUs. Disclosures for the two types of non-current asset are also similar.

Current accounting methods lead to some inconsistencies and suggestions have been made by interested groups for additional disclosures. The IASB does not have any current plans to address these issues.

 ## Further reading

Anderson, N. (2004) Value judgments, *Accountancy*, November 2004: 86–87. Why read? The article illustrates the practical difficulties of valuing intangible assets acquired in a business combination.

IASB (International Accounting Standards Board) (2004) IAS 38 *Intangible Assets*, revised March 2004. London: IASB.

ICAEW (Institute of Chartered Accountants in England and Wales) (2009) *Developments in New Reporting Models*, pp. 20–27. Available at: http://www.icaew.com (accessed 14 October 2012). Why read? The highlighted pages explore why the issue of accounting for intangibles has always prompted criticism in the context of financial reporting models.

Skinner, D. J. (2008) *Accounting for Intangibles – A Critical Review of Policy Recommendations*. Presented at ICAEW Information for Better Markets Conference, 17–18 December 2007. Why read? A critical evaluation of the arguments for reforming accounting methods applied to intangible assets.

 ## Bibliography

Arsenal Holdings plc (2008) *Annual Report, 2008*. London: Arsenal Holdings.

IASB (International Accounting Standards Board) (2001) *The Framework for the Preparation and Presentation of Financial Statements*, April 2001, London: IASB.

IASB (International Accounting Standards Board) (2004) IAS 38
Intangible Assets, revised March 2004. London: IASB.

IASB (2009) Exposure Draft *Fair Value Measurement*, May 2009. London: IASB.

ICAEW (Institute of Chartered Accountants in England and Wales) (2003)
New Reporting Models of Business – Proposals for Reform, pp. 51–57.
Available at: http://www.icaew.com (accessed 14 October 2012).

ICAEW (Institute of Chartered Accountants in England and Wales) (2009) *Developments in New
Reporting Models*, pp. 20–27. Available at: http://www.icaew.com (accessed 14 October 2012).

International Valuation Standards Board (2010) *International Valuation Guidance
Note No. 4 – Valuation of Intangible Assets*. Available at: http://www.iasplus.
com/en/binary/ivsc/0901ivscedivgn4.pdf (accessed 14 October 2012).

Leadbetter, C. (2000) *New Measures for the New Economy*. Report produced
by the Centre for Business Performance for the ICAEW. London: ICAEW.

Meritum (2001) *Guidelines for Managing and Reporting on Intangibles – Intellectual Capital
Report*. Report produced by Meritum, a group of European researchers brought together under
the auspices of the EU. Available at: http://www.pnbukh.com/ (accessed 14 October 2012).

Nokia Corporation (2010) *Annual Report, 2009*. Espoo: Nokia.

PricewaterhouseCoopers (2009) *Making Sense of a Complex World – IAS 36 Impairment of
Assets - A Discussion Paper on the impact on the Telecoms Industry*. Paper produced for the
PwC telecommunications industry accounting group (TIAG). London: PricewaterhouseCoopers.

RICS (Royal Institution of Chartered Surveyors) (2006) *Valuation of Intangible Assets –
Four Case Studies*. Available at: http://www.rics.org (accessed 14 October 2012).

Rolls-Royce plc (2010) *Annual Report, 2009*. London: Rolls-Royce.

Shire plc (2010) *Annual Report, 2009*. St Helier: Shire.

Skinner, D. J. (2008) *Accounting for Intangibles – A Critical Review of Policy Recommendations*.
Presented at ICAEW Information for Better Markets Conference, 17–18 December 2007.

Vodafone Group plc (2010) *Annual Report, 2010*. Newbury: Vodafone.

 ## Questions

● Quick test

1 A company is developing improved production processes and has recruited a manager to
head up the team responsible for this. The manager is on an annual salary of £64,000. The
company has also incurred costs of £50,000 in training the personnel and now has a highly
skilled team.

Discuss whether the company has any intangible assets, as defined by IAS 38 *Intangible
assets*.

2 Warmington plc produces a range of children's toys, and markets and sells them under its
internally developed brand, KidzToys. The brand is now highly respected and the products are
regarded as 'must have' toys.

On 1 July 20X3 Fraser plc acquired the whole of Warmington plc for £50 million. At this date a
brand valuation expert valued the KidzToys brand at £15 million on the basis of a useful life of
5 years. Other net assets were deemed to have a fair value of £25 million.

Required

Assuming that the goodwill arising on the acquisition of Warmington was not impaired at 30 June 20X4, what amounts for intangible assets should be recognised in Fraser plc's consolidated financial statements at 30 June 20X4 in respect of this transaction?

●● Develop your understanding

3 (a) Company Alpha acquires Company Beta in a business combination. Beta manufactures goods in two distinct lines of business: sporting goods and electronics. Gamma, a customer of Beta, purchases both sporting goods and electronics from Beta, which has a contract with Gamma to be its exclusive provider of sporting goods, but has no such contract for the supply of electronics. Both Beta and Alpha believe that only one overall customer relationship exists between Beta and Gamma.

(b) Company Delta acquires Company Epsilon in a business combination on 31 December 20X5. Epsilon does business with its customers solely through purchase and sales orders. At 31 December 20X5, Epsilon has a backlog of customer purchase orders from 60% of its customers, all of whom are recurring customers. The other 40% of Epsilon's customers are also recurring customers. However, as of 31 December 20X5, Epsilon has no open purchase orders or other contracts with those customers.

Required

For each scenario determine whether there are identifiable intangible assets in these business combinations.

4 On 1 January 20X2 a company acquires computer software specific to a project for £200,000. Although the project is in its early stages, and is not expected to make profits or positive cash flows for a number of years, the company will start to use the software straight away; it is estimated it has a useful life of 10 years. The company negotiated to defer the payment to the supplier until 1 January 20X4. The company currently pays interest on its borrowings at 6% per annum.

Required:

Show how this transaction would be accounted for at 1 January 20X2 and in the financial statements of the company for the year ended 31 December 20X2.

5 (a) On 1 January 20X1 a broadcasting company with a 31 December financial year end acquires a broadcasting licence for £360,000 that is renewable every 10 years if the holder provides at least an average level of service to its customers and complies with the relevant legislative requirements. The licence may be renewed indefinitely at little cost. At the date of acquisition, the licence has been renewed twice by the previous owner and it will require renewing again on 1 January 20X6. The acquiring company intends to renew the licence indefinitely and evidence supports its ability to do so. Historically, there has been no compelling challenge to the licence renewal. The technology used in broadcasting is not expected to be replaced by another technology at any time in the foreseeable future.

(b) On 1 January 20X3 the licensing authority decides that it will no longer renew broadcasting licences, but will auction the licences when the renewal is due. The broadcasting company expects to hold the licence until this date and will then decide whether it will bid for the licence.

Required:

Determine the useful life of the broadcasting licence, and discuss the subsequent accounting treatment at the two dates 1 January 20X1 and 20X3.

● ● ● Take it further

6   Airpro plc is a newly established company in the business of providing engineering and operational support services to aircraft manufacturers.

Airpro plc has received a confirmed order from a well known aircraft manufacturer to develop new designs for ducting the air conditioning of their aircraft. For this project, Airpro needed funds totalling £1 million. It was able to obtain this funding from two venture capitalists at the start of 20X6.

During 20X6 Airpro incurred the following expenditures in respect of this research and development project:

January	Paid £175,000 toward salaries of the technicians (engineers and consultants).
March	Incurred £250,000 toward cost of developing the duct and producing the test model.
June	Paid an additional £300,000 for revising the ducting processes to ensure that product could be introduced in the market.
August	Developed, at a cost of £80,000, the first model (prototype) and tested it with the air conditioners to ensure its compatibility.
October	A focus group of other engineering providers was invited to a conference of the introduction of this new product. Cost of the conference aggregated to £50,000.
December	The development phase was completed and a cash flow budget was prepared. Net profit for the year was estimated to equal £900,000.

Required

Discuss the proper accounting treatment of the various costs incurred in the financial statements of Airpro plc for the year ended 31 December 20X6, in accordance with IAS 38 *Intangible Assets*.

7   On 31 December 20X6 Jolyon Pharmaceuticals plc acquired the whole of the share capital of Gillet Ltd for a total consideration of £10 million. Gillet Ltd had been involved in the research and development of a drug to help asthma sufferers. By 31 December 20X6 Gillet had written off to profit and loss total research and development costs of £500,000, as the criteria for recognition of any of the costs as an intangible asset had not yet been met. At the date of acquisition, Jolyon Pharmaceuticals estimated the fair value of the asthma drug project at £800,000 and agreed to provide funding to support its further development.

During 20X7 and 20X8 work on this project continued, and Gillet incurred further costs of £900,000 in 20X7 and £1 million in 20X8 up to 31 October—the costs being incurred evenly over the years. On 31 March 20X8 the drug was approved by the regulatory authorities, at which point Gillet considered that it was also commercially viable. On 1 November 20X8 the drug started being marketed and sold. Gillet estimates the product to have a useful life of 10 years.

Required:

Explain how the costs relating to this drug project should be accounted for in the consolidated financial statements of Jolyon Pharmaceuticals plc for the years ended 31 December 20X7 and 20X8. Justify your answer by reference to IAS 38 *Intangible assets*.

   Visit the Online Resource Centre for solutions to all these end of chapter questions plus visual walkthrough solutions. You can test your understanding with extra questions and answers, explore additional case studies based on real companies, take a guided tour through a company report, and much more. Go to the Online Resource Centre at **www.oxfordtextbooks.co.uk/orc/maynard/**

12

Current assets

➤ Introduction

The main current assets of businesses are inventories, receivables, and bank and cash balances. Other current assets arise in the normal course of accounting for business transactions, for example prepayments and short-term investments. Those businesses engaged in long-term service and construction contracts will have asset balances relating to work not yet completed or work not yet billed to customers. Accounting for many current assets is straightforward and arises from the application of the underpinning accruals concept, for example the recording of an account receivable when a sale is made on credit or the calculation of a prepayment for, say, insurance.

Current assets are key in assessing the liquidity and efficiency of working capital management of a business; thus, it is important that the figures are as accurate as possible and comparable.

However, there are accounting issues relating to some of these current assets. The recognition of accounts receivable is obviously related to when revenue is recognised, and this has been discussed in Chapter 7. Inventories and long-term contracts vary from business to business, so to ensure the accounting is consistent these assets have their own accounting standards, International Accounting Standard (IAS) 2 *Inventories* and IAS 11 *Construction Contracts*. These standards are discussed in detail in this chapter.

★ Learning objectives

After studying this chapter you will be able to:

- understand the importance of consistent accounting methods for the various current assets businesses hold
- understand the main valuation principles for inventories, and explain how cost and net realisable value are determined
- explain the accounting methods for receivables as a financial asset
- understand the approach taken by IAS 11 *Construction Contracts* in accounting for construction contracts, and be able to calculate income statement and statement of financial position figures for a construction contract in various stages of completion.

✔ Key issues checklist

- ❏ The definition of a current asset.
- ❏ The use of current assets in the assessment of a company's liquidity.
- ❏ Accounting for inventories:
  - ❏ issues with validating the physical presence of inventories
  - ❏ the key valuation principles for inventories—lower of cost and net realisable value and first-in, first-out.
- ❏ Accounting for receivables as a financial asset—cost less impairment losses.
- ❏ Accounting for construction contracts:
  - ❏ what is a construction contract
  - ❏ the main issue of accounting for construction contracts—the recognition of revenue and costs over the relevant accounting periods
  - ❏ the stage of completion method for contracts where the outcome can be estimated reliably
  - ❏ loss-making contacts and contracts where the outcome cannot be estimated reliably
  - ❏ resulting balances for the statement of financial position
  - ❏ criticisms of the current IAS 11 and changes to come.
- ❏ Disclosures for different current assets.

12.1 Definition of and significance of current assets

An asset is defined as:

> ...a resource controlled by the entity as a result of past transactions and from which future economic benefits are expected to flow to the entity...

> *(IASB, 2010: para. 4.4)*

Users of financial statements need to be able to distinguish between those assets which are long-term resources, and those which are continuously circulating and changing as working capital. Businesses therefore separate non-current assets from current assets on their statements of financial position and thus highlight assets which are expected to be realised within the current operating cycle. This enables users to assess the liquidity of a business.

Reminder *Liquidity is the ability of a business to meet its liabilities as they fall due. An analysis of the liquidity of a business involves an assessment of what makes up working capital or net current assets (i.e. current assets—current liabilities), which is needed by all businesses in order to finance day-to-day trading activities. The efficiency of the management of working capital is also important in an assessment of liquidity. Various financial ratios relevant to this assessment are discussed in Chapter 5.*

Assets are defined as current in IAS 1 *Presentation of Financial Statements* when:

(a) a business expects to realise the asset, or intends to sell or consume it, in its normal operating cycle;

(b) a business holds the asset primarily for the purpose of trading;

(c) a business expects to realise the asset within twelve months after the reporting period; or

(d) the asset is cash or a cash equivalent (as defined in IAS 7 *Statement of Cash Flows*) unless the asset is restricted from being exchanged or used to settle a liability for at least twelve months after the reporting period.

Current assets therefore include inventories, receivables and cash, and cash equivalents. The operating cycle is the time it takes between the acquisition of the asset and its ultimate conversion into cash or cash equivalents. Although some businesses may have a normal operating cycle longer than 12 months, the inventories and receivables arising in this cycle are still classified as current. Assets held primarily for trading will include some financial assets; however, the accounting treatment of these is beyond the scope of this textbook.

12.2 Inventories

12.2.1 Significance of inventories

Inventories are a significant current asset on the statements of financial position of most businesses which produce and/or sell goods. For example:

- J Sainsbury plc 2011 (supermarket)—inventories (£812 million) 48% of total current assets (£1,708 million), by far the largest current asset

- Nestlé Group 2010 (food and consumables manufacturer)—inventories (CHF 7,925 million) 20% of total current assets (CHF 38,997 million)

- Rolls-Royce plc 2010 (manufacturer)—inventories (£2,429 million) 25% of total current assets (£9,824 million).

Inventories for retailers and distribution companies encompass goods purchased and held for resale, and for manufacturers' inventories include finished goods produced, work in progress being produced, and also materials and supplies yet to be used in the production process. A service provider can also have inventories which are the costs of the service for which the provider has not yet recognised the related revenue.

The under-/overvaluation of inventories can have a material impact on the calculation of profits—if inventories are undervalued, profits are reduced; if inventories are overvalued, profits are increased.

Financial reporting in practice 12.1 | Rolls-Royce plc, 2010

Rolls-Royce plc 2010 results show the company made a net profit before tax of £702 million. Closing inventories are valued at £2,429 million.

A 5% error in inventory valuation (5% × £2,429 million = £121 million) would mean a 17% error in profit before tax (£121 million/£702 million = 17%).

For some companies, a small error in inventories may convert a profit into a loss.

An error in inventory one year also has a knock-on effect on next year's profit, as one year's closing inventory becomes next year's opening inventory.

12.2.2 Issues with accounting for inventories

Key issues relating to the accounting for inventories are:

- the physical existence of inventories
- whether the business actually controls the asset
- measurement (or valuation), which is what IAS 2 *Inventories* addresses.

Many frauds or accounting scandals have concerned inventories, as illustrated by the following cases.

 Examples of inventory-related accounting scandals

1 US case of McKesson & Robbins (1938)—fictitious inventories conveniently 'abroad' in Canada (note the auditors did not perform a physical check).

2 UK case of the GEC/AEI takeover (1967)—a forecast profit of £10 million turned into an actual loss of £4.5 million, where much of the difference related to the valuation of inventories.

3 UK case of Pergamon Press, a Maxwell company (1969)—significant differences in inventory valuation leading to a reduction in audited profits.

Companies may be tempted into 'managing' the physical presence of inventories in order to 'manage' earnings, and cases have been known of companies shipping goods to customers early or having goods in transit so that they are not physically present at any premises. This may be relatively easy if this occurs between companies in the same group. Consignment inventories (e.g. goods received from a supplier or sent to a customer on a sale or return basis) and the inclusion of obsolete inventories can also be used to manipulate recorded physical quantities. Auditors have to be alert to these issues and also be particularly careful that a company has accounted for the year end cut-off correctly. This means a check has to be made that purchases recorded before and after the year end match inventories on hand or goods not included in inventories, respectively, and that goods sold before the year end are not included in inventories.

12.2.3 Measurement of inventories

The key issue in the measurement of inventories is the amount of cost to be recognised as an asset and carried forward to be matched against the related revenues. Thus, the underpinning principle of valuation is that of accruals, but, as an asset, inventories should not be carried at amounts in excess of their value to the business. So IAS 2 requires inventories:

> …to be measured at the lower of cost and net realisable value.

(IASB, 2003: para. 9)

Inventories where this requirement does not apply are shown in Table 12.1.

12.2.4 Cost of inventories

The criteria for determining whether a cost can be included in the cost of inventories are similar to those set out in IAS 16 *Property, Plant and Equipment* for the cost of an item of property, plant and equipment.

> Cost shall comprise all costs of purchase, costs of conversion and other costs incurred in bringing the inventories to their present location and condition.

(IASB, 2003: para. 10)

Table 12.1 Businesses where the measurement requirement of IAS 2 does not apply

Type of business	Valuation method used
Producers of agriculture, forest products, agricultural produce after harvest, minerals and mineral products	Net realisable value
Commodity brokers and traders	Fair value less costs to sell

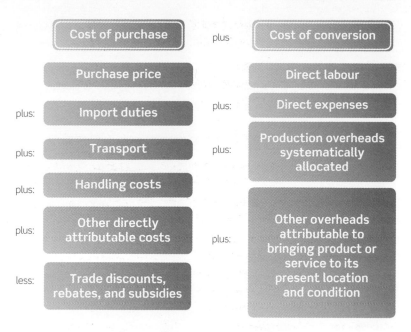

Figure 12.1 Components of cost of purchase and cost of conversion

In other words, all costs which have been incurred in getting the inventory to its particular state of completion wherever located are part of the cost. Costs of purchase and costs of conversion are defined in Figure 12.1.

Techniques such as absorption costing or activity based costing, which are used to allocate fixed production overheads to the cost of products for management accounting purposes, are therefore incorporated into financial reporting measurement requirements. The allocation of these production overheads should be based on the normal capacity of the business, which is the level of production that the business expects to achieve under normal circumstances. If production is lower than usual, or machinery is not used, the amount of fixed overhead allocated to each unit of production is not increased; these unallocated overheads are recognised as an expense. However, if production is abnormally high, the amount of overhead allocated to each unit of production is lower and this is not increased to normal levels, otherwise inventories would be measured at greater than cost.

 Worked example 12.1: to calculate the cost of inventory, including capacity considerations

The Staybright Company plc has inventories of finished goods at 31 December 20X5 and has gathered the following information in relation to these:

	£
Cost of materials	32,000
Labour	1,000 hours @ £8.00 per hour
Other variable overheads	1,400

Fixed production overheads incurred

1 October 20X5 – 31 December 20X5	80,000
Selling and distribution expenses	20,000

The number of hours worked in the period 1 October 20X5–31 December 20X5 was 18,000. During December 2,000 hours of work were lost because of an industrial dispute.

Required:
Calculate the cost of Staybright's finished goods at 31 December 20X5.

The cost of inventories at 31 December 20X5 is determined as follows:

	£
Cost of materials	32,000
Labour (1,000 × £8.00)	8,000
Variable overheads	1,400
Fixed overheads $\dfrac{£80,000}{20,000 \text{ hours}} \times 1,000$	4,000
Cost of inventories	45,400

Note 1: Selling and distribution costs are not a cost of production and so are not included.
Note 2: The allocation of the fixed production overheads to the costs of conversion is based on the normal capacity of the production facilities, in other words 20,000 hours.

12.2.5 Cost methods

The costs of specific or specialised inventories can usually be identified separately. However, where there are large numbers of inventories which cannot be distinguished from each other (e.g. a container of the same sized bolts), the cost is determined by using the **first-in, first-out (FIFO)** or **weighted average cost methods**. The FIFO method assumes a rational approach to the use of inventories in that the items purchased or produced first are sold first, so that the inventories remaining at the end of the accounting period are those which were most recently purchased or produced. Under the weighted average cost method, the cost of each item is the weighted average of the cost of similar items at the beginning of a period and the cost of similar items purchased or produced during the period.

Other costing methods may be used by businesses for internal management accounting reasons, and include:

● last-in, first-out (LIFO)
● replacement cost
● current purchase price.

These are not permitted to be used for cost purposes under IAS 2. However, many businesses carry their inventories at **standard cost** and retailers will often use selling price minus gross margin. Provided these methods approximate to cost, they may be used to establish the cost for valuation purposes.

Worked example 12.2: to show the calculation of FIFO and average cost

Glazier plc has 100 units of raw material X on hand at 1 March 20X7, which had cost £10 per unit. The following transactions in material X occurred in the month of March:

3 March	Purchases	80 units at £12 per unit
8 March	Used in production	60 units
15 March	Purchases	70 units at £11 per unit
18 March	Used in production	110 units

Required:

Compute the cost of inventory of material X at 31 March 20X7 on the following bases:

(i) First-in, first-out

(ii) Weighted average.

(i) *First-in, first-out*

		Purchases		Used		Balance		
		No.	Cost	No.	Cost	No.		£
1 March	On hand	100	£10			100	£10	1,000
3 March	Purchases	80	£12			80	£12	960
						180		1,960
8 March	Used			60	£10	40	£10	400
						80	£12	960
						120		1,360
15 March	Purchases	70	£11			40	£10	400
						80	£12	960
						70	£11	770
						190		2,130
18 March	Used			40	£10			
				70	£12	10	£12	120
				110		70	£11	770
						80		890

Cost of inventory at 31 March 20X7 under FIFO method is £890.

(ii) *Weighted average*

		Purchases		Used		Balance		
		No.	Cost	No.	Cost	No.		£
1 March	On hand	100	£10			100	£10	1,000
3 March	Purchases	80	£12			80	£12	960
						180	£10.89	1,960
8 March	Used			60	£10.89	120	£10.89	1,307

15 March	Purchases	70	£11			120	£10.89	1,307
						70	£11	770
						190	£10.93	2,077
18 March	Used			110	£10.93	80	£10.93	874

Cost of inventory at 31 March 20X7 under weighted average method is £874.

12.2.6 Net realisable value

Net realisable value (NRV) is defined as

> ...the estimated selling price in the ordinary course of business less the estimated costs of completion and the estimated costs necessary to make the sale.

(IASB, 2003: para. 6)

A number of reasons may cause the NRV of inventories to fall below cost. For example, there may be a permanent fall in the market price of inventories, inventories may physically deteriorate or become obsolete, or the business may deliberately decide to sell below cost, perhaps to dispose of high inventory levels or seasonal items. In addition, costs of completing the inventory or estimated costs to make the sale may have increased. NRV is subjective as it is based on future estimates.

The effect of writing down inventory to NRV is to recognise a loss on inventory before any sale has actually occurred; this may appear to contradict the matching principle. However, it is consistent with the view that the carrying amount of assets should not be in excess of amounts expected to be realised from their sale or use.

 Example of the effect of writing inventory down to NRV

An inventory item was purchased by a retailer in December 20X0 for £150 and usually retails for £200. Before the 31 December financial year end the company slashes selling prices by 50%.

At 31 December the inventory item's NRV is £100, which is lower than the cost of £150. By writing down the inventory item to £100, the retailer has recognised a loss of £50 in 20X0.

If the inventory item is sold in 20X1, the value of £100 will be matched to the sale price of £100, and no profit or loss will be recognised.

The determination of the lower of cost and NRV is done inventory item by inventory item, unless, for example, it is impracticable to evaluate items of inventory from others produced from the same production process that have similar purposes or end uses.

Raw materials held for use in the production of inventories are not written down below cost if the finished products in which they will be incorporated are expected to be sold at a price at or above cost. However, if this is not the case, the NRV of the raw materials needs to be considered; the best estimate of this may be replacement cost.

 Worked example 12.3: to show cost versus NRV calculations

The Standard Mix Company plc has the following items in inventories at its year end:

Item	Cost (£)	Selling price (£)
A	7,000	10,000
B	8,400	10,200
C	9,200	10,400

Item A is ready for immediate resale.

Item B is also ready for sale, but, owing to falling demand, a 25% special discount will be offered.

Item C requires packaging before it can be sold; this cost is estimated at £1,800.

Required:

Calculate the value of inventories to be included in the company's year end financial statements.

Item	Cost £	NRV	£	Lower of cost and NRV £
A	7,000		10,000	7,000
B	8,400	10,200 − (25% × 10,200)	7,650	7,650
C	9,200	10,400 − 1,800	8,600	8,600
	24,600		26,250	23,250

The cost versus NRV comparison is performed for each item of inventory separately; therefore, the value of inventory for financial reporting purposes is £23,250.

12.2.7 Disclosures

Information about the carrying amount of different categories of inventories and the extent of the changes in these assets is useful to users of financial statements in their assessment of liquidity. Although companies can choose the categories that are appropriate to their business, common classifications are:

- merchandise
- production supplies
- materials
- work in progress
- finished goods.

The accounting policies adopted by the company, including the cost formula used, are also disclosed. This tends to be similar for most companies. The amount recognised as an expense during the period, in other words cost of sales, is required to be disclosed. Companies that choose to analyse expenses according to their nature for the format of their income statements (see Chapter 4 for details of this), do not actually include this figure. Details of amounts of inventory write-down to net realisable value or reversals of write-downs are also to be disclosed.

Financial reporting in practice 12.2   Rolls-Royce plc, 2010

Rolls-Royce plc includes the following accounting policy in relation to the valuation of inventories. The note to the financial statements showing a breakdown of inventory categories and other disclosures is also included.

Accounting policy - Inventories

Inventories and work in progress are valued at the lower of cost and net realisable value on a first-in, first-out basis. Cost comprises direct materials and, where applicable, direct labour costs and those overheads, including depreciation of property, plant and equipment, that have been incurred in bringing the inventories to their present location and condition. Net realisable value represents the estimated selling prices less all estimated costs of completion and costs to be incurred in marketing, selling and distribution.

Note 11 - Inventories

	2010 £m	2009 £m
Raw materials	377	358
Work in progress	943	820
Long-term contracts work in progress	42	61
Finished goods	1,024	1,163
Payments on account	43	30
	2,429	2,432
Inventories stated at net realisable value	202	138
Amount of inventory write-down	135	83
Reversal of inventory write-down	2	5

12.3 Receivables

Receivables is a financial asset as defined by IAS 32 *Financial Instruments: Presentation* as it represents a contractual right to receive cash in the future. Its accounting treatment is therefore governed by IAS 39 *Financial Instruments: Recognition and Measurement*. Although these two accounting standards are outside the scope of this textbook, the accounting methods for financial assets as it relates to receivables will be explained briefly.

IAS 39 requires that financial assets are measured at amortised cost less impairment losses. Amortised cost is effectively the net present value of the asset, in other words a discounted cash flow figure, which has taken into account amounts repaid. It requires a discount factor to be used, which should be 'the effective interest rate', an interest rate that the business has to estimate. The amounts actually received would then be allocated between the repayment of the principal and the effective interest earned.

 Example of accounting for the amortised cost

A business sells a machine for £100,000 and allows a year's credit before the customer has to pay. Assume an interest rate of 8%.

The receivable (and revenue from the sale) would be recorded at the present value of £100,000/1.08 = £92,593:

		£	£
Debit	Receivables	92,593	
Credit	Sales revenue		92,593

When the customer settles its debt, the £100,000 would be repaying this principal with the balance being accounted for as interest received:

		£	£
Debit	Bank	100,000	
Credit	Receivables		92,593
Credit	Interest received (8% x £92,593)		7,407

This seems to imply that all receivables should be discounted to their present value, which, in practice, would be extremely cumbersome for businesses to do. Most trade receivables are also very short-term, in other words due for repayment within trading terms, which are usually 30 or 60 days, or, in some cases, 90 or 120 days. Trade receivables are therefore discounted only when the impact of accounting for the time value of money would have a significant impact on the financial statements. (Note that exposure draft ED 2011/6 *Revenue from Contracts with Customers*, which is discussed in Chapter 7, proposes that an adjustment for the time value of money need only be done if the period between the transfer of the goods or services and the expected receipt of all or substantially all of the consideration is greater than one year.)

Financial reporting in practice 12.3

This is indicated by GKN in its accounting policy for financial assets in its 2010 annual report.

Financial assets and liabilities

The carrying value of other financial assets and liabilities, including short term receivables and payables, are stated at amortised cost less any impairment provision unless the impact of the time value of money is considered to be material.

For receivables, the impairment losses referred to in IAS 39's measurement requirements relate to whether there has been an event or events which will have an impact on the estimated future cash flows of the financial asset, in other words whether the receivable is considered to be collectible or not. This leads to the accounting for the provision for doubtful debts, as described in Chapter 1. (Note the proposed change in the presentation of any provision for doubtful debts contained in ED 2011/6 *Revenue from Contracts with Customers*. It is proposed that the change in the provision be presented immediately after the revenue line in the income statement.)

12.3.1 Disclosures

Companies are required to provide information about which receivables may be impaired, in other words which are subject to consideration for a provision, plus details of the impairment provision. Many do this by giving information about overdue debts, as illustrated by Nestlé in its 2010 financial statements.

Financial reporting in practice 12.4

Note 6. Trade and other receivables

6.1 By type

In millions of CHF	2010	2009
Trade receivables	8,899	9,425
Other receivables	3,184	2,884
	12,083	12,309

The five major customers represent 9% (2009: 9%) of trade and other receivables, none of them exceeding 4% (2009: 4%).

6.2 Past due and impaired receivables

In millions of CHF	2010	2009
Not past due	10,522	10,554
Past due 1–30 day	742	916
Past due 31–60 days	273	341
Past due 61–90 days	121	130
Past due 91–120 days	107	134
Past due more than 120 days	727	685
Allowance for doubtful receivables	(409)	(451)
	12,083	12,309

6.3 Allowance for doubtful receivables

In millions of CHF	2010	2009
At 1 January	451	444
Currency retranslations	(52)	4
Allowance made during the year	94	139
Amounts used and reversal of unused amounts	(84)	(93)
Reclassified as held for sale	–	(43)
At 31 December	409	451

Based on the historic trend and expected performance of the customers, the Group believes that the above allowance for doubtful receivables sufficiently covers the risk of default.

12.4 Construction contracts

Construction companies engage in the building of 'products', such as buildings, roads, bridges, pipelines, tunnels, and other complex pieces of plant and machinery. The main difference between these products and inventories dealt with by IAS 2 is that their very nature means that the construction activity usually falls into different accounting periods, and the date at which the contract is entered into and the date when the activity is completed may be a number of years apart. The question arises as to whether the products produced as a result of a construction contract should be accounted for as inventory? In other words, should the ongoing costs be accounted for as work-in-progress and valued according to IAS 2, with any profit only being recognised once the completed product has been 'sold' or passed to the customer?

The result of this would be that construction companies would build up huge current assets as a contract progressed and then recognise (probably large) one-off profits once the contract was completed at intervals of potentially a number of years. This would lead to financial statements including large fluctuations in profits and asset balances from year-to-year, which would, therefore, be incomparable. This accounting treatment would also fail to be faithfully representative of the extent of the contract activity and performance of the company during an accounting period.

IAS 11 *Construction Contracts* therefore specifies how construction contracts should be accounted for. Its focus is from the perspective of the statement of comprehensive income, as it addresses the primary issue of the allocation of contract revenue and contract costs to the accounting periods in which the construction work is performed. Balances for the statement of financial position, representing amounts either due from or due to customers, are the result of these accounting methods. In this sense this accounting standard, which has remained largely unchanged for many years, is different from other accounting standards. These focus on the asset and liability figures, with resulting changes passing through the statement of comprehensive income. This is one of its criticisms and will be addressed when it is replaced by being subsumed into the new standard on Revenue Recognition, which is discussed in Chapter 7.

Note that IAS 11 also applies to contracts for the rendering of services which are directly related to the construction of the asset, for example the services of project managers or architects, and also contracts for the destruction or restoration of assets.

12.4.1 Terminology associated with a construction contract

Before the accounting for construction contracts is discussed, the terminology associated with the contract needs to be explained. The contractor will negotiate a contract with a customer to deliver the final product or groups of related products for a price. This selling price is often termed the contract price. The contract may be a fixed price contract or a cost plus contract. The latter category is where the contractor is reimbursed for costs plus either a percentage of these costs or a fixed fee.

In the case of a fixed price contract the final contract price may well be different from the initial price which would have been based on judgements and estimates made at the time of negotiation. The estimates will often need to be revised as the contract progresses and uncertainties are resolved, which may lead to cost escalations. Changes to the contract price agreed by the customer are termed variations.

A contractor may incur additional costs as a contract progresses, for example from delays in completing planned work, or from errors in specifications or design. The contractor will usually seek to recover these from the customer; these amounts are termed claims.

Over the course of a contract, the contractor will bill the customer on account—these are termed progress billings. The timing of and the amounts which are billed may be specified in the contract or be subject to external assessors, such as architects, who assess the stage of the completion of the construction and approve the amounts which can be billed. The progress billings are usually subject to retentions, which are amounts which the customer is not obliged to pay until certain conditions specified in the contract have been met. An example of this would be until defects in the construction have been rectified.

A customer may pay amounts to the contractor before certain work is performed—these amounts are called advances. A customer may also pay additional amounts to the contactor in excess of the contract price if specified performance targets are met or exceeded, for example for early completion of the contract. These amounts are termed incentive payments.

12.4.2 Contract revenues and costs

Given all the estimates and uncertainties surrounding construction contracts, a basic principle of accounting for contract revenue is that it should only be included if:

(i)   It is probable that the revenue will be recoverable from the customer

(ii) The amount of the revenue can be measured reliably.

Particular care must therefore be taken in the case of variations, claims, and incentive payments to ensure that these principles are adhered to.

Contract costs are either:

(a) Costs relating directly to the specific contract

(b) Costs that are attributable to general contract activity, but which do not directly relate to a specific contract

(c) Other costs specifically chargeable to the customer under the terms of the contract.

Costs relating directly to the contract may include:

- costs of materials consumed
- site labour, and site supervisors' wages and salaries
- depreciation for plant and equipment used in the contract
- lease rentals for hired plant and equipment
- costs incurred in the shifting of plant, equipment, and materials to and from the construction site
- costs of design and technical assistance
- costs of rectification work.

If income is realised, say from the sale of any surplus materials or plant and equipment, this is deducted from the contract costs rather than being included in revenue.

General contract activity costs that are not directly related to a specific contract should be allocated to the specific contract using a systematic and rational basis, and based on the normal level of construction activity. (Note this is the same principle as the allocation of production overheads to the cost of inventory—see section 12.2.4) Examples of such costs include:

- insurance
- design costs
- technical assistance
- other construction overheads.

Costs excluded specifically from any such allocation include:

- marketing and selling costs
- general and administrative costs for which the reimbursement is not specified in the contract
- research and development costs for which the reimbursement is not specified in the contract
- depreciation of plant and equipment lying idle (and not used in any particular contract).

 Example of cost allocation

A construction company incurs £500,000 in annual rental expense for the office space occupied by a group of engineers and architects, and their support staff. The company utilises this group to act as the quality assurance team that overlooks all contracts undertaken by the company. Annual costs of electricity, water, and maintenance of the office space occupied by this group are £200,000.

These costs cannot be attributed to a specific contract. However, they relate to the general contract activity of the company and should be allocated across all the company's contracts using a systematic and rational basis of allocation, for example:

- labour hours utilised in each contract
- contract revenue.

12.4.3 Accounting for construction contract revenues and costs

Where the outcome of a contract can be estimated reliably, contract revenue and contract costs can be recognised while the contract is in progress. The amounts should reflect the contact activity carried out during the accounting period and is achieved by reference to the stage of completion of the contract at the end of the accounting period. The method is also known as the **percentage of completion method** and is the same as how revenue is currently recognised from service contracts (see Chapter 7). Expected losses on a contract are recognised immediately in full.

The principles behind the recognition of revenue and expenses given in the International Accounting Standards Board's (IASB) *Conceptual Framework* are applied in determining whether 'the outcome of a contract can be estimated reliably'. For both fixed price and cost plus contracts the following must be satisfied:

(i)   It is probable economic benefits associated with the contract will flow to the company

(ii) Contract costs attributable to the contract can be identified clearly and measured reliably

For fixed price contracts the following additional requirements need to be met:

(iii) Total contract revenue can be measured reliably

(iv) Contract costs to complete the contract and the stage of completion of contract at the end of the accounting period can be measured reliably.

IAS 11 provides a little more guidance as to when it would be considered that reliable estimates can be made. A company would be required to demonstrate it had an effective internal financial budgeting and reporting system. The construction contract itself would have to be agreed by both parties and establish each party's enforceable rights, the contract price, and terms relating to payments.

However, as a principles-based accounting standard it is essentially left to the judgement of management to determine whether the outcome of a contract can be estimated reliably. In practice it is highly unlikely that a company with a contract in its very early stages would determine that its outcome could be estimated reliably, but there is no given percentage stage of completion above which this would be considered the case.

The stage of completion of a contract may be determined in a variety of ways, depending on the nature of the contract and the particular company. Companies should be consistent and apply the selected method to all their contracts. Suggested methods given in IAS 11 are:

(a)   The proportion of costs incurred for work performed in relation to total contract costs

(b)   Surveys of work performed

(c)   Completion of a physical proportion of work.

House-building companies may use a chart of stage of completion which indicates the physical stage of a house (e.g. foundations complete, first floor windows reached, roof on, etc.) and converts this to a standard stage of completion in percentage terms.

This percentage stage of completion is then applied to total revenue and total costs to give the cumulative revenues, and costs which can be recognised in profit and loss since the contract commenced. By this process revenue is being matched with the contract costs incurred in reaching the stage of completion. If estimates of revenues or costs change, the totals are revised for the period in which the change is made in accordance with IAS 8 *Accounting Policies, Changes in Accounting Estimates and Errors*.

Each separate accounting period's revenue and costs is calculated by deducting revenue and costs recognised in the previous accounting periods.

For example, if the stage of completion is determined by the proportion of costs incurred to date—method (a)—contract revenue recognised in a particular accounting period is calculated as follows:

$$\frac{\text{Costs to date}}{\text{Cumulative costs incurred} + \text{estimated costs to complete}} \times \text{Contract price} - \text{Revenue previously recognised}$$

In this case, certain costs should be excluded from costs incurred to date, for example contract costs that relate to future activity and payments made in advance to subcontractors prior to performance of the work by subcontractor.

Worked example 12.4: to show the recognition of contract revenue and costs

Bilbo Builders plc is involved in long-term construction contracts and has one contract which began in 20X8. The following figures for the years ended 31 December 20X8 and 20X9 are relevant:

	20X8 £	20X9 £
Total contract price	1,000,000	1,000,000
Costs incurred to 31 December	320,000	630,000
Estimated costs to completion	480,000	210,000
Progress billings	360,000	700,000
Value of work certified at 31 December *	390,000	730,000

Assume all progress billings have been paid by the customer.

* Value of work certified represents a valuer's assessment of the value of the contact completed by 31 December each year at selling prices.

Required:
For the financial years 20X8 and 20X9 calculate the amounts to be recognised as revenue and cost of sales.

20X8

Step 1

Check that the contract is not a loss-making contract.

	£000	£000
Contract price		1,000
Contract costs		
Incurred to date	320	
Estimated costs to completion	480	800
Estimated profit		200

Step 2

Calculate the percentage stage of completion at 31 December.

Assume that the company chooses to calculate the stage of completion on the proportion of costs incurred to date.

$$\text{Stage of completion} = \frac{320}{800} = 40\%$$

Step 3

Apply this percentage to total contract revenue and costs to calculate the cumulative revenue and costs that can be recognised to 31 December. As this is the first year of the contract these are the amounts to be recognised in 20X8's statement of comprehensive income.

		£000
Revenue	40% × £1,000,000	400
Cost of sales		320
Recognised profits less recognised losses		80

20X9

Step 1

Check that the contract remains a profit making contract.

	£000	£000
Contract price		1,000
Contract costs		
Incurred to date	630	
Estimated costs to completion	210	840
Estimated profit		160

Step 2

Calculate the percentage stage of completion at 31 December using the same method.

$$\text{Stage of completion} = \frac{630}{840} = 75\%$$

Step 3

Apply this percentage to total contract revenue and costs to calculate the cumulative revenue and costs that can be recognised to 31 December 20X9. Deduct the revenue and costs recognised previously in 20X8.

		£000
Revenue	(75% × £1,000,000) – £400,000	350
Cost of sales	£630,000 – £320,000	310
Recognised profits less recognised losses		40

Note: in total profit of £80,000 + £40,000 = £120,000 has been recognised. This makes sense as it represents 75% of the revised total contract profit (£120,000/£160,000 = 75%).

12.4.4 Loss-making contracts

IAS 11 requires that if it is probable that total contract costs will exceed total revenue, the expected loss is recognised as an expense immediately. This is consistent with the IASB's recognition principles for expenses. Losses represent decreases in economic benefits and are recognised in the income statement when they can be measured reliably.

 Worked example 12.5: to show the accounting for a loss-making contract

Based on the scenario used in Worked example 12.4, assume the contract figures for the years 20X8 and 20X9 are as follows:

	20X8	20X9
	£	£
Total contract price	1,000,000	1,000,000
Costs incurred to 31 December	320,000	630,000
Estimated costs to completion	780,000	510,000
Progress billings	360,000	700,000
Value of work certified at 31 December	390,000	730,000

Required:
For the financial years 20X8 and 20X9 calculate the amounts to be recognised as revenue and cost of sales.

20X8

Step 1

Check whether the contract is a loss-making contract.

	£000	£000
Contract price		1,000
Contract costs		
Incurred to date	320	
Estimated costs to completion	780	1,100
Estimated loss		(100)

This needs to be recognised in full in 20X8.

Step 2

Calculate the percentage stage of completion at 31 December.

$$\text{Stage of completion} = \frac{320}{1,100} = 29\%$$

Step 3

Apply this percentage to total contract revenue to calculate the cumulative revenue that can be recognised to 31 December.

A loss of £100,000 needs to be recognised, so the expenses recognised become the balancing figure to ensure this.

		£000
Revenue	29% × £1,000,000	290
Cost of sales	Balancing figure	390
Recognised profits less recognised losses		(100)

20X9

Step 1

Check the total contract profit or loss.

	£000	£000
Contract price		1,000
Contract costs		
Incurred to date	630	
Estimated costs to completion	510	1,140
Estimated loss		(140)

An additional contract loss of £40,000 needs to be recognised in 20X9 (£100,000 has been recognised in 20X8).

Step 2

Calculate the percentage stage of completion at 31 December.

$$\text{Stage of completion} = \frac{630}{1,140} = 55\%$$

Step 3

Apply this percentage to total contract revenue to calculate the cumulative revenue that can be recognised to 31 December and deduct the contract revenue recognised previously in 20X8.

As before, costs recognised become the balancing figure.

		£000
Revenue	(55% × £1,000,000) − £290,000	260
Cost of sales	Balancing figure	300
Recognised profits less recognised losses		(40)

12.4.5 Contracts whose outcomes cannot be estimated reliably

If the outcome of the contract cannot be estimated reliably, the accounting treatment is as follows:

(a) Contract costs are recognised as an expense in the period they are incurred

(b) Revenue is recognised only to the extent of contract costs incurred that it is probable will be recoverable.

Thus, either zero profit or a loss will be recognised for these contracts. This should be recognised, even if actual work has not yet commenced.

 Worked example 12.6: to show the accounting for a contact in early stages of completion

Based on the scenario used in Worked example 12.4, assume the contract figures for the years 20X8 and 20X9 are as follows:

	20X8	20X9
	£	£
Total contract price	1,000,000	1,000,000
Costs incurred to 31 December	80,000	630,000
Estimated costs to completion	720,000	210,000
Progress billings	70,000	700,000
Value of work certified at 31 December	100,000	730,000

Required:
For the financial years 20X8 and 20X9 calculate the amounts to be recognised as revenue and cost of sales.

20X8

Step 1

Check that the contract is not a loss-making contract.

	£000	£000
Contract price		1,000
Contract costs		
Incurred to date	80	
Estimated costs to completion	720	800
Estimated profit		200

Step 2

Calculate the percentage stage of completion at 31 December.

$$\text{Stage of completion} = \frac{80}{800} = 10\%$$

This is a contract clearly in the early stages of completion. Assume that the company determines it cannot estimate its outcome with sufficient certainty.

Step 3

Contract costs incurred are recognised with contract revenue restricted to this amount.

		£000
Revenue	Balancing figure	80
Cost of sales		80
Recognised profits less recognised losses		–

20X9

Step 1

Check that the contract remains a profit making contract.

	£000	£000
Contract price		1,000
Contract costs		
Incurred to date	630	
Estimated costs to completion	210	840
Estimated profit		160

Step 2

Calculate the percentage stage of completion at 31 December.

$$\text{Stage of completion} = \frac{630}{840} = 75\%$$

Step 3

Apply this percentage to total contract revenue and costs to calculate the cumulative revenue and costs that can be recognised to 31 December 20X9. Deduct the revenue and costs recognised previously in 20X8.

		£000
Revenue	(75% × £1,000,000) – £80,000	670
Cost of sales	£630,000 – £80,000	550
Recognised profits less recognised losses		120

12.4.6 Accounting for the remaining balances on the statement of financial position

The double-entry bookkeeping for contract costs as they are incurred is:

Debit   Contract cost account (a statement of financial position account)

    Credit   Accounts payable/bank

At the financial year end the revenue and costs to be recognised in the income statement are calculated as demonstrated in the previous section and accounted for as follows:

Debit   Contract cost account

    Credit   Contract revenue (I/S)

Debit   Contract costs (I/S)

    Credit   Contract cost account

The net result of these two entries to the contract cost account is that the contract recognised profit (or loss) is debited (credited for a loss).

As progress billings are made, the accounting for this is as follows:

Debit   Accounts receivable

    Credit   Contract cost account

and, as the customer pays, the normal accounting treatment is:

Debit   Bank

    Credit   Accounts receivable

After this accounting treatment, the balance remaining on the contract cost account is made up as follows:

	Contract costs incurred	X
Add/less:	Contract profits/losses recognised to date	X
Less:	Progress billings	(X)
		X

This balance may be positive (a debit balance) or negative (a credit balance). If positive it represents gross amounts due from customers and is included in the statement of financial position as a current asset. If the balance is negative, possibly because progress billings have exceeded the aggregate of costs incurred plus recognised profits or losses, it represents gross amounts due to customers and is included as a current liability.

Worked example 12.7: to show the statement of financial position balances

Using the figures from Worked example 12.4:

	20X8	20X9
	£	£
Total contract price	1,000,000	1,000,000
Costs incurred to 31 December	320,000	630,000
Estimated costs to completion	480,000	210,000
Progress billings	360,000	700,000
Value of work certified at 31 December	390,000	730,000

Assume all progress billings have been paid by the customer.

Required:
Calculate the amounts to be shown in the statements of financial position at 31 December 20X8 and 20X9.

From the solution to Worked example 12.4:

	20X8	20X9
Profit recognised	£80,000	£40,000

Statement of financial position balances (note these are calculated on a cumulative basis):

	20X8	20X9
	£000	£000
Contract costs incurred	320	630
Recognised profits less recognised losses	80	120
	400	750
Less: progress billings	360	700
Gross amounts due from customers (presented as a current asset)	40	50

Note that even if the contract were a loss-making contract or one where the outcome could not be estimated reliably and zero profit was recognised, the accounting for the statement of financial position balances would follow the same process.

12.4.7 Disclosures

The disclosures for construction contracts are not very onerous. To enable an assessment of the profitability of contracts entered into and a comparison of different construction companies' results, disclosure of their accounting policies for the recognition of contract revenue and how the stage of completion of contracts in progress is determined is required. In addition, companies should disclose:

(a) The amount of contract revenue recognised in the period

(b) For contracts in progress at the end of the period:

   (i) The aggregate of costs incurred and recognised profits (less losses) to date

   (ii) The amount of advances received

   (iii) The amount of retentions.

All contracts should be accounted for separately with profitable contracts not being netted off with loss-making profits.

Financial reporting in practice 12.5   Balfour Beatty plc, 2011

Balfour Beatty plc is a company which undertakes in long-term construction projects as one of its activities. Its 2011 Annual Report and Accounts include the following details.

Principle accounting policies continued

1.7 Construction and service contracts

When the outcome of individual contracts can be estimated reliably, contract revenue and contract costs are recognised as revenue and expenses respectively by reference to the stage of completion at the reporting date. The stage of completion is measured by the proportion of the value of work done to the total value of work under the contract. Full provision is made for all known or expected losses on individual contracts once such losses are foreseen. Revenue in respect of variations to contracts, claims and incentive payments is recognised when it is probable it will be agreed by the client. Profit for the year includes the benefit of claims settled on contracts completed in previous years.

1.8 Pre-contract bid costs and recoveries

Pre-contract costs are expensed as incurred until it is virtually certain that a contract will be awarded, from which time further pre-contract costs are recognised as an asset and charged as an expense over the period of the contract. Amounts recovered in respect of pre-contract costs that have been written-off are deferred and amortised over the life of the contract.

Note 19 Construction contracts

	2011 £m	2010 £m
Contracts in progress at reporting date:		
Due from customers for contract work *	604	591
Due to customers for contract work *	(576)	(651)
	28	(60)

The aggregate amount of costs incurred plus recognised profits; less recognised losses; for all contracts in progress that had not reached practical completion at the reporting date was £16,910m (2010: £18,839m).

*These amounts are disclosed separately in current assets and current liabilities respectively. There is no set-off permitted under IAS 11.

The company includes disclosure of the amount of contract revenue recognised in the period in its segmental analysis where construction services are a reportable segment.

12.4.8 Issues with IAS 11

The statement of financial position balances are one of the key criticisms of accounting for construction contracts under IAS 11. As can be seen from the worked examples, the resulting current asset balance balances bear little relation to any of the figures given in the scenario, and unless the accounting methods are followed through and understood, the balances have little meaning in themselves. The inclusion of profit in the balances seems counterintuitive to the historic cost principle.

Remember also that these balances incorporate judgements made by management about whether the outcome of a contract can be foreseen with any degree of certainty. Additionally, they include inaccuracies inherent in making estimates about future costs to be incurred or amounts which may be recoverable from customers on contracts which may take years to complete.

IAS 11's approach to the recognition of profit as a contract progresses can also be said to contribute to income smoothing. While this may be preferable for investors rather than widely fluctuating profits, it is questionable in relation to the underpinning principles of relevance and faithful representation. Consistency in a company's approach to the accounting for all of its contracts is therefore very important so that the company cannot be accused of manipulating its forecasts and estimates to achieve 'expected' or 'required' profits.

12.4.9 Changes to come

As discussed in Chapter 7, IAS 11 is due to be replaced with a new standard on revenue recognition.

Reminder *A five-step approach will be applied to all contracts with customers:*

1   *Identify the contract with the customer*

2   *Identify the separate performance obligations in the contract*

3   *Determine the transaction price*

4   *Allocate the transaction price to the separate performance obligations*

5   *Recognise revenue when a performance obligation is satisfied.*

While a contract may have to be divided into separate performance obligations, many contracts will be treated as a single performance obligation. The exposure draft (ED) proposes basing revenue recognition on the transfer of control to the customer, with revenue from construction contracts probably being recognised over time. If this is the case, the output or input methods suggested for measuring the progress towards a performance obligation are similar to the current methods recommended by IAS 11 for estimating the stage of completion of a contract. In addition, the proposals relating to loss-making contracts or contracts in early stages of completion are very similar to IAS 11. In practice it is likely that the ED's proposals will produce similar results to the current IAS 11 approach to accounting for construction contracts.

Summary of key points

An assessment of the liquidity of a company requires consistent information relating to the current assets that a company holds. Inventories vary so much in nature between companies that this is particularly important. There are accounting standards for the measurement of inventories (IAS 2 *Inventories*) and how to account for construction contracts (IAS 11 *Construction Contracts*) to help ensure this, and accounting for receivables—a financial asset—is incorporated in accounting standards for financial instruments.

The key principle underpinning inventories is that they should be valued at the lower of cost and NRV. Cost for manufacturers includes costs of converting the materials purchased into the final products and uses management accounting techniques to allocate manufacturing overheads to the products. NRV is the expected selling price less costs to complete the product and costs to be incurred in selling the goods. Inventory valuation is based on the FIFO or standard cost approach, with most other bases of valuation not permitted, unless they approximate to FIFO. Lower of cost and NRV is consistent with the principle that the carrying amount of assets should not be in excess of amounts expected to be realised from their sale or use.

Construction contracts, by their nature, take a number of years to complete, and so the main issue dealt with by IAS 11 is the recognition of contract revenue and costs over these periods. This approach to the accounting treatment takes an income statement approach and is based on the principle of matching to reflect the activity undertaken by a company. It also leads to income smoothing, and resulting statement of financial position balances that may require some explanation and understanding.

For contracts whose outcome can be estimated reliably the revenue and costs are recognised on the basis of their stage of completion, with this determined by methods such as the proportion of costs incurred in relation to total estimated costs or the proportion of revenue earned in relation to total revenue. For any contract where the estimated overall outcome is a loss, this loss must be recognised in full immediately. Contracts where the outcome cannot be estimated reliably, such as contracts in very early stages of completion, revenues are restricted to the costs incurred, which will be recoverable from the customer.

Accounting for construction contracts is similar to the current accounting treatment of long-term service contracts, currently addressed by IAS 18 *Revenue*. Deliberations are currently being held by the IASB to replace this standard. The new standard will incorporate the accounting for all long-term contracts, and so IAS 11 will ultimately disappear as a standard in its own right. However, the accounting methods for long-term contracts under the proposed ED are likely to be fairly similar to those in the current standard.

 ## Further reading

IASB (International Accounting Standards Board) (2003) IAS 2 *Inventories*. London: IASB.

IASB (International Accounting Standards Board) (2004) IAS 11 *Construction Contracts*. London: IASB.

Bibliography

Balfour Beatty (2011) *Annual Report and Accounts, 2010*. London: Balfour Beatty.

GKN plc (2011) *Annual Report and Accounts, 2010*. Redditch: GKN.

IASB (International Accounting Standards Board) (2003) IAS 2 *Inventories*. London: IASB.

IASB (International Accounting Standards Board) (2004) IAS 11 *Construction Contracts*. London: IASB.

IASB (International Accounting Standards Board) (2010) *Conceptual Framework for Financial Reporting 2010*. London: IASB.

IASB (International Accounting Standards Board) (2011a) Exposure draft ED/2011/6 *Revenue from Contracts with Customers*. London: IASB.

IASB (International Accounting Standards Board) (2011b) Exposure draft ED/2011/6 *Revenue from Contracts with Customers*, Illustrative examples. London: IASB.

IASB (International Accounting Standards Board) (2011c) Exposure draft ED/2011/6 *Revenue from Contracts with Customers*, Basis for conclusions. London: IASB.

IASB (International Accounting Standards Board) (2011d) Revised exposure draft snapshot: *Revenue from Contracts with Customers*. London: IASB.

ICAEW (Institute of Chartered Accountants in England and Wales) (2012) *Revenue from Contracts with Customers FAQ*. London: ICAEW.

Nestlé (2011) *Financial Statements, 2010*. Vevey: Nestlé.

Rolls-Royce Group plc (2011) *Annual Report, 2010*. London: Rolls-Royce.

 Questions

Quick test

1   Indicate which of the following costs would be included in the cost of inventory according to IAS 2 *Inventories*:

- discounts on purchase price
- interest charge for late payment
- import duties
- recoverable value added tax (VAT)
- irrecoverable tax
- quality certificates
- insurance during transit from supplier
- depreciation of factory
- costs of leasing machinery
- cost of factory canteen
- research on new products
- costs of extra scrap/waste
- sales department salaries

- purchase department salaries
- maintenance of factory
- rebuilding of factory
- audit fees
- costs of using patent.

2 Tomac Enterprises commenced the manufacture of lockable petrol caps on 1 July 20X5. By 31 December 20X5, when the half-yearly financial reports were prepared, 2,000 complete petrol caps and 200 half-finished (as regards materials, labour, and factory overheads) petrol caps were produced. No orders from customers had yet been taken. Costs in the six-month period were as follows:

	£
Materials consumed	1,650
Labour	2,160
Production overheads	390
Administrative overheads	270
	4,470

At 31 December 20X5 it was estimated that the sale value of each completed petrol cap was £2.75.

At this date, the firm also held stocks of raw materials as follows:

	Cost £	Net realisable value £
Material X	1,200	1,370
Material Y	300	240
Material Z	530	680

Required:

Acceptable valuations at 31 December 20X5 for financial reporting purposes for:

(i) materials to be consumed

(ii) assets in the process of production

(iii) assets held for sale.

3 Byson Ltd is an established company operating in the highly competitive business of manufacturing domestic appliances. Its best-selling product is a vacuum cleaner, the 'Byson Dust Buster 400'.

A standard dust buster has the following costs:

	£
Direct labour and materials	58
Bought-in components	25
Factory overhead costs	18
Royalty on sale payable to owner of a patent	12

For 1,000 dust busters the other overhead costs are £14,000 made up as follows:

	£
Salary and office costs of production director	4,000
General office administration	2,500
Selling and distribution costs	7,500

The selling and distribution costs include a fixed commission of £4 per vacuum cleaner payable to the salesmen.

The advertised selling price of this model has recently been reduced to £119 due to increased competition.

Required:

(a) Calculate the unit value of closing inventory for the Byson Dust Buster 400 on the basis of IAS 2 *Inventories*. State any assumptions you have made.

(b) IAS 2 *Inventories* states that the cost of inventory includes production overheads and other overheads. Explain the principle on which the inclusion of these costs is based and how these costs should be allocated to units of inventory.

4   On 1 July 20X6 Pentose Construction plc entered into a contract to construct a bridge over a river. The agreed price of the bridge is £5 million and construction is expected to be completed on 30 June 20X8. Pentose incurred the following costs in relation to this contract by 31 December 20X6:

	£000
Materials , labour, and overheads	1,200
Specialist plant acquired 1 July 20X6	800

The value of the work certified at 31 December 20X6 has been agreed at £2.2 million and the estimated cost to complete (excluding plant depreciation) is £1 million. The specialist plant will have no residual value at the end of the contract and should be depreciated on a monthly basis. Progress billings by 31 December 20X6 total £570,000. Pentose recognises profits on uncompleted contracts on the basis of value of work completed.

Required:

Discuss the accounting treatment of this contract in accordance with IAS 11 *Construction Contracts*, and show the resulting figures which would appear in the income statement for the financial year ended 31 December 20X6 and statement of financial position at this date.

●● Develop your understanding

5   Tintagel plc produces one product, sharp stones, which it manufactures from rocks bought from a company in Wales. Two tonnes of stones are produced from three tonnes of rocks. During the year Tintagel plc purchased rocks in loads of 4,000 tonnes, the purchase price being fixed at £210 per tonne, with delivery and handling charges per load of £10,000.

Direct production costs throughout the year were £40 per tonne of sharp stones produced. Production capacity exists to process 5,000 tonnes of the stones per week; fixed production costs were £45,000 per week. General management costs for the year were £2,500,000.

The sharp stones sell for £449 per tonne. Loading costs are £15 per tonne and delivery is subcontracted at an annual cost of £210,000. During the year Tintagel plc sold 70,000 tonnes of sharp stones.

At the year end Tintagel plc had the following inventories:

Rocks	12,000 tonnes
Sharp stones	2,000 tonnes

There were no inventories in the process of production.

Required:

Calculate the value of inventories at the year end in accordance with IAS 2.

6   A construction contractor has a fixed price contract for £9,000,000 to build a bridge. The initial amount of revenue agreed in the contract is £9,000,000. The contractor's initial estimate of contract costs is £8,000,000. It will take three years to build the bridge.

By the end of year 1, the contractor's estimate of contract costs has increased to £8,050,000.

In year 2, the customer approves a variation resulting in an increase in contract revenue of £200,000 and estimated additional contract costs of £150,000. At the end of year 2, costs incurred include £100,000 for standard materials stored at the site to be used in year 3 to complete the project.

The contractor determines the stage of completion of the contract by calculating the proportion that contract costs incurred for work performed to date bear to the latest estimated total contract costs. A summary of the financial data during the construction period is as follows:

	Year 1	Year 2	Year 3
	£000	£000	£000
Initial amount of revenue agreed in contract	9,000	9,000	9,000
Variation in revenue	–	200	200
Total contract revenue	9,000	9,200	9,200
Contract costs incurred to date	2,093	6,168	8,200
Estimated costs to complete	5,957	2,032	–
Total estimated costs	8,050	8,200	8,200
Advances from customer	100	–	–
Progress billings to date	2,160	6,400	9,200

Required:

For this contract, calculate the amount of profit (or loss) which would be shown for each year and show how the contract would appear on the statements of financial position.

7   One of Fladbury Construction plc's ongoing major contracts is the construction of a dual carriageway and tunnel through the Malvern Hills. Construction started in late summer 20X3, and is still ongoing. Details of this contract at the company's year ends of 31 December 20X3, 20X4, and 20X5 are as follows:

	20X3	20X4	20X5
	£m	£m	£m
Total contract price	250	260	275
Work certified to 31 December	10	105	230
Costs incurred to 31 December	16	140	255
Estimated costs to completion	174	62	30
Progress billings	5	90	200

During 20X4 the main drilling machine had to undergo major overhaul and repair owing to the nature of the rock encountered. A variation in contract price was agreed. Similar problems continued in the first half of 20X5 and a further variation in contract price was agreed with the customer. Negotiations to increase the contract price further had broken down by the end of December 20X5.

Required:

Calculate the amounts to be included in the income statements and statements of financial position of Fladbury Construction plc for the years ended 31 December 20X3, 20X4, and 20X5 in relation to this contract.

8 (a) Explain the concepts that underpin the requirements of IAS 11 *Construction Contracts*.

(b) Wickhams plc specialises in bridge construction and has two contracts in progress at its year end, 31 March 20X8. Contract details extracted from the company's costing records at 31 March 2008 were as follows:

	Stour Bridge	Avon Bridge
	£000	£000
Total contract selling price	7,000	4,000
Work certified to date	4,200	450
Costs to date	3,500	1,200
Estimated costs to completion	1,500	3,150
Progress billings	5,000	250

Construction on the Stour Bridge started in April 20X6. Work certified to date at 31 March 20X7 was £2,800,000 and the appropriate amount of profit was recognised for the year ended 31 March 20X7. No changes to the total estimated contract selling price or costs occurred between the start of the construction and 31 March 20X8.

However, on 11 April 20X8, the customer's surveyor notified Wickhams plc of a fault in one of the bridge supports constructed during a severe frost in January 20X8. This will require remedial work in May 20X8 at an estimated additional cost of £400,000.

Construction on the Avon Bridge started in June 20X7.

Wickhams plc estimates the stage of completion of its contracts on the basis of the value of work certified at each year end.

Required:

For both contracts calculate the amounts to be included in the income statement and statement of financial position of Wickhams plc for the year ended 31 March 20X8.

●●● Take it further

9   Harness Technology plc designs, constructs, and installs wind turbine systems. The company compiles its accounts on the basis of relevant international standards and its financial year end is 31 December. You are being asked to compile the inventory information and relevant contract revenue, expenditure, and profit information for the statement of financial position and income statement based on the following information.

(i)   The company produces two types of engine cooling system, the ZX100 and the ZX150, which are generally sold to customers who experience system problems and need replacement parts. The ZX100 is a now outdated, but still usable, model, which has been superseded by the ZX150 model. The inventory count at 31 December 20X8 confirmed that there were 300 turbine blades (spare parts) in stock and 100 engine cooling systems in stock (20 ZX100s and 80 ZX150s). It is estimated that owing to the ZX100 being technically superseded by the ZX150, the 20 ZX100s are likely to sell for 60% of their usual selling price.

Twelve blades which were not included in the inventory count are in transit under an arrangement where the buyer pays transportation costs and legal ownership has already passed to the customer. It is anticipated that 50 of the blades will need very minor repairs costing £150 (per blade) to make them usable (due to damage through poor storage). The rest of this inventory is in good condition and likely to be sold at existing market prices in the future.

Standard information is provided in Table 12.2 to assist you in determining the total value for the inventory which should be included in the statement of financial position and income statement.

(ii)   Harness Technology plc has recently begun work on a large wind turbine system, the MidGreen project, in the Midlands. The company is contracted to design, build, and install the system. Work began in September 20X8 and is expected to be completed by January 20Y0. The agreed price of the contract was £55 million and the original estimated cost of the project was £38 million.

Table 12.2 Figures for Question 9 (i)

	Blades (per unit)	ZX100 (per unit)	ZX150 (per unit)
Direct labour and materials	£350	£125	£125
Bought-in components*	£175	£250	£300
Factory overhead	£200	£110	£110
Head office general administrative overhead	£45	£40	£40
Selling price	£1,000	£600	£750

* Each unit cost (blade, ZX100 and ZX150) includes £10 per unit transport cost incurred in transporting the components to Harness Technology's factory.

By November 20X8 the company had to revise its estimate of the total direct costs and now estimates this as £38.5 million. In addition, research costs not specified in the contract are £400,000 as at the 20X8 year end. At the end of December 20X8 materials costing £500,000 have been paid for and are in stock ready for use in 20X9. The client pays £5 million every quarter after the contract has reached the 20% completion stage (the point at which revenue may begin to be recognised) and has paid the first instalment on 15 Dec 20X8. Actual contract costs incurred to date are £10 million.

The company determines the stage of completion of the contract by calculating the proportion that contract costs incurred for work performed to date bear to the estimated total contract costs.

Required:

Based on all the information given:

(a) Calculate the total figure for inventory on the 20X8 statement of financial position for Harness Technology plc

(b) Show the amounts that would be included as revenues and costs in the income statement for the year ended 31 December 20X8 in respect of the MidGreen Project

(c) Explain the basic principles involved in the valuation of inventory and contracts for the financial statements. Include in your explanation:

(i) The basic principles underlying IAS 2 *Inventories*

(ii) The basic principles underlying IAS 11 *Construction Contracts*.

Visit the Online Resource Centre for solutions to all these end of chapter questions plus visual walkthrough solutions. You can test your understanding with extra questions and answers, explore additional case studies based on real companies, take a guided tour through a company report, and much more. Go to the Online Resource Centre at
www.oxfordtextbooks.co.uk/orc/maynard/

13

Liabilities

➤ **Introduction**

Liabilities encompass many items. These range from normal trade payables for goods that have been delivered and not yet paid for, to accruals for overhead expenses incurred not yet billed, to liabilities under leasing arrangements and pension schemes, and debt instruments. The accounting for some of these liabilities is set out in various accounting standards, some of which are included in this textbook, but some of which are outside its scope. Accounting for current and deferred taxation, and the resulting tax liabilities is discussed in Chapter 9; liabilities arising from construction contracts are discussed in Chapter 12; and liabilities under leasing arrangements are discussed in Chapter 14.

This chapter deals mainly with provisions and contingent liabilities. These arise when there is uncertainty as to the amount or the timing of the settlement of the liabilities. These uncertainties, together with the fact that the settlement is in the future, result in the accounting for these liabilities requiring estimates and much judgement. To ensure there is some consistency of treatment, International Accounting Standard (IAS) 37 *Provisions, Contingent Liabilities and Contingent Assets* specifies when a provision should be recognised, gives guidance as to its measurement, and addresses what should happen in increasing cases of uncertainty.

Confirmation of the existence and measurement of liabilities, and, in some cases, the measurement of assets and other transactions, may occur after the end of the financial year. A question arises as to what extent a company should change its financial statements as a result of what happens after the statement of financial position date. IAS 10 *Events after the Reporting Period* addresses this and its requirements are discussed at the end of this chapter.

★ Learning objectives

After studying this chapter you will be able to:

● understand the key problems in accounting for liabilities and how these are addressed by accounting standards

● understand the relationship between liabilities, provisions, and contingent liabilities, and explain their accounting treatment

● explain the accounting treatment of contingent assets

● understand the impact on the financial statements of events that happen after the financial year end.

✔ Key issues checklist

❑ Definition of a liability.

❑ Issues with the definition—reliance on estimates and judgement.

❑ Impact of accounting for liabilities improperly.

❑ Criteria for the recognition of a provision.

❑ Methods for the measurement of a provision.

❑ Accounting for operating losses, restructuring, and onerous contracts.

❑ Contingent liabilities and their relationship to provisions.

❑ Contingent assets and their accounting treatment.

❑ Disclosures required for provisions, contingent liabilities, and contingent assets.

❑ Potential changes to the accounting for provisions and contingent liabilities.

❑ The critical period after the end of the financial year before the financial statements are authorised for issue.

❑ Adjusting and non-adjusting events, and their treatment in the financial statements.

❑ The going concern assumption.

13.1 Accounting for liabilities

13.1.1 Key issues in accounting for liabilities

The International Accounting Standards Board's (IASB) definition of a liability as given in its *Conceptual Framework* is:

> A liability is a present obligation of the entity arising from past events, the settlement of which is expected to result in an outflow from the entity of resources embodying economic benefits.
>
> *(IASB, 2010: para. 4.4(b))*

The definition of a liability mirrors the *Framework*'s definition of an asset.

🛈 **Reminder** *The definition of an asset is a resource controlled by the entity as a result of past events and from which future economic benefits are expected to flow to the entity.*

One of the key issues in accounting for liabilities is that the outflow of resources is going to happen in the future, after the date of the statement of financial position. By the time the financial statements have been published the outflow may not yet have occurred. For liabilities such as trade payables this may not present a problem for recognition and measurement; however, this may be less clear-cut for other transactions and situations, and gives rise to a number of questions:

- What exactly is meant by a present obligation?
- How definite does the expectation of the outflow of resources have to be?
- What is meant by resources embodying economic benefits?

Even if these recognition questions are resolved, there may be uncertainty surrounding how much will be paid to settle the liability and therefore how the outflow of resources is valued.

Companies have, in the past, accounted for liabilities on the grounds of prudence, which used to be considered one of the fundamental underpinning principles of financial reporting. Management of companies have taken this further and used the uncertainties of accounting for the future and liabilities to manipulate profits. This is commonly referred to as 'big bath' accounting.

Example of 'big bath' accounting

In October 20X6, following years of declining profits, a company undergoes a management buy-out (MBO), which is funded by venture capitalists. A period of restructuring is commenced by the new management team, who consider a prudent estimate for restructuring costs to be £2 million. The draft financial statements at 31 December 20X6 show a large loss.

An argument for accounting for this situation on the basis of prudence, which was not unknown in the past, follows:

1 20X6 is a 'bad year' already

2 So it does not matter so much if 20X6's results are made *even worse* by including large (prudent) **provisions** for restructuring costs which will be incurred in 20X7:

   Dr   Restructuring expenses   £2 million

     Cr   Provisions (Liability)   £2 million

3 In 20X7, as these costs are actually incurred, they are charged against the provision (assume these amount to £1.5 million):

   Dr   Provisions   £1.5 million

     Cr   Bank   £1.5 million

4 This leaves a large credit balance on the provisions account, which is no longer required at 31 December 20X7

5 This will be written back to profit and loss in 20X7:

Dr   Provisions   £0.5 million

 Cr   Profit   £0.5 million

The result of this is that the 20X7 financial statements are much improved by this credit to profit, which will please the venture capital firm and demonstrate that the new management team are performing well!

The above accounting is clearly not acceptable if financial statements are to faithfully represent the financial performance and position of a company. To counter this type of abuse of accounting for liabilities, the IASB has clarified some of the terms included in its definition of a liability.

13.1.2 Terms used in the definition of a liability

Present obligation

One key characteristic of a liability is that there is a present obligation that arises from a past event. An obligation is a duty or responsibility to act or perform in a certain way. This may be a legal obligation which is enforceable as a result of an enforceable contract or statutory requirement, for example the purchase of goods or the receipt of a service. However, obligations can also be constructive, where usual business custom and practice creates an expectation that a business has accepted certain responsibilities. An example of this could be if a business usually carries out repair work on products it has supplied even after the expiry of the warranty period.

Past event

The past event means that a transaction which has triggered the obligation must have occurred before the date of the statement of financial position. For example, goods must have been received, or a bank loan which will be repaid at some future date must have been received. This past event is termed the obligating event. A future commitment does not give rise to a liability.

 Example of a past event versus future commitment

A company's directors decide to acquire a property in the future, which is recorded in board minutes. However, this does not give rise to a present obligation. This is a future commitment only and a contract would need to have been signed for a past event to have occurred.

Outflow of resources

The settlement of a liability does not have to be in the form of a cash payment. The outflow of resources embodying economic benefits could refer to:

- the transfer of assets, through an exchange
- the provision of services, e.g. repairs under a warranty
- the replacement of one liability with another, e.g. the rolling over of a loan
- the conversion of a liability to equity, such as convertible debt instruments.

However, the very nature of a liability often leads to uncertainty surrounding the timing and amount of the outflow, and therefore the measurement (or value) of the liability. The settlement is going to be in the future, and may not have occurred by the time the statement of financial position is drawn up and made available for users. Some liabilities may not be settled for many years and require increased estimation, for example the liabilities for the clean-up of land contaminated by drilling for oil may be settled 20 or 30 years after the drilling commences.

Liabilities where there is uncertainty surrounding timing and amount of the settlement are known as provisions. Note that the term provision is sometimes used in connection with depreciation, impairment, and doubtful debts to indicate the amount deducted from the value of the related asset. However, the term provision is to be used in this chapter in connection with the particular type of liability detailed. IAS 37 *Provisions, Contingent Liabilities and Contingent Assets* was issued by the IASB to deal with the issues surrounding the recognition and measurement of provisions.

13.2 Provisions

13.2.1 Recognition of a provision

As a subset of liabilities, the criteria for the recognition of a provision in the financial statements satisfy the basic definition of a liability. There are three criteria, all of which must be met, otherwise a provision cannot be included in the statement of financial position.

1   The company has a present obligation as a result of a past event.

2   It is probable that an outflow of resources embodying economic events will be required to settle the obligation.

3   A reliable estimate can be made of the amount of the obligation.

What is meant by a present obligation and obligating event has already been discussed. A couple of further examples to illustrate this discussion follow.

 Examples of whether obligating events exist

1   A company in the oil industry causes contamination, but cleans up only when required to do so under the laws of the particular country in which it operates. One country in which it operates has

had no legislation requiring cleaning up and the entity has been contaminating land in that country for several years. At 31 December 20X0 it is virtually certain that a draft law requiring a clean-up of land already contaminated will be enacted shortly after the year end.

The obligating event is the contamination of the land.

2 Under new legislation, a company is required to fit smoke filters to its factories by 30 June 20X1. At 31 December 20X0 the company has not fitted the smoke filters.

There is no obligation because there is no obligating event either for the costs of fitting smoke filters or for fines under the legislation. The company could avoid this future expenditure by its future actions, for example by changing its method of operation.

The second criterion for the recognition of a provision is that the outflow of resources must be probable, in other words more likely than not to occur. In probability terms this means that the probability should be greater than 50%. This clearly introduces subjectivity into the question of recognition, as there are no clear-cut guidelines as to the likelihood of an outflow occurring. The meaning of an outflow of resources embodying economic resources was discussed earlier.

The final criterion is that a reliable estimate of the value of the outflow of resources can be made. In most cases this should be possible, as IAS 37 specifies that this amount should be the best estimate at the statement of financial position date. As for the second criterion the uncertainties surrounding this estimate introduce subjectivity which requires management judgement. Experience of similar events and transactions, or independent expert advice, such as legal advice, may have to be called for. Evidence from events that occur after the financial reporting date may also be used. (Note: events after the reporting period are discussed further in section 13.5.)

13.2.2 Measurement of a provision

The best estimate is explained by IAS 37 as the amount a business would rationally pay to settle the obligation. This implies it would take a sensible course of action after considering all factors. However, uncertainties should be taken into consideration. Table 13.1 provides explanations and examples of what is meant by the best estimate for different types of obligation.

The risks and uncertainties surrounding many provisions should be taken into account when determining the best estimate. Risk affects the estimates of the amount(s) of the possible outcome(s). When judgements are made companies should ensure that provisions are not understated. However, IAS 37 is quite clear in stating that risk should not be overstated and uncertainties should not justify excessive provisions.

In estimating future costs, companies should take into account the effect of future changes in technology or new legislation provided there is sufficient objective evidence that these will alter the costs.

Table 13.1 The best estimate for different types of obligation

Obligation	Best estimate	Example
(a) A single obligation	The individual most likely outcome	A company has to carry out repair work in plant it has supplied which it estimates at £1,000. This may be the most likely outcome, but the company should consider additional possible outflows if these initial repairs do not solve the problem. The company may decide to increase the amount of the provision.
(b) A large population of possible obligations	All obligations are weighted by their associated probabilities and an expected value is calculated	A company sells goods with a warranty under which customers are covered for the cost of repairs detected within a year of purchase. Different amounts of repair costs should be weighted by their respective probabilities of occurrence. The provision is the sum of these weighted outcomes.
(c) A continuous range of possible obligations	The mid-point of the range	A company is being sued for damages due to defective products and have been found liable. Lawyers advise the damages may range from £200,000 to £400,000. The company may determine the provision at £300,000.

13.2.3 Use of present value

The settlement of some provisions may not arise for a number of years, for example the clean-up of contaminated land by an oil company. IAS 37 specifies that if the time value of money is material, the amount of the provision should be the present value of the expenditures required to settle the obligation. In other words, a discounted cash flow basis is used for measurement purposes. This introduces yet more subjectivity into the measurement of the provision. Firstly, the question of what is meant by material requires judgement by management.

 Reminder *Material information is defined in the Conceptual Framework as that whose omission or misstatement could influence decisions taken by a user. This is discussed further in Chapter 1. Materiality will be different for different users.*

The second question raised by the discounting requirement is what discount rate should be used to carry out the calculation. IAS 37 specifies that this should be:

> ...a pre-tax rate (or rates) that reflect(s) current market assessments of the time value of money and the risks specific to the liability.

(IASB, 2005: para. 47)

So that the effect of risk is not double-counted, the rate should not reflect risks for which future cash flow estimates have been already been adjusted.

 Worked example 13.1: to show a provision involving discounted cash flow

At 31 December 20X0 Cleaner Energy plc, a company involved in nuclear activities, estimates that it will incur decommissioning costs of £900 million in 60 years' time. The pre-tax discount rate for this liability has been estimated at 2%.

Required:

(a) Calculate and show the accounting for the provision for decommissioning costs at 31 December 20X0.

(b) Show the effect of small changes in the estimates used in estimating the provision.

(c) Assuming no changes in estimates, show the accounting for the provision for decommissioning costs at 31 December 20X1.

(a) The provision for decommissioning should be recorded at

$$£900\,\text{million} \times \frac{1}{(1.02)^{60}} = £274.3\,\text{million}$$

		£	£
Debit	Decommissioning expenses	274.3 million	
Credit	Provision		274.3 million

(b) Note that only small changes in the discount rate or the estimate of the year of decommissioning lead to significant changes in the provision.

(i) If the discount rate used is 2.5%, the provision would be

$$£900\,\text{million} \times \frac{1}{(1.025)^{60}} = £204.6\,\text{million}$$

(ii) If the activities extend for a further 5 years, the provision would be

$$£900\,\text{million} \times \frac{1}{(1.02)^{65}} = £248.4\,\text{million}$$

(c) Each year the provision is recalculated and, as the provision is nearer in time, it will increase. Assuming no changes in the initial estimates, this unwinding of the discount rate is accounted for as a finance charge in the statement of comprehensive income.

Assuming original estimates, at 31 December 20X1 the provision would be

$$£900\,\text{million} \times \frac{1}{(1.02)^{59}} = £279.8\,\text{million}$$

		£	£
Debit	Finance costs (279.8 – 274.3)	5.5 million	
Credit	Provision		5.5 million

[This can also be calculated as 2% × £274.3 million = £5.5 million]

13.2.4 Particular circumstances included in IAS 37

IAS 37 addresses a number of particular circumstances which may be considered to give rise to provisions and which have been misused by companies in past years (see Example of 'big bath' accounting in section 13.1.1). The first of these is future operating losses. The standard is very clear that no provision should be recognised for these. Essentially, these are estimates of the future, not arising as a result of past events, and so they are not liabilities. Forecast operating losses may indicate that certain operating assets are impaired and so companies should be aware of this when considering impairment testing. (See Chapter 10 for a discussion of impairment.)

The second issue that is specifically discussed by IAS 37 concerns costs of restructuring. Restructuring is a general term which could encompass all sorts of activities, including redundancies, relocations, reorganisations, and other disruption to normal business activities. IAS 37 defines restructuring as a programme that is planned and controlled by management, and which materially changes either:

(a) The scope of business undertaken by the company

(b) The manner in which the business is conducted.

This could include the sale or termination of part of the business, and closure of business locations, relocations of business activities from one region or country to another, and changes in management structures, such as the elimination of a layer of management.

In order to recognise a provision for restructuring costs, the three criteria for the recognition of a provision must be fulfilled. This requires a company to have a constructive obligation to restructure, which, in turn, would require some formal evidence, such as a detailed plan for the restructuring. Such a plan would include details of which part of the business was to be restructured, anticipated, and realistic dates for the various stages, and estimates of the nature and amount of expenditure. A constructive obligation also requires there to be a valid expectation in those affected that the restructuring will be carried out, so the plan must have been communicated to the relevant employees. A board decision to carry out the restructuring programme is insufficient in itself to give rise to a provision. However, the restructuring activities need not have actually started.

IAS 37 gives guidance as to the costs that may be included in determining the provision for restructuring. These must be necessary costs arising directly from the restructuring and not costs associated with the ongoing activities of the company.

Examples of costs which could be included in the provision are:

- termination of leases
- disposal of surplus inventories
- remuneration of employees engaged in the restructuring activities
- redundancy costs.

Costs specifically excluded are:

- retraining or relocating continuing staff
- marketing
- investment in new systems and distribution networks
- future operating losses.

The third item addressed specifically by IAS 37 is the requirement for a provision to be recognised for the obligations under an onerous contract. Many contracts into which businesses enter are for specific lengths of time, and establish rights and obligations for each of the parties involved. Some contracts can be cancelled without compensation being required by any party. An onerous contract is one in which this is not possible and where the resulting unavoidable costs of meeting the terms of the contract exceed any benefits expected to be received under it. In this case a provision is recognised and is measured at the least net cost of exiting from the contract. What this means is that it is assumed a business would take a rational approach to either:

(i)   fulfilling the terms of the contract

(ii) not fulfilling the terms and incurring fines or penalties

and would choose the option which had the lower cost.

 Example of an onerous contract

A company operates profitably from a factory that it has leased under an operating lease. During December 20X0 the company relocates its operations to a new factory. The lease on the old factory continues for the next four years. It cannot be cancelled and the factory cannot be re-let to another user.

Consider the criteria for the recognition of a provision.

1   There is a legal obligation on the company to make the lease payments arising from the obligating event which is the signing of the lease contract.

2   When the lease becomes onerous in December 20X0, an outflow of resources embodying economic benefits is probable.

3   The amount of the provision can be estimated as the lower of:

   (a) the best estimate of the unavoidable lease payments

   (b) the penalties to be incurred if the company 'walks away' from the contract.

13.2.5 Disclosures

To assist users' understanding of the amounts included in the financial statements as provisions, companies are required to explain the nature of the provisions recognised and the expected timing of the outflows, together with an indication of the uncertainties surrounding these. This may include details of assumptions which have been made about the future.

Companies will naturally wish to exercise caution about these disclosures. For example, if a company is required to include a provision for damages because it anticipates losing an ongoing court case, it will clearly wish to minimise the amount of the provision, and be very careful about the language used in the provisions note so that admission of liability is not necessarily apparent. In practice, companies will use, and auditors will rely on, legal professionals to assist in the drafting of such information. IAS 37 permits companies not to disclose information if it is considered that it could seriously prejudice the position of the company in a dispute with other parties. However, in this case the company would still be required to disclose the general nature of the dispute together with the fact that, and the reason why, full details have not been disclosed.

Companies often list provisions as one of the areas where significant estimates have been made and judgement exercised.

Financial reporting in practice 13.1   BP plc, 2010

Oil companies, such as BP, will normally have significant provisions relating to the decommissioning of their production facilities and pipelines, and future environmental clean-up costs. BP plc's 2010 Annual Report, its first after the Gulf of Mexico oil spill, which occurred during May to August 2010, contains a very lengthy provisions disclosure note, which itself refers to substantial descriptions of the oil spill disaster contained elsewhere in the report.

BP's total provisions at 31 December 2009 of US$14,630 million leapt to a total of US$31,907 million at 31 December 2010. These included provisions relating to the assessment of environmental damage ($809 million), spill response clean-up costs ($1,043 million), litigation and claims ($10,973 million) and US Clean Water Act penalties ($3,510 million).

The explanations of the provisions, particularly in relation to the litigation and claims, are worded in very careful language, to give nothing away. The note indicates that the company has used its previous history and experience to estimate the amounts provided for, but acknowledges that 'actual costs could ultimately be significantly higher or lower than those recorded as the claims and settlement process progresses'. A range of possible outcomes is given as $6 billion to $13 billion.

Companies are also required to disclose for each class of provision a reconciliation of the balance at the start of the year to the balance at the end of the year which shows:

(a) Additional provisions made during the year, including increases to existing provisions

(b) Amounts charged against the provision during the year

(c) Any amounts reversed during the year because the provision is no longer required or can be reduced

(d) The increase in any provision included at present value as a result of the outflow being one year closer

(e) The effect of any changes in the discount rate used for provisions which have been included at present value.

This is illustrated by the provisions disclosure note in Marks & Spencer plc's 2011 financial statements.

Financial reporting in practice 13.2   **Marks and Spencer plc, 2011**

Note 24 Provisions

	2011 £m	2010 £m
At start of year	**51.1**	103.8
Provided in the year	**10.8**	5.1
Released in the year	**(1.7)**	(14.2)
Utilised during the year	**(15.4)**	(43.4)
Exchange differences	**(0.1)**	(0.2)
At end of year	**44.7**	51.1
Analysis of provisions:		
Current	**22.7**	25.6
Non-current	**22.0**	25.5
Total provisions	**44.7**	51.1

The provisions are primarily comprised of one-off costs related to the strategic restructure in the UK in 2008/09, including onerous leases.

The current element of the provision primarily relates to costs relating to the property exit costs and redundancies.

The non-current element of the provision relates to store closures, primarily onerous leases, and is expected to be utilised over a period of ten years.

13.3 Contingent liabilities

13.3.1 Definition

As discussed earlier a company will only recognise a provision if the three criteria are met:

1 The company has a present obligation as a result of a past event

2 It is probable that an outflow of resources embodying economic events will be required to settle the obligation

3 A reliable estimate can be made of the amount of the obligation.

Given that the last two criteria in particular are highly subjective, there is scope for companies to 'manage' the inclusion or exclusion of provisions. So what happens if:

- there is some doubt about whether a present obligation exists
- it is less than 50% probable, but there is still some possibility that an outflow of resources will be required
- a reliable estimate of the obligation cannot be made?

If companies could just ignore the possibilities that a liability may exist, this would not provide faithfully representative information of the company's financial position to users. IAS 37 therefore includes another category of liability, a **contingent liability**, which it defines as:

> A possible obligation that arises from past events and whose existence will be confirmed only by the occurrence of one or more uncertain future events not wholly within the entity's control; OR
>
> A present obligation which is not recognised because:
>
> - it is not probable that an outflow of resources will be required to settle the obligation; or
> - the amount of the obligation cannot be measured with sufficient reliability.
>
> *(IASB, 2005: para. 10)*

In other words a contingent liability is a form of provision where there is considerable doubt and uncertainty about its existence or value. Given these uncertainties, contingent liabilities are not recognised in the financial statements, but are required to be disclosed within a separate disclosure note. Only if the possibility of an outflow of resources is considered remote is no disclosure required. What is meant by remote is not defined in IAS 37; no suggested probability percentage is given below which something would be considered remote. However, the use of this word implies that an event would have to be highly unlikely.

13.3.2 Relationship between provisions and contingent liabilities

Clearly, the relationship between provisions and contingent liabilities is close. They are both concerned with the same sorts of issue, with the question of inclusion in the financial statements, or disclosure, or no disclosure resting on how likely a future event may turn out to be, or how certain an estimate of the amount is. The flowchart shown in Figure 13.1 demonstrates this. If items are classified initially as contingent liabilities, they must be continually kept under review to determine whether the likelihood of an outflow becomes probable, or the outcome of events makes estimates more reliable. If so, what is classified initially as a contingent liability may become a provision in a later accounting period.

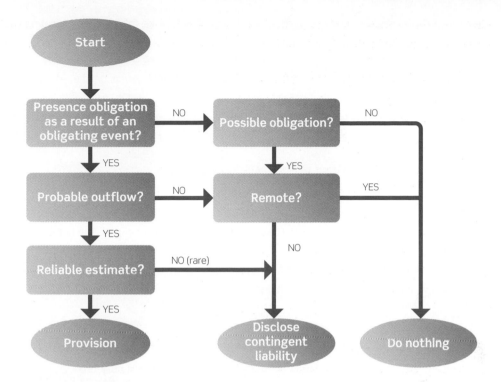

Figure 13.1 Accounting for provisions and contingent liabilities

Worked example 13.2: to show a provision versus a contingent liability

After a wedding reception held at a hotel, Abbey Park Hotel plc, in December 20X0, ten people died as a result of food poisoning. Legal proceedings are started in December seeking damages from the hotel for supplying the food which caused the poisoning, but the company disputes any liability.

Up to the date of authorisation for the issue of the financial statements for the year to 31 December 20X0, the hotel's lawyers advise that it is probable that the hotel will not be found liable.

However, when the hotel prepares the financial statements for the year to 31 December 20X1, its law-yers advise that, owing to developments in the case, it is probable that the company will be found liable.

Required:
Discuss the accounting treatment of this situation in the financial statements of Abbey Park Hotel plc for the years ended 31 December 20X0 and 20X1.

The obligating event was the wedding reception held in December 20X0. Following the flowchart in Figure 13.1:

At 31 December 20X0

1 *Is there a present obligation as a result of the obligating event?*

No—although there is an obligating event, there is no present obligation as the company disputes the liability and the lawyers advise it is probable that the hotel will not be found liable.

2 *Is there a possible obligation as a result of the obligating event?*

Yes—the lawyers advise it is only probable that the hotel will not be found liable, indicating that there may be some possibility.

3   *Is the outflow of resources (i.e. payment of damages) considered remote?*

As there is no definition of remote, the answer to this will probably rest on the advice of the lawyers.

Unless this is considered very unlikely, the company would have to disclose a contingent liability in a note to its financial statements. If it was sufficiently unlikely, then the company would make no mention of the event at all.

At 31 December 20X1

1   *Is there a present obligation as a result of the obligating event?*

Yes—events have moved on and the advice of the lawyers has now changed. The hotel company now has an obligation.

2   *Is there a probable outflow of resources?*

Yes—the lawyers are advising it is probable the hotel company will be found liable and therefore have to pay damages.

3   *Can a reasonable estimate be made of the amount?*

It is likely that an estimate of the damages could be made and the lawyers would, again, advise.

The company will have to include a provision in its statement of financial position at 31 December 20X1, including a corresponding expense in its income statement. The amount would be the best estimate, as discussed earlier in the chapter.

13.3.3 Contingent assets

Although this is a chapter on liabilities, contingent assets are included in IAS 37, and, as the name suggests, relate to contingent liabilities. The definition of a contingent asset mirrors that of a contingent liability.

> A possible asset that arises from past events and whose existence will be confirmed only by the occurrence of one or more uncertain future events not wholly within the entity's control...

(IASB, 2005: para. 10)

Contingent assets arise from unplanned or other unexpected events that give rise to the possibility of an inflow of economic benefits to a company. The inflow may be in the form of cash, but does not have to be. A classic example of a contingent asset is where a company is involved in a legal dispute and is claiming damages from a third party.

If the outcome of the future event is virtually certain, resulting in an inflow of benefits, then the related asset is not a contingent asset, as the criteria for the recognition of an asset are met. The accounting for this situation would be:

Debit   Asset (Receivable)

Credit   Income

If the outcome is anything less than virtually certain, then an asset is not recognised, as this may result in the recognition of income that may never be realised. However, if it is considered probable that an inflow of resources will result, the company should include the contingent asset in a disclosure note. The meaning of probable is the same as for provisions above, in other words more than 50% likely.

13.3.4 Contingent liabilities versus contingent assets

Table 13.2 shows that the accounting treatment for contingent liabilities and assets is not symmetrical. It could therefore be argued that it is biased.

Table 13.2 Comparison of the accounting treatment of contingent liabilities and contingent assets

Likelihood of outflow/inflow	Accounting treatment	
	Liability	Asset
Virtually certain	Recognise	Recognise
Probable	Recognise provision	Disclose contingent asset
Possible	Disclose contingent liability	No disclosure
Remote	No disclosure	No disclosure

Worked example 13.3: to show the accounting treatment of a contingent liability and a contingent asset

A claim has been made against Delta Construction plc for injury suffered by a pedestrian in connection with building work by the company. The company's legal advisors have confirmed that Delta Construction will probably have to pay damages of £200,000. Legal advisors go on to advise that a claim can be made against the building subcontractors for £100,000.

Required:
Discuss the accounting treatment of these issues.

The claim against the company and the counter-claim made by the company are treated separately following the principle that assets and liabilities should not be offset.

Claim of £200,000 against the company

1 The company has a present obligation as a result of a past event (the injury suffered).
2 Legal advisors are advising that there is a probable outflow of resources.
3 There is a reliable estimate of the amount (£200,000).

The three criteria for the recognition of a provision are met, so the company will record a provision for £200,000:

Debit   Expenses
 Credit   Provision

Claim of £100,000 by the company

There is the possibility that the company may recover an amount from the building company (a possible asset). This, however, is contingent upon the company actually making the claim and then the outcome of any legal discussion, or possibly a court case. The outcome is clearly uncertain and not within the control of the company.

This situation therefore gives rise to a contingent asset. The probability of an inflow of resources (the receipt of the £100,000) needs to be estimated. If it is considered probable, i.e. more than 50% likely, the company will disclose this as a note to the financial statements. However, if it is considered less than 50% probable, then no mention will be made in the financial statements.

13.3.5 Disclosures of contingent liabilities and contingent assets

For both contingent liabilities and contingent assets the disclosure notes should provide information about:

1   The nature of the contingent liability or asset

2   An estimate of their financial effect

3   Details relating to the uncertainties.

For contingent assets it is important that the disclosures do not give misleading indications of the likelihood of income arising.

It needs to be made clear where contingent liabilities arise from the same set of circumstances as provisions that have been made.

Financial reporting in practice 13.3	BP plc, 2010

This last point is particularly illustrated in the case of the disclosures made by BP concerning the Gulf of Mexico oil spill, which has been provided as an example for provisions earlier. Not only is there extensive discussion of the provisions the company has made, the company has included a lengthy contingent liability note. The contingent liabilities relate mainly to further lawsuits which had been brought or may still be brought in the future by individuals, corporations, and governmental entities for claims for personal injury, wrongful death, commercial or economic injury, breach of contract, and violations of statute as a result of the oil spill. As many of these lawsuits were at the very early stages of proceedings at the time the financial statements were completed, BP claimed that it was not possible to arrive at a reliable estimate and hence a provision could not be made.

BP also includes disclosures of contingent assets related to the oil spill, as it is claiming reimbursement for costs it has incurred and will suffer from two other co-owners of the oil well.

13.4 Issues with IAS 37 and its future

As one of its convergence projects with the US Financial Accounting Standards Board (FASB), in 2005 the IASB issued an Exposure Draft (ED) of a new accounting standard to replace IAS 37. It had identified three key issues with the standard which it wants to address.

1   Inconsistencies with other IRFSs in the treatment of the 'probability of outflows'

Under IAS 37 a provision is recognised only if it is probable (more likely than not) that there will be an outflow of resources. If it is less than likely a contingent liability is disclosed (unless the likelihood is considered remote). These recognition criteria are inconsistent with treatment of liabilities in IFRS 3 *Business Combinations* and IAS 39 *Financial Instruments: Recognition and Measurement.* Companies may therefore not be recognising some material liabilities in their financial statements.

2   Convergence with FASB

IAS 37 and US generally accepted accounting principles (GAAP) differ in how the costs of restructuring a business are treated. IAS 37 requires a provision to be recorded for the total costs of restructuring when it announces or starts to implement a restructuring plan. In contrast, US GAAP requires a provision to be recorded for the individual costs only when the business has incurred the costs.

3   Improvement in the measurement of liabilities

The IASB considers that the measurement of liabilities in IAS 37 is unclear and there is evidence of different measures being used by businesses. Provisions are required to be measured at the 'best estimate' of the expenditure required to settle the obligation. Companies interpret this in different ways as follows:

●   the most likely outcome

●   the weighted average cost of all possible outcomes (expected value)

●   the minimum or maximum amount in a range of outcomes.

In addition, IAS 37 does not specify the costs the business should include in the measurement which has lead companies in practice to include different costs. For example, some companies include only incremental costs, while others include all direct costs, and others a proportion of overheads.

The IASB received many comments on its proposals, in particular that its proposals on the measurement of liabilities lacked clarity. This resulted in the IASB issuing a further ED on *Measurement of Liabilities in IAS 37* in 2010. The key proposals contained in this are:

●   uncertainty about the amount and timing of the outflow of resources should be included by using a measurement that reflects their expected value, i.e. the probability-weighted average of the outflows for the range of possible outcomes

- the measurement of a liability should be the amount an entity would rationally pay at the measurement date to be relieved of the liability. This would be the lower of:
  - an estimate of the present value of the outflow of resources
  - the amount the entity would pay to cancel the obligation
  - the amount the entity would pay to transfer the obligation to a third party
- provisions for restructuring should be recorded for each individual cost only when the entity incurs that cost
- provisions for the payment of cash to a counterparty (e.g. to settle a legal dispute) should include associated costs such as legal fees
- a provision for undertaking a future service (e.g. decommissioning plant at the end of its life) would use as the estimate of outflows the amounts the entity would pay a contractor at a future date, and not the internal costs that the entity would incur if it undertook this work itself.

There have been many dissenting voices against the removal of the 'probability of outflows' recognition criterion. The implication of the proposals is that the amount recognised for a liability would not be an estimate of an actual amount that the company would pay, but a probability-weighted figure, as illustrated by the following example.

 Worked example 13.4: to show the measurement of a liability under the ED

Britoil plc, an oil production company, owns and operates an oil rig. Existing environmental laws oblige rig owners to dismantle rigs that have reached the end of their useful lives. Rig owners cannot cancel such obligations, or transfer them to third parties. However, there are contractors that provide dismantling services for rig owners. A contractor would charge $125,000 to dismantle the oil company's rig now, in a way that complies with existing environmental laws. The rig has an estimated remaining useful life of 10–15 years. The current 10- and 15-year risk-free rates of interest are, respectively, 6% and 5.5% each year.

Measurement of the liability is at the present value of the outflows required to fulfil the obligation. The outflows are the amounts the company estimates a contractor would charge at the end of the rig's life to dismantle the rig at that time. This is estimated by taking the current price of $125,000 and estimating future price increases—based on knowledge and experience of the market, and possible technological developments. The estimates are based on existing legal requirements.

Suppose the company identifies six outcomes that represent a reasonable estimate of the distribution of possible outcomes:

Outcome	Useful life	Estimated outflow ($)	Discount rate	Estimated probability
1	10 years	200,000	6%	5%
2	10 years	225,000	6%	25%
3	10 years	275,000	6%	20%
4	15 years	230,000	5.5%	5%
5	15 years	260,000	5.5%	25%
6	15 years	340,000	5.5%	20%

Required:

Calculate the value of the liability for dismantling the oil rig at the end of its estimated useful life.

Probability-weighted average of the present value of the six outcomes would give the measurement of the liability:

Outcome	Estimated outflow ($)	Discounted outflow ($)	Estimated probability	Present value ($)
1	200,000	111,679	5%	5,584
2	225,000	125,639	25%	31,410
3	275,000	153,559	20%	30,712
4	230,000	103,025	5%	5,151
5	260,000	116,463	25%	29,116
6	340,000	152,297	20%	30,459
				132,432
Risk adjustment (rational payment to be relieved of risk of uncertainties in prices)—say 5%				6,622
Liability recognised				139,054

The IASB has published further details of how the new proposals would relate to lawsuits, an area which particularly concerns respondents to the ED. Despite intentions to publish the new standard by the end of 2010, this did not happen and there has been no further movement on the project. The project is paused until the IASB concludes its ongoing deliberations about its future work plan.

13.5 Events after the reporting period

In accounting for provisions and contingent liabilities, estimates of the future are required to be made. Information from events and transactions which arise after the date of the statement of financial position is therefore relevant in helping determine these. A question which arises in connection with this is how long after the end of an accounting period should a company have to be aware of events and transactions which may affect amounts or disclosures included in the financial statements? Should details of an unexpected event, such as a fire at the company's premises, be included in the financial statements?

The answer to the last question is yes. If financial statements are to provide relevant information to the users then information about significant or material events which could affect their decisions, even those that occur after the end of the financial year, should be incorporated into the financial statements. To ensure consistent treatment of such items IAS 10 *Events after the Reporting Period* sets out when actual figures in the financial statements should be changed and the disclosures that should be provided.

13.5.1 Definition of events after the reporting period

A typical timeline for the production and publication of a company's financial statements is shown in Figure 13.2.

For listed companies the date that the directors authorise the issue of the financial statements to the shareholders will typically be 2–3 months after the end of the financial year, with the annual general meeting (AGM) held a few weeks after this.

 Example to illustrate the period in which events are required to be noted

Consider the following information for a company:

- year end: 31 December 20X0
- preparation of financial statements completed: 15 February 20X1
- board of directors meeting: 18 February 20X1 (at the meeting the board approve the financial statements and authorise them for issue)
- AGM held: 28 March 20X1 (at the AGM the shareholders approve the financial statements)
- the approved financial statements are filed by the company (as per Company legislation) on 6 April 20X1.

A significant event occurred on 7 March 20X1 which it is considered would alter an investor's opinion on the financial position of the company. Should this be included in the financial statements?

Events after the reporting period are defined in IAS 10 as:

> Those events, both favourable and unfavourable, which occur between the end of the reporting period and the date on which the financial statements are authorised for issue by the board of directors.
>
> *(IASB, 2004: para. 3)*

There are two types of event after the reporting period, classification of which determines the accounting treatment. These are outlined in Table 13.3.

A condition is a transaction or item that has happened. So an adjusting event may confirm this or provide information that helps determine its measurement. A non-adjusting event is a material transaction or item that occurs in the period after the end of the financial year and before the financial statements are authorised for issue, information about which needs

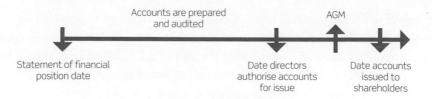

Figure 13.2 A timeline for the production and publication of financial statements

Table 13.3 Types of events after the reporting period and their accounting treatment

Type of event	Accounting treatment
Adjusting Events that provide evidence of conditions that existed at the end of the reporting period	Adjust the financial statements to reflect the adjusting event
Non-adjusting Events that are indicative of conditions that arose after the reporting period	Do not adjust the financial statements, but provide details of the event in a disclosure note

to be provided to the users as it may affect decisions they may make. The disclosures should include the nature of the event and an estimate of its financial effect or, if this is not possible, a statement that such an estimate cannot be made.

 Worked examples 13.5: of events after the reporting period

Company Beta has a financial year end of 30 June 20X5 and authorised the issue of its financial statements to shareholders on 31 October 20X5. The following events have occurred.

Required:
Determine whether they are adjusting or non-adjusting and what the relevant accounting treatment should be.

1   On 31 July 20X5 Beta was advised by the liquidator that a customer who owed £150,000 at 30 June 20X5 was insolvent. The liquidator advised that he would be paying all of this customer's creditors 10p for every pound owed and estimated this would be paid in September 20X5.

2   Beta's inventory at 30 June 20X5 includes a line of products valued at cost at £100,000. Owing to declining economic trends in the market, this inventory was not able to be sold during July 20X5. On 10 August 20X5 Beta entered into an agreement to sell the entire line of inventory to a competitor for £80,000.

3   In July 20X5 Beta acquired a factory building for £2 million. Negotiations with the seller had commenced in April 20X0.

4   Beta has a portfolio of investments valued at market value at 30 June 20X5 at £600,000. The market value of these investments fell to £450,000 as of 31 October 20X5 as the stock market declined.

All events have occurred in the period between the end of the financial year and the date of authorisation of the issue of the financial statements.

1   This is an adjusting event since the receivable balance of £150,000 was the condition in existence at the end of the financial year. The details from the liquidator provide information about the measurement of the receivable.

Adjustment required is to write-off the element of the debt which will not be received (0.9 × £150,000):

		£	£
Debit	Bad debts expense	135,000	
Credit	Receivables		135,000

2   This is an adjusting event as the inventory was in existence at the end of the financial year. The sale after the end of the year provides information about its net realisable value (NRV).

Adjustment required is to write down the value of this line of inventory to its NRV (i.e. reduce it to £80,000):

		£	£
Debit	Cost of sales	20,000	
Credit	Inventory (SoFP)		20,000

3   The condition is the purchase of the factory building and this happened after the end of the financial year. Although negotiations with the seller had been ongoing before 30 June 20X5, intention to acquire the building does not give rise to a condition that had actually happened. (Beta could always pull out of the negotiations.)

This is a non-adjusting event. The acquisition, however, would be considered a material item and so a note should be provided in the financial statements describing the transaction and its financial effect.

4   The decline in the market value of the investments does not normally relate to their condition at the end of the financial year. It reflects circumstances that have arisen subsequently.

This is a non-adjusting event. The investments remain at their year end valuation of £600,000. The decline in the value is likely to be considered material and so disclosure about the fall in the market value would be made in a note to the financial statements.

An example of the disclosures relating to a non-adjusting event arising after the end of the financial year is given.

Financial reporting in practice 13.4	Arsenal Holdings plc, 2010

Note 29 – Post balance sheet events

Player transactions

Since the end of the financial year a subsidiary company, Arsenal Football Club plc, has contracted for the purchase and sale of various players. The net cost resulting from these transfers, taking into account the applicable levies is £6.5 million. These transfers will be accounted for in the year ending 31 May 2011.

Note – Arsenal Holding's PBIT (profit before interest and tax) for year ended 31 May 2010 was £74 million, so the cost represents 9% of PBIT.

13.5.2 Dividends

Final dividends for a financial year which are declared after the end of the year are not liabilities because at the date of the year end there is no obligation for an outflow of resources. This is so even if a final dividend is expected by shareholders. If the dividends are declared before the date the financial statements are authorised for issue to the shareholders, the dividends are disclosed in the notes in accordance with IAS 1 *Presentation of Financial Statements*.

| Financial reporting in practice **13.5** | | J Sainsbury plc, 2011 |

10 Dividends

	2011 pence per share	2010 pence per share	2011 £m	2010 £m
Amounts recognised as distributions to equity holders in the year:				
Final dividend of prior financial year	10.20	9.60	189	167
Interim dividend of current financial year	4.30	4.00	80	74
	14.50	13.60	269	241

After the balance sheet date, a final dividend of 10.80 pence per share (2010: 10.20 pence per share) was proposed by the Directors in respect of the 52 weeks to 19 March 2011, resulting in a total final proposed dividend of £201 million (2010: £189 million). The proposed final dividend has not been included as a liability at 19 March 2011.

13.5.3 Going concern assumption

The going concern assumption is one of the fundamental principles of financial reporting as detailed in Chapter 2.

⬤ **Reminder** *Going concern means it is assumed an entity will continue in existence for the foreseeable future. If the entity intends to liquidate or materially curtail the scale of its operations, the financial statements may have to be prepared on a different basis, possibly by valuing the assets and liabilities on a break-up basis.*

IAS 1 requires a company to disclose if there are material uncertainties related to events or conditions that may cast significant doubt upon the company's ability to continue as a going concern. These events or conditions may arise after the end of financial year. For example, there may be a sudden deterioration in operating results and financial position caused by economic conditions or the company may fail to renew its overdraft facility with its bank. The directors of the company will need to be alert to this and consider if the going concern assumption is still appropriate. If not, then IAS 10 requires a fundamental change to the basis of accounting, which would mean the assets and liabilities would be valued on a break-up basis.

Going concern matters have received particular attention since the financial crisis with the UK's Financial Reporting Council publishing advice for both listed and non-listed companies in its *Going Concern and Liquidity Risk: Guidance for Directors of UK Companies 2009*. This sets out three categories of the going concern status for companies and the resulting disclosures and basis of accounting as shown in Table 13.4.

Table 13.4 Assessment of going concern and relevant disclosures

Conclusion	Resulting disclosures
No material uncertainties related to events or conditions that may cast significant doubt about the ability of the company to continue as a going concern have been identified.	Going concern is presumed in preparing financial statements. Disclosure will need to be made about liquidity risk, other uncertainties, and key assumptions concerning going concern as necessary. Disclosure of principal risks and uncertainties will be needed in the directors' reports of companies other than small companies.
Material uncertainties related to events or conditions that may cast significant doubt about the ability of the company to continue as a going concern have been identified, but the going concern basis remains appropriate.	Disclosures explaining the specific nature of the material uncertainties that may cast significant doubt and explaining why the going concern basis has still been adopted. Other disclosures will have to be made as described previously.
The going concern basis is not appropriate as the company has no realistic alternative but to cease trading or go into liquidation, or the directors intend to cease trading or place the company into liquidation.	Disclosures explaining the basis of the conclusion and the accounting policies applied in preparing the financial statements on other than a going concern basis and any uncertainties about the carrying amounts of assets and liabilities.

Note that directors of UK listed companies are required by Listing Rules to include in their annual financial report a statement that the business is a going concern, together with supporting assumptions or qualifications as necessary.

In March 2011 the Financial Reporting Council (FRC) launched a further inquiry, headed by Lord Sharman, to identify lessons for companies and auditors addressing going concern and liquidity risks and to recommend any necessary measures to improve the existing reporting regime and related guidance for companies and auditors. The inquiry published its final proposals in June 2012. These are discussed in Chapter 4. Essentially, the recommendations suggest much more guidance should be provided to directors in terms of how they assess whether their company is a going concern, requiring them to integrate the assessment with their business planning and risk management processes. The proposals suggest that the above three-category approach to going concern is too specific, and that going concern and discussion of this, and the risks a company faces, are much more nuanced. Better disclosures about what the risks faced by a company are and how they have been assessed should be provided.

An example of the current statutory requirement for listed companies for a statement regarding going concern is provided in Financial reporting in practice 13.6. Note this is before the implementation of any of Sharman's recommendations. The company does relate their assessment of going concern to consideration of the risks it faces, but, as in many cases, the company refers to other places in their annual report where these issues are discussed.

Typically, this results in information about how companies have assessed their going concern position being scattered in various parts of their report, making it difficult for users to obtain a coherent and comprehensive picture.

Financial reporting in practice 13.6 — Dixons Retail plc, 2010/11

Going concern (from the Directors Report)

In considering the going concern basis for preparing the financial statements, the directors have considered the Company's objectives and strategy, risks and uncertainties in achieving its objectives and its review of business performance which are all set out in the Business Overview, Strategic Summary and Performance Review sections of this Annual Report and Accounts. The Group's liquidity and funding arrangements are described in notes 17 and 22(f) to the financial statements as well as in the funding section of the Performance Review and the directors consider that the Group has significant covenant and liquidity headroom in its borrowing facilities for the foreseeable future.

Accordingly, after reviewing the Company's expenditure commitments, current financial projections and expected future cash flows, together with the available cash resources and undrawn committed borrowing facilities, the directors have considered that adequate resources exist for the Company to continue in operational existence for the foreseeable future. Accordingly, the directors continue to adopt the going concern basis in preparing the financial statements.

Summary of key points

Accounting for liabilities has, in the past, been abused by companies on the grounds of prudence. The IASB no longer states prudence as an underpinning concept to the preparation of financial statements, and provides the criteria for the recognition of a liability in its *Conceptual Framework*. However, uncertainties about whether there is to be a settlement of an obligation and the amount at which this is to be made always exist for many liabilities, and this requires estimates and judgements about the future. This is the key issue with the accounting for many liabilities.

Certain liabilities are dealt with by specific accounting standards. IAS 37 *Provisions, Contingent Liabilities and Contingent Assets* addresses liabilities not the subject of these other standards where there is uncertainty about the timing and the amount of the outflow of resources. It sets out three criteria which have to be met for a provision to be included in the financial statements. However, these criteria themselves are based on judgement. For instance, the probability of a future event happening has to be assessed and estimates about the value also have to be made. The recognition or not of provisions can have a significant impact on a company's financial statements as profit may be reduced, and key liquidity ratios and debt covenants affected.

IAS 37 further explains the treatment and disclosures of potential liabilities which are not yet recognised as a provision because they are contingent upon the outcome of a future event which is not within the control of the company. These contingent liabilities also arise because the probability of an outflow of resources is considered less than likely or because the amount of the outflow cannot be estimated reliably. In these cases financial statements would be rendered unreliable if amounts were included in them. However, users need to know about these potentially large obligations, and so companies are required to make disclosures with sufficient details to provide users with this relevant information.

Contingent assets are also considered by IAS 37, and the asymmetrical treatment of contingent liabilities and contingent assets should be noted.

The current accounting for provisions and contingent liabilities is inconsistent with some other international accounting standards' requirements and US standards. The IASB and US FASB have been working on proposals for a new standard and issued the latest version of an ED in 2010. However, the project is currently paused.

Given that so much of the accounting for liabilities and provisions relies on judgements about what may happen after the end of the financial year, the chapter concludes by considering how companies should deal with such events. IAS 10 *Events after the Reporting Period* specifies the critical period in which companies have to be aware of these events, and the definitions and resulting accounting treatment for adjusting and non-adjusting events. Consideration of going concern is a crucial current issue and companies are required to consider this carefully in their review of these events.

Further reading

IASB (International Accounting Standards Board) (2004) IAS 10 *Events after the Reporting Period*. London: IASB.

IASB (International Accounting Standards Board) (2005) IAS 37 *Provisions, Contingent Liabilities and Contingent Assets*. London: IASB.

Bibliography

Arsenal Holdings plc (2010) *Annual Report 2010*. London: Arsenal Holdings.

BP plc (2011) *Annual Report and Form 20-F, 2010*. London: BP.

Dixons Retail plc (2011) *Annual Report and Accounts, 2010/11*. Hemel Hempstead: Dixons Retail.

IASB (International Accounting Standards Board) (2004) IAS 10 *Events after the Reporting Period*. London: IASB.

IASB (International Accounting Standards Board) (2005) IAS 37 *Provisions, Contingent Liabilities and Contingent Assets*. London: IASB.

IASB (International Accounting Standards Board) (2010) *Conceptual Framework*. London: IASB.

FRC (Financial Reporting Council) (2009) *Going Concern and Liquidity Risk: Guidance for Directors of UK Companies*. London: FRC.

FRC (Financial Reporting Council) (2011) *The Sharman Inquiry, Going Concern and Liquidity Risks: Lessons for Companies and Auditors, Preliminary Report and Recommendations of the Panel of Inquiry*. London: FRC.

FRC (Financial Reporting Council) (2012) *The Sharman Inquiry: Going Concern and Liquidity Risks: Lessons for Companies and Auditors, Final Report and Recommendations of the Panel of Inquiry*. London: FRC.

J Sainsbury plc (2011) Annual Report and Financial Statements, 2011. London: J Sainsbury.

Marks and Spencer plc (2011) Annual Report and Financial Statements, 2011. London: Marks and Spencer.

💬 Questions

● Quick test

1   The following events occurred before the financial statements were approved for release to shareholders by the directors of the respective companies.

Required:

Discuss whether they should be classified as adjusting or non-adjusting events occurring after the end of the reporting period.

(a)   One month after the year end, a company received notification advising that the large balance on a receivable would not be paid as the customer was being wound up. No payments are expected from the customer or receiver.

(b)   Before the financial statements of a company are finalised, a defect was found in the material used in some batches of Product X awaiting shipment to an overseas customer. It was discovered that these were the only batches affected and that they were all manufactured in the last week of the financial year. As a result, the customer was offered a 40% discount on the agreed price. This was accepted and the sale proceeded at a value of £60,000. The value placed on the inventory in question in the year end accounts was £80,000.

(c)   At the end of the reporting period, a company is negotiating with its insurance provider about the amount of an insurance claim that it had filed. Within 3 weeks of the financial reporting date, the insurance provider agreed to pay £200,000.

(d)   A serious fire occurred one week after the end of the financial year for a furniture manufacturing company. The company's entire inventory of recliner chairs were water damaged during this incident and, before the audit of the financial statements was complete, they were sold for £20,000 to an overseas customer. The cost of the chairs was £45,000.

(e)   A company took delivery of a new machine from the USA in the last week of the financial year. It was discovered almost immediately afterwards that the supplier of the machine had filed for bankruptcy and would not be able to honour the warranties and repair contract on the new machine. Because the machine was so advanced, it was unlikely that any local entity could provide maintenance cover.

2   Portia plc is currently defending two legal actions:

(a)   An employee, who suffered severe acid burns as a result of an accident in Portia's factory, is suing for £20,000, claiming that the directors failed to provide adequate safety equipment. Portia's lawyers are contesting the claim, but have advised the directors that they will probably lose.

(b)   A customer is suing for £50,000, claiming that Portia's hair care products damaged her hair. Portia's lawyers are contesting this claim and have advised that the claim is unlikely to succeed.

Required:

Explain whether, and how much, Portia plc should provide for these legal claims in its financial statements.

3   Xanver plc has the following two legal claims outstanding:

●   a legal action against Xanver claiming compensation of £200,000, filed in February 20X7. Xanver has been advised that it is probable that the liability will materialise

● a legal action taken by Xanver against another entity claiming damages of £300,000, started in March 20X7. Xanver has been advised that it is probable that it will win the case.

Required:

How should Xanver plc report these legal actions in its financial statements for the year ended 30 April 20X7?

●● Develop your understanding

4   Explain which one(s) of the following would require a provision to be created by Abel plc at the end of its reporting period, 31 October 20X5:

(a) Under new legislation, businesses are required to fit smoke filters to their factories by 30 April 20X5. At 31 October 20X5 Abel has not fitted the smoke filters

(b) Abel makes refunds to customers for any goods returned within 30 days of sale and has done so for many years, even though it has no legal obligation to do so

(c) On 12 October 20X5 the board of Abel decided to close down a division. By 31 October 20X5 the decision was not communicated to any of those affected and no other steps were taken to implement the decision.

Would your answer change if by 20 October 20X5 a detailed plan for closing down the division was agreed by the board, letters were sent to customers warning them to seek an alternative source of supply, and redundancy notices were sent to the staff of the division?

5   Discuss whether the legal requirement for an airline to overhaul its aircraft once every three years means that a provision for the costs of doing so should be recognised?

6   Discuss the treatment of the following items in the respective companies' financial statements.

(a) Borax plc has always paid bonuses to its two directors based on 5% of profit before tax. The draft financial statements at 31 March 20X1 include a gross bonus amounting to £11,500 each following the resolution to pay a bonus based on the draft figures on 20 March 20X1. This bonus is not paid until the financial statements are approved because of various adjustments that are often incorporated in the final accounts. The accounts are approved by the board of directors four months after the year end and, because of a large write-down of inventory, the profits have reduced to an extent that the gross bonus should only be £4,500 each.

(b) Carstairs plc is a supermarket that operates four different business divisions: groceries, mobile telephone provision, Internet service provision, and domestic appliances. Each division is material to the financial statements of the company. The financial year end is 31 March 20X3 and the financial statements have not yet been authorised for issue. On 30 June 20X3 the company's directors decided that because of extremely difficult trading conditions, and a heavy loss, it would discontinue the domestic appliances division. This announcement was made on 1 July 20X3.

7   Balti plc sells refrigerators and freezers, and provides a one-year warranty against faults occurring after sale. Balti estimates that if all goods with an outstanding warranty at its statement of financial position date of 31 March 20X6 need minor repairs the total cost would be £3 million. If all the products under warranty needed major repairs the total cost would be £12 million. At 31 March 20X7 these amounts have risen to £3.5 million and £13 million respectively.

Based on previous years' experience, Balti estimates that 85% of the products will require no repairs, 14% will require minor repairs, and 1% will require major repairs.

During the year ended 31 March 20X7 actual costs of repairs under the warranty amounted to £480,000.

Required:

Explain the accounting treatment of the warranty in Balti plc's financial statements for the year ended 31 March 20X7, quantifying figures which would appear in the income statement and statement of financial position.

●●● Take it further

8 Warwick Refreshments runs a brewing business. In February 20X4, the accounts for the year 31 December 20X3 are being finalised. The following issues remain outstanding.

(a) A customer bought a glass of Warwick Best Beer in a local bar during October 20X3 and became ill. The customer is suing the bar and Warwick Refreshments. The case has not yet come to court and, although the entity's solicitors believe they will win the case, the directors offered an out-of-court settlement of £10,000 as a goodwill gesture. Under the terms of the offer, each side would meet their own costs, which, in the case of Warwick Refreshments, are £1,500 up to December 20X3. This entire amount had been paid by the year end. The customer has not yet formally accepted the offer.

(b) A consignment of hops costing £95,000 was delivered to the brewery on 20 December 20X3. The supplier has not yet issued an invoice.

(c) Bottles of the entity's beers are supplied by Bottlebank. Five years ago, in order to secure supplies, Warwick Refreshments gave a guarantee over a £3,000,000 10-year bank loan taken out by Bottlebank. The guarantee is still in force. Bottlebank's latest accounts indicate net assets of £6.8 million, and it has not breached any of the terms and conditions of the loan.

(d) Owing to a faulty valve, a batch of beer was inadvertently discharged into a river instead of into the bottling plant in March 20X3. Warwick Refreshments paid a fine of £20,000 in July 20X3 for an illegal discharge. It is also responsible for rectifying any environmental damage. To 31 December 20X3, £200,000 had been paid. The extent of further expenditure is uncertain, although it is estimated to be between £100,000 and £140,000.

Required:

Explain how each of the above items should be treated in the financial statements of Warwick Refreshments for the year ended 31 December 20X3.

9 On 1 October 20X5, Havant Oil plc acquired a newly constructed oil platform at a cost of £30 million together with the right to extract oil from an offshore oilfield under a government licence. The terms of the licence are that Havant Oil will have to remove the platform (which will then have no value) and restore the sea bed to an environmentally satisfactory condition in ten years' time when the oil reserves have been exhausted. The estimated cost of this on 30 September 20Y5 will be £15 million. An appropriate discount rate to use for Havant Oil is 10%. Discount factors using this rate at different time periods are as follows:

Time period	Discount factor
7	0.513
8	0.467
9	0.424
10	0.386

On 1 October 20X8 the oil platform suffered an accident and was completely destroyed. The accident caused an oil spill in the approximate area causing significant damages to the environment. As a result of the accident, the government licence was revoked and Havant Oil was informed by authorities that it was unlikely to obtain the licence again for the offshore oilfield. Havant Oil was also ordered to remove the remains of the platform and restore the sea bed within one year.

The finance director of Havant Oil gathered the following information after the accident:

1   The cost of the removal of the platform and restoration of the sea bed is re-estimated at £10 million

2   The engineers have estimated the clean-up of the oil spill will require an additional £50 million

3   Preliminary estimates indicate that £20 million may be recoverable from Havant Oil's insurance policy

4   The fishermen in the nearby area have filed a class action against Havant Oil claiming £300 million of damages. Havant Oil has instructed its lawyers to commence negotiations with the fishermen to try and settle an amount outside of court. The lawyers believe the final compensation may be significantly less than the original claim.

Required:

(a) Discuss the difference between a liability, provision, and contingent liability.

(b) In relation to IAS 37 *Provisions, Contingent Liabilities and Contingent Assets*, discuss the accounting treatment of the acquisition of the oil platform under the government licence in the financial statements of Havant Oil plc for the year ended 30 September *20X6*, showing amounts which would appear in the statement of financial position and income statement for that year as appropriate.

(c) Discuss and quantify, where appropriate, how Havant Oil plc should account for the oil spill and related events in the financial statements for the year ended 30 September *20X9*.

 Visit the Online Resource Centre for solutions to all these end of chapter questions plus visual walkthrough solutions. You can test your understanding with extra questions and answers, explore additional case studies based on real companies, take a guided tour through a company report, and much more. Go to the Online Resource Centre at **www.oxfordtextbooks.co.uk/orc/maynard/**

14

Leasing

➤ Introduction

The financial position of a company may be improved by increasing asset values and reducing liabilities. The exclusion of certain long-term liabilities from a company's statement of financial position, commonly called off balance sheet financing, has been a continuing issue for companies, the users of their financial statements and accounting standard setters for a number of decades. Over the years companies have sought to structure transactions involving debt to ensure that their accounting treatment was in line with current accounting practice, but the debt could be kept off the statement of financial position. To counter this accounting standard-setters have issued and revised various standards to ensure that financial statements faithfully reflect the commercial substance of all financial transactions and items.

One of the major areas that gives rise to off balance sheet financing is leasing, whereby companies acquire the use of non-current assets for a period of time in return for a series of payments. Prior to the issue of accounting standards on leases companies argued that because they did not own the assets neither the assets nor the obligations for the payments appeared on their statements of financial position. International Accounting Standard (IAS) 17 *Leases* partially addresses this by requiring leases to be classified as either finance or operating. If an asset is acquired under a finance lease, the asset should be recognised on the statement of financial position together with the related obligation for the payments. Operating leases remain 'off balance sheet' and payments under the lease agreement are accounted for like rental expenses.

This chapter explores the definitions of the two types of leases and the resulting accounting methods in both the lessee's and lessor's financial statements in more detail. There is also discussion of the International Accounting Standards Board's (IASB) continuing attempts to address the issue of operating leases still remaining off balance sheet through the issue of a new accounting standard.

★ Learning objectives

After studying this chapter you will be able to:

- understand what off balance sheet financing is and its implications for financial reporting
- explain the distinction between finance and operating leases, and be able to demonstrate the accounting methods for the two different types of lease for both lessees and lessors
- explain what a sale and leaseback transaction is, and its accounting treatment
- discuss the problems with IAS 17 and the issues raised by the proposals contained in the Exposure Draft (ED) of a standard to replace this.

✔ Key issues checklist

- ❑ What is off balance sheet financing and its effect on financial statements.
- ❑ What is a lease.
- ❑ The principles-based approach to accounting for leases as given in IAS 17.
- ❑ The distinction between finance leases and operating leases.
- ❑ Significant lease terminology definitions—lease term, the inception and commencement of a lease, minimum lease payments, guaranteed and unguaranteed residuals, discount rates.
- ❑ Accounting for a finance lease for a lessee.
- ❑ Accounting for an operating lease for a lessee.
- ❑ Disclosures in the financial statements of lessees.
- ❑ Accounting for a finance lease for a lessor.
- ❑ Accounting for an operating lease for a lessor.
- ❑ Disclosures in the financial statements of lessors.
- ❑ Sale and leaseback transactions where the lease is a finance lease or an operating lease.
- ❑ The problems IAS 17 has left unresolved.
- ❑ The key proposals of ED/2010/9 *Leases* (August 2010) and criticisms of these.

14.1 Off balance sheet financing

14.1.1 Why is off balance sheet financing an issue?

Off balance sheet financing refers to situations where some, or all, of a business's debt obligations are not recognised on the statement of financial position. If a company has obligations which are not recognised, then its financial statements cannot be said to be faithfully representative, are misleading, and, at worst, fraudulent. The statement of financial position is used by users to evaluate the financial health of a business. A company with lower levels of debt may look more attractive to potential investors than one with high debt. As discussed in Chapter 5, debt balances are included in key financial ratios, such as return on capital employed and gearing. If debt can be excluded from the statement of financial position these ratios will appear improved.

Reminder *Return on capital employed (ROCE) is a key measure of return to investors. Gearing measures the balance of debt and equity financing and is an indicator of risk for an equity investor.*

 Example of the effect of off balance sheet finance on accounting ratios

Assume a company's summarised statements of financial position including and excluding £1,500 of long-term debt are as follows. From the rules of double-entry if the debt (a credit balance) is not recognised, then a debit balance (which could be an asset or a loss) is also not recognised. Assume, in this case, a corresponding asset is also excluded.

	Including debt £	Excluding debt £
Non-current assets	4,000	2,500
Current assets	2,500	2,500
	6,500	5,000
Equity	1,800	1,800
Long-term debt	1,700	200
Current liabilities	3,000	3,000
	6,500	5,000

Assume the company's profit before interest and tax for the year then ended was £400.

ROCE	$\dfrac{\text{PBIT}}{\text{Equity} + \text{LT debt}}$	$\dfrac{400}{3,500} = 11.4\%$	$\dfrac{400}{2,000} = 20\%$
Gearing	$\dfrac{\text{Debt}}{\text{Equity}}$	$\dfrac{1,700}{1,800} = 94.4\%$	$\dfrac{200}{1,800} = 11.1\%$

The company's ROCE is higher and its gearing is lower when the debt and corresponding asset are excluded from the statement of financial position.

14.1.2 Leases

The main topic of this chapter which gives rise to off balance sheet financing is leases, where one company (the lessee) acquires the right to use an asset for a period of time in return for a payment or series of payments to another company (the lessor), which retains legal ownership of the asset. Leasing as a means of obtaining the use of assets grew enormously in the latter half of the twentieth century. Prior to any standards dealing with this, the accounting treatment followed the legal form, and the asset remained on the books of the lessor. The lessee's financial statements showed neither the asset nor the obligation for the payments, and the payments were accounted for as rental expenses.

It is reported that in the USA, in the 1970s, billions of dollars of leased items were not shown on the books of companies, a situation of which investors began to be increasingly critical. In the UK, the issue received particular attention after the collapse of a major tour operator, Court Line, in 1974. This revealed that the company had undisclosed aircraft lease obligations of £millions; obligations which were much greater than the failed company's reported net assets.

IAS 17 *Leases* which partially addresses this off balance sheet issue was based on accounting standards which had been introduced in both the USA in the 1970s and the UK in the 1980s. Under IAS 17 the accounting treatment of certain lease arrangements, termed **finance leases**, requires the assets and the related obligations to be recognised on the statement of financial position. However, this still leaves many lease arrangements, termed **operating leases**, off balance sheet. The IASB has been working for a number of years to address this, with the issue of an ED for a new accounting standard to replace IAS 17. The proposals are for substantially all leases to be brought on balance sheet. This is discussed in more detail at the end of this chapter.

14.1.3 Other transactions involving off balance sheet finance

The collapse of the US energy giant, Enron, in 2001 revealed substantial off balance sheet financing. An outline of the case is given in Chapter 3. Enron used rules based US accounting standards to avoid consolidating (in other words, including) special purpose entities (SPEs) in its financial statements. The SPEs, which Enron essentially controlled, had been used by the company to hide huge losses and debts.

The issue of control of one entity by another is at the heart of the question of which entities' results and net assets should be included in a company's consolidated financial statements. The IASB completed a major programme of work in this area in 2011, and issued a new suite of accounting standards dealing with consolidated financial statements and other business combinations. IFRS 10 *Consolidated Financial Statements* addresses the key question of control, which is discussed in Chapter 15.

Other arrangements that have given rise to off balance sheet finance include sale and leaseback arrangements, inventories sold under consignment, debt factoring, and the securitisation of assets. Broadly, these all involve the 'sale' of assets, with related obligations being incurred to re-acquire the assets in the future. IAS 17 includes details of how to account for a sale and leaseback arrangement. The IASB has addressed the issue of the potential for an asset and obligation to be off balance sheet from the other types of transactions by considering what constitutes a sale and when revenue from a sale should be recognised. Accounting for revenue is spelt out in IAS 18 *Revenue*. This takes a principles-based approach by requiring that revenue should be recognised if the 'risks and rewards' of ownership are passed to the acquirer. The proposed new accounting standard for revenue also takes a principles-based approach, with the recognition of revenue from a sale being based on transfer of control. This is more consistent with the latest approach to consolidations. These matters are discussed in detail in Chapters 7 and 15.

Other complex transactions in financial instruments are evolving continuously and some of these result in companies being able to avoid recognising all their debts on their statements of financial position. The IASB is continuing to work on accounting standards on financial instruments.

14.1.4 Principles-based approach

As seen from the earlier discussion, off balance sheet financing may arise from a variety of items and transactions, and different accounting standards have been developed and then revised, sometimes a number of times, to deal with these different areas. The IASB's approach is to produce standards which are based on the principles contained in its *Conceptual Framework,* including substance over form.

🛈 **Reminder** *Substance over form, as discussed in Chapter 2, means that accounting should be in accordance with the economic or commercial reality of a transaction rather than its legal form. This will help ensure that financial statements convey information that is faithfully representative of the underpinning transactions and items.*

Principles-based standards should ensure that no 'rules' or 'bright lines' are created either side of which an obligation would be recognised and not recognised, respectively, and which would have the effect of actually influencing the way a transaction is set up. Accounting standards should reflect the transactions of businesses and not influence their structure.

Consistency between standards is also important. As discussed, the new standards and proposals for revised standards that have been issued are addressing this. The issue of control of an asset (which has a related liability) is crucial in ensuring this consistent approach.

🛈 **Reminder** *The definition of an asset given in the Conceptual Framework includes the term control.*

14.2 Leases

14.2.1 Using assets

Companies acquire assets for long-term use in different ways. A company may purchase an asset outright, in which case legal ownership passes to it from the seller. The company can then do what it wishes with the asset as it obtains all the risks and rewards that come with ownership, and the asset is accounted for as a non-current asset.

However, for various reasons, including lack of available cash, or for tax efficiency reasons, a company may hire or lease an asset for a period of time by making regular payments over the period of the hire or lease. Legal ownership remains with the hirer or lessor, but the company gains economic benefits from the use of the asset. In a hire purchase agreement, ownership passes to the company at the end of the agreement, once the final payment has been made.

The commercial substance of this transaction is that the company has, over the period of the agreement, acquired the use of a non-current asset and may acquire some, or all, of the risks and benefits as if the company owned the asset. The asset is used in a similar manner to other non-current assets, even though, legally, it belongs to the hirer or lessor.

The substance over form principle implies that an asset acquired under a hire or lease arrangement should be capitalised. This accounting treatment also follows from the IASB's definition of an asset (note that 'control' does not mean ownership):

> An asset is a resource controlled by the entity as a result of past transactions and from which future economic benefits are expected to flow to the entity...
>
> *(IASB, 2010c: para. 4.4)*

14.2.2 Classification of leases

When the first accounting standards requiring the capitalisation of leases were being produced, the accounting standard-setters at the time appeared to recoil from introducing a requirement for the capitalisation of all leases. To reduce the impact on the thousands of affected companies' statements of financial position and accounting ratios, a distinction was drawn between a finance lease and an operating lease with different accounting treatments for each. Finance leases were required to be on balance sheet and operating leases remained off balance sheet. (The effect was still dramatic, with subsequent falls in share prices.)

The definition of a finance lease is given as one which

> ...transfers substantially all the risks and rewards incidental to ownership [to the lessee].
>
> *(IASB, 2005: para. 4)*

All other leases are classified as operating leases.

The commercial substance of a lease agreement needs to be considered carefully to differentiate between a finance lease and an operating lease. As with many other areas in financial reporting, this leads to judgement needing to be exercised. The risks of owning an asset include possible losses resulting from the asset lying idle or because it has become technologically obsolete, or variable returns from the use of the asset as economic conditions alter. Rewards resulting from owning an asset include profitable returns or gains from an appreciation in value. So if these result from using an asset, then it is considered similar to owning the asset and the asset should be included in the statement of financial position.

To help in the classification IAS 17 provides examples of certain typical conditions in lease agreements, which may indicate that a lease is a finance lease. These generally indicate that the leased asset will be used only by one lessee, who will probably retain the asset at the end of the lease term.

(a) the lease transfers ownership of the asset to the lessee by the end of the lease term;

(b) the lessee has the option to purchase the asset at a price that is expected to be sufficiently lower than the fair value at the date the option becomes exercisable for it to be reasonably certain, at the inception of the lease, that the option will be exercised;

(c) the lease term is for the major part of the economic life of the asset even if title is not transferred;

(d) at the inception of the lease the present value of the minimum lease payments amounts to at least substantially all of the fair value of the leased asset; and

(e) the leased assets are of such a specialised nature that only the lessee can use them without major modifications.

Operating leases, however, are much more like rental agreements, with the probability that an individual asset will be leased to a number of different lessees under agreements covering shorter time frames.

Not all the conditions have to be present in a lease arrangement; indeed, only one may be, but all clauses in the agreement need to be considered together. Other factors which may indicate the lease should be classified as finance are:

(a) if the lessee can cancel the lease, the lessor's losses associated with the cancellation are borne by the lessee;

(b) gains or losses from the fluctuation in the fair value of the residual accrue to the lessee (for example, in the form of a rent rebate equalling most of the sales proceeds at the end of the lease); and

(c) the lessee has the ability to continue the lease for a secondary period at a rent that is substantially lower than market rent.

 Examples of classification

1 A company leases the machine tools it uses in its manufacturing processes. Legal title is transferred to the company after three years.

This may be a finance lease because title is transferred, and the company enjoys the risks and rewards of ownership as it uses the tools.

2 A company leases a car for a salesman for a five-year period, after which the car will be returned to the lessor and scrapped.

This may be a finance lease as the lease term is for the full useful economic life of the asset.

3 A company leases a photocopier. The present value of the **minimum lease payments** is £3,000, but the fair value of the asset is £12,000.

This may be an operating lease as the fair value of the asset is much higher than the minimum lease payments.

4   A company acquires some equipment made bespoke to its specifications. If the equipment were to be sold to a third party it would require substantial modification.

This may be a finance lease as only the lessee can use the equipment without major modifications.

The lease classification is made at the inception of the lease, which is when the terms of the lease, including the financial settlement, are agreed. This may be the contract signing date or, if earlier, the date when the main terms were agreed. The date of inception of a lease may be different from the date of commencement of the lease; the difference between these two dates is important. The lease is classified at the date of inception and, in the case of a finance lease, values for the asset and liability are determined at this date. The date of commencement is the date when the lessee is able to use the leased asset. For example, a company leasing a building may move in several months after the lease contract was agreed. Values determined at inception are not recognised in the financial statements until the commencement date. In many cases, the dates are not far apart.

14.2.3 Minimum lease payments

One of the most persuasive conditions used to indicate a lease is a finance lease is that the present value of the minimum lease payments amounts to at least substantially all of the fair value of the leased asset (condition (d) in the first list in section 14.2.2). The use of the words 'substantially all' is interesting here. IAS 17 was written after the UK's accounting standard on leases was issued and is based largely on this standard. The UK standard at the time included a similar condition, but included a precise 90% cut-off instead of the words 'substantially all'. What this has meant in practice is that UK companies often apply this 90% rule to determine whether a lease agreement is a finance or operating one, and, indeed, structure leases so that perhaps only 89% is reached, meaning the lease can be treated as operating.

Minimum lease payments require careful definition as the type of payments does vary from lease to lease. Minimum lease payments here are defined as the payments over the lease term that the lessee is required to make, but the following are excluded:

●   contingent rentals (i.e. payments that are not fixed in amount, but are based on a future factor which may change, e.g. a percentage of future sales)

●   costs for services and taxes to be paid by, and reimbursed to, the lessor

●   other amounts guaranteed by the lessee or by a party related to the lessee.

The lease term also requires definition, as leases may be extended after an initial period. The lease term here means the non-cancellable period for which the lessee has contracted to lease the asset, plus any further period in which the lessee has the option to extend the lease, provided that at the start of the whole arrangement it is reasonably certain that the lessee will take this option.

In practice during the initial lease period the lease will either be non-cancellable or will be cancellable only under certain conditions, for example on the payment of a heavy settlement figure. During this period the amounts payable will be sufficient to repay to the lessor the cost of the equipment plus interest thereon. During any subsequent extension period the lease may be cancellable at any time at the lessee's option. The rentals during this period will probably be of a nominal amount (sometimes referred to as a 'peppercorn rent').

 Worked example 14.1: to show a minimum lease payments calculation

Jana plc enters into an agreement to lease a machine for five years at an annual rent of £1,000 payable at the end of each year. The cash price for the machine if purchased would be £3,605.

(Assume the machine has zero residual value at the end of the five years and also assume a discount rate of 12%.)

Required:

Calculate the present value (PV) of the minimum lease payments and use this to determine the type of lease.

The present value of the minimum lease payments is calculated as:

Payment £		Discount factor	PV £
1,000	×	1/(1.12)	893
1,000	×	1/(1.12)^2	797
1,000	×	1/(1.12)^3	712
1,000	×	1/(1.12)^4	636
1,000	×	1/(1.12)^5	567
			3,605

(Alternatively, discount or annuity tables could be used.)

The present value of the minimum lease payments at £3,605 is compared with the fair value of the asset at the inception of the lease, which is given by the cash price of the machine of £3,605.

As the two figures are the same, the 'substantially all' condition is satisfied and (in the absence of information about other clauses in the lease agreement) the lease would be accounted for as a finance lease.

14.2.4 Leases of property

When property is leased, separate consideration needs to be given to the land and the buildings. A characteristic of land is that it usually has an indefinite economic life and legal title to the land may not pass to the lessee at the end of the lease term. If this is the case, the lease of the land will be treated as an operating lease because the lessee is not receiving substantially all of the risks and rewards incidental to ownership. If title to the land does pass to the lessee at the end of the lease term, it is likely that the land lease would be classified as a finance lease. The lease of the buildings will be classified as finance or operating according to the criteria discussed previously.

However, this may result, as it often does in practice, in the land lease being treated as an operating lease, while the buildings lease is treated as a finance lease. The minimum lease payments will then need to be allocated between the two leases. This is done in proportion to the relative fair values of the leasehold interests in the land element and the buildings element at the inception of the lease. If this cannot be done, then both elements are treated as finance leases unless it is clear that both leases are operating leases.

14.3 Accounting for leases in lessees' financial statements

Figure 14.1 summarises the accounting treatments of finance and operating leases specified in IAS 17. These are discussed in detail below.

14.3.1 Finance leases

The commercial substance of a finance lease is that the lessee is acquiring the economic benefits of the leased asset for the major part of its economic life in return for a entering into an obligation to make series of payments to the lessor. The asset is therefore capitalised, just as any

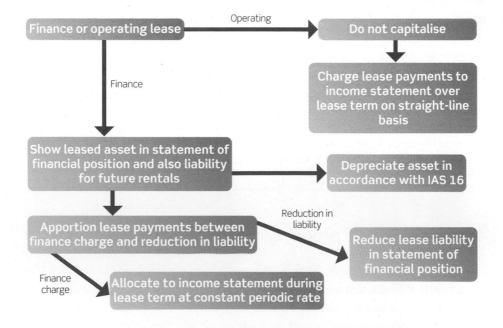

Figure 14.1 **Accounting treatment of finance and operating leases for lessees**

other asset for which legal title has been obtained is capitalised, and a liability is recognised for the future lease payments. The value at which these are recognised initially is the same for both the asset and the liability, is measured at the inception of the lease, and is the lower of:

- the fair value of the leased asset
- the present value of the minimum lease payments.

In order to calculate the minimum lease payments, a discount rate is required. If it is possible to determine this, this should be the **interest rate implicit in the lease**, in other words the discount rate that ensures:

Present value of (minimum lease payments + unguaranteed residual value)

= fair value of leased asset + initial direct costs of lessor

(Note: in this calculation the unguaranteed residual value and the initial direct costs of the lessor are often taken as zero.)

Any initial direct costs incurred by the lessee, such as negotiating and securing the lease arrangement, are added to the asset amount.

The double-entry required at the commencement of a finance lease is therefore:

Debit   Non-current asset

Credit   Lease obligation

As with any other non-current asset, once it has started to be used, depreciation has to be accounted for. To be consistent with all other owned assets, this is applied in accordance with IAS 16. (See Chapter 10 for full details of depreciation.) The method of depreciation will, therefore, reflect the pattern of usage of the asset. The life that is used is the shorter of the lease term and the useful economic life of the asset. If it is reasonably certain that the lessee will obtain ownership of the asset at the end of the lease term, then the expected useful life is used for the calculation of depreciation.

As lease payments are made, these are not expensed, but are apportioned between the finance charge inherent in the payments and the reduction of the outstanding liability. IAS 17 requires that the finance charge is calculated so as to give a constant periodic rate of interest on the remaining liability balance. In other words, as the liability reduces, the interest expense reduces. Payments on a lease are a constant amount each payment period, so this will mean that the split between interest portion and the capital portion will change over the lease term, with higher interest charges in earlier periods. Calculations to show this using the **actuarial method** (or **effective interest method**) are given in Worked example 14.2, but, in practice, a lessee may use some form of approximation to simplify the calculations, such as the sum-of digits method.

The double-entry for accounting for the lease payments is as follows:

Debit   Lease obligation   }   with full payment

Credit   Bank   }

Debit	Finance charge	}	with interest element
Credit	Lease obligation	}	

Any payments made for contingent rents are charged as expenses in the year they are incurred:

Debit	Lease expense
Credit	Bank

 Worked example 14.2: to show the finance lease accounting

Able plc leases a computer from TG Finance plc. The terms of the lease are that Able plc pays four annual rental payments of £10,000 each, with the first payment being made on 1 January 20X3. Thereafter, the computer can be rented indefinitely for a nominal sum of £1 per year. The cost of the computer new would be £34,868, and the interest rate implicit in the lease is 10% per year.

Required:

(a) Determine whether the lease is a finance lease or an operating lease

(b) If relevant, compute the amount of the lease obligation to be shown at the end of each year in the statement of financial position

(c) Show how the lease would be accounted for in Able plc's financial statements for the year ended 31 December 20X3.

(a) The determination of whether the lease is a finance or operating lease should look for indications that the risks and rewards of ownership have passed to the lessee. Here, the lease term can be extended indefinitely for a minimal sum, which IAS 17 states is an indication of a finance lease.

In addition, the present value of the minimum payments is 4 × £10,000 discounted using a 10% discount rate = £34,868, which is equal to (i.e. more than substantially all) the fair value of the computer.

The asset is therefore capitalised and a liability recognised for £34,868, the fair value of the computer, which is the same as the present value of the minimum lease payments.

(b) The calculation of the finance charge and the amount by which the lease obligation is reduced each year is achieved by drawing up a table tracking the lease obligation balance as follows:

Year	Obligation at start of year	Instalment	Obligation after instalment	Interest @ 10%	Obligation at end of year
	£	£	£	£	£
20X3	34,868	(10,000)	24,868	2,487	27,355
20X4	27,355	(10,000)	17,355	1,736	19,091
20X5	19,091	(10,000)	9,091	909	10,000
20X6	10,000	(10,000)	–		

(c) The accounting at the commencement of the lease to capitalise the asset and recognise the lease obligation is:

		£	£
Debit	Asset	34,868	
Credit	Lease obligation		34,868

The first payment is accounted for as:

		£	£
Debit	Lease obligation	10,000	
Credit	Bank		10,000

At the end of the year, the finance charge is calculated and accounted for as:

		£	£
Debit	Finance charge	2,487	
Credit	Lease obligation		2,487

Depreciation would also be accounted for. Given that there is no indication whether the asset would be used for a period different to the lease term, the asset would be depreciated over the lease term of 4 years (£34,868/4 = £8,717):

		£	£
Debit	Depreciation expense	8,717	
Credit	Accumulated depreciation		8,717

The resulting figures in the financial statements at 31 December 20X3 are therefore as follows:

Statement of financial position at 31 December 20X3

Non-current assets	£
Asset cost	34,868
Accumulated depreciation	8,717
Net book value	26,151

Lease liability

The total balance remaining at the end of the year is given in the table in part (b) as £27,355. This is split between the amount due within one year (current liability) and the amount due after more than one year (non-current liability). These figures can be obtained from the table.

Look at the figures in the next year line (i.e. the 20X4 line). The payments on this lease are being made in advance each year. Once the payment has been made, the balance on the obligation is £17,355. This figure is the amount due after one year, the non-current liability. The current liability is therefore the difference between the total £27,355 and £17,355, in other words £27,355 – £17,355 = £10,000.

(Note the calculation has been spelt out this way, so that the similarity between leases where payments are made in advance and those where payments are made in arrears can be seen—see Worked example 14.3.)

	£
Current liability	10,000
Non-current liability	17,355

Income statement for the year ended 31 December 20X3

There are two figures relating to this lease which will be included in the income statement:

	£
Finance charge (from table)	2,487
Depreciation expense	8,717

Contrast the Worked example 14.2 with one where the lease payments are made in arrears.

 Worked example 14.3: to show a finance lease liability with payments in arrears

On 1 January 20X0, at the start of its financial year, Jones plc enters into an agreement to lease a cutting machine for a period of four years. Assume that this is a finance lease and that the relevant figures are given as follows:

- annual payment of £20,000 made on 31 December each year
- interest rate implicit in lease 8%
- fair value of machine at inception of lease £66,244 (which is equivalent to the present value of the minimum lease payments).

Required:
Calculate the total lease obligation at 31 December 20X0, and show the split of this into current and non-current liabilities.

The lease obligation table is drawn up as follows. Note the order of the columns which follows the sequence of items to be accounted for—interest for the year is charged before the annual payment is made.

Year	Obligation at start of year	Interest @ 8%	Obligation after interest	Payment	Obligation at end of year
	£	£	£	£	£
20X0	66,244	5,300	71,544	(20,000)	51,544
20X1	51,544	4,124	55,668	(20,000)	35,668
20X2	35,668	2,853	38,521	(20,000)	18,521
20X3	18,521	1,482	20,003*	(20,000)	–

* Rounding difference.

At 31 December 20X0 the total lease obligation is £51,544. In order to calculate the split of this between current and non-current, as before, look at the figures in the 20X1 line. The obligation after the payment is £35,668. This is the non-current liability. The balance of £51,544 – £35,668 = £15,876 is the current liability. (Note this is because of the £20,000 payment to be made in 20X1, £4,124 will be taken as the finance charge.)

14.3.2 Finance lease disclosures

Amounts capitalised as non-current assets and the lease obligations are not netted off on the statement of financial position, as this would defeat the purpose of the accounting treatment and not be faithfully representative.

In the property, plant and equipment disclosure note, details of the carrying amount of assets held under finance leases must be indicated, often by a footnote such as:

Of the total carrying amount of £X, £Y relates to assets held under finance leases.

Other than this, all disclosures relating to property, plant and equipment required by IAS 16 are applicable to assets leased under finance leases.

For the liability IAS 17 requires disclosure of future lease payments, split between amounts due:

- within 1 year
- within 2–5 years
- after more than 5 years.

This disclosure must be given in two ways:

- on a gross basis—this shows gross future lease payments for each of the three time-period categories and then deducts as a single figure the future periods' finance charges. The resulting figure is the total lease obligation figure included in liabilities
- on a present value basis—this excludes from each of the three time-period categories the finance charges allocated to future periods.

If there are contingent rentals these need to be disclosed along with details of the basis on which these have been calculated. Other details of lease agreements, such as renewal or purchase options and any restrictions imposed should be provided to enable users to understand the implications of the company entering into the agreements.

 Example of disclosures of finance lease liabilities

Based on Worked example 14.2 of a finance lease, the disclosures relating to the lease liability at 31 December 20X3 would be as follows.

Gross basis

	£
Finance lease liabilities include gross lease payments due within:	
1 year	10,000
2–5 years	20,000
	30,000
Less: finance charges allocated to future periods (£1,736 + £909)	(2,645)
	27,355

Present value basis

	£
Finance lease liabilities include amounts due within:	
1 year	10,000
2–5 years (balancing figure)	17,355
	27,355

Financial reporting in practice 14.1   British Airways, 2010

The annual report of British Airways 2009/10 discloses the following in relation to finance leases.

Note 14: Property, plant and equipment

£ million	Fleet	Property	Equipment	Total
Net book amounts				
31 March 2010	**5,739**	**920**	**245**	**6,904**
31 March 2009	*5,996*	*971*	*266*	*7,233*
Analysis at 31 March 2010				
Owned	2,581	904	225	**3,710**
Finance leased	2,196		17	**2,213**
Hire purchase arrangements	770			**770**
Progress payments	71	16	3	**90**
Assets not in current use*	121			**121**
	5,739	**920**	**245**	**6,904**

Details of the finance lease obligations are included within the notes relating to financial instruments.

Note 30: Financial risk management objectives and policies

The table below analyses the Group's financial assets and liabilities into relevant maturity groupings based on the remaining period at the balance sheet to the contractual maturity date. The amounts disclosed in the table are the contractual undiscounted cash flows and include interest.

£ million	Within 6 months	6–12 months	1–2 Years	2–5 years	More than 5 years	Total
Cash and cash equivalents	786					**786**
Other current interest-bearing deposits	833	95				**928**
Trade receivables	499					**499**
Interest-bearing loans and borrowings:						
Finance lease and hire purchase obligations	(286)	(182)	(201)	(708)	(1,618)	**(2,995)**
Fixed rate borrowings	(47)	(36)	(83)	(485)	(455)	**(1,106)**
Floating rate borrowings	(49)	(71)	(113)	(317)	(174)	**(724)**
Trade and other payables	(1,219)					**(1,219)**
Derivative financial instruments:						
Cross currency swaps			(1)	(2)	(2)	**(5)**
Forward currency contracts	17	4				**21**
Fuel derivatives	24	20	27			**71**
Forward currency contracts	(3)					**(3)**
At 31 March 2010	**555**	**(170)**	**(371)**	**(1,512)**	**(2,249)**	**(3,747)**

14.3.3 Operating leases

As discussed previously, an operating lease is any lease other than a finance lease. The accounting for these leases is straightforward as it follows the legal form. In other words, the lease payments are recognised as an expense and IAS 17 specifies that this should be on a straight-line basis over the lease term unless another systematic basis is more representative of the lessee's use of the asset. Payments may follow a different pattern, in which case normal accounting for accruals and prepayments will ensue.

Given that these leases are off balance sheet, no amounts are recognised in the financial statements for the obligations. However, disclosures of these commitments are required to help users evaluate the financial obligations of companies under these lease arrangements. As for finance leases the future minimum lease payments are broken down into amounts due:

- within 1 year
- within 2–5 years
- after more than 5 years.

Further disclosures include amounts expensed in profit and loss, and a general description of the company's significant leasing arrangements.

Financial reporting in practice 14.2   Air France–KLM, 2011

As with many airlines, Air France–KLM finances its acquisition of aircraft through lease arrangements. At its financial year end of 31 March 2011, the company's financial statements disclosed the following obligations under these lease agreements.

£ millions	Capital (i.e. finance) leases	Operating leases
Flight equipment (including aircraft)	3,926	4,650
Buildings	300	1,824
Other property, plant and equipment	140	–
	4,366	6,474

This example serves to illustrate large amount of off balance sheet financing present in companies such as airlines.

14.4 Accounting for leases in lessors' financial statements

Under IAS 17, accounting for leases in the financial statements of lessors is more-or-less a mirror image of the accounting by lessees. The same definitions and guidance for the classification of a lease as finance or operating apply to lessors. For finance leases, the asset is derecognised (in other words sold to the lessee) and a profit or loss on sale is recognised at this point. The entitlement to receive lease payments is recognised as a receivable. For operating leases, the asset remains in the financial statements of the lessor and the receipt of the lease payments is recognised as income on a straight-line basis over the period of the lease.

Figure 14.2 summarises the IAS 17 requirements.

14.4.1 Finance leases

Under a finance lease substantially all the risks and rewards incidental to ownership are transferred by the lessor to the lessee and, therefore, the asset is derecognised (i.e. removed from the lessor's statement of financial position). The lease payment receivable is treated as a repayment of principal together with finance income to reimburse and reward the lessor for its investment and services. The lease payment receivable is recognised initially at an amount equal to the net investment in the lease. The net investment in a lease is defined as:

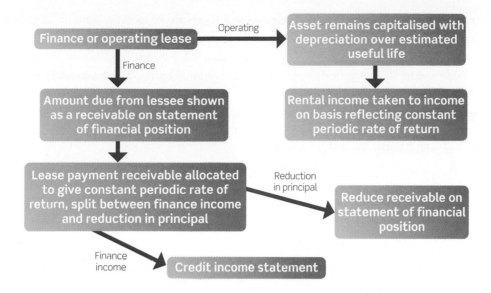

Figure 14.2 Accounting treatment of finance and operating leases for lessors

Present value of gross investment in lease

= Present value of (minimum lease payments receivable by the lessor plus any unguaranteed residual value accruing to the lessor)

At the end of the lease term, the lessee may guarantee that the asset will have a certain value. This is a guaranteed residual value. However, the lease arrangement may also include a figure for the residual value based, say, on expected market values. This is an unguaranteed residual value as it may never be realised; however, it is taken into account by the lessor when the lease is settled and in calculating the lease payment receivable.

The discount rate to be used in calculating the present value is based on the interest rate implicit in the lease. This has the same definition as for lessee accounting (see above).

The double-entry at the commencement of the lease is therefore as follows.

Derecognition of asset:

| Debit | Cost of sales | } | with carrying amount of asset |
| Credit | Asset | } | |

Sale of asset under finance lease agreement:

| Debit | Lease payment receivable | } | at net investment in lease |
| Credit | Sales revenue | } | |

A lessor will probably incur initial direct costs, for example commission, legal fees, and other costs of negotiating and setting up a lease. For lessors other than manufacturers and dealers, which are discussed in section 14.4.2, these initial costs are included in the initial measurement of the finance lease receivable and therefore reduce the amount of income recognised over the lease term.

As lease payments are received they are apportioned between a reduction in the lease receivable and finance income on a systematic and rational basis, so that a constant periodic rate of return on the lessor's net investment in the lease is achieved. This is done by carrying out the same form of calculation as for lessees in allocating their payments under a finance lease between a reduction in the lease liability and the finance charge. The actuarial method is the one which will achieve this.

The double-entry for this is as follows:

Debit	Bank	}	with full receipt
Credit	Lease payment receivable	}	
Debit	Lease payment receivable	}	with interest element
Credit	Finance income	}	

Worked example 14.4: to show the accounting for a finance lease in the financial statements of a lessor

Crystal Finance plc leased an asset to Bengal Ltd with the following terms:

Lease term	4 years
Inception of lease	1 January 20X1
Annual payments in advance	£10,000
Residual value of asset guaranteed by lessee	£6,000
Expected residual value at end of lease	£8,000
Fair value of the asset	£38,966
Interest rate implicit in the lease	10%

The unguaranteed residual value is £2,000 (i.e. £8,000 – £6,000).

Required:
Assuming this is a finance lease, show the accounting treatment of the lease in the financial statements of Crystal Finance plc for the year ended 31 December 20X1.

The net investment in the lease is calculated as follows:

Date		Gross investment	Discount factor (10%)	Net investment
		£		£
1.1.X1	Instalment 1	10,000	1	10,000
1.1.X2	Instalment 2	10,000	1/1.1	9,091
1.1.X3	Instalment 3	10,000	$1/1.1^2$	8,264

1.1.X4	Instalment 4	10,000	$1/1.1^3$	7,513
31.12.X4	Guaranteed residual value	6,000	$1/1.1^4$	4,098
Minimum lease payments		46,000		38,966
31.12.X4	Unguaranteed residual value	2,000	$1/1.1^4$	1,366
		48,000		40,332

A lease receivable table can be drawn up similar to the one drawn up for the lease obligation in the lessee's books:

Year	Receivable at start of year	Instalment	Receivable after instalment	Interest @ 10%	Receivable at end of year
	£	£	£	£	£
20X1	40,332	(10,000)	30,332	3,033	33,365
20X2	33,365	(10,000)	23,365	2,337	25,702
20X3	25,702	(10,000)	15,702	1,570	17,272
20X4	17,272	(10,000)	7,272	727	7,999*

* At the end of the lease term, the balance on the receivable equates to the expected residual value of the lease of £8,000 (ignore the rounding difference of £1).

Detailed bookkeeping for the first year is as follows. At the commencement of the lease, the lease payment receivable is set up as the net investment in the lease:

		£	£
Debit	Lease payment receivable	40,332	
Credit	Revenue		40,332

The first receipt reduces the lease payment receivable:

		£	£
Debit	Bank	10,000	
Credit	Lease payment receivable		10,000

At the end of the year, interest is accounted for:

		£	£
Debit	Lease payment receivable	3,033	
Credit	Finance income		3,033

Financial statement extracts for 20X1

	£
Income statement	
Finance income	3,033
Statement of financial position	

Non-current assets

Finance lease receivable (read from the 20X2 line in the table)   23,365

Current assets

Finance lease receivable (£33,365 – £23,365)   10,000

Note: the solution has separated the amount receivable according to the normal non-current/current asset definition. In practice, lessors, if they are financial institutions, will usually present their statement of financial position on
a liquidity basis and the receivable will be a single figure, with further analysis in the notes.

14.4.2 Manufacturers or dealers

The accounting treatment of finance leases by a manufacturer or a dealer who acquires assets
to lease to others is slightly different to that described previously. The reason for this is that
such companies often offer artificially low interest rates on the lease arrangement to attract
customers. If this were the case, the net investment in the lease would be inflated and the
company would recognise an artificially high profit on the sale of the asset at the commencement of the lease. This would also not be consistent with profits earned if the lessor made an
outright sale of the asset.

So, the following figures are used in the accounting:

1   The revenue recognised at the lease commencement should be the lower of the fair
    value of the asset and the present value of the minimum lease payments computed
    using a market interest rate

2   The cost of sale recognised at the lease commencement should be the lower of the
    cost of the asset, or its carrying amount if different, less the present value of any
    unguaranteed residual value

3   Costs incurred in negotiating and setting up the lease are accounted for as an expense
    at the lease commencement because these costs are mainly related to earning the
    selling profit.

 Worked example 14.5: to show the accounting for a finance
lease for a car dealer

On 1 January 20X2 a dealer sold a car for £30,000, payable either in full on delivery or by three annual
payments in advance at 0% finance. Each payment was therefore £10,000. The dealer had purchased
the car from the manufacturer for £24,000. The market rate of interest was 6%. The purchaser chose
the interest-free option.

(Assume zero residual values.)

Required:

What amounts should the dealer recognise in its income statement for the year ended 31 December 20X2 and in its statement of financial position at that date?

The car dealer has an asset with a carrying amount of £24,000.

The present value of the minimum lease payments is calculated as:

	Payment £	Discount factor (6%)	£
1.1.X2	10,000	1	10,000
1.1.X3	10,000	1/1.06	9,434
1.1.X4	10,000	$1/1.06^2$	8,900
			28,334

At the commencement of the lease, the following are recognised in the income statement:

	£
Revenue	28,334
Cost of sales	24,000
Gross profit	4,334

The lease payment receivable will be recognised at 1 January 20X2 at £28,334. The first two years of the receivable can be tracked as follows:

Year	Receivable at start of year £	Instalment £	Receivable after instalment £	Interest @ 6% £	Receivable at end of year £
20X2	28,334	(10,000)	18,334	1,100	19,434
20X3	19,434	(10,000)	9,434		

Also recognised in the 20X2 income statement is finance income of £1,100.

In the statement of financial position at 31 December 20X2, the car dealer will have a lease receivable of £19,434 split £9,434 non-current asset and £10,000 current asset.

14.4.3 Finance lease disclosures

Again, the IAS 17 disclosures for finance leases for lessors mirror the disclosures required by lessees. For the receivable, the future lease payments to be received should be split between amounts receivable:

- within 1 year
- within 2–5 years
- after more than five years.

This disclosure must be given both:

- on a gross basis, i.e. showing gross future lease receipts for each of the three time-period categories, then deducting as a single figure the future periods' finance income to arrive at the total lease receivable
- on a present value basis, which excludes from each of the three time-period categories the finance income allocated to future periods.

The future periods' finance income is useful to users as it provides an indication of future income.

Additional disclosures include:

- the unguaranteed residual values accruing to the benefit of the lessor
- contingent rentals which have been included as income in the year
- a general description of the lessor's material leasing arrangements.

Financial reporting in practice 14.3 — Lloyds Banking Group, 2011

The annual report and accounts of Lloyds Banking Group include finance lease receivables in loans and advances to customers. Details of these are provided in the disclosure note relating to this balance.

Loans and advances to customers include finance lease receivables, which may be analysed as follows:

	2011 £m	2010 £m
Gross investment in finance leases, receivable:		
Not later than 1 year	1,168	1,358
Later than 1 year and not later than 5 years	2,754	2,522
Later than 5 years	6,355	7,218
	10,277	11,098
Unearned future finance income on finance leases	(2,391)	(2,603)
Rentals received in advance	(56)	(183)
Commitments for expenditure in respect of equipment to be leased	(30)	(21)
Net investment in finance leases	7,800	8,291

The net investment in finance leases represents amounts recoverable as follows:

	2011 £m	2010 £m
Not later than 1 year	724	986
Later than 1 year and not later than 5 years	2,307	1,965
Later than 5 years	4,769	5,340
Net investment in finance leases	7,800	8,291

Equipment leased to customers under finance leases primarily relates to structured financing transactions to fund the purchase of aircraft, ships and other large individual value items. During 2011 and 2010 no contingent rentals in respect of finance leases were recognised in the income statement. The allowance for uncollectable finance lease receivables included in the allowance for impairment losses is £92 million (2010: £287 million).

14.4.4 Operating leases

For an operating lease the lease term is, by definition, shorter than the asset's useful life. As for lessees the accounting for an operating lease for a lessor is very straightforward. The asset remains in the financial statement of the lessor according to its nature. If it is an item of property, plant and equipment it is depreciated in accordance with IAS 16 and is subject to impairment reviews as per IAS 36.

The receipts are accounted for as income and recognised on a straight-line basis over the period of the lease term, even if receipts are not made on this basis. If another systematic and rational basis is more representative of the time pattern in which the benefit from the leased asset is receivable, this should be used. The initial direct costs incurred by lessors in negotiating and arranging an operating lease should be added to the carrying amount of the leased asset and recognised as an expense over the lease term through depreciation.

Disclosure should be made of the future minimum lease payments split between amounts due:

- within 1 year
- within 2–5 years
- after more than 5 years.

14.5 Sale and leaseback transactions

A sale and leaseback transaction involves the owner of an asset selling it, usually to a finance house or bank, and simultaneously leasing it back. These arrangements provide companies with the opportunity to release capital tied up in the business's assets to enable investment in other opportunities or to return it to shareholders. In essence, a company acquires cash in exchange for a commitment to make regular lease payments without losing use of the asset.

A sale and leaseback transaction can result in either a finance lease or an operating lease, as determined by applying the principles contained in IAS 17. As the accounting treatment of the transaction depends on this categorisation, this decision is critical.

14.5.1 Finance leases

If the lease part of a sale and leaseback transaction results in a finance lease, the risks and rewards of ownership remain with the company that made the original sale and the transaction is effectively a means of this company obtaining finance using the asset as security. The recognition of a profit on the sale of the asset would therefore not faithfully represent the transaction. Any excess of sales proceeds over the carrying amount of the asset is therefore deferred and amortised over the lease term. The finance lease is then accounted for in the usual way.

 Worked example 14.6: to show the accounting for a sale and leaseback transaction as a finance lease

Gradgrind plc owns an asset with a carrying amount of £79,000 that it sells to Beta Finance plc on 1 January 20X4 for its fair value of £100,000. Gradgrind immediately leases the asset back from Beta Finance for its remaining economic life of 3 years at £36,000 per year payable in advance. Assume an interest rate of 8%.

Required:
Show the accounting treatment of this transaction in the financial statements of Gradgrind plc for the year ended 31 December 20X4.

On sale of the asset, the following accounting entries are made:

		£	£
Debit	Bank	100,000	
Credit	Asset		79,000
	Deferred revenue		21,000

The present value of the minimum lease payments totals £100,197 (i.e. £36,000 + £36,000/1.08 + £36,000/1.08^2), so this lease is accounted for as a finance lease in the usual way. At the commencement of the lease the accounting entries are:

		£	£
Debit	Asset	100,000	
Credit	Lease liability		100,000

(Note: amount is the lower of the present value of the minimum lease payments and the fair value of the asset.)
The first payment under the lease is made:

		£	£
Debit	Lease liability	36,000	
Credit	Bank		36,000

At the end of the year, 31 December 20X4, depreciation and the interest are accounted for:

		£	£
Debit	Depreciation (100,000/3)	33,333	
Credit	Asset		33,333
Debit	Finance charge (see working)	5,120	
Credit	Lease liability		5,120

In addition, the deferred income is amortised to profit and loss:

		£	£
Debit	Deferred revenue (21,000/3)	7,000	
Credit	Profit and loss		7,000

Income statement for the year ended 31 December 20X4

	£
Depreciation expense	(33,333)
Finance charge	(5,120)
Release of deferred income	7,000

Statement of financial position at 31 December 20X4

	£
Non-current assets:	
Cost	100,000
Accumulated depreciation	(33,333)
	66,667
Non-current liabilities:	
Lease obligation (see working)	33,120
Deferred income	7,000
Current liabilities:	
Lease obligation	36,000
Deferred income	7,000

Working

Year	Obligation at start of year	Instalment	Obligation after instalment	Interest @ 8%	Obligation at end of year
	£	£	£	£	£
20X4	100,000	(36,000)	64,000	5,120	69,120
20X5	69,120	(36,000)	33,120		

The effect of this, as illustrated in Worked example 14.6, is that the asset has effectively been revalued to its fair value of £100,000, with the accounting treatment of this rather different to that permitted under IAS 16 for the revaluation of property, plant and equipment (see Chapter 10 for full details). The figure net of the new depreciation expense and the deferred income release (£33,333 – £7,000 = £26,333) is the same as the original depreciation expense (£79,000/3 = £26,333).

The effective commercial transaction of the company receiving a loan based on the security of the asset has not entirely been reflected by the accounting set out in IAS 17.

14.5.2 Operating leases

The commercial reality of a sale and leaseback involving an operating lease is that a real sale has taken place as the risks and rewards of ownership pass to the finance company, and the seller's intentions are to continue to use the asset for only a portion of its remaining useful life. For example, a business may sell its current premises and then lease them back for a year while it builds new premises, using the sale proceeds to finance this. Thus, a profit or loss on sale (sale proceeds minus carrying amount) should be recognised. However, the accounting for this becomes more complex depending on the sale value of the asset.

If the sale price is at fair value, the profit or loss on sale should be recognised immediately in profit or loss. If the sale price is different from fair value, different rules apply:

1   If the sale price is below fair value and future lease payments are at market levels, any profit or loss is recognised immediately.

    Even though lease payments are set at market levels, the sale price might be below fair value because the company is desperate for cash and so accepts a low sale price to alleviate its liquidity problems. Under these circumstances it is appropriate that the whole loss on disposal should be recognised immediately.

2   If the sale price is below fair value and the loss is compensated for by future lease payments at below market levels, the loss is deferred and amortised in proportion to the lease payments over the period for which the asset is expected to be used.

3   If the sale price is above fair value, the excess over fair value is deferred and amortised over the period for which the asset is expected to be used.

14.6 Future accounting for leases

14.6.1 Issues with IAS 17

As discussed at the start of this chapter, one of the intentions of IAS 17 was to prevent off balance sheet financing resulting from leasing arrangements. However, the distinction was drawn between finance and operating leases, leaving the latter off balance sheet. This remains an issue. Although companies are required to make disclosures of future obligations arising under operating leases, this is not a substitute for actual recognition of the assets and liabilities of these agreements. Based on these disclosures, investors may make arbitrary adjustments to include the assets and liabilities of operating leases in their calculations of financial ratios, such as gearing and return on capital, which can then be used in company comparisons. However, these adjustments can only ever be estimates, and there is evidence to suggest that users would like operating leases brought onto balance sheets.

Companies also structure lease agreements in order to avoid the 'substantially all' transfer of risks and rewards, resulting in similar leases being accounted for differently from company to company. UK studies have revealed that average operating lease commitments are over 10 times that of reported finance lease obligations, and a ball-park figure of off balance sheet gross operating lease obligations of $94 billion for the top 50 UK companies has been quoted. Sir David Tweedie, former chairman of the IASB, who retired in June 2011, is reputed to have said that he wished to fly in an airplane that was actually reflected in the financial statements of the airline company!

14.6.2 Exposure Draft ED/2010/9 *Leases* August 2010

The IASB, as part of its convergence project with the US Financial Accounting Standards Board (FASB), has been working on a new leasing standard for many years. It finally issued an ED in August 2010, which triggered an unprecedented number of comment letters.

The objective of the ED is that the accounting for leases should provide information about the amounts, timing, and uncertainty of cash flows. The ED's main proposals, together with some of the key comments and criticisms, are shown in Table 14.1.

14.6.3 Where to next?

The IASB has been deliberating over the many comments it has received on, and criticisms of, the ED. In addition, it has held many public meetings and carried out outreach work around the world. The results of all of this consultation, which is still ongoing, is that the IASB is reaching conclusions about the accounting treatment of some of the issues which are different to those contained in the ED. The IASB has stated that it is, therefore, going to re-expose these decisions by issuing an updated ED, which is expected in late 2012.

One decision that is unlikely to change is that what have been known as operating leases for many years will finally be brought onto the statements of financial position of companies. Thus, this cause of off balance sheet financing will finally be removed.

Table 14.1 Proposals of ED/2010/9 *Leases*

	Proposal	Comment/criticism
1	The distinction between finance and operating leases will be removed, with all leasing agreements appearing on the statement of financial position of lessees as assets and liabilities.	Broad support from most users, although property-owning companies, ranging from Tesco to Oxfam, have protested, in particular. This will affect all leases covering aircraft and ships through vehicle fleets to the lease of non-core assets, such as photocopiers, and some businesses claim it will add cost and undue complexity to financial accounting.
2	There is some simplification in the requirements for short-term leases of one year or less.	This will create a 'bright-line' and companies may structure leases accordingly.
3	The definition of a lease is that the lessee has acquired the 'right to use' a specified asset for a period of time in exchange for consideration.	The 'right-of-use' model is generally accepted. However, it is inconsistent with the definition of an asset in the IASB's *Conceptual Framework*.
4	Intangible assets are excluded from the ED as the IASB has stated it wishes to consider broader issues relating to the accounting for intangible assets first.	Inconsistent treatment of tangible and intangible assets.

Lessee accounting

5	The asset and liability are recorded at a probability-weighted present value of lease payment outcomes. In determining these outcomes the payments include estimates of contingent rentals, residual value guarantees, and term option penalties. The lease term is taken as the longest possible period that is more likely than not to occur.	The measurement of the assets and liability are based on the inclusion of a number of estimates and, because they are weighted by their respective probabilities, the resulting values do not actually represent outflows of cash. The measurements are complex and highly subjective.
6	The estimates included in the measurements should be reassessed each year if there are indications that they have changed.	Practically, this is an administratively burdensome requirement.

Lessor accounting

7	Two alternative models are proposed, dependent upon whether the risks or benefits of the underlying asset have been transferred to the lessee.	It is inconsistent to have one method of accounting for leases by lessees and two methods for lessors. The risk and benefit criteria do not apply to lessee accounting.
8	If the risks or benefits have been transferred, the asset is derecognised (sold to the lessee) and the statement of financial position will show the expected residual value in the asset, together with a receivable for the right to receive the lease payments.	This is similar to the current IAS 17 accounting treatment of finance leases for lessors.

Table 14.1 (Continued)

	Proposal	Comment/criticism
9	If the risks or benefits have not been transferred, the performance obligation approach applies. The asset remains on the statement of financial position and, in addition, a receivable for the right to receive the lease payments is recognised together with a liability to permit the lessee to use the asset.	Two assets, plus a liability, are recorded for the same transaction. The asset will be capitalised in both the lessee's and lessor's financial statements.

Summary of key points

Off balance sheet accounting, one of the most significant financial accounting problems of the later twentieth and twenty-first centuries, is when financing obligations do not appear on companies' statements of financial position. The types of financial transaction and arrangement which give rise to this are various, but the result is that companies' financial positions, and gearing and return on capital ratios appear better than they would if the debt were recognised.

Leasing arrangements give rise to off balance sheet financing. The current accounting standard, IAS 17 *Leases*, classifies leases as either finance or operating. Operating leases remain off balance sheet, although disclosures of obligations under this type of lease do have to be made. A transfer of risks and rewards of ownership model is used to distinguish between the two types of lease; if these are transferred to the lessee then the lease is a finance lease, otherwise the lease is an operating lease. This inevitably involves a subjective judgement, so a key method by which this may be determined is to evaluate whether the present value of the minimum lease payments is at least substantially all of the fair value of the asset. Many companies have taken substantially all to mean around 90%, thus creating a 'bright line', which is contrary to the intentions of this principles-based standard.

For lessees the accounting for finance leases requires the asset and liability to be included on the statement of financial position at the lower of the present value of the minimum lease payments and the fair value of the asset. The asset is depreciated and the payments are split between a repayment of the liability and an interest charge. The interest is calculated so as to provide a constant periodic rate of interest on the remaining liability balance.

Operating leases are accounted for as hire arrangements with all lease payments being expensed in profit and loss.

The accounting treatment of lease agreements for lessors is virtually a mirror image of that for lessees. For finance leases the asset is sold to the lessee, so it is removed from assets and a receivable is recognised at the present value of the minimum lease payments receivable plus any unguaranteed residual value accruing to the lessor. As lease payments are received these are split between a reduction of the receivable and finance income, which is calculated so as to provide a constant periodic rate of interest on the remaining receivable balance.

For operating leases, the risks and rewards of ownership remain with the lessor, and so the asset remains in the lessor's books, with the receipt of lease payments being accounted for as rental income in the income statement.

IAS 17 is due to be replaced, with the IASB and the US FASB working on a revised standard which will remove the distinction between finance and operating leases and, for lessees, require them all to be accounted for the same way and brought onto balance sheets. An ED was issued in 2010, but, as a result of many comments and criticisms, mainly in connection with measurement issues, the proposals are being rethought, and will be re-exposed. A new standard will therefore not be issued in the very near future.

 ## Further reading

IASB (International Accounting Standards Board) (2005) IAS 17 *Leases*. London: IASB.

IASB (International Accounting Standards Board) (2010) Exposure Draft *Snapshot: Leases*, August 2010. London: IASB.

 ## Bibliography

Air France–KLM (2012) *Annual Report 2010–11*. Tremblay-en-France: Air France–KLM.

Anon. (2010) Lease of strife, *Financial Times* (4 August 2010).

British Airways plc (2010) *Annual Report and Accounts, 2009/10*. London: British Airways.

Christodoulou, M. (2011) Tesco and Sainsbury's attack lease accounting proposals, *Accountancy Age*, Available at http://www.accountancyage.com (accessed 18 December 2012).

Drake, J. (2011) A Step too far: Are the IASB's leases proposals just too complicated?, *By All Accounts*, January: 15.

Hughes, J. (2009) Leasing: Attempt to close a false divide, *Financial Times* (4 February 2009).

Hussey, R. and Ong, A. (2011) IAS 17: Is it fatally flawed?, *International Accountants*, May: 12–15.

IASB (International Accounting Standards Board) (2005) IAS 17 *Leases*. London: IASB.

IASB (International Accounting Standards Board) (2010a) ED/2010/9 *Leases*, August 2010. London: IASB.

IASB (International Accounting Standards Board) (2010b) Exposure Draft *Snapshot: Leases*, August 2010. London: IASB.

IASB (International Accounting Standards Board) (2010c) *Conceptual Framework*. London: IASB.

Lloyds Banking Group (2012) *Annual Report and Accounts, 2011*. Edinburgh: Lloyds Banking Group.

Poole, V. (2010) No pain, no gain. Available at: http://www.accountancyage.com (accessed 18 December 2012).

 ## Questions

● Quick test

1   (a) Explain what 'off balance sheet financing' is and how IAS 17 *Leases* addresses this issue.

     (b) Dawlish plc entered into a lease for its computer system commencing 1 April 20X6. The terms of the lease are that Dawlish pays four annual rental payments of £150,000 each, with the first payment made on 1 April 20X6. Thereafter, the computer can be rented indefinitely for a nominal sum of £1 per year. The cost of the computer new would have been £523,028 and the finance cost implicit in the lease is 10% per year. Dawlish expects to use the computer system for 5 years.

Required:

Discuss the accounting treatment of this transaction in the accounts of Dawlish plc for the years ended 31 March 20X7 and 20X8, and calculate the relevant statement of financial position and income statement values to be shown.

2   On 1 January 20X0, Power Tools plc acquired use of a machine that normally sells for £3,000,000. Owing to cash flow constraints Power Tools entered into a lease agreement with the machine supplier to pay six semi-annual instalments of £700,000 over the next 3 years starting on 30 June 20X0. The half-yearly interest rate implicit in the lease is 10%. The machine would normally be expected to last 3 years. Power Tools is required to insure the machine and cannot return it to the lessor without severe penalties.

Required:

(a) Describe whether the lease should be classified as an operating or finance lease.

(b) Show the effect of the lease on the income statement and statement of financial position of Power Tools plc for the year ended 31 December 20X0.

3   Conex plc is the lessee of an asset on a non-cancellable lease contract with a primary term of three years from 1 January 20X7. The rental is £5,404 per quarter, payable in advance. The lessee has a right after the end of the primary period to continue to lease the asset as long as the company wishes at a rent of £1 per year. The lessee bears all maintenance and insurance costs. The leased asset could have been bought for cash at the start of the lease for £55,404. The rate of interest implicit in the lease is 3% per quarter. The company expects to continue to employ the asset for one year after the end of the primary term and uses the straight-line method of depreciation.

Required:

Show the amounts relating to this agreement to be included in the financial statements of Conex plc for the relevant years.

4   (a) Discuss the difference between a finance lease and an operating lease, and explain why this distinction is important in financial reporting.

    (b) Nottingham plc, whose year end is 31 March 20X4, manufactures shoes. On 1 April 20X3 the company entered into an agreement with Capital Finance plc for the lease of a new machine. Terms of the lease include:

        (i)   Neither party can cancel

        (ii) Nottingham plc is to have responsibility for maintenance

        (iii) Six instalments of £45,000 are payable half-yearly in advance.

    The cash price of the machine on 1 April 20X3 was £240,000 and the machine is expected to have a life of 5 years. The rate of interest implicit in the lease is 5% semi-annually.

    Required:

    Discuss the accounting treatment of this transaction in the accounts of Nottingham plc for the year ended 31 March 20X4, and calculate the relevant statement of financial position and income statement values to be shown.

●● Develop your understanding

5   IAS 17 *Leases* is used to prevent off balance sheet financing abuses for leasing transactions.

Discuss what off balance sheet financing is, why it is important that this issue is tackled, and how the international accounting standard-setters have addressed the issue to date.

(You should use leases and other transactions giving rise to off balance sheet financing as examples to illustrate your answer.)

6   (a) IAS 17 *Leases* distinguishes between two types of lease: finance and operating; and stipulates different accounting treatments for each.

Discuss the requirements of IAS 17 in relation to the principle of 'substance over form'.

(b) Ferrars plc, which has an accounting year end of 31 December 20X7, entered into the following lease agreements with other companies in 20X7:

(i) On 1 January 20X7 Ferrars leased a specialised machine (Machine X) on a non-cancellable lease contract from Willoughby plc. On that date the machine had a fair value of £503,030. Ferrars estimates that the useful life of the machine is six years.

Details of the lease are:

● term of lease—six years

● six-monthly lease payment, payable in arrears on 30 June and 31 December—£60,000

● six-monthly implicit interest rate—6%

● Ferrars to bear all maintenance and insurance costs.

(ii) Ferrars leased another machine (Machine Y) from Darcy plc on 1 January 20X7. The lease term is 3 years with 3 instalments of £84,000 payable to Darcy on 1 January each year. The expected useful life of this machine is 6 years. At the end of the lease period Machine Y will be transferred back to Darcy. The fair value of the machine at 1 January 20X7 was £300,000 and the annual interest rate implicit in this lease is 12%.

Ferrars plc uses the straight-line method of depreciation for its machinery and estimates the residual value of all machines as zero.

Required:

(a) Discuss the accounting treatment of the two leases in the financial statements of Ferrars plc.

(b) Show the relevant income statement and statement of financial position figures for the two leases for Ferrars plc for the year ended 31 December 20X7.

7   Alpha plc has entered into the following sale and leaseback transactions, details of which are provided as follows.

(i) Alpha sold an asset with carrying amount of £8,000 to Beta plc at £10,000 and immediately leased back the asset under a finance lease. The fair value of the asset is £10,000.

(ii) Alpha sold an asset with carrying amount of £8,000 to Gamma plc at £10,000 and immediately leased back the asset under an operating lease. The fair value of the asset is £10,000.

(iii) Alpha sold an asset with carrying amount of £12,000 to Delta at £10,000 and immediately leased back the asset under an operating lease. The fair value of the asset is £15,000.

(iv) Alpha sold an asset with carrying amount of £8,000 to Epsilon at £15,000 and immediately leased back the asset under an operating lease. The fair value of the asset is £10,000.

Required:

Explain how Alpha plc should account for each sale and leaseback transaction under IAS 17.

●●● Take it further

8 On 1 January 20X8, Shilton plc sold a machine that had a carrying amount in its financial statements of £400,000 to Bucknor plc for its fair value of £497,000. Shilton immediately leased the machine back under the following conditions:

(i) The term of the lease is 4 years non-cancellable

(ii) The annual rental is £125,000 payable at the beginning of the year

(iii) The future economic life of the equipment is estimated to be 5 years

(iv) The machine is to be sold to Shilton for £50,000 at the end of the lease term

(v) The interest rate implicit in the lease is 8%

(vi) Shilton depreciates all its equipment on a straight-line basis.

Required:

(a) Discuss how the lease should be classified for both the lessor and the lessee.

(b) Prepare the journal entries and show how this lease transaction should be reported in the income statement and statement of financial position of Shilton plc for the year ended 31 December 20X8.

9 On 1 January 20X4 Carston plc acquired an asset for its fair value of £75,979 and immediately leased it out to Bollington Ltd for 4 years under a finance lease with the following lease terms:

● annual payments of £20,000 paid on 1 January each year

● residual value of asset guaranteed by the lessee £7,500

● expected residual value at end of lease £9,000

● interest rate implicit in the lease 10%

● direct costs incurred by lessor at start of lease £500.

Carston's depreciation policy for similar assets is 40% per annum on a reducing balance basis.

Required:

(a) Show the figures which would appear in the financial statements of Carston plc in relation to this lease agreement for the year ended 31 December 20X4.

(b) If there were significant restrictions on what the lessee was allowed to do with the asset, the lease would be classified as an operating lease. Using the same figures, show how the lease would be presented in the financial statements of Carston plc for the year ended 31 December 20X4.

10 Surefast plc owns the office building it occupies. The company intends to move into newer premises which are to be built on a nearby site. In order to finance the construction, the company is negotiating a sale and leaseback agreement with Goodrich plc for its current office building. Goodrich has offered Surefast two options.

	Option 1	Option 2
Period of leaseback	3 years	3 years
Purchase price payable by Goodrich	£2.73 million	£3 million
Annual rental payable by Surefast	£210,000	£300,000

The current market value of the office building is approximately £2.85 million and the current carrying amount of the depot in Surefast's statement of financial position is £2.4 million. The market rental for Surefast's offices is estimated to be £250,000 per year.

Required:

Show how each of the above options would impact Surefast's profit or loss for the next 3 years.

Visit the Online Resource Centre for solutions to all these end of chapter questions plus visual walkthrough solutions. You can test your understanding with extra questions and answers, explore additional case studies based on real companies, take a guided tour through a company report, and much more. Go to the Online Resource Centre at **www.oxfordtextbooks.co.uk/orc/maynard/**

Part 5

Consolidated financial statements

Chapter 15 Subsidiaries

Chapter 16 Associates, joint arrangements, and statements of cash flow

15

Subsidiaries

Today, the modern global economy is driven by complex, multi-entity organisations with their shares listed on multiple international stock markets. Investors in these markets require information about the corporations as a whole, and thus need financial statements which represent fairly the combination of the different organisations.

Arguably, the rise of consolidated financial reporting may be considered one of the most important accounting developments of the twentieth century. Consolidated financial statements have developed since the early 1900s to combine the financial statements of more than one entity so that they reflect the entities' investments in each other and combinations of their businesses. The financial results and position of the combined entities are therefore presented as those of a single entity.

This chapter examines accounting for simple parent and subsidiary business combinations, where one company acquires control of another. The recent changes that the International Accounting Standards Board (IASB) has introduced with the issue of its latest accounting standards in this area:

- International Financial Reporting Standard (IFRS) 10 *Consolidated Financial Statements*
- IFRS 12 *Disclosure of Interests in Other Entities*

are discussed, together with the requirements of the other accounting standards that are still applicable:

- International Accounting Standard (IAS) 27 *Separate Financial Statements*
- IFRS 3 *Business Combinations*.

The focus of the chapter is on the techniques of preparation of the consolidated statement of financial position, the consolidated income statement, the consolidated statement of comprehensive income, and the consolidated statement of changes in equity. The preparation of the consolidated statement of cash flows is discussed in Chapter 16.

After studying this chapter you will be able to:

- understand the need for consolidated financial statements
- understand the different categories of investment by one company in another and how different accounting treatments result
- explain when a parent/subsidiary relationship exists, and how and why the question of control is central to this
- prepare a consolidated statement of financial position, statement of comprehensive income, and statement changes of equity for a simple group structure, including a parent company and one or more subsidiaries, using the acquisition method
- discuss the disclosures required by reporting companies.

✔ **Key issues checklist**

- ❑ Categories of investments by one company in another.
- ❑ The need for consolidated financial statements.
- ❑ The single entity concept.
- ❑ The definition of a subsidiary.
- ❑ The key question—control—and issues relating to how this is determined.
- ❑ The acquisition method of preparing consolidated financial statements for a simple group structure of a parent plus one or more subsidiaries:
  - ❑ consolidated statement of financial position
  - ❑ consolidated income statement and statement of comprehensive income
  - ❑ consolidated statement of changes in equity.
- ❑ Consideration and its valuation.
- ❑ Goodwill on acquisition.
- ❑ Subsidiary fair values in acquisition accounting.
- ❑ The two alternative methods for the valuation of non-controlling interest (NCI) in the consolidated financial statements.
- ❑ Pre- and post-acquisition reserves.
- ❑ Preference shares and other debt instruments acquired by the parent company.
- ❑ Intra-group transactions and balances.
- ❑ Unrealised profit in inventories.
- ❑ Acquisition of a subsidiary part-way through the latest accounting period.
- ❑ Disclosures required by IFRS 12.

15.1 Categorisation of investments

It is normal commercial practice for businesses to make investments in other businesses as part of their overriding strategies. Investments can be in corporations or unincorporated businesses and range from minor investments to earn some investment income to full purchase or takeover. Mergers and acquisitions (M&A) activity is on a vast scale—up to the end of quarter three of 2011, global M&A activity totalled US$1,785 billion. Given the size of this activity it is therefore imperative that accounting for the resulting business combinations is based on sound principles, is consistent, and faithfully represents the relationships of the combined businesses.

Broadly, there are three categories of investment of one company in another according to the degree of influence or interest that the investing company (the investor) has over or in the investee company, as shown in Table 15.1. Different accounting methods result dependent upon the categorisation of the investee.

15.1.1 Limited influence

The simple investment is, as its name suggests, the simplest to account for. This situation arises where one company holds a small proportion of the shares in another company for investment purposes. The investor is only concerned with the operations and financial results of the investee to the extent of the investment income (dividends) that it receives, and the effect of the investee's share price. It plays no part in the management of the investee company.

The accounting for this investment follows, in that the investor shows the investment as a financial asset on its statement of financial position. This is measured at cost or in accordance with IFRS 9 *Financial Instruments* and IAS 39 *Financial Instruments: Recognition and Measurement*. In the income statement dividends are recognised as finance income when the right to receive the dividend has been established.

15.1.2 Partial influence

Partial influence can be obtained either by a company acquiring a certain number of shares in another to give it significant influence over the investee, or by a company acquiring its investment with other investors and control of the investee company being shared amongst all the investors. The investor has more than merely a passive interest in the operations and financial results of the investee, and the accounting treatment of either the associate or the joint arrangement reflects this. This is the subject of Chapter 16.

Table 15.1 Categories of investment of one company in another

Degree of influence	Limited influence	Partial influence		Total influence
Nature of interest	Acquirer has a *passive interest* in acquiree	Acquirer exercises *significant influence* over acquiree	Acquirer *shares control* of acquiree *jointly* with others	Acquirer *controls* acquiree
Resulting category	Simple investment	Associate	Joint arrangement	Subsidiary

15.1.3 Total influence

Total influence is the topic of this chapter. The investor, the parent company, obtains control over the investee, which is termed a subsidiary. What is meant by control, which is at the heart of the consolidation question, is discussed in section 15.2. Where control exists, consolidated financial statements are prepared which incorporate the subsidiary's financial results, assets, liabilities, and cash flows with the parent's. These financial statements are sometimes referred to as group accounts. The method of accounting is called the acquisition method, which is set out in IFRS 3 *Business Combinations*.

15.1.4 The need for consolidated financial statements

 Worked example 15.1: to show the need for consolidated financial statements

Suppose Company P owns 100% of the share capital of company S, which gives it control. In the first year of trading of both companies the following transactions occur:

● P buys goods for £2,000 and sells them to S for £4,000

● P requires S to mark up the goods by 100% and sell them back to P for £8,000

● P then gets S to distribute all its profit by dividend.

These transactions can be represented as shown in Figure 15.1.

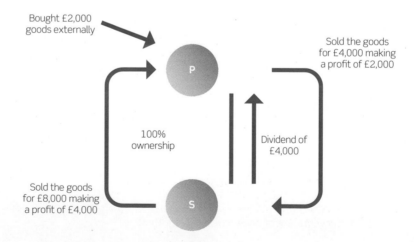

Figure 15.1 Transactions between two companies

P and S are two separate companies, and are legally required to prepare their own individual financial statements. The income statements of these companies will appear as follows:

	P		S	
	£	£	£	£
Sales		4,000		8,000
Purchases	10,000		4,000	
Closing inventory	(8,000)		–	
Cost of sales		(2,000)		(4,000)
Net profit		2,000		4,000
Dividends received		4,000		–
Dividends paid		–		(4,000)
Retained profit		6,000		–

If the investors in company P received P's individual financial statements only, they may anticipate a dividend of up to £6,000 as a result of these transactions. If company P marked up the goods again, sold them on to S, which did the same and sold them back to P, and so on, company P could appear to make an ever increasing amount of profit! Clearly, this is misleading and does not represent the economic reality of the situation.

The initial scenario is that company P has bought some goods and still has them at the end of the financial period. The financial statements that the investors in company P receive should reflect this position and not show bogus profits. As company P controls company S, consolidated financial statements, which include the financial transactions of the two companies taken together as if they were one, would reflect the commercial reality and be faithfully representative of this.

Consolidated financial statements are therefore designed to extend the reporting entity to include other entities which are subject to its control. This means that the assets, liabilities, and activities of subsidiary companies are treated as if they were part of the parent company's own net assets and activities. The overall aim is to present the financial results and position of the reporting company, and its subsidiaries, the group, as if they were those of a single entity. The shareholders in the parent company become the group shareholders, and are interested in the consolidated financial statements. The financial results and position of the individual parent company become mainly irrelevant.

However, the parent company and all its subsidiary companies are separate legal entities, and are required by UK legislation to prepare and file individual financial statements. When a group annual report is prepared, the consolidated financial statements and the parent company's individual financial statements are both included. The subsidiaries' individual financial statements are not part of this.

Many listed groups will consist of the parent company, which is a public listed company, with the subsidiary companies being private limited companies. The group financial statements are required to include information about the subsidiary companies so that the users understand the composition of the group.

Financial reporting in practice 15.1　　　　　|　J Sainsbury plc, 2011　|

J Sainsbury plc's 2011 financial statements contain the following information about its subsidiary companies.

Note 13 - Investments in subsidiaries

The Company's principal operating subsidiaries, all of which are directly owned by the Company, are:

	Share of ordinary allotted capital and voting rights	Country of registration or incorporation
JS Insurance Ltd	100%	Isle of Man
JS Information Systems Ltd	100%	England
Sainsbury's Supermarkets Ltd	100%	England

All principal operating subsidiaries operate in the countries of their registration or incorporation, and have been consolidated up to and as at 19 March 2011. The Company has taken advantage of the exemption in s410 of the Companies Act 2006 only to disclose a list comprising solely of the principal subsidiaries. A full list of subsidiaries will be sent to Companies House with the next annual return.

15.2 Control

15.2.1 Ownership versus control

The definition of a subsidiary company is fundamental to the preparation of consolidated financial statements. When consolidated financial statements were originally introduced in the early part of the twentieth century, this was determined by reference to legal owner-ship. If an investing company owned more than 50% of the voting share capital of another company, it was deemed to control the investee, as resolutions at the annual general meeting (AGM) are passed by simple majority.

This ownership model generally sufficed for determining control until the 1970s. However, from this time, it became more common for companies to set up other entities in which they had little or no legal ownership interest, but which they effectively controlled. These entities, sometimes referred to as **special purpose entities** (SPEs), could be used to undertake borrowings, which, because the entity was not 'controlled' according to the legal ownership model, would not be consolidated into the statement of financial position of the 'parent' company. The effect could be a case of off balance sheet financing, an illustration of which is provided in Figure 15.2.

In the situation illustrated in Figure 15.2 the sponsor may hold a minority of the equity of the SPE or none of it, and may or may not retain a beneficial interest. The sponsor may

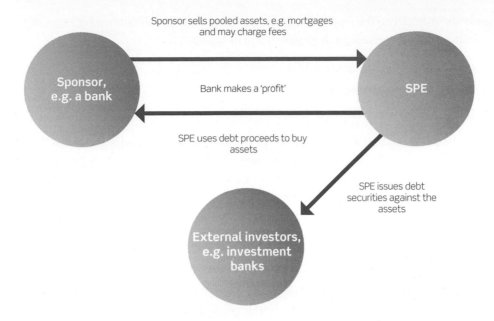

Figure 15.2 Example of a special purpose entity

appoint an independent fund manager. However, if the sponsor retains the right to modify decision-making powers and liquidate the SPE, then effective control is present.

The case of Enron comes to mind when considering this form of off balance sheet financing. Enron hid its losses and vast debts in various entities in which it had minimal ownership interest, but which it did control. According to the narrowly drawn rules contained in the US accounting standards at the time, which were based on the concept of legal ownership, the entities were not consolidated in Enron's financial statements, with the result that Enron's financial results and position appeared much better than it really was. Once Enron had collapsed, its SPEs came to light, leading to questions being raised about the rules-based nature of the accounting standards. Critics said at the time that this type of disaster could not have happened within a principles based regulatory environment where the issue of ownership versus control would have been resolved by following the substance over form approach.

15.2.2 IASB business combinations project

Ever since it was formed in 2001, the IASB has been working on a consolidations project to improve the quality of accounting for business combinations and address the diversity that has existed in practice. The project has been conducted in a number of phases, with the latest being in conjunction with the US Financial Accounting Standards Board (FASB). Over the years this has resulted in many revisions to the international accounting standards dealing with business combinations, which were assumed in 2001, and the issue of others to replace standards withdrawn. The project was given impetus by the global financial crisis of 2007–8, and culminated in the issue of three new IFRSs in May 2011:

- IFRS 10 *Consolidated Financial Statements*
- IFRS 11 *Joint Arrangements*
- IFRS 12 *Disclosure of Interests in Other Entities*.

IFRS 10 is the standard which addresses the definition of control and requires that the same control criteria is applied to all entities. It has replaced those parts of IAS 27 *Separate Financial Statements* that dealt with control and SIC-12 *Consolidation – Special Purpose Entities*. IFRS 12 requires enhanced disclosures of the composition of group structures, the relationships a reporting company has with other entities, specifically those with special purpose or **structured entities**, and the risks companies are exposed to from their involvement with such entities.

For the vast majority of companies with straightforward investments, these new standards will not alter whether they are consolidated or not. However, other companies with more complex investments will have to consider the revised requirements carefully. These latter investments are largely outside the scope of this textbook. Companies have been given some time in which to assimilate the new standards, as they are not required to be adopted until the first accounting periods beginning on, or after, 1 January 2013.

15.2.3 Definition of control

The definition of control now has three elements, all of which must be present:

- power over the investee from existing rights
- exposure, or rights, to variable returns from the investee
- the ability to use power to affect the amount of the investor's returns that the investor receives.

Power is the ability of the investor to direct those activities which significantly affect the investee's returns—termed the relevant activities. It arises from rights, which may be straightforward to identify (e.g. through holding more than 50% of voting rights) or may be more complex (e.g. through one or more contractual arrangements).

A company which holds less than the majority of voting rights of the investee may still have control, which would lead to the consolidation of the investee. All facts and circumstances would need to be considered and, as critics have already pointed out, significant judgement exercised. Examples of other factors could be:

- where the investee is a structured entity, in other words one which has been designed so that voting rights are not the dominant factor in deciding who controls the entity—e. g., voting rights may relate only to administrative matters and the key activities which affect returns are directed by means of contractual arrangements

- where the investor has substantive potential voting rights, in other words the investor has the practical ability to exercise its voting rights even though they may not be exercisable

- where the investor is an agent and its principal has delegated decision-making authority to the agent.

IFRS 10 contains extensive application guidance to assist companies in determining whether they control and have power over another entity. One area in particular that is addressed is where the investor holds less than the majority of the voting rights, but it has the practical ability to direct the relevant activities unilaterally owing to the size and dispersion of the other shareholders' holdings.

 Examples of power with a significant minority shareholding

Consider the following situations:

1 Company A holds 45% of the voting rights of company B. The remaining voting rights are held by many other shareholders, none individually holding more than 1% of the voting rights.

2 Company A holds 45% of the voting rights of company B. Two other investors each hold 26% of the voting rights of B. Three other shareholders own 1% each.

3 Company A holds 45% of the voting rights of company B. Eleven other shareholders each hold 5% of the voting rights of B.

Does company A have power over company B?

1 On the basis of the absolute size of its holding and the relative size of the other shareholdings, company A has a sufficiently dominant voting interest to give it power. It would be unlikely that the other dispersed shareholders would have arrangements where they would consult each other or be able to make collective decisions.

2 In this case, the two shareholders holding 26% of the voting rights could easily cooperate at the AGM, and prevent company A from directing the relevant activities of company B. Company A could therefore not be said to have power over company B.

3 Here, the absolute and relative sizes of the various shareholdings are less conclusive. In practice, if there are no arrangements in place whereby the 11 shareholders each holding 5% of the voting rights could consult each other or make collective decisions, then it may be difficult for them to do so and prevent company A from being able to direct the relevant activities.

   However, the fewer the parties that would need to act together to outvote company A, the more reliance needs to be placed on other facts and circumstances to determine whether A has power over B. The history of the pattern of voting by these other shareholders could be examined to see whether they do turn up and vote at all, or whether they always vote in a particular way. IFRS 10 does not provide any bright lines in terms of percentages that would have to be held, or minimum numbers of small minority shareholders. Professional judgement would have to be exercised in this sort of case.

Another area in which application guidance is provided is where rights that the investor has give an investor power over its investee. Examples provided in IFRS 10 include:

(a) Rights to appoint, reassign or remove members of an investee's key management personnel who have the ability to direct the relevant activities – usually the board of directors

(b) Rights to appoint or remove another entity that directs the relevant activities

(c) Rights to direct the investee to enter into, or veto, or make changes to, transactions for the benefit of the investor

(d) The existence of a management contract which gives the investor the ability to direct the relevant activities

Even if contractual rights to carry out the aforementioned do not exist, if the investor has the ability to do so, then this would provide some evidence of power, which could be considered together with any rights that the investor does hold.

15.3 Exemptions from the preparation of consolidated financial statements

IFRS 10 has not changed the situations where a parent company, which has an investment in a subsidiary company, does not have to prepare consolidated financial statements. All of the following must apply:

1   The parent is a wholly-owned or partially-owned subsidiary of another entity itself, and all its other owners do not object to consolidated financial statements not being prepared

2   The parent's ultimate or any intermediate parent produces financial statements that comply with IFRS and are available for public use

3   The parent's debt or equity instruments are not traded in a public market

4   The parent does not file its financial statements with a securities commission or other regulatory organisation for the purpose of issuing any class of instruments in a public market.

15.4 Consolidation techniques

Financial reporting in practice 15.2   J Sainsbury plc, 2011

The accounting policies of Sainsbury's contain a typical note relating to the basis of consolidation:

The acquisition method of accounting is used to account for the acquisition of subsidiaries by the Group. The cost of acquisition is measured as the fair value of the assets given, equity instruments issued and liabilities incurred or assumed at the date of exchange, plus costs directly attributable to the acquisition. Identifiable assets and liabilities acquired are measured at fair value at the acquisition date. The excess of cost over the fair value of the Group's share of identifiable assets and liabilities acquired is recorded as goodwill.

Investments in subsidiaries are carried at cost less any impairment loss in the financial statements of the Company.

Sainsbury's accounting policy note includes some important terminology which refers to the methods used in consolidation:

- acquisition method
- cost of acquisition measured at fair value
- fair value measurement of subsidiary's identifiable assets and liabilities
- goodwill
- impairment loss.

These will be discussed and illustrated in detail together with other techniques of consolidation in the remainder of this chapter. The preparation of a consolidated statement of financial position will be considered first, as many consolidation techniques will be addressed in the preparation of this statement. The method for consolidating a subsidiary company set out in IFRS 3 *Business Combinations* is called the **acquisition method**.

15.4.1 Consideration

To acquire an investment in another company consideration is given in return. This consideration can be in the form of cash or shares, or possibly some other assets, or a combination of these. If there is a cash element to the consideration, this may be deferred or be based on some future performance criteria. The underpinning principle is that the consideration, whatever its type, is measured at fair value.

If cash is given at the date of acquisition then the fair value is the amount of cash. The fair value of deferred cash is its discounted present value. The fair value of any shares given will be the market value of the shares, which will exist for a listed company, and may have to be estimated if not readily available.

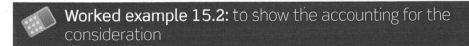

Worked example 15.2: to show the accounting for the consideration

The summarised statement of financial position of Dukes plc at 1 January 20X0 is set out as follows:

	£000
Non-current assets	
Property, plant and equipment	500

Current assets	250
Total assets	750
Equity	
Share capital (£1 shares)	300
Retained earnings	260
	560
Current liabilities	190
Total equity and liabilities	750

On 1 January 20X0 Dukes acquired 100% of the shares of Spring Ltd for £150,000 and gained control.

Required:

Prepare the statement of financial position of Dukes immediately after the acquisition if:

(a) Dukes acquired the shares for cash

(b) Dukes issued 50,000 equity shares of £1 each. At the date of issue the market value of these shares was £3 each.

Dukes plc

Statement of financial position at 1 January 20X0

	(a) Cash acquisition £000	(b) Share exchange £000
Non-current assets		
Property, plant and equipment	500	500
Investment in Spring	150	150
Current assets	100[1]	250
	750	900
Equity		
Share capital (£1 shares)	300	350[2]
Share premium	–	100[2]
Retained earnings	260	260
	560	710
Current liabilities	190	190
	750	900

Notes

1   Cash has decreased by £150,000.

2 The fair value of the 50,000 shares issued is £3 per share. The shares are therefore being issued at a premium of £2 per share.

15.4.2 Date of acquisition

The date of acquisition is the date on which the acquirer obtains control of the acquiree and is generally the date on which the acquirer legally transfers the consideration, acquires the assets, and assumes the liabilities of the acquiree—sometimes referred to as the closing date. However, an acquirer might obtain control on a date that is either earlier or later than the closing date if, for example, there is a written agreement which provides that the acquisition date precedes the closing date. All facts and circumstances need to be considered in identifying the acquisition date.

15.4.3 Acquisition method

Consolidated financial statements present the financial information about the group as a single economic entity. The basic rules of preparation are as follows.

1 The parent company combines the financial statements of itself and its subsidiaries line by line by adding together like items of assets, liabilities, income, and expenses.

2 The carrying amount of the parent's investment in each subsidiary and the parent's portion of equity of each subsidiary are eliminated, which will usually result in goodwill on acquisition arising.

3 Non-controlling interests (NCI) in the profit or loss of consolidated subsidiaries for the reporting period are identified.

4 NCI in the net assets of consolidated subsidiaries are identified separately from the parent's ownership interests in them.

5 Measurement of the subsidiaries' assets and liabilities are at their fair value at the date of acquisition.

15.4.4 Consolidated statement of financial position

The chapter is initially going to deal with consolidated statements of financial position. Taking the simplest case first where the investing company acquires 100% of the equity share capital of the investee, the rules given in section 15.4.3 may be presented as shown in Figure 15.3.

The consolidated statement of financial position in final form shows the total net assets controlled by the group, including 100% of the net assets of the subsidiary, which are valued at fair value as at the date of acquisition, and the ownership interest in these, which here is only the shareholders of P—the group shareholders.

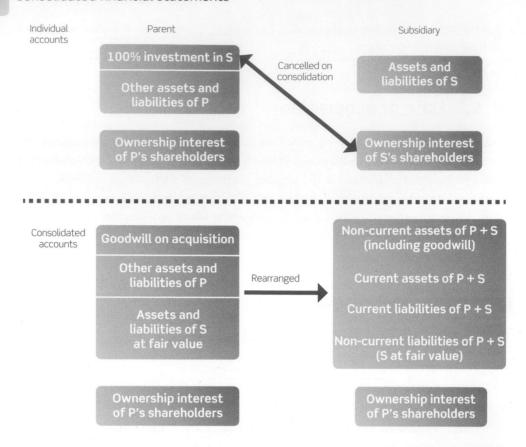

Figure 15.3 Consolidation of statements of financial position: 100% investment

Worked example 15.3: to show the preparation of a consolidated statement of financial position with 100% investment in a subsidiary

P plc has just bought 100% of the shares of S Ltd. The two statements of financial position are as follows:

	P plc	S Ltd
	£	£
Investment in S Ltd	600	
Net assets	400	600
	1,000	600
Share capital	500	200

Retained earnings	500	400
	1,000	600

(Assume that the book values of the net assets in S are equivalent to their fair values.)

Required:
Prepare the consolidated statement of financial position at the date of acquisition.

The investment can be considered as P paying £600 to acquire control of £600 worth of net assets of S. S's net assets equate to its equity, so the investment cancels out with S's equity:

	£
Consideration	600
S's equity	600
	–

The resulting consolidated statement of financial position is as follows:

	£
Net assets (P + S)	1,000
Equity	
Share capital (P only)	500
Retained earnings (P only)	500
	1,000

The group controls net assets valued at £1,000 and the ownership interest in these is all the group shareholders'.

15.4.5 Non-controlling interest (NCI)

As discussed previously, a parent–subsidiary relationship will usually result if the investor acquires more than 50% of the voting rights, which means more than 50% of the equity share capital. So if the investor acquires a proportion of equity shares in S which is less than 100%, but more than 50%, there will remain a minority group of shareholders in S who do not have control, as illustrated by Figure 15.4.

The consolidated statement of financial position will include all the net assets controlled by the group, including 100% of the net assets of the subsidiary at fair value as at the date of acquisition, and the ownership interest in these net assets. This ownership interest, however, will now include that of the non-controlling shareholders in S. This can be represented as shown in Figure 15.5.

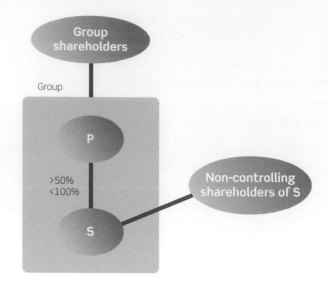

Figure 15.4 Illustration of non-controlling interest

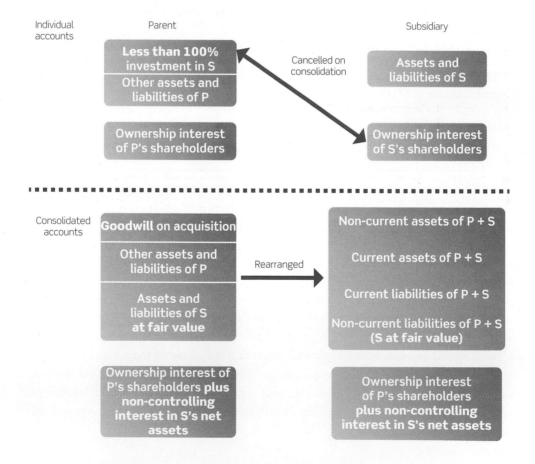

Figure 15.5 Consolidation of statements of financial position: less than 100% investment

Worked example 15.4: to show the preparation of a consolidated statement of financial position with less than 100% investment in a subsidiary

The statements of financial position of P plc and S Ltd are as follows, immediately after P has acquired the shares in S:

	P plc	S Ltd
	£	£
Investment in S Ltd (800 shares)	2,400	
Net assets	2,300	3,000
	4,700	3,000
Share capital (£1 equity shares)	2,000	1,000
Retained earnings	2,700	2,000
	4,700	3,000

(Assume that the book values of the net assets in S are equivalent to their fair values.)

Required:

Prepare the consolidated statement of financial position at the date of acquisition.

P has acquired 80% (800/1,000) of the equity share capital of S. P still controls S, but there is an NCI in S of 20%.

The value of the investment in S is compared with 80% of the net assets (= 80% of the equity) of S as follows:

	£
Consideration	2,400
Net assets acquired (80% × 3,000)	2,400
	–

The ownership interest of the non-controlling shareholders (NCI) in the net assets of S needs to be shown in the consolidated statement of financial position as:

NCI   = 20% of net assets (= 20% of equity)
        = 20% × £3,000
        = £600

The resulting consolidated statement of financial position is as follows:

	£
Net assets (P + S)	5,300
	5,300
Equity	
Share capital (P only)	2,000
Retained earnings (P only)	2,700

	4,700
NCI	600
	5,300

The group controls net assets valued at £5,300, and there is ownership interest in these from the group shareholders valued at £4,700 and from the 20% non-controlling shareholders in S valued at £600.

15.5 Goodwill on acquisition

As demonstrated in the Worked example 15.4, on the acquisition of a subsidiary, the cost of investment, which is measured at fair value, is compared with the parent's share of the fair value of the assets acquired. In this example the two amounts are the same. However, the acquirer is usually prepared to pay a premium for its investment and thus there will be a resulting excess (debit) balance. This premium represents a payment made by the acquirer in anticipation of future economic benefits from assets that it controls, but that are not identified individually and recognised separately in the subsidiary company in the acquisition process.

The amount therefore fulfils the definition of an asset given in the IASB's *Conceptual Framework* and can thus be recognised as a non-current intangible asset in the consolidated financial statements. The asset is **goodwill arising on acquisition**, and is recognised and accounted for according to the requirements of IAS 38 *Intangible Assets* (see Chapter 11).

 Worked example 15.5: to show goodwill on acquisition

P plc acquires 600 shares in S Ltd and the following statements of financial position are drawn up immediately:

	P plc	S Ltd
	£	£
Investment in S Ltd	1,500	
Net assets	2,500	2,000
	4,000	2,000
Share capital (£1 equity shares)	1,000	1,000
Retained earnings	3,000	1,000
	4,000	2,000

(Assume that the book values of the net assets in S are equivalent to their fair values.)

Required:

Prepare the consolidated statement of financial position at the date of acquisition.

P has acquired 60% (600/1,000) of S's equity share capital. Comparing the consideration transferred for the investment with the share of net assets acquired gives the following:

	£
Consideration	1,500
Net assets acquired (60% × £2,000)	1,200
Goodwill on acquisition	300

P has paid a premium for its share of the net assets because it must expect to gain future benefits from this investment.

The NCI in S Ltd is calculated in the same way as before:

NCI   = 40% of net assets of S (= 40% of equity)

       = 40% × £2,000

       = £800

The resulting consolidated statement of financial position is as follows:

	£
Intangible assets	
Goodwill	300
Other net assets (P + S)	4,500
	4,800
Equity	
Share capital (P only)	1,000
Retained earnings (P only)	3,000
	4,000
NCI	800
	4,800

🔵 **Reminder—goodwill annual impairment test** *Goodwill acquired in a business combination is never amortised, but is tested each year for impairment. For the purpose of its impairment testing, goodwill is allocated to the cash-generating units (CGUs) expected to benefit from the combination, which are then tested for impairment. Any impairment loss is allocated first to goodwill and then to the net assets of the CGU. Any impairment loss passes through the consolidated income statement. (See further example in Chapter 11.)*

15.5.1 Goodwill calculation per IFRS 3 *Business Combinations*

Using the previous example's figures, an alternative method of calculating goodwill could be shown as:

	£
Consideration	1,500
Plus: NCI at acquisition (40% × 2,000)	800
	2,300
Less: Net assets at acquisition (100% × 2,000)	(2,000)
Goodwill on acquisition	300

The resulting goodwill figure is exactly the same, but it is calculated here in accordance with how IFRS 3 defines goodwill:

The acquirer shall recognise goodwill as of the acquisition date measured as the excess of (a) over (b) below:

(a) the aggregate of:

   (i) the consideration transferred measured in accordance with this IFRS, which generally requires acquisition-date fair value;

   (ii) the amount of any non-controlling interest in the acquiree measured in accordance with this IFRS; and

   (iii) in a business combination achieved in stages, the acquisition-date fair value of the acquirer's previously held *equity interest* in the acquiree.

(b) the net of the acquisition-date amounts of the identifiable assets acquired and the liabilities assumed measured in accordance with this IFRS.

(IASB, 2012: para. 32)

Note: (a) (iii) is outside the scope of this textbook, so will be ignored in all future calculations.

In the figures shown below the NCI is valued at its proportionate share of the subsidiary's net assets. When IFRS 3 was revised in 2008, as a result of conclusions reached from the joint IASB/US FASB business combinations project, an alternative method of valuing the NCI was introduced. This method is that NCI can be valued at fair value – in other words at the market value of the shares if this exists.

The effect of this is that NCI in the statement of financial position will be a different value and include its share of the goodwill in the subsidiary.

 Worked example 15.6: to show non-controlling interest (NCI) valued at fair value

P plc acquired 60% of the equity shares of S plc and gained control. At the date of acquisition the summarised statements of financial position of the two companies were as follows:

	P plc	S plc
	£000	£000
Investment in S	90	
Other net assets	270	80
	360	80
Equity		
Share capital (£1 shares)	200	50
Share premium	–	20
Retained earnings	160	10
	360	80

Note

The total of the fair value of the net assets of S plc at acquisition was £120,000. The market value of a £1 share in S at the date of acquisition was £2.75.

Required:

Calculate goodwill arising on acquisition if P values the NCI at:

(a) the fair value of the separable net assets

(b) fair value.

(a)

	£000
Consideration	90
Plus: NCI at acquisition (40% × £120,000)	48
	138
Less: Net assets at acquisition (100% × £120,000)	(120)[1]
Goodwill on acquisition	18

(b)

	£000
Consideration	90
Plus: NCI at acquisition (40% × 50,000 × £2.75)	55
	145
Less: Net assets at acquisition (100% × £120,000)	(120)[1]
Goodwill on acquisition	25

Notes

1 Note this figure in the goodwill calculation is the same under both methods.

So what gives rise to the difference in the two NCI values?

(a) Under method (a), the net assets of S are identified and fair valued separately. A total of these separate fair value figures is calculated and the NCI's share of this total is used in the consolidated financial statements.

(b) Under method (b), the fair value of company S as a whole is used, which is what is reflected in the market price of its shares. The valuation of a company as a whole will include assets which cannot be recognised separately in S's financial statements, in other words internally generated goodwill. So the NCI, calculated as its proportion of the fair value of the company as a whole, will therefore include its share of S's goodwill.

In Worked example 15.6, this can be seen as follows:

	£000
Fair value of S's separable net assets	120.0
Internally generated goodwill	
(not recognised in S's financial statements)	17.5 (balancing figure)
Fair value of S (50,000 × £2.75)	137.5

Under method (b) the NCI includes 40% of S's internally generated goodwill:

40% × £17,500 = £7,000

which is the difference between the NCI figures in (a) and (b) (£55,000 − £48,000 = £7,000).

Since this latter option of valuing NCI was introduced by a revision to IFRS 3 only in 2008, it is not used much by UK companies—it is more common in the USA. Most examples in this textbook therefore require NCI at acquisition to be valued at the fair value of the separable net assets of the subsidiary.

15.5.2 Negative goodwill

Although not very common, goodwill on acquisition may be negative. In this case the acquirer has effectively paid less than the value of its share of the net assets of the acquiree. This is termed a 'bargain purchase' and may arise in practice through a forced sale of the acquiree. The resulting credit balance of goodwill is a gain and is recognised in the consolidated income statement in the year in which the acquisition occurs, and therefore increases consolidated profit and retained earnings.

15.5.3 Multiple investments

A separate goodwill calculation is performed for each investment in a subsidiary—in practice the investments will be on different dates. Negative goodwill is never netted off with positive goodwill. The different NCI balances from different investments will be calculated separately, but combined to give one balance in the consolidated financial statements.

15.5.4 Other issues relating to the goodwill calculation

As part of accounting for the acquisition process, the acquiring company is encouraged to identify and value intangible assets in the subsidiary, even if these are not permitted to be recognised in the subsidiary's own individual financial statements under IAS 38 *Intangible Assets*. For example, internally generated assets not meeting the recognition criteria of IAS 38 or the subsidiary's brands may be identified as separable assets and be able to be measured reliably at fair value. These assets will be recognised as such in the consolidated financial statements and subsequently accounted for according to IAS 38. Note that they will continue to be excluded from recognition in the subsidiary's own financial statements. (See Chapter 11 for further details of intangible assets.)

The intentional effect of this is to reduce the value given to goodwill arising on acquisition. Rather than having a large goodwill balance, calculated as the difference between the consideration and the parent's share of what is recognised in the subsidiary's financial statements on acquisition, the identification and inclusion of exactly what has been acquired in the consolidated financial statements increases their transparency. Users are informed better and the faithful representation of the financial statements is enhanced.

IFRS 3 details some further exceptions to the recognition and measurement of other assets and liabilities of the acquired company at acquisition. Most of these concern items which are outside the scope of this textbook; however, there are a couple which should be noted.

1. Where the subsidiary company has contingent liabilities (see Chapter 13 for full details of contingent liabilities), and they are present obligations that arise from past events and their fair value can be measured reliably, they are recognised as a liability of the subsidiary in the goodwill calculation and consolidated financial statements. This is contrary to IAS 37 *Provisions, Contingent Liabilities and Contingent Assets*, as the liability is recognised, even if it is not probable that an outflow of resources embodying economic benefits will be required to settle the obligation.

   ⚑ **Reminder** *A contingent liability is in IAS 37 defined as:*

   (a) *a possible obligation that arises from past events and whose existence will be confirmed only by the occurrence or non-occurrence of one or more uncertain future events not wholly within the control of the entity; or*

   (b) *a present obligation that arises from past events but is not recognised because:*

     (i) *it is not probable that an outflow of resources embodying economic benefits will be required to settle the obligation; or*

     (ii) *the amount of the obligation cannot be measured with sufficient reliability.*

   It is not recognised in the financial statements, but is disclosed in a note to the financial statements.

2   Assets classified as held for sale in the subsidiary's financial statements at the date of acquisition are valued at fair value less costs to sell, in accordance with IFRS 5 *Non-current Assets Held for Sale and Discontinued Operations*, rather than fair value.

15.6 Consolidated statement of financial position after acquisition date

In all examples considered so far, the consolidated statement of financial position has been drawn up at the date of acquisition. However, parent companies need to present consolidated financial statements at all subsequent financial year ends.

15.6.1 Post-acquisition fair value adjustments

The statement of financial position will include the subsidiaries' net assets as of the date the financial statements are drawn up, but these values will incorporate any adjustments which were made at the date of acquisition to the subsidiaries' net assets to fair value. This may include:

- increases or decreases in property, plant and equipment, and other assets which are still held

- increases or decreases in the property, plant and equipment accumulated depreciation as a result of the revaluation to fair value.

15.6.2 Pre- and post-acquisition reserves

The consolidated reserves (including consolidated retained earnings) will only include changes in the subsidiaries' reserves which have arisen after the date of acquisition. Pre-acquisition reserves, which cancel out in calculation of goodwill, are not available for distribution to the group shareholders.

Adjustments to the consolidated retained earnings will have to be made to account for:

- increased or decreased depreciation on revalued property, plant and equipment

- the realisation of profits or losses from inventories which were revalued to fair value at acquisition and which have subsequently been sold.

The NCI will take its share of any fair value adjustments as they affect values of assets and liabilities of the subsidiary.

Worked example 15.7: to show the accounting for pre- and post-acquisition retained earnings

On 1 January 20X3 P plc acquired 80% of the ordinary share capital of S Ltd for £150,000 cash. The statements of financial position of the two companies at 31 December 20X3 were as follows:

	P plc	S Ltd
	£000	£000
Property, plant and equipment (PPE)	400	70
Investment in S	150	
Other net assets	220	40
	770	110
Equity share capital (£1 shares)	200	30
Retained earnings	570	80
	770	110

On 1 January 20X3 the retained earnings of S were £50,000. On this date the fair value of S's PPE was £20,000 in excess of the book values. S depreciates its PPE using the straight-line method and, at 1 January 20X3, these assets had a remaining useful life of ten years.

Required:
Prepare the consolidated statement of financial position at 31 December 20X3.

If S had included the revaluation of its PPE to fair value in its financial statements, it would have made the adjustment:

		£000	£000
Debit	PPE	20	
Credit	Revaluation reserve		20

The goodwill calculation incorporates this and becomes:

	£000
Consideration	150
Add: NCI share of [*FV of net assets* of subsidiary]	
[= Share capital + reserves including notional	
revaluation reserve *at date of acquisition*]	
20% × [30 + 50 + 20]	20
	170
Less: FV of net assets of subsidiary (30 + 50 + 20)	(100)
Goodwill	70

The fair value adjustment to S's PPE means that additional annual depreciation of £20,000/10 = £2,000 has to be accounted for in the consolidated financial statements:

- in consolidated PPE—in this example one year's additional accumulated depreciation
- in consolidated retained earnings
- and it affects the NCI balance.

Working 1—PPE

	£000
P	400
S	70
Fair value adjustment	20
Less: additional depreciation	(2)
	488

Working 2—Consolidated retained earnings

	£000
P	570
P's share of post-acquisition retained earnings of S	
adjusted for additional depreciation	
80% × [(80 – 50) – 2]	22.4
	592.4

Working 3—NCI

	£000
S's net assets at 31 December 20X3	110
Fair value adjustment	20
Additional depreciation	(2)
	128
NCI share 20% × 128	25.6

Consolidated statement of financial position

	£000
Goodwill	70
Property, plant and equipment	488
Other net assets (P + S)	260
	818
Equity share capital	200

Retained earnings		592.4
		792.4
NCI		25.6
		818

15.7 Acquisition of preference shares and other financial instruments in the subsidiary

15.7.1 Preference shares

The acquisition of preference shares of the subsidiary does not affect the question of control, as preference shares (usually) do not carry voting rights or possess rights to reserves. However, the consideration for the preference shares may not equate to their par value and therefore goodwill on acquisition may arise. If the preference shares are acquired at the same time as the equity shares, the calculation of this goodwill is subsumed within the calculation of goodwill on the purchase of the equity shares.

The proportion of preference shares not held by the parent company forms part of NCI and is measured at the appropriate percentage of the par value of the shares. This is amalgamated with other NCI balances.

Any other reserves in the subsidiary's accounts are divided between the parent's share and the NCI's share according to the percentage ownership of the equity shares.

 Worked example 15.8: to show preparation of a consolidated statement of financial position including preference shares

P plc has purchased 800 equity shares and 40 preference shares in S Ltd. S Ltd's issued share capital comprises £200 in equity 20p shares and £100 in £1 preference shares. The statements of financial position of the two companies immediately after the acquisition of the shares by P are as follows:

	P plc	S Ltd
	£	£
Investment in S Ltd	950	
Net assets	50	600
	1,000	600
Equity		
Equity shares	450	200

Preference shares	50	100
Retained earnings	500	300
	1,000	600

At the date of acquisition, the fair values of S Ltd's net assets were £750.

Required:

Prepare the consolidated statement of financial position at the date of acquisition.

% shareholdings

Ordinary shares	800/(200 × 5*)	80%
Preference shares	40/100	40%

* S Ltd's equity shares are 20p shares, so £1-worth of share capital equates to 5 shares. S Ltd has issued £200-worth of equity shares.

The shareholdings can be represented as shown in Figure 15.6.

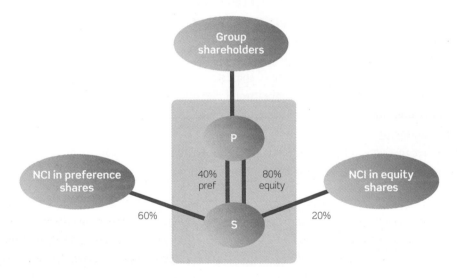

Figure 15.6 Group structure

Working—goodwill

	£	£
Consideration		950
Add: NCI in fair value of net assets of S		
Equity share capital	200	
Retained earnings	300	
Fair value adjustment	150	
20% × 650	130

Preference share capital	60% × 100	60
		1,140
Less: Fair value of net assets of S		750
Goodwill		390

Consolidated statement of financial position

	£
Goodwill	390
Other net assets (50 + 600 + 150)	800
	1,190
Equity	
Equity shares (P only)	450
Preference shares (P only)	50
Retained earnings (P only)	500
	1,000
NCI (130 + 60)	190
	1,190

15.7.2 Other financial instruments

Like preference shares, the acquisition of debentures or bonds or other forms of long-term debt in the subsidiary does not affect the question of control. If the acquisition occurs at the same time as the acquisition of equity and possibly preference shares, the cost of the instruments to the parent will be part of the consideration in the calculation of goodwill so that any premium or discount is dealt with in goodwill. The intercompany loan will be cancelled out in the consolidated statement of financial position (see section 15.8).

Any portion of the debt instruments not acquired by the parent at the date of acquisition is not part of NCI though. This remains as a liability in the consolidated statement of financial position.

15.8 Intragroup transactions and balances

It is very common for companies with the same group to trade with each other. For example, a group may comprise a manufacturing company, a distribution company and a retailer. Other assets may be bought and sold between the group companies, and it is also usual for the parent company to charge management fees to the subsidiary companies it controls, possibly to reflect the time the directors and senior management personnel of the parent have spent directing and controlling the operations of the subsidiary.

As seen in Worked example 15.1, which demonstrated the need for consolidated financial statements, transactions between group companies should not be reflected in the consolidated accounts. Given that each company records the transactions in their own individual financial statements, the consolidation process requires adjustments to be made to cancel these out.

A sale from one group company to another is a purchase in this other company's accounts; thus, for consolidated financial statements purposes, the sale will cancel out with the purchase. Any management charge will be recorded as fee income in the parent's accounts, which will cancel out on consolidation with the management fee expenses in the subsidiaries' accounts.

These transactions are likely to be on credit terms, and so receivable and payable balances will exist between the group companies. In the statement of financial position these intragroup balances are cancelled out. The consolidated financial statements will therefore show the transactions and resulting balances of the group as a single entity.

 Example of intragroup receivables and payables

P plc owns 75% of the equity share capital of S Ltd.

1   P plc sells goods to S Ltd and at the financial year end S owes P £50,000.

   P plc will have the balance of £50,000 included in its trade receivables and S Ltd will have a corresponding £50,000 included in its trade payables.

   When the consolidated statement of financial position is drawn up, £50,000 will be deducted from both trade receivables and trade payables.

2   Suppose just before the year end, S Ltd sends a cheque to P plc for £20,000 as part settlement of its liability, but P does not receive this until a few days into the new financial year.

   P will still have a balance of £50,000 included in its trade receivables, but the trade payables balance in S's accounts will now be £30,000. The two balances will not fully cancel each other out.

   This situation is referred to as **cash-in-transit**. The cash is accounted for in the consolidated financial statements as if it had been received by P plc by the financial year end. So consolidated bank balances are increased by £20,000 and P's trade receivables are reduced by £20,000:

Debit   Bank
  Credit   Trade receivables

The resulting intragroup trade receivable and trade payable of £30,000 now cancel out on consolidation.

15.8.1 Unrealised profit in inventories

The cancellation of these transactions will not affect consolidated profits. However, consider the situation where one group company makes a profit from the sale of goods to another and some of these goods are on hand in the buyer's inventories at the consolidated statement of financial position date. The profit element included in the value of these inventories needs to be eliminated on consolidation as it has not yet been realised by selling the goods on outside the group.

 Example of unrealised profit in inventories

Company S is a subsidiary of company P. During the year, P purchases goods for £160. P sells these goods onto S for £280. By the end of the year S has sold three-quarters of these goods to customers outside the group.
   This may be represented by Figure 15.7.

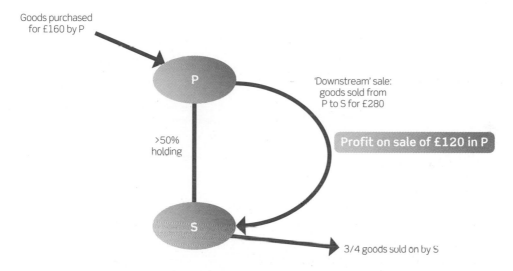

Figure 15.7 Intragroup trading and unrealised profit in inventories

   At the year end one-quarter of the goods remain in S's inventories. These had cost S $1/4 \times 280 = £70$. The concept of the group being a single entity means that the consolidated financial statements should reflect the cost of the goods to the group, which is $1/4 \times 160 = £40$.
   The profit element of £30 (£70 – £40) is therefore eliminated from consolidated inventories. As unrealised profit, it is also eliminated from P's profits.

   Now consider the situation using the same figures, but reversing the direction of the sale so that it is an **upstream sale** from S to P, with the inventories in P's accounts and S having made the profit. The profit element of £30 is still eliminated from consolidated inventories. The unrealised profit has to be eliminated from S's profits, which means that the NCI in S take its share of this unrealised profit.

   Note: care should be taken when calculating the unrealised profit on inventories. Details may be provided in the form of a gross profit/margin percentage or a mark-up. Gross profit/margin is a percentage based on selling price, while mark-up is a percentage based on cost.

Example of gross margin versus mark-up

1   Goods are sold for £600 at a mark-up of 25%

Profit included = **25/125** × £600 = £120

2   Goods are sold for £1,000 giving a gross margin of 25%

Profit included = **25/100** × £1,000 = £250

 Worked example 15.9: to show the accounting for intragroup balances and unrealised profit in inventories

P plc acquired 60% of the shares of S Ltd on 31 December 20X5. The two statements of financial position at 31 December 20X6 are as follows:

	P plc		S Ltd	
	£	£	£	£
Non-current assets		280		150
Investment in S Ltd		160		
		440		
Current assets				
Inventories	240		220	
Receivables	200		130	
Bank	60		30	
		500		380
Total assets		940		530
Equity				
Share capital		200		100
Retained earnings		400		160
		600		260
Payables		340		270
Total equity and liabilities		940		530

At the date of acquisition the retained earnings of S Ltd were £70. At this date, the fair values of S's non-current assets were determined as £50 greater than their carrying amounts with an estimated remaining useful life of 10 years. S uses the straight-line method of depreciation.

During 20X6 P plc sold goods which had cost £160 to S Ltd for £280. Of these goods, S had sold three-quarters by 31 December 20X6.

At 31 December 20X6 S Ltd owed P plc £50.

Required:

Prepare the consolidated statement of financial position at 31 December 20X6.

Workings

Working 1—goodwill

	£
Investment	160
Add: NCI in fair value of net assets of S at acquisition	
= 40% × (share capital + reserves + fair value adjustment at date of acquisition)	
= 40% × (100 + 70 + 50)	88
	248
Less: Fair value of net assets of S at acquisition	(220)
Goodwill	28

Working 2—unrealised profit in inventories

Sale from P to S—'downstream' sale.

Eliminate unrealised profit of £30 from closing inventories and consolidated retained earnings.

Working 3—intercompany debt

Intercompany debt of £50 eliminated from consolidated receivables and payables.

Working 4—non-current assets

	£
P	280
S	150
Plus: fair value adjustment	50
Less: additional fair value depreciation (£50/10)	(5)
	475

Working 4—consolidated retained earnings

	£
P plc	400
Less: unrealised profit in inventories	(30)
Plus: share of S's post-acquisition retained earnings adjusted for fair value depreciation 60% × (160 − 70 − 5)	51
	421

Working 5—non-controlling interest (NCI)

	£
NCI share of S's net assets at 31 December 20X6 adjusted for fair values	
40% × (260 + 50 − 5)	122

Consolidated statement of financial position at 31 December 20X6

		£	£
Non-current assets			475
Goodwill			28
			503
Current assets			
Inventories	(240 + 220 – 30)	430	
Receivables	(200 + 130 – 50)	280	
Bank	(60 + 30)	90	
			800
Total assets			1,303
Equity			
Share capital	(P only)		200
Retained earnings			421
			621
NCI			122
Payables	(340 + 270 – 50)		560
Total equity and liabilities			1,303

15.9 Consolidated income statement

As discussed earlier, the consolidated financial statements for a parent and its subsidiary companies are prepared using the acquisition method. For the income statement this means that all like items of income and expenses are added together line by line. Note, as for assets and liabilities, 100% of the subsidiaries' income and expenses are included, irrespective of whether the shareholding of the parent in the subsidiaries is less than 100%. Remember the parent controls its subsidiaries, so it controls their profits completely.

Intercompany trading activities as described in section 15.8 have to be eliminated so that the results of the group as a single entity are shown. This will also include elimination of dividends received by the parent from the subsidiaries.

Consolidation items that have been seen so far in this chapter as adjustments to consolidated retained earnings will be included under an appropriate heading in the consolidated income statement. These will include:

- the provision for unrealised profit in closing inventories
- additional depreciation on the subsidiaries' non-current assets revalued to fair value at the date of acquisition
- goodwill impairment.

The NCIs in the profit or loss of consolidated subsidiaries for the reporting period are identified and shown at the foot of the income statement.

If a subsidiary company is acquired part-way through the reporting period, the income and expenses of the subsidiary are only included from the date of acquisition. This may require time-apportionment of these items.

 Worked example 15.10: to show the preparation of a consolidated income statement

P plc purchased 80% of the ordinary shares in S Ltd on 1 January 20X1. Income statements of the companies for the year ended 31 December 20X2 are as follows:

	P plc		S Ltd	
	£000	£000	£000	£000
Revenue		640		330
Cost of sales		410		200
Gross profit		230		130
Distribution costs	35		20	
Administrative expenses	70	105	55	75
Profit from operations		125		55
Income from investments		28		–
Profit before tax		153		55
Tax		26		10
Profit for the year		127		45

Notes

1 During 20X2 S sold goods, which had cost it £20,000, to P. S marked up these goods by 50%.

2 By the year end 30% of these goods had not been sold by P.

3 During 20X2 S paid total dividends of £35,000.

4 At the date of acquisition the fair values of S's non-current assets were £100,000 greater than their book values. S uses a 10% straight-line depreciation policy.

Required:
Prepare the consolidated income statement for the year ended 31 December 20X2.

Working 1—investment income

The first item to check is whether the investment income in P's income statement is completely from dividends received from S or whether there is any other investment income from sources external to the group.

$$\text{Intragroup dividend} = 80\% \times \text{S's dividend}$$
$$= 80\% \times £35,000$$
$$= £28,000$$

This is equivalent to the investment income in P's income statement. Hence, P's income from investments is cancelled out on consolidation.

Working 2—intercompany sales

	£
Cost of intercompany sales	20,000
Mark-up	10,000
Selling price	30,000

£30,000 is eliminated from both sales and purchases (S's sale is P's purchase).

Working 3—unrealised profit in inventories

P's closing inventories must be reduced to the cost to the group.

Thirty per cent of the £10,000 profit from the intercompany sale is deducted from closing inventories. This has the effect of *increasing* consolidated cost of sales by £3,000.

The sale is an 'upstream' sale from S to P. Thus, the NCI in S takes its share of the elimination of this profit element.

Working 4—fair value depreciation

The additional depreciation on the larger fair values of S's non-current assets is included in the consolidated income statement.

$$\text{Additional depreciation} = 10\% \times £100,000 = £10,000$$

Working 5—NCI in S's profit

	£000
S's profit after tax	45
Less: unrealised profit in inventories	(3)
Less: additional FV depreciation	(10)
	32

NCI in S's profit = 20% × 32,000 = £6,400

P plc's consolidated income statement for the year ended 31 December 20X2

		£000	£000
Revenue	(P + S – intercompany)		
	(640 + 330 – 30)		940
Cost of sales	(P + S – intercompany		

	+ unrealised profit in inventories)		
	(410 + 200 − 30 + 3)		583
Gross profit			357
Distribution costs	(35 + 20)	55	
Administrative expenses	(70 + 55 + FV depreciation 10)	135	
			190
Profit before tax			167
Tax	(26 + 10)		36
Profit for the year			131
Attributable to:			
Shareholders of the group (balancing figure) *			124.6
NCI			6.4
			131

* Note that the NCI in S's net profit is calculated first. The profit attributable to the group shareholders is the balancing figure.

15.9.1 Consolidated statement of comprehensive income

As discussed in Chapter 4, the income statement is either presented on its own with a statement of other comprehensive income and losses as an additional statement, or the income statement forms part of the statement of comprehensive income. Chapter 4 indicated that the main item of other comprehensive income within the scope of this textbook related to the surpluses or deficits on revaluations of property, plant and equipment (see Chapter 10 for details of these).

For the purpose of this textbook, consolidated statements of comprehensive income will, therefore, be limited to only including items arising from property, plant and equipment revaluations in the parent company. Note that if this were to be included, the interest in the group's profit for the year and in the group's total comprehensive income from the group's shareholders and the NCI should be disclosed, as shown by the example in Chapter 4.

15.10 Consolidated statement of changes in equity

🅘 **Reminder** *The consolidated statement of changes in equity shows the changes in the equity balances over the course of the financial year. The closing balances on this statement are transferred to the equity section of the statement of financial position.*

Chapters 1 and 4 discuss this statement in detail.

The consolidated statement of changes in equity requires a column showing the changes in NCI over the year. If a subsidiary has been acquired during the financial year this column will also have to include any NCI valued at the date of acquisition. A pro forma consolidated statement of changes in equity is shown in the Example statement.

 Example statement

Company XXX

Consolidated statement of changes in equity for the accounting period

	Share capital £000	Share premium £000	Retained earnings £000	NCI £000	Total £000
At start of year	XX	XX	XX	XX	XX
On acquisition of subsidiary				XX	XX
Profit for year [1]			XX	XX	XX
Dividends paid [2]			(XX)	(XX)	(XX)
At end of year	XX	XX	XX	XX	XX

[1] The figures for the profit for the year are the figures from the bottom section of the income statement.

[2] The dividends deducted from consolidated retained earnings are dividends paid to the group shareholders. The dividends deducted from the NCI column are the NCI's share of dividends paid by the subsidiaries.

 Worked example 15.11: to show the preparation of a consolidated statement of changes in equity

Using the details given in the income statement in Worked example 15.10, further information is as follows.

1   The equity account balances of P and S at 31 December 20X1 were as follows:

	P plc £000	S Ltd £000
Equity share capital	150	80
Share premium	60	–
Retained earnings	129	140
	339	220

2   At the date of acquisition S's retained earnings were £90,000.

3   During the year ended 31 December 20X2 P paid total dividends of £50,000.

Required:

Prepare the consolidated statement of changes in equity for the year ended 31 December 20X2.

Working 1—consolidated retained earnings at 1 January 20X2

Remember, this is a statement of financial position balance, so the workings are as detailed in section 15.6.2.

	£000
P	129
P's share of S's post-acquisition retained earnings *at 1 January 20X2*	
adjusted for accumulated fair value depreciation	
80% × (140 − 90 − 1 year × 10)	32
	161

Working 2—NCI at 1 January 20X2

Remember, this is also a statement of financial position balance, so the workings are as detailed in section 15.4.5.

	£000	£000
NCI share of S's net assets at fair value *at 1 January 20X2*		
[Remember net assets at fair value = equity + fair value adjustment]		
Share capital	80	
Retained earnings	140	
Fair value adjustment	100	
Fair value accumulated depreciation (1 year × 10)	(10)	
	20% × 310	62

Working 3—dividends paid

Dividends paid to the group shareholders of £50,000 will be deducted from consolidated retained earnings.

Dividends paid to the NCI in S = 20% × £35,000 = £7,000

Consolidated statement of changes in equity for the year ended 31 December 20X2

	Share capital £000	Share premium £000	Retained earnings £000	NCI £000	Total £000
At 1 January 20X2	150	60	161	62	433
Profit for year			124.6	6.4	131
Dividends paid			(50)	(7)	(57)
At 31 December 20X2	150	60	235.6	61.4	507

The balances at 31 December 20X2 are the balances which will be transferred to the statement of financial position.

These balances can be checked as follows.

Consolidated retained earnings at 31 December 20X2

	£000	£000
P (129 + 127 – 50)		206
P's share of S's post-acquisition retained earnings *at 31 December 20X2* adjusted for unrealised profit in inventories and accumulated fair value depreciation:		
Post-acquisition retained earnings ((140 + 45 – 35) – 90)	60	
Unrealised profit in inventories	(3)	
Fair value accumulated depreciation (2 years × 10)	(20)	
80% × 37		29.6
		235.6

NCI at 31 December 20X2

	£000	£000
NCI share of S's net assets at fair value *at 31 December 20X2*		
Share capital	80	
Retained earnings (140 + 45 – 35)	150	
Unrealised profit in inventories	(3)	
Fair value adjustment	100	
Fair value accumulated depreciation (2 years × 10)	(20)	
20% × 307		61.4

15.11 Disclosures in the financial statements

In its latest accounting standards relating to consolidations, the IASB produced a separate standard specifically addressing disclosures—IFRS 12 *Disclosure of Interests in Other Entities*. This details the disclosures required for all categories of investments by one company in another, except for simple investments, which are dealt with by IFRS 7 *Financial Instruments: Disclosures*. Users of financial statements had been constantly requesting improvements to the disclosure of a company's interests in other entities to help identify the profit or loss and cash flows available to the investing company, and to determine the value of a current or future investment. The 2007 global financial crisis also highlighted a lack of transparency about the risks to which a company was exposed from its involvement with special purpose and structured entities.

IFRS 12 therefore combines disclosure requirements for interests in subsidiaries, associates, joint arrangements and unconsolidated structured entities. Those relating to associates and joint arrangements are discussed further in Chapter 16.

Importantly for users, the significant judgements and assumptions a company has made in determining the nature of its interest in another entity or arrangement, and in determining the type of joint arrangement in which it has an interest must be disclosed. The impact of this is that where the determination of control, in other words the question of whether an investee is a subsidiary and should be consolidated, is not straightforward—the reporting company has to explain the basis for its decisions.

If a company has interests in a structured entity that it does not consolidate, then it must provide sufficient information to enable users:

(a) to understand the nature and extent of its interests in unconsolidated structured entities; and

(b) to evaluate the nature of, and changes in, the risks associated with its interests in unconsolidated structured entities.

Quantitative and qualitative information is required to explain the interest in the entities, together with the company's maximum exposure to losses which may arise from the investments.

15.11.1 Disclosures of interests in subsidiary companies

Disclosures of interests in subsidiary companies are required to enable users of the consolidated financial statements:

(a) to understand:

(i) the composition of the group; and

(ii) the interest that non-controlling interests have in the group's activities and cash flows; and

(b) to evaluate:

    (i) the nature and extent of significant restrictions on the parent company's ability to access or use assets, and settle liabilities, of the group;

    (ii) the nature of, and changes in, the risks associated with the parent's interests in consolidated structured entities;

    (iii) the consequences of changes in the ownership interest in a subsidiary that do not result in a loss of control; and

    (iv) the consequences of losing control of a subsidiary during the reporting period.

This will include factual information about a subsidiary and a summary of its financial information. However, there is again a focus on the provision of information about the risks arising from the investments.

Financial reporting in practice 15.3   Barclays plc, 2011

Note: for its 2011 financial statements, Barclays applied IAS 27 *Consolidated and Separate Financial Statements* and SIC 12 *Consolidation – Special Purpose Entities (SPEs)*, the accounting standards applicable for these financial statements. Therefore, not all of the aforementioned disclosures will be seen in this example.

Accounting policy – Consolidation

The consolidated financial statements combine the financial statements of Barclays PLC and all its subsidiaries. Subsidiaries are entities over which it has control of the financial and operating policies through its holdings of voting shares and SPEs, which are consolidated when the substance of the relationship between the Group and the entity indicates control. The control assessment for special purpose entities includes an assessment of the Group's exposure to the risks and benefits of the entity. The consolidation of SPEs is considered at inception, based on the arrangements in place and the assessed risk exposures at that time. The initial consolidation analysis is revisited at a later date if:

- the Group acquires additional interests in the entity;
- the contractual arrangements of the entity are amended such that the relative exposures to risks and rewards change; and
- the Group acquires control over the main operating and financial decisions of the entity.

  Intra-group transactions and balances are eliminated on consolidation and consistent accounting policies are used throughout the Group for the purposes of the consolidation.

  Changes in ownership interests in subsidiaries are accounted for as equity transactions if they occur after control has already been obtained and they do not result in loss of control.

  Details of the principal subsidiaries are given in Note 40.

Note 40 – Investments in subsidiaries

Principal subsidiaries for the Group are set out below. This list has been revised to include those subsidiaries that are significant in the context of the Group's business, results or financial position.

Country of registration or incorporation	Company name	Nature of business	Percentage of equity capital held (%)
England	Barclays Bank PLC	Banking, holding company	100
England	Barclays Bank Trust Company Limited	Banking, securities industries and trust services	100
England	Barclays Stockbrokers Limited	Stockbroking	100
England	Barclays Capital Securities Limited	Securities dealing	100
England	FIRSTPLUS Financial Group PLC	Secured loan provider	100*
Isle of Man	Barclays Private Clients International Limited	Banking	100*
Japan	Barclays Capital Japan Limited	Securities dealing	100
Kenya	Barclays Bank of Kenya Limited	Banking	68.5*
South Africa	Absa Group Limited	Banking	55.5*
Spain	Barclays Bank SA	Banking	100*
USA	Barclays Capital Inc.	Securities dealing	100
USA	Barclays Bank Delaware	US credit card issuer	100
USA	Barclays Group US Inc.	Holding company	100*

The country of registration or incorporation is also the principal area of operation of each of the above subsidiaries. Investments in subsidiaries held directly by Barclays Bank PLC are marked*. Full information of all subsidiaries will be included in the Annual Return to be filed at UK Companies House.

Although the Group's interest in the equity voting rights in certain entities listed below may exceed 50%, or it may have the power to appoint a majority of their Boards of Directors, they are excluded from consolidation because the Group either does not direct the financial and operating policies of these entities, or another entity has a controlling interest in them. Consequently, these entities are not controlled by Barclays:

Country of registration or incorporation	Company name	Percentage of ordinary share capital held %	Equity shareholders' funds £m	Retained profit for the year £m
UK	Fitzroy Finance Limited	100	–	–
Cayman Islands	Palomino Limited	100	1	–

Summary of key points

With one or two exceptions, consolidated financial statements are required to be drawn up for a parent company and its subsidiary companies—the group—as if the group were a single entity. The key issue in determining whether the investee company is a subsidiary or not, and therefore whether it should be consolidated or not, is that of control. The issue of control has been the subject of much deliberation by the IASB and is the main subject of the IASB's recent accounting standard IFRS 10 *Consolidated Financial Statements*, in which it is defined as having three elements for the investor:

- power over the investee
- exposure or rights to variable returns from the investee
- ability to use power to affect the reporting company's returns.

In the vast majority of situations within the scope of this textbook, control is present through the parent company holding more than 50% of the voting or equity share capital of the subsidiary. However, a principles-based definition of control is very important, not least to eliminate the possibilities of entities which are controlled and not being consolidated, which could lead to off balance sheet financing and financial statements not being faithfully representative.

The chapter has discussed and provided examples of the preparation of a consolidated statement of financial position, income statement, statement of comprehensive income, and statement of changes in equity. The techniques of consolidation follow the acquisition method and require that all assets, liabilities, income, and expenses of the parent company and its subsidiaries are combined line-by-line, with the subsidiaries' figures being incorporated at their fair value at the date of acquisition. The effects of intragroup trading and other activities are eliminated, and if the acquisition is made part-way through the most recent accounting period, only the post-acquisition profit and loss elements of the subsidiary are included. If the parent company holds less than 100% of the voting share capital of a subsidiary company, then there is NCI in this company, which is shown in all consolidated statements.

At the date of acquisition, if the fair value of the consideration plus the NCI in the subsidiary exceeds the fair value of the identified separable net assets of the subsidiary, then goodwill on acquisition arises. This fulfils the definition of an intangible asset and it is recognised in the consolidated financial statements. It is not amortised, but is tested annually for impairment.

The latest accounting standards require that investing companies explain the judgements they made in determining whether to consolidate or exclude from consolidation their interest in other entities. In addition, they should evaluate and disclose their exposure to risk from their consolidated subsidiaries and interests in unconsolidated structured entities.

 ## Further reading

IASB (International Accounting Standards Board) (2011a) IAS 27 *Separate Financial Statements*. London: IASB.

IASB (International Accounting Standards Board) (2011b) IFRS 10 *Consolidated Financial Statements*. London: IASB.

IASB (International Accounting Standards Board) (2012) IFRS 3 *Business Combinations*. London: IASB.

Bibliography

Barclays plc (2012) *Annual Report, 2011*. London: Barclays.

Boulton, J. (2011) *Profit alert!*, ICAEW By All Accounts.

Bloomberg, *M&A Rankings*, Q3 2011.

Bryer, R. (2011a) *Consolidated Accounts I: Theory and Regulations*. Working paper. Coventry: Warwick Business School.

Bryer, R. (2011b) *Consolidated Accounts II: Fair Value Accounting for Acquisitions and Investments*. Working paper. Coventry: Warwick Business School.

Bryer, R. (2012) *Consolidated Accounts III: IFRS 10 and the Problem of Control*. Working paper. Coventry: Warwick Business School.

Davies, A. (2011) A weighty subject *Accountancy* 148 (1420). Available online by subscription only at www.accountancylive.com.

IASB (International Accounting Standards Board) (2011a) IAS 27 *Separate Financial Statements*. London: IASB.

IASB (International Accounting Standards Board) (2012) IFRS 3 *Business Combinations*. London: IASB.

IASB (International Accounting Standards Board) (2011b) IFRS 10 *Consolidated Financial Statements*. London: IASB.

IASB (International Accounting Standards Board) (2011c) IFRS 12 *Disclosure of Interests in Other Entities*. London: IASB.

IASB (International Accounting Standards Board) (2011d) *Effect Analysis: IFRS 10 Consolidated Financial Statements and IFRS 12 Disclosure of Interests in Other Entities*. London: IASB.

IASB (International Accounting Standards Board) (2011e) *Project Summary and Feedback Statement: IFRS 10 Consolidated Financial Statements and IFRS 12 Disclosure of Interests in Other Entities*. London: IASB.

ICAEW Institute of Chartered Accountants in England and Wales (2010) IFRS Factsheet: *IFRS 3 revised*. London: ICAEW.

J Sainsbury plc (2011) *Annual Report and Financial Statements, 2011*. London: J Sainsbury.

Questions

Quick test

1   P plc acquires all the shares in S Ltd and the following statements of financial position are immediately drawn up. Prepare the consolidated statement of financial position. You may assume that the fair values of S Ltd's net assets are equivalent to their book values.

	P plc	S Ltd
	£	£
Investment in S Ltd	29,000	
Non-current assets	5,000	12,000
Current assets		
Inventories	4,000	6,000

Receivables	3,000	4,000
Cash and cash equivalents	1,000	2,000
	8,000	12,000
Total assets	42,000	24,000
Equity		
Equity share capital (£1 shares)	25,000	15,000
Retained earnings	14,000	3,000
	39,000	18,000
Current liabilities	3,000	6,000
Total equity and liabilities	42,000	24,000

2   P plc buys 100% of the equity share capital of S Ltd when S has a credit balance on its retained earnings of £300. The statements of financial position of the two companies at a later date are as follows:

	P plc	S Ltd
	£	£
Investment in S Ltd	1,800	
Net assets	1,500	1,500
	3,300	1,500
Equity share capital	2,000	1,000
Retained earnings	1,300	500
	3,300	1,500

Prepare the consolidated statement of financial position at this later date. You may assume that the fair values of S Ltd's net assets were equivalent to their book values at the date of acquisition.

3   Marks plc acquired 10,000 shares in Spencer Ltd on 1 January 20X2 when the retained earnings of Spencer were £5,000. At 31 December 20X4 the statements of financial position of the two companies are as follows:

	Marks plc	Spencer Ltd
	£	£
Non-current assets		
Property, plant and equipment	85,000	11,000
Investment in Spencer Ltd	17,000	
	102,000	
Current assets	214,000	33,000

Total assets	316,000	44,000
Share capital (£1 equity shares)	100,000	10,000
Retained earnings	40,000	9,000
	140,000	19,000
Current liabilities	176,000	25,000
Total equity and liabilities	316,000	44,000

Prepare the consolidated statement of financial position of Marks plc at 31 December 20X4. You may assume that the fair values of Spencer Ltd's net assets were equivalent to their book values at the date of acquisition.

4 P plc acquired shares in S Ltd on 1 April 20X3 when the retained earnings of S Ltd were £2,200. The statements of financial position at 31 March 20X5 are as follows:

	P plc	S Ltd
	£	£
Investment in S Ltd (2,750 shares)	4,850	
Net assets	26,650	7,700
	31,500	7,700
Share capital (£1 equity shares)	30,000	5,000
Retained earnings	1,500	2,700
	31,500	7,700

Prepare the consolidated statement of financial position at 31 March 20X5. You may assume that the fair values of S Ltd's net assets were equivalent to their book values at the date of acquisition.

●● Develop your understanding

5 The following statements of financial position have been prepared at 31 December 20X8.

	Smith plc	Jones Ltd
	£	£
Non-current assets		
Property, plant and equipment	85,000	18,000
Investment: 120,000 shares in Jones	60,000	
	145,000	
Current assets	160,000	84,000
Total assets	305,000	102,000

Equity share capital (20p shares)	100,000	30,000
Retained earnings	70,000	25,000
	170,000	55,000
Current liabilities	135,000	47,000
Total equity and liabilities	305,000	102,000

Smith plc acquired its holding in Jones Ltd on 31 December 20X7, when Jones' retained earnings stood at £20,000. At this date, the fair value of items of property, plant and equipment was estimated as being £10,000 higher than their book value. The remaining life of these assets at 31 December 20X7 was estimated at five years and Jones uses the straight-line method of depreciation.

Prepare the consolidated statement of financial position of Smith plc at 31 December 20X8.

6   Morecombe plc acquired 8,000 equity shares and 6,000 preference shares in Wise Ltd on 31 December 20X3 when the retained earnings of Wise Ltd were £25,000. The following statements of financial position were prepared at 31 December 20X6:

	Morecombe plc	Wise Ltd
	£	£
Investments: shares in Wise Ltd		
Preference shares	5,000	
Equity shares	35,000	
	40,000	
Sundry net assets	160,000	70,000
	200,000	70,000
Called up share capital		
Equity shares of £1 each	20,000	10,000
Preference shares of £1 each	100,000	20,000
Retained earnings	80,000	40,000
	200,000	70,000

Prepare the consolidated statement of financial position of Morecombe plc at 31 December 20X6. You may assume that the fair values of Wise Ltd's net assets were equivalent to their book values at the date of acquisition.

7   On 30 June 20X4, Ant plc acquired 60% of the equity share capital and 20% of the preference share capital of Dec Ltd for £95,000 and £15,000 respectively. At the date of acquisition the fair values of Dec's property, plant and equipment, which had a carrying value of £160,000, was estimated at £200,000. Dec Ltd depreciates its property, plant and equipment on the straight-line method, and the assets' remaining useful lives were estimated at 8 years. Also, at the date of acquisition the balance on Dec's retained earnings was £50,000 and the balance on the share premium account was £9,000.

The following statements of financial position have been prepared at 30 June 20X8.

	Ant plc	Dec Ltd
	£	£
Non-current assets		
Property, plant and equipment	220,000	170,000
Investment: shares in Dec Ltd	110,000	
	330,000	
Current assets	270,000	186,000
Total assets	600,000	356,000
Equity		
Equity shares of £1 each	200,000	90,000
Preference shares of £1 each	–	40,000
Share premium account	25,000	9,000
Retained earnings	150,000	80,000
	375,000	219,000
Current liabilities	225,000	137,000
Total equity and liabilities	600,000	356,000

Prepare the consolidated statement of financial position of Ant plc at 30 June 20X8.

8   P plc bought 40,000 shares in S1 Ltd and 27,000 shares in S2 Ltd on 31 December 20X2. The
following statements of financial position were drafted at 31 December 20X3.

	P plc	S1 Ltd	S2 Ltd
	£	£	£
Investments in subsidiaries			
S1 Ltd 40,000 shares	49,000		
S2 Ltd 27,000 shares	30,500		
Non-current assets	90,000	38,200	31,400
Net current assets	80,500	19,200	14,600
	250,000	57,400	46,000
Share capital (£1 equity shares)	200,000	50,000	36,000
Retained earnings			
At 1 January 20X3	11,000	3,000	4,800
Profit/(loss) for 20X3	16,000	(1,600)	3,400
	27,000	1,400	8,200
General reserve	23,000	6,000	1,800
	250,000	57,400	46,000

Draw up the consolidated statement of financial position for P plc at 31 December 20X3. You may assume that the fair values of both S1 Ltd's and S2 Ltd's net assets were equivalent to their book values at the date of acquisition.

9   Draw up a consolidated statement of financial position at 31 December 20X5 from the following:

	P plc	S Ltd
	£	£
Investment in S Ltd		
6,000 shares acquired 31/12/20X4	9,700	
Other non-current assets	9,000	5,200
	18,700	5,200
Current assets		
Inventories	3,100	7,200
Receivables	4,900	3,800
Bank	1,100	1,400
	9,100	12,400
Total assets	27,800	17,600
Equity share capital (£1 shares)	20,000	10,000
Retained earnings		
At 31 December 20X4	6,500	3,500
(Loss)/profit for 20X5	(2,500)	2,000
	4,000	5,500
Current liabilities	3,800	2,100
Total equity and liabilities	27,800	17,600

At 31 December 20X5 S Ltd owes P plc £600.

During 20X5 P plc sold goods to S Ltd for £500. P had marked up these goods by £200. Twenty-five per cent of these goods were still in inventory at the statement of financial position date.

You may assume that the fair values of the net assets of S Ltd at the date of acquisition were equivalent to their book values.

10   You are presented with the following information from the Seneley group of companies for the year ended 30 September 20X6:

	Seneley	Lowe	Wright
	£000	£000	£000
Non-current assets	225	300	220
Investments—shares in group companies:			
Lowe Ltd	450		

Wright Ltd		130	
		580	
Current assets			
Inventories		225	150	45
Trade receivables		240	180	50
Cash and cash equivalents		50	10	5
		515	340	100
Total assets		1320	640	320
Equity share capital		800	400	200
Retained earnings		200	150	50
		1,000	550	250
Current liabilities		320	90	70
Total equity and liabilities		1,320	640	320

Additional information:

(a) The authorised, issued, and fully paid share capital of all three companies consists of £1 equity shares

(b) Seneley purchased 320,000 shares in Lowe on 1 October 20X3 when Lowe's retained earnings were £90,000

(c) Seneley purchased 140,000 shares in Wright on 1 October 20X5 when Wright's retained earnings were £60,000

(d) During the year to 30 September 20X6 Lowe had sold goods to Seneley for £15,000. These goods had given Lowe a gross profit of 40%, and Seneley still had half these goods in inventories at 30 September 20X6. For all other intragroup trading, the inventories had been sold on outside the group by 30 September 20X6

(e) Included in the respective trade payable and trade receivable balances at 30 September 20X6 were the following intercompany debts:

- Seneley owed Wright £5,000
- Lowe owed Seneley £20,000
- Wright owed Lowe £25,000.

Required:

Prepare the Seneley group's consolidated statement of financial position at 30 September 20X6.

You may assume that the fair values of the net assets of Lowe and Wright at the date of acquisition were equivalent to their book values.

● ● ● Take it further

11 B plc acquired 200,000 of the ordinary shares of A Ltd on 30 November 20X2 when the retained earnings of A amounted to £15,000. The statements of financial position of the two companies at 30 November 20X4 are as follows:

	B plc	A Ltd
	£	£
Non-current assets		
Property, plant and equipment		
Cost	140,000	100,000
Accumulated depreciation	(32,000)	(34,390)
	108,000	65,610
200,000 shares in A Ltd (cost)	63,000	
	171,000	
Current assets		
Inventories	17,000	13,390
Receivables	10,000	11,000
Bank	2,000	–
	29,000	24,390
Total assets	200,000	90,000
Equity		
Equity share capital (20p shares)	100,000	50,000
Retained earnings	80,000	30,000
	180,000	80,000
Current liabilities		
Bank overdraft	–	3,000
Payables	20,000	7,000
	20,000	10,000
Total equity and liabilities	200,000	90,000

The fair value of A's property, plant and equipment at 30 November 20X2 was £86,000, when its book value was £81,000. (A depreciates its assets at an average rate of 10% on the reducing balance method.)

During the year ended 30 November 20X4 B purchased goods from A for £30,000. A had marked up these goods by 25%. B had sold two-thirds of these goods to external customers by the statement of financial position date. At 30 November 20X4 A had a receivable of £2,500 in its books representing the amount due from B. B had paid this on 28 November.

The impairment review at 30 November 20X4 estimated the recoverable amount of goodwill to be £3,000. There had been no impairment at 30 November 20X3.

Required:

Prepare the consolidated statement of financial position at 30 November 20X4.

12 The following information relates to the Brodick group of companies for the year to 30 April 20X7:

	Brodick plc	Lamlash Ltd	Corrie Ltd
	£000	£000	£000
Revenue	1,100	500	130
Cost of sales	(630)	(300)	(70)
Gross profit	470	200	60
Administrative expenses	(105)	(150)	(20)
Investment income	30	–	–
Profit before tax	395	50	40
Tax	(65)	(10)	(20)
Profit after tax	£ 330	£ 40	£ 20

Additional information:

1 The issued share capital of the group is as follows:

Brodick plc: £5,000,000 (£1 ordinary shares)

Lamlash Ltd: £1,000,000 (£1 ordinary shares)

Corrie Ltd: £200,000 (50p ordinary shares).

2 Brodick plc purchased 800,000 shares in Lamlash Ltd on 1 May 20X0 when the retained earnings of Lamlash amounted to £56,000. At 1 May 20X6 Lamlash's retained earnings were £106,000.

3 Brodick plc purchased 240,000 shares in Corrie Ltd on 1 May 20X4 when the retained earnings of Corrie amounted to £20,000. At 1 May 20X6 Corrie's retained earnings were £30,000.

4 Lamlash and Corrie trade with Brodick and, during the year, intercompany sales totalled £40,000 and £10,000 respectively. One-quarter of the goods sold by Lamlash to Brodick is still in Brodick's inventories at the year end. Lamlash earns a 30% gross margin on its intercompany sales.

5 Adjustment to the fair values of the net assets of Lamlash and Corrie was required on their respective dates of acquisition, but the adjustments were not put through the books. Lamlash's net assets' fair value was £100,000 greater than their book value and Corrie's net assets' fair value was £50,000 greater than their book value. Additional depreciation expense each year of £10,000 and £5,000 in Lamlash and Corrie, respectively, is required as a result of this.

6 The companies paid the following dividends during the year ended 30 April 20X7:

Brodick: £200,000

Lamlash: £30,000

Corrie: £10,000.

7 Brodick's retained earnings at 1 May 20X6 were £460,000.

8 No company has any reserve accounts other than retained earnings.

Required:

Prepare the Brodick group of companies' consolidated statement of comprehensive income and consolidated statement of changes in equity for the year ended 30 April 20X7.

13 You are presented with the following summarised information for Norbreck plc and its subsidiary, Bispham Ltd:

Statements of comprehensive income for the year ended 30 September 20X7

	Norbreck plc	Bispham Ltd
	£000	£000
Revenue	1,700	450
Cost of sales	(920)	(75)
Gross profit	780	375
Administrative expenses	(300)	(175)
Investment income	40	–
Profit before tax	520	200
Tax	(30)	(20)
Profit after tax	£ 490	£180

Statements of financial position at 30 September 20X7

	Norbreck plc	Bispham Ltd
	£000	£000
Non-current assets		
Property, plant and equipment	1,280	440
Investments: shares in group company	500	–
	1,780	440
Current assets		
Inventories	300	250
Receivables	200	150
Cash and cash equivalents	40	30
	540	430
Total assets	2,320	870
Equity		
Equity share capital (£1 shares)	900	400
Retained earnings	720	220
	1,620	620
Current liabilities		
Trade payables	80	160
Other creditors	160	70
	240	230
Provisions for liabilities and charges	460	20
	700	250
Total equity and liabilities	2,320	870

Additional information:

1 Norbreck plc acquired 320,000 shares in Bispham Ltd on 1 October 20X4 when Bispham's retained earnings were £40,000.

2 At this date, the fair values of Bispham's property, plant and equipment were agreed as £150,000 greater than their book values. These values were not incorporated into Bispham's books. Bispham has a 10% straight-line depreciation policy.

3 Bispham has sold goods to Norbreck during the year for £50,000, which included a 25% mark-up on cost. At the year end one-fifth of these inventories are still held by Norbreck.

4 The review for impairment of goodwill arising on acquisition made at 30 September 20X7 revealed that there was an impairment loss of £8,000.

5 Retained earnings at 30 September 20X6 for Norbreck and Bispham were £320,000 and £90,000 respectively.

6 Dividends paid by the companies during the year ended 30 September 20X7 were Norbreck £90,000 and Bispham £50,000.

Required:

Prepare Norbreck plc's consolidated statement of comprehensive income and statement of changes in equity for the year ended 30 September 20X7, and a consolidated statement of financial position at that date.

14 The following financial statements have been drawn up for Old plc, Field Ltd and Lodge Ltd.

Income statements for the year ended 30 April 20X6

	Old plc	Field Ltd	Lodge Ltd
	£000	£000	£000
Revenue	1,250	875	650
Opening inventories	90	150	80
Purchases	780	555	475
Closing inventories	(110)	(135)	(85)
Cost of sales	760	570	470
Gross profit	490	305	180
Distribution costs	(125)	(85)	(60)
Administrative expenses	(28)	(40)	(72)
Profit from operations	337	180	48
Investment income	(88)	–	–
Profit before tax	425	180	48
Tax	(125)	(75)	(20)
Profit for the year	£ 300	£ 105	£ 28

Statement of changes in equity for the year ended 30 April 20X6— retained earnings

	Old plc	Field Ltd	Lodge Ltd
	£000	£000	£000
At 1 May 20X5	30	40	50
Profit for the year	300	105	28
20X5 final dividend paid	(45)	(35)	(15)
20X6 interim dividend paid	(68)	(44)	(15)
At 30 April 20X6	£ 217	£ 66	£ 48

Other information:

(a) The share capital of the companies is as follows:

	Old plc	Field Ltd	Lodge Ltd
Equity shares of £1 each	£450,000	£350,000	£200,000

(b) Old plc acquired the whole of the ordinary shares in Field Ltd many years ago when Field's retained earnings were £6,000, and 120,000 shares in Lodge Ltd on 1 August 20X5.

(c) Profits of all three companies are deemed to accrue evenly throughout the year.

(d) Field Ltd paid its interim dividend on 31 July 20X5.

(e) Lodge Ltd paid its 20X5 final dividend on 30 June 20X5 and its 20X6 interim dividend on 14 November 20X5.

(f) Field Ltd sells goods for resale to Old plc. The following goods purchased from Field are included in Old's inventories:

At 1 May 20X5	£36,000
At 30 April 20X6	£40,000

The gross profit for Field Ltd on sales of these goods is 25%.

Total sales in the year by Field Ltd to Old plc were £150,000.

Required:

Prepare the consolidated income statement for Old plc and its subsidiaries for the year ended 30 April 20X6 and the consolidated retained earnings column as it would appear in the consolidated statement of changes in equity for the year ended 30 April 20X6.

Assume the fair values of the net assets of Field Ltd and Lodge Ltd were equivalent to their book values at the date of acquisition.

15 The following financial statements have been drawn up for Gold plc and Silver Ltd at 31 December 20X8.

Income statements for the year ended 31 December 20X8

	Gold plc	Silver Ltd
	£000	£000
Revenue	4,250	900
Cost of sales	(2,300)	(150)
Gross profit	1,950	750
Administrative expenses	(750)	(350)
Investment income	170	–
Profit before tax	1,370	400
Tax	(275)	(40)
Profit for the year	1,095	360

Statement of changes in equity for the year ended 31 December 20X8—retained earnings

	Gold plc	Silver Ltd
	£000	£000
At 1 January 20X8	300	100
Profit for the year	1,095	360
Dividends paid: equity	(270)	(100)
preference	–	(120)
At 31 December 20X8	1,125	240

Statements of financial position at 31 December 20X8

	Gold plc	Silver Ltd
	£000	£000
Non-current assets		
Property, plant and equipment	3,200	980
Investments	1,250	–
	4,450	980
Current assets		
Inventories	750	500
Receivables	500	300
Cash and cash equivalents	100	60
	1,350	860
Total assets	5,800	1,840

Equity

Equity share capital (£1 shares)	2,250	700
6% Preference share capital (£1 shares)	–	200
Retained earnings	1,125	240
	3,375	1,140

Current liabilities

Trade payables	1,075	320
Other payables	200	340
	1,275	660
Provisions for liabilities and charges	1,150	40
Total equity and liabilities	5,800	1,840

Additional information:

(a) The cost of Gold's investment in Silver is made up as follows:

	£000
560,000 ordinary shares	1,000
150,000 preference shares	250
	1,250

(b) The shares were acquired on 1 January 20X6 when the retained earnings of Silver amounted to £112,000.

(c) At this date the fair values of Silver's property, plant and equipment were £100,000 greater than their book values. Silver uses an average depreciation policy of 30% reducing balance on its non-current assets.

(d) A review for impairment of goodwill at 31 December 20X8 requires goodwill to be written down to £300,000. No previous write-downs have been required.

(e) Gold and Silver do not trade with each other, but included in Gold's revenue and Silver's administrative expenses is a management charge of £200,000. £50,000 is owing from Silver to Gold at 31 December 20X8.

Required:

Prepare Gold plc's consolidated income statement and consolidated statement of changes in equity for the year ended 31 December 20X8 and a consolidated statement of financial position at that date.

Visit the Online Resource Centre for solutions to all these end of chapter questions plus visual walkthrough solutions. You can test your understanding with extra questions and answers, explore additional case studies based on real companies, take a guided tour through a company report, and much more. Go to the Online Resource Centre at www.oxfordtextbooks.co.uk/orc/maynard/

16

Associates, joint arrangements, and statements of cash flow

➤ Introduction

This chapter examines the accounting methods required when an investing company exerts partial influence over its investee company. It can do this individually or enter into an arrangement with other investors whereby they jointly control the investee. Individually, the investor does not control the investee and thus consolidation is not appropriate; however, its investment is more than just a passive one. Alternative methods of accounting to demonstrate this are required.

If the investing company individually can demonstrate significant influence over the investee company, this latter company is classified as an associate and the equity method of accounting is used. If the investing company has entered into a joint arrangement with other investors, the arrangement needs to be classified as either a joint operation or a joint venture, and different accounting methods follow. A joint venture uses the equity method of accounting.

The recent issue of new accounting standards in the area of consolidated financial statements included a replacement standard for joint arrangements—International Financial Reporting Standards (IFRS) 11 *Joint Arrangements*—and resulted in a revision to International Accounting Standard (IAS) 28, which deals with associates. This standard is now entitled *Investments in Associates and Joint Ventures*. Disclosure issues for associates and joint arrangements are contained in the new IFRS 12 *Disclosure of Interests in Other Entities*.

Similar to Chapter 15, the focus of the chapter is on the techniques of accounting for associates and joint ventures in the consolidated income statement, the consolidated statement of comprehensive income, the consolidated statement of changes in equity, and the consolidated statement of financial position by the equity method. The accounting for other joint operations is also discussed. In addition the techniques of the preparation of a consolidated statement of cash flows are included to complete the consolidated financial statements.

After studying this chapter you will be able to:

- understand what an associate, a joint operation, and a joint venture are, and the accounting methods for each
- prepare consolidated financial statements and account for associates and/or joint ventures using the equity method
- explain the disclosure requirements for associates and joint arrangements
- prepare a consolidated statement of cash flows.

✔ **Key issues checklist**

- ❑ The definitions of an associate and significant influence.
- ❑ Exemptions from accounting for an associate.
- ❑ The **equity method of accounting**.
- ❑ The issues of goodwill and impairment for associates.
- ❑ Preparation of a consolidated income statement, consolidated statement of changes in equity, and consolidated statement of financial position for a group including an associate.
- ❑ Disclosures for associates.
- ❑ Joint arrangements and joint control.
- ❑ Joint operations and the resulting accounting method.
- ❑ Joint ventures and the resulting accounting method.
- ❑ Disclosures for joint arrangements.
- ❑ Preparation of a consolidated statement of cash flows for a group involving subsidiaries and associates, including where acquisitions have occurred during the year.

16.1 Associate companies

16.1.1 Categorisation of investments

Chapter 15 discussed the categorisation of an investment of one company in another according to the degree of influence or interest that the investing company (the investor) has over or in the investee company. A reminder of the categories is given in Table 16.1.

Chapter 15 demonstrated how consolidated financial statements are prepared for a simple group of companies consisting of a parent and one or more subsidiary companies.

This chapter deals with the situations where the investing company has partial, not total, influence over the investee. For an individual investing company this is where it has significant influence. If this is the case, then the investee is termed an associate and the equity method of accounting is used for the investment.

Table 16.1 Categories of investment of one company in another

Degree of influence	Limited influence	Partial influence		Total influence
Nature of interest	Acquirer has a *Passive interest* in acquiree	Acquirer exercises *significant influence* over acquiree	Acquirer *shares control* of acquiree *jointly* with others	Acquirer *controls* acquiree
Resulting category	Simple investment	Associate	Joint arrangement	Subsidiary

16.1.2 Significant influence

Significant influence is defined in IAS 28 as:

> ...the power to participate in the financial and operating policy decisions of the investee, but is not control of joint control of those policies.

(IASB, 2011: para. 3)

Significant influence is presumed if the investor holds 20% or more of the voting share capital of the investee, unless it can clearly be demonstrated that this is not the case. The holding can be direct or indirect, for example through a subsidiary company, as illustrated in Figure 16.1.

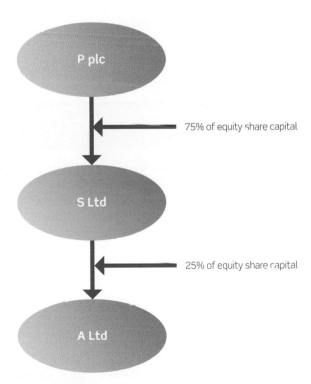

Figure 16.1 Indirect holding of an associate

In this situation P plc's effective ownership of A Ltd is only 19% (75% × 25%). However, the 25% holding in A Ltd by S Ltd would be presumed to give S significant influence over A. As P controls S, it therefore controls this 25% investment in A. The P plc group's consolidated financial statements therefore includes the parent, P and subsidiary, S, with A included in the consolidated accounts as an investment in an associate.

Conversely, if the investing company holds less than 20% of the voting share capital, it is presumed that significant influence does not exist, unless this can be demonstrated clearly. Evidence of significant influence could be from one or more of the following:

(a) representation on the board of directors

(b) participation in policy-making processes, including participation in decisions about dividends or other distributions

(c) material transactions between the investor and investee

(d) interchange of managerial personnel

(e) provision of essential technical information.

Similar to the question of control and whether one company is a subsidiary of another as discussed in Chapter 15, management's judgement may have to be exercised to determine whether significant influence does exist. If the investor holds convertible financial instruments that give it potential voting rights which are currently exercisable, these will also need to be taken into account into the determination of whether significant influence exists.

In addition the distribution of the shareholding of the remaining voting shares should be considered. A substantial or even majority ownership by another investor does not necessarily preclude the investing company from having significant influence.

 Worked example 16.1: to illustrate the issue of significant influence

Sefi Ltd has issued equity share capital of £10 million in 25p shares. Enterprise plc has held 12 million of these shares since it acquired them on 1 April 20X5 when a director of Enterprise was appointed to the board of Sefi. At 31 December 20X7 the remaining equity shares in Sefi were owned by many separate investors. In March 20X8 Rocket plc, a company unrelated to Enterprise plc, bought 22 million shares from these shareholders. From this date the director of Enterprise lost her seat on Sefi's board.

Required:
Explain, with reasons, the accounting treatment Enterprise should adopt for its investment in Sefi in its financial statements for the two years ending 31 December 20X7 and 20X8.

31 December 20X7

Total no. of equity shares of Sefi = 10 million × 4 = 40 million

Enterprise's holding = 12 million/40 million = 30%

There is a presumption that Enterprise plc exercises significant influence over Sefi Ltd. This is enhanced by a director of Enterprise sitting on the board of Sefi. Sefi would be accounted for as an associate of Enterprise plc.

31 December 20X8

The position from March 20X8 is that although Enterprise still owns 30% of Sefi's shares, Sefi has become a subsidiary of Rocket, as this company has acquired more than 50% of Sefi's shares (22 million/40 million = 55%). Sefi is now under the control of Rocket; therefore, it is difficult to see how Enterprise can now exert significant influence over Sefi. The fact that Enterprise has lost its seat on Sefi's Board appears to reinforce this point. Unless Enterprise can provide evidence that it still has significant influence over Sefi, it is likely that the investment in Sefi would no longer be accounted for as an associate, but would be treated under IAS 39 *Financial Instruments: Recognition and Measurement*. It will cease to be equity accounted from the date of loss of significant influence. Its carrying amount at that date will be its initial recognition value under IAS 39 and thereafter carried at fair value.

16.1.3 Exemptions from accounting for an associate

The same conditions are required for an investing company not to account for its investment in an associate using the equity method as for a company not to consolidate a subsidiary. All the following must apply:

1   The investing company is a wholly- or partially-owned subsidiary of another entity itself and all its other owners do not object to consolidated financial statements not being prepared

2   The investing company's ultimate or any intermediate parent produces financial statements that comply with IFRS and are available for public use

3   The investing company's debt or equity instruments are not traded in a public market

4   The investing company does not file its financial statements with a securities commission or other regulatory organisation for the purpose of issuing any class of instruments in a public market.

There are also alternative accounting methods where the investment in an associate is held by an entity that is a venture capital organisation or a mutual fund, unit trust, or other similar entity. These are outside the scope of this textbook.

16.1.4 The equity method of accounting

As the investing company has significant influence over the investee, the investor has an interest in the associate's performance and return on its investment, which extends beyond the receipt of dividends. The distributions received may, in any event, bear little relation to the performance of the associate. The equity method of accounting for an associate therefore extends the scope of the investor's financial statements to include its share of the associate's profits or losses. This provides more informative reporting of the investor's net assets and profit or loss.

In practice this means the following for the preparation of financial statements:

(a) On the statement of financial position the investment in the associate is recognised initially at cost, and the carrying amount is then adjusted to include the investor's accumulated share of the profits or losses, and other comprehensive income of the associate since the date of acquisition. Dividends received from the associate reduce the carrying amount of the investment.

Retained earnings includes the investor's accumulated share of the profits or losses of the associate since the date of acquisition. Other reserves, such as a revaluation reserve, will include the investor's share of the changes in the associate's reserves since the date of acquisition.

(b) In the statement of comprehensive income, the investor's share of the associate's profit or loss after tax for the accounting period is included in one line, usually prior to the subtotal of profit before tax. The associate's profit or loss after tax is adjusted:

(i) For the elimination of unrealised profit in inventories resulting from an upstream sale from the associate to the investor

(ii) For additional, or a reduction in, depreciation based on the fair values of property, plant and equipment (PPE) at the acquisition date

(iii) If the investment in the associate was made during the year. In this instance only the investor's share of the profit or loss after tax which has arisen since the acquisition date is included. This may be done on a time-apportionment basis.

The investor's share of unrealised profit in inventories remaining at the financial year end from sales of goods between the investor and the associate is eliminated from gross profit. (See Chapter 15 for a full discussion of unrealised profit in inventories.)

Any impairment losses are also included in profit and loss—see further discussion in section 16.1.5.

The investor's share of any other comprehensive income of the associate is included in other comprehensive income.

(c) In the statement of changes in equity the retained earnings figures will include the investor's share of the post-acquisition profits and losses of the associate. Note that non-controlling interest (NCI) figures are unaffected by any investment in associates.

16.1.5 Goodwill and impairment losses

Goodwill relating to an associate is not accounted for separately under the equity method of accounting. If, at the date of acquisition, there is an excess of the cost of the investment over the investing company's share of the fair value of the net assets of the associate then this 'goodwill' is not accounted for separately. It is included in the carrying amount of the investment as it is inherent within the cost of the investment.

However, if there is an excess of the investing company's share of the fair value of the net assets of the associate over the cost of the investment, this is added to the net profit or loss of the associate in the year of acquisition. It therefore increases the investing company's share of the associate's profit (or reduces the investing company's share of the associate's loss) in this year.

As goodwill is not recognised separately, it is not tested for impairment. However, the carrying amount of the investment as a whole is tested for impairment in accordance with IAS 36 *Impairment of Assets*. Thus, if there are indications that the investment may be impaired, its recoverable amount (the higher of value in use and fair value less costs to sell) has to be determined and compared with the carrying amount. IAS 28 gives some guidance as to how the value in use should be estimated as follows:

(a) The investor's share of the present value of the estimated future cash flows expected to be generated by the associate, including the cash flows from its operations, plus the proceeds from the ultimate disposal of the investment, or

(b) The present value of the estimated future cash flows expected to be received from dividends paid to the investor, plus the proceeds from the ultimate disposal of the investment.

Helpfully, IAS 28 advises that if appropriate assumptions are made, these two methods should give the same result. As for all impairment testing, there is a huge reliance on management's estimates and assumptions.

16.1.6 Classification as held for sale

If an investment in an associate, or a portion thereof, meets the criteria to be classified as held for sale, then the investing company is required to apply the accounting set out in IRFS 5. This is discussed in detail in Chapter 6.

🔵 **Reminder** *An asset or a disposal group is classified as held for sale if there is a formal commitment to disposal with evidence of positive steps taken towards this before the year end. The sale must be expected to be completed within a year. If classified as held for sale, the asset or disposal group is valued at the lower of carrying amount and fair value less costs to sell.*

 Worked example 16.2: to show the accounting for an associate in consolidated financial statements

Alpha plc is a company with subsidiary undertakings. It also has 25% of the equity share capital of Beta Ltd. This was bought for £100,000 on 1 January 20X0 when Beta had retained earnings of £20,000 and when the fair value of Beta's PPE was £30,000 in excess of its carrying amount. The PPE had a remaining useful life of 10 years at this date.

The following are the financial statements of the Alpha group and Beta Ltd. Note that the Alpha group financial statements have already consolidated Alpha plc and its subsidiaries.

Income statements for the year ended 31 December 20X3

	Alpha plc and subsidiaries (consolidated) £000	Beta Ltd £000
Revenue	540	200
Cost of sales	(370)	(130)
Gross profit	170	70
Distribution costs	(20)	(3)
Administrative expenses	(40)	(8)
Investment income from Beta Ltd	10	–
Profit before tax	120	59
Tax	(28)	(16)
Profit for the year	92	43
Attributable to:		
Owners of Alpha	80	
NCI	12	
	92	

Extracts from statements of changes in equity for the year ended 31 December 20X3

	Alpha plc and subsidiaries (consolidated)		Beta Ltd
	Retained earnings £000	NCI £000	Retained earnings £000
At 1 January 20X3	35	44	53
Profit for year	80	12	43
Dividends paid	(40)	(6)	(40)
At 31 December 20X3	75	50	56

Statements of financial position at 31 December 20X3

	Alpha plc and subsidiaries (consolidated) £000	Beta Ltd £000
PPE	115	142
Investment in Beta Ltd (at cost)	100	–
Goodwill	30	–

Other net assets	180	114
	425	256
Share capital	300	200
Retained earnings	75	56
	375	256
NCI	50	–
	425	256

Required:

Prepare the full consolidated financial statements of the Alpha group at 31 December 20X3.

Workings

(a) The investment income from Beta Ltd is eliminated on consolidation.

(b) Share of profit of associate for income statement	£000
Beta profit after tax	43
Fair value depreciation (£30/10)	(3)
	40

Alpha's share = 25% × £40,000 = £10,000

(c) Investment in associate	£000
Cost	100
Plus: share of post-acquisition adjusted retained earnings of Beta	
25% × (56 – 20 – 4 × 3)	6
	106

(d) Retained earnings at 1 January 20X3	£000
Alpha plus subsidiaries	35
Plus: share of post-acquisition adjusted retained earnings of Beta	
25% × (53 – 20 – 3 × 3)	6
	41

Consolidated income statement for the year ended 31 December 20X3

			£000
Revenue	)		540
Cost of sales	)		(370)
Gross profit	)	(Alpha and subsidiaries only)	170
Distribution costs	)		(20)
Admin expenses	)		(40)

		110
Share of profit of associate (W2)		10
Profit before tax		120
Tax	(Alpha + subsidiaries only)	28
Profit for the year		92
Attributable to:		
Owners of Alpha	(Balancing figure)	80
NCI		12
		92

Consolidated statement of changes in equity for the year ended 31 December 20X3

	Share capital £000	Retained Earnings £000	NCI £000	Total £000
At 1 January 20X3	300	41	44	385
Profit for year		80	12	92
Dividends paid		(40)	(6)	(46)
At 31 December 20X3	300	81	50	431

Consolidated statement of financial position at 31 December 20X3

		£000
Goodwill		30
PPE	(Alpha + subsidiaries only)	115
Investment in associate		106
Other net assets	(Alpha + subsidiaries only)	180
		431
Share capital		300
Retained earnings		81
		381
NCI		50
		431

16.1.7 Disclosure requirements

The disclosure requirements for associates are included in IFRS 12 *Disclosure of Interest in Other Entities*. The investing company is required to disclose information that enables the users to evaluate:

(a) the nature, extent and financial effects of its interests in associates, including the nature and effects of any contractual relationships with the other investors in the associates, and

(b) the nature of, and changes in, the risks associated with these interests.

Note that, as for disclosures relating to subsidiaries, there is now an emphasis on disclosing the risks associated with the investments.

The disclosure requirements, again as for subsidiaries, include factual information about material associate companies, including whether the nature of the activities conducted by these associates are strategic to the investing company's activities. Summarised financial information of the associates should be shown and the method of accounting disclosed.

Financial reporting in practice 16.1 | Tesco plc, 2011

Note: for its 2011 financial statements, Tesco has applied the previous version of IAS 28 *Investments in Associates*, the accounting standards applicable for these financial statements. Therefore, not all of the aforementioned disclosures will be seen in this example.

Accounting policy - Joint ventures and associates

A joint venture is an entity in which the Group holds an interest on a long-term basis and which is jointly controlled by the Group and one or more other venturers under a contractual agreement.

An associate is an undertaking, not being a subsidiary or joint venture, over which the Group has significant influence and can participate in the financial and operating policy decisions of the entity.

The Group's share of the results of joint ventures and associates is included in the Group Income Statement using the equity method of accounting. Investments in joint ventures and associates are carried in the Group Balance Sheet at cost plus post-acquisition changes in the Group's share of the net assets of the entity, less any impairment in value. The carrying values of investments in joint ventures and associates include acquired goodwill.

If the Group's share of losses in a joint venture or associate equals or exceeds its investment in the joint venture or associate, the Group does not recognise further losses, unless it has incurred obligations to do so or made payments on behalf of the joint venture or associate.

Unrealised gains arising from transactions with joint ventures and associates are eliminated to the extent of the Group's interest in the entity.

Note 13 - Interests in joint ventures and associates

The Group uses the equity method of accounting for its interest in joint ventures and associates. The following table shows the aggregate movement in the Group's investment in joint ventures and associates:

	Joint ventures £m	Associates £m	Total £m
At 28 February 2009	49	13	62
Additions	83	–	83
Foreign currency translation	9	–	9
Share of post-tax profits of joint ventures and associates	29	4	33
Income received from joint ventures and associates	(34)	(1)	(35)

(continued)

(continued)

	Joint ventures £m	Associates £m	Total £m
At 27 February 2010	136	16	152
Additions	88	86	174
Foreign currency translation	(5)	–	(5)
Share of post-tax profits/(losses) of joint ventures and associates	65	(8)	57
Income received from joint ventures and associates	(60)	(2)	(62)
At 26 February 2011	224	92	316

Associates

The Group's principal associates are:

	Business activity	Share of issued share capital, loan capital and debt securities	Country of incorporation and principal country of operation
Greenergy International Limited*	Fuel Supplier	34%	England
Tesco Underwriting Limited*	Insurance	49.9%	England

* Held by an intermediate subsidiary.

On 18 May 2010 the Group acquired an additional 13% of the ordinary share capital of Greenergy International Limited for a cash consideration of £16m, taking the Group's holding to 34%.

The share of the assets, liabilities, revenue and profit of the Group's associates, which are included in the Group financial statements, are as follows:

	2011 £m	2010 £m
Assets	535	156
Liabilities	(452)	(142)
Goodwill	9	2
	92	16
Revenue	1,551	473
(Loss)/profit for the year	(8)	4

The accounting period ends of the associates consolidated in these financial statements range from 31 December 2010 to 28 February 2011. The accounting period end dates of the associates are different from those of the Group as they depend upon the requirements of the parent companies of those entities.

There are no significant restrictions on the ability of associated undertakings to transfer funds to the parent, other than those imposed by the Companies Act 2006.

16.2 Joint arrangements

For a variety of reasons companies may enter into contractual arrangements with other companies to work together. Reasons may include the production of a particular product, or the exploration of whether oil and gas resources exist, or the delivery of a government contract. In some instances the companies party to the arrangement may set up another entity for the purpose of carrying out the work. Irrespective of the structure or legal form of the arrangement, the principle behind the accounting for **joint arrangements** set out in IFRS 11 *Joint Arrangements* is that it should reflect the rights and obligations that the companies have as a result of the arrangement.

IFRS 11 has changed the approach to the accounting for joint arrangements as set out in its predecessor standard. The old IAS 31 *Interests in Joint Ventures* was considered unsatisfactory by the International Accounting Standards Board (IASB) and not faithfully representational of many joint arrangements. Choices in accounting methods were also allowed by the standard, which had led to similar arrangements being accounted for differently, thus making comparisons difficult for users.

IRFS 11 defines a joint arrangement as an arrangement in which two or more parties have joint control. Joint control is a contractually agreed sharing of control by the parties and requires the unanimous consent of all the parties sharing control in decisions that are made about the arrangement's activities. The unanimity of the consent of all the parties is important when considering the issue of control —if this is not unanimous this would raise questions about whether there was a parent/subsidiary relationship with one party perhaps controlling the decision-making.

In practice, joint arrangements can take very many different forms, but for accounting purposes two different types are defined which lead to different accounting methods being applied. The two types are joint operations and joint ventures.

16.2.1 Joint operations

A joint operation is defined as a joint arrangement whereby the parties that have joint control have rights to the assets and obligations for the liabilities that relate to the arrangement. The parties to the arrangement are called joint operators. The assets and liabilities of a joint operation may be legally acquired and incurred, respectively, by a separate entity set up by the joint operators; however, if the details of the arrangement specify the parties' rights to the assets and obligations for the liabilities, then the arrangement will still be classified as a joint operation.

A joint operator accounts for a joint operation by including in its own individual financial statements:

(a) its share of any assets held jointly;

(b) its share of any liabilities incurred jointly;

(c)   its share of the revenue from the sale of the output by the joint operation; and

(d)   its share of any expenses incurred jointly.

If a joint operator enters into a transaction with the joint operation, then, as for the accounting for associate companies, there must be the elimination of interoperation profits so that the commercial reality of the transaction is reflected. So, for example, if the joint operator sells or contributes assets to the joint operation, the commercial reality of this is that the joint operator is conducting this transaction with the other joint operators. The joint operator recognises any gains and losses only to the extent of the other parties' interests in the joint operation. If, however, the transaction is, for example, the sale of inventory or an item of PPE from the joint operator to the joint operation, and the sale provides evidence of a reduction in the net realisable value of the assets or of an impairment loss, then the joint operator should recognise these losses fully.

If a joint operator purchases assets from the joint operation, it does not recognise its share of any gains or losses arising from this transaction until it resells these assets to a third party. If, however, the purchase price provides evidence of a reduction in the net realisable value of the assets or of an impairment loss, then the joint operator should recognise its share of these losses.

There may be parties that participate in a joint operation and have rights to the assets and obligations for liabilities, but which do not have joint control. These parties should also account for their share of the operation's assets, liabilities, revenue, and expenses.

16.2.2 Joint ventures

The other type of joint arrangement is a joint venture. This is defined by IFRS 11 as a joint arrangement whereby the parties that have joint control have rights to the net assets of the arrangement. The implication of the term 'net assets' in this definition is that the parties, referred to as joint venturers, have rights to an investment in the arrangement rather than for specific assets and liabilities.

It might appear that a consequence of this definition, together with the definition of a joint operation, would be that if the joint arrangement's activities were conducted through a separate entity, this would lead to the arrangement being classified as a joint venture. However, this is not necessarily the case, and the IASB has been careful to emphasise the principle of the accounting methods for joint arrangements, namely that it should reflect the rights and obligations that the companies have as a result of the arrangement.

The difference may be summarised by Figure 16.2.

If an arrangement is classified as a joint venture, then the accounting treatment follows the definition. Having an interest in the net assets of an investee is faithfully represented by using the equity method in accordance with IAS 28 *Investments in Associates and Joint Ventures*. Thus, the accounting for joint venture is the same as accounting for an associate, as detailed in section 16.1. Critics have pointed out that having significant influence over an investee is different to having joint control, although both now result in the same accounting method.

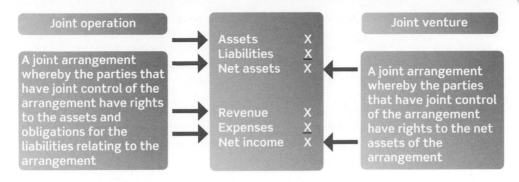

Figure 16.2 The difference between a joint operation and a joint venture

The IASB responded by indicating that the equity method of accounting for joint ventures did reflect a company's interest in the net assets of an investee and, at the time IFRS 11 was being drafted, the board was not considering any changes to the equity method being used for associates.

 Example of the classification of a joint arrangement

Alpha and Beta are two companies whose businesses are the provision of many types of public and private construction services. They set up a contractual arrangement to work together for the purpose of fulfilling a contract with a government for the design and construction of a road between two cities. The contractual arrangement determines the participation shares of Alpha and Beta, and establishes joint control of the arrangement.

The parties set up a separate company, Zeta, through which to conduct the arrangement. Zeta, on behalf of Alpha and Beta, enters into the contract with the government. In addition, the assets and liabilities relating to the arrangement are held in Zeta. The main feature of entity Zeta's legal form is that Alpha and Beta, not Zeta, have rights to the assets and obligations for the liabilities of this company.

The contractual arrangement between Alpha and Beta additionally establishes that:

(a) The rights to all the assets needed to undertake the activities of the arrangement are shared by Alpha and Beta on the basis of their participation shares in the arrangement

(b) Alpha and Beta have several, and joint, responsibilities for all operating and financial obligations relating to the activities of the arrangement on the basis of their participation shares

(c) The profit or loss resulting from the activities of the arrangement is shared by Alpha and Beta on the basis of their participation shares.

For the purposes of coordinating and overseeing the activities, Alpha and Beta appoint an operator, who will be an employee of one of the companies. After a specified time, the role of the operator will rotate to an employee of the other company. Alpha and Beta agree that the activities will be executed by the operator's employees on a 'no gain or loss' basis.

In accordance with the terms specified in the contract with the government, Zeta invoices the construction services to the government on behalf of the parties.

Required:
Discuss whether this arrangement should be classified as a joint operation or a joint venture, and explain the consequential accounting method.

The joint arrangement is carried out through a separate company, Zeta, but the legal form of Zeta does not confer separation between Alpha and Beta and Zeta. In other words, the assets and liabilities held in Zeta are the assets and liabilities of Alpha and Beta. This is reinforced by the terms agreed by Alpha and Beta in their contractual arrangement, which state that these companies have rights to the assets, and obligations for the liabilities, relating to the arrangement that is conducted through Zeta. The joint arrangement is therefore a joint operation.

Alpha and Beta each recognise in their financial statements their share of the assets (e.g. PPE, and accounts receivable) and their share of any liabilities resulting from the arrangement (e.g. accounts payable to third parties) on the basis of their agreed participation share. Each also recognises its share of the revenue and expenses resulting from the construction services provided to the government through Zeta.

16.2.3 Disclosure requirements

The disclosures for interests in joint arrangements, in other words both joint operations and joint ventures, are set out in IFRS 12, and are identical to those for associates. These have been detailed in section 16.1.7.

Financial reporting in practice 16.2   Tesco plc, 2011

In its 2011 Annual Report and Financial Statements, extracts of which are provided in Financial reporting in practice 16.1, Tesco lists its principal joint ventures, all except one of which are in property development. It also provides summarised financial information about them as follows.

Note 13 - Interests in joint ventures and associates

The share of the assets, liabilities, revenue and profit of the joint ventures, which are included in the Group financial statements, are as follows:

	2011 £m	2010 £m
Non-current assets	2,720	2,216
Current assets	577	359
Current liabilities	(1,957)	(411)
Non-current liabilities	(1,123)	(2,041)
Goodwill	7	1
Cumulative unrecognised losses	–	12
	224	136
Revenue	369	355
Expenses	(304)	(326)
Profit for the year	65	29

The unrecognised share of losses made by joint ventures during the financial year was £7m (2010 – £3m).

16.3 Consolidated statements of cash flow

These two chapters on consolidated financial statements conclude by considering the final financial statement, the consolidated statement of cash flows. IAS 7 *Statement of Cash Flows* governs the preparation and presentation of a statement of cash flows, and this applies equally to individual company and consolidated statements of cash flow. The aim of a consolidated statement of cash flows is to show the cash inflows and outflows of the group with third parties.

The statement of cash flows for an individual company was discussed in detail in Chapter 4 and an example of its preparation demonstrated. This preparation was from the two statements of financial position at the beginning and end of the financial year and this same approach will be taken for consolidated financial statements.

Reminder *A statement of cash flows shows the historical changes in cash and cash equivalents, classifying cash flows as arising from:*

- *operating activities*
- *investing activities*
- *financing activities.*

It reconciles opening and closing cash and cash equivalents balances, where cash equivalents are defined as short-term, highly liquid investments that are readily convertible to known amounts of cash and which are subject to an insignificant risk of changes in value.

Used in conjunction with the rest of the financial statements, a statement of cash flows provides information about:

- *the changes in the net assets of an entity*
- *an entity's financial structure (including its liquidity and solvency)*
- *its ability to affect the amounts and timing of cash flows in order to adapt to changing circumstances and opportunities.*

Cash flow information is useful in assessing the ability of the entity to generate cash and cash equivalents.

For consolidated statements of cash flows the following additional items need to be considered:

1   Dividends paid to the NCI in subsidiaries are disclosed separately and classified as financing activities

2   Any impairment of goodwill arising on the acquisition of a subsidiary is added back in the reconciliation of profit before tax to cash flows from operating activities

3   The net cash effect of the acquisition (or disposal) of a subsidiary is disclosed separately under investing activities. The net cash effect is the cash paid (or received) net of the cash balances the subsidiary has at the date of acquisition or disposal.

If there are investments in associates or joint ventures accounted for by the equity method, the cash flows shown in the consolidated statement of cash flows are restricted to the cash flows between the investor and the investee, in other words to dividends and advances. So, additional items are:

4   Dividends received from associates that are disclosed separately and classified as investing activities

5   Cash payments (and receipts) to acquire (and dispose of) associates, respectively, that are classified under investing activities.

 Example of how cash flows from an investment in an associate would be included in the consolidated statement of cash flows

The following is an extract from the consolidated income statement of the Baxter plc group for the year ended 31 December 20X7:

	£000
Group profit from operations	273
Share of profit of associates	60
Profit before tax	333
Income tax expense	(63)
Profit for the year	270

The consolidated statements of financial position at 31 December 20X7 and 20X6 show the following:

	20X7	20X6
	£000	£000
Non-current assets		
Investment in associate	552	528

Baxter plc has only one associate company, in which it has invested since 20X3.

Required:
In relation to the investment in the associate, what figure(s) will be included in the consolidated statement of cash flows for the Baxter plc group for the year ended 31 December 20X7?

The share of profit of the associate of £60,000 does not represent a cash flow, so must be subtracted in the reconciliation of profit before tax to cash flows from operating activities.

The only cash flow from holding the investment in the associate is from any dividends paid by the associate and received by the investor. This is calculated from reconciliation:

	£000
Opening investment in associate	528
Add: Share of profit of associate	60

Less: Dividend received from associate	(36)	Balancing figure
Closing investment in associate	552	

A separate line item, dividends received from associate £36,000, will be included in the consolidated statement of cash flows—under cash flows from investing activities.

16.3.1 Acquisition or disposal of subsidiaries

As indicated in section 16.3 the net cash effect of acquisition or disposal of a subsidiary is shown as a separate line item under investing activities.

 Example of the cash effect of the acquisition of a subsidiary

P plc acquired 75% of S Ltd by issuing 250,000 £1 shares at their fair value of £2.50 per share and £200,000 in cash. At the date of acquisition the cash and cash equivalents in S Ltd's statement of financial position amounted to £30,000.

Required:
What figure would be included for the acquisition of a subsidiary under investing activities in P plc's consolidated statement of cash flows?

Acquisition of subsidiary S Ltd, net of cash acquired = £200,000 – £30,000
$$= £170,000$$
This would be shown as a cash outflow, i.e. the figure would be in brackets.

Care should be taken when calculating the movements in individual asset and liability balances not to double-count the effects of the acquisition or disposal of a subsidiary during the accounting period. The consolidated asset or liability balances may have increased or decreased, not from any cash flow, but because the subsidiary's assets or liabilities were added to or deducted from the consolidated figures.

Subsidiary *acquired* in the period	*Subtract* PPE, inventories, receivables, payables, etc. at the date of acquisition from the movement on these items.
Subsidiary *disposed of* in the period	*Add* PPE, inventories, receivables, payables, etc. at the date of acquisition from the movement on these items.

 Example of the calculation of additions to property, plant and equipment (PPE)

An extract from the consolidated statement of financial position of P plc at 31 December is as follows:

	20X7 £000	20X6 £000
PPE	500	400

During 20X7 P plc acquired 80% of the equity share capital of S Ltd. At the date of acquisition, S Ltd's assets included PPE with an estimated fair value of £75,000.

There were no disposals of PPE in the year. Depreciation of £25,000 was charged to the consolidated income statement.

Required:

Calculate the amount to be disclosed as 'Purchase of property, plant and equipment' under cash flows from investing activities in the consolidated statement of cash flows.

If there had been no acquisition of S during the year, the purchase of PPE would have been obtained from the reconciliation:

	£000	
Opening balance	400	
Add: purchases	125	Balancing figure
Less: depreciation	(25)	
Closing balance	500	

However, £75,000 of the PPE at 31 December 20X7 is from S's acquired PPE—this is not a cash flow. So the reconciliation becomes:

	£000	
Opening balance (P only)	400	
Add: acquisition of S's PPE	75	
Add: purchases	50	Balancing figure
Less: depreciation	(25)	
Closing balance	500	

A cash outflow of £50,000 would be shown for 'Purchases of property, plant and equipment' under cash flows from investing activities in the consolidated statement of cash flows.

16.3.2 Worked example of a consolidated statement of cash flows

 Worked example 16.3: to show the preparation of a consolidated statement of cash flows

On 1 October 20X8 P plc acquired 90% of S Ltd by issuing 100,000 shares at their fair value of £2 per share and paying £100,000 in cash. At that time the fair values of the net assets of S Ltd were as follows:

	£000
PPE	190
Inventories	70
Trade receivables	30

Cash and cash equivalents	10
Trade payables	(40)
	260

The consolidated statements of financial position of P plc at 31 December were as follows:

	20X8 £000	20X7 £000
Non-current assets		
PPE	2,500	2,300
Goodwill	66	–
	2,566	2,300
Current assets		
Inventories	1,450	1,200
Trade receivables	1,370	1,100
Cash and cash equivalents	76	50
	2,896	2,350
Total assets	5,462	4,650
Equity attributable to owners of the parent		
Equity share capital (£1 shares)	1,150	1,000
Share premium account	650	500
Retained earnings	1,791	1,530
	3,591	3,030
NCI	31	–
	3,622	3,030
Current liabilities		
Trade payables	1,690	1,520
Income tax payable	150	100
	1,840	1,620
	5,462	4,650

The consolidated income statement for the year ended 31 December 20X8 was as follows:

	£000
Revenue	10,000
Cost of sales	(7,500)
Gross profit	2,500
Administrative expenses	(2,080)
Profit before tax	420

Income tax expense	(150)
Profit for the year	270
Profit attributable to:	
Owners of P plc	261
NCI	9
	270

The retained earnings in the consolidated statement of changes in equity for the year ended 31 December 20X8 were as follows:

	Retained earnings £000
Balance at 1 January 20X8	1,530
Profit for the period	261
Balance at 31 December 20X8	1,791

You are also given the following information:

1 Depreciation charged to the consolidated income statement amounted to £210,000.
2 There were no disposals of PPE during the year.

Required:
Prepare a consolidated statement of cash flows for P plc for the year ended 31 December 20X8 under the indirect method in accordance with IAS 7 *Statement of Cash Flows*. Provide the note which shows the reconciliation of profit before tax to cash generated from operations.

Workings

1 Check whether there is any impairment of goodwill.

On the acquisition of S Ltd, goodwill would have been calculated as

	£000
Consideration	300
Add: NCI in fair value of net assets of S Ltd 10% × 260	26
	32
Less: fair value of net assets of S Ltd	(260)
	66

This is the balance in the statement of financial position at 31 December 20X8, hence there has been no impairment of goodwill.

2 Net cash paid for the acquisition of the subsidiary.

	£000
Total consideration	300
Less: non-cash consideration (100,000 × £2)	(200)
Less: cash of S at acquisition	(10)
Cash out flow for acquisition	90

3 Cash paid for the purchase of PPE.

	£000
Balance at 31 December 20X7	2,300
On acquisition	190
Less: depreciation	(210)
	2,280
Additions (balancing figure)	220
Balance at 31 December 20X8	2,500

4 Proceeds from the issue of share capital.

	£000
Ordinary share capital at 31 December 20X8	1,150
Share premium at 31 December 20X8	650
	1,800
Ordinary share capital at 31 December 20X7	1,000
Share premium at 31 December 20X7	500
	1,500
Difference (1,800 – 1,500)	300
Shares issued on acquisition of subsidiary	(200)
Other shares issued during year for cash	100

5 Dividend paid to NCI.

It is helpful to think of the NCI column of statement of changes in equity column.

	£000
NCI on acquisition	26
NCI for the year—from consolidated income statement	9
	35
Dividend paid to NCI (balancing figure)	(4)
Balance at 31 December 20X8	31

Reconciliation of profit before tax to cash generated from operations

		£000
Profit before taxation		420
Add back: Depreciation		210
		630
Increase in trade receivables	(1,370 – 1,100 – 30)	(240)
Increase in inventories	(1,450 – 1,200 – 70)	(180)
Increase in trade payables	(1,690 – 1,520 – 40)	130
Cash generated from operations		340

Consolidated statement of cash flows for the year ended 31 December 20X8

	£000	£000
Cash flows from operating activities		340
Income taxes paid (100 + 150 – 150)		(100)
Net cash from operating activities		240
Cash flows from investing activities		
Acquisition of subsidiary S Ltd, net of cash acquired	(90)	
Purchase of PPE	(220)	
Net cash used in investing activities		(310)
Cash flows from financing activities		
Proceeds from issue of share capital	100	
Dividend paid to NCI	(4)	
Net cash from financing activities		96
Net increase in cash and cash equivalents		26
Cash and cash equivalents at beginning of year		50
Cash and cash equivalents at end of year		76

16.3.3 Disclosures

The disclosures for statements of cash flow are discussed in Chapter 4. Where there have been acquisitions or disposals of subsidiaries during an accounting period, the following additional disclosures are required:

(a) Total purchase price/disposal consideration

(b) Portion of purchase price/disposal consideration discharged by means of cash and cash equivalents

(c) Amount of cash and cash equivalents in subsidiary acquired or disposed of

(d) Amount of other assets and liabilities in subsidiary acquired or disposed of, summarised by major category.

The separation of cash flows arising from acquisitions and disposals of subsidiaries assists users in distinguishing these amounts from the cash flows arising from the other operating, investing, and financing activities.

Financial reporting in practice 16.3   Tesco plc, 2011

An extract from Tesco's statement of cash flows for the 52 weeks ended 26 February 2011 includes the following highlighted items relating to group cash flows:

	2011	2010
Cash flows from investing activities		
Acquisition of subsidiaries, net of cash acquired	(89)	(65)
Proceeds from sale of property, plant and equipment	1,906	1,820
Purchase of property, plant and equipment and investment property	(3,178)	(2,855)
Proceeds from sale of intangible assets	3	4
Purchase of intangible assets	(373)	(163)
Increase in loans to joint ventures	(219)	(45)
Decrease in loans to joint ventures	25	–
Investments in joint ventures and associates	(174)	(4)
Investments in short-term and other investments	(1,264)	(1,918)
Proceeds from sale of short-term investments	1,314	1,233
Dividends received	62	35
Interest received	128	81
Net cash used in investing activities	(1,859)	(1,877)
Cash flows from financing activities		
Proceeds from issue of ordinary share capital	98	167
Increase in borrowings	2,175	862
Repayment of borrowings	(4,153)	(3,601)
Repayment of obligations under finance leases	(42)	(41)
Dividends paid to equity owners	(1,081)	(968)
Dividends paid to non-controlling interests	(2)	(2)
Own shares purchased	(31)	(24)
Net cash from financing activities	(3,036)	(3,607)

Note 33 Business combinations and other acquisitions

Business combinations

On 18 June 2010 the Group acquired the trade and certain assets and liabilities of 2 Sisters Food Group, Inc. for consideration of £52m. On 19 July 2010 the Group acquired 100% of the ordinary share capital of Wild Rocket Foods, LLC for consideration of £64m. The table below sets out the provisional analysis of the net assets acquired and the fair value to the Group in respect of these two acquisitions.

	Pre-acquisition carrying values	Fair value adjustment	Provisional fair values on acquisition
	£m	£m	£m
Non-current assets	45	7	52
Current assets	9	(1)	8
Current liabilities	(6)	(1)	(7)
Non-current liabilities	(8)	(11)	(19)

(continued)

(continued)

	Pre-acquisition carrying values £m	Fair value adjustment £m	Provisional fair values on acquisition £m
Net assets acquired	40	(6)	34
Goodwill arising on acquisition			82
			116
Consideration:			
Cash			45
Non-cash			71
Total consideration			116

 ## Summary of key points

An investing company can exert partial influence over an investee company either on its own, through having the power to participate in the financial and operational decisions of the investee, or by entering into a contractual arrangement with other investors and forming a joint arrangement. In order for the financial statements of the investor to be faithfully representative of these situations, they need to reflect more than just the cost of the investment and the distributions received from the investee company.

In the first case if the investing company has significant influence over the investee, which is presumed if the holding of equity shares is more than 20%, although there are other indicators, the investee is termed an associate and the equity method of accounting is used. This means the investor's financial statements will include its share of the associate's profits or losses, and the investment on the statement of financial position will include the investor's share of the cumulative profits and losses of the associate since the date of acquisition.

A joint arrangement requires the parties to the arrangement to have joint control. This means they have to reach unanimous agreement over decisions about the running of the arrangement. There are two types of joint arrangement for accounting purposes and different accounting results depending on the categorisation. The first is a joint arrangement where the parties have rights to the assets and obligations for the liabilities of the arrangement. A joint operator includes in its financial statements its share, as specified in the agreement, of the specific assets, liabilities, income, and expenses of the operation.

A joint venture is the other type of joint arrangement. This is where the parties have rights to the net assets of the arrangement and thus is more like an investment in the arrangement. A joint venturer accounts for this investment by the equity method.

The final section of the chapter demonstrates the preparation of a consolidated statement of cash flows, indicating how cash flows of a group consisting of subsidiaries and associates are accounted for and presented.

 ## Further reading

IASB (International Accounting Standards Board) (2011a) IAS 28 *Investments in Associates and Joint Ventures*. London: IASB.

IASB (International Accounting Standards Board) (2011b) IFRS 11 *Joint Arrangements*. London: IASB.

IASB (International Accounting Standards Board) (2004) IAS 7 *Statement of Cash Flows*. London: IASB.

Bibliography

IASB (International Accounting Standards Board) (2004) IAS 7 *Statement of Cash Flows*. London: IASB.

IASB (International Accounting Standards Board) (2011a) IAS 28 *Investments in Associates and Joint Ventures*. London: IASB.

IASB (International Accounting Standards Board) (2011b) IFRS 11 *Joint Arrangements*. London: IASB.

Tesco plc (2011) Annual Report and Financial Statements, 2011. Cheshunt: Tesco.

Questions

● Quick test

1   The draft statements of financial position at 31 December 20X6 of three companies are set out as follows:

	Lanchester Ltd	Norman Ltd	Thorne Ltd
	£000	£000	£000
PPE	300	100	160
Investments at cost			
18,000 shares in Norman	100	–	–
18,000 shares in Thorne	30	–	–
Other net assets	320	160	80
	750	260	240
Equity			
Equity shares of £1 each	250	30	60
Retained earnings	400	180	100
	650	210	160
Long-term loans	100	50	80
	750	260	240

The shares in Norman Ltd were acquired on 1 January 20X4 when its retained earnings were £70,000. At this date the fair value of its PPE was £40,000 greater than the book value and the average life of these assets remaining was 8 years.

The shares in Thorne Ltd were acquired on 1 January 20X6 when its retained earnings were £30,000. At this date the fair value of its PPE was £20,000 greater than the book value and the average life of these assets remaining was 5 years.

Both companies use the straight-line method of depreciation.

Required:

Prepare the consolidated statement of financial position at 31 December 20X6.

2   Aroma plc, a company with 100% owned subsidiaries, purchased 30% of Therapy Ltd on 1 July 20X0. At all times, Aroma participates fully in Therapy's financial and operating policy decisions.

The equity of Therapy Ltd at acquisition was as follows:

	£000
Share capital	1,000
Revaluation reserve	100
Retained earnings	450
	1,550

Income statements for the year ended 30 June 20X4

	Aroma plc group £000	Therapy Ltd £000
Revenue	5,000	3,000
Cost of sales	(3,000)	(1,500)
Gross profit	2,000	1,500
Expenses	(790)	(440)
Profit from operations	1,210	1,060
Investment and interest income	55	–
Finance charges	(50)	(10)
Profit before tax	1,215	1,050
Tax	(400)	(350)
Profit after tax	815	700

Aroma plc and Therapy Ltd paid total dividends of £300,000 and £50,000, respectively, during the year.

Statements of financial position at 30 June 20X4

	Aroma plc group £000	Therapy Ltd £000
Non-current assets		
Goodwill	800	
PPE	3,200	3,500
Investment in Therapy Ltd	1,000	
	5,000	

Current assets		
Inventories	670	430
Receivables	500	395
Cash and cash equivalents	130	215
	1,300	1,040
Total assets	6,300	4,540
Equity		
Equity share capital	2,000	1,000
Revaluation reserve	1,000	500
Retained earnings	2,550	2,470
	5,550	3,970
Current liabilities	750	570
Total equity and liabilities	6,300	4,540

Therapy's revaluation reserve at 1 July 20X3 was £400,000.

Required:

Prepare the consolidated income statement and consolidated statement of changes in equity for the year ended 30 June 20X4 and the consolidated statement of financial position at this date.

3   Two property management companies, Hafford plc and Lysters plc, set up a separate company, Fairfax Ltd, for the purpose of acquiring and operating a shopping centre. The contractual arrangement between Hafford and Lysters establishes joint control of the activities that are conducted in Fairfax. The main feature of Fairfax's legal form is that the company, not Hafford and Lysters, has rights to the assets, and obligations for the liabilities, relating to the arrangement. These activities include the rental of the retail units, managing the car park, maintaining the centre and its equipment, such as lifts, and building the reputation and customer base for the centre as a whole.

The terms of the contractual arrangement are such that:

(a) Fairfax owns the shopping centre. The contractual arrangement does not specify that Hafford and Lysters have rights to the shopping centre.

(b) Hafford and Lysters are not liable in respect of the debts, liabilities, or obligations of Fairfax. If Fairfax is unable to pay any of its debts or other liabilities, or to discharge its obligations to third parties, the liability of each party to any third party will be limited to the unpaid amount of that party's capital contribution.

(c) Hafford and Lysters have the right to sell or pledge their interests in Fairfax.

(d) Hafford and Lysters each receive a share of the income from operating the shopping centre (which is the rental income net of the operating costs) in accordance with its interest in Fairfax.

Required:

Discuss whether this arrangement should be classified as a joint operation or a joint venture, and explain the consequential accounting method.

●● Develop your understanding

4   The abbreviated accounts of three companies are as follows.

Income statements for the year ended 31 December 20X6

	Hartleys plc	Samuel Smith Ltd	Adnams Ltd
	£000	£000	£000
Profit from operations	26	30	20
Investment income from Samuel Smith Ltd	6		
Investment income from Adnams Ltd	4		
Profit before tax	36	30	20
Tax	9	11	7
Profit after tax	27	19	13

Statements of financial position at 31 December 20X6

	Hartleys plc	Samuel Smith Ltd	Adnams Ltd
	£000	£000	£000
Non-current assets			
PPE	163	74	11
30,000 shares in Samuel Smith Ltd	45		
4,000 shares in Adnams Ltd	7		
	215		
Current assets	11	36	25
Total assets	226	110	36
Equity			
Called up share capital (£1 shares)	100	40	10
General reserve	60	–	–
Retained earnings	37	27	13
	197	67	23
Current liabilities			
Payables	20	32	6
Tax payable	9	11	7
	29	43	13
Total equity and liabilities	226	110	36

The following additional information is provided:

(a)   Hartleys plc purchased its investments 2 years ago when the retained earnings of Samuel Smith Ltd and Adnams Ltd were £12,000 and £8,000 respectively.

(b)   The companies do not trade with each other.

(c)   The book values and fair values of the non-current assets of the investee companies at the respective dates of acquisition were as follows:

	Book value	Fair value
Samuel Smith Ltd	£62,000	£66,000
Adams Ltd	£10,000	£12,000

The fair values have not been incorporated into the companies' accounts. Both companies use a 10% straight-line depreciation method.

Assume the fair values of the other net assets of these companies were not materially different from their book values at the time of the acquisitions.

(d) The companies paid the following dividends during the year:

Hartleys £10,000, Samuel Smith £8,000, and Adnams £10,000.

Required:

Prepare the consolidated statements of comprehensive income and changes in equity for the year ended 31 December 20X6, and a consolidated statement of financial position at that date.

(Note: for the consolidated statement of changes in equity, retained earnings at the start of the year will need to be derived.)

5   The income statements and the retained earnings columns from the statements in changes in equity for the year ended 31 March 20X6, and the statements of financial position at 31 March 20X6 of three companies, Worcester plc, Pershore Ltd, and Evesham Ltd, are as follows.

Income statements for the year ended 31 March 20X6

	Worcester plc	Pershore Ltd	Evesham Ltd
	£000	£000	£000
Revenue	10,630	4,260	5,870
Cost of sales	7,760	3,200	4,110
Gross profit	2,870	1,060	1,760
Distribution costs	730	275	590
Administrative expenses	1,290	405	760
	2,020	680	1,350
Profit from operations	850	380	410
Income from investments	71	–	–
Finance costs	(225)	(15)	(94)
Profit before tax	696	365	316
Income tax	160	80	70
Profit for the year	536	285	246

Statements of changes in equity—retained earnings for the year ended 31 March 20X6

	Worcester plc	Pershore Ltd	Evesham Ltd
	£000	£000	£000
At 1 April 20X5	4,863	975	2,430
Profit for the year	536	285	246

Dividends paid	(144)	(90)	(66)
At 31 March 20X6	5,255	1,170	2,610

Statements of financial position at 31 March 20X6

	Worcester plc £000	Pershore Ltd £000	Evesham Ltd £000
Assets			
Non-current assets			
PPE	8,400	2,070	3,810
Investments	3,975		
	12,375		
Current assets			
Inventories	1,860	645	1,440
Trade and other receivables	1,785	960	1,875
Cash and cash equivalents	450	–	675
	4,095	1,605	3,990
Total assets	16,470	3,675	7,800
Equity			
Equity shares (£1 shares)	3,000	750	2,400
6% Irredeemable preference shares (£1 shares)	900	–	300
Share premium	1,840	195	–
Retained earnings	5,255	1,170	2,610
	10,995	2,115	5,310
Liabilities			
Current liabilities			
Bank overdraft	–	375	–
Trade and other payables	1,725	1,185	1,290
	1,725	1,560	1,290
Non-current liabilities			
Debentures	3,750	–	1,200
Total liabilities	5,475	1,560	2,490
Total equity and liabilities	16,470	3,675	7,800

Additional information:

(a) The balance on Worcester plc's Investment account is made up as follows:

	£000
450,000 shares in Pershore Ltd	1,725
840,000 equity shares in Evesham Ltd	2,250
	3,975

(b) Worcester plc purchased its investment in Pershore Ltd on 1 April 20X4 when the balance on Pershore's retained earnings was £810,000. At this date the fair value of Pershore's PPE was £2,100,000, while the book value was £1,500,000.

(c) Worcester plc purchased its investment in Evesham Ltd on 1 April 20X5, when the balance on Evesham's retained earnings was £2,430,000. At this date the fair values of Evesham's PPE was £5,400,000, while the book value was £4,500,000.

(d) The fair values of all other net assets in Pershore and Evesham at the respective dates of acquisition can be assumed to be equal to their book values.

(e) Assume Pershore and Evesham use an average depreciation method of 10% straight-line.

(f) Pershore Ltd issued its preference shares when it was first formed. Since 1 April 20X4 and 1 April 20X5 there have been no movements in share capital in Pershore Ltd and Evesham Ltd respectively.

(g) Worcester, Pershore, and Evesham trade with each other. During the year ended 31 March 20X6 Worcester and Evesham purchased goods from Pershore for £2,450,000 and £85,000, respectively, which Pershore had marked up by 25%. At the year end, Worcester's inventories included some of these goods, which had cost it £780,000.

(h) Worcester and Evesham's accounts payable include amounts owing to Pershore of £180,000 and £45,000 respectively. Pershore's accounts receivable show £320,000 due from Worcester and £45,000 from Evesham.

Required:

Prepare Worcester plc's consolidated income statement and consolidated statement of changes in equity for the year ended 31 March 20X6, and its consolidated statement of financial position at that date.

6 Companies Fyfield plc and Gresham plc have set up a strategic and operating agreement (the framework agreement) in which they have agreed the terms according to which they will conduct the manufacturing and distribution of a product (product P) in different markets.

The companies have agreed to conduct manufacturing and distribution activities by establishing joint arrangements, described as follows.

(1) *Manufacturing activity*: Fyfield and Gresham have agreed to undertake the manufacturing activity through a joint arrangement (the manufacturing arrangement). The manufacturing arrangement is structured in a separate company, Mixit Ltd, whose legal form causes it to be considered in its own right (i.e. the assets and liabilities held in Mixit are the assets and liabilities of Mixit and not the assets and liabilities of Fyfield and Gresham). In accordance with the framework agreement, Fyfield and Gresham have committed themselves to purchasing the whole production of product P manufactured by the manufacturing arrangement in accordance with their ownership interests in Mixit. Fyfield and Gresham subsequently sell product P to another arrangement, jointly controlled by the two parties themselves, that has been established exclusively for the distribution of product P, described as follows. Neither the framework agreement nor the contractual arrangement between Fyfield and Gresham dealing with the manufacturing activity specify that Fyfield and Gresham have rights to the assets, and obligations for the liabilities, relating to the manufacturing activity.

(2) *Distribution activity:* Fyfield and Gresham have agreed to undertake the distribution activity through a joint arrangement (the distribution arrangement). The companies have structured the distribution arrangement in a separate company, Donna Ltd, whose legal form causes it to be considered in its own right (i.e. the assets and liabilities held in Donna are the assets and liabilities of Donna, and not the assets and liabilities of Fyfield and Gresham). In accordance with the framework agreement, the distribution arrangement orders its requirements for product P from Fyfield and Gresham according to the needs of the different markets where the distribution arrangement sells the product. Neither the framework agreement nor the contractual arrangement between Fyfield and Gresham dealing with the distribution activity specifies that these companies have rights to the assets, and obligations for the liabilities, relating to the distribution activity.

In addition, the framework agreement establishes:

(a) That the manufacturing arrangement will produce product P to meet the requirements that the distribution arrangement places on Fyfield and Gresham

(b) The commercial terms relating to the sale of product P by the manufacturing arrangement to Fyfield and Gresham. The manufacturing arrangement will sell product P to Fyfield and Gresham at a price agreed by Fyfield and Gresham that covers all production costs incurred. Subsequently, Fyfield and Gresham sell the product to the distribution arrangement at a price agreed by Fyfield and Gresham

(c) That any cash shortages that the manufacturing arrangement may incur will be financed by Fyfield and Gresham in accordance with their ownership interests in Mixit.

Required:

Discuss whether this arrangement should be classified as a joint operation or a joint venture, and explain the consequential accounting method.

●●● Take it further

7   The financial statements for the year ended 30 June 20X5 of Strauss plc, Cook Ltd, and Anderson Ltd at are given as follows.

Income statements for the year ended 30 June 20X5

	Strauss plc £000	Cook Ltd £000	Anderson Ltd £000
Revenue	5,090	2,650	1,530
Cost of sales	2,955	2,075	1,105
Gross profit	2,135	575	425
Distribution and administration expenses	1,775	415	195
Profit from operations	360	160	230
Income from investments	66	–	–
Profit before tax	426	160	230
Income tax expense	168	35	50
Profit after tax	258	125	180

Extracts from the statements of changes in equity for the year ended 30 June 20X5

	Retained earnings		
	Strauss plc	Cook Ltd	Anderson Ltd
	£000	£000	£000
Balance at 1 July 20X4	472	165	510
Profit for the year	258	125	180
Dividends paid	(100)	(20)	(200)
Balance at 30 June 20X5	630	270	490

Statements of financial position at 30 June 20X5

	Strauss plc	Cook Ltd	Anderson Ltd
	£000	£000	£000
Non-current assets			
PPE	1,580	1,090	820
Investments			
In Cook Ltd	950		
In Anderson Ltd	370		
	2,900		
Current assets			
Inventories	830	450	390
Accounts receivable	970	410	370
Cash and cash equivalents	70	–	150
	1,870	860	910
Total assets	4,770	1,950	1,730
Equity			
Share capital	2,000	600	500
Share premium	800	100	–
Retained earnings	630	270	490
	3,430	970	990
Current liabilities			
Bank overdraft	–	30	–
Accounts payable	780	750	580
Corporation tax	560	200	160
	1,340	980	740
Total equity and liabilities	4,770	1,950	1,730

Additional information:

(a) The investments in Cook and Anderson were made as follows:

	Nominal value of ordinary share capital	No. of shares acquired	Date of acquisition	Retained earnings at date of acquisition
Cook	£1	480,000	1.7.20X3	£110,000
Anderson	20p	625,000	1.7.20X4	£510,000

Since 1 July 20X3 and 1 July 20X4 there have been no movements in share capital in Cook Ltd and Anderson Ltd respectively.

(b) The book values and fair values of the PPE of Cook at the date of acquisition of its shares by Strauss were £810,000 and £960,000 respectively. At this date the expected remaining useful life of these assets was estimated at five years. The fair values of all other net assets in Cook can be assumed to be equivalent to their book values.

(c) During the year ended 30 June 20X5 Cook and Anderson purchased goods from Strauss for £375,000 and £150,000 respectively. Strauss earned a gross margin of 40% from these transactions. At the year end Cook had one-third of the goods it had purchased in its inventories and owed Strauss £75,000. Anderson had one-quarter of the goods it had purchased in its inventories.

(d) At 30 June 20X5 a review for impairment found that the recoverable amount of the goodwill arising on the acquisition of Cook was £100,000. In all other reviews for impairment of goodwill, no adjustments to goodwill values had been necessary.

(e) Assume that Strauss values the non-controlling interest using the proportion of net assets method.

Required:

Prepare the following financial statements for the Strauss plc group:

(i) The consolidated income statement for the year ended 30 June 20X5

(ii) The retained earnings and non-controlling interest columns of the consolidated statement of changes in equity for the year ended 30 June 20X5

(iii) The consolidated statement of financial position at 30 June 20X5.

8 (a) In the context of accounting for business combinations, discuss the difference between an acquiring company having:

(i) significant influence

(ii) control

over the acquiree company and explain the different accounting treatments that result.

(b) The income statements of three companies, Hexham plc, Colwell Ltd, and Alston Ltd, for the year ended 30 June 20X7 and their statements of financial position at that date are as follows.

Income statements for the year ended 30 June 20X7

	Hexham	Colwell	Alston
	£000	£000	£000
Revenue	5,268	1,950	1,449
Cost of sales	(3,531)	(1,458)	(1,173)
Gross profit	1,737	492	276
Distribution costs	(846)	(243)	(153)
Administrative expenses	(417)	(90)	(87)
Profit from operations	474	159	36
Income from shares in group companies	42	–	–
Finance charges	(45)	–	(12)
Profit before tax	471	159	24
Taxation	(96)	(36)	(6)
Profit for the year	375	123	18

Statements of financial position at 30 June 20X7

	Hexham	Colwell	Alston
	£000	£000	£000
Non-current assets			
PPE	705	198	222
Investment in Colwell Ltd	378		
Investment in Alston Ltd	75		
	1,158		
Current assets			
Inventories	435	120	168
Receivables	603	156	183
Cash and cash equivalents	166	96	–
	1,204	372	351
Total assets	2,362	570	573
Equity			
Equity shares of £1 each	450	90	150
Share premium	195	60	–
Retained earnings	472	195	(57)
	1,117	345	93

Non-current liabilities	450	–	150
Current liabilities			
Bank overdraft	–	–	108
Payables	795	225	222
	795	225	330
Total equity and liabilities	2,362	570	573

Additional information

(a) Hexham plc acquired 63,000 shares in Colwell Ltd on 1 July 20X5 when Colwell's retained earnings were £126,000 and the balance on its share premium was £60,000.

(b) At 1 July 20X5 the fair values of Colwell's non-current assets were £240,000 whereas the net book values were £180,000. The assets had an estimated remaining useful life of 10 years at this date. The fair values of all other net assets were equivalent to their book values.

(c) Hexham plc acquired 60,000 shares in Alston Ltd on 1 January 20X7. Alston's profits for the year ended 30 June 20X7 may be assumed to have arisen evenly over the year.

(d) At 1 January 20X7 the fair values of Alston's net assets can be assumed to be equal to their book values.

(e) During the year ended 30 June 20X7 Hexham sold goods to Colwell for £75,000, earning a 40% gross profit on this transaction. One quarter of these goods was still in Colwell's inventories at the year end.

(f) At 30 June 20X7 Hexham's trade receivables include an amount owing from Colwell of £30,000.

(g) The review for impairment of goodwill at 30 June 20X7 indicated that goodwill on acquisition should be written down to £100,000.

(h) During the year ended 30 June 20X7 Hexham and Colwell paid dividends of £80,000 and £60,000 respectively. Alston did not pay any dividends during the year.

Required:

Prepare Hexham plc's consolidated income statement and statement of changes in equity for the year ended 30 June 20X7 and a consolidated statement of financial position at that date.

9 The following are extracts from the consolidated financial statements of Tahir plc and one of its wholly owned subsidiaries, Amex Ltd, the shares in which were acquired on 31 October 20X8.

Statements of financial position at:

	Tahir plc Group		Amex Ltd
	31 December 20X8	31 December 20X7	31 October 20X8
ASSETS	£'000	£'000	£'000
Non-current assets			
PPE	4,764	3,685	694
Goodwill	42	–	–
Investments in associates	2,195	2,175	–

Current assets			
Inventories	1,735	1,388	306
Receivables	2,658	2,436	185
Cash and cash equivalents	43	77	7
Total assets	11,437	9,761	1,192
EQUITY AND LIABILITIES			
Equity			
Equity share capital	4,896	4,776	400
Share premium account	216	–	–
Retained earnings	2,458	2,000	644
Non-current liabilities			
Loans	1,348	653	–
Current liabilities			
Payables	1,915	1,546	148
Bank overdrafts	258	406	–
Taxation	346	380	–
Total equity and liabilities	11,437	9,761	1,192

Consolidated income statement for the year ended 31 December 20X8

	£'000
Profit before interest and tax	546
Share of profit of associates	120
Profit before tax	666
Income tax expense	126
Profit for the period	540
Profit attributable to:	
Owners of Tahir plc	540
Non-controlling interest	–
	540

The following information is also given:

(a) The consolidated figures at 31 December 20X8 include Amex Ltd.

(b) Depreciation charged on PPE during the year was £78,000. Additions to PPE, excluding PPE acquired on the acquisition of Amex Ltd, were £463,000. There were no disposals.

(c) The cost on 31 October 20X8 of the shares in Amex Ltd was £1,086,000. This was satisfied by Tahir plc issuing £695,000 unsecured loan stock at par, 120,000 ordinary shares of £1 each at a value of 280p each, and £55,000 in cash.

(d) No write down of goodwill was required during the period.

(e) Total dividends paid by Tahir plc during the period amounted to £63,000.

Required:

Prepare the following:

(i) A consolidated statement of cash flows for Tahir plc for the year ended 31 December 20X8 using the indirect method

(ii) A note reconciling profit before tax to cash generated from operations

(iii) A note showing the effect of the subsidiary acquired in the period.

Visit the Online Resource Centre for solutions to all these end of chapter questions plus visual walkthrough solutions. You can test your understanding with extra questions and answers, explore additional case studies based on real companies, take a guided tour through a company report, and much more. Go to the Online Resource Centre at **www.oxfordtextbooks.co.uk/orc/maynard/**

Part 6
Conclusion

Chapter 17 Interpretation of financial statements revisited

17

Interpretation of financial statements revisited

➤ Introduction

For a user to understand companies' financial statements a sound approach to their interpretation using all relevant information is required. This chapter revisits interpretation of financial statements, which was introduced in Chapter 5. It uses the basic analytical tools discussed in Chapter 5 together with details of what constitutes published financial statements, and the accounting methods used in the recognition and measurement of many of the key figures in the financial statements. This is material that has been covered in other chapters.

A model for interpretation which uses all of this information, the CORE approach (context, overview, ratios, and evaluation), is discussed and illustrated by use of a full example of the interpretation of a single company, J Sainsbury plc.

Much of the approach to this interpretation will apply to company-to-company comparisons also. If this is the interpretation being performed, the contextual information is vital to an understanding of the differences between the companies.

After studying this chapter you will be able to:

● understand and be able to perform an interpretation of companies' published financial statements using a variety of techniques and information.

❑ The CORE approach to the interpretation of financial statements.
❑ Context
  ❑ external and internal environments.
❑ Overview
  ❑ horizontal and trend analyses
  ❑ other significant information in the annual report.
❑ Ratio calculations
  ❑ categories of ratios
  ❑ companies' key performance indicators (KPIs)
  ❑ operating segments.
❑ Indicators of financial distress.
❑ Evaluation.
❑ The effect of recognition and measurement methods.
❑ The effect of and changes in accounting policies.
❑ Comprehensive case study.
❑ Use of databases.

17.1 Interpretation of financial statements in the context of material covered in the textbook

Chapter 5 provided details of some analytical techniques that can be used in the interpretation of the financial statements of a company. The methods covered in that chapter were horizontal analysis, vertical analysis, and ratio analysis. It was emphasised there that these were techniques to be used as part of an interpretation, and that a full interpretation of financial statements requires an understanding of far more than some line-by-line comparisons and ratio calculations. The bases for the recognition and measurement of different figures need to be understood, and to be meaningful; any interpretation must be set in the context of the company's internal and external environments.

If all previous chapters have been studied, readers should now have knowledge and understanding of what constitutes published financial statements, and the accounting methods used in the recognition and measurement of many of the key figures in the financial statements. The information contained in accounting policies and disclosure notes, which explain, enhance, and provide a breakdown of the aggregated figures on the face of the financial statements, has also been discussed throughout the textbook.

An annual report of a company, however, does not just contain financial statements and related notes. A UK company publishes a wealth of narrative information in the first half of its annual report, which includes its own interpretation of the company's financial performance and position. There is also much information about how the financial results and position have been achieved, the company's governance regime, and its environmental and social policies. All of this is to enable the users to assess the long-term success of the business. Details of these issues have been discussed in detail in Chapter 3.

17.2 A CORE approach

A framework for the interpretation of the financial statements of a company can be represented as shown in Figure 17.1.

This four-stage CORE (context, overview, ratios, and evaluation) approach ensures that any interpretation will focus on areas that are important, and take into account external and internal influences on the financial data presented in the financial statements. The stages are discussed in more detail in the following sections.

As highlighted in Chapter 5, it is crucial that the purpose of the interpretation and the user's needs are used to direct the interpretative techniques employed and the areas investigated.

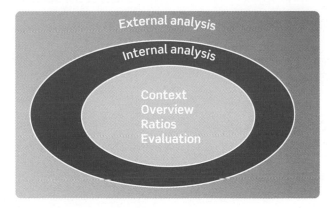

Figure 17.1 CORE analysis in strategic performance appraisal. Adapted from *Management Accounting Research*, vol.4, Moon and Bates, 'Core analysis in strategic performance appraisal', pp.139–152, Copyright (1993), with permission from Elsevier.

17.2.1 Context

Before any meaningful interpretation of financial statements can be performed, it is essential to understand the context in which the company is operating. Context here means the external and internal environments, and events that could influence the financial performance and position of a company.

Many external factors and influences can be identified by consideration of the following:

- What does the company do?
- In which markets does it compete?
- What is its position in its markets?
- What are the market structures?
- How do the main players compete?
- Recent industry/sector performance
- Recent economic and political developments, e.g. inflation, interest, and exchange rates
- Review of specific 'news' about the company being analysed.

By identifying the company and the sectors in which it operates, some broad expectations about what the financial statements might look like can be derived. A review of the actual financial statements against these expectations could then highlight anomalies or areas requiring investigation. For example, a retail chain would be expected to have high property assets and/or property lease expenses, high inventories, and relatively low receivables. An international airline company would be expected to have high values for plant and equipment (aircraft, although many of these will be off balance sheet, spare parts, etc.), some property, average receivables, and low inventories. Note that companies operate in many different sectors and provide details of which it identifies as its main ones in the segmental information it discloses. See Chapter 6 for further details of the disclosure requirements of operating segments.

Internal factors are things a company controls and relate to developments in the company's own strategic positioning within its sector, and steps it takes which influence its performance. To identify these factors the following questions need to be considered:

- What is the company's strategy?
- How does the company compete?
- What changes have occurred recently?
  - Changes in activities might include the mix of business, major new contracts, new products or processes, acquisitions, or disposals
  - Changes in strategy might include market positioning, or taking a balanced scorecard approach
- Review of specific 'news' about the company and its competitors.

Again, the actual effect of any of these on the financial performance and position should be compared with the expected effect, which will help confirm figures or identify areas requiring further investigation.

 Examples of external and internal context

How might the following factors affect the financial performance and position of a company?

1 A competitor starts selling a new, upgraded product.

This external factor might cause the sales revenue from the company's existing product to be affected. If the improved product's selling price is set too high, then revenues may not suffer; however, if the new product's selling price is set carefully, sales may be taken away from the company and revenues fall.

2 A company takes the decision to close the data processing function and outsource this operation, possibly overseas.

This internal factor will have implications for the financial performance and position of the company, as property, plant and equipment is disposed of affecting assets and capital; higher profit margins are achieved from lower salary costs; and the influence of exchange rates may have to be accounted for.

17.2.2 Overview

Before plunging into detailed ratio analysis, this stage provides an overview of the financial performance and the position the company is in at the end of the financial year. It is about reviewing trends in key figures in the financial statements through horizontal and trend analyses—techniques that were discussed in Chapter 5.

Reminder

1 Horizontal analysis compares key figures in the financial statements with the comparative year's figures, selecting those which are of particular interest for the purposes of the analysis. The aim of this is to gain a 'feel' for the financial performance and position of the company at least for the later year compared with the previous year and to direct attention to areas which require additional investigation. The key figures will usually include revenue, operating profit, profit before tax, and certain key assets and liabilities.

2 As conclusions drawn from an overview of just two years' worth of figures may be distorted by one-off figures in either year, trend analysis extends horizontal analysis to more years of data to establish a longer trend in changes. Companies publish key figures for the past five years (sometimes ten years) in their annual report.

It is essential to be aware of significant, one-off events within any period under review as these can distort comparisons or trends. Examples of these could include mergers or acquisitions, share issues, reorganisations, and natural catastrophes, such as floods. Some companies may disclose the financial effect of these separately on the face of the statement of comprehensive income under the heading of exceptional items, as discussed in Chapter 6; however, this would be a voluntary disclosure method. Other companies may refer to the effect in the notes.

In performing the overview, any changes in accounting policies need to be taken into account, as, again, the comparison or trend may be distorted if this has occurred. Changes in accounting policy are highlighted in financial statements and are discussed in more detail in Chapter 4. For company-to-company comparisons, it is essential to take into account the differences in accounting policies. Further discussion of how different accounting policies may affect the financial data to be analysed is included later in this chapter.

An overview of financial statements should also include an overview of other significant information contained in the annual report. For example:

- Is the audit opinion unqualified, in other words clean?
- Have there have been changes in key personnel?
- What does the company identify as its principal risks?
- Where have significant estimates or judgements been made?

17.2.3 Ratios

The third stage in the interpretation of a set of financial statements is to calculate financial ratios. Not all ratios need to be calculated for every analysis. As detailed in Chapter 5 the categorisation of ratios will help different groups of users determine which will be relevant for the purposes of their particular analysis. The ratios explained in Chapter 5 are summarised in Table 17.1

This is a typical set of financial ratios; however, there will be other ratios which may be calculated to meet the aims of the interpretation. For example, for companies in the pharmaceutical or telecommunications industries, ratios of intangible non-current assets to tangible non-current assets can reveal information about the underlying stability of the companies' capital. Ratios which incorporate non-financial data may also be relevant, for example the ratio of sales revenue to number of employees or sales revenue to floor area may be relevant in a retail company.

Interpreters should also look at the KPIs that companies themselves define in their annual report and how these are calculated. Clearly, these ratios have significance for the company.

The actual figures to be used in the numerator and denominator of ratios should be considered carefully. For example, a company may have different categories of non-current liability on its statement of financial position, including provisions, deferred tax, pension fund liabilities, and long-term borrowings. In determining the denominator of the ratio return on capital employed (profit before interest and tax/equity + long-term debt), care must be taken that only the appropriate figure for long-term debt is included and that also any current portion of the debt, which will be included in current liabilities, is also included.

In addition, ratios can be calculated for the different operating segments that the company has defined. This is discussed in more detail in Chapter 6.

Table 17.1 Typical financial ratios used in interpretation

Ratio category	Ratios
Profitability Effectiveness in generating profits	• Return on capital employed • Asset turnover • Net profit margin • Gross profit margin • Expenses as a percentage of sales
Liquidity Ability to meet liabilities when they fall due	• Current ratio • Liquid ratio
Efficiency/activity Effectiveness of use of business assets	• Asset turnover • Inventory turnover • Receivables collection period • Payables payment period
Gearing Financial structure	• Gearing • Financial leverage • Interest cover
Investor/stock market Returns to investors	• Return on equity (ROE) • Earnings per share (EPS) • Price/earnings ratio (PE ratio) • Dividend per share • Dividend cover • Dividend yield • Total shareholder returns

17.2.4 Ratios to indicate financial distress

A number of the ratios given in section 17.2.3 taken together may indicate that a company is in financial difficulties. Falling profitability ratios do not in themselves mean a company is in financial difficulties, but, collectively with other ratios, there may be indicators of future problems. For example, if profitability and liquidity are both falling, gearing increasing, and interest cover falling, the company may have difficulties meeting future debt servicing requirements. This could mean renegotiations with debt providers are needed or, worse, the company is put into administration or liquidators are called in.

There have been a number of attempts to develop a scoring system which would indicate that a company was in financial difficulties—a score below a certain target providing this indication. The original Z-score was developed by Professor Altman in 1968 and combines a number of weighted financial ratios as follows:

$$Z = 0.012R_1 + 0.014R_2 + 0.033R_3 + 0.006R_4 + 0.999R_5$$

where:

R_1 = working capital/total assets

R_2 = retained earnings/total assets

R_3 = earnings before interest and tax/total assets

R_4 = market capitalisation/book value of debts

R_5 = sales/total assets.

A score of 3.0 and above is considered to be a sign of a healthy company, whereas a score of below 1.8 is considered to mean the company is very likely to fail. The range in the middle is a 'grey area'.

A number of alternative Z-scores have subsequently been developed, but there are limitations to all of these models arising from different measurement and classification methods used by companies and the fact that they are based on historical data. In practice they are not widely used.

Other non-financial information should be considered, together with the financial ratios, and, collectively, these may give indications of a company in difficulties. Non-financial information could include:

- changes in senior management, particularly if unexpected
- high staff turnover
- recent changes in auditors or other financial advisors
- renewal of bank overdraft facilities with less favourable terms and conditions
- applications for loans from other than mainstream lenders
- a reduction in the company's credit rating.

A-scores have been developed that attempt to quantify non-financial indicators by weighting them and producing an overall score out of 100. An A-score will group the indicators under three headings—defects, mistakes, and symptoms. Defects relate to management structure, decision-making, accounting systems, and response to change. Mistakes are concerned with gearing and trading levels. Symptoms are poor financial ratios. A score above 25 indicates a company in difficulties.

17.2.5 Evaluation

The evaluation stage is the interpretation of all the information gathered in the previous three stages. Consistency between the data collected, ratios calculated, and conclusions reached in each stage needs to be checked, together with ensuring that areas highlighted as requiring investigation in one stage have been followed through.

As comparisons of ratios from one period to another, or one company to another, are made, the bases of the figures used in the ratios have to be considered. For example, what figures are included in the numerator and denominator, what changes/differences have occurred in these figures, and what effect will this have on the ratio? Knowledge of the valuation basis of the figures included in the ratio may affect the interpretation, as discussed in section 17.3. It is also important to understand the relationship between ratios, such as given by the Du Pont pyramid of operating ratios; one ratio may give one interpretation of the state of the business, but it needs to be supported by other ratios.

The business and financial reviews included in the narrative sections of a company's annual report will often provide some useful evaluation of the company's financial performance and position. Although the reliability of this information could be questioned, as it has been produced by the company, it will have been reviewed by the external auditors to provide assurance that it is at least consistent with the financial statements.

17.3 The effect of recognition and measurement issues, and accounting policies on interpretation

The bases of the figures which are used in analytical techniques and ratios must be fully understood so that an appropriate interpretation is made. This means that the accounting methods concerning recognition and measurement issues of all figures used should be considered in the evaluation. This will also encompass understanding the accounting policies the company or companies have used. Significant changes in accounting policies will affect comparative figures and trends, but this information should be available as these changes are required to be disclosed.

It is now a number of years since the 2005 requirement for all European Union (EU) companies to use International Financial Reporting Standards (IFRS). Although companies at the time produced one year's financial statements according to both IFRS and their national generally accepted accounting principles (GAAP), they were not required to adjust all figures in their five-year data, so a good trend analysis was difficult. However, it should be remembered that other countries have adopted IFRS more recently, and also that the IASB is continually updating and reissuing accounting standards. The first time a company uses a new or reissued standard there may be a significant effect on comparative figures. For example, if the proposed requirement for all leases to be capitalised is introduced in the forthcoming reissue of the leases accounting standard, this will have an enormous effect on asset and liability figures in the financial statements of many companies (see Chapter 14 for further details of leases).

A summary of the recognition and measurement issues included in this textbook which may affect the interpretation of financial statements is given in this section. It should always be remembered that many figures are based on management's best estimates or judgement, and so the interpretation of these figures may be more suggestive than absolute. Companies are required to disclosure the areas where significant estimates and judgement have been applied. See Chapter 6 for further discussion of this topic.

The summary also includes some reminders of information included in financial statements which may be useful in an interpretation.

17.3.1 Income statement and statement of comprehensive income

Revenue

● This will be an aggregate figure from many different sources, activities, and companies in a group.

● The accounting policy should provide details of the bases for the recognition of the different revenue types.

● Revenue from the different operating segments is disclosed (IFRS 8).

Discontinued operations

● The financial result from discontinued operations is disclosed separately on the face of the statement of comprehensive income. This comprises the net profit/loss from the operation plus any profit or loss from the sale of the operation or impairment loss from revaluation of the net assets if still held at the year end. A breakdown of these figures is included in a disclosure note.

● This may also be useful for predictions of future results.

One-off or exceptional items

● As discussed previously these will distort comparatives and trends.

● Companies are required to disclose these separately if they are considered material and relevant to an understanding of the company's financial performance.

● Companies may elect to disclose them separately on the face of the statement of comprehensive income.

Operating segments

● The disclosures for operating segments are very useful to break down the aggregate figures included on the face of the main financial statements.

● From the information required to be disclosed, certain financial ratios on a segment-by-segment basis can be calculated and compared.

- The segments are chosen by management to fit in with how they organise and manage their business, so will not necessarily be comparable from one company to another.

Adjustments to the fair value measurement of assets and liabilities, including impairment losses

- Certain assets and liabilities, mainly financial instruments, are measured each year end at fair value with the changes passing through profit and loss. Arguably, these changes have little to do with the financial performance of a business.

- Impairment losses and their reversal may pass through profit and loss. These may arise from external factors which have little to do with the financial performance of the business.

Earnings per share

- Remember, basic and diluted earnings per share (EPS) is disclosed on the face of the income statement, and a disclosure note provides details of its calculation. There is no need to recalculate these figures!

17.3.2 Statement of changes in equity

All changes in equity balances are shown in this statement, including all transactions with the shareholders. It is therefore useful in understanding ratios that use equity in their denominator, for example return on capital employed, return on equity, and gearing.

17.3.3 Statement of financial position

Property, plant and equipment

- The accounting policy will disclose information about depreciation methods and rates used for the different classes of assets. Remember these are based on estimates. This information will help in an understanding of the depreciation expense in profit and loss, assets' ages, and when assets are expected to be replaced.

- Decreases in the estimates of the useful economic life of non-current assets will lower the reported carrying amount. Although such a change in estimate would imply the assets of the business are wearing out faster than expected (seen as not a good development), ratios with net asset in the denominator would improve owing to the lower asset value.

- If the business replaces failing assets with new ones, increasing its operating capacity or using improved technology, such ratios will decline.

- A comprehensive disclosure note shows all movements in non-current assets by class over the year, so significant acquisitions and disposals can be identified.

- There are two alternative measurement models available and although most UK companies use the historic cost model, some may choose the revaluation model for some classes of assets. If the latter method is used, the depreciation expense and profit will be affected. Various disclosures are required which enable comparison to the historic cost model.

- Whether the companies are property-owning or not needs to be established for company-to-company comparisons.

- Property, plant and equipment will include assets capitalised under finance leases, but not assets held under operating leases.

Intangible assets

- Companies that can recognise intangible assets through direct purchase or acquisition of companies in which intangible assets can be identified are not directly comparable to companies that generate their own intangible assets where the recognition criteria may not be satisfied.

- Goodwill included in financial statements only arises from the acquisition of a subsidiary. Thus, companies that grow organically are not directly comparable to those that grow through acquisitions.

- Much judgement is required in determining when internally generated intangible assets can be recognised.

- As for property, plant and equipment, two alternative measurement models are available—historic cost or revaluation.

- Accounting for amortisation varies according to the type of intangible asset.

Inventories

- Inventories will include materials, work-in-progress, and finished goods, and this breakdown is disclosed.

- Companies will have many different inventory lines subject to different internal purchasing policies. This information will not necessarily be disclosed.

- The accounting policy will disclose the measurement method which will usually be the lower of cost and net realisable value.

Receivables

- Management's attitude to credit risk will affect the amount included as a provision for irrecoverable debts; this may change over time.

Construction contract amounts owed by or owed to customers

- For construction companies these balances may be assets or liabilities.
- The method to determine the recognition of revenues and profits is disclosed in the accounting policy, but may vary from company-to-company.

Current liabilities

- Current liabilities will include various balances including bank overdrafts, accounts payable, accruals, provisions, deferred income, tax payable, construction contract balances, and the current portion of any long-term liabilities, such as long-term borrowings and finance leases. All these are very different in their nature.
- Management's judgement has to be exercised, particularly in the recognition and measurement of provisions.

Debt

- The current portion of long-term debt should be included in any ratio which includes debt.
- Companies often use the term 'net debt', which is interest-bearing loans less cash and bank balances and marketable securities. The reason for this is that net debt is the figure that represents the outcome of treasury management policies.

Non-controlling interest

- This should not be included in the figure of equity which is used in various ratios.

17.3.4 Statement of cash flows

- This should be used in any interpretation of liquidity and availability of cash and cash equivalents.
- The reconciliation of profit before tax to cash flows generated from operating activities is particularly useful in the interpretation of the management of working capital.
- Horizontal and trend analysis is less meaningful for this statement as some cash inflows and outflows will not be regularly recurring items and will vary in amount from transaction to transaction, e.g. cash outflows to acquire property, plant and equipment or proceeds from the issue of shares.

- Some further financial ratios use cash flows from operating activities, e.g.:

$$\frac{\text{Net operating cash flows}}{\text{Net profit}}$$ An indication of the quality of profits—this ratio indicates the extent to which profits are 'real' rather than the result of possibly creative accounting methods.

$$\frac{\text{Net operating cash flows}}{\text{Current liabilities}}$$ An alternative liquidity ratio—this ratio gives an indication of the ability to meet current obligations.

17.4 Case study

A comprehensive analysis of the 2011 financial statements of J Sainsbury plc now follows, which will demonstrate many of the techniques discussed. Note that this is not the only approach to the interpretation that could be taken. It is principally for an equity investor or a potential investor, but, for completeness, assesses all areas.

J Sainsbury is one of the leading UK supermarkets with stores solely in the UK. The financial statements are available from their website at www.j-sainsbury.co.uk. For convenience the main financial statements for the group (income statement, statement of comprehensive income, balance sheet, and cash flow statement) have been included at the end of the chapter. Some of the analysis, however, uses information contained in other parts of the annual report and financial statements for 2011.

17.4.1 External environment

For the purposes of this exercise a full analysis of the external environment has not been performed. However, the period covered by the financial statements (52 weeks ended 19 March 2011 and the comparative 52 weeks ended 20 March 2010) was one of a challenging economic environment, as cost of living increases impacted on consumers' disposable income and job uncertainties for many prevailed. Thus, many customers shopped around looking for the best value. Sainsbury's operates in a very competitive business sector with main rivals being Tesco, Asda, and Morrisons, and has a 16% share of this market—its share marginally increasing from the previous year.

One key external factor that affects one of Sainsbury's major products is the impact of oil prices and fuel taxes on petrol sales. Over the period covered by the financial statements these have increased.

17.4.2 Internal environment

An assessment of this will start from identifying exactly what Sainsbury's strategic objectives and business are, and if there have been any significant changes to these in 2011. This information is gathered principally from the narrative reports contained in the company's annual report.

Sainsbury's strategic objectives are not defined in these terms in the annual report. However, the company's business model defines five areas of focus for its business and the company reviews its operations under these headings:

- great food at fair prices
- accelerating the growth of complementary non-food ranges and services
- reaching more customers through additional channels
- growing supermarket space
- active property management.

The products offered by Sainsbury's are groceries, complementary non-food ranges (household goods/furniture, clothing, books, home textiles, entertainment, electricals), access to advice and products related to home energy (insulation and solar panels), and financial services (through Sainsbury's Bank). The company operates a total of 934 stores comprising 557 supermarkets and 377 convenience stores. The complementary non-food products and services are available in many of the stores. An Internet-based home delivery shopping service is also available to over 93% of UK households. The company jointly owns Sainsbury's Bank with Lloyds Banking Group, and has two property joint ventures with Land Securities Group plc and the British Land Company plc.

Non-food sales (which are possibly higher margin) grew more than three times faster than food sales, with some areas growing in excess of 20%. The convenience business has grown and Sainsbury's opened a further 47 convenience stores in 2011. The online groceries business also grew in 2011, with annual sales up by more than 20%.

Gross supermarket space has increased by 15.9% since March 2009, with an additional 8.5% added in 2011 from the opening of 21 new stores, 24 extensions, and 47 convenience stores.

Sainsbury's states that it is continually looking for methods to streamline its operations and keep a tight control on operating costs. The company has achieved savings on paper, packaging materials, transport miles travelled, and energy from its focus on environmental matters, which is one of its underpinning values; these should lead to lower costs.

The company is constantly looking for ways to generate value from its property portfolio. Approximately 65% of its properties are freehold with the remainder being leasehold. The company generated £275 million of proceeds from the sale and leaseback of property considered to have no further development potential.

17.4.3 Summary of Sainsbury's context

What do we expect the financial statements to show from this review of the external and internal environments?

A supermarket, by its nature, is likely to have:

- high levels of land and buildings
- a negative working capital cycle

- low receivables
- fairly low levels of inventories
- low margins and high turnover
- relatively stable profit/revenue patterns.

Sales in 2011 should have grown from the addition of the new stores and increases in petrol prices, but the difficult trading environment may have meant customers turned to low-cost supermarkets, such as Aldi. Sainsbury's green initiatives and focus on efficiencies may have countered inflationary pressures on costs, and increased sales from non-food items may cause increased margins; however, the picture of profit margins is mixed.

Large additions to property are expected, but there will also be large disposals from the sale and leaseback transactions. Funding of the additions will need to be analysed.

17.4.4 Overview

Changes in key figures in the financial statements from 2010 to 2011 are now calculated and reviewed.

 Worked example 17.1: to show selection and calculation of changes in key figures in Sainsbury's financial statements from 2010 to 2011

	2011 £m	2010 £m	Change
Revenue	21,102	19,964	+5.7%
Operating profit (PBIT)	851	710	+19.9%
Underlying operating profit[1]	738	671	+10.0%
Profit before tax	827	733	+12.8%
Underlying profit before tax[1]	665	610	+9.0%
Profit after tax	640	585	+9.4%
Shareholders' funds (equity)	5,424	4966	+9.2%
Net debt (as defined by Sainsbury's)	1,814	1549	+17.1%
Capital employed (defined here as equity plus net debt)	7,238	6,515	+11.1%
Non-current assets	9,678	9,002	+7.5%
Current assets	1,708	1,797	−4.9%
Current liabilities	2,942	2,793	+5.3%
Net cash and cash equivalents movement (net decrease/ increase as a percentage of opening balance)	−40%	+39%	

No. of shares	1,871 m	1,860 m	+0.6%
Closing share price[2]	351p	330p	+6.4%

(Note: closing 2009 share price was 313p.)

1 Sainsbury's breaks down its profit before tax on the face of the income statement into 'underlying profit before tax' plus other items. All profit measures included in Sainsbury's KPIs also use this measure of profit.

Underlying profit before tax is defined as profit before tax before any profit or loss on the disposal of properties, investment property fair value movements, impairment of goodwill, financing fair value movements, International Accounting Standard (IAS) 19 pension financing element, and one-off items that are material and infrequent in nature. In other words, Sainsbury's is stripping out of its key profit measure all items that do not relate to its core (underlying) supermarket activity.

2 Share price is not available from the financial statements.

Five year data

	2011	2010	2009	2008	2007
Sales[3] (including VAT, including fuel) (£m)	22,943	21,421	20,383	19,287	18,518
Increase on previous year (%)	7.1	5.1	5.7	4.1	6.9[4]
Indexed[5]	132	124	118	111	107
Underlying operating profit – retailing (£m)	738	671	616	535	429
Increase on previous year (%)	10.0	8.9	15.1	24.7	21.9[4]
Indexed[5]	210	191	175	152	122
Underlying profit before tax (£m)	665	610	519	434	339
Increase on previous year (%)	9.0	17.5	19.6	28.0	38.9[4]
Indexed[5]	273	250	213	178	139
Earnings per share					
Underlying basic (pence)	26.5	23.9	21.2	17.4	13.0
Increase on previous year (%)	10.9	12.7	21.8	33.8	36.8[4]
Proposed dividend per share (pence)	15.1	14.2	13.2	12.0	9.75
Number of outlets at financial year end	934	872	792	823	788
Sales area (000 sq ft)	19,108	17,750	16,703	16,191	15,715
Net increase on previous year (%)	7.7	6.3	3.2	3.0	3.6[4]
Indexed[5]	126	117	110	107	104
No. of new stores	68	89	29	35	40
Sales intensity (including VAT)					
Sales per sq ft (£ per week)	20.04	20.42	20.01	19.69	19.30

3   Note that Sainsbury's reports and discusses a number of different sales measures:

- sales including value added tax (VAT) and including fuel
- sales including VAT and excluding fuel
- like-for-like sales (which excludes sales from new stores which were not in operation in the previous year).

One of its KPIs is like-for-like sales, including VAT, excluding fuel.

Sales, as reported in the income statement, would be total sales, including fuel, but excluding VAT.

The company itself highlights the following increases in sales over the past five years (presumably from 2006):

- like-for-like sales 22.7%
- total sales 33.4%.

4   The 2006 financial statements have had to be obtained in order to calculate the 2007 increase on the previous year. These show:

- sales   £17,317 million
- underlying operating profit—retailing   £352 million
- underlying profit before tax   £244 million
- earnings per share—underlying basic   9.5 pence
- sales area   15,166,000 sq ft.

5   Indexation is explained in Chapter 5. The base year used here is 2006.

Preliminary comments

An investor should find this overview positive. The income statement reveals that all profit figures have increased in 2011 and have exceeded the increase in revenue, indicating a better financial performance in 2011 compared with 2010. The statement of financial position appears marginally stronger in 2011 with increases in assets, offset by increases in liabilities, resulting in a net increase in shareholders' funds.

Over the past five years all measures of sales show steady increases. The increase in profit measures has outstripped the increase in sales, indicating that expenses have not risen at the same rate as the increase in sales. However, the rate of increase of profit and earnings per share has fallen over the five years. Although Sainsbury's has invested heavily in new stores each year, sales per square foot has increased only marginally.

Further detailed analysis using ratios is required to draw full conclusions.

Other information obtained from an overview reveals that the audit report is unqualified and that there have been some changes in key personnel at board level, although not the chairman and chief executive.

There have been no changes in accounting policies or any new accounting standards which the company considers would have a significant impact on the financial statements. The areas which Sainsbury's details as requiring significant judgement and estimates are as follows:

- goodwill impairment—goodwill is immaterial
- impairment of assets—there have been no impairments of assets in 2011
- post-employment benefits—comprise 11% (2010: 14%) of non-current liabilities

- provisions—immaterial amounts in current and non-current liabilities
- income taxes.

17.4.5 Ratios

The calculation of a set of financial ratios from a published set of financial statements is more complex than for financial statements presented in an exam question. Questions always arise about which figures to include or exclude under a particular heading. It should be remembered that there are no absolute definitions of ratios. Consistency in calculation from one period to the next, or from company to company, or from ratio to ratio should be maintained as far as possible, and the interpretation should be of the ratios that have been calculated.

In the calculation of the following ratios, various questions have been asked to illustrate this; although the ratios have been calculated in a particular way, these are not the only solution.

17.4.6 Shareholder ratios

$$\text{Return on equity} \qquad \frac{\text{Profit attributable to equity holders}}{\text{Equity}}$$

$$2011 \quad \frac{640}{5,424} = 11.8\% \qquad 2010 \quad \frac{585}{4,966} = 11.8\%$$

$$\text{EPS} \qquad \frac{\text{Profit attributable to equity holders}}{\text{No. of equity shares}}$$

- This is disclosed on the face of the income statement, but should basic or fully diluted be used in an analysis?

  Basic EPS is usually used for trend analysis of performance, and incorporates all elements of profit and loss. Diluted EPS is a theoretical figure based on the maximum number of shares that could be in issue if all options are converted. Sainsbury's also discloses underlying EPS based on its definition of underlying profit.

2011			2010		
	Basic	34.4p		Basic	32.1p
	Diluted	33.8p		Diluted	31.6p
	Underlying basic	26.5p		Underlying basic	23.9p
	Underlying diluted	26.1p		Underlying diluted	23.6p

$$\text{Dividend per share} \qquad \frac{\text{Dividends}}{\text{No. of equity shares}}$$

- Should this ratio use dividends paid, which comprises the previous year's final dividend and the current year's interim, or dividends for the current year?

Dividends recognised in the statement of changes in equity are dividends paid in the financial year, i.e. the 2010 final dividend and the 2011 interim dividend. It is more usual to calculate this ratio using the 2011 dividends—both interim and final—the latter is disclosed in note 10. This is also what the company has done in its headline financial summary figure on page 1.

- At what point should the number of shares be taken?
  The number of shares has varied over the year, so in calculating this ratio the weighted average has been used as disclosed in note 9 to the financial statements.

  2011 $4.30 + 10.8 = 15.1p$ *2010* $4.0 + 10.2 = 14.2p$

Dividend cover	$\dfrac{\text{Profit attributable to equity holders}}{\text{Total dividends}}$

- Which dividends should be included?
  As mentioned previously, it is more usual to include the same year's interim and final dividends in calculating this ratio. The ratio provides information about how well these dividends are covered by the 2011 profits and what proportion is being paid out as a dividend as opposed to being reinvested in the business.

  2011 $\dfrac{640}{(80 + 201)} = 2.28$ *2010* $\dfrac{585}{(74 + 189)} = 2.22$

PE ratio	$\dfrac{\text{Market price per share}}{\text{Earnings per share}}$

  2011 $\dfrac{351}{34.4} = 10.2$ *2010* $\dfrac{330}{32.1} = 10.3$

Total shareholder returns	$\dfrac{\text{Change in share price} + \text{dividend}}{\text{Opening share price}}$

- What if the share price is volatile and opening or closing share price was affected by an abnormal event that did not persist throughout the year?
  If the share price is volatile at the year end and the effect seems to be temporary, then it might be necessary to use share price at a different point, which is considered more representative of the long term picture.

  2011 $\dfrac{(351 - 330) + 15.1}{330} = 10.9\%$ *2010* $\dfrac{(330 - 313) + 14.2}{313} = 10.0\%$

17.4.7 Profitability

Return on capital employed	$\dfrac{\text{Profit before interest and tax (PBIT)}}{\text{Capital employed}}$

- Is PBIT, or operating profit, the best measure to use?

The operating profit has increased by nearly 20% in 2011; however, a significant part of this is a result of an increase in 'other income', which is the profit from the disposal of properties.

- Why does this ratio exclude the finance income/costs?

  As discussed in Chapter 5, this is to ensure that the numerator and denominator are consistent. Most companies, such as Sainsbury's, will have equity and debt funding for their operations, and therefore a ratio including both of these in the denominator has more meaning. The numerator should be a profit figure before any returns to the providers of funding.

- The financial review and KPIs use 'underlying operating profit'—would this be a better measure to use than PBIT?

  Remember—underlying operating profit excludes the following items from the profit (return) figure:

  - profit on sale of properties
  - fair value movements in investments and financial instruments
  - revaluation of joint ventures.

  The name suggests that Sainsbury's considers this a profit measure from its main underlying operations, that of a supermarket. The primary objective of such a business is not to make profits from buying and selling properties, although it will necessarily deal with a lot of property in the course of its business. So there are arguments for and against including this item in the profit figure for this ratio.

  Changes in the valuation of certain assets (the fair value movements) are not connected to a supermarket's key business, and Sainsbury's has little control over these, so it would be appropriate to exclude these figures.

  The exclusion or inclusion of the share of profits from joint ventures depends on two things. Firstly, what is the nature of the joint ventures? Are their operations similar enough to the parent company's for it to make sense to include them and does the management of Sainsbury's have enough control over the operations to hold them accountable for the results? Secondly, to what are the ratios to be compared and to what use are the ratios to be put? Are results from joint ventures included in the comparative figures? Is this ratio about assessing the return from the company's core business or is it about assessing the performance of the group as a whole?

- How should capital employed be defined?
  Capital employed is Equity + Debt.

- How should debt be defined?
  The notes to the financial statements show that borrowings consist of loans, loan notes, bonds, bank overdrafts, and finance lease obligations, so the current and non-current figures for borrowings would be a reasonable figure to use.
  Note that the Chief Financial Officer's definition of capital employed in the financial review is 'average of opening and closing net assets before net debt', where:

Net assets = Total assets minus total liabilities (or equity)

'Before net debt' means add back net debt. Net debt is defined in the financial statements (note 27) as:

Borrowings, bank overdrafts and financial derivative liabilities net of cash and cash equivalents, financial derivative assets and interest-bearing financial assets and deposits...

An alternative ratio to return on capital employed is return on net assets.

Return on net assets	$\dfrac{\text{Profit before interest and tax (PBIT)}}{\text{Total assets} - \text{current liabilities}}$

This raises further questions.

- Should net assets include intangible assets?
  Most commercial financial analysis systems (such as DataStream or FAME) exclude intangible assets on the grounds that their valuation is subjective and they are not recognised consistently from company to company. In some cases these assets have a very different character to the other assets included in capital employed.

- Should net assets include investment in joint ventures?
  Here, consistency with the numerator should be maintained. If the share of profits from joint ventures is included in the numerator profit, then the investment in joint ventures must be included in the denominator. Otherwise, both should be excluded. Arguments are detailed previously as to whether profit from joint ventures should be included or not.

- Should net assets include financial assets and derivative financial instruments?
  Again, consistency with the numerator should be maintained. If income from the financial assets and derivatives is included in the numerator, the asset should be included in the denominator.

- Should net assets include deferred tax assets?
  Similarly, this comes down to whether we want to class tax assets as an income-generating asset. However, deferred tax largely represents a timing difference in tax cash flows which does not really fit in with the idea of an asset which generates income, as in operating profits.

- Should net assets include non-current assets held for sale?
  This depends on whether the ratio is being used to look backwards, i.e. what return was generated from all net assets held by the business in the year which includes assets held for sale, or forwards, i.e. the ratio is to be used to forecast future returns when these assets are likely to be held no longer.

Return on capital employed	$\dfrac{\text{Profit before interest and tax (PBIT)}^{1}}{\text{Capital employed}^{2}}$

Using:

1 Underlying PBT per income statement with finance income deducted and finance costs added back

2 Equity plus current and long-term borrowings.

$$2011 \quad \frac{665 - 32 + 116}{5,424 + 74 + 2,339} = 9.6\% \qquad 2010 \quad \frac{610 - 33 + 148}{4,966 + 73 + 2,357} = 9.8\%$$

Alternative:

$$Return\ on\ capital\ employed \quad \frac{Profit\ before\ interest\ and\ tax\ (PBIT)^3}{Capital\ employed^4}$$

Using:

3 PBIT per income statement, i.e. before interest and share of profits from joint ventures

4 NCA + CA – CL, excluding intangible assets, investments in joint ventures, financial assets and liabilities, assets held for sale.

$$2011 \quad \frac{851}{[(9,678 - 151 - 502 - 176 - 29) + (1,708 - 52) - (2,942 - 59)]} = 11.2\%$$

$$2010 \quad \frac{710}{[(9,002 - 144 - 449 - 150 - 20) + (1,797 - 43) - (2,793 - 41)]} = 9.8\%$$

Per the financial review in the annual report, ROCE is defined as:

$$\frac{Underlying\ profit\ before\ interest\ and\ tax^5}{Average\ capital\ employed^6}$$

5 Includes underlying share of post-tax profit from joint ventures.

6 Average of opening and closing net assets before net debt (i.e. equity with net debt added back).

$$2011 \quad \frac{738 + 24}{(5,424 + 1,814 + 4,966 + 1,549) / 2} = 11.1\%$$

$$2010 \quad \frac{671 + 18}{(4,966 + 1,549 + 4,376 + 1,671) / 2} = 11.0\%$$

$$\textbf{Asset turnover} \quad \frac{Revenue}{Net\ assets^7}$$

● The same issues identified earlier apply to the definition of net assets. Should assets that do not directly generate revenue, such as financial instruments and joint ventures, be excluded?

7 Using same definition as in the earlier second calculation of ROCE:

$$2011 \quad \frac{21,102}{7,593} = 2.8 \qquad 2010 \quad \frac{19,964}{7,241} = 2.8$$

$$\textbf{Net profit margin} \quad \frac{Profit\ before\ interest\ and\ tax\ (PBIT)^{8\,or\,9}}{Revenue}$$

● The same issues arise for this ratio as identified earlier in relation to defining the profit figure.

8   Using the income statement figure:

$$2011 \quad \frac{851}{21{,}102} = 4.0\% \qquad\qquad 2010 \quad \frac{710}{19{,}964} = 3.6\%$$

9   Using underlying profit before interest and tax from the financial review:

$$2011 \quad \frac{762}{21{,}102} = 3.6\% \qquad\qquad 2010 \quad \frac{689}{19{,}964} = 3.5\%$$

Gross profit	$\dfrac{\text{Gross profit}}{\text{Revenue}}$

$$2011 \quad \frac{1{,}160}{21{,}102} = 5.5\% \qquad\qquad 2010 \quad \frac{1{,}082}{19{,}964} = 5.4\%$$

17.4.8 Liquidity

Current ratio	$\dfrac{\text{Current assets}}{\text{Current liabilities}}$

Liquid ratio	$\dfrac{\text{Current assets} - \text{inventories}}{\text{Current liabilities}}$

- These ratios assume that all current assets can be liquidated at their statement of financial position values in order to settle all current liabilities in a short time frame. Is this reasonable here?

  Sainsbury's current assets include derivatives, which it may not be possible to liquidate immediately. The best way to judge liquidity is usually to study the cash flow statement. In the case of Sainsbury's, overall cash balances decreased from £834m to £500m, a decrease of 40%, whereas in the previous year they increased by £235m.

$$2011 \quad \text{Current} \quad \frac{1{,}708}{2{,}942} = 0.58 \qquad 2010 \quad \text{Current} \quad \frac{1{,}797}{2{,}793} = 0.64$$

$$2011 \quad \text{Liquid} \quad \frac{1{,}708 - 812}{2{,}942} = 0.30 \qquad 2010 \quad \text{Liquid} \quad \frac{1{,}797 - 702}{2{,}793} = 0.39$$

17.4.9 Management efficiency

Inventory holding period	$\dfrac{\text{Inventories}}{\text{Cost of sales}} \times 365$

- Should year end or average inventories be used?
  Year end inventory may not be representative of usual inventory levels because of the time of year or the company deliberately running down inventories at the year end (to assist with inventory checks). Average inventory is a far better measure to use for this ratio; however, it is not available from the financial statements. The

average of inventory at the beginning and end of the year may be better than just year end inventory, but with only two years' worth of financial statements available, a comparative calculation for 2010 will not be possible.

$$2011 \quad \frac{812}{19,942} \times 365 = 15 \text{ days} \qquad 2010 \quad \frac{702}{18,882} \times 365 = 14 \text{ days}$$

$$\textbf{Payables payment period} \quad \frac{\text{Trade payables}}{\text{Credit purchases}} \times 365$$

- Care should be taken as to which payables figure is used.
  The figure on the face of the statement of financial position includes trade payables, other payables (such as amounts owing for wages, VAT, employment taxes), and accruals. The ratio is giving users an indication of the time Sainsbury's takes to pay its suppliers for goods, hence only trade payables are relevant. The figure should be taken from the notes to the financial statements (note 19).

- Is credit purchases able to be derived?
  Credit purchases is not available from the financial statements. Provided opening and closing inventory levels are not significantly different, purchases may be able to be approximated by cost of sales. However, other direct costs must also be included in cost of sales, as administrative expenses per the income statement does not include all staff costs. Without knowing the allocation of expenses to the line items in the income statement, the ratio, as calculated, is not completely representative of the length of time taken to pay suppliers.

$$2011 \quad \frac{1,836}{19,942} \times 365 = 34 \text{ days} \qquad 2010 \quad \frac{1,782}{18,882} \times 365 = 34 \text{ days}$$

Note that the receivables collection period has not been calculated as it is not significant for a retailer. Although there is a sizeable receivables figure on the face of the statement of financial position, and there are some trade receivables, the balance consists mainly of other receivables, and prepayments and accrued income.

17.4.10 Gearing

$$\textbf{Gearing ratio} \quad \frac{\text{Debt}^{\,10\,\text{or}\,11}}{\text{Equity}}$$

- The question of how debt is defined is discussed previously in relation to capital employed.
  Borrowings from the face of the statement of financial position could be used or, alternatively, Sainsbury's provides its own definition and calculation of net debt.

10 Using current and non-current borrowings:

$$2011 \quad \frac{74 + 2,339}{5,424} = 44.5\% \qquad 2010 \quad \frac{73 + 2,357}{4,966} = 48.9\%$$

11 Using Sainsbury's definition of net debt:

$$2011 \quad \frac{1,814}{5,424} = 33.4\% \qquad 2010 \quad \frac{1,549}{4,966} = 31.2\%$$

Financial leverage	$\dfrac{\text{Total capital employed (net assets)}^{12}}{\text{Shareholders' funds}}$

- This ratio is intended to measure what proportion of Sainsbury's net assets is financed by equity and, by implication, what proportion by debt. It provides a measure of the exposure of the company to the risk of fixed return and fixed term finance. However, is it reasonable to regard everything that is not equity as debt?
- Should all assets be included?

  See earlier discussion relating to return on capital employed.

12 Using net assets as total assets minus current liabilities:

$$2011 \quad \frac{(11,399 - 2,942)}{5,424} = 1.56 \qquad 2010 \quad \frac{(10,855 - 2,793)}{4,966} = 1.62$$

Interest cover	$\dfrac{\text{Profit before interest and tax}}{\text{Interest (finance costs)}}$

$$2011 \quad \frac{851}{116} = 7.3 \qquad 2010 \quad \frac{710}{148} = 4.8$$

17.4.11 Other KPIs

Sainsbury's includes two other KPIs in its annual report which are not included in any of the aforementioned figures:

Net capital expenditure
2011   £880 m   2010   £915 m
Operating cash flow
2011   £1,138 m   2010   £1,206 m

17.4.12 Segmental analysis

Sainsbury's operating segments are 'determined on information provided to the operating board to make operational decisions on the management of the group'. They are given as:

- retailing (supermarket and convenience)
- financial services (Sainsbury's bank joint venture)
- property investment.

Their comparative sizes and importance to the company's operating performance are given as follows:

	Assets	Profits
	%	%
Retailing	96	93
Financial services	1	1
Property investment	3	6

Clearly, retailing is the dominant segment, and the others are of relatively minor importance and are support activities for the main business. Note that these other two segments fall below the 10% threshold and are therefore disclosed voluntarily by Sainsbury's, presumably on the basis that they are subject to separate internal reporting and decision-making processes.

A return on assets ratio (using profit before tax as the profit measure) for the different operating segments shows:

	2011		2010	
Retailing	767/10,897	7.0%	595/10,406	5.7%
Financial services	11/115	9.6%	7/102	6.9%
Property investment	49/387	12.7%	131/347	37.8%

However, the effect of the differences between the returns of these segments on the overall financial statements is minimal given the overwhelming size of the retailing segment.

17.4.13 Evaluation

Summary of ratios	2011	2010
Return on equity	11.8%	11.8%
Earnings per share—basic	34.4p	32.1p
Earnings per share—underlying basic	26.5p	23.9p
Dividend per share	15.1p	14.2p
Dividend cover	2.28	2.22
PE ratio	10.2	10.3
Total shareholder returns	10.9%	10.0%
Return on capital employed (using equity and borrowings)	9.6%	9.8%
Return on net assets	11.2%	9.8%
Asset turnover (using net assets)	2.8	2.8
Net profit margin (using income statement PBIT)	4.0%	3.6%
Underlying net profit margin	3.6%	3.5%
Gross profit	5.5%	5.4%
Gearing (Sainsbury's definition of net debt)	33.4%	31.2%

Financial leverage	1.56	1.62
Interest cover	7.3	4.8
Current ratio	0.58	0.64
Liquid ratio	0.30	0.39
Inventory holding period	15 days	14 days
Payables payment period	34 days	34 days

Evaluation

Sainsbury's overarching business is the supermarket retail business in which it sells groceries, complementary non-food products, home energy-related products, petrol, and financial services. Sainsbury's revenues, profits, and returns to shareholders have been growing for the past few years, with 2011 being no exception, despite the challenging economic climate. Profit growth has generally been higher than growth from revenues. In 2011 growth in revenues from non-food items outstripped increases from groceries. For an investor these are pleasing figures; however, the detailed ratio analysis indicates that, in fact, the 2011 performance has been very similar to 2010. The statement of financial position appears marginally stronger in 2011.

A more detailed evaluation of 2011 compared with 2010 follows.

Shareholders' perspective

There has been no change in return on equity, although basic EPS has increased by 7.2%. Profit after tax and equity have both increased at the same rate (approximately 9%) with the increase in equity principally being from retained profits. The number of shares has increased by less than 1% resulting in a larger increase in basic EPS.

Note that underlying basic EPS has increased by 10.9% and dividends for the year have increased in cash terms. The dividend cover ratio shows a fairly consistent dividend/profit retention policy.

The increase of 6.4% in the share price over 2011 has not matched the increase in EPS, but has been closer to the increase in profits. Therefore, the PE ratio has fallen marginally. However, this should also be set against generally suppressed stock markets over the period.

Profitability

The return ratios (ROCE and RONA) have varied according to how they are defined. However, the impact of the other income figures on the results should be noted and the return ratios based on underlying profits are less impressive. A closer examination of capital employed (net assets) reveals that there have been significant purchases of property, plant and equipment, whereas current assets have, in fact, decreased mainly because of the fall in cash and cash equivalents. Note that this ties in with the cash flow statement, which shows negative cash flow from investing and financing activities, despite the release of cash from the sale and leaseback of properties.

Sainsbury's achieved a higher net profit margin in 2011 than in 2010; however, the underlying operating profit margin shows no significant increase. The revenue generated from the use of the assets, as shown by the asset turnover ratio, was identical in both years. Thus, the increase in ROCE can be said to be due to increased profit margins and not from more effective use of assets in generating revenues. Further analysis shows a small improvement in the gross margin and administrative expenses rising at a lower rate than revenues.

Finance costs have fallen, but this is possibly a result of the fall in interest rates in the economy rather than any managerial decisions made by the company. The fall in the share of post-tax profits from the joint ventures is also significant and requires further investigation.

Gearing

The gearing ratio indicates that in both 2011 and 2010 approximately 70% of net assets were funded by equity. Sainsbury's own definition of net debt, used in the gearing ratio, has netted off cash and cash equivalents with debt, and as cash has decreased significantly, this has influenced this ratio. Whichever definition of gearing is used, Sainsbury's can be considered a fairly low-geared company, which is also reflected in the interest cover, which indicates it can comfortably cover the debt-servicing costs out of operating income, particularly with the fall in finance costs as discussed previously.

Liquidity

As with all supermarkets, Sainsbury's has net current liabilities, and current and liquid ratios well below 1, which are marginally lower in 2011 than in 2010. This does not necessarily indicate liquidity problems as cash pours into the retail outlets every day and Sainsbury, like other large supermarkets, may require long payment terms from many of its suppliers. Both the current and liquid ratios have decreased in 2011 mainly because of the decrease in cash and cash equivalents, as discussed earlier. There have also been increases in inventories and trade receivables, which have had a negative impact on operating cash flow.

The working capital management ratios for inventory and payables are very similar in 2011 and 2010, probably as one would expect.

Risks

Sainsbury's is not in a risky business sector and does not have significant risky investments. The company appears to have considered its principal risks and has taken steps to mitigate against these including regular reviews.

Conclusion

- A relatively low-risk business showing continued growth.
- Maintenance of a positive financial performance despite the economic background.
- Some improvement in shareholder returns.

These facts should lead an investor to consider this an investment in Sainsbury's a sound one. An investor looking for a company advocating sustainability issues should also note that Sainsbury prides itself on its focus on its corporate responsibility commitments and claims they are at the heart of its policies and decision-making.

17.5 Industry statistics—use of databases

There are a number of databases which contain company and average industry sector financial ratios, such as FAME and DataStream. While these are undoubtedly very useful in the interpretation of the financial statements of companies, care should be exercised in the use of the ratios included therein. It is important to understand how the database has defined the ratios and also which figures have been used in their calculation. As can be seen from the discussion for Sainsbury's, there are alternative definitions and ways of calculating many ratios.

 ## Summary of key points

Interpretation of financial statements requires more than an analysis of financial data. This chapter has set out an approach which starts with a review of the external environment in which a company is operating, followed by a review of internal factors that may affect its financial performance and position. Interpretation can only be meaningful if set in these contexts.

The next stage in interpretation is to carry out an overview of the financial data through horizontal and trend analyses, taking into account one-off or exceptional items and events that could affect an individual year's figures. If the interpretation is using published annual reports of companies, this overview stage should also consider the effect of other significant information which is contained in the narrative reports.

The calculation and analysis of financial ratios are at the heart of any interpretation, but this should be directed towards the required interpretation for the particular user. To properly interpret ratios, the user must take into account the changes or differences in the individual figures that make up a ratio, the bases of valuation and any changes or differences in these, and the relationships between ratios. This interpretation should be set in the context of the information gathered from the review of the external and internal environments and the overview of the financial statements themselves.

 ## Further reading

Moon, P. and Bates, K. (1993) 'Core analysis in strategic performance appraisal', *Management Accounting Research*, 4, 139–152. Why read? This expands upon the approach to financial statement analysis taken in this chapter.

 ## Bibliography

J Sainsbury plc (2011) *Annual Report and Financial Statements, 2011*. London: J Sainsbury. [Reproduced by kind permission of Sainsbury's Supermarkets Ltd. The opinions expressed are those of the author.]

Moon, P. and Bates, K. (1993) Core analysis in strategic performance appraisal, *Management Accounting Research*, 4, 139–152.

Questions

●●● Take it further

1   Pink plc and Goldie plc are competing companies operating UK mobile phone networks for personal and business customers. There is increased regulatory pressure on the pricing of mobile phone tariffs within the telecommunications industry and, with the strong competition between companies, this leads to competitive pricing structures.

Extracts from the annual reports of the two companies are as follows:

Income statements for the latest financial years

	Pink	Goldie
	£m	£m
Revenue	2,695	5,220
Cost of sales	(1,595)	(2,990)
Gross profit	1,100	2,230
Selling and distribution costs (see note 1)	(190)	(430)
Administrative expenses	(150)	(290)
Impairment losses (see note 2)	(1,000)	–
(Loss)/profit from operations	(240)	1,510
Finance costs	(75)	(160)
(Loss)/profit before taxation	(315)	1,350
Tax	(195)	(460)
(Loss)/profit for the year	(510)	890

Final dividends of 6.5p per share (Pink) and 6.2p per share (Goldie) were disclosed in the financial statements.

Statements of financial position at the year ends

	Pink		Goldie	
	£m	£m	£m	£m
ASSETS				
Non-current assets				
Property, plant and equipment		1,600		3,060
Intangibles		4,615		10,780
		6,215		13,840
Current assets				
Inventories	15		30	
Trade receivables	460		990	

Cash and cash equivalents	620		450	
		1,095		1,470
Total assets		7,310		15,310
EQUITY & LIABILITIES				
Equity				
Issued capital—£1 ordinary shares		1,335		2,660
Share premium		2,600		5,180
Other reserves		270		470
Retained earnings		115		1,580
Shareholders' equity		4,320		9,890
Non-current liabilities				
Borrowings	2,060		4,070	
Provisions	20		30	
		2,080		4,100
Current liabilities				
Trade payables	565		700	
Taxation and other liabilities	345		620	
		910		1,320
Total equity and liabilities		7,310		15,310

Note 1

Pink plc spent £10 million in this financial year on new advertising and sports sponsorship to boost brand awareness.

Note 2

The impairment losses of £1,000 million included in the operating profit of Pink plc arise from a fall in the estimated fair values of the company's goodwill and other intangible assets, such as operating licences. The estimation of fair values is an issue involving significant management judgement.

Required:

Produce a report for a potential equity investor which compares the financial performance, financial position and liquidity of Pink plc and Goldie plc.

Your report should include:

● an overview of the financial information provided

● calculations of appropriate ratios

● an evaluation of the financial performance, financial position, and liquidity of the two companies in comparison with each other

● conclusions and recommendations for the potential investor, which should also include details of further information that you consider should be obtained to enhance the analysis.

2 Hawtons plc is a long established and well-known producer and retailer of luxury confectionery, specialising in chocolate. The company supplies its products through 379 shops and cafés, 250 franchises, plus Internet and mail order services. The annual report states that the company's long-term goals are:

- to re-establish Hawtons as the undisputed leading premium chocolate brand in the UK
- to increase its share of the UK chocolate market by more than 50%
- to increase all year round business to reduce dependency on Christmas and Easter
- to improve operating profit margins
- the selective development of export sales.

The statements of financial position, comprehensive income and cash flows for Hawtons are shown as follows.

Hawtons plc: statements of financial position at 30 June

	20X8 £000	20X7 £000
Non-current assets		
Intangible assets	4,786	5,950
Property, plant and equipment	64,084	66,378
	68,870	72,328
Current assets		
Inventories	24,307	18,202
Trade and other receivables	15,155	12,628
Cash and cash equivalents	1,088	2,858
	40,550	33,688
Total assets	109,420	106,016
Equity		
Ordinary shares	6,835	6,811
Share premium account	13,750	13,551
Retained earnings	14,450	14,524
	35,035	34,886
Non-current liabilities		
Borrowings	5,295	6,692
Deferred tax liabilities	2,750	2,512
Retirement benefit obligations	15,965	15,417
Other non-current liabilities	2,612	1,996
Provisions	586	478
	27,208	27,095
Current liabilities		
Borrowings	24,057	22,577
Trade and other payables	22,014	19,859

	984	1,418
Tax payable	984	1,418
Provisions	122	181
	47,177	44,035
Total equity and liabilities	109,420	106,016

Hawtons plc: Income statements for the years ended 30 June

	20X8 £000	20X7 £000
Revenue	208,122	185,989
Cost of sales	(103,017)	(86,022)
Gross profit	105,105	99,967
Operating expenses	(95,918)	(91,923)
Other operating income	1,139	808
Operating profit	10,326	8,852
Finance income	45	61
Finance costs	(1,901)	(1,832)
Profit before taxation	8,470	7,081
Taxation	(2,402)	(1,785)
Profit for the year	6,068	5,296
Earnings per share		
Basic	9.1p	8.0p
Diluted	9.0p	7.9p

Hawtons plc: statements of other comprehensive income and expense for the years ended 30 June

	20X8 £000	20X7 £000
Profit for the year	6,068	5,296
Other comprehensive income/expense		
Actuarial (loss)/gain in the defined benefit pension scheme	(2,148)	1,510
Movement of deferred tax on actuarial (loss)/gain in the defined benefit pension scheme	601	(453)
Effect of reduction in tax rate	–	(342)
Net other comprehensive (expense)/income	(1,547)	715
Total comprehensive income for the year	4,521	6,011

Hawtons plc: statements of cash flow for the years ended 30 June

	20X8	20X7
	£000	£000
Cash flows from operating activities	11,481	14,600
Cash flows from investing activities		
Proceeds from sale of property, plant and equipment	262	400
Purchase of property, plant and equipment	(5,680)	(5,030)
Net cash used in investing activities	(5,418)	(4,630)
Cash flows from financing activities		
Net proceeds from issue of ordinary shares	223	748
Interest paid	(1,831)	(1,849)
Interest received	37	25
Capital element of finance lease rental payments	(3,712)	(4,526)
Borrowings advanced	2,000	3,000
Dividends paid	(4,550)	(4,512)
Net cash used in financing activities	(7,833)	(7,114)
Net (decrease)/increase in cash and cash equivalents and bank overdrafts	(1,770)	2,856
Cash and cash equivalents at beginning of period	2,858	2
Cash and cash equivalents at end of period	1,088	2,858

Notes to the financial statements

(i) The intangible assets of the company are pieces of computer software, some of which have been acquired externally and some of which were generated internally. The amortisation charge for these assets, which amounted to £2.018 m in 20X8 and £1.973 m in 20X7, is recognised in cost of sales within the income statements.

(ii) The dividends paid by the company were a 1.95p per share interim dividend and a 4.85p final dividend in both years.

(iii) The mid-market price of the ordinary shares at 29 June 20X7 (the last dealing day prior to 30 June 20X7) was 175p and at 27 June 20X8 (the last dealing day prior to 28 June 20X8) was 114p. The range for the period was from 112p to 200p.

(iv) The number of shares in issue was 6.835 m at 30 June 20X8 and 6.811 m at 30 June 20X7.

Required:

You are considering including Hawtons plc in your investment portfolio. Analyse the performance of the company during the two years 20X8 and 20X7 and assess whether it is likely to be a worthwhile investment.

3 Obtain the 2011 Annual Report and Accounts for Next plc, which are available from www.nextplc.co.uk.

Required:

Using the analysis of the financial performance of Next plc as completed for Question 8 in Chapter 6, which used the company's segmental information, carry out a full interpretation of Next plc's financial statements for the year ended 29 January 2011.

4   Obtain the most recent financial statements of two companies operating in the same business sector. Carry out a comparative analysis of the two companies' financial statements, paying particular attention to the effect of any significant differences in the companies' recognition and measurement policies.

Case Study: To assist with your understanding of the Case Study in Chapter 17, extracts from the main financial statements of Sainsbury's *Annual Report and Financial Statements, 2011* are reproduced here.

Financial reporting in practice **17.1**	J Sainsbury plc, 2011

Group income statement for the 52 weeks to 19 March 2011

	Note	2011 £m	2010 £m
Revenue	4	**21,102**	19,964
Cost of sales		**(19,942)**	(18,882)
Gross profit		**1,160**	1,082
Administrative expenses		**(417)**	(399)
Other income		**108**	27
Operating profit	5	**851**	710
Finance income	6	**32**	33
Finance costs	6	**(116)**	(148)
Share of post-tax profit from joint ventures	14	**60**	138
Profit before taxation		**827**	733
Analysed as:			
Underlying profit before tax		**665**	610
Profit on disposal of properties	3	**108**	27
Investment property fair value movements	3	**39**	123
Financing fair value movements	3	**7**	(15)
IAS 19 pension financing credit/(charge)	3	**3**	(24)
One-off items	3	**5**	12
		827	733
Income tax expense	8	**(187)**	(148)
Profit for the financial year		**640**	585
Earnings per share	9	**pence**	pence
Basic		**34.4**	32.1

Diluted		**33.8**	31.6
Underlying basic		**26.5**	23.9
Underlying diluted		**26.1**	23.6

Group statement of comprehensive income for the 52 weeks to 19 March 2011

	Note	2011 £m	2010 £m
Profit for the period		640	585
Other comprehensive income/(expense):			
Net actuarial gains/(losses) on defined benefit pension scheme	30	29	(173)
Available-for-sale financial assets fair value movements:			
Group		14	43
Joint ventures		2	24
Cash flow hedges effective portion of fair value movements:			
Group		(8)	(3)
Joint ventures		2	–
Current tax on items recognised directly in other comprehensive income	8	(1)	16
Deferred tax on items recognised directly in other comprehensive income	8	(5)	21
Total other comprehensive income/(expense) for the period (net of tax)		33	(72)
Total comprehensive income for the period		673	513

Group balance sheets at 19 March 2011 and 20 March 2010

	Note	2011 £m	2010 £m
Non-current assets			
Property, plant and equipment	11	8,784	8,203
Intangible assets	12	151	144
Investments in joint ventures	14	502	449
Available-for-sale financial assets	15	176	150

(continued)

(continued)

Other receivables	17	**36**	36
Derivative financial instruments	29	**29**	20
		9,678	9,002
Current assets			
Inventories	16	**812**	702
Trade and other receivables	17	**343**	215
Derivative financial instruments	29	**52**	43
Cash and cash equivalents	26b	**501**	837
		1,708	1,797
Non-current assets held for sale	18	**13**	56
		1,721	1,853
Total assets		**11,399**	10,855
Current liabilities			
Trade and other payables	19	**(2,597)**	(2,466)
Borrowings	20	**(74)**	(73)
Derivative financial instruments	29	**(59)**	(41)
Taxes payable		**(201)**	(200)
Provisions	22	**(11)**	(13)
		(2,942)	(2,793)
Net current liabilities		**(1,221)**	(940)
Non-current liabilities			
Other payables	19	**(120)**	(106)
Borrowings	20	**(2,339)**	(2,357)
Derivative financial instruments	29	**–**	(2)
Deferred income tax liability	21	**(172)**	(144)
Provisions	22	**(62)**	(66)
Retirement benefit obligations	30	**(340)**	(421)
		(3,033)	(3,096)
Net assets		**5,424**	4,966
Equity			
Called up share capital	23	**535**	532
Share premium account	23	**1,048**	1,033
Capital redemption reserve	24	**680**	680
Other reserves	24	**(213)**	(242)

Retained earnings	25	**3,374**	2,963
Total equity		**5,424**	**4,966**

Group cash flow statement for the 52 weeks to 19 March 2011

	Note	2011 £m	2010 £m
Cash flows from operating activities			
Cash generated from operations	26	**1,138**	1,206
Interest paid		**(126)**	(111)
Corporation tax paid		**(158)**	(89)
Net cash generated from operating activities		**854**	1,006
Cash flows from investing activities			
Purchase of property, plant and equipment		**(1,136)**	(1,036)
Purchase of intangible assets		**(15)**	(11)
Proceeds from disposal of property, plant and equipment		**282**	139
Acquisition of and investment in subsidiaries, net of cash acquired	12	**(1)**	–
Investment in joint ventures		**(2)**	(2)
Investment in financial assets		**(50)**	(10)
Interest received		**19**	18
Dividends received		**1**	2
Net cash (used in) investing activities		**(902)**	(900)
Cash flows from financing activities			
Proceeds from issuance of ordinary shares		**17**	250
Repayment of short-term borrowings		**(11)**	(36)
Proceeds from long-term borrowings		**45**	235
Repayment of long-term borrowings		**(61)**	(74)
Repayment of capital element of obligations under finance lease payments		**(3)**	(2)
Interest elements of obligations under finance lease payments		**(4)**	(3)
Dividends paid	10	**(269)**	(241)
Net cash (used in)/generated from financing activities		**(286)**	129
Net (decrease)/increase in cash and cash equivalents		**(334)**	235
Opening cash and cash equivalents		**834**	599
Closing cash and cash equivalents	26	**500**	834

Visit the Online Resource Centre for solutions to all these end of chapter questions plus visual walkthrough solutions. You can test your understanding with extra questions and answers, explore additional case studies based on real companies, take a guided tour through a company report, and much more. Go to the Online Resource Centre at **www.oxfordtextbooks.co.uk/orc/maynard/**

TERMINOLOGY CONVERTER

Term used in this book	Equivalent terms	Explanatory note
Statement of financial position	Balance sheet	The term statement of financial position is the one used by international accounting standards, but IAS 1 does permit entities to use the alternative name, balance sheet.
Statement of comprehensive income	Statement of profit or loss and other comprehensive income	The latest name for this statement is the statement of profit or loss and other comprehensive income. IAS 1 does permit entities to use the alternative name, statement of comprehensive income. As the name change has not yet been endorsed by the EU, few companies will be using the latest name.
Income statement	Profit and loss account Statement of profit or loss	The term income statement was the one used in IAS 1 for companies that chose to present this as a separate statement. Many UK listed companies use income statement. The 2011 change to IAS 1 has almost reverted back to the original name of this statement, but this will not be seen yet, as detailed above.
Statement of cash flows	Cash flow statement	A minor change to the IAS 1 name. IAS 1 does permit the alternative cash flow statement.
Carrying amount	Book value	
Equity shares	Ordinary shares	
Nominal value	Par value	Alternative terms widely used.
Liquid ratio	Acid test ratio, or Quick ratio	
Nominal ledger	General ledger	

Accounting standards Authoritative statements issued by independent standard-setting bodies detailing how transactions and other events should be reflected in the financial statements.

Accounting Standards Board (ASB) The independent standard-setting body in the UK. Accounting standards issued by the ASB are called Statements of Standard Accounting Practice (SSAPs) and Financial Reporting Standards (FRSs) and are applicable to UK non-listed companies. The Accounting Council, a sub-council of the Financial Reporting Council, took over this role in July 2012.

Accrual accounting/accruals principle The effects of transactions and other events and circumstances on a business's economic resources and claims are accounted for in the periods in which those effects occur, even if the resulting cash receipts and payments occur in a different period.

Acquisition method The method of accounting used to account for the acquisition of subsidiaries by an acquirer company.

Actuarial method/effective interest method The method used to apportion payments made by a lessee under a finance lease between the finance charge and the reduction of the outstanding liability so as to produce a constant periodic rate of interest on the remaining balance of the liability.

Amortisation The term used for depreciation of intangible assets. (See depreciation.)

Asset A resource controlled by the entity as a result of past events and from which future economic benefits are expected to flow to the entity. Assets are classified as non-current (held for long-term use) or current (continuously changing as business is conducted).

Associate A company over which its investor company can demonstrate significant influence. This is usually evidenced by a shareholding of 20–50% of its equity shares.

Association of Chartered Certified Accountants (ACCA) A global professional accountancy body offering a professional accountancy qualification. A member of the Consultative Committee of Accountancy Bodies.

Audit An examination of the financial and other related statements of a company by an independent member of a Recognised Supervisory Body in order to express an opinion whether the statements are prepared, in all material respects, in accordance with an applicable financial reporting framework.

Auditing Practices Board (APB) A former part of the UK's Financial Reporting Council with responsibilities for issuing auditing standards for use by auditors. Its work has now been taken over by the Audit and Assurance Council.

Authorised share capital The maximum share capital a company may issue as detailed in its Memorandum of Association.

Basic earnings per share Profit or loss attributable to ordinary equity holders (i.e. profit or loss after tax and after preference dividends) divided by the number of ordinary shares outstanding during the period.

Capital The residual interest in the assets of an entity after deducting all its liabilities. It represents the owners' investment in the entity.

Carrying amount The value of an asset or liability recognised in the financial statements.

Cash and cash equivalents The term used for bank and cash balances in a statement of financial position. Cash is cash on hand and demand deposits. Cash equivalents are short term, highly liquid investments that are readily convertible to known amounts of cash and which are subject to an insignificant risk of changes in value.

Cash-generating unit The smallest identifiable group of assets that generates cash inflows which are largely independent of cash inflows from other assets or groups of assets. Used in testing for impairment.

Cash-in-transit A payment by one entity to another at the financial year end which has been recorded as cash out by the paying entity, but which has not been recorded as cash in by the receiving entity.

Chartered Institute of Management Accountants (CIMA) A global professional accountancy body offering a professional accountancy qualification especially for management accountants.

Company An entity with a separate legal identity from the owners, where the owners' liability is limited to the amount they have invested. Ownership is evidenced by the holding of shares in the limited liability company.

Comparable information An enhancing qualitative characteristic of financial information. Information is more useful if it can be compared from year-to-year and from business to business.

Construction contract A contract negotiated specifically for the construction of an asset or a combination of assets that are closely interrelated or interdependent in terms of their design, technology, and function, or their ultimate purpose or use. Contracts often last for more than one year. Construction contracts may be fixed price or cost-plus.

Contingent liability A possible liability that is not recognised in the statement of financial position because of uncertainties surrounding its existence or value.

Current tax The amount of income taxes payable or recoverable in respect of the taxable profit (tax loss) for an accounting period.

Debit and credit The type of bookkeeping entry made to an account or the nature of the balance on an account at the end of an accounting period.

Decision-usefulness The principal objective of financial accounting and reporting advocated by the IASB, which is to provide financial information about the reporting entity that is useful to existing and potential investors, lenders, and other creditors in making decisions about providing resources to the entity.

Deferred tax An accounting measure representing income taxes payable or recoverable in the future relating to transactions which have already taken place.

Depreciable amount The cost of an asset, or other amount substituted for cost, less its residual value.

Depreciation The systematic allocation of the depreciable amount of an asset over its useful life.

Diluted earnings per share (EPS) An alternative EPS ratio using figures which assume that convertible instruments are converted, that options or warrants are exercised, or that equity shares are issued upon the satisfaction of specified conditions.

Directors The individuals appointed by the shareholders to run and manage a company.

Distributable profits A company's accumulated, realised profits (which have not previously been distributed or capitalised) less its accumulated, realised losses (which have not previously been written off in a reduction or reorganisation of its share capital), and which are available for a distribution, such as a dividend, to shareholders. Generally distributable profits comprise revenue reserves.

Dividends A distribution to shareholders as a return to them for their investment in the company. Dividends may be interim, which are paid part way through the financial year, or final (also called proposed dividends), which are proposed by the directors after the end of the financial year and paid during the following year.

Double-entry bookkeeping The method used to record financial transactions in a financial accounting system. Every transaction has an effect on two (or more) accounts and is recorded to ensure the balance of the statement of financial position.

Downstream and upstream sales Sales of items from a parent company to its subsidiary companies (downstream) or from the subsidiary companies to the parent (upstream).

Elements Assets, liabilities, equity, income, and expenses—the building blocks of financial statements. All financial transactions are expressed as changes to one or more of these items.

Enhancing qualitative characteristics Characteristics that will improve the usefulness of relevant and faithfully represented financial information. The enhancing characteristics are comparability, verifiability, timeliness, and understandability.

Equity method of accounting The term for capital for a company comprising share capital and reserves. Equity is the residual interest in the assets of the entity after deducting all its liabilities.

Equity shares Shares that are not preference shares and do not have any predetermined dividend amounts. An equity share entitles the owner to a vote in matters put before shareholders in proportion to their percentage ownership in the company.

Equity method of accounting The method of accounting used by an investor company to include its share of an associate's or joint venture's profits or losses.

Exceptional items Financial transactions or items which are unusual owing to their nature or their size, and which an entity may wish to present separately in its financial statements.

Expectations gap The lack of understanding by a user of an assurance report (such as an audit report) of the assurances actually being provided or the work done in making the assurances.

Fair value The price that would be received to sell an asset or paid to transfer a liability in an orderly transaction between market participants at the measurement date.

Faithfully representative information A fundamental qualitative characteristic of information. Faithfully representative information should be as complete as possible, neutral, and free from error.

Finance lease A lease that transfers substantially all the risks and rewards incidental to ownership of an asset.

Financial Accounting Standards Board (FASB) The accounting standard-setting body in the USA. Accounting standards issued by the FASB are applicable to all US non-governmental entities. The standards are officially recognised as authoritative by the Securities and Exchange Commission (SEC).

Financial asset Any asset that gives a contractual right to receive cash or another financial asset from another entity; or to exchange financial assets or financial liabilities with another entity under conditions that are potentially favourable to the entity.

Financial instrument Any contract that gives rise to a financial asset of one entity and a financial liability or equity instrument of another entity.

Financial liability Any liability that is a contractual obligation to deliver cash or another financial asset to another entity; or to exchange financial assets or financial liabilities with another entity under conditions that are potentially unfavourable to the entity.

Financial Reporting Council (FRC) The UK's independent regulator responsible for promoting high quality corporate governance and reporting. The body sets standards for corporate reporting and monitors and enforces accounting and auditing standards. It also oversees the regulatory activities of the professional accountancy bodies and operates independent disciplinary arrangements for public interest cases involving accountants.

Financial Reporting Review Panel (FRRP) A former part of the UK's Financial Reporting Council with responsibilities for ensuring that the annual accounts of public companies and large private companies comply with the requirements of the Companies Act 2006 and applicable accounting standards. Its work has now been taken over by the Monitoring Committee.

Financial Reporting Standards (FRSs) Accounting standards issued by the UK's Accounting Standards Board (ASB).

Financial Services Authority (FSA) An independent body that regulates the financial services industry in the UK. It has a wide range of rule-making, investigatory, and enforcement powers

First-in, first-out (FIFO) A method of valuing inventory which assumes that oldest inventories are used or sold first, thus leaving the newest inventories on hand.

Fundamental qualitative characteristics Qualitative characteristics which make financial information useful to users. The fundamental characteristics are relevance and faithful representation.

Generally accepted accounting principles (GAAP) The standard framework of accounting guidelines used in any given jurisdiction. It includes statutory requirements, mandatory guidelines, such as accounting standards, and underpinning principles.

Going concern The underlying assumption of financial statements. It assumes an entity will continue in operation for the foreseeable future and that it has neither the intention nor the need to liquidate or curtail materially the scale of its operations.

Goodwill Intangible items that are not recognised in an entity's financial statements and which contribute to the value of an entity as a whole being greater than the carrying amounts of its net assets.

Goodwill arising on acquisition The only goodwill recognised in financial statements. It is an asset representing the future economic benefits arising from other assets acquired in a business combination that are not individually identified and separately recognised.

Hedge A finance technique to minimise the risks of changes in expected fair values or future cash flows of financial transactions and items.

Historic cost A measurement basis for assets and liabilities. It uses the amount of cash paid or the fair value of the consideration given to acquire an asset at its acquisition, or the amount of proceeds received in exchange for an obligation, or the amounts of cash or cash equivalents expected to be paid to satisfy a liability.

Horizontal analysis An analytical technique involving the calculation and comparison of changes in line items in the financial statements over successive years.

Impairment loss The amount by which the carrying amount of an asset or a cash generating unit exceeds its recoverable amount.

Income statement The financial statement which shows the total of income less expenses (i.e. profit or loss) excluding items in other comprehensive income. The income statement may be presented separately or as part of the statement of comprehensive income.

Institute of Chartered Accountants in England and Wales (ICAEW) A professional accountancy body providing financial knowledge and guidance to the global accountancy and finance profession. The body offers a professional accountancy qualification, the ACA. A member of the Consultative Committee of Accountancy Bodies.

Intangible asset An identifiable non-monetary asset without physical substance.

Interest rate implicit in the lease (imputed interest rate) The discount rate that, at the inception of the lease, causes the aggregate present value of (a) the minimum lease payments and (b) the unguaranteed residual value to be equal to the sum of (i) the fair value of the leased asset and (ii) any initial direct costs of the lessor.

International Accounting Standards (IASs) Accounting standards that were issued by the International Accounting Standards Committee (IASC), the predecessor of the IASB, and which were adopted by the IASB upon its formation.

International Accounting Standards Board (IASB) The independent international body with responsibility for setting international accounting standards.

International Federation of Accountants (IFAC) A New York-based global organisation for the accountancy profession which develops and promotes international standards in the areas of auditing and assurance, quality control, ethics, accounting education, and public sector accounting, and has as members national accountancy organisations.

International Financial Reporting Standards (IFRSs) Accounting standards issued by the International Accounting Standards Board since its formation.

Inventories Assets held for sale in the ordinary course of business; or in the process of production for such sale; or in the form of materials or supplies to be consumed in the production process or in the rendering of services.

Investment property Property held by the owner or by the lessee under a finance lease to earn rentals or for capital appreciation or both.

Irredeemable preference shares Preference shares which cannot be redeemed during the lifetime of the company.

Joint arrangement An arrangement, usually in connection with two or more parties working together to invest in a business venture, of which the parties have joint control. Joint arrangements can be joint operations or joint ventures.

Lease An agreement whereby the lessor conveys to the lessee in return for a payment or series of payments the right to use an asset for an agreed period of time.

Liability A present obligation of the entity arising from past events, the settlement of which is expected to result in an outflow from the entity of resources embodying economic benefits. Liabilities are classified as current (due for settlement within one year of the date of the statement of financial position) and non-current (due after one year).

Liquidity The ability of an entity to meet its debts as they fall due.

Market to book ratio A ratio comparing the market value of a company (no. of shares × market price per share) to its book value (total assets minus total liabilities).

Market value The price at which an asset would trade in a competitive auction setting such as on a stock market.

Materiality An aspect of relevance that relates to the nature or size or both of information. Information is material if its omission or misstatement influences the decision made by a user.

Measurement The valuation of an item.

Minimum lease payments Payments over the lease term that the lessee is required to make, excluding contingent rent, costs for services and taxes to be paid by and reimbursed to the lessor.

National Insurance A system of contributions paid by employees and employers in the UK towards the cost of certain state benefits. It is an employment tax.

Net book value The cost of an asset, or other amount substituted for cost, minus its accumulated depreciation or amortisation.

Net realisable value The estimated selling price of an asset in the ordinary course of business less the estimated costs of completion and the estimated costs necessary to make the sale.

Nominal value The unit value of a share which is determined when a company is first formed.

Nominal ledger Part of the financial accounting system which comprises all the accounts of the entity in which are recorded all the individual financial transactions.

Off balance sheet financing The practice by which transactions involving debt are structured to ensure that their accounting treatment is in line with current accounting practice but the debt is kept off the statement of financial position.

Operating lease Any lease other than a finance lease.

Other comprehensive income Items of income and expense that are not recognised in profit and loss (i.e. the income statement) as required or permitted by IFRSs, and are included in the statement of comprehensive income.

PAYE Pay-as-you-earn is a tax payment method in which an employer deducts income tax (and National Insurance, if applicable) from an employee's taxable wages or salary and pays it to the tax authorities.

Percentage of completion method The method by which revenues and expenses relating to a construction contract or the rendering of a service are recognised in the income statement to reflect the contract activity carried out during the accounting period. This is achieved by reference to the stage of completion of the contract at the end of the accounting period.

Pre-acquisition reserves The reserves of a subsidiary or associate company at the date of the acquisition of their shares by the acquirer.

Preference shares Shares that have a predetermined dividend amount. A preference share does not entitle the owner to a vote in matters put before shareholders.

Present value A measurement basis for assets and liabilities. It uses the present discounted value of the future net cash inflows or outflows that the asset is expected to generate or that are expected to be required to settle the liability in the normal course of business.

Primary user group Existing and potential investors, lenders, and other creditors.

Principles based accounting standards Accounting standards based on a conceptual framework that consists of a hierarchy of underpinning principles. The accounting methods specified by the standards reflect the economic reality of transactions and items and require the balanced exercise of judgement in their application.

Private and public limited companies A public limited company (plc) is one whose shares may be traded publicly on stock markets. A private limited (Ltd) company's shares are not able to be traded publicly.

Property, plant and equipment Tangible items that are held for use in the production or supply of goods or services, for rental to others, or for administrative purposes, and are expected to be used during more than one period.

Prospective adjustments to financial statements A prospective adjustment is one which is made in the current accounting period even if it relates to changes to estimates made in previous accounting periods.

Provision A liability of uncertain timing or amount.

Prudence An accounting principle which requires that, when making judgements and estimates, better evidence is needed for the recognition of assets and income compared to liabilities and expenses.

Qualifying asset An asset that necessarily takes a substantial period of time to get ready for its intended use or sale.

Recognition The process of incorporating in the statement of financial position or income statement an item that meets the definition of an element and satisfies the criteria for recognition.

Recoverable amount The amount the company could recover through either the use or the sale of the asset. The recoverable amount is the higher of the value in use of the asset, and the fair value less costs to sell of the asset.

Redeemable preference shares Preference shares which can be redeemed (i.e. the company can buy them back from the shareholder) on, or after, a period fixed for redemption under the terms of issue.

Relevant information A fundamental qualitative characteristic of information. Relevant information affects the decisions made by users and will either confirm evaluations or be used in making predictions about an entity.

Research and development costs Research costs are those relating to original and planned investigation undertaken with the prospect of gaining new scientific or technical knowledge and understanding.

Development costs arise from the application of research findings or other knowledge to the production of new or substantially improved products, processes, or services.

Reserves Any part of shareholders' equity, except for share capital. Reserves represent amounts that are retained in the company and not distributed to the shareholders.

Residual value The estimated amount that an entity would currently obtain from the disposal of an asset, after deducting the estimated costs of disposal, if the asset were already of the age and in the condition expected at the end of its useful life.

Retained earnings A reserve representing the amount of net profits (or losses) not paid out as dividends, but retained by a company to be reinvested in its business.

Retrospective adjustments to financial statements A retrospective adjustment is one where the financial statements are drawn up as if the adjustment had always been applied. All affected previous and comparative figures are restated. It only arises from a change in accounting policy or the correction of a material error.

Revaluation reserve A reserve that records the surplus created when assets are revalued to fair value.

Rules based accounting standards Accounting standards containing numerous specific requirements and much detailed implementation guidance in an attempt to address as many potential contingencies as possible.

Separate business entity An underpinning concept of financial reporting which requires that whatever form a business entity takes, or whatever its legal status, it reports the financial affairs of itself only.

Share capital The portion of a company's equity that is obtained by selling shares to a shareholder. The statement of financial position share capital line item shows the sum of the nominal values of all shares issued.

Share premium The excess of the market value of a share over its nominal value. Share premium is a reserve on the statement of financial position.

Shareholders The investors in a company.

Special purpose entities (SPEs) A legal entity of some type created to fulfil narrow, specific, or temporary objectives, such as to finance a large project. SPEs are used typically by companies to isolate themselves from financial risk.

Standard cost The planned cost of the products, components or services produced in a period.

Statement of cash flows The financial statement which shows the inflows and outflows of cash and monetary assets deemed to be equivalent to cash over the accounting period. The inflows and outflows are classified under operating, investing, and financing activities.

Statement of changes in equity The financial statement which shows all changes in the equity balances over the accounting period.

Statement of comprehensive income The financial statement which shows the changes in equity that have arisen from the transactions of a company other than with the owners in their capacity as owners. It includes both profits and losses, shown in the income statement part, and other comprehensive income.

Statement of financial position The financial statement showing the assets, liabilities and capital of an entity at a particular point in time.

Statements of Standard Accounting Practice (SSAPs) Accounting standards that were issued by the UK Accounting Standards Committee (ASC), the predecessor of the ASB, and which were adopted by the ASB upon its formation.

Stewardship An objective of financial accounting and reporting which is to provide financial information about the reporting entity in order to assess how efficiently and effectively the entity's management and governing board have discharged their responsibilities to use the entity's resources.

Structured entities An entity that has been designed so that voting rights are not the dominant factor in deciding who controls the entity.

Subsidiary An entity that is controlled by another entity. This is usually evidenced by a shareholding of more than 50% of its equity shares.

Substance over form An underpinning concept of a principles based financial reporting system which requires that items and transactions are accounted for according to their economic or commercial substance, rather than their legal form.

Tax base The amount attributed to an asset or liability for tax purposes and which reflects the tax consequences that will occur when the carrying amount of the asset or liability is recovered or settled.

Temporary differences The difference between the carrying amount of an asset and its tax base which gives rise to a deferred tax liability or asset. Temporary differences can be taxable or deductible.

Timely information An enhancing qualitative characteristic of financial information. The more recent the information, the more useful it is.

Trial balance A list of all the balances drawn from the nominal ledger accounts at a particular point in time.

Understandable information An enhancing qualitative characteristic of financial information. Information which is classified, characterised, and presented clearly and concisely is more useful.

Unrealised profit in inventories The profit element included in the value of inventories remaining in a parent or subsidiary company at the end of the accounting period which were purchased from another group company.

Unwinding of a discount rate The effect of the change in the discount factor applied to the measurement of a liability using a discounted cash flow basis from the beginning of a year to the end of the year.

Useful life The period over which an asset is expected to be available for use by an entity; or the number of production or similar units expected to be obtained from the asset by an entity.

Value in use The present value of the future cash flows expected to be derived from the use of an asset.

VAT (Value added tax) The tax added to the sales price of goods and services.

Verifiable information An enhancing qualitative characteristic of financial information. The better the evidence supporting a transaction or item, the more reliable the information.

Vertical analysis An analytical technique involving the comparison of financial statements which have been expressed in a common size (i.e. in percentages of a key figure taken from the statements).

Weighted average cost method A method of valuing inventory where the cost of each item is the weighted average of the cost of similar items at the beginning of a period and the cost of similar items purchased or produced during the period.

Working capital Net current assets or liabilities (i.e. current assets minus current liabilities).

INDEX

A

A-scores 666
absorption costing 459
accountability 55–6
  audit 98–102
  audit committee 98
  internal control 97–8
  risk 97
  UK Corporate Governance Code
    95–7
accounting 3
  policies 163, 166–7, 236–7, 245,
    667–72
  see also IAS 8 *under* Interna-
    tional Accounting Standards
  standards 24, 57, 58–66, 69–70
Accounting Standards Board (ASB)
  59, 60, 67
Accounting Standards Committee
  (ASC) 60, 61
accruals principle 9, 12, 27 33, 128,
  235, 343, 458
  depreciation 28–9
  non-current assets, disposal of
    31–3
  prepayments 27–8
  reducing balance depreciation
    30–1
  straight-line depreciation 29–30
acid test ratio *see* liquid ratio
acquisition method 562, 568, 571
activity based costing 459
activity ratios 197
actuarial method (effective interest
    method) 531
adjusting event 510–11
advances from customers 469
advertising commissions 291
AEI 60
aggregation 129–30
aggressive earnings management
  284
Ahold 332–3
amortisation 143, 166, 465, 466,
  548, 670

intangible assets 437, 438–40,
  441, 443, 446
Arsenal Holdings plc 239, 432–3,
  512
assets 6, 75, 76, 77, 135–6, 173, 297,
  525–6
  contingent 504–6
  deferred tax 351–2, 363
  exceptions to recognition of
    deferred tax 350–1
  fair value less costs to sell 396–7
  financial 561
  held for sale 245
  net 200, 210, 421, 623
  operating life of 410
  qualifying 381
  return on 199, 448
  taxation 343–5, 347–8, 349, 350,
    359
  total 199
  turnover 199, 200, 202
  value in use of 396–7
  see also current assets;
    impairment of assets;
    intangible assets;
    inventories; non-current
    assets; property, plant and
    equipment; receivables;
    tangible assets
associate companies 256, 617,
  618–28, 632, 634–5
  classification as held for sale
    623–6
  consolidated financial statements
    623–6
  disclosure requirements 626–8
  equity method 621–2
  exemptions from accounting 621
  goodwill 622–3
  IAS 28 *Investments in Associates*
    70, 423, 617, 619, 623, 630
  impairment losses 622–3
  indirect holding 619
  investments, categorisation of
    618–19

limited influence 619
partial influence 619
significant influence 619–21
total influence 619
Association of Chartered Certified
  Accountants (ACCA) 61,
  112
audit/auditors 55, 98–102, 118–19,
  449
Auditing Practices Board (APB) 101

B

balance sheet *see* statement of
  financial position
Balfour Beatty plc 480
Barclays plc 600–1
Barings Bank 90
best estimate 495–6, 507
BG Group plc 245–6
big bath accounting 492–3
board of directors 92–3
bonus element of rights issue 321–2
bonus fraction 320
bonus issue 311, 319
book value *see* carrying amount
BP plc 500, 506
brand name 430, 435, 444, 447–8
British Airways plc 536–7
buildings 406
  see also property, plant and
    equipment
business combinations 641–2
  IFRS 3 *Business Combinations* 70,
    423, 429, 430, 507, 559, 562,
    569, 578–81
business-to-business comparisons
    and ratio analysis
    limitations 217

C

Cadbury Committee/Report 90, 92,
  94, 98, 104
capacity considerations 459
capital 6
  allowances 343

capital (*continued*)
  expenditure 684
  working 6–7, 204, 207–9, 456
  see also equity; return on capital
      employed; statement of
      changes in equity
capitalisation versus write-off of
    expenditure 422
carrying amount 29, 384–5, 403,
    433, 622–3
  intangible assets 421, 437–8, 440,
      441, 442
cash
  basis 343
  and cash equivalents 10, 152, 153
  deferred 285
  flow statement *see* statement of
      cash flows
cash flows 151, 153–6, 381, 396–7,
    411, 496–8, 505, 623
  future 127, 150, 164, 165–6
  inflows 72–3, 75, 150–1, 396, 397
  operating 684
  outflows 396, 397, 495, 505–6,
      507–8, 581, 671
  projected 411
  see also statement of cash flows
cash-generating units (CGUs) 247,
    400, 401, 402, 409, 441, 577
Chartered Institute of Management
    Accountants (CIMA) 61, 117
claims 468
classification as held for sale 623–6
closing date 571
Co-ordinating Group on Audit and
    Accounting Issues 101
cohesiveness 172
combined operations and ratio
    analysis limitations 217
common size statements *see* vertical
    analysis
Companies Act (2006) 24, 57, 58,
    59, 111, 267
  published financial statements
      127, 134
company financial accounting 24
comply or explain approach 106
computer software 166, 444
Conceptual Framework (IASB)
    70–7, 79, 127, 128, 147, 150
  current assets 471, 525
  elements of financial statements
      74–5

fair value 75–7
going concern assumption 74
intangible assets 424, 425, 426
liabilities 491–2, 496
objectives of financial
    reporting and qualitative
    characteristics 72–3
property, plant and equipment
    378
published financial statements
    127, 128, 147, 150
reporting entity 73–4
revenue 282, 283–4, 288
subsidiaries 576
taxation 351, 359–60
consideration 569–71
consignment sales 291
consolidated financial statements
    268–70, 562–4, 588, 617,
    623–6
  *IAS 27 Consolidated and Separate
      Financial Statements* 423,
      559, 600
  *IFRS 10 Consolidated Financial
      Statements* 524, 559, 566,
      567–8
  see also control; goodwill on
      acquisition; intragroup
      transactions and balances
consolidated income statements
    (profit and loss account)
    239, 314, 332–3, 637–8
  associate companies 625–6
  subsidiaries 577, 592–5
consolidated retained earnings 591,
    597, 598
consolidated statement of cash flows
    633–42
  disclosures 640–2
  subsidiaries 635–6
  worked example 636–40
consolidated statement of changes
    in equity 595–8, 626, 638
consolidated statement of
    comprehensive income 595
consolidated statement of financial
    position 571–6, 637
  associate companies 626
  preference shares 585–7
  subsidiaries 582–5, 592
consolidation techniques 568–76
  acquisition date 571
  acquisition method 571

consideration 569–71
  non-controlling interest (NCI)
      573–6
  subsidiaries 600
construction contracts 284, 303,
    467–82
  amounts owed by or owed to
      customers 671
  disclosures 479–80
  in early stages of completion
      476–7
  future changes 481–2
  loss-making 474–5
  remaining balances on statement
      of financial position 478–9
  revenues and costs 469–74
  stage of completion 470, 471–2,
      481
  terminology 468–9
  whose outcomes cannot be
      estimated reliably 476–7
  see also IAS 11 *under*
      International Accounting
      Standards
constructive obligation 498
content of published financial
    statements 131–2
context 662–3, 673–4
contingent assets 504–6
  see also IAS 37 *under*
      International Accounting
      Standards
contingent liabilities 501–6, 507,
    581
  definition 501–2
  disclosures 506
  and provisions 502–4
  see also IAS 37 *under*
      International Accounting
      Standards
contracts 334
  costs 302
  with customers *see* ED 2011/6
      (*Revenue from Contracts
      with Customers*)
  in early stages of completion
      481–2
  fixed price 468, 471
  forward 334
  loss-making 481
  onerous 499
  service 480
  see also construction contracts

control 564–5, 566–8
  internal 97–8
  transfer of 296–7, 303
  see also subsidiaries
convertible financial instruments
    324–5, 620
CORE (context, overview, ratios and
    evaluation) approach 659,
    661–7
  context 662–3, 673–4
  evaluation 666–7, 685–7
  external factors 395, 662, 663
  internal factors 395–6, 662–3
  overview 663–4, 674–7
  ratios 664–6
corporate collapses 88–9, 150
corporate governance 87–92
  definition 87–8
  ineffective 88–92
  reporting 88, 106–7
  *see also UK Corporate Governance
    Code*
corporate sustainability 107–13
  environmental and social
    responsibility 109–10
  key factors 108–9
  present day 110
  reporting 110–13
corporation tax 24, 342, 344–5
cost
  approach 389
  average 461–2
  basis 447
  borrowing 381–2
  of capital 77
  constraint 17
  construction contracts 469–74,
    480
  of conversion 459
  decommissioning 410
  development 349, 434–5, 436
  historical 8, 75, 77, 433, 670
  initial 426–7
  model 388, 404, 437
  plus contract 468, 471
  property, plant and equipment
    380–1
  of purchase 459
  restructuring 498–9, 507
  of sales method 143–6
  scrapping 410
  standard 460
Court Line 524

current assets 7, 204, 454–82
  definition and significance 455–6
  disclosures 466–7
  receivables 464–7
  see also construction contracts;
    inventories
current liabilities 8, 133, 199,
    204–5, 671
current tax 342, 343–6
  IAS 12 *Income Taxes* 359–60
customer bases/lists 440, 444

D
databases 688
debt 209, 671
  bad and doubtful 34–7, 466
  finance 209
  intercompany 591
  net debt 209–11, 671, 679–81,
    683–4, 687
  see also gearing
decommissioning costs 410
deferral 548
deferred cash 285
deferred income approach 383
deferred tax 342, 346–56, 362–3
  calculation 355–6
  definition 346–7
  exceptions to recognition of
    deferred tax assets and
    liabilities 350–1
  IAS 12 *Income Taxes* 359–60
  income smoothing effect 357–9
  recognition 347, 353–4, 355–6
  recoverability of asset 351–2
  right of offset 354–6
  tax base of asset or liability
    347–8
  tax rate used in measurement 352
  taxable and deductible temporary
    differences 349–50
  unrecognised 364
denominators 664, 667
depreciable amount 439
depreciated replacement cost
    approach 389
depreciation 11, 143, 406
  accruals principle 28–9
  accumulated 29–33, 384, 388,
    391–3, 398–400, 407–8
  associate companies 622
  charge 402
  current assets 531

elimination of accumulated
    depreciation on revaluation
    392
  fair value 594
  grossing up of cost and
    accumulated depreciation
    392–3
  intangible assets 435, 438
  leasing 545, 548
  methods 405
  property, plant and equipment
    166, 383–8, 410
  rates 405
  reducing balance 30–1
  straight-line 29–30
  subsidiaries 582
  sum of digits method 29, 387
  taxation 343, 349
  units of production method 29,
    385, 387
  see also revaluation
derecognition 402–3, 442, 538
development costs 349, 434–5, 436
diluted earnings per share 322–9,
    330, 334
  contingently issuable shares 325–6
  control number 327
  convertible instruments 324–5
  definition 322–3
  dilutive and antidilutive potential
    ordinary shares 326–9
  share options and warrants 323–4
diminishing balance method *see*
    reducing balance method
direct holding 619
directors 24, 94, 99
  report 95–6, 128
disaggregation 172
disclosures 78, 617
  associate companies 626–8
  consolidated statements of cash
    flow 640–2
  construction contracts 479–80
  contingent assets 506
  contingent liabilities 506
  current assets 466–7, 537–8
  discontinued operations and
    non-current assets held for
    sale 245–6
  earnings per share 330–3
  entity-wide 258–9
  events after the reporting period
    514

disclosures *(continued)*
finance lease 535–7, 543–5
financial instruments 599
government assistance 69, 382
intangible assets 432–3, 442–8
inventories 463–4
joint arrangements 632
leasing 545
liabilities 500–1
operating segment reporting
255–9, 261–2
property, plant and equipment
405–9
provisions 501
remuneration 104
revenue 292, 320–3
subsidiaries 599–601
taxation 360–5
see also IFRS 12 *under*
International Financial
Reporting Standards; related
party disclosures
discontinued operations and non-
current assets held for sale
173, 241–52, 668
accounting for discontinued
operations 247–51
accounting for non-current assets
held for sale 243–5
change of plans 245
definition of discontinued
operation 246–7
definition of non-current assets
held for sale 242–3
disclosures 245–6
IFRS 5 *Non-Current Assets Held
for Sale and Discontinued
Operations* 70, 241, 247,
251–2, 375, 405, 411, 425,
582, 623
judgement in classification 251
proposed changes to accounting
251–2
discount factor 465
discount rate 243, 396–7, 529, 531
discounted cash flow 381, 496–8
disposal group 242
disposal proceeds 31–3, 403, 442
dividends 24, 622, 633, 634, 639,
677–8
cover 214
events after reporting period
512–13

final or proposed 26
interim 26
limited companies' financial
statements 26–7
ordinary and preference 26
paid 597
per share 214
yields 214
Dixons Retail plc 515
dot.com boom 313, 420–1
double-entry bookkeeping 18–19,
345–6
downstream sale 589
Du Pont pyramid of operating ratios
667

E

earnings before interest, tax,
depreciation, and
amortisation (EBITDA) 199
earnings per share 212–13, 216,
310–35, 669
accounting standard, necessity
for 313
basic 311, 315, 323–6, 330, 334,
677
bonus issue of shares 319–20
definition 311–12
definition of earnings 313–15
definition of shares 317
disclosures 330–3
IAS *Earnings Per Share* 20, 212,
310, 313, 317, 319–20, 330,
333–4
importance 312
issue and repurchase of shares at
fair value 318
rights issue of shares 320–1
see also diluted earnings per share
efficiency ratios 197, 206–9
asset turnover 200
inventory turnover 206–7, 208
payables payment period 207,
208
receivables collection period 207,
208
working capital cycle 207–9
employee benefits *see* IAS 19 *under*
International Accounting
Standards
Enron 68, 88–90, 98, 114, 284, 524,
565
entities 4–5, 77

separate 4–5
small and medium-sized 59, 66–7
special-purpose 67, 524, 564–5,
566
structured 566
environmental responsibility 109–10
equity 136, 209
method 617, 618, 621–2, 627,
630–1, 634
(ordinary) shares 24–5, 330, 334
plus non-current liabilities 199
reserve 390
return on 211–12
errors 168–70
see also IAS 8 *under* International
Accounting Standards;
retrospective application
estimates 164–6, 167–8, 236–7,
384, 623
see also best estimates; IAS
8 *under* International
Accounting Standards
estimates of useful life 168, 387–8,
444
ethics 114–19
in business 114–16
financial performance 116
professional bodies 117–19
European Union (EU) 77–8, 342,
667
evaluation 666–7, 685–7
events after reporting period
509–15
adjusting events 510–11
definition 510–12
disclosures 514
dividends 512–13
going concern assumption 513–15
*IAS 10 Events After the Reporting
Period* 69, 490, 509, 513
non-adjusting events 510–11
exceptional items *see* one-off or
unusual items
exit price *see* fair value
expectations gap 99
expected useful life 29, 385, 396
see also useful life
expenses 9, 235
as percentage of sales 201
time-apportioning 27, 28
Exposure Draft (ED) 252
Exposure Draft (ED) 2010/9 *Leases*
549, 550–1

Exposure Draft (ED) 2011/6
    *Revenue from Contracts with
    Customers* 280–2, 294–304,
    465–6, 481–2
  allocation of transaction price
    to separate performance
    obligations 299–301
  contract costs 302
  disclosures 320–3
  effect of 303–4
  identification of contract with
    customer 295
  identification of separate
    performance obligations in
    contract 295–6
  onerous performance obligations
    301–2
  performance obligations satisfied
    at a point in time 298–9
  performance obligations satisfied
    over time 297–8
  satisfaction of performance
    obligations 296–7
Exposure Draft (ED) *Measurement
    of Liabilities* 508–9
external indicators 395, 662, 663

F
fair value 75–7, 78, 165, 243, 285,
    334, 404–5
  adjustments 582, 669
  associate companies 622, 623
  current assets 528
  depreciation 594
  hierarchy 389
  IFRS 13 *Fair Value Measurement*
    70, 75, 243, 285, 388, 405,
    428, 430
  intangible assets 428, 430, 435,
    437–8, 447
  issue and repurchase of shares
    at 318
  leasing 548
  less costs to sell 244–5, 402, 405,
    458
  non-controlling interest (NCI)
    valued at 578–80
  property, plant and equipment
    388–9, 390, 397, 406, 410
  revenue 285, 300
  subsidiaries 569, 571, 582, 584
  taxation 349
faithful representation 15, 68

Finance Act 341
finance charge 531
Financial Accounting Standards
    Board (FASB) 53, 59, 63,
    69, 71–2, 251, 252
  business combinations project
    565
  intangible assets 449
  Norwalk Agreement 62
  see also International Accounting
    Standards Board/Financial
    Accounting Standards
    Board convergence project
Financial Accounting Standards
    (FASs) 69
financial instruments 78
  IAS 32 *Financial Instruments:
    Presentation* 70, 317, 324,
    423, 464
  IAS 39 *Financial Instruments:
    Recognition and
    Measurement* 70, 77, 465,
    466, 507, 561, 621
  IFRS 7 *Financial Instruments:
    Disclosures* 70, 599
  IFRS 9 *Financial Instruments* 70,
    243, 561
financial ratios 210, 523, 549, 665–6
  see also efficiency ratios; gearing;
    investor ratios; liquidity
    ratios; profitability ratios;
    return on capital employed
Financial Reporting Council (FRC)
    57, 61, 105, 129, 513–14
  Effective Company Stewardship
    101–2, 105–7
Financial Reporting Review Panel
    (FRRP) 78, 260
Financial Reporting Standard for
    Smaller Entities (FRSSE)
    59, 67
Financial Reporting Standards
    (FRSs) 24, 59, 61
financial reporting system 53–80
  company legislation 57–8
  Conceptual Framework 70–7
  high quality 55–6
  International Accounting
    Standards Board (IASB)
    65–7
  International Accounting
    Standards (IASs) 58–64
  regulatory framework 56–7, 59

see also International Financial
    Reporting Standards
Financial Services Authority (FSA)
    92, 106
financial statements 5–10, 20–3,
    37–42, 74–5, 100
  cash flows *see* statement of cash
    flows
  of changes in equity *see* statement
    of changes in equity
  consolidated 562–4, 588, 617,
    623–6
  of financial position *see* statement
    of financial position
  of profit or loss *see* income
    statement
  of profit or loss and other
    comprehensive income *see*
    statement of comprehensive
    income
  see also IAS 1 *Presentation of
    Financial Statements under*
    International Accounting
    Standards; interpretation of
    financial statements; notes
    to the financial statements;
    published financial
    statements
first-in, first-out (FIFO) method
    460–2, 464
five-year data 195–6, 316, 667
fixtures, equipment and vehicles 406
footballers as intangible assets
    432–3, 512
foreign exchange rates 69
free from error 15
FTSE 350 companies 94, 95, 116
function of expense method 143–6
future commitments 493
future operating losses 498
future trading profits 352

G
gearing 197, 209–13, 523, 665,
    683–4, 687
GEC/AEI takeover 60, 457
general ledger, *see* nominal ledger
generally accepted accounting
    principles (GAAP) 59, 61,
    62, 63, 237, 443, 507, 667
  published financial statements
    162, 171
GKN plc 141–3, 466

Global Reporting Initiative (GRI)
110, 111
glossary 700–6
going concern assumption 74,
128–9, 513–15
goodwill 400–1, 409, 670
on acquisition 576–82
associate companies 622–3
on consolidation 395
impairment 577, 633, 638
intangible assets 427–9, 441, 443
negative 580
subsidiaries 571, 582, 583, 585,
586–7, 591
taxation 350–1
government grants 382–3
Greene King plc 256–8
gross basis 200–2, 399, 535–6, 544,
589–90
group accounts *see* consolidated
financial statements
guaranteed residual value 539

H
Hampel Report 105
hedge accounting 78
Higgs Report 94
hire purchase agreement 526
historical cost 8, 75, 77, 433, 670
horizontal analysis 189–92, 660,
663, 671
House of Lords Economic Affairs
Committee report 98, 102,
129

I
impairment 166
forecast operating losses 498
of goodwill 166
intangible assets 432, 440–1
losses 243, 437, 465–6, 622–3,
630, 669
property, plant and equipment
409, 410–11
reviews 545
see also external indicators;
impairment of assets;
internal indicators
impairment of assets 394–402
accounting for results of
impairment test 398–400
cash-generating units (CGUs) 400,
401

definition 394–5
goodwill 400–1
IAS 36 *Impairment of Assets* 70,
375, 395, 396, 440, 545, 623
impairment test 396–8
requirement for impairment test
395–6
reversal of impairment losses
401–2
incentive payments 469
income 9, 235
deferred income approach to
government grants 382–3
smoothing 357–9
taxes 342, 365
see also IAS 12 *under* International Accounting Standards
see also income statement
income statement (profit and loss
account) 3, 9–10, 140–3,
240, 249–50, 313–14, 315,
668–9
leasing 534, 547
nominal ledger 18
prudence 35, 36
published financial statements
127, 140, 141–2, 143, 144–6,
154, 169
taxation 345–6, 361–2
worked example 11–12, 21, 22, 41
see also consolidated income
statement
indefinite useful/economic life 395,
529
indirect holding 619
industry statistics—databases 688
inflationary effect 216
influence, total 561, 562, 619
information 15, 16–17, 131, 216,
263–4
asymmetry 88
initial costs 426–7
input methods 297–8, 389, 481
Institute of Chartered Accountants
in England and Wales
(ICAEW) 57, 117
*Recommendations on Accounting
Principles* 60
Reporting with Integrity 114–15,
116
insurance contracts *see* IFRS 4 *under*
International Financial
Reporting Standards

intangible assets 152, 419–50, 581,
670
acquired in business combination
427–30
amortisation and useful life
438–40
current accounting and reporting,
acceptability of 448–9
derecognition 442
disclosures 442–8
fair value 430
finite lived 443
goodwill 441, 571–2, 576–80
IAS 38 *Intangible Assets* 70,
423–7, 430, 433–5, 440,
446–7, 576, 581, 627
identifiable 424
impairment 440–1
importance of accounting for
420–1
with indefinite useful lives 395,
409
initial measurement 426–7
International Accounting
Standards Board (IASB)
current position 449
issues in accounting 421–3
measurement issues 423, 437–42
not yet available for use 395
recognition 425–6
recognition issues 422
see also internally generated
intangible assets
intellectual property rights 439
inter-reserve transfer 438
intercompany debt 591
intercompany sales and purchases
594
interest
capitalisation of 406
cover 210–11
-free credit period and revenue
285–6
rates 411, 465, 531, 539
internal indicators 395–6, 662–3
internally generated intangible
assets 431–7
cost 435–7
development 433–5
research 433
International Accounting Standards
Board (IASB) 59, 61–2, 63,
65–7, 71–2, 77, 79, 667

business combinations project
  395, 565–6
current assets 474, 521, 524, 526
decision-usefulness approach
  235
earnings per share 334
intangible assets 449
liabilities 493, 507, 509
Presentation of Items of Other
  Comprehensive Income
  (Amendments to IAS 1) 148
principles based standards 68–9
property, plant and equipment
  404
published financial statements
  162
reporting performance 252, 264
subsidiaries 559
see also Conceptual Framework
International Accounting Standards
  Board (IASB)/Financial
  Accounting Standards
  Board (FASB) convergence
  project 71–2, 75, 78, 549
earnings per share 333–4
leasing 549
published financial statements
  130, 170–1
reporting performance 241, 280
revenue 294, 304
International Accounting Standards
  Committee (IASC) 61, 62,
  71, 342
International Accounting Standards
  (IASs) 24, 58–64, 67, 69–70
1 *Presentation of Financial*
  Statements 61, 69, 111, 448,
  456, 512, 513, 538
  comparative information and
    consistency 131
  materiality and aggregation
    129–30
  notes to financial statements
    161, 163, 164, 165, 168
  offsetting 130
  published financial statements
    127–31, 132, 133, 134, 137,
    138, 143, 170, 171, 173
  reporting performance 235,
    237, 247
  taxation 354
  true and fair/present fairly
    127–8

underpinning principles 128–9
2 *Inventories* 69, 134, 404, 423,
  454, 458, 467
7 *Statement of Cash Flows* 69,
  127, 150–3, 156, 171, 456,
  633
8 *Accounting Policies, Changes in*
  Accounting Estimates and
  Errors 69, 163, 167, 168,
  345, 387, 441, 471
10 *Events after the Reporting*
  Period 69, 490, 509, 513
11 *Construction Contracts* 69,
  404, 423, 454, 468, 471, 474,
  481–2
  revenue 280–1, 290, 292, 294,
    302, 303
12 *Income Taxes* 69, 243, 340,
  342, 347–8, 350, 353–4, 356,
  359–60, 423
14 *Segment Reporting* 252, 260
16 *Property, Plant and Equipment*
  69, 134, 243, 375, 378, 383,
  385, 389–90, 394, 402, 404,
  458
  leasing 531, 535, 545, 548
17 *Leases* 69, 404, 423, 521, 524,
  527–8, 531–2, 535, 537, 543,
  545, 548–50
18 *Revenue* 69, 280–1, 285–94,
  296, 302, 303, 403, 525
  advertising commissions 219
  consignment sales 219
  criticisms 293–4
  disclosures 292
  lay away sales 219
  measurement of revenue
    285–6
  rendering of services 289–91
  sale of goods 287–9
  servicing fees included in price
    of product 219
  subscriptions to publications
    219
  transactions 286–7
19 *Employee Benefits* 69, 162,
  243, 266, 423, 675
20 *Accounting for Government*
  Grants and Disclosure of
  Government Assistance 69,
  382
21 *Effects of Changes in Foreign*
  Exchange Rates 69

23 *Borrowing Costs* 69, 381
24 *Related Party Disclosures* 70,
  264, 267
26 *Accounting and Reporting*
  by Retirement Benefit Plans
  70
27 *Consolidated and Separate*
  Financial Statements 70,
  423, 559, 600
28 *Investments in Associates and*
  Joint Ventures 70, 423, 617,
  619, 623, 630
29 *Financial Reporting in*
  Hyperinflationary
  Economics 70
31 *Interests in Joint Ventures* 629
32 *Financial Instruments:*
  Presentation 70, 317, 324,
  423, 464
33 *Earnings Per Share* 70, 212,
  310, 313, 317, 319–20, 330,
  333–4
34 *Interim Financial Reporting* 70
36 *Impairment of Assets* 70, 375,
  395, 396, 440, 545, 623
37 *Provisions, Contingent*
  Liabilities and Contingent
  Assets 70, 110, 301, 304,
  490, 494–6, 498–500, 502,
  504, 507–9, 581
38 *Intangible Assets* 70, 423–7,
  430, 433–5, 437, 440, 446–7,
  576, 581, 627
39 *Financial Instruments:*
  Recognition and
  Measurement 70, 77, 465,
  466, 507, 561, 621
40 *Investment Property* 70, 243,
  375, 403, 404
41 *Agriculture* 70, 243
and the International Accounting
  Standards Board (IASB)
  61–2, 65–7
terminology 59
United States acceptance of 62–5
International Federation of
  Accountants (IFAC)
Defining and Developing an
  Effective Code of Conduct for
  Organisations 119
Handbook of the Code of Ethics
  for Professional Accountants
  117–18

International Financial Reporting
  Standards (IFRSs) 24, 59,
  62–5, 67, 69, 71, 75–6, 127–8,
  131, 134, 137, 139, 162–4,
  167, 171, 667
  1 *First-time Adoption of
    International Financial
    Reporting Standards* 70, 423
  2 *Share Based Payment* 70, 266,
    323
  3 *Business Combinations* 70, 423,
    429–30, 507, 559, 562, 569,
    578–81
  4 *Insurance Contracts* 70, 243,
    423–4
  5 *Non-Current Assets Held for Sale
    and Discontinued Operations*
    70, 241, 247, 251–2, 375, 405,
    411, 425, 582, 623
  6 *Exploration for and Evaluation of
    Mineral Resources* 70, 423
  7 *Financial Instruments:
    Disclosures* 70, 599
  8 *Operating Segments* 70, 252–4,
    258, 260–1, 263, 265, 668
  9 *Financial Instruments* 70, 243,
    561
  10 *Consolidated Financial
    Statements* 70, 524, 559, 566,
    567–8
  11 *Joint Arrangements* 70, 566,
    617, 629, 630–1
  12 *Disclosure of Interests in Other
    Entities* 70, 559, 566, 599,
    617, 626, 632
  13 *Fair Value Measurement* 70, 75,
    243, 285, 388, 405, 428, 430
  audit opinion 99
  consequences of global adoption
    77–8
  corporate governance 86
  Foundation 65, 79
  future of 78–9
  Interpretations Committee 66, 69
  principles based 67–70
  for small- and medium-sized
    entities (SMEs) 59, 61, 67
interpretation of financial statements
    184–218, 659–88
  A-scores 666
  analytical techniques 186–9
  business information 186
  efficiency ratios 206–9

five-year data 195–6
gearing 209–11
horizontal analysis 189–92
income statements 668–9
industry statistics—databases 688
liquidity ratios 197, 203–6
purpose of analysis 185–6
questioning 'why' 186
ratio analysis 196–7, 216–17,
  664–6
ratios to indicate financial distress
  665–6
recognition and measurement
  issues and accounting
  policies 667–72
statement of cash flows 671–2
statement of changes in equity 669
statement of comprehensive
  income 668–9
statement of financial position
  (balance sheet) 669–71
vertical analysis 192–5
Z-scores 665–6
see also CORE approach; investor
  ratios; J Sainsbury plc case
  study; profitability ratios
intragroup transactions and balances
  587–92
inventories 134, 163, 204–5, 456–64,
  670
  adjustment to consolidated
    retained earnings 582
  consignment 458
  cost 458–62
  disclosures 463–4
  first-in, first-out (FIFO) method
    460–2
  IAS 2 *Inventories* 69, 134, 404,
    423, 454, 458, 467
  issues with accounting 457–8
  measurement 458
  net realisable value (NRV) 462–3
  obsolete 458
  scandals 457
  significance of 456–7
  turnover ratio 206–7, 208
  unrealised profit in 588–92, 594,
    622
  weighted average cost method
    460–2
investments 268–9, 560–4, 618–19,
  622
  in an associate company 634–5

see also IAS 28 *under* Interna-
    tional Accounting Standards
  consolidated financial statements
    562–4
  income (dividends) 561, 593–4
  limited influence 561
  multiple 580–1
  partial influence 561
  property 78, 403–5, 406
    see also IAS 40 *under* Interna-
      tional Accounting Standards
  simple 561
  in subsidiaries 600–1
  total influence 561, 562
investor ratios 211–16
  dividend cover 214
  dividend per share 214
  dividend yield 214
  earnings per share 212–13
  price/earnings ratio (P/E)
    213–14
  return on equity 211–12
  total shareholder returns 215–16
investor/stock market 197, 665

J
J Sainsbury plc 112–13, 139–40,
    199, 210
  current assets 456
  earnings per share 316
  income taxes 365
  liabilities 513
  one-off or unusual items 238
  property, plant and equipment
    406–7
  subsidiaries 564, 568–9
  underlying profit 139–40, 238,
    316, 674–7, 681–2, 686
  see also J Sainsbury plc case study
J Sainsbury plc case study 659, 672–87
  context 673–4
  efficiency 682
  evaluation 685–7
  external environment 672
  gearing 683–4, 687
  income statement 676
  internal environment 672–3
  liquidity 682, 687
  management efficiency 682–3
  net capital expenditure 684
  operating cash flow 684
  overview 674–7
  profitability 678–82, 686–7

ratios 677
risks 687
segmental analysis 684–5
shareholder ratios 677–8
shareholders' perspective 686
statement of cash flows 671
statement of changes in equity
    669, 678
statement of financial position
    (balance sheet) 676
strategic objectives 672–3
JD Wetherspoon plc 239–41, 402
joint arrangements 617, 629–32
    IFRS 11 Joint Arrangements 70,
        566, 617, 629, 630–1
joint control 629
joint operations/joint operators 617,
    629–30, 631–2
joint ventures 256, 617, 627–8, 629,
    630–1, 632, 634, 679
    IAS 28 Investments in Associates
        and Joint Ventures 70, 423,
        617, 619, 623, 630
judgements 68, 164–6, 236–7, 251,
    410 11, 620, 670, 671

K
key performance indicators (KPIs)
    664
Kingfisher plc 268–70
KPMG 108, 109, 112

L
land 29, 406, 529–30
lay away sales 219
leasing 68, 521–52
    assets 525–6
    buildings 530
    classification 526–8
    contingent rentals 528, 535, 544, 550
    date of commencement 528
    date of inception 528
    Exposure Draft (ED)/2010/9
        Leases 549, 550–1
    finance lease 521, 524, 526–8,
        549, 550
    guaranteed residual value 539
    IAS 17 Leases 69, 404, 423, 521,
        524, 527–8, 531–2, 535, 537,
        543, 545, 548–50
    land 530
    minimum lease payments 527,
        528–9, 530–1

off balance sheet financing 522–5
operating leases 521, 524, 526–8,
    529–30, 538, 549, 550
principles-based approach 525
property 529–30
sale and leaseback transactions
    545–8
term 528–9
unguaranteed residual value 531,
    539, 542, 544
see also actuarial (effective interest)
    method; lessees' financial
    statements; lessors' financial
    statements
legislation of companies see
    Companies Act (2006)
Lehmans 89
Lenzing AG 249–51, 315
lessee accounting 550
lessees' financial statements 530–8
    finance lease disclosures 535–7
    finance leases 530–5
    operating leases 537–8
lessor accounting 550–1
lessors' financial statements 538–45
    finance lease disclosures 543–5
    finance leases 538–42
    manufacturers or dealers 542–3
    operating leases 539, 545
leverage see gearing
liabilities 6, 75, 76, 77, 466, 490–516,
    669
    best estimate 495–6
    big bath accounting 492–3
    current 8, 204, 671
    deferred tax 362–3
    discounted cash flow 497–8
    exceptions to recognition of
        deferred tax 350–1
    Exposure Draft (ED) Measurement
        of Liabilities 508–9
    finance lease 535–6
    IAS 37 Provisions, Contingent
        Liabilities and Contingent Assets
        70, 110, 301, 304, 490, 494–6,
        498–500, 502, 504, 507–9, 581
    key issues 491–3
    leasing 533–5
    measurement 507
    non-current 8
    obligations 495–6
    onerous contract 499
    outflow of resources 493–4

past event versus future
    commitment 493
present obligation 493
present value 496–8
property, plant and equipment
    380–1
provision, measurement of 495–6
provision, recognition of 494–5
published financial statements
    135–6, 173
taxation 343–5, 347–8, 349, 350,
    351, 359
see also contingent liabilities;
    events after reporting period
licence fees 444
limited companies' financial
    statements 23–7
limited influence 561, 619
liquid ratio 204–5
liquidity 5, 133, 456, 665, 682, 687
    ratios 197, 203–6
    risks 129, 514
listed companies 58, 514
listing rules 55, 514
Lloyds Banking Group plc 544–5
loyalty scheme accruals 166

M
McKesson & Robbins 457
management efficiency 682–3
management reporting and
    controlling systems 258
manufacturers or dealers 542–3
mark-up 589–90
market approach 389
market price 318
market value 25, 406, 448
    expected 539
    for non-cash consideration 432
market-to-book ratios 421
Marks and Spencer plc 99–101,
    136–7, 161, 165–6, 331, 501
Marston's plc 362–3, 394, 409
matching 235, 289
materiality/material information
    14–15, 129–30, 496
    material transaction 510
Maxwell 89, 98, 114
measurement issues 75
    effect on interpretation 667–72
mergers and acquisitions (M&A)
    561
minimum lease payments 527, 530–1

mixed valuation model approach 77
Myners' review 105

N

narrative reports 86–7, 97
National Insurance (NI) 342
nature of expense method 140–1
Nestlé 361–2, 364, 456, 466–7
net assets 200, 210, 421, 623
net operating cash flows to current
    liabilities ratio 672
net operating cash flows to net profit
    ratio 672
net present value *see* present value
net realisable value (NRV) 433, 458,
    462–3, 464, 630
netting-off method 383
Next plc 128, 134–6, 165, 364–5
ninety percent rule 528
Nokia Corporation 431
nominal amount (peppercorn rent)
    529
nominal ledger 17–18
nominal value 25, 137
nominations committee 95
non-adjusting event 510–11
non-controlling interest (NCI)
    573–6, 584, 591, 594, 597,
    598, 639, 671
    subsidiaries 571, 581, 582, 585,
      589, 593, 596
    valued at fair value 578–80
non-current assets 7, 29, 456, 526, 591
    disposal of 31–3
    held for sale 405, 407
      see also discontinued operations
        and non-current assets held
        for sale
      see also IFRS 5 *under* Interna-
        tional Financial Reporting
        Standards
non-financial data ratios 664, 666
non-listed companies 58, 59
norms, reliance on and ratio analysis
    limitations 217
notes to the financial statements
    161–70
    accounting policies 163
    changes in accounting estimates
      167–8
    changes in accounting policies
      166–7
    errors 168–70

estimates, judgements and risks
    164–6
numerators 664, 667

O

objectives of financial reporting 72–3
obligation 493, 494–6, 498, 581
    see also performance obligations
off balance sheet 67, 521, 522–5, 526,
    537, 549, 564–5
offsetting 130, 354–6
on balance sheet 526
one-off, significant or material events
    509, 663–4
one-off or unusual items 139,
    237–41, 664, 668
onerous contract 499
onerous performance obligations
    301–2
operating cash flow 684
operating cycle 133, 283, 456
operating profit *see* profit before
    interest and tax
operating segment reporting 252–63,
    668–9
    definition 253
    disclosures 255–8
    entity-wide disclosures 258–9
    IAS 14 *Segment Reporting* 252, 260
    IFRS 8 *Operating Segments* 70,
      252–4, 258, 260–1, 263, 265,
      668
    reportable operating segments
      253–5
    uses in analysis 261–3
options 334
ordinary shares *see* equity shares
other comprehensive income 137–8,
    158, 362
    see also statement of
      comprehensive income
outflows 495, 505, 507–8, 581
output methods 297–8, 481
overview 663–4, 674–7
ownership versus control 564–5

P

par value *see* nominal value
parent company 563
partial influence 561, 619
past events 493, 581
payables 588
    payment period 207, 208

PAYE (pay-as-you-earn) 342
payments in arrears 534–5
percentage stage of completion
    method 470, 471
performance obligations 295–6, 304,
    481
    see also under Exposure Draft (ED)
      Revenue from Contracts with
      Customers
Pergamon Press 60, 457
permanent differences 343, 357
possible obligation 581
post balance sheet events 512
post-retirement benefits 166
power as part of control 566
power with significant minority
    shareholding 567–8
preference shares 24–5, 26, 27, 317,
    585–7
present obligation 493, 581
present value 75, 496–8, 535–6
    current assets 528
    discounted 569
    leasing 539, 544
    value in use for associate
      companies 623
    see also value in use
price/earnings ratio (P/E) 213–14,
    312, 313
primary user group 72–3
principal–agent problem 88, 103
principles-based approach 67, 68–9,
    73, 118, 525, 565
private limited company 23, 24, 563
probability recognition criterion 425
probability-weighted average 508–9
production overheads 459
professional bodies and ethics 117–19
profit
    before interest and tax (PBIT)
      142–3, 198, 200
    and cash flow, difference between
      11–13, 151
    distributable 26
    gross margin 200–2, 589–90
    net margin 199, 200, 201–2, 203,
      448
    unrealised in inventories 588–92,
      594, 622
profit and/or loss 432
    account *see* income statement
    associate companies 622
    and taxation 342–3

profit/earnings (P/E) ratio 216
profitability 197–8, 217, 479, 665,
    678–82, 686–7
profitability ratios 197, 198–203,
    665
  asset turnover 200
  expenses as percentage of sales
      201
  gross profit margin 200–1
  net profit margin 200, 203
  relationship between 201–3
  return on capital employed
      (ROCE) 198–9, 202–3
  return on net assets 199
progress billings 468–9, 478
property
  leasing 529–30
  valuation 394
property, plant and equipment 134,
    163, 375–412, 536, 584,
    669–70
  associate companies 622
  borrowing costs 381–2
  cost 380–1
  definition 377–8
  depreciation 166, 383–8
  derecognition 402–3
  disclosures 405–9
  estimates of useful life 387–8
  fair value 388–9
  government grants 382–3
  impairment 394–402
  initial measurement 380–3
  initial recognition 378–9
  investment properties 403–5
  judgements 410–11
  measurement models 78
  non-current assets held for sale
      405
  recognition of subsequent
      expenditure 379–80
  revaluation 389–94, 548
  significance 376–7
  subsidiaries 582
  understanding of information
      409–11
  see also impairment of assets;
      IAS 16 under International
      Accounting Standards
prospective application 167
provisions 502–4
  disclosures 500–1
  for doubtful debts 34–7

IAS 37 Provisions, Contingent
    Liabilities and Contingent
    Assets 70, 110, 301, 304, 490,
    494–6, 498–500, 502, 504,
    507–9, 581
  measurement 495–6
  recognition 494–5
  see also big bath accounting; best
      estimate; future operating
      losses; onerous contract;
      restructuring costs
prudence 33–7
public limited company 23
public listed company 24, 563
published financial statements
    125–74
  IAS 1 Presentation of Financial
      Statements 127–31
  notes to the financial statements
      161–70
  proposed changes to presentation
      170–3
  structure and content 131–2
  see also statement of cash flows;
      statement of changes
      in equity; statement of
      comprehensive income;
      statement of financial position

Q

qualitative characteristics 13–17, 72–3
  comparable information 15–16
  cost constraint 17
  enhancing 13–14
  faithful representation 15
  fundamental 13–14
  materiality 14–15
  relevant information 14
  timely information (timeliness) 16
  understandable information
      16–17
  verifiable information 16
quality, measures of 77
quick ratio see liquid ratio

R

ratio analysis 196–7, 664–6
  limitations 216–17
ratios 664–6, 677
  market-to-book 421
  non-financial data 664, 666
  and off balance sheet financing
      523

see also efficiency ratios; financial
    ratios; gearing; liquidity
    ratios; investor ratios;
    profitability ratios; return on
    capital employed
realisable (settlement) value 75
realised gains and losses 147
receivables 34–7, 134, 464–7, 588,
    670
  allowance for doubtful receivables
      467
  collection period 207, 208
  past due and impaired 467
  trade 466
  see also provision for doubtful
      debts
recognition 74–5, 422, 425–6, 435,
    446–7, 667–72
reconciliation 156, 343, 442, 639
recoverable amount 394–5, 402, 411
  associate companies 623
  intangible assets 440
  see also impairment of assets
recycling 148
reducing balance method of
    depreciation 29
refunds 166
  sales 288–9
related party disclosures 263–70
  definition of related party 264–6
  disclosures 266–70
  IAS 24 Related Party Disclosures
      70, 264, 267
  information, necessity for 263–4
  transaction, definition of 266
relevant activities 76, 566
relevant information 14–15
remuneration 24, 102–4
rendering of services revenue 289–91
replacement cost, gross 399
reporting 3
  corporate governance 106–7
  corporate sustainability 110–13
  entity 73–4
  financial 4
  see also reporting performance
reporting performance 233–70
  accruals concept 235
  balance sheet approach to profit
      recognition 235–6
  estimates, judgement and choices
      of accounting policies 236–7
  one-off or unusual items 237–41

reporting performance *(continued)*
  see also discontinued operations
       and non-current assets held
       for sale; operating segment
       reporting; related party
       disclosures
research and development 349, 433,
     437
reserves 24, 136, 582–5
  consolidated 582
  pre- and post-acquisition 582–4
residual value 384, 385, 388, 398–9,
     410, 439, 539
  expected 29
  see also guaranteed residual value;
       unguaranteed residual value
restructuring costs 498–9, 507
retained earnings 24
  associate companies 622
  consolidated 591, 597, 598
retentions 469
retirement benefit costs 349
retrospective application 167
retrospective information 216
return on assets 199, 448
return on capital employed (ROCE)
     198–9, 448, 523, 664, 669,
     678–81
return on equity 211–12
return on net assets (RONA) 199,
     680
revaluation 388, 389–94, 398–9, 408,
     410, 670
  intangible assets 437–8, 440,
       442–3, 447
  reserve 282, 622
revenue 280–305, 668
  advertising commissions 219
  consignment sales 219
  criticisms 293–4
  disclosures 292
  lay away sales 219
  measurement of revenue 285–6
  rendering of services 289–91
  sale of goods 287–9
  servicing fees included in price
       of product 219
  subscriptions to publications
       219
  transactions 286–7
  construction contracts 469–74
  current assets 525
  definition 282–3

property, plant and equipment
     403
  recognition 283–4, 303
  sale of goods 287–9
  see also Exposure Draft 2011/6
       *Revenue from Customers
       with Contracts*; IAS 18 *under*
       International Accounting
       Standards; sales refunds
rights issue 320–1
risk 97, 164–6, 497, 687
  corporate governance 87, 90
  corporate sustainability 109
  going concern 129
  liquidity 129, 514
  management 95, 98, 115, 536–7
  reporting of 96, 106–7, 162,
       165–6, 260
  and reward, transfer of 303, 526,
       538, 549
  and uncertainty 165, 495
  see also accountability
Rolls-Royce plc 162–3, 258–9, 431
  current assets 457, 464
  intangible assets 437
  property, plant and equipment
       407–8
royalty revenue 282, 291, 349
rules based accounting 68, 524, 565

S
sale of goods revenue 287–9
sale and leaseback transactions
     finance leases 546–8
     operating leases 548
sale and leaseback transactions
     545–8
sale, measurement of costs associated
     with 289
sale and repurchase agreements 288
sale or return basis 288, 299
sales, intercompany 594
sales refunds 288–9
scrapping costs 410
segmental analysis 684–5
  see also operating segment
       reporting
selling price (contract price) 460, 468
sensitivity analysis 165
separability (identifiable) criterion
     432
separate business entity 4–5
shareholders 23

institutional 91, 103–4, 106
  perspective 686
  relations with 104–6
  total returns 215–16
  see also accountability; corporate
       governance; investor ratios;
       principal–agent problem;
       stewardship; *UK Corporate
       Governance Code*
shares and share capital 24–6, 134,
     136, 639
  market value 25
  new shares 136
  nominal value 25
  premium 25–6
  share buy-back 137
  share price 216, 561
  see also bonus issue; earnings per
       share; rights issue
Sharman Inquiry 129
  see also going concern assumption
Shire plc 431, 439
significant influence 619–21
significant minority shareholding
     567–8
small- and medium-sized entities
     (SMEs) 59, 66–7
social responsibility 109–10
special-purpose entities (SPEs) 67,
     524, 564–5, 566
spectrum fees 444
standard cost 460
statement of cash flows 10, 12, 24,
     150–61, 205–6, 671–2
  analytical techniques 188–9
  direct and indirect methods of
       reporting cash flows from
       operating activities 153–6
  full statement 156–60
  horizontal analysis 191, 192
  IAS 7 *Statement of Cash Flows* 69,
       127, 150–3, 156, 171, 456, 633
  proposed structures 172
  simple statement example 150–1
  see also consolidated statement of
       cash flows
statement of changes in equity 10,
     24, 41, 148–50, 158, 170, 669
  analytical techniques 187
  associate companies 622, 624
  consolidated 595–8, 626, 638
  property, plant and equipment
       390

see also IAS 1 *Presentation of Financial Statements under* International Accounting Standards

statement of comprehensive income 10, 132, 137–48, 668–9
    analytical techniques 187
    associate companies 622
    consolidated 595
    construction contracts 468
    definition 137–8
    earnings per share 330
    function of expense method 143–6
    horizontal analysis 190, 191
    nature of expense method 140–1
    necessity for 147–8
    presentation 138–40
    pro forma 146–7
    property, plant and equipment revaluations 390
    proposed structures 172
    reporting performance 235
    vertical analysis 192–3
    see also IAS 1 *Presentation of Financial Statements under* International Accounting Standards; income statement; other comprehensive income

Statement of Financial Accounting Standard (SFAS) 131 260
statement of financial position (balance sheet) 3, 6–8, 12–13, 21–3, 42, 246, 669–71
    analytical techniques 188
    associate companies 622, 624 5
    consideration 570–1
    consolidated 571–3, 582
    construction contracts and remaining balances 478–9
    current and non-current classifications 133
    horizontal analysis 190–1, 192
    leasing 533–4, 547
    Marks and Spencer plc 136–7
    Next plc 135–6
    nominal ledger 18
    non-current assets held for sale 405
    presentation 134
    profit recognition 235–6
    proposed structures 172
    prudence 36, 37
    published financial statements 132–8, 154–5, 158–60

and ratio analysis limitations 217
    share capital 134
    subclassifications 134
    taxation 345–6
    vertical analysis 193–4
    see also consolidated statement of financial position; IAS 1 *Presentation of Financial Statements under* International Accounting Standards

statement of profit or loss *see* income statement

statement of profit or loss and other comprehensive income *see* statement of comprehensive income

Statements of Interpretation (SICs) 69
Statements of Standard Accounting Practice (SSAPs) 24, 59, 61
stewardship 5, 56, 72–3, 87–8
stock market values 421
straight-line depreciation method 29–30, 386, 388, 434, 439, 444
    leasing 537, 538, 545
structure of published financial statements 131–2
structured entities 566
subscriptions to publications 219
subsidiaries 559–602
    acquisition or disposal 635–6
    consolidated income statement 592–5
    consolidated statement of changes in equity 595–8
    consolidated statement of comprehensive income 595
    consolidated statement of financial position after acquisition date 582–5
    control, definition of 566–8
    disclosures in financial statements 599–601
    exemptions from preparation of consolidated financial statements 568
    fair value adjustments, post-acquisition 582
    goodwill on acquisition 576–82
    IASB business combinations project 565–6
    intragroup transactions and balances 587–92

investments, categorisation of 560–4
    multiple investments 580–1
    negative goodwill 580
    non-controlling interest (NCI) 578–80, 584
    ownership versus control 564–5
    power with significant minority shareholding 567–8
    preference shares 585–7
    property, plant and equipment 584
    reserves, pre- and post-acquisition 582–5
    retained earnings, consolidated 584
    see also consolidated financial statements; consolidation techniques
substance over form 68, 287, 525, 526
sum of digits method 29, 387, 531

T
T accounts 18–19
tangible assets 664
    see also in particular property, plant and equipment
taxation 24, 340–66
    corporation tax 24, 342, 344–5
    disclosures 360–5
    IAS 12 *Income Taxes* 69, 243, 340, 342, 347–8, 350, 353–4, 356, 359–60, 423
    income tax 342, 365
    permanent differences 343
    planning opportunities 352
    reconciliation of accounting profit to taxable profit 344
    tax base 347
    temporary differences 343, 347, 349–50, 352, 356
    users' interpretation of 365–6
    see also current tax; deferred tax
temporary differences 343, 347, 349–50, 352, 356
Tesco plc 627–8, 632, 640–2
time-apportionment 593, 622
timely information (timeliness) 16
transaction price 299–301
trend analysis 195–6, 663, 671, 677
trial balance 19–20
true and fair 57–8, 68, 99, 127–8, 237
Turnbull Report 97

U

UK Corporate Governance Code 90, 92–106
  accountability 95–7
  accountability: audit 98–102
  accountability: audit committee 98
  accountability: internal control 97–8
  accountability: risk 97
  board of directors 92–3
  effectiveness 94–5
  leadership 93–4
  remuneration 102–4
  shareholders, relations with 104–6
UK Stewardship Code 91, 105–6
unadjusted quoted prices 389
  see also fair value
uncertainty of future events 164, 581
  see also contingent assets;
      contingent liabilities
underlying profit before tax 139–40,
    238, 316, 674–7, 681–2, 686
  see also J Sainsbury plc case study
unguaranteed residual value 531,
    539, 542, 544

United States 59, 79, 94, 421, 524,
    565, 580
  acceptance of International
      Accounting Standards 62–4
  Concepts Statements 70–1
  Sarbanes–Oxley Act 90
  Securities and Exchange
      Commission (SEC) 62, 63
  see also Financial Accounting
      Standards Board
units of production method 29, 387
unrealised gains or losses 147
unrealised profit in inventories
    588–92, 594, 622
upstream sale 589, 622
useful life 29, 383, 396, 405, 410,
    438–40, 443
  indefinite 440, 441, 529
  unlimited 384
  see also estimates of useful life;
      expected useful life

V

value
  added tax (VAT) 342
  realisable 75

in use 396, 398, 402
  see also fair value; market value;
      net realisable value; present
      value; residual value
verifiability 16, 410–11
vertical analysis 192–5, 660
Vodafone Group plc 153, 292, 431,
    443–6
voting rights 566–7, 573
voting shares 600, 619, 620
  see also equity (ordinary) shares

W

Walker Report 97, 105
warranties 304
warrants 334
working capital 6–7, 204, 207–8,
    456
  cycle 207–8
  management 207, 671
WorldCom 377
writing down allowances *see* capital
    allowances

Z

Z-score 665–6